A FIFTIETH ANNIVERSARY PUBLICATION

SOME HISTORIANS
OF MODERN EUROPE

THE UNIVERSITY OF CHICAGO PRESS · CHICAGO
THE BAKER & TAYLOR COMPANY, NEW YORK; THE CAMBRIDGE UNIVERSITY
PRESS, LONDON; THE MARUZEN-KABUSHIKI-KAISHA, TOKYO, OSAKA,
KYOTO, FUKUOKA, SENDAI; THE COMMERCIAL PRESS, LIMITED, SHANGHAI

SOME HISTORIANS
OF MODERN EUROPE

ESSAYS IN HISTORIOGRAPHY BY FORMER STUDENTS
OF THE DEPARTMENT OF HISTORY OF
THE UNIVERSITY OF CHICAGO

EDITED BY

BERNADOTTE E. SCHMITT

ANDREW MACLEISH DISTINGUISHED SERVICE PROFESSOR
OF MODERN HISTORY

THE UNIVERSITY OF CHICAGO PRESS
CHICAGO · ILLINOIS

PREFACE

SOME of these essays were first prepared in a course on the historiography and bibliography of modern Europe which I offer to graduate students in history. Others have been written especially for this volume by older scholars who completed a somewhat similar course under the late James Westfall Thompson when he was still a professor in the University of Chicago. The subject of each essay was agreed upon by the author and myself. In the case, however, of several historians who would naturally be included in such a volume, I could unfortunately find no one willing to write on them. The essays are now published as a feature of the Fiftieth Anniversary Celebration of the University of Chicago not only because of their intrinsic interest but also with the object of giving former students some share in the Celebration.

It has become a commonplace that each generation writes its own history. Not only does the discovery and publication of new records add to or correct existing information, but the interpretation of the evidence depends on the spirit of the age. In the last fifty years or so the old manner of writing history as a record of politics, diplomacy, and war has been largely replaced by the social or economic approach. More recently, two other tendencies have been coming to the front. One has been the emphasis laid on the history of ideas; the other, a willingness to abandon a narrow, national outlook and to try to write history from the point of view of world-developments. By the year 2000 still other orientations may well have been found.

The essays in this volume treat of European historians of modern Europe whose work has been done in the last two generations and who are not mentioned in those classics of historiography, Eduard Fueter's *Geschichte der neueren historiographie* (1911) and G. P. Gooch's *History and historians in the nineteenth century* (1913).

Historians of six countries are included, but no clear principle of selection can be indicated. Many fields of history are represented, and, in several cases, conflicting points of view about the same field. But there is no real unity about the essays, for the excellent reason that these twenty-two persons were men of strong personality and individuality who had little in common except devotion to history. What the essays do prove is that it is possible to have many approaches to history and that there are about as many "philosophies of history" as there are historians. This I am convinced of from my acquaintance with five of the twenty-two: Hans Delbrück, Élie Halévy, Sir Richard Lodge, Albert Mathiez, and Harold Temperley.

My part in this enterprise has been strictly limited. I did, indeed, offer a few general suggestions to the contributors as to what was wanted, but I carefully refrained from trying to impose a formula. Hence the great variety of treatment exhibited by the essays. My editorial duties have been restricted almost entirely to harmonizing spellings, capitalizations, references, and the like. I take this opportunity to express to all the contributors my deep appreciation of the co-operative spirit which they uniformly displayed and to thank them for the zeal with which they have, one and all, endeavored to make this volume possible.

BERNADOTTE E. SCHMITT

November 11, 1941

TABLE OF CONTENTS

TABLE OF CONTENTS

LIST OF ABBREVIATIONS

Books and articles mentioned in footnotes without indication of the author are written by the subject of the essay.

AHR	American historical review
CHR	Cambridge historical review
CR	Contemporary review
DNB	Dictionary of national biography
EHR	English historical review
HZ	Historische Zeitschrift
JMH	Journal of modern history
RH	Revue historique
SR	Slavonic review

I

RAFAEL ALTAMIRA (1866——)

JOHN E. FAGG*

MEN of learning in Spain have frequently been conscious of an obligation to their less erudite compatriots. They have sought to diffuse knowledge both of the outside world and of Spanish past grandeur in the hope of stimulating a national revival. One of the most public spirited of these missionary-intellectuals is Rafael Altamira y Crevea, whose outstanding contribution has been a monumental history of Spanish civilization. He believed that humanity usually behaved in line with its conception of experience, in accordance with its historical memory, and that, therefore, it should at least know the facts about its past. An investigator who observed the highest standards of research, he was eager to simplify and to popularize the results of his inquiries. To him the historian's duty was first to arrive at the truth and then to communicate it to the lay reader.†

Born in Alicante on February 10, 1866, of undistinguished parentage, Altamira was well known in Spanish intellectual circles by the time he was twenty-one. As a student at the University of Valencia he was singled out by the remarkable mental powers, the personality, and the industry that were to characterize him

* San Saba, Tex.; sometime Henry Milton Wolf fellow in history.

† His chief writings in the field of history are: *Historia de la propiedad comunal* (Madrid, 1890), *La enseñanza de la historia* (Madrid, 1895), *Historia de España y de la civilización española* (4 vols.; Barcelona, 1900–1911; rev. ed., 1913–14), *Cuestiones de historia del derecho y de legislación comparada* (Madrid, 1914), and chapters on Spain in the *Cambridge medieval history* and the *Cambridge modern history*. Many of his essays and lectures are included in *De historia y arte* (Madrid, 1898), *Psicología del pueblo español* (Madrid, 1902), *Temas de historia de España* (Madrid, 1929), and *Cuestiones modernas de historia* (Madrid, 1935).

through life. His activities ranged from political agitation as a republican and anticlerical to publishing novels, literary criticisms, and articles on historical subjects and pedagogical questions.[1] In common with most Spanish men-of-letters, he was fated to study law, and in 1886 he went to Madrid to complete his studies under the direction of Spain's leading professors. Readily accepted into a group of prominent scholars and public men, including such figures as Azcárate, Giner de los Ríos, and Salmerón, the gifted young Valencian was soon one of their peers.

Altamira's career took the shape it was to hold in the atmosphere of the last decade of the nineteenth century. Spain was dormant in most respects; but her intelligentsia were alive to the currents of thought that were altering world-outlook, and, above and beyond the sphere of politics, they sought to divert them into the peninsula. From his youth, Rafael Altamira labored enthusiastically in the self-imposed task of popularizing the historical, literary, and sociological trends with which he was in touch. With unswerving confidence he preached that Spain could rise again as a great civilization if her citizens accepted the proper instruction. It was not unnatural that a man of his temperament and wide interests should embrace the "new history" or that there should be many aspects of his career other than historian. In his chief life-mission, however, that of promoting national regeneration, he was primarily concerned as a student of the past.

Until he won a chair in 1897 at the University of Oviedo by means of the Spanish custom of competition, Altamira was scarcely a professional historian. He delivered public lectures on historical subjects, published a few articles on legal history, and regularly contributed bibliographical essays to the *Revue historique* and the *Jahresberichte der Geschichtswissenschaft*. But, as secretary of the national pedagogical museum, most of his efforts were devoted to educational reform. He also founded and edited the *Revista crítica de historia y literatura españolas, portuguesas, y hispano-americanas*, a unique little journal which proved a boon to Spanish scholars during its brief career. Altamira's appetite for work was not satisfied until he had published several novels, countless literary criticisms, and fugitive articles in the republican press. With abundant enthusiasm for all branches of his activity—literature, education, history, and law—he won some distinction in each.

His excursions into literature, which for a time furnished part of his livelihood, did not bring Altamira renown. None of his novels even approached success on the book market, although one was deemed to show promise.[2] In 1907 he finally abandoned literature for concentration on his historical and other interests, but he continued to regard it somewhat nostalgically as blessed relief from the unlovely features of human conduct contemplated by the historian.[3] His literary criticisms were numerous and, for the most part, meritorious. His reviews were said to be distinguished for their reflection and justice;[4] his guiding principle was that the critic should "have a heart."[5] But neither was his reputation in this field outstanding nor has it endured. Through his literary interests, however, he came to associate with other Spanish writers and scholars, such as Leopoldo Alas, Menéndez y Pelayo, Unamuno, Pérez Galdós, and Menéndez Pidal. If his literary efforts affected his historical writing in later years, its influence was probably salutary, for his style of composition, hopelessly awkward in his first attempts, improved markedly as he continued writing. And it is likely that the attentive study he devoted to national and European literature further equipped him as a historian of culture.

Acutely conscious of the influence exercised by historical knowledge or misinformation on the thoughts and actions of nations, Altamira believed that history should inform the individual of his true juncture with the evolution of world-civilization. He appeared to consider the pedagogical function of a historian as inseparable from his capacity as an investigator of the past. His early maturity in questions of education was revealed in a book he circulated privately in 1891 and published four years later, *La enseñanza de la historia*. The reception of this work abroad was favorable,[6] and in Spain it became the principal guide in matters of historical methodology and pedagogy. He urged, among other things, that students be taught history from their beginning school years, on the grounds that it would awaken the critical spirit, imbue a respect for truth, provide a sense of perspective, and form habits of reaching conclusions through factual knowledge.[7] Although its power of example might be weak, Altamira insisted that history maintained the traditional spirit of a people and inspired sentiments and ideals of vast importance in the present.[8] It would condition the approach of the public to contemporary problems with a consciousness of the peculiarities of the nation's development.

The methods of teaching proposed in *La enseñanza de la historia* recalled in many respects the ancient conception that history was a mode of inquiry. Altamira would have each youth work with documents, make excursions to sites of famous events of the past, and study monuments, inscriptions, and relics.[9] As he considered every phase of the past within the proper scope of history, he would encourage students to undertake personal investigations of the sources in any field, provided they learned to think in terms of evolutionary development. Aware of the continuity of civilization and trained in the best techniques of historical method, they should become capable citizens. Veritably, Altamira considered every man his own historian.

In comparison with the educational policies in other countries, which he analyzed with characteristic thoroughness, Altamira described conditions in Spain as "detestable."[10] The universities suffered from politics and bureaucracy, and the lower schools from dry rot. The state of the archives and libraries was discouraging to scholarly enterprises. In the case of history-teaching, students were fed mischievous legends long discarded by specialists and were compelled to memorize passages of rhetorical beauty. Textbooks embalmed absurd myths which misinformed Spaniards and antagonized foreigners. Furthermore, Altamira complained, there was in existence no creditable book on the history of Spanish civilization. He called for such a work—a lucid, accurate survey primarily for students and the general public but also acceptable to scholars. And, he stipulated, only a Spaniard who was saturated with the spirit of the past was adequately qualified for the task.[11] One may well conjecture that he had himself in mind.

To remedy those shortcomings in Spanish education Altamira worked indefatigably during much of his lifetime. From his university days on he published articles and books on pedagogy, expounded his liberal ideas in lectures, and participated in international congresses.[12] As secretary of the pedagogical museum from 1889 until 1897, he was active in educational reform work and in the campaign to overcome the blight of illiteracy. When he went to Oviedo as a professor of history he instituted the seminar method and carried out other favorite ideas that brought student and teacher into co-operative research. More spectacular was his foundation of the university extension, by means of which the assumed blessings of enlightenment were carried to the unlettered workmen of Asturias and Santander. When he held the post of director-general of primary teaching from 1911 to 1913, Altamira energetically pushed his program for revitalizing the system of public education. Academic duties, he preached, were national duties.[13] As for the history book of Spanish civilization, whose absence he had lamented, that, too, was to be provided by the active professor at Oviedo.

Altamira attained full stature as a historian-patriot of national importance after the disastrous events of 1898. In that year the catastrophic defeat suffered by Spain at the hands of the United States spoke with crashing eloquence of the decadence and isolation of the peninsular kingdom. Many of the intellectuals were jolted into patriotic introspection, and out of the prevailing despondency they undertook to bring about a national renaissance. This so-called "generation" of 1898 proposed to borrow selectively from other civilizations, to look into the Spanish past for instruction, and, by means of stimulating artistic activity, to rejuvenate the genius of Spain. Much of the literature they produced was devoted to a searching analysis of the spirit of the people and the potentialities of the national character. The humili-

ating defeat of 1898 had wrenched Altamira's soul,[14] and he
joined this movement, which to some extent he had anticipated—
his role to be that of a historian who resurrected the achievements of the past in order to counteract discouragement as to the
future.

His chief production in the ensuing patriotic campaign was a
collection of essays mistitled *Psicología del pueblo español*, the purpose of which was to discover whether or not Spain still possessed
a "right to life."[15] As befitted a "scientific" historian, Altamira
concentrated much less on a psychological appraisal of the people than on the effect of historical evolution. Analyzing the
Hispanophobe writings of the past, he was astonished at the
strength of the legends that blackened the Spanish name with
acts of cruelty and bigotry. More than ever he was convinced
that both native and foreign historians had perpetuated fables
that imbued in Spaniards grotesque notions of the factors in the
past which had brought them to their present state. The decadence of Spain he considered the result not of temperamental
weakness but of misguided economic activities.[16] In addition, unfortunate distractions at critical moments had ruinously dispersed
national energy and had thus accelerated the decline.[17] Certainly there was nothing deficient in Spanish cultural and intellectual contributions, although the driving force that had once
dominated Europe and subdued a new world had almost dried
up. The burden of the message of *Psicología del pueblo español* was
that a survey of the past indicated that Spain's national character
was wholesome, that she was still capable of greatness.

While he often labeled himself a patriot, Altamira was no ego-
tistical nationalist, disdainful of other lands and aggressively
proud of his own. On the contrary, he was a pacifist who believed
that each people should be free to cultivate its own distinctive
note in the concert of civilization. He once translated Fichte's
Reden an die deutsche Nation in the hope that the German philosopher's appeal would stir the Spanish as it had the Prussians a century before, but he was careful to reject the militaristic-imperial-
istic implications of the work.[18] Misoneism and flamboyant pa-

triotism were repugnant to him. His "patriotic campaign," a strand of varied interests manifest throughout his career, consisted only of the harmless desire to arouse the Spanish to the value of foreign ideas and to inspire them with their truly remarkable accomplishments in the past.

Altamira's historical writing was rarely disfigured by undue attributions to Spain, and he was not a genuine nationalistic historian. If he presumed to edify his countrymen with an abstract of their civilized existence, it was not to flatter them. Nor did he expect to discover ironclad principles of conduct in the past. Rather, he hoped to correct misconceptions in the national self-consciousness and to lay the foundation of the future on the basis of earlier achievements. The Spanish people were geared to a psychology of failure after the 1898 debacle, and the hopeful historian believed most firmly that the work of regeneration could not proceed until credit had been restored to their history.[19] To be sure, he had once complained that no scholarly book for this purpose was available, but at last he was ready to fill the need.

Altamira's preparations for a history of Spanish civilization gathered momentum during the depth of the malaise following the events of 1898. His original impulse was admittedly didactic, but soon fascination with the work was alone enough to impel him to continue.[20] The task was indeed formidable, however compelling his inspiration, for it was difficult enough in any case to clear the way in cultural and social history. In Spain, however, the chaotic state of archives and libraries made the obstacles all the more forbidding. Vital monographs on certain important phases of history were lacking, thus necessitating a large amount of investigation on his part. Hallowed national legends cluttered his path, to mislead him if they were accepted and to haunt him if he passed them over. Apparently he did without the aid of research assistants and collaborators. And the work was carried on during years when duties as a professor, publicist, and man-of-letters diverted the full force of his energy.

His qualifications for the undertaking were likewise imposing. He was familiar with the latest aids in methodology employed by foreign historians, and he had read widely in history in addition to his various bits of research. His breadth of information and his vast capacity for assimilating data were refined by a solid wisdom. That Altamira was not exclusively a professional historian was probably advantageous. for he brought to the task the perspective and originality of a man of extensive interests. Thus he was enabled to treat widely varied aspects of history intelligently, if not with equal authority.

The first volume of Altamira's *Historia de España y de la civilización española* was published in 1900. A distinctive work, it traced the evolution of Spain from primitive times through the middle ages. The reception of this volume on the part of specialists in history was enthusiastic, and he was urged to continue the work.[21] Yet in the preface he had disclaimed any pretensions that it was erudite or exhaustive; he modestly presented it as a manual for use in secondary schools and for the general public. The second volume, completing the period of Ferdinand and Isabella, appeared in 1902. The third and longest, published in 1906, was originally intended to bring the work to a close, but it only finished up the reign of the House of Austria. Other activities and fatigue because of the colossal labor involved delayed the final volume until 1911.[22] With it the narrative terminated at the year 1808.

Altamira declined to treat recent history in this set because the sources were too overwhelming,[23] certainly not because he hesitated to touch contemporary subjects. Since he could not be prevailed upon to carry this particular study down to the present, it was eventually done by another historian.[24] In the course of three decades it was corrected, revised, and sent through two more editions. Condensations of it were published in several languages, the English version becoming available in 1918 with Professor Charles E. Chapman's *A history of Spain*, based on Altamira's four volumes. The *Historia de España* was the most famous production of Spanish historical scholarship abroad at the time; more than twenty years passed before it came to be superseded in part by the more elaborate work of Antonio Ballesteros.[25] In Spain its renown was such that an editor could justly refer to it as a national enterprise.[26]

The organic concept of Spanish civilization and the hierarchy of organization indicated Altamira's almost uniform mastery of the field. The work was nearly mathematically proportioned; and the aims of simplicity, factual presentation, and cautious interpretation were evident throughout. Significantly enough, the first sentence announced that Spain was located on a peninsula in the extreme southwest of Europe. In such an elementary and clear fashion the history of Spain until the chosen termination point of 1808 was subjected to close scrutiny. Political and diplomatic events were treated dutifully at the beginning of each period, but without the details usually lavished on them by the earlier historians. Then the little essays on the manifold topics ensued. Usually they were generalizations of monographs, although in many cases Altamira had extracted new and instructive facts in his own investigations. Such varied phases of a civilization as law, society, institutions, military establishments, women, education, subject peoples, ecclesiastical affairs, commerce, art, industry, philosophy, architecture, scholarship, and many others were illuminated with skill. By no means were they discussed as incidental to the course of civilization; instead they were given ample sections of each volume.

Although most of the work was purely descriptive, the author ventured to set forth guiding interpretations. They were not obtrusive, however, for Altamira endeavored to achieve his effect by piling facts upon facts until the general lines were, or should be, obvious. The details he amassed tended to indicate his position on the Romanization of Spain, the role of the Visigoths, the importance of the municipalities, the expulsion of the Jews, and the activities of the Catholic Inquisition—all controversial issues among historians at that time. A prominence unorthodox in a Spanish history was given to the achievements of the Moors and Arabs. The chapters on the middle ages threw light into many a dim corner, while ancient myths were ignored or relegated disdainfully to their proper niche. In handling the history of the church, Altamira was objective and frank; he was prudent enough to document the shortcomings he described. He broke tradition in granting considerable space to economic matters, but he did not often interpret the past according to the materialistic view. Other innovations in the work were the adequate consideration devoted to the colonial empire and the refreshingly indulgent treatment of French influence in eighteenth-century Spain. Himself a man of enthusiasm, Altamira could narrate the exploits of others with sympathy. He had a gift for portraying the opinions and actions of individuals, no matter how unpopular as historical characters, in their setting, with the result that their attitudes were shown as comprehensible or even inevitable.

From flaws his set was by no means exempt. This grandiose synthesis of hundreds of aspects of Spanish history was naturally subject to errors of detail and inference. Painstaking though he was, Altamira was far from being an expert in all the ages he studied. His discussion of the Moorish period in particular was later deemed deficient.[27] He treated political and military history sketchily, if not contemptuously. On the other hand, the descriptions of the various topics in each period in every region of the Spanish possessions were at times repetitious and encyclopedic. He reached no happy solution of the problems involved in listing the illustrious men of science and literature, and some sections were only catalogues of names. And perhaps too often he speculated on might-have-beens at critical junctures in the past.

Altamira's circle of admirers widened as each volume of his *Historia de España* appeared. His work won the warm approval of his countrymen, although certain ecclesiastics and aristocrats found parts of it displeasing. His conscience as a historian could be amply satisfied, for modern methods of style, organization, and criticism had been observed. The various themes of Spanish history had been correlated with one another and treated as evolutionary forces, in accordance with the dictum he had once laid down in *La enseñanza de la historia*. Furthermore, his liberal political and religious prejudices were rarely offensive to objective students; neither diatribes nor eulogies had a place in his work. In spite of his much advertised patriotism, the sober pages seldom smacked of nationalistic distortion of the truth. The educator in Altamira could well regard the set as a success, for it was filled with cross-references and other teaching aids for the benefit of students. He could hardly be disappointed if his volumes had surpassed their mere pedagogical aim and had become a famous work of history. And yet the *Historia de España* surprisingly approached failure in one respect. In presenting a "scientific" book of history, replete with details, Altamira was too confident that it would suggest its own conclusions, and he neglected to write large in order to emphasize the broad lines of development. Its effect in guiding the Spanish nation in the tradition of its past was diminishing by the author's evident apprehension that he should appear to be shouting.

Another of Rafael Altamira's chief interests in life has been the Pan-Hispanic movement for the furtherance of greater intimacy between Spain and her estranged daughters in the western hemisphere. His association with it dates back to 1895, and in subsequent years he has been active as a historian and publicist in its promotion. The animosity borne by the Spanish-speaking nations of the new world toward the mother-country was, he was early convinced, in large part the product of fancied historical grievances.[28] Even in the peninsula it was fashionable for liberals to vilify the work of Spain in colonization. Irritated at this persistence of the "black legend," he attempted to set the record as straight as possible in the *Historia de España*. This work was, as he once noted with pride,[29] one of the first books of national history to consider the colonial empire as an integral part of Spanish civilization, and Altamira was among the earliest of the leftist writers to vindicate the imperial achievements of his country. Although his sections devoted to the new world in the *Historia de España* were compendious, they served to inter many a poisonous legend of Spanish misgovernment and cruelty.

His researches in Hispanic-American history were otherwise not significant. But he dedicated much effort to making source material available for the use of other scholars. He compiled a bibliography of colonial history[30] and published a large collection of constitutions and texts of legislation.[31] Always desirous of raising standards, he cautioned historians against the indiscriminate use of the old chronicles as source material of equal value,[32] and late in life he accepted the responsibility of directing the edition of documents and monographs for the history of Spanish America.

Convinced, as he was, that Spain's colonial record had been great and creditable, Altamira made known the possibilities of the harvest and recruited scholars to gather it. In an address to the American Historical Association, for example, he dwelt upon the superficial nature of historical studies of the field and called attention to the rich and almost undisturbed archives of the Indies at Seville.[33] While he held the chair of professor of the civil and political institutions of America at the University of Madrid he directed his students in ambitious research projects in Hispanic-American history. It seems likely, however, that some of Altamira's disciples carried a surplus of patriotism into their work, for too often recent Spanish scholars have mistaken the letter of legislation in behalf of the colonies for its fulfilment. When foreign historians published books on Spanish imperial history they received a cordial salute from the "restorer" of the history of Spain. Not only did their findings contribute to the fund of historical information, but his beloved *patria* usually emerged with a cleaner reputation.

Regarding Latin America as a proving-ground where the Spanish people were demonstrating their vitality anew,[34] Altamira was full of projects to stimulate the intellectual communion of Spaniards on both sides of the Atlantic. He was long a publicist for the Pan-Hispanic movement, and in 1908 he was entrusted with an important good-will mission to learned groups in the western hemisphere. His receptions as he lectured in Argentina, Uruguay, Chile, Peru, Mexico, and Cuba were flattering,[35] and his tour was considered a spectacular success for Pan-Hispanism. In the first years of his propagandist career he restricted the aims of the movement to a spiritual reconquest of the former empire.

But encouraging results in that direction later led him to sponsor diverse political and economic arrangements to solidify the Spanish-speaking world.[36] While this work was not out of harmony with his ideal of a historian who was at the same time an active patriot, his ardor was somewhat unrestrained, and his writings were unworthy of his scholarly gifts.

Altamira's erudite production in legal history was far more substantial than his Hispanic-American studies, and his works brought him great prestige as a jurist. More often than not his professorial duties were concerned with the history of law and institutions. He was elected president of international juridical societies, he served as arbitrator for the government in labor disputes, and he won awards for his research. The crowning honor came in 1920, when he was commissioned, along with other distinguished jurists, by the Council of the League of Nations to draw up a plan for the Permanent Court of International Justice. Having publicized the Allied cause in Spain during the war of 1914–18,[37] he was now moderately optimistic about the potentialities of world-peace machinery.[38] For some years after 1922 he was a judge on the Permanent Court of International Justice at The Hague.

His doctoral dissertation, *La historia de la propiedad comunal*, marked Altamira as a member of the illustrious liberal school of Spanish jurists. His research was thorough, his enunciation of legal ideas bold. From the first he hoped to demolish illusions that institutions were not mutable,[39] and he skilfully, though hurriedly, traced the evolution of common property through the centuries. While teaching at the University of Oviedo, he published various bits of research in articles and a preliminary study of the history of law.[40] An attractive monograph on the life and customs in his natal region of Alicante won a prize from the Academy of Political and Moral Sciences.[41] A work published under the title of *Cuestiones de historia del derecho y de legislación comparada*, containing summaries of his own lecture courses and a survey of Spanish law, was warmly approved by foreign scholars.[42] In the *Historia de España* the recurring themes of jurisprudence in the different periods of Spanish history were discussed with a fulness that bordered on emphasis. Altamira's treatment of legal history was distinctive at the time for his conception of law as a vital expression of national life springing from social requirements.

Long a steadfast upholder of scientific methodology in historical research, Altamira struggled to improve Spanish standards through his own teaching and writings. His smaller historical works attested to his own observance of refined critical methods. He even went to the extreme of conducting lengthy battles for authority among sources in the very pages of his early studies. The *Historia de España* was primarily a work of generalization, and footnote citations to sources were not employed. But documents were inserted in the text when the author seemed to anticipate that verification of his points would be required. Customs and institutions were considered along with documents as relics of historical significance. At the end of the last volume was a bibliography which, in spite of its brevity and the modest value he placed on it,[43] was for years a leading guide to the materials of the history of Spain. His other bibliographical articles and collections were valuable to students, but he was not able to fill his early aspiration for an exhaustive study of the sources of Spanish history.[44]

Possibly as a result of his reaction against the rhetorical and philosophical sallies of the older historians, Altamira's literary style was factual and subdued. His first works were made disagreeable by involved sentences, some of them more than two hundred words long. But his skill increased with practice, and by the time he composed the *Historia de España* his style was lucid and his arrangement logical. He did not often attain eloquence, but neither was his effectiveness vitiated by a self-conscious striving for effect. Unadorned and straightforward, his literary technique also was governed by standards of common sense and good taste.

Altamira declared in his first book that historical research had its own finality independent of application in the present,[45] but in many of his works he admitted a preoccupation with contemporary affairs. He never weakened in his stand that solutions of modern questions could assuredly be suggested by a scientific scrutiny of experience;[46] historical studies were an erudite pastime if they did not serve to guide humanity in the light of its past development. For a consciousness of history was imbedded in the minds of men. They often turned to it for precedents and records of experience, which affected, if they did not actually direct, social and national opinion. Thus it was essential, Altamira urged in his inaugural address to the Real Academia de la Historia, to narrow the chasm between the information of the specialists and the impressions of the public.[47]

The position of the historian in his own age was therefore one of great influence, for his publications helped to shape the course of events in the present and in the future. Altamira was convinced that behind the research of the historian, whether he always realized it or not, lay the yearning to discover the best means of improving humanity.[48] These he was more likely to strike if he worked the mine of all-embracing history of civilization. Once he had fitted the minuscule fragments of the past into a comprehensible picture, he should present it in simple form so that even the uncultured could participate in the maintenance of the traditional spirit. As exemplified by his lifelong activities and his nearly sixty volumes of writings, Altamira's own career was in keeping with that conception. Not only did he preach to his colleagues that the historian was a man of great moral and political responsibility,[49] but he himself took quite seriously his role as a guide to his fellow-men in everyday affairs.

In speaking upon one occasion of the philosophy of history,[50] Altamira posited questions as to whether there was an end toward which humanity was moving blindly, perhaps directed by something transcendental to itself. He complained that most historians had dodged the true problems of philosophy, but he did not attempt to formulate a system of speculation to define and predict the course of mankind. That there was an eternal striving toward liberty, sincerity, and justice he did once affirm,[51] and in the substratum of his history of Spanish civilization this vein can be detected. But he hesitated to inquire whether these long-ings tended to triumph in conflicts with opposing forces for fear, he said, that the answer would be in the negative.[52] Progress in its highest form he considered the awakening of humanity to the idealistic qualities behind its actions, and the experience of history demonstrated that such progress had been made—but only in certain features.[53] For the element of evil was still undominated and defiant in such moral aberrations as envy, anger, cupidity, ambition, and the craving for luxury. In spite of a "clamor for the ethical basis to life, a demand for the reign of justice in the sphere of jurisprudence, of the good in the sphere of morality,"[54] he doubted that men could purge themselves of those natural impulses.

As Altamira entered old age his impressive range of activities hardly diminished. He labored at revising his prolific writings and publishing them in a set of *obras completas*. He continued to direct students in historical research and to publicize his various causes. An eminent historian of world-wide reputation, he was invited to give courses at such European universities as Cambridge, Oxford, London, Brussels, the Sorbonne, the Collège de France, and in Spanish intellectual centers, where he was always a prized guest. Having addressed learned audiences both in the United States and in Latin America, he was well known in the New World as an inspiring and brilliant orator. His very appearance and personality were in keeping with the distinguished position he held in scholarly circles. Tall, erect, slender, and handsome, he typified Spanish dignity. He was respected for his character and for his unswerving idealism; and, with it all, he was unassuming, kindly, and beloved of his friends.

In a lecture delivered in the United States in 1912 the historian of Spanish civilization expressed pessimism concerning the future of human civilization in general. His contemplation of the past had stirred him with the victory of man over nature and the consequent betterment of certain social and material aspects of life. But, he mused, might not all these advances be "doomed to immolation before a sudden metamorphosis of human thought and opinion"—illogical, perhaps, but not unprecedented?[55] Between the enormous disproportion in achievements in the material order and those of the ethical there lay spirit-chilling perils. And, he added, "who can escape the bitter confession that moral development is still exiguous, that customs are not improving all around, and that the higher ethical doctrines remain untranslated into action in the practical life of the majority?"[56]

Rafael Altamira witnessed events in his later years that may have justified in his mind those forebodings. In common with men great and humble the world over, he saw the aspirations he cherished for humanity frustrated. If the spread of public education and the popular diffusion of history had results, they could scarcely have been those he had anticipated. His ideal Spain appeared on the stage in 1931, but it perished in agony soon after making its bow. The Pan-Hispanic movement of which he had been a guiding spirit altered its temper and aggressively increased its aims. Having labored in international peace arrangements and proclaimed the conciliation of peoples, he saw his efforts mocked as the world again plunged down the cascades to war.

Futile as Altamira's designs for his contemporary world may have proved, his work as a historian has a lasting value. His books were profoundly influential in clarifying the national traditions of Spain, and his career was a boon to Spanish scholarship. Even with the corrosion that the passing of time and new findings wreak on the authority of the facts and interpretations he set forth, his books form a general structure of knowledge that is hardly weakened. History he wrote, taught, and even preached. Not often in recent times has its value been affirmed with more spirited consistency than it has by Rafael Altamira.

NOTES

1. *Diccionario enciclopédico hispano-americano de literatura, ciencias, y artes* (28 vols.; Barcelona, 1887–99), XXIV, 125.

2. *Revue hispanique*, I (1894), 214

3. *Arte y realidad* (Barcelona, 1921), p. 10.

4. Prologue of Leopoldo Alas in *Mi primera campaña* (Madrid, 1893), p. x.

5. *De historia y arte*, p. 252.

6. *RH*, XLVIII (1891), 450, and *AHR*, I (1896), 316–18.

7. *La enseñanza de la historia*, p. 11.

8. *Ibid.*, pp. 370–71.

9. *Ibid.*, pp. 413–16.

10. *Ibid.*, p. 457.

11. *Ibid.*, pp. 350–51.

12. *Enciclopedia universal ilustrada europeo-americana* (Apéndice, 10 vols.; Barcelona, 1930–33), I, 418–20.

13. *Psicología del pueblo español*, p. 196.

14. *Ibid.*, p. 11.

15. *Ibid.*, p. 13.

16. *Ibid.*, p. 127.

17. *Ibid.*, p. 129.

18. *Ibid.*, p. 11.

19. *Ibid.*, p. 139.

20. *Manuel de historia de España* (Madrid, 1934), preface, p. 18.

21. *RH*, LXXXVII (1904), 156–58, and *Revista crítica de historia y literatura*, V (1900), 382–85.

22. Reviews by Desdevises du Dezert, in *RH*, CIX (1912), 158–63, and in *Revue hispanique*, VI (1900), 522–25, and IX (1902), 528–32.

23. *Historia de España y de la civilización española*, III, 741–42 (advertencia).

24. Pío Zabala y Lera, *Historia de España y de la civilización española*, Vol. V (Barcelona, 1930).

25. *Historia de España y de su influencia en la historia universal* (8 vols.; Barcelona, 1918–34).

26. Zabala, editor's note.

27. *AHR*, XXIV (1919), 720–21.

28. *La huella de España en América* (Madrid, 1924), p. 14.

29. *Escritos patrióticos* (Madrid, 1929), p. 75.

30. *Bibliographie d'histoire coloniale (1900–30): Espagne* (Paris, 1932).

31. *Constituciones vigentes ... y colección de textos para el estudio de la historia de las instituciones de América* (5 vols.; Madrid, 1926).

32. *La huella de España en América*, p. 57.

33. *AHR*, XV (1910), 476.

34. *La huella de España en América*, p. 44.

35. *Mi viaje a América* (Madrid, 1911).

36. His other chief books of this nature are *Cuestiones hispano-americanos* (Madrid, 1900), *España en América* (Valencia, 1908), *España y el programa americanista* (Madrid, 1917), *La política de España en América* (Valencia, 1921), and *Ultimos escritos americanistas* (Madrid, 1929).

37. *La guerra actual y la opinión española* (Barcelona, 1915).

38. *La sociedad de las naciones y el proyecto del tribunal permanente de justicia internacional* (Madrid, 1920).

39. P. 36.

40. *Historia de derecho español: cuestiones preliminares* (Madrid, 1903).

41. *Derecho consuetudinario y economía popular de la provincia de Alicante* (Madrid, 1905).

42. *RH*, CXVIII (1915), 375–76, and *AHR*, XX (1914), 185–86.

43. *Historia de España*, IV, 457.

44. Preface of R. Altamira to B. Alonso Sánchez, *Fuentes de la historia española* (Madrid, 1919).

45. *Historia de la propiedad comunal*, p. 36.

46. *De historia y arte*, p. 165.

47. *Cuestiones modernas de historia*, p. 163.

48. "The theory of civilization," *Rice Institute pamphlet* (Houston, Texas, 1915), III, 282.

49. *AHR*, XXI (1915), 10.

50. "The problem of the philosophy of history," *Rice Institute pamphlet*, III, 256–78.

51. "Philippe II d'Espagne," *Hommes d'état* (3 vols.; Paris, 1937), II, 513.

52. *La huella de España en América*, p. 207.

53. "The theory of civilization," *loc. cit.*, p. 307.

54. *Ibid.*, p. 311.

55. *Ibid.*, pp. 297–98.

56. *Ibid.*, pp. 299–300.

II

SIR WILLIAM ASHLEY (1860–1927)

JANET L. MacDONALD*

THE extensive development of graduate study in this country during the past half-century has vastly increased the amount of formal training available, the facilities for research, and the extent of information in each special field; but it has, perhaps unconsciously and certainly unfortunately, tended to minimize the importance of teaching. The great majority of graduate students spend the rest of their lives teaching, but many of them do so with the conviction that the time spent on this and on administrative work is time lost, and that research—too often with no specifications as to its nature or importance—is the only worthy occupation for a scholar. To those who believe this, the career of William James Ashley must appear as a melancholy warning. Some of Ashley's historical work represents the results of original research, but more is based on recognized secondary authorities or is a synthesis of the writings of other scholars, and the first decade of his maturity gave promise of a greater scholarly future than he ever achieved. He never completed his most important historical work, *Introduction to English economic history and theory*. Almost forty years lie between the publication of its first volume in 1888 and the appearance in 1927 of *The bread of our forefathers*, and, with the exception of the publication of the second volume of the *Introduction* in 1893, nothing appeared during these years which was the result of original research into any considerable aspect of history. His importance as a historian rests, therefore, not so much on the originality of what he wrote as on the originality of the field in which he worked and of the method which he employed.

* Assistant professor of history, Hollins College.

20

He was one of the greatest and one of the most determined advocates of the study of economic history, a study so unrecognized when he was a young tutor that he himself said that when he began to talk about Gustav von Schmoller, "I suspect some of my friends almost supposed I had invented him." A tremendous amount of his time and energy went to gaining recognition for the importance and intrinsic merit of the field of economic history, and it was over thirty years before he could say thankfully that "the study of specifically economic history is no longer an individual eccentricity, calling almost for an apology."[1]

His interest in a new field led him to participate in that time-consuming academic activity, curriculum reform. "He three times (at Toronto, Harvard and Birmingham) created so new an academic department that he had to begin by explaining his conception of the meaning of his subject."[2] From 1888 to 1892 he was professor of political economy and constitutional history in the University of Toronto, and he took an active interest not only in the administration of his department but also in Canadian politics. In 1892 he became the first professor of economic history at Harvard University; and when, in 1900, he accepted an invitation to become chairman of the faculty of commerce in the new University of Birmingham, he had to devote the major share of his energy and intellect to the development of a new type of education and to an enlargement of his statements as to the nature of economic history, rather than to scholarly research. Yet nothing is more certain than that Ashley, himself, never regretted this work, and this very lack of regret throws an interesting light on the man and on his attitude toward historical research.

William James Ashley was not descended from the class which usually produced university tutors. He was born in London in 1860, and his father, James Ashley, was a journeyman hatter, a skilled artisan who plied his trade with difficulty in an age of mechanized industry. A family background of hard work, economic insecurity, and puritanism contributed two elements to the son's personality which remained important throughout his life: one was his keen sense of the reality of economic problems, and the other was his conviction of the existence of spiritual realities. A young man whose father was threatened with loss of work because of the use of machines was not likely to be unaware of the problems of the displacement and mobility of labor. Consequently, the opinions in regard to the "laboring classes" held by many of his academic associates seemed artificial to him:

> When a distinguished Oxford tutor long ago . . . . began to talk . . . . about the "Proletariate" it was remarked that his knowledge of the "Proletariate" was derived exclusively from the observation of his college scout. I have sometimes thought of late that the notions of the labouring classes entertained by the barristers who write for the papers are derived from their contemplation of the laundresses in their chambers.[3]

From the evangelical and puritanical background of his home he derived not a rigid code of conduct but a lasting conviction of the existence of ultimate good and of a purpose in the universe. He grew up in a family which took for granted the supreme reality and importance of spiritual values, and he remained a man "to whom the reality and supremacy over all others of ethical and social issues was almost an axiom of thought which he was incapable of doubting."[4] As a result, he made a continual effort to use his knowledge in the service of society, and he was convinced that such service was the duty not only of the Christian but also of the scholar. In the last years of his life a number of his addresses were collected and published under the title *The Christian outlook: sermons of an economist*,[5] in which he refers with feeling to the necessity for a union of expert knowledge with a desire to serve mankind. But for all that, he had too realistic and too active a mind to be attracted by purely emotional humanitarianism. Speaking on the text, "Seek ye first the Kingdom of God," he said:

> A glow of emotion, a warm feeling inside one, a moist eye as social ideals rise before our imaginations, these are not "seeking." "Seeking" is a toilsome, and it may be, a long endeavor of brain as well as of heart. . . . . The union of knowledge with an active regard for the well-being of our fellows is the most difficult of human ideals.[6]

Ashley was educated at two small private schools—a Wesleyan elementary school and St. Olave's Grammar School in South-wark. In the latter, but largely without the assistance of its masters, he prepared himself for the examination for the Brackenbury scholarship at Balliol. It was at this time that he attended a series of lectures on the Stuart period given by S. R. Gardiner, "one of the few saints among historians." His first attempt for the scholarship was unsuccessful, but with assistance from St. Olave's and from a parochial trust he went up to Oxford in the fall of 1878 and entered St. Edmund's Hall, where he remained until, having won the Brackenbury in November, 1878, he entered Balliol.

As a student, Ashley was painstaking and thorough, so much so that one of his tutors, James Franck Bright, was moved to remark: "You needn't go back to protoplasm, Ashley." In 1881 he took a first class in history and for the next four years lived in Oxford, in the most straitened circumstances, as coach and tutor. Without money, without family influence, without social experience and poise, he made four unsuccessful attempts to secure a fellowship at one of the colleges. Not until 1885, when he was elected a fellow of Lincoln College, was he able to enter his chosen profession.

In later years he himself said that the greatest influences on his historical study had been Bishop Stubbs, whom he knew only through his books; Arnold Toynbee, whose lectures he attended at Oxford; and Gustav von Schmoller, with whose work he became acquainted on visits to Germany in 1880, 1883, and 1884. Twenty years later he described to an Oxford audience how his academic life found its direction under the guidance of Toynbee and how he had

listened . . . . to Toynbee's lectures on the Industrial Revolution, and how that slim, graceful figure seemed to tremble and his hands were nervously strained together, as he tried to make us realize how vast and awful a revolution it had been.[7]

When he approached Toynbee for permission to attend his lectures, the latter advised Ashley to take some one problem (i.e., wages) and, beginning with Adam Smith, read each of the classical economists on that subject and try to discover how and *why* the theory in regard to it had changed. It was this emphasis on the why that turned Ashley away from what he came to consider the arid field of economic theory to the fertile field of economic history. "In these talks he first came to see that economic doctrine could be studied historically and first encountered the dynamic as contrasted with the static view of economic theory and fact."[8]

Schmoller furnished the method for the studies which Toynbee had inspired. From him Ashley learned to combine "unceasing investigation of detail with the sacred and undying passion for generalization." Something of the meticulousness of German scholarship is apparent in Ashley's lifelong insistence that historical generalizations could not be based on the interpretation of a few words or phrases but must rest on the evidence of all the sources. In dedicating to Schmoller his *Surveys: historic and economic*, Ashley wrote: "I have received more stimulus and encouragement from your writings than from those of any other; encouragement in the effort, which academic and popular opinion renders so difficult, to be an economist without ceasing to be an historian."[9]

To the study of economic history Ashley brought not only the precepts of Toynbee, the method of Schmoller, and the practical sense of reality which his background gave to all economic problems but also certain personal convictions with regard to the prevailing theories of his time. In general, he distrusted all theories; they were too simple, too perfect, or too unreal; therefore, he was not swept away by any of the intellectual faiths of the nineteenth century. His belief in evolution was tempered by his belief in ultimate goodness; to him evolution meant change, but change for the better. He held this conviction unconsciously but so strongly that, in his daughter's opinion, it made it impossible for him to accept the theory that the manorial system had originated in a free village community, because he could not believe that a free community could ever have sunk into serfdom. He found a certain amount of truth in Karl Marx, but he believed that Marx's theory of value was wrong and that the evolution of social and economic institutions had been and would continue to be much slower and more complex than Marx taught. Future changes in the structure of society would come about not solely through class warfare but through certain practices of private industry, notably concentration of ownership and management, and through the assumption of new functions by the government. He was unconvinced of the soundness of economic determinism; just as he could not accept for all towns and all manors the mark or the free village community theories, so he maintained that he had "yet to see any considerable part of the history of mankind explained as the exclusive result of material conditions."[10] Trade-unionism won his ardent and consistent support and influenced his attitude toward contemporary economic problems. Because of this, he was opposed to all schemes of profit-sharing and believed that any increased profits of industry should be passed on to labor in the form of a general increase in wages.[11]

He was never an adherent of any school of history—such an allegiance would have been impossible for a man with his distrust of theories—but before he left Oxford he was clear in his own mind as to why he had chosen to study economic history and as to what method he intended to use.

The more one reads, the more one distrusts the picturesque. I won't deny there is such a thing—but there is vastly less of it, and it is of a very different sort, than is usually imagined. I care for history and economic history in particular, because it tells me of the life of the people. . . . . One is bound constantly to generalize; to try to discover the *meaning* of institutions, their growth and decay, their relation to one another. And thus one gets into the way of regarding the whole of human history as having a meaning, as not being purposeless, as moving to some goal. . . . . Therefore, it seems to me that the work of the *Economist* should be, (i) the investigation of economic history—no facts are too remote to be without significance for the present . . . . and (ii) the examination of modern industrial life *in the piece*. We can leave to the Cambridge people hair-splitting analysis of abstract doctrine.[12]

This conception of his task was amplified by his later work and writings, but it was never modified in substance.

The greater part of Ashley's historical work was done between 1881 and 1900. His first published work was an essay on *James and Philip van Artevelde*,[13] which won the Lothian prize in 1882; it was followed by an article on "Feudalism" contributed to *Essays introductory to the study of English constitutional history*,[14] *The early history of the English woollen industry*,[15] and the completion of Part I, *The middle ages*,[16] of his *Introduction to English economic history and theory*. These works, together with an introduction to Mrs. Ashley's translation of Fustel de Coulanges' *The origin of property in land*,[17] with Part II, *The end of the middle ages*[18] of the *Introduction*, and with *Surveys: historic and economic*,[19] which were published during his years at Harvard, constitute his chief historical writings, present his beliefs in regard to the middle ages, and illustrate his historical method.

James and Philip van Artevelde is important largely as his first essay in medieval history. Eighteen years later, in a review of Henri Pirenne's *Geschichte Belgiens*, Ashley was obviously amused to "revive the recollections of my own juvenile and wooden performance" and to observe "how trustfully I followed in 1882 the leading of Georg von Maurer and . . . . found the germs of the later town system in an imaginary mark-community."[20] His knowledge of the sources of medieval history is shown not only by the essay "Feudalism" but also by *Edward III and his wars, 1327–1360*,[21] a small volume of selections from Froissart, Jehan le Bel, Knighton, Adam of Murimuth, and Robert of Avesbury.

It is, however, on *An introduction to English economic history and theory* that Ashley's reputation as a scholar rests. Actually, the title represents a hope rather than an accomplishment, because only Parts I and II of the first volume of what Ashley designed to be a complete economic history were ever published, and even these omit a discussion of certain topics. The study had been inspired by "the idea of an orderly evolution of society . . . . which . . . . had the effect of opening to the economist undreamt-of perspectives of the past and the future." Although Ashley was never an adherent of any particular school of history, he had his articles of faith nonetheless, and he states his position clearly in the preface to the *Introduction*. Political economy was a body not of absolutely true doctrines but of more or less valuable theories and generalizations, and the science was not born fully armed from the brain of Adam Smith but had varied with every age. Consequently, theories and institutions of the past must be judged in relation to the past. "Modern economic theories are, therefore, not universally true; they are true neither for the past, when the conditions they postulate did not exist, nor for the future, when, unless society becomes stationary, the conditions will have changed." From this dogma he derives not only his treatment of economic history but also his disagreement with the classical economists and with all those who would find "laws" for economic life.

The treatment of the subject matter in the *Introduction* is topical rather than chronological; certain periods are dealt with in greater detail than others; and some of the chapters are summaries of the work of English or continental scholars, while others represent the results of Ashley's own work. The first volume discusses the origin of medieval land tenure and of town life and describes the economic theory and legislation of the age. Ashley was a determined opponent of those who found the origin of the manor in a free village community. The free tenants of the later middle ages were not survivals of an earlier system of free ownership but originated in the elevation of the villeins as a result of the enclosure and renting of portions of the waste and of the lord's demesne. This contention was reiterated and amplified in his introduction to Fustel de Coulanges' *Origin of property in land*. He applied Fustel's criticisms of the general theory to England and concluded that "there is absolutely no clear documentary evidence for the free village community in England"; the theory was a product of the romanticism of the nineteenth century, which lauded the virtues of primitive society and which had satisfied, "during a period of democratic change," that "most unscientific but most English desire, the desire for precedent." Consequently, "an extension of the suffrage rose far above mere expediency when it became a reconquest of primitive rights."[22]

His position on the origin of towns and of the guild organizations in them was much less clear. He had surrendered his allegiance to the theory of Georg von Maurer that the towns were outgrowths of original free mark-communities, but he advanced no new explanation; rather, he was content to warn students that no one theory would fit all European towns, that later documents could not be used to prove the existence of similar conditions in earlier centuries, and that, above all, the question must be studied in the light of all the documentary evidence and not on the basis of a few phrases in one or two documents.

> We may be sure . . . . that when we do arrive at a satisfactory explanation of the growth of medieval institutions, it will be based, not on an elaborate interpretation of three or four phrases, but on the unmistakable teaching of the whole current of our documentary evidence; and also that we cannot hope for an intelligible history, either of law or of constitutions, unless we can form to ourselves some sort of picture of the daily life of the men who lived under the law.[23]

Medieval economic theory and legislation was a reflection of the age and not a set of eternally true principles. The reasonableness of the "just price" had been obscured for modern economists by their theory of "value in use"—a concept which was foreign to the medieval mind. To the former, value was subjective; it was what each individual purchaser cared to give for a thing. To the medieval theorist it was something objective, outside the will of the individual purchaser or seller and attached to the thing itself.[24] Likewise, the opposition to usury could be partly explained by the fact that the conditions under which loans were contracted differed from those of today, and it found its ultimate justification in the teaching that "a man has not the right to do what he likes with his own." There was little opportunity for investment in the middle ages, and most loans were made in times of stress and protected by ample security; hence, Ashley, true to his belief that theories usually reflect contemporary conditions, found the medieval attitude reasonable.[25]

The scope and nature of the *Introduction* was considerably enlarged in Part II, and each topic was treated in greater detail, with a greater wealth of references to English sources. The major part of the book was the result of original research on town life, the craft guilds, the woolen industry, the agrarian revolution, and the relief of the poor. The final chapter, a summary of continental writing on the canon law, was typical of Ashley's work in bringing foreign research to the attention of English scholars.

In Ashley's opinion, never since the Norman conquest had English towns been entirely free from the rights of the crown, the church, or some noble. He traced in detail the relation of the merchant guilds and the city government, which he believed had in most places "already coalesced" by the fourteenth century, and the development of the craft guilds and their struggles with the city. A national economy began to appear in the fourteenth century, but there was no actual decline in the prosperity of the towns as a result of this; the frequent ordinances of the sixteenth century with regard to the destruction of tumble-down urban dwellings are a sign not of failing prosperity but of the fact that the wealthier merchants were improving their social position by the purchase of country estates rather than by building town houses.

The principal weakness of Ashley's analysis of the end of the middle ages lay in his inability to decide whether the fourteenth century was a period of relative prosperity or distress and what had been the effect of the Black Death and the Peasants' Revolt on the position of the urban and agricultural worker. His analysis of the decline of the craft guilds suffered because of this. The most valuable contribution to urban history was his discussion of the actual effect of the confiscation of the chantries in the sixteenth century. Their disendowment accelerated the decline of the crafts but did not destroy them because only the funds used for religious purposes were confiscated. He defends the guilds from the charge of oppressive regulations, pointing out that the rules were neither so oppressive as they seem to modern eyes nor so regularly enforced. At all events, "in the absence of a strong national government, the individual artisan or trader needed the support of an organized body to protect him against the violence of the powerful; and with protection necessarily went control."[26]

In discussing the agrarian revolution he attacked with vigor the theory that the Black Death and the Peasants' Revolt ended manorialism; the substitution of pasturage for tillage had been slowly taking place during the preceding century, and this evolution continued long after the fourteenth century. It was his firm belief, expressed here and elsewhere, that the villein had no legal security of tenure against his lord:

> From 1450 to 1550, enclosures meant to a large extent the actual dispossession of the customary tenants by their manorial lords. This took place, either in the form of the violent ousting of the sitting tenant, or of a refusal on the death of one tenant to admit the son.

This view was attacked by his contemporaries, and Ashley later admitted that the copyholder of the sixteenth century may have had some legal rights, but he did not change his position in regard to the customary tenants. He analyzed in detail the statements of Glanvill (d. 1190) and Littleton (1422–81) on the legal position of the villein and insisted that they all presented him as without *legal* rights no matter what his customary position may have been.

> The law as we find it in Coke, which does give the customary tenant a security of tenure, must be regarded as itself the product of the *Sturm und Drang* of the preceding century and a half. . . . . Until comparatively modern days, the cultivators of the soil were always in a condition of serfdom, and held their lands at the arbitrary will of their lords. For centuries the lord knew of no other way of getting his land cultivated and had no wish to get rid of a tenant . . . . custom tended to harden into law; and it was just on the point of becoming law, when a change in the economic situation, and the increasing advantage of pasture over tillage, prompted the lords to fall back on their old rights. Then followed a struggle between *a legal theory becoming obsolete*, but backed by the influence of the landowners, and *a custom on its way to become law*, backed by public sentiment and by the policy of the Government.[27]

The long chapter on the relief of the poor is rich in illustrations of medieval philanthropic policies, the effectiveness of which Ashley believed had been greatly exaggerated. The monasteries had given little actual relief, many of the thirds of tithes, which were supposed to be devoted to charity, having been diverted to other causes. Most relief was afforded by the "hospitals"—in reality, almshouses as well—by bequests in the wills of private individuals and by relief from craft guilds and fraternities. The apparent increase in poverty in the sixteenth century was due not to the disappearance of any or all of these but to a succession of bad harvests and to the agrarian revolution. The Elizabethan poor law provided no adequate remedy for this situation because, like all similar medieval legislation, it was based on the theory that reasonable employment existed, if laborers would take it; and it aimed at assuring an adequate supply of labor and eliminating mendicancy rather than at the relief of the poor. This attitude was not altered until, in the sixteenth century, towns like Ypres, Augsburg, and Strassburg accepted the provision of relief as a public duty.

In spite of the fact that this second volume represented far more original research than the previous one, there are still many gaps in the account; foreign trade is not mentioned, and many aspects of the fourteenth century are ignored. The great merit of the *Introduction* lies in the fact that it opened up a new field; it used with care and respect those sources with which the author was familiar, and it presented to English students, in a clear, simple, and unpretentious style, the results of continental scholarship. It was Ashley's achievement that he entered a new field; it was inevitable that his work should, in later years, be found scanty and insufficient on many points. He himself would have been the first to recognize this and the first to wish that his work might serve as an inspiration for further study rather than as a definitive account of the period.

Ashley's ability to synthesize and criticize with restraint and objectivity the work of other scholars is admirably illustrated by the *Surveys: historic and economic*, a collection of articles and book reviews on the study of economic history, of medieval agrarian and urban conditions, and of the relations of England and America in the eighteenth century. In the most important article on medieval agrarian conditions, a critique of Vinogradoff's *Villeinage in England*, Ashley again attacked the theory of the free village community, pointing out with astringent humor that it was a comparative newcomer in England; it had not appeared in Hallam but had first been spread by Maine and Stubbs.

It appealed to many of the strongest feelings of academic men. It was new, and therefore enlightened; on the other hand, the example of Dr. Stubbs showed that it was compatible with great learning and unimpeachable Conservatism. Moreover it was admirably adapted to the exigencies of the modern tutorial method."[28]

To his mind, Freeman and Stubbs had been guilty of carrying "back into the past the ideas of equality and self-government which have characterized our own age."[29] But although he disagreed with this theory and accepted the validity of Fustel de Coulanges' criticisms, he was also aware of the gaps in the latter's investigations.

In the medieval manor there were two elements, the *seigneurial*—the relations of the tenants to the lord; and the *communal*—the relations of the tenants to one another. The mark theory taught that the seigneurial was grafted on to the communal. The value of the work of M. Fustel de Coulanges and of Mr. Seebohm is in showing that we cannot find a time when the seigneurial element was absent. . . . . But the communal element is still an unsolved mystery . . . . nothing is more characteristic of the later manor than *week-works*. . . . . But such week-works do not appear in medieval documents until A.D. 622.[30]

In the same spirit in which Vinogradoff's work had been reviewed, the essay on "The beginnings of town life in the middle ages" criticizes the work of Flach, Varges, Pirenne, and Keutgen. He considered Flach's work on the early middle ages important but maintained that there was no contemporary evidence that the town constitutions grew out of the right of *sauveté;* and, although he agreed with Varges's contention that the burg, around which many towns grew up, was a place of defense, he believed that burgs could and did exist without walls. Pirenne's great contribution, in Ashley's eyes, was his insistence that the origins of towns had not varied in different nations but were to be found in the same economic forces, operating everywhere. The later divergences between French and German towns were "due, not to differences of race, but to the difference between France and Germany in the strength of the central authority."[31] However, he criticized Pirenne for failing to account for the extension of town privileges to other than merchant groups.

The *Surveys* contain Ashley's only work in the field of modern history, "The Tory origins of free trade policy"; and two articles on Anglo-American relations: "The commercial legislation of England and the American colonies, 1660–1760" and "American smuggling." The first of these found the reason for the Tory support of free trade at the end of the seventeenth century not in their allegiance to any theory but in their opposition to the Whigs, who favored the prohibition of trade with France in 1678. The second article advanced the conclusion that, with the exception of the Molasses Act of 1733, "the English commercial legislation did the colonies no harm prior to 1760; and the English connection did them much good." "American smuggling" was written in reply to Arthur H. Johnson, who had attacked Ashley's conclusions and claimed that the existence of a wide smuggling trade proved that English commercial legislation was harmful to the colonies. After a detailed analysis of the various types of colonial trade, Ashley maintained his opinion that the trade with England was natural and not forced, and that, "with the exception as always of the molasses business—the bulk of the American import trade was strictly legal, because the colonials had no interest that it should be otherwise." Both of these latter studies show a familiarity with the sources for colonial history, but there is a lack of a complete mastery of details and of that comprehension of the atmosphere of an age which Ashley had achieved so well in his work on the middle ages. He fails to note that, although colonial trade with England increased after the War of Independence, it did so at a much slower rate than formerly; and, after all, to except "the molasses business" is to omit a very large share of commercial activity.[32]

With the publication of the *Surveys* Ashley's historical work ceased for over a decade. He threw himself into the creation of the faculty of commerce at Birmingham, into the education of businessmen and the clarification of political issues that had an economic significance.

He had been slowly preparing himself for this change. Even as a student at Oxford, he had been critical of the highly theoretical nature of contemporary economics, and he never had any sympathy or admiration for the lamentable academic tendency of turning "a branch of knowledge into an esoteric mystery, hidden from the vulgar by a special vocabulary."[33] In later years he went so far as to doubt whether a familiarity with classical economic theory was essential to an understanding of the economic factors in society; Charles Booth's *Life and labour of the people of London* was good economics, but no knowledge of theory was required to understand it. Ashley's entire work was done in the belief that economic theories reflected the conditions of the period which gave them birth and that the authenticity and reasonableness of these theories could not be judged until a vast deal of minute and concrete details about the past had been collected. In his inaugural address at Harvard in 1893, he had urged his students to undertake this work of collecting. Admitting that the historical record was imperfect in many respects, he nonetheless begged them to turn their attention from the "laws" of production, distribution, and exchange and to cultivate "a sacred passion for the observation of real life."[34]

For years he had devoted himself to the first of the goals he had set as a student, "the investigation of economic history"; now he turned to the second of his goals, "the examination of modern industrial life in the piece." By reason of his attacks on the economic theorists he had been led to differentiate between two types of economics: one, which he called "political economics," dealt with a statement of general theories which might guide a statesman; the other, "business economics," dealt with the practical problems which arise in the handling of any industrial or commercial enterprise. Both were, in his estimation, fit subjects for university instruction, but he insisted that instruction should be given by men who were well informed on the facts of economic life. In the conclusion of his Harvard address he gives expression to the belief which goes far to explain his surrender of historical research.

The general cultivated public . . . . wants to know how individuals and episodes are related to some large whole, and what the *significance* of it all has been. If scholars competently trained will not try to satisfy this natural and laudable desire, incompetent writers *will*. . . . . The historian and the economist may expel Nature with the fork of the Seminary and the Deductive Method; but Nemesis stands very near the shoulder of "Pure Economics" or "Pure History"—and in America it usually calls itself "Sociology."[35]

It was with this determination to impart to the ordinary man —and in Ashley's case this was the businessman—the scholar's conception of the significance of the economic history of England that Ashley went to the University of Birmingham. The businessman would not send his son to the university without reasonable assurance that he would return to business; consequently, the course offered a study of specific business problems as well as a survey of the industrial and commercial organization in England and other countries. Although not "ashamed to be frankly and nakedly utilitarian" in the curriculum, Ashley saw no reason why the businessman could not benefit from a cultural, as well as a practical, training. "The man who learns Spanish to sell to the Spaniards may use it to read Cervantes and the man who learns Chemistry to make soap may still be capable of appreciating the Atomic Theory."[36]

The faculty of commerce began its work with eight students, and its enrolment at no time exceeded eighty. As a teacher, Ashley was respected but was held in awe by his students; his extreme caution, his determination to state all the facts on all sides of a question, made his lectures slow and ponderous. But for the possibility and worth of this type of business education he taught and wrote and lectured for a quarter of a century, and to it went the energy which might have gone to historical research. Consequently, his writing is concerned with immediate economic and political problems. He edited a series of lectures on *British industries* and *British dominions*,[37] and he published a study on *The adjustment of wages* and numerous articles on gold and prices and on trade-unions.

With but one exception the work of this period does not contribute directly to historical knowledge, but it does throw light on

Ashley's ideas as an economic historian. He had become convinced of the necessity for the adoption of a protective tariff for England and of imperial preference, and his years in Canada had deepened this conviction.

> By upbringing and sympathies I am a Liberal. As an economist, my main interest has always been in the condition of the working classes. But the general opinions expressed [here] were formed long before I returned to England, and while I was still a teacher, first in a Canadian and then in an American university.[38]

To assist the Conservative campaign for tariff reform he wrote *The tariff problem* and *The progress of the German working classes in the last quarter of a century*.[39] Protection might entail a temporary loss, but national and imperial interests and the necessity of securing a permanent market would overbalance this.

> The question of the *productive* powers of a country, and their possible development is far more important than that of *present values;* it might be well worth while to incur a loss for a time in order to secure a more than proportionate future gain.[40]

On the other hand, the maintenance of free trade in England would encourage the growth of cheap labor industries and lead to the exhaustion of national "capital" by the export of coal, the destruction of the iron and steel industries, and an increasing import of food.

> And while London and a few other great towns will become ever larger agglomerations of labouring population, the rest of England will remain an agreeable place of residence for rentiers . . . . and will flourish on the "tourist industry." And . . . . the history of Holland will have been repeated.[41]

The consolidation of the empire by means of a preferential system was one of his dearest desires, and he had become convinced in Canada that the increasing independence of the dominions could be arrested only by creating some material interest in union. Despite his interest in the problem, his discussion of the means by which imperial preference might be achieved is the weakest part of his presentation because he minimizes the extent of industrialization in the dominions and its effect on their policy.

The progress of the German working classes was written because "the advocates of tariff inaction commonly allege that the condition of the German people is such as properly to deter Great Britain from any departure from its present policy." The volume, with its careful analysis of a multitude of statistics, illustrates his caution as a historian and his lack of dogmatism, even in political writing. He does not distort the facts to prove a thesis but admits, for example, that the increase in the wages of the German agricultural worker was due, in all probability, not to the tariff but to a scarcity of labor. Once again, he points out the influence of conditions on theories and notes that socialists like Bernstein were renouncing the theory of "the constant and inevitable tendency towards the progressive impoverishment of the masses" not because they could not accept it but rather "because it has become glaringly untrue."[42]

However, the chief interest for the historian in this discussion lies in Ashley's attack, in the opening chapters of *The tariff problem*, on the classical economists. He condemned them for their support of laissez faire in all fields, industrial as well as commercial, and for their maintenance of the fiction of "freedom of contract." Since they were unacquainted with the conditions of contemporary industry and commerce, their doctrines could not be blindly applied to it.

His most interesting writing on this subject appeared in 1909, when he edited and wrote a lengthy introduction to John Stuart Mill's *Principles of political economy*. This was a meticulous task; the printed text was that of 1871, but the extremely full footnotes indicated every change of text from previous editions and the date when these changes occurred. In Ashley's opinion, Mill's economics "remained those of his father down to the end of his life . . . . ; he sought to surround it, so to speak, with a new environment." After his father, the greatest influences on his work had been Coleridge, Comte, and his wife.

By confining, as he did, the term "science" to the abstract arguments, and leaving the determination of its relation to actual conditions to what he himself calls "the sagacity of conjecture," Mill undoubtedly exercised a profound influence on the subsequent character of economic writing in England.

And there is no doubt left in the reader's mind that Ashley considered this portion of Mill's influence unfortunate.[43]

Two academic honors were conferred on Ashley in the years before the war. In 1910 he received an honorary doctorate of philosophy from the University of Berlin, "the distinction which, of all others, he was most certain to prize";[44] and, in 1912, he delivered a series of lectures before the Colonial Institute of Hamburg which, when published as *The economic organization of England*,[45] became his most popular and most read book. It was in work of this type, a popular but scholarly synthesis of existing knowledge, that Ashley excelled. There is nothing new in information or original in treatment, and there are some gaps in the story and some minor errors in fact; but with clearness and masterly simplicity he draws the picture of the agrarian, urban, and commercial organization of England from the thirteenth to the nineteenth century. He avoids the tortuous questions of the origins of the manor and the relations of the merchant and craft guilds; he confines his description of early industry to the manufacture of woolen cloth, and he makes no mention of the great increase in trade under the Tudors or of the navigation acts. But there is a sweep and assurance to the survey and a charm of style which still commend it not only to the expert but also to the layman. It awakens in the minds of its readers a regret that academic and political activity had made it impossible for Ashley to complete his *Introduction to English economic history and theory*, but it reflects his continuing interest in economic problems and the increased sureness of his understanding and touch.

Because of his admiration for Germany and her scholars, from whom he had "first caught the infection of the scientific spirit," the outbreak of war in 1914 was to him "a special and personal grief."[46] He had been distressed at the tension between the two countries, and in his lectures at Hamburg he had pleaded for Anglo-German friendship. The megalomania of certain German writers had, as he wrote in his introduction to the English edition of Friedrich Naumann's *Central Europe*, made him wonder "whether German writers . . . . do not sometimes forget that a good many people outside Germany can read German." He had no doubt as to the justice of Britain's cause, and throughout the war he served on numerous government and private committees which studied the German food supply, retail coal prices, trade relationships after the war, food prices, and agricultural wages. As a committee member he was conciliatory and practical, and he regretted that the members "ranged themselves into sides, more or less in accordance with their views with regard to Government intervention in general" than with regard to the particular problem under study. For him, one of the few consoling features of the war was the increased activity of the government in all fields of economic work. He welcomed this "intelligent direction of the nation at home to the welfare of the whole" as the death blow to laissez faire.[47]

His war work, which led to a knighthood in 1917, did not divert him from academic interests. He was made vice-chancellor of the University of Birmingham, and until his death, in 1927, he continued his writings in favor of business education along with his service on government commissions and the production of his final work, *The bread of our forefathers*. On current economic questions his opinions did not change. From June, 1919, when he was appointed a member of the Royal Commission on Agriculture, until ill health forced his resignation from the Committee on Industry and Trade in November, 1926, he continued to work for tariff reform. In a memorandum submitted at the time of his resignation he stated that he was of the opinion "that had Mr. Chamberlain's then [1903] policy been carried out, this country would have been in a better position to confront the post-war difficulties." The crucial fact was that Britain "had lost . . . . a large part of its foreign market" and that, since her cost of production was high because her industries did not operate on so large a scale as the American, and because the strength of trade-unionism made the wage scale less flexible, the adoption of a low general tariff, on all articles other than raw materials, was essential. To protect Britain against dumping, which Ashley always regarded not as a depraved commercial policy but as the "perfectly normal outcome of a business situation," he would invoke the Safeguarding of Industries Act. No remedy for the situation could be found in the nationalization of the depressed industries, because they were largely dependent on a foreign market; and, if no change occurred in England's fiscal policy, she would have to face the burden of recurring depressions and increased unemployment.[48]

The report, in 1923, of the Agricultural Tribunal of Investigation expressed his attitude toward the problems of the English farmer. He supported the tribunal's recommendation of a government subsidy for all arable land and of an additional subsidy for land planted in wheat. Although the tribunal was unable to agree on the question of an agricultural tariff, Ashley's previous writings make it clear that he would have approved of this, especially if it could have been devised in such a way as to aid the cause of imperial unity.

In his last historical work, published posthumously, *The bread of our forefathers*,[49] Ashley returned to his first love, the economic history of the middle ages. The study, whose purpose was to trace back to medieval times the cultivation of cereals and to test the truth of the belief that the medieval Englishman had eaten a wheaten rather than a rye loaf, illustrates all his care in investigation, all his caution and critical use of sources, and also all his sureness of judgment. From the evidence of agricultural writers, the "Improvers," from market records, and from the corn certificates of the sixteenth and seventeenth centuries (which had not been published hitherto), Ashley concluded that by the Tudor period wheat was being used by the gentry and rye by the peasants and that the former was grown in enclosed farms and the latter in open fields. Carrying the problem back into medieval times, he attacked the writers who had claimed that the English loaf was wheaten throughout this period. He offered evidence that the Latin word for rye had been given its classical, rather than its medieval, meaning by later writers and, hence, was mistranslated, and that Thorold Rogers' figures on medieval production referred only to the bailiffs' accounts of the cultivation of the demesne and

give us absolutely no direct information at all concerning the cultivation of by far the greater part of the arable land of the country . . . . all that remaining in the hands of the peasants, of the small freeholders and of the lesser lords of the manor.[50]

He was not so successful in the use of monastic records; these, at least on the surface, seemed to show that the bread of the monasteries was wheat. Although Ashley did not deny this, he insisted that considerable rye was used, especially by the almoners. The earlier cultivation and the wider use of wheat in England was due to the unique three-part organization of English agriculture— landlord, tenant-farmer, and laborer—which made available the capital necessary for improvement.

A country like Germany, which at the beginning of the medieval period is a rye-growing and a rye-eating land, continues to be in the main a rye-growing and a rye-eating land, because it continues to be a country of peasant proprietors. . . . . On the other hand, in England, rye yields much earlier to wheat, although far more slowly than is commonly supposed, largely because in England capitalist farming first developed.[51]

In many ways *The bread of our forefathers* might stand as a perfect monument to Ashley, the historian. It is concerned with the field of his greatest historical interest and contribution, the economic life of the middle ages; it is the product of a study of detailed information—he does not approach the period with any conclusion which he is determined to make the evidence substantiate, but he studies a wide range of minute details and formulates his general conclusion with caution but also with firmness. Finally, the problem with which he dealt is essentially a practical one; it is not a question of medieval theory that he wishes to investigate but a question of fact. Twenty years before, in his lectures on the adjustment of wages, he had said:

For all save those exceptional individuals who have a gift for abstract speculation—I recognize that it is a real gift, but I am sure that it is very exceptional —the chief duty of the professional economist . . . . is the ascertainment of the facts of actual life.[52]

No words can describe better than his own, as a younger man, the unremittent desire for exact information, the moderation of opinion, and the wish to inspire further study rather than to be accounted himself the discoverer of absolute truth, which informs all his work.

> These are only provisional conclusions of one who has tried to take a general view of a very wide subject. You will not think of them as "ex cathedra" pronouncements, but as a preliminary survey of a field of investigation on which I trust some of you will enter. . . . . If I have not used in this course the language of economic ethics, it is because I think the great need of our own day is for absolutely colourless economic dynamics. Before we set about judging the forces at work, we have to learn what they are.[53]

In comparison with many historians Ashley's work is small in bulk, but his influence was widespread. He taught in three countries; he held the first chair of economic history in the world; and he founded a school of commerce. It is because he devoted a quarter of a century to urging students to ascertain what "the forces at work are" that he made such a limited factual contribution to our knowledge of the past. But he bears a major share of the credit for having familiarized English students with German research and method and for having turned economics from theoretical to historical interests. His greatest service as a historian lay in his emphasis on the nature of the field to be studied and the method of study which was essential, rather than in great contributions to knowledge as a result of his own investigations.

NOTES

1. "Comparative economic history and the English landlord," *Economic journal*, XXIII (1913), 165–66.

2. Anne Ashley, *William James Ashley: a life* (London, 1932), p. 10 (cited hereafter as "Ashley").

3. *The adjustment of wages: a study in the coal and iron industries of Great Britain and America* (London, 1903), pp. 10–11.

4. Ashley, p. 13.

5. London, 1925.

6. *Ibid.*, pp. 42, 60.

7. *Surveys: historic and economic* (London, 1900), p. 431.

8. Ashley, pp. 18–24.

9. *Surveys*, dedication.

10. *Ibid.*, pp. 26–27.

11. "Profit-sharing," *Quarterly review*, CCXIX (1913), 509–30.

12. Letter to Margaret Hill (Mrs. Ashley), 1881, Ashley, pp. 33–35.

13. London, 1883.

14. H. O. Wakeman and Arthur Hassall (eds.), (London, 1887), pp. 45–112.

15. Baltimore, 1888; review by W. Cunningham, *EHR*, III (1888), 567.

16. London, 1888.

17. London, 1890.

18. London, 1893.

19. London, 1900; reviewed by Charles H. Hull, *AHR*, VI (1900–1), 793–96.

20. *Surveys*, p. 239.

21. London, 1887.

22. Fustel de Coulanges, *The origin of property in land*, trans. Margaret Ashley (London, 1890), pp. viii, xiii.

23. *Introduction*, Part I, chap. ii; review of Rudolph Sohm, *Entstehung des deutschen Stadtwesens* in *EHR*, VII (1892), 341.

24. *Introduction*, Part I, p. 140.

25. *Ibid.*, I, 155–59.

26. *Ibid.*, II, 168.

27. *Ibid.*, pp. 273–78; "The character of villein tenure," *Annals of the American Academy of Political and Social Science*, I (1890–91), 412–25.

28. *Surveys*, pp. 40–41.

29. *Ibid.*, p. 86.

30. Fustel, p. xlii.

31. *Surveys*, p. 201.

32. *Ibid.*, pp. 320–60.

33. Ashley, p. 66.

34. *Surveys*, pp. 6–20.

35. *Ibid.*, p. 30.

36. "The universities and commercial education," *North American review*, CLXXVIII (1903), 32–35.

37. London, 1903, 1908.

38. *The tariff problem* (London, 1903), pp. v–vi.

39. London, 1904; reviewed very critically in *Nation*, LXXVIII (1904), 236–37.

40. *Tariff problem*, pp. 25–26.

41. *Ibid.*, pp. 112–13.

42. *German working classes*, p. 140.

43. J. S. Mill, *Principles of political economy*, ed. W. J. Ashley (London, 1909), pp. ix–xxi.

44. Ashley, p. 144.

45. London, 1914.

46. *The war and its economic aspects* ("Oxford pamphlets," No. 44 [Oxford, 1914]), p. 3.

47. Ashley, pp. 150–57; reviewed by J. H. Clapham, *EHR*, **XXX** (1915), 188–89; E. P. Cheyney, *AHR*, **XXI** (1915–16), 142–44; Conyers Read, *Journal of political economy*, **XXIII** (1915), 289–92.

48. Ashley, pp. 165–71; *Business economics* (London, 1926), p. 30.

49. Oxford, 1928; reviewed by A. L. Dunham, *AHR*, **XXXIV** (1928–29), 320–21.

50. *Bread of our forefathers*, p. 87.

51. *Ibid.*, p. 145.

52. *Adjustment of wages*, pp. 7–8.

53. *Ibid.*, p.185.

III

ALPHONSE AULARD (1849–1928)

JAMES L. GODFREY*

TODAY the world is in a revolutionary movement which threatens to leave its imprint upon action and thought in just as indelible a manner as did the French Revolution of a century and a half ago. From one point of view the present revolution may be considered the true counterrevolution to that which brought the eighteenth century to a close, for in many respects the values and ideas created and fostered then have just now been challenged by new social and political conceptions. This fact in itself should direct the attention of the student back to that most formative period of western European culture when the men of those countries and that time entered upon a heritage that now seems on the point of exhaustion. Those who do turn their attentions back will soon be conscious of the fact that they have incurred a debt to Alphonse Aulard, who, more than anyone else, has been responsible for the excellent work in writing and in documentation that has characterized the historical treatment of the French Revolution over the last fifty years.

Scholars of the French Revolution in this country would have little difficulty in agreeing that the major portion of their deference should go to Aulard and Albert Mathiez; these two men seem to dominate the historical work on the period just as Danton and Robespierre seemed for a time to dominate the period itself. The analogy may be even more finally drawn, for it is well known that Aulard considered himself the champion of Danton, while Mathiez portrayed the virtues of the incorruptible Robespierre. This favoritism gives a clear insight into the personal feelings of the

* Instructor in history, University of North Carolina.

two authors as they consider the Revolutionary period. It seems apparent that Aulard would have been content had the Revolution abated before the apogee of internal violence was reached under Robespierre, if the gains that had been made could have been solidified under Danton's capacity for compromise; while Mathiez, without the advent of Robespierre and his connotations of economic and social change, would have considered the entire movement as incomplete—the beginning of a syllogism that refused to continue itself beyond the minor premise. The basis for a lively feud[1] becomes obvious, and even yet it is difficult not to take sides, for the Revolutionary movement is eloquent in its appeal to partisanship. It is possible, however, without entering this controversy, to judge Aulard on the basis of his historical influence, his methodology, his success as a teacher, his devotion to scholarship, his products of research, and the great impetus which he gave to the study of history of the Revolution. Most of these qualities and contributions Aulard shares with few peers; their common residence in one personality explains why Aulard is usually considered as "the grand old man" of French Revolutionary history.

Of Aulard's early life but little has been ascertained.[2] He was born on July 19, 1849, at Monthron in Charente. His father was an inspector of secondary education. Economically, the family was probably of the lower middle class but with a more pretentious claim to an intellectual rating. It is known that young Alphonse studied at the College of Sainte-Barbe and at the Lycée Louis-le-Grand in Paris. At the age of eighteen he entered the École Normale Supérieure, where his studies were interrupted by his voluntary enlistment (although legally exempt) for service in the Franco-German War. The following year, 1871, he became an *aggrégé des lettres*. He spent the period following graduation in the south of France, serving successively as professor of humanities at the lycées of Nîmes and Nice. In 1877 he received the degree of *docteur ès lettres*, submitting for his thesis one paper in Latin on Asinius Pollion, under the title of *De Caii Asinii Pollionis vita et scriptis*, and one in French on Leopardi, the Italian poet.

It is interesting to note that Aulard's formal training was in literature, where he showed promise, rather than in history, where he achieved fame. Between 1878 and 1884 he served as professor of French literature at Aix, Montpellier, Dijon, and Poitiers. After this extensive apprenticeship in the provinces, he returned to Paris in 1884 as professor of rhetoric at the Lycée Janson-de-Sailly. The following year the municipality of Paris endowed at the University of Paris a chair of the history of the French Revolution, which Aulard accepted and filled with distinction until his retirement in 1922.

That a person prepared in literature should be appointed to an important chair in history must have been a matter of chagrin in historical circles. The election, however, was justified not only by future hopes but by past performances. Aulard had devoted a great portion of his time spent in the provinces to research in the history of the Revolutionary period. In 1882 he began to publish a series entitled *L'éloquence parlementaire pendant la Révolution française*.[3] The work, by later standards, was modest enough, but it was favorably received at the time as embodying a pleasing and impartial presentation of the legislative aspects of selected figures in the Revolutionary assemblies.[4] In a later (1905) and extended edition of the book Aulard admits that he approached his first study from a literary point of view and that many errors were incorporated in the text; but the work had virtue, for it was undertaken at a time when there existed but "few examples of the application of the historical method to the Revolutionary period." In 1884 Aulard began his contributions to journals, publishing with some success under the name of "Santhonax" in Clemenceau's journal *Justice*.[5] And so it was not a man entirely unknown and unvouched for who in 1885 honored the municipality of Paris by his acceptance of its generosity.

Why did Aulard turn from his first chosen field to devote his talents to historical research, and why in the Revolutionary period? Georges Lefebvre suggests that a solution might be found in the fact that Aulard belonged to a generation which from 1870 to 1875 had struggled to form a parliamentary and secular democracy in France.[6] The study of the Revolutionary period might be calculated to constitute the most effective historical background for such an attempt; it was the period of French history which best exhibited, shorn of its popular excesses, the political society which a depressed and humiliated France sought to recapture. The study of such a period during the years following the Franco-German War would certainly have the psychological compensation of contemplating more glorious days. In addition, the study of parliamentary figures from the standpoint of their speeches might, with some courtesy, be considered as a legitimate interest for a teacher of French literature. Then, again, it may be that the journalistic tendencies of Aulard—those who regarded him from the opposite side of the historical fence were very vocal in their opinion that Aulard was essentially a journalist—led him to an examination of the Constituent Assembly, sensing that he would find there political sentiments which could be useful in consolidating the Third Republic.

There is another item in this conversion which must be mentioned. Aulard was, in the better sense of the word, a nationalist. He possessed too much intellectual integrity, he had too sane a perspective on the fluctuations of both private and national life, to feel personally humiliated by his country's defeat of 1870–71. Yet he was conscious that as a result of the ill fortunes of war French culture experienced a sickening sag, that the public mind lost tone and resilience. France needed to be revived—and one of the first therapeutic aids to revival was teaching.[7] Add to that belief in the efficacy of teaching, Aulard's personal attitude toward history, and one can estimate the strong intellectual and emotional tug which must have drawn Aulard from the formal study of literature to the more utilitarian (politically) study of history. Léon Cahen, a contemporary professional colleague, classifies Aulard as the spiritual son of Michelet, Quinet, and the men of '48, for whom history was the highest form of human culture, the foundation of political science, and the basis of progress.[8] Surely here was an opportunity that a man of Aulard's convictions and predilections could scarcely have refused: the occasion, a psychopathic depression of the national ego; the therapeutic method, teaching; and the therapeutic dose, history. In any case, it is not so strange that Aulard turned to the study of French Revolutionary history as it was that Revolutionary history waited for his turning.

Since Aulard placed such a premium upon the ministration of teaching, it should be of interest, now that he was in Paris and on his way to becoming the center of a historical constellation, to observe his methods and something of his successes as a teacher. As occupant of the new chair created by the Paris municipality, Aulard delivered his first lecture on March 12, 1886.[9] From that time until his retirement in 1922 he was actively engaged in imparting to others the attitudes and methods which, watered by his own genius, had been made to bear rich fruit for himself.[10] This does not mean that Aulard was concerned with indoctrination. Such an imputation would have been received by him with a sense of aggrievement; he was too aware of the changing evaluations of scholarship, of the evolution of all sciences, and of the ephemeral character of facts and ideas—"the definitive of today is the provisional of tomorrow"[11]—to seek to set the intellectual bonds too tightly. The object of teaching, according to his conviction, was "to purify the passions through the action of the intelligence." His ideal was that of Dante, "une lumière intellectuelle pleine d'amour."[12] The result and comfort of work should be the joy of understanding—an understanding which comprehended not only the texts but—perhaps more important and certainly more difficult—the men themselves. Such a general attitude has enough of "sweetness and light" to be appealing; enough of intellectual integrity and toughness—when one considers the character of the man—to be a formidable and compelling intellectual discipline.

We are told by Pierre Flottes, a professional colleague, in the issue of La Révolution française devoted to the memory of Aulard, that Aulard discounted the role of memory. For him the "good life," intellectually, resided not in the retention of details but in the power of analysis, in the possession of "l'esprit de finesse." He never reproached a student for not knowing a thing. "If he does not know it, it is perhaps because he has a bad memory! It may be that he has not had time to learn it! There are so many things to learn."[13] This intellectual compassion, this generosity of attitude, represented a deliberate choice on the part of Aulard. To him it was of great value to catch what he considered to be the essence of things; he would have been derelict in his duty—in his mission—had he not allowed his students the same latitude.

The fact that Aulard emphasized the quality of analysis rather than that of tenacious memory must not be interpreted to mean that he possessed no rigorous standards or that he was lax in his methodology. Camille Bloch, the general secretary of the Société de l'Histoire de la Révolution, who delivered modest reminiscences at the funeral of Aulard, has recalled that Aulard at the beginning of an academic year habitually passed to his classes the following observations:

Always use the sources; say nothing that one does not know from the originals; write nothing without producing the appropriate references; avoid assertions without proof; work from the texts; distinguish between the important and interesting facts and those that are insignificant and without interest; emphasize the former and neglect the latter; estimate the value of a historical fact in terms of its degree of influence upon the evolution of the individual, group, or society that is being studied; present the facts in an impartial and objective manner; in publishing that which is new [inédit] the pertinent facts should not be buried beneath that which is insignificant and of the character of rubbish [fatras]; and, finally, let the research be long and the results short.[14]

It would not, I think, be irreverent to refer to these admonitions as "M. Aulard's decalogue for historical study."

These would be virtues enough for a teacher, but to them must be added certain qualities which, while not professional in character, serve to adorn the profession. Albert Mathiez, the most brilliant student to know Aulard as a teacher, has recorded that he was cordial with his students, that he used his Sundays to receive and counsel those who studied under him.[15] Easily approachable, he appears as a democrat by birth and instinct as well as by reason. Those who knew him appreciated this quality, and one friend remembered him for these few words spoken when he gave a small sum of money to a needy student: "It is an occasion when a small sum of money can save a man."[16] From his mind, his spirit, and his pocket he gave to those who came seeking him.

So far, most of the evidence for Aulard's ability as a teacher has been of the inferential variety; for those who must have the pragmatic test of accomplished results, the evidence is no less convincing. Mathiez assures us that Aulard had a very productive influence on his students and cites in affirmation a short list of works, the inspiration for which came from Aulard. They comprise: *L'Isle de France sous Decaen*, by Henri Prentout; *Fouché*, by Louis Madelin; *Jeanbon Saint-André*, by Léon Lévy-Schneider; and *Phillippeaux* and *Histoire de le théophilanthropie*, by Paul Mautouchet.[17] In addition, Professor Louis Gottschalk, recently described by an academic rival of Oxford as the leading exponent of the Mathiez school in America, considers Mathiez himself as one of the most persuasive arguments for the thesis that Aulard was a great teacher.[18] In the perverse world of education it is considered —and correctly so—something of a triumph to have been the teacher of the man who later does more than anyone else to question the definitive quality of your work and to threaten you in the role of the leading authority. On this particular score the evidence is fairly complete and consistent—Aulard was a great teacher.

Aulard, however, was no academic orchid seeking his sustenance from the air. He paid for his success in the good hard coin of devoted and consistent work. From the time in southern France when as a teacher of French literature Aulard first began to consider seriously the historical sources of the French Revolution, he was never for long free from the fascination which the documents of the Revolutionary period held for him. Always he seems to have worked with a triple purpose: to understand the documents; to use them faithfully in his accounts of the Revolution; and to make them, as far as possible, available for the students who were to follow him. In the first lecture delivered from his new post, Aulard reviewed the work that had been done in Revolutionary history and lamented the sad lack of scientific documentation. His spirits were sustained, however, by the knowledge that with some regrettable exceptions the documents remained and could be made to yield their true evidence to an unimpassioned investigator.[19] Ample room there was for this, for he estimated that not over a fourth or a third of the documents pertaining to the period had even been catalogued. And so he set for himself the task not only of portraying the Revolution but of making available its remnants as his chief witnesses, speaking their testimony to any who might inquire of them.

From the man to his writings is but a natural step, for Aulard faithfully reflected in his writings the qualities and ideas which characterized him as a teacher. The only thing surprising is the fact that a man who gave so much time to his teaching should have produced, as writer and editor, the vast quantity of careful work that now bears his name. It must have been that in a fortunate mental synthesis he combined the two so that they aided, rather than hindered, each other, for the catalogue of the Bibliothèque Nationale lists under his name some sixty volumes. Even when the appropriate discount is made for the works that were merely edited, almost thirty volumes remain. This is even more imposing when one considers the rigor of his method and the historical worth of his contribution. And as this long and fruitful life expressed itself in scholarly work, it is only fair to say that Aulard maintained with remarkable consistency his personal attitude toward the Revolution—there seems to have been some subtlety of association that enabled them to draw the best from each other.

Indeed, it may be said that the Revolution occupied for Aulard something of the place that social cynics usually attribute to a satisfactory wife of several years' standing. He took "her" seriously; he considered himself "her" official defender; and for "her" contributions to his intellectual and emotional happiness he repaid "her" by a lifelong devotion. To him the French Revolution represented the most important era in the history of

France,[20] for he saw it not as a period but as a continuous process which had its origins before 1789 and which was still moving toward fulfilment. According to Mathiez, he held the view that the Revolution was not made but was in a process of making itself.[21] The period of Revolution proper he described as a mirror held before France in which she could discern her true lineaments. "Without the Revolution, one would have never known that our nation could be all at once so lusty [*forte*] and so sensitive [*sensible*], so gay and so sad, so loving and so irritable, so generous and so dreadful."[22] He aptly summed it up when he concluded that for France to know the Revolution was for her to know herself.

Having established for himself the position of the Revolution, Aulard warned that the historian approaching the subject should do so with clean hands. Partisanship should be avoided; judgments *en bloc* should yield themselves to a more selective method. This is rigorous enough, but, as is so often the case with Aulard, it is subject to a softening touch: "He who does not sympathize with the Revolution sees only the surface. In order to understand it, it is necessary to love it."[23] Such an attitude, such an affection toward any subject, would bring its own rewards in the shape of fervor and emotional zeal in the actual process of the work; and, truly, sympathy is almost a necessary condition to a fair understanding. Yet it is questionable if such an attachment would yield appreciable dividends in the way of impartiality and objectivity. It is said that whom the Lord loveth, he chasteneth. But could Aulard do the same? Or did he feel for certain aspects of his subject emotional predilections that predisposed him in his judgments? And Aulard realized fully that judgment was a legitimate province of the historian.[24] This is not an indictment of Aulard; if anything, it is an indictment of the fallacy of a complete objectivity, and a preparation for an exposition of how Aulard's personality—his emotional affinities—influenced, to a degree beyond that encompassed by the term "purely scientific," his reactions to the study of Revolutionary history.

For the purpose of explaining more fully Aulard's attitude toward the Revolution, we may do violence to chronology and select not his first published works but his *Histoire politique de la Révolution française*.[25] This work, published in 1901, gives such a complete picture of the historian of the Revolution that it is necessary to consider his lesser works of authorship only *en passant* in order to care for a few specialized views. Of all the works which Aulard could call his own in the sense that they took their being from the impact of facts upon his mind, this was his favorite one— and even here, in justice to Aulard's appreciation of the transitory nature that works of scholarship carry about them, it should be said that he pledged his claim to lasting recognition not upon this book but upon a work which he edited and which will be mentioned later.

It is doubtful if many historical contributions have been made in which the contributor was in more complete control of the technical apparatus of his craft than was Aulard in offering his political history to the world of scholars and to the public.[26] Twenty years of research in the sources made their valuable contribution to the narrative,[27] while invaluable experience as a teacher, author, and editor was utilized to adorn the tale. Within the chronological limitations of the period between 1789 and 1804 Aulard proposed to depict the political history of the Revolution "au point de vue des origines et du développement de la démocratie et de la république," It seemed clear to him that "la conséquence logique du principe de l'égalité, c'est la démocratie. La conséquence logique du principe de la souveraineté nationale, c'est la république."[28] In such a limitation Aulard recognized the hazard that critics would accuse him of painting but a partial picture: of leaving out items and influences that had a legitimate—some would say, paramount—claim to consideration; of neglecting to present the information that would show, alongside the political, the socioeconomic manifestations of the movement. This could not be avoided: history is very demanding, and life is short; there must be a limitation to the material in the sources that can be thoroughly covered in a lifetime. In this regard Aulard wrote:

Si on n'est pleinement satisfait ni de ma méthode ni de mon plan, j'espère qu'on aura du moins, quant à ma documentation, une sécurité, qui vient de la nature de mon sujet. Je veux dire qu'on n'aura pas à craindre qu'il m'ait été matériellement impossible de connaître toutes les sources essentielles. Il n'en est pas de même pour d'autres sujets. L'histoire économique et sociale de la Révolution, par exemple, est dispersée en tant de sources qu'il est actuellement impossible, dans le cours d'une vie d'homme, de les aborder toutes ou même d'en aborder les principales.[29]

There is little doubt, however, that Aulard in selecting the political field for his efforts was at the same time doing that which was most congenial with his intellectual interests and tastes.

Having once set his goal, Aulard proceeded with some persuasiveness. The acquisition of a democratic republic, which characterized, according to Aulard, the French government from 1792 to 1795, was not a march of events in which logic played a large part. To the author, events unfolded themselves, ideas germinated and grew, from the mutual interaction of men and circumstances—an interaction which on its political side exhibited "ni unité de plan, ni continuité de méthode, ni suite logique dans les divers remaniements de l'édifice politique."[30] From this welter of interacting forces came the "ups and downs" of the graph of historical events, as now this, now that, combination of men and circumstances dominated the scene. An excellent illustration of the manner in which Aulard viewed these manifestations was his belief that the establishment of the democratic republic was the true revelation of the Revolutionary movement; yet in 1789, when the movement was already well under way, he failed to discern anywhere in France the semblance of a republican party. The men were there who were perfectly capable of such a government, but circumstance had not as yet claimed them for its own. Not until the king sought the eastern border in the flight to Varennes did circumstances and men combine for the formation of a truly republican party. Probably, in the short run, Aulard would not have subscribed to any historical doctrine which contemplated an orderly and logical marshaling and fulfilling of historical events. The possibilities of combination were too infinite. It is also possible, however, that as one lengthened the period under consideration Aulard would have admitted an increasing possibility not for the elimination of, but for the reduction of, the operation of chance. His contention that the Revolutionary process continued through the France of his day may be taken to indicate that, in the long run, certain patterns and combinations tend to predominate. While this is far from affording the historian a foundation from which he can view without trepidation the symmetrical unfolding of sequences, it, at least, gives some assurance for the patient and long-lived that there is in history, the magnetic effect of a trend which eventually will make itself felt and establish a compulsive force about which the events of history will cluster.

To Aulard must go considerable credit for predicating his treatment of the Revolution upon fairly sound consideration of the external relationships of France during the period. The invasions were largely responsible for Revolutionary government and the Terror, though there is a possibility that Aulard attributed too much significance to the military troubles in his explanation of this period of the Revolution. If the character of man is an active factor, along with circumstances, in the determination of events, then it is all too probable that events cannot be explained in terms of one alone. To the provinces also goes a liberal portion of Aulard's attention. We must credit Aulard with his view of the Revolution as not born of a doctrine but imposed as a fact,[31] and the contribution that came from his distribution of emphasis between Paris and the provinces as centers of the Revolutionary movement.[32]

This political history is the chief opus of its author. The faults that characterize it will also characterize him. Great though Aulard is when considered as a whole, he is not flawless in detail. While Aulard prided himself upon his methodology and his assiduous cultivation of the documents, it is reasonably doubtful whether his method of selection was that best calculated to give a true picture. The citations in the political history—in fact, in most of Aulard's works—are overwhelmingly from the official reports. While no one would begrudge the historian the comfort and assurance that such sources give, it must be pointed out that official sources, especially during a revolutionary period, are to be regarded with some suspicion. They are too apt to deal with propaganda, too inclined to place either the best or the worst construction on important acts; such documents, before being admitted into the text of history, should be most carefully evaluated. This matter of excessive reliance on official documents has made Aulard fair game for more than one critic; H. Chobaut,[33] writing in a rival journal and under a rival flag, cites it as one of the dangers that must be guarded against when reading Aulard, while Augustin Cochin, in defense of Taine, administers to Aulard a critical drubbing equaled only by that previously administered by Aulard to Taine.[34] The result of this method has been to make of Aulard's work more of a façade than what a great work of history, in the modern sense, should be.

Another indictment has been offered in the charge that Aulard paid too much attention to ideas and not enough to personalities. That a work of history should show concern for the intellectual attributes of the subject it treats is in itself a matter for congratulations, but there is the danger that one will forget that the basis for intellectual manifestations is in the personalities of the men who make ideas and in the personality of the age that influences the men. This must be considered, and considered seriously, if the resultant treatment is to be more than an abstraction of an abstraction. Aulard has too little concerned himself with the intricacies and irrationalities of personality.

Perhaps as a result of the previous lack, it is true that Aulard has not enough occupied himself with the diverse social groups that comprise the whole of society. Just as there was too great emphasis placed upon official documents, it is possible to say that the author placed too great an emphasis upon what might be termed an "official group." This prevented an adequate appreciation of all the forces that combined in forming the specific movement that Aulard describes so well.

These faults are not minor ones; they would have crushed a smaller man. But, fortunately, faults may be considered as relative to virtues: as the latter increase, the former decrease. Even the most sadistic critic must admit that, despite the maladies that beset the historical person of Aulard, he will live. His work had sufficient vitality to conquer for itself one of the strongest of the entrenched positions, and it would seem that that which it conquered it can hold against all, save possibly the historical revulsions which time may bring.

Although the *Histoire politique* must obviously overshadow the other historical works of Aulard, he would not be entirely without credit if he depended upon them alone. His minor works often strike a rich vein of Revolutionary history and bring from the genius of Aulard a very welcome illumination of dark corners. One of his earlier attempts was *Le culte de la raison et le culte de l'Être suprême*,[35] a monograph which, though short, is indispensable in any serious study of Revolutionary religious aberrations.[36] About a decade later, undoubtedly stirred by the nature and spirit of the clerical question in France,[37] Aulard added another volume on the subject of religious history during the Revolutionary period with the publication of *La Révolution française et les congrégations*.[38] This additional venture was not well advised, for his treatment of the religious question was not lacking in superficiality, especially in the view that the French people were not deeply attached to the Catholic church. It is quite possible that Aulard, through his personal sympathies that were undoubtedly stirred by the controversy about him, allowed himself certain liberties more in keeping with his occasional role as a polemnist than with that of a historian. In 1905 a new and revised edition of his work on Revolutionary oratory was issued, and in 1911 he made a contribution to the history of the Napoleonic period with *Napoleon Ier et la monopole universitaire*.[39] It was undoubtedly with great pleasure that Aulard came to the conclusion that the educational policy of Napoleon, instead of bolstering his personal position and his government, actually contributed to the downfall of both. With the publication of *La Révolution française et la régime féodal*[40] Aulard entered still another field. He had always been conscious of the fact that his work in the history of the Revolution lacked those elements of economic history which younger writers were using to such good effect. This work may be considered a belated effort to repair this deficiency. Although Aulard assumed no special competence in economic history, he was always interested in it and played an important part on the committee charged with the collection and publication of materials relating to the economic history of the Revolutionary period. In addition to these formidable publications, all during this period Aulard was collecting the articles that he contributed to periodicals, especially his own *La Révolution française*, and issuing them as volumes in a series entitled *Études et leçons sur la Révolution française*.[41] Beyond this one finds him making contributions to the following journals: *Justice, Matin, Journal, Dépêche de Toulouse, Populaire* (Nantes), *l'Heure, Nouvelles Littéraires, l'Œuvre, Progrès civique, Quotidien, l'Ère nouvelle,* and *Lumière*.[42] Under the pressure of such an accomplishment the quality of the work done represents a tribute to Aulard's rich endowment in industry and in genius.

One of the great interests of Aulard's professional career was to make the documents of the Revolutionary period available to students. This was not merely a side line to Aulard's work; it was of equal rank with his teaching and writing. Indeed, there is reason to suppose that Aulard considered it, in the final analysis, the most important aspect of his work. He is said to have considered his work in editing the documents of the Committee of Public Safety[43]—*Recueil des actes du Comité de Salut Public, avec la correspondance officielle des représentants en mission*—as that most likely to prevent his contributions to history from perishing.[44]

Such a belief reflected sound judgment on the part of Aulard. The work (comprising twenty-six large volumes) is of the highest importance; it constitutes an indispensable collection of documents for the study of the Revolution. The Committee of Public Safety was the most important governmental body during the period of Revolutionary government; its decrees and reports, along with the reports sent to it by the deputies on mission, are matters of paramount concern. Most of these documents are chronologically arranged and reprinted in full, though some, of less importance, are only summarized. An attempt on the part of Chobaut to treat this work as a hodgepodge in which the material and the immaterial are jumbled together, shows not only a critical viciousness but an embarrassing lack of judgment.[45] There must be at least fifty thousand documents in the collection either given in full or summarized; that some should be more important than others is patent. The importance of any one document, however, depends as much on the subject which the researcher is studying as it does upon the intrinsic worth of the document itself. The collection is a monument to skill and industry; its completeness must be considered as a vindication rather than as an indictment of Aulard's scholarship.

As companion pieces Aulard has offered *La société des Jacobins: recueil des documents puur l'histoire de club des Jacobins de Paris*,[46] and three shorter collections dealing with the municipal history of the city of Paris under the titles: *Paris pendant la réaction thermidorienne et sous le Directoire, Paris sous le Consulat*, and *Paris sous le premier Empire*.[47] While less extensive than the series of volumes on the Committee of Public Safety, they all represent work that needed to be done. The documents on the Jacobin Club are especially important in view of the fact that the club for the greater part of its existence occupied a semiofficial position in the political structure. It will be noticed that practically all of this documentary material appeared before Aulard wrote his political history and offered tangible proof of intense industry during the twenty years which he claimed to have spent in the archives.

Another great historical service of Aulard's was his editorship of *Le Révolution française*, a professional journal devoted to the publication of work done in the Revolutionary period. This journal had been founded in 1881 by Dide and Charavay; Aulard assumed the editorship in 1887 and exerted such an influence upon its character that the personalities of the journal and its editor tended to blend. The maintenance, in full vigor, of such a journal, offering, as it did, a publisher for meritorious work, was a steady incentive for students of the period. It is interesting to note that the first differences between Aulard and Mathiez appeared over the interpretation which should have been made in an article submitted by Mathiez to the journal.[48] Also in connection with his editorial duties, Aulard prepared much private literature for publication, the list including such works as: *Mémoires secrets de Fournier l'Américain*,[49] *Notes historiques* ... of Delbrel,[50] and the *Mémoires de Chaumette sur la révolution du 10 août 1792*.[51] With the completion of this appreciation of Aulard as an editor, there remains but one other phase of his activities for our consideration.

Aulard was also something of a public man. At all times he seems to have given freely of himself to academic and social movements in which he believed. His activities on academic committees were considerable and of high order. During the course of his life he served in the following capacities: in the ministry of public instruction Aulard was president of the section on modern history; at the ministry of foreign affairs he was a member of the committee on diplomatic archives and the committee for the publication of the diplomatic documents on the origin of the war of 1914;[52] he was a member of the committee for publication of the history of the city of Paris; and he served with considerable interest and assistance on the committee for the collection and publication of documents relating to the economic history of the French Revolution. In the professional historical societies outside that of his own field he held a membership in the Société d'Histoire Moderne, the Société d'Histoire de la Guerre Mondiale, and the Société d'Histoire de la Révolution de 1848.

In the sociopolitical groups Aulard identified himself with several that attracted his sympathies. He was at one time vice-president of the Ligue Française des Droits de l'Homme et du Citoyen and a member of the council of the Fédération Internationale des Ligues des Droits de l'Homme. He served as both president and vice-president of the Mission Laïque Française. His interest in peace and his prestige secured for him the presidency of the Association Française pour la Société des Nations, and in 1927 he presided over an international union of national associations.[53] His death, in the fall of the same year, closed a career that had been given without stint to his colleagues, his people, and the world.

A final paragraph which catches and holds for display the man who was Alphonse Aulard is very difficult. He was a person who lived with some intensity; such people are not easy to impale with rigid formulas. It is difficult also to determine whether or not Aulard should be considered a truly great historian. As a thinker he would have profited from a little more brilliance; as a writer a trifle more of grace and suavity of style would have been an appreciable benefit; as a craftsman a more latitudinarian use of the sources would have contributed to his finality. What patience, interest, and skill, combined with a deep feeling for the historical, can do, Aulard did. Great or not, he continues to dwarf the many who have followed him, though they have added height by standing upon his shoulders. Great or not, the day is long hence when serious works on the French Revolution will not bear citations from the works written and edited by Aulard. Until such a time comes let those who use him do him honor.

NOTES

1. See the anecdote recounted in the introduction to Hermann Wendel, *Danton* (New Haven, 1935). Aulard's explanation of why he championed Danton is an interesting one. He saw in Danton the spirit of the embattled Revolution, the incarnation of the national defense against all of its foes. This picture of Danton had been understood before by such men as Villaume, Despois, Bougeart, and Sorel, but harm had been done by the fact that Auguste Comte and his disciples had distorted the character of Danton by presenting an untrue Danton—free of error but lacking on the positive side. Aulard thus felt it his mission to rescue Danton from the dialectic of the positivists. An account of this can be found in "Auguste Comte et la Révolution française" in *La Révolution française*, XXIV (1893), 5–9.

2. For a biographical skeleton of Aulard's life and activities see "Notice biographique," *La Révolution française*, LXXXI (1928), 293 ff. Also *Grande encyclopédie*, IV (Paris, *s.d.*), 671.

3. Vol. I, *Les orateurs de l'Assemblée Constituante* (Paris, 1882); Vols. II, III, *Les orateurs de la Legislative et de la Convention* (Paris, 1885–86).

4. Ch. Bemont, "Bulletin historique," *RH*, XXX (1886), 395.

5. A. Mathiez, "M. Aulard, historien et professeur," *La Révolution française*, LV (1908), 59. Also *Grande encyclopédie*, IV, 671. In *La Révolution française*, XII (1887), 670–72 ,will be found an interesting list of ninety-five articles under the title "Lundis révolutionnaires" published from Dec. 29, 1884, through Dec. 27, 1886, in *Justice*. These articles include, among other subjects, some treatment of the following men: Taine, Danton, Marat, Dubois-Crancé, Quinet, Dufour, Jullien de Paris, Couthon, Robespierre, Vergniaud, Billaud-Varennes, Legendre, Hérault de Sechelles, Ba-

zire, Desmoulin, Saint-Just, Barère, Ducos, Royer-Fonfrède, Guadet, Isnard, Lanjuinais, Fauchet, Fauriel, Moreau, Carrier, Lindet, and Babeuf.

6. G. Lefebvre, "L'œuvre historique d'Albert Mathiez," *Annales historiques de la Révolution française*, IX (1932), 194.

7. L. Cahen, "Alphonse Aulard," *Revue universelle*, I (1929), 304.

8. *Ibid.*, p. 303.

9. "Leçon d'ouverture du cours d'histoire de la Révolution française à la faculté des lettres de Paris," *Études et leçons sur la Révolution française*, I (Paris, 1901), 3–39.

10. The most interesting information—though of an impersonal nature—concerning Aulard as a teacher is contained in a report prepared by himself and published under the title, "L'enseignement de l'histoire de la Révolution française à la Sorbonne (1886–1911)," in *La Révolution française*, LXI (1911), 442–55. This article lists the subjects considered in the public course each year from 1886 through 1911 and reveals the rich variety of Aulard's work. Some of his outstanding students and their publications are given along with the publications of the author and many interesting items concerning his professional relationships with students.

11. A. Mathiez, *loc. cit.*, p. 58.

12. E. Herriot, *La Révolution française*, LXXXI (1928), 306–7.

13. P. Flottes, "Aulard professeur," *La Révolution française*, LXXXI (1928), 341. This immensity of what there was to know may have left Aulard with the opinion that too much time was frequently spent on learning that which it was not necessary to know. At least he carried on a running fight against the requirement that the minor thesis submitted for the *doctorat* be in Latin when the work done is in modern and contemporary history. This point was brought up in the notices that Aulard wrote on the examinations of Philippe Sagnac ("Le doctorat de M. Sagnac," *La Révolution française*, XXXVI [1899], p. 7) and Paul Gautier ("Le doctorat de M. Paul Gautier," *ibid.*, XLIV [1903], 174–75). Evidently, Aulard felt that his criticisms had possessed some weight, for the same article stated that the University Council would take up the question at its session in June, 1903. He pointed out that the *petite thèse* is now written in French ("Le doctorat de M. Arnaud," *ibid.*, XLVIII [1905], 49). To have helped in this reform is to have spread one's benefactions to an undoubtedly eager group of students.

14. These advisory remarks are a very free translation of Bloch's arrangement of them. See C. Bloch, "Notre Deuil," *La Révolution française*, LXXXI (1928), 291–92.

15. *Loc. cit.*, p. 53. Professor M. B. Garrett, of the University of North Carolina, was kind enough to share with the writer his impressions of Aulard gained from a Sunday afternoon call. He confirms the opinion that Aulard had an abundance of sympathy and patience. A picture of Aulard (*La Révolution française*, LXXXI [1928] facing p. 289) reveals that he had a delightfully French appearance.

16. Flottes, *loc. cit.*, p. 341.

17. Mathiez, *loc. cit.*, p. 53.

18. L. Gottschalk, "Professor Aulard," *JMH*, I (1929), 86.

19. "Leçon d'ouverture," *Études et leçons*, I, 18–28.

20. *Ibid.*, p. 6.

21. *Loc. cit.*, p. 60.

22. *Études et leçons*, I, 6.

23. *Ibid.*, p. 16.

24. *Ibid.*, p. 12.

25. Paris, 1901. The copy most frequently found in American libraries is a translation with notes made by Bernard Miall from the third French edition: *The French Revolution, a political history, 1789–1804* (New York, 1910).

26. James Harvey Robinson, after pointing out the difficulties of a partisan and emotional nature which beset the period, commends Aulard's fairness and judgment and adds the glowing tribute that "there is no reason to suppose that anyone in the world knows more than he about the sources" (*Political science quarterly*, XXVI [1911], 133–41). It is unfortunate, however, that Aulard's principal work should have reached the English and American reader through such a bad translation. Robinson complains in the critical article just quoted of the bad translation by Miall—a judgment partly concurred in by H. E. Bourne in *AHR*, XVI (1910–11), 386.

27. *Histoire politique*, p. x.

28. *Ibid.*, p. iii.

29. *Ibid.*, p. ix.

30. *Ibid.*, p. vii.

31. *Revue historique*, LXXVII (1901), 368.

32. A good statement of this point of view is found in a speech given by Aulard on June 9, 1900 (just before the publication of the *Histoire politique*) at the general meeting of the Congrès des Sociétés Savantes. This speech was subsequently printed as "L'histoire provinciale de la France contemporaine," *La Révolution française*, XXXVIII (1900), 481–99. The relationship is clearly set forth: "On est d'accord à comprendre que, dans l'histoire comme dans la réalité, Paris et la province sont inséparables, qu'on ne connaît vraiment la France que quand on la considère en ces deux éléments, qui se pénètrent et se mêlent sans cesse, et que, puisqu'on connaît assez bien l'histoire de Paris, il est temps d'étudier l'histoire de la province d'une manière complète et méthodique" (*ibid.*, p. 484).

33. H. Chobaut, "L'œuvre d'Aulard et l'histoire de la Révolution français," *Annales historiques de la Révolution française*, VI (1929), 2–3.

34. A. Cochin, *La crise de l'histoire révolutionnaire* (Paris, 1909), pp. 21 ff. This attack upon Taine as a historian is so well known through Aulard's *Taine, historien de la Révolution française* (2d ed.; Paris, 1908), that one is apt to get the impression that Aulard had a critical viciousness that operated against the work of anyone whom he did not consider a professional historian. As a pleasant contrast to this one might read the words of praise that Aulard has for Jean Jaurès in "M. Juarès historien de la Révolution," *La Révolution française*, XLIII (1902), 289–99.

35. Paris, 1892.

36. This work received the following description from a German critic: "Der Werth des Buches liegt nicht in dieser künstlichen, ganz willkürlichen Hypothese, sondern in der Erzählung des Thatsächlichen, in der Sammlung zahlreicher historische Notizen über jenen kurzlebigen revolutionären Kultus in Paris und in dem Provinzen" (*HZ*, LXIX [1892], 562).

37. F. M. Fling, "Some recent works on the French Revolution," *AHR*, X (1904–5), 889.

38. Paris, 1903.

39. Paris, 1911.

40. Paris, 1919.

41. 9 vols.; Paris, 1901–24.

42. "Notice biographique," *La Révolution française*, LXXXI (1928), 294.

43. 26 vols.; Paris, 1889–1923. Despite its great length, this marvelous collection was never fully completed.

44. Bloch, *loc. cit.*, p. 312.

45. Chobaut, *loc. cit.*, p. 2.

46. 6 vols.; Paris, 1889–97. This collection was made under the auspices of the municipal council of Paris and is compiled from numerous sources, many of them newspapers.

47. 5 vols., Paris, 1898–1902; 4 vols., Paris, 1903–9; Paris, 1912.

48. *Annales historiques de la Révolution française*, IX (Paris, 1932), p. 219. This is in a letter from Mathiez to Gottschalk dated Paris, Nov. 23, 1930.

49. Paris, 1890.

50. Paris, 1893.

51. Paris, 1893.

52. Aulard interestingly enough contributed to various periodicals a number of articles on the subject of the war of 1914. These were collected and issued under the title: *La guerre actuelle commentie par l'histoire; vues et impressions au jour le jour (1914–1916)* (Paris, 1916). There was also a later volume entitled: *1914–1918; histoire politique de la grande guerre, publie sous la direction de A. Aulard ... avec la collaboration de E. Bouvier ... et A. Ganem* (Paris, 1924).

53. Most of this material is from "Notice biographique," *La Révolution française*, LXXXI (1928), 293 ff. The complete list includes membership in a few groups not mentioned in this essay.

IV

BENEDETTO CROCE (1866——)

RICHARD V. BURKS*

CROCE is one of the best-known intellectuals of our time. He is, according to a former compatriot, more widely known outside his native land, at least in scholarly circles, than any Italian thinker since Galileo.[1] Troeltsch regards him as "one of the most distinguished and most characteristic thinkers of the present day."[2] His principal works have been translated into English, French, and German and, in some instances, even into Russian and Japanese. Within Italy herself he looms up as a sort of national monument, equivalent in importance to the universities. His absence from the ranks of Fascism constitutes one of the great question marks for Italian youth.[3] His system of thought has provoked bitter criticism and unmeasured approval; it is "as clear as a starless night,"[4] says one, while another judges it the "highest conquest in contemporary thought."[5]

In either case the system is significant. In its origins it was part of the rising tide of Neo-Romanticism, which latterly found political expression in Fascism; indeed, a former disciple of the philosopher argues that the Italian dictator borrowed many of his ideas from Croce's writing.[6] As a system, Croce's philosophy reveals affinities with Bergson's creative evolution, with Sorel's syndicalism, even with Dewey's instrumentalism, and its basic conception of time is related to Einstein's theory of relativity, which appeared almost simultaneously.[7] But the system is significant for the historian as well as for the philosopher. Croce has attempted what amounts to a Copernican revolution in historical

* Instructor in history, Wayne University.

thought. According to his way of thinking, all knowledge is historical knowledge, philosophy is merely the methodology of history, science is infinitely inferior to history as a method of getting at the truth, and history, far from being a pleasant but impractical form of erudition, is an activity without which civilization could not exist.

Croce's interests are catholic and his energy prodigious. In expounding his "Copernican revolution" he has written some fifty books, not only on aesthetics, ethics, and logic, but also on the history of modern European and Italian literature and civilization and on the history and theory of historiography. He once undertook to publish critical editions of all the chief Italian writers. Continued by others, this monumental series, when completed, will contain six hundred volumes.[8] For nearly forty years, furthermore, he has edited, and for the most part written, an internationally recognized scholarly journal.

Croce's conception of history is very difficult and is to be understood only in terms of a wide variety of factors which went to shape his life. First of all, there is his upbringing, which was distinctly conservative and upper class and to which can be traced the conservative liberal coloring he gives his Romantic philosophy. He was born near Naples on February 15, 1866, as the period of the Risorgimento drew to a close. His parents belonged to the landed gentry, and one of his grandfathers had been a high magistrate under the Bourbons. One uncle was professor of philosophy at the University of Naples. Another was a member of parliament and leader of the Right. In his household in Rome young Croce spent three years, learning politics from the conservative liberals who frequented his uncle's drawing-room.[9]

As for his formal education, it was Catholic and classical. As a boy he attended a religious boarding-school; and while he eventually reacted to the priestly teachings by becoming an atheist,[10] his acquaintance with scholastic philosophy left an indelible mark on his style of presentation, which is notable for distinctions so subtle that they exhaust both the subject matter and the reader, and for a tendency to slip into casuistry when the author is hard pressed. So classical was his training that today he is the only outstanding philosopher who is either ignorant of or indifferent to science, which, as a means of grappling with reality, he persistently subjects to contemptuous ridicule. At the University of Rome he registered in jurisprudence, but he spent most of his time in the library working on his own and frequented Labriola's lectures on ethics, which interested him tremendously. Add to this considerable research abroad, especially in Germany, where he acquired a knowledge of positivist historical method,[11] and we have an education largely oriented toward human, rather than cosmic, problems.

Concerning human problems, Croce was free to write in an unorthodox fashion. An earthquake (1883) snuffed out the lives of his parents and his only sister and left him a very wealthy landowner. Economic independence not only strengthened his conservative liberal tendencies, but it also helps explain his prodigious scholarly output; and, above all, it meant that his career was to remain unaffected by the traditions of universities and professors, for both of whom he retains a magnificent contempt.[12] Croce's wealth has also protected him against Mussolini, who no doubt finds inconvenient the withering, if indirect, blasts which issue from the philosopher's pen.

Croce could afford to be a heretic, but it was not until the nineties that he began to take advantage of this unusual freedom. His first period of creative activity, roughly 1886–92, was thoroughly traditional in character. He was a local historian, according to his own account reveling in an erudite positivism.[13] He produced three works of importance: *La rivoluzione napoletana del 1799*,[14] *I teatri di Napoli dal Rinascimento alla fine del secolo decimottavo*,[15] and the delightful *Storie e leggende napoletane*.[16] But with this antiquarianism, as he later came to call it, he soon became dissatisfied. Striking out into broader fields, he projected a history of Italian culture from the Renaissance to modern times, and he began by studying the cultural relations of Italy with neighboring countries, producing thus *La Spagna nella vita italiana durante la Rinascenza*.[17] But the work seemed endless, and ultimately, in desperation, he plunged into the theoretical problems which were at the bottom of his dissatisfaction. What was history? Was it art or science or merely erudition? The nineties were marked by a kind of personal intellectual crisis which gave a permanent twist to Croce's mentality.[18]

In a broad way this crisis meant merely that he was alive to the incipient revolt in western thought against positivism, naturalism, and realism.[19] At this time radium was smashing scientific determinism, Euclid was giving way before inconceivable but perfectly consistent geometries, history in Germany was beginning its tantalizing struggle with the problem of relativism, expressionistic art was defying the tenets of impressionism. For the first time question marks were placed after the basic assumptions underlying western civilization. Croce may also have been sensitive to the notion, everywhere prevalent, that Italy was culturally decadent and had been so since the great fires of the Renaissance burned low. Perhaps unconsciously he wished to win for Italy a positive role in the intellectual life of Europe. Certainly his unbounded popularity derives in part from the feeling of educated Italians that in him they possess an original thinker who is, at the same time, Italian.[20] But Croce's system is far more than a nationalistic effulgence. Its roots dig deep into the Romanticism of the early nineteenth century.

The thinkers who really influenced the construction of Croce's systematic philosophy were Vico, De Sanctis, Marx, and Hegel. All of them were Romanticists or possessed marked Romantic strains. The first two, Neapolitans like himself, were important to him partly for patriotic reasons, and he later set out to win for them recognition as thinkers of the first rank.[21] Vico's *Scienza nuova*, written early in the eighteenth century, was, in Croce's view,[22] highly critical of the Enlightenment and foreshadowed the historicism of the Romanticists. History is the sum total of knowledge, it argued, for "we know only what we do": "action and truth are mutually convertible."[23] De Sanctis, a literary critic of the Risorgimento, from whom Croce derived his expressionistic theory of art,[24] continually harped on the theme that "erudition without philosophy is neither criticism nor history but mere formless matter."[25]

As for the Germans, their influence on Croce was more subtle and also more pronounced. The introduction of Marxism in Italy in the 1890's, Croce feels, was the immediate occasion for the Romantic revival there, and he himself coquetted with socialism for a time.[26] Before long, however, he had produced a volume of essays (*Materialismo storico ed economica marxistica*)[27] in which he came to the conclusion not only that Marxism was a bad philosophy of history but that all philosophies of history were bad. Among other things, he pictured economic determinism as a soft-minded surrender to the suggestions of the new industrial environment and valuable only in so far as it called the attention of historians to a hitherto neglected class of facts. This critique of socialism, according to its author, was largely influencial in provoking that crisis in Latin socialism which led to syndicalism on the one hand, and to Italian revisionism on the other.[28]

Croce did not become conscious of how much he owed to Hegel until he had already begun his systematic exposition of the *Filosofia come scienza del spirito*. In a broad way Vico had anticipated the German thinker's philosophy of history, while De Sanctis had borrowed heavily from his aesthetic theories, and everyone knows what Marx owed to his master. Furthermore, Giovanni Gentile, Croce's intimate and collaborator in the publication of the review *La critica* (founded in 1903), was an out-and-out Hegelian. For the first time Croce began to study Hegel himself,[29] that magician who had attempted to reconcile Romanticism with the theories of the Enlightenment, who had held that all that exists is rational and that history is a gradual unfolding of the idea of liberty. Long arguments with Gentile convinced Croce that Hegel's identification of philosophy and the history of philosophy was acceptable in the sense that philosophy and historiography were identical. At the same time Croce was influenced by the Romantic activism of Sorel, though to what extent it is difficult to say. At least he translated Sorel's *Reflections on violence* and accompanied the book with a flattering preface. And he was much preoccupied with the notion that, in politics, the only standard is success.[30]

Roughly, Croce spent the first fifteen years of the twentieth century elaborating his *Filosofia come scienza del spirito*. It was idealistic, romantic, historicist. It was the very antithesis of the systems of Spencer and Comte. The first volume was on art: *Estetica come scienza dell' espressione e linguistica generale*.[31] It remains the most famous of Croce's works, and the author himself thinks that it

inspired everything of importance that was produced in the field of philosophical and historical study, criticism of poetry, music, and the fine arts, linguistic studies, legal and economic science, the history of thought and civilization, and religious and educational controversies; thus, after an interval of two centuries, it recovered for Italian thought an active part in the thought of Europe, and even a kind of primacy in certain branches of study.[32]

The other works in the series were: *Logica come scienza del concetto puro*,[33] *Filosofia della pratica: economica ed etica*,[34] and *Teoria e storia della storiografia*.[35] The bent of the man's mind is also revealed by the fact that during the same period he wrote *La filosofia di Giambattista Vico*,[36] *Ciò che è vivo e ciò che è morto della filosofia di Hegel*,[37] and *Storia della storiografia italiana nel secolo decimonono ai giorni nostri*.[38]

The coming of Fascism was the last of the influences which played a leading role in shaping Croce's philosophy and history. In a sense, his system had prepared the way for Fascism, emphasizing, as it did, the importance of action, the autonomy of politics, and the relativity of values. Borgese argues acidly that Fascism was the only logical conclusion to be drawn from *Filosofia come scienza del spirito;* that from Croce, Mussolini himself learned that idealism meant a world which is what the will makes it; and that Machiavelli was profoundly right.[39] A writer more in sympathy with Fascism avers that Mussolini's political system merely gave practical realization to the ideas of Vico, Gentile, and Croce.[40] For his part the Neapolitan sage denies his parenthood, arguing that with the foundation of *La critica* he had fought the irrational and morbid elements in the new Romanticism, denouncing futurism in art, the new cult of nationalism in politics, and in philosophy actual idealism, Gentile's creation, now the official philosophy of the Fascist state.[41] True that at first Croce lent his vast prestige to the support of Mussolini's regime. Equally true that in 1924 he broke with Mussolini. It may have been, as Borgese suggests, that this was merely a revolt of sentiment outraged by Fascist tactics[42]—the Matteoti murder, for example.

The breach with Mussolini was a courageous act, only possible in view of Croce's economic independence and his tremendous popularity. Sonnino had named him senator in 1910, and in 1920 Giolitti had included him in his cabinet as minister of public instruction. The universities numbered many men who counted themselves his students or followers. The world-wide indignation aroused when a band of ruffians broke into Croce's library one night revealed to Mussolini the danger of making a martyr out of the philosopher, who, for his part, did not relish the thought of exile and so expressed himself by indirection. Croce's followers did not fare so well. Gentile, now an enemy, suggested to Mussolini a Fascist oath for university professors and in this way eventually rid the universities of Croce's adherents.[43]

Since 1924 the master has been reconstructing his philosophy in a more liberal direction. Surrounded by his books (he has collected one of the finest private libraries in the world), his family of five, and a small circle of intimates, this unprepossessing septuagenarian—short, blondish, bespectacled—has lashed out at Fascism with a cold and scholarly fury. But the most important works of his later years—*Storia d'Italia dal 1871 al 1915*,[44] *Storia d'Europa nel secolo decimonono*,[45] and *Storia come pensiero e come azione*[46] —are not only scarcely veiled attacks on Fascism; they are also attempts to reconcile Neo-Romantic and liberal-positivistic conceptions of history. To this task Croce brings a tremendous erudition, a prodigious memory, and a facile pen. Yet it is not easy to reconcile the cult of facts and objectivity with a subjectivism as rigid as ever stalked this earth, a complete disdain for philosophy of history with a history conceived of as philosophy, a halting faith in gradual progress, and a stuffing of the whole time process into the present. Perhaps Croce has attempted a stride greater than his legs are long. Certainly his personal failings—supreme egotism; extreme pettiness; above all, his tendency to hold to intellectual positions out of personal dislike—have marred the result. Yet, whatever one may think of his synthesis, Croce is the only important thinker of our time to have made such an attempt.

What is fundamental in Croce's history is his conception of time. For the average historian time flows. He speaks of the "stream of time" and conceives of himself as living in a present which has taken the place of the past and is also distinct from a yet unborn future. The past is dead. It is of little importance to anyone save himself. He can describe it on paper or in a lecture hall; he can peruse its remains; he may speculate on its significance; but it is still something not here and not now, it is a reality outside himself, extending backward to the mists of creation. The past is a cause which has ceased to exist except in so far as the present is its mechanical effect. Time is eternal, and the present is merely a moment.[47]

For Croce time stands still. The present is eternal and includes all time within itself. Past and future are not separate from the present but are part of it. They exist only now, and therefore only in the mind, as ideas of things that have happened or will happen. That the average historian thinks the past is dead is due to the fact that time is measured by a spatial clock. But it is consciousness, rather than the present, which is momentary. Time is not extension; it is rather duration. Past and future are purely psychological subdivisions within the present.[48] All that is— be it the French Revolution or the Fascist revolution or a planned-for revolution—is now. All history, that of paleolithic and medieval times as well as that of recent times, is contemporary history. "Contemporaneity is not the characteristic of a class of histories . . . . but an intrinsic characteristic of every history."[49] Cut off from the past, the present loses all meaning.[50] Witness the victim of amnesia.

If the average historian should reply that this is one of those metaphysical propositions which makes no practical difference, Croce would say that it is not metaphysical and that it makes a world of difference. The proposition that the present is eternal makes reality a creature of consciousness. It does this because it makes space an aspect of time and represents ordinary objective three-dimensional reality as a product of the momentary character of consciousness. So-called "objective reality" becomes a theoretical construction of the mind. This fictitious reality has the practical use of creating fixed points in a world of flux—fixed by projection "forward" and "backward" from a momentary consciousness. It has the practical use of everyday orientation, but it is not the true reality.[51]

The true reality, according to Croce, is subjective; it is mental, and mind is activity. Activity may be classified as either theoretical or practical. There is the act of knowing and the act of doing. We know in two ways. First of all we visualize the individual thing—that is to say, we create the thing known. Such visualization is aesthetic intuition and is the first and basic activity of the mind. When we think about the thing visualized there is, in the second place, logical activity; and from this empirical-logical basis we proceed to practical activity, which is either economic or moral. Thus for Croce there are four categories or activities inherent in the nature of the mind: aesthetic, logical, economic, and ethical; and each category is expressed in typical forms and is dominated by a particular value.[52] Aesthetic activity expresses itself in art and language, and its value is beauty. Logical activity takes the form of philosophy and history, and its value is truth. Economic activity realizes itself in such things as government, science, the production of goods; it aims at the useful. Ethical activity finds outlet in moral codes, social reforms, and the like; and its value or aim is the good.[53] As we shall see, this conception of the categories influences decisively Croce's theory of the nature and function of history.

Croce's notion of the eternal present leads him not only to identify reality and mind, but also to identify history and knowledge. Knowledge consists of facts, and facts are always things that have happened. They are memories of completed actions and so belong to that division of the eternal present which we call "the past." Furthermore, all knowledge is knowledge of the concrete. Things are just exactly as they happened; each event or action—each fact, that is to say—is unique. Every work of art is different from every other work of art; every dictatorship, from every other dictatorship. There is no knowledge which is not historical, and none that is not knowledge of individual things.[54]

On the basis of this conception of knowledge, Croce argues that history is not, and can never become, science. For science abstracts from concrete human activity its physical and mathematical aspects, treats these as realities independent of the mind, and, by assuming that they remain constant and uniform, creates empirical generalizations, the so-called "laws of nature."[55] Science is not knowledge, because all its procedures go contrary to the nature of reality, which is subjective and not objective, concrete and not abstract, diverse rather than uniform. If it be objected that science works, that it builds bridges, solves the problem of communications, cures the sick, Croce replies: "Exactly so." The natural sciences are practical and not theoretical activities; they "are not directed to action, but *are*, themselves, actions";[56] they are fictitious constructions of the mind for practical purposes and have nothing to do with truth. Proof of this assertion is that the sciences must conform to the true reality in order to work; they must apply their abstract generalizations and empirical concepts to specific bridges, railways, illnesses.[57]

Nor is history a social science, for these disciplines, in so far as they are not history—that is to say, in so far as they attempt to ape the methods of physical science—Croce also relegates to the sphere of practical activity and sets aside as not concerned with knowledge. Sociology, for example, attempts to correlate slum areas and the distribution of wealth—both abstractions from particular slum areas and particular aggregates of wealth. Economics posits a "law" of supply and demand, a generalization possible only if we assume—what is not true—that there exists an abstract economic man motivated solely by considerations of prof-it.[58] Some well-meaning souls have even attempted to consider history a science. As an example Croce cites Taine, whose *Origines de la France contemporaine* was intended as a medical prescription for his sick and troubled country, fumbling for a new constitution after the disaster of 1871. The new constitution, Taine thought, should be suited to the peculiar traits and circumstances of the French people, and the formula might be obtained by a case study of the patient. Applying the methods of science, Taine produced a study of a dangerous malady, more familiarly known as "rationalism," an explanation of France in terms of race, circumstance, geographical features and (what Croce calls) other mythological nonsense. When asked for specific recommendations—Taine's contemporaries were aware of his project—he could only say: "Don't look for simple solutions," or "On this particular question I do not have enough details."[59] Croce emphasizes that social science merely *attempts* to ape the methods of physical science. It cannot do so with real success because only the mathematical and physical constructs of the mind offer a sound basis for abstraction. Nor is history art, for art is intuition or, to use an equivalent term, expression—simply and purely expression. There is nothing intellectual or logical about it, so that by definition it fails to fulfil the requirements of knowledge.[60]

History is instead philosophy, or, to be more accurate, philosophy is the methodology of history.[61] To borrow a phrase from Durant, history is philosophy in motion.[62] As Croce puts it, "philosophy is history, since history is the reality or consciousness of all that happens, and this reality does not achieve its full consciousness apart from the category of philosophy which always accompanies it."[63] To state the proposition another way, history is experience; philosophy, the elucidation of the concepts which make it possible to understand experience. Technically, this doctrine of the identity of philosophy and historical method rests on Croce's logic—the "science of the pure concept"—which identifies the historical judgment, the judgment of fact, and the definition. The subject of any proposition is always a historical fact; the predicate, always a universal or concept. This argument rests, in turn, on a sort of scholastic theory of the universal, namely, that the universal exists only and entirely in every particular.[64] In lay terms the substance of the matter is this: Fact and interpretation are not essentially different. They are implicit in each other. All facts are historical; all interpretations philosophical. It is impossible to know something and yet not understand it. As no historical problem can be understood without reference to the concepts worked out by philosophy, so no philosophical problem can be solved except in relation to the facts. Otherwise we are left with a useless record of brute facts, as in the case of the professional historian, or with endless disputes over meaningless abstractions, as in the case of the professional philosopher.[65]

The Crocean union of philosophy and history is not, however, to be taken as a philosophy *of* history. Such constructs are fantastic. On this point Croce agrees profoundly with the orthodox historian, though for different reasons. In Croce's way of thinking philosophies *of* history are all based on an elementary error, on a dualism of fact and interpretation. They ignore the meanings implicit in the facts and superimpose on these facts an arbitrary interpretation, usually for moral or economic, i.e., for practical purposes. The philosopher of history takes the schematic devices of history—divisions according to time, space, and classes of facts —and attempts to transform these fictions into concepts.

Let us look at the books of "philosophy of history" and observe this process of arbitrary judgment and confusion. In one the Orient will be identified with "immediate consciousness," Rome with "abstract generality" or with the "state," the German world with the "unity of the individual and the universal," of "worldliness" and "spirituality." In another the Orient will be identified with the "infinite," Greco-Roman antiquity with the "finite," and the Christian age with the "synthesis of the finite and the infinite. . . . ." Not dissimilarly proceed philosophies of history which adopt materialistic concepts or pseudo-categories, as that of the Marxists, which identifies the ancient era with the concept of "slave economy," the medieval era with that of "serf economy," the modern era with "capitalist economy," and the future with the "socialization of the means of production"; or the ethnic, which treats in a similar fashion the geographic and linguistic groupings of peoples, fantastically converting them into pure races, constant and perpetual in their being, dividing these into inferior and superior, and identifying them with the idea of virtue and vice, of spiritual forces and the contrary defects—heroism, prowess, religiousness, speculative and artistic capacity, and baseness, irreligiousness, mental weakness, selfishness, and so on.[66]

Philosophy of history is thus a species of allegory, pretending to discover the true history under the apparent and often attempting to forecast the history of the future. Both Christianity and Marxism, to take significant examples, place at the end of the historical process the catastrophic birth of a static state of perfection. Nothing, avers Croce, could be more grotesque than interpretations of this character. Like all dualisms, philosophy of history is an intellectual monstrosity. Fact and interpretation are certainly distinguishable, but they are also inseparable.[67]

From this point of view, the old problem of objectivity is seen in a new light. For Croce there is no such thing as objectivity as it is conceived of by the orthodox historian, as a problem of being fair-minded and impartial in the interpretation of the facts which he finds in the documents. Not that Croce thinks historians should make moral judgments or plead the cause of a political party or some other interest group. Moral judgments and party history belong to practical, not theoretical, activity. We must not confuse the categories. As no painting can ever be morally good or bad but is solely beautiful or ugly, so no event can be judged on ethical grounds, since it can be only significant or insignificant. Similarly, party history is a form of economic activity, to be judged only in terms of its success; as propaganda it may be effective or ineffective, but it is always propaganda, never history. Ultimately all error, both theoretical and practical, is the result of confusing the categories.[68]

The weakness of orthodox objectivity lies not so much in its avowed ideals as in its superficiality. It rightly avoids moral judgments, party prejudice, and philosophy of history, but on the mistaken ground that truth consists in the mere presentation of facts. This kind of objectivity is in reality a screen for intellectual naïveté. Ranke's histories—and there are no better examples—

were not investigations of urgent theoretical or speculative problems but were merely accounts, organized in terms of empirical or pseudo-concepts, such as the state. Their naïveté is well illustrated by the *History of the papacy in the sixteenth and seventeenth centuries*, in which the ancient monarchy is treated as moribund, without significance in modern times, a corpse which Ranke gleefully takes it upon himself to bury at the very moment Bismarck was being worsted in the *Kulturkampf*.[69] What Ranke failed to see was that the reality which he wished to describe *wie es eigentlich gewesen* was not extrinsic to himself but a construction of his own mind and that, therefore, true objectivity coincides with an awareness of the irremediable subjectivity of all knowledge. The mere presentation of facts is chronicle; and professional historians, "who are usually professors or other simple-minded people,"[70] are chroniclers and not historians. Following the example set by Ranke, they eschew theories and stick to the facts, observe the most scrupulous exactness, and substitute these things for the trouble of serious thought. What they produce is not knowledge but a practical preparation for future knowledge. Chronicle becomes history only when it is apprehended by a thinking mind, only when the facts are infused with thought.[71] The historian who would be more than a chronicler must realize that history is the gnosiological horizon perceived at a given moment in the time process. All divisions and periods are constructions within that horizon and possess exactly as much validity and objective necessity as the moment, the point of view, possesses. All interpretations are a process of self-understanding having meaning and truth only in and for the moment.[72] Only by accepting the subjective character of reality and grappling with it intelligently, that is to say, systematically, can the work of the historian be profound and meaningful, and only in this way can it be truly objective.

Obviously, Croce thinks that the orthodox historian places far too much emphasis on the critical evaluation of the documents. Certainly one must insist on factual accuracy, but factual accuracy is not truth. Even miracles cannot be rejected on the basis of attested evidence, since they are supported by the same kind of testimony that makes certain a treaty of peace. Attested evidence, furthermore, is always uncertain, owing to the possibility of the discovery of new documents. Truth always requires intrinsic, never extrinsic, reasons;[73] it is not a one-to-one correspondence of events and statements about events but a matter of logical coherence. "True history is that of which an interior verification is possible."[74] In short, documents, as the term is ordinarily used, are relatively insignificant. Diplomas, charters, and diaries do not furnish us with the raw material of history but with "those secondary particulars which it would not be worth while to make the effort of keeping alive and complete in the mind."[75]

The historian's real document is his own mentality, which is a historical formation containing within itself the whole of history. Historiography (philosophy) consists in a clarification and qualification of our remembrance of that which we did, of that which did the humanity which is in us. If documents are to be considered the raw material of history, the term must be extended to include

all the works of the past yet recallable in written words, in musical notations, in pictures and sculpture and architecture, in technical discoveries, in the transformations made in the surface of the earth, in those made in the depths of the soul, or in political, moral, religious institutions, in the virtues and in the sentiments little by little formed in the course of centuries and yet alive and at work within us. These are the documents which, gathered from time to time in our spirit, uniting with acquired conviction and with our thoughts and sentiments, make possible the knowledge of what has happened by a sort of Platonic "anamnesis," or rather by virtue of the Vichian principle of the convertibility of truth and action, whence man, who has created history, always knows it, re-creating it in thought.[76]

The writing of history thus consists in reliving an action so that it becomes a part of our own experience. Beyond a certain point the study of documents becomes superfluous because the recalling has already taken place. And the absence of evidence on some points hardly interferes with the search for truth, no more than in the case of the individual who, in recalling his own past, has forgotten the date of such and such an event but is no less aware of what he has been, which is the reality of what he is now.[77] "History is not something we have, it is something we are."[78]

It is upon the thinking out of truth rather than on the study of the documents that Croce would have the orthodox historian place the emphasis. For Croce the essential thing in a history book is its logical unity, its formulation and solution of some urgent theoretical problem arising out of the necessity for action. Methodology, in so far as it is a preparation for this systematic work, must concern itself with conceptual apparatus, with the definition of such concepts as Renaissance and medieval, with the problem of periodization, with the different kinds of history. For Croce, of course, all such conceptual apparatus hangs on the nature and relation of the categories. There are, for example, only four distinct kinds of history—history of art, of thought, of ethical and economic action, the last-named variety including what the orthodox historian would call "political history."[79] Beyond these, or rather as the quintessence of these, is ethicopolitical history, which

is the story of the human mind and its ideals in so far as they express themselves in theories and in works of art, in practial and moral actions. Considered especially as moral and practical action, it is the record of the human *ethos*, which I have chosen to designate as *ethico-politics* in order to make it clear that, as distinguished from mere political history, it has its life-germ in the moral consciousness; and, as distinguished from the mere history of moral ideas, it includes politics, economics, and every other form of practical activity. . . . . To use academic and doctrinal terms . . . . ethico-political history is the union of the *History of Civilization*, arising principally in the eighteenth century, with the old *Political History* or *History of the State*, revived and restated in Germany in the nineteenth century—the union of *Kulturgeschichte* and *Staatsgeschichte;* but a profound unity and not an eclectic juxtaposition such as is usually practiced in those books in which there have been casually appended to the chapters on political history, treatments of religious, scientific, moral, cultural, or other types of history.[80]

What ethicopolitical history really is can be made clear only if we analyze Croce's conception of the historical process.

The Crocean process is a truly Heraclitean flux. Change alone is permanent, or rather the categories alone are permanent, for it is they which make it possible to recognize change. The categories introduce an order into the process, but an order very different from that which the orthodox historian conceives of. In Croce's process there is no causality. The notion of cause is foreign to history because it is a product of science and has its function in that field. No historian has ever succeeded in writing history in terms of cause and effect; he has succeeded only in adding to his account the terminology of causality in order to make a show of scientific learning. Causality is a fallacious explanation because it requires a reality external to the mind. Past actions must be regarded as material, rather than as psychological, facts and then booked up mechanically with present actions in the vain hope of explaining them.[81] Even in science the principle of causation

is not a formula of explanation but a description of certain relations given by empirical observations, and therefore of certain operations to produce certain facts which from time to time it is of use to reproduce or to know by what means they are reproduced in order to be able to prevent them in case of necessity. But when [the principle] is divorced from its context and distorted to furnish arguments and explanations concerning reality and history, its inadequacy is immediately revealed in the appearance of an infinite regress in which one cause always depends on another, and from which there is no issue except most assuredly by degrading it altogether to the level of a phenomenology of an ultimate cause, which is transcendent, and therefore either obviously unknown or posited as known by an act of the imagination.[82]

The truth is that a reality wholly mental cannot be explained in terms of a fictitious objective reality created by mind itself. Proof is to be found in the inability of the historian to predict. When asked to forecast, he always ends up muttering something trite about "the complexity of the factors involved,"[83] which really means that the activity of the mind is unpredictable because thought is self-determining.

There is no causality in history, nor does history repeat itself. Even if the temporal-spatial situation alone is different, we are confronted with something new; every event has an unconfoundable physiognomy. The illusion of repetition arises from the misuse of the principle of classification, from an attempt to make classification mean in history what it means in science by conceiving as basic and significant groupings which in history can only be mnemonic conveniences. Considered as material things, facts can be classified; but as the mental entities which they really are, they cannot be classified because each is unique.[84]

There is no causation, and there is no recurrence. Yet the flux does have a pattern. It develops dialectically as a continuous synthesis of opposites. It is, in the first place, a synthesis of permanence and change. Things endure only because they develop. Man is always the same, and culture always different. New ideas become solidified in institutions against which creative thinkers and revolutionaries always rebel.[85] The flux, in the second place, is a continuous synthesis of good and evil, a perpetual overcoming of evil with good. Invasion, famine, plague, anarchy—these are the things against which men build fortifications, cultivate fields, undertake sanitary arrangements, just as against the mystery of the unknown, the fear of the future, and the misery of sorrow they invent religions and philosophies, write poetry and music. Civilization is a perpetual struggle against the perpetual danger of a relapse into barbarism.[86] "We are obliged continuously to reachieve with our labor and with our sufferings all that we have inherited from those who have gone before us."[87] Decadence and disintegration are the preparation of a new way of life, and the decline of the ancient world will remain a mystery until it is viewed as the emergence of a new and Christian civilization.[88] In the third place, the flux is a synthesis of truth and error, a dynamic progression in which every logical proposition is true at the time of its conception but untrue in succeeding time-situations when it becomes part of other and more inclusive truths. *Veritas filia temporis*—and yet it is not a question of a gradual approximation of definitive truth or of a complete submersion of truth in the time process. The universals used in qualifying particulars are absolute because they depend on the unchanging categories, but the particulars which are judged are always changing. The dialectical flux gives us a truth at the same time relative and absolute.[89]

But the dialectical process not only has a pattern; it also has meaning; it has direction: it is progress. Again it is a very un-orthodox progress, for it consists not in a gradual and ulti-mately definitive eradication of war, poverty, ignorance, and other evils. In Croce's way of thinking, a perfect state, which would result from the elimination of evil, is inconceivable; it would mean the solution of all man's problems, and in this situa-tion life itself would become a contradiction in terms. The goal is not outside but within the historical process. It is reached at every moment, but at the same time not reached because every attainment creates the need for a new one. Progress is the in-clusion of that which precedes in that which follows, and only in the sense that nothing occurs in history without fruit does history attain a superior level and realize an improvement. The last is *ipso facto* the best.[90]

The improvement consists in a greater degree of liberty, i.e., in the creation of new and richer forms of life, in the recognition and promotion in one's self and others of that humanity which is the true creative force. Liberty realizes itself in every thought and every action which has the character of truth, goodness, utility, or poetry.[91] To a greater or lesser extent, therefore, liberty exists in every age. Certainly the society of ancient Athens was based on slavery, but that does not detract from the greatness of the works produced by those Athenians who were free. Certainly the "liberties" of medieval Italian towns were the privileges of a few, but within their sphere these liberties produced a great art and a great literature. True enough, the monarchies of early modern times were absolute, but their historic function was to destroy medieval privilege and localism and so prepare the way for the greatest age of liberty so far—the nineteenth century. Now as law and government, now as opposition and rebellion, liberty is always with us; and the story of its fortunes is history[92]—more particularly, ethicopolitical history.

A final point concerning the role which written history plays in the historical process: The orthodox historian tends to regard historical erudition as interesting but useless, as a kind of knowl-edge having value only in and for itself. Croce argues that without historical erudition (i.e., without knowledge) there would be no historical process. The dependence of man on his knowledge of the past is for Croce obvious.[93] The ordinary individual remembers an appointment he made yesterday for today, a debt he contracted last year and due today, a marriage celebrated ten years ago, the anniversary of which falls today; and on the basis of this knowledge he takes action. It is much the same with society. Who can deny the connection between our morality and our conception of the origins of Christianity, or between our political practices and our knowledge of the origins of the constitution, or between our present foreign policy and our experiences in the last world war? "Historical erudition has the end of keeping alive the knowledge which human society has of its own past, that is to say, of its present, which is to say, of itself."[94] Croce's argument is that we are interested in past facts because they have a direct bearing on our present problems, that historiography is an attempt to answer pressing questions, that it is

an act of comprehension and of intelligence, aroused by a need of practical life which cannot be satisfied by passing over into action if first the fantasms and the doubts and the obscurity, against which it struggles, are not dispersed, thanks to the positing and resolution of a theoretical problem, which is that act of thought. The seriousness of a need of practical life gives it the necessary presupposition— be that a moral need, that is, of knowing in what circumstances one is placed in order that inspiration and action and the good life may issue forth; or a purely economic need, such as the selection of the proper means. . . . .[95]

Historiography, in other words, provides the theoretical basis for all practical action.[96]

This doctrine is a bit difficult. Croce does not mean that historiography is useful as a means of social control. Elaboration of symbols, indoctrination of the masses with a particular political faith (as, for instance, in the teaching of history in the public schools), analysis of social and economic structure with a view to curative legislation—these are practical, and not theoretical, actions. History is not social science. Nor does Croce mean that theoretical activity (historiography) determines the nature of practical action, that the connection between them is causal.

Practical action has its origin in the will, which is "free by definition." The function of historiography is to clear the way for the will by giving meaning to the situation and outlining choices. While the act has an ideal correspondence with the preceding theory, it is always a new and different act, provoking new and different theories. Historiography is that part of the historical process which makes possible (but does not determine) all practical activity.[97] Nothing, therefore, could be more significant in our time of crisis than a truly profound and systematic book of history.

It is a tradition among historians that philosophy of history reduces itself either to a collection of truisms or a collection of words; in any case, it scarcely affects the actual writing of history. Croce's works constitute an exception to the tradition. Whatever one may think of his ideas, it is certainly true that they affect profoundly his historical writings. Such ethicopolitical histories as that of *Italy 1871–1915* and that of *Europe in the nineteenth century* are hardly comprehensible except in the light of the conceptions outlined in the foregoing pages. What could be more incomprehensible, more unorthodox, than an interpretation which views the nineteenth century as essentially an age of religious struggles?

The work on Italy is an attack on Fascism. It undertakes to disprove the Fascist view of pre-war Italian history as an era of decline and to deny, by implication, the belief that Fascism represents the birth of a new and greater Italy. Croce begins with what he regards as the facts: pre-war Italy was progressive and liberal; and her achievements, if less stirring than those of the Risorgimento, were equally significant. In the forty-five years before 1915 Italy created a constitutional monarchy, pushing aside her antiquated aristocracy and ending the rule of priests and police, so that politics were no longer a matter of intrigues and arrests but came out into the open, into the chambers, which were elected by a well-nigh universal suffrage, with the assistance of a free press, free speech, and freedom of assembly. Pre-war

Italy, in the second place, began an economic expansion un-paralleled in her history: the beginnings of industrialization and an overseas empire, a foreign trade which increased 118 per cent in one ten-year period, a population which rose from twenty-five millions in 1861 to thirty-five millions in 1911. In the third place, Italy developed a stable social order. A common Italian life gradually took the place of the separate lives of the provinces. Illiteracy was reduced to 38 per cent. A law for compulsory ele-mentary education was adopted, if not enforced. There was ex-tensive social legislation and, above all, an absence of social con-flicts. Through participation in parliamentary government, re-publicanism and socialism lost their revolutionary edge. Through the policy of a free church in a free state the formation of a clerical party was prevented. There was no sign of anti-Semitism, and the notion of class warfare had to be introduced from abroad, and class hatreds artificially fostered. Politically, socially, and eco-nomically, pre-war Italy, far from being in a state of decline, was "in the making."[98]

Yet, despite all this progress—and Croce concedes this much to the Fascists—the Italians were convinced that as a nation they were a failure. They felt that their heroic age was over, that they now had no mission to perform. The fall of the Right (1876) and the breakup of the bi-party system seemed to prove that they were unable to govern themselves, while the seizure of Tunis by France and the disaster to Italian arms at Adowa indicated that in international affairs Italy counted for nothing. This feeling of inferiority was accentuated by comparisons with Germany. Lib-erty, it was said, was born in the German forests, and a truly free people could spring only from Teutonic stock. The Italians were an old and worn-out people. Like the other Latin races, they were predestined to spiritual subjection to the Catholic church, while politically they were condemned to oscillate between or-dered absolutism and undisciplined democracy. Or, contrari-wise, it was argued that Italy was a young and inexperienced na-tion, who had acquired her liberal institutions at a stroke (and largely through luck), and that this was the reason for her incompetence.[99] In any case, the Italians were agreed that they were a third-rate people.

And Italian politics, Croce holds, were largely determined by this feeling of inferiority. Crispi's ministry (1887–96) can be explained in no other way. The Italians regarded Crispi as a strong man, capable of making something of Italy, though exactly what was not quite clear. Whatever it was, Crispi set out to accomplish it with furious energy; and when he directed his attention to attainable ends, he achieved much, as in the case of social legislation and local government. But for the most part he involved Italy in unnecessary difficulties. Wild rumors led him to start a quarrel with France, and this precipitated a tariff war which so adversely affected Italian finances that he had to retire from office temporarily. He made colonial commitments far beyond Italy's resources, and this led to Adowa and his own fall. His use of authoritarian methods, especially with regard to the socialists, eventuated in a bloody rising in Milan and four years of crisis during which it seemed for a time that Italy might adopt an autocratic regime. But it is not only Crispi, it is also the seizure of Tripoli, and Italy's entrance into the late war,[100] and, by implication, the post-war Fascist regime itself, which Croce would explain chiefly in terms of the Italian inferiority complex.

The explanation of this paradox, these tremendous accomplishments and this profound sense of humiliation, springs straight from Croce's theory of the categories. The idea that the Italians were a third-rate people was, he says, an illusion, or rather a pack of illusions. In fact, pre-war Italy lacked a mission because historical missions are myths. In fact, transformism meant merely that it is impossible to organize political parties in terms of the philosophical principles of conservation and change. In fact, the "failure" of Italian foreign policy meant only that the establishment of German hegemony fundamentally altered the character of international politics, so that the earlier liberal motifs (the freedom of peoples, for example), which had brought Italy into existence, were replaced with industrial and balance-of-power considerations which Italy could not really accept. The racial theories Croce hardly bothers to dismiss. The real cause of Italy's sense of frustration he finds in her cultural decadence, which was as menacing as her political, social, and economic achievements were promising. For it was this same cultural decadence which gave birth to Fascism. The liberal tradition in Italy—so runs his argument—was of recent origin and not yet firmly rooted. Italy's free institutions were a body of political devices rather than a living faith. Nor could they become otherwise until they possessed a profound theoretical basis. But it was precisely this basis that failed to develop, owing first to positivism and then to irrationalism.[101]

In a way, Italy was not to blame, for her cultural decadence was common to the whole of Europe; it was in reality a crisis in faith and moral ideals, occasioned to begin with by the decline of philosophy, that is to say, the Romantic idealism of the early nineteenth century. In the place of idealism there emerged an arrogant positivism which gradually destroyed all faith in the true human values. For positivism substituted the scientific for the speculative method, sought to explain such things as beauty and love in psychological terms, adopted an agnostic attitude toward everything that could not be demonstrated in a laboratory, and reduced man to the level of an animal. With the decline of philosophy the whole of culture became stagnant. History tended to become chronicle. Political science concerned itself with constitutional mechanisms. Theories of education were full of hygiene and medicine and empty of spiritual values. Literature, taking Zola as a model, gave itself over to the portrayal of human animality and filled the horizon with social diseases. The intellectual world was painfully small and narrow, superficial, confused, lacking the power of synthesis,[102] certainly incapable of providing liberalism with that theoretical structure it so badly needed.

The reaction which set in about 1890 promised something better. It began with the introduction in Italy of Marxian socialism, which induced the intelligentsia, hitherto concerned with surface phenomena, to refocus their attention on underlying realities. Historians, for example, began now to study movements and institutions as the expression of economic needs and class struggles. Marxism was, indeed, a wholly fallacious body of doctrines, but it was certainly better than the philosophic vacuum on which the positivists had prided themselves, and, what was more, it led to a renewed study of idealism. This was, obviously, a move in the right direction; had it become the dominant tendency, there might still be a liberal Italy. But, unfortunately, Croce and his disciples were a minority; the Romantic revival plunged almost immediately into a morbid and irrational idealism, which expressed itelf in such monstrosities as intuitionism, pragmatism, and futurism. The truth was that industrialism and Bismarckism had enfeebled the moral consciousness of Italy and Europe, and so made impossible a healthy and rational idealism. Consequently, the younger generation turned to imperialism, nationalism, and syndicalism. War and dictatorship came to be viewed as praiseworthy, while liberalism was regarded as a handicap to a nation which aspired to the position of a world-power.[103] The Fascist regime, Croce feels but dares not say, far from representing a rebirth of a decadent Italy, is itself a cesspool of intellectual confusion, moral despair, and cultural disintegration.

In his *History of Europe in the nineteenth century* Croce projects this interpretation of recent history on a much broader and more philosophic plane. This work is primarily concerned with refuting the notion that Fascism constitutes a distinct Weltanschauung, a political and social faith which is capable of taking the place of liberalism. Croce's argument amounts to an analysis of the fundamental forces at work in the nineteenth and twentieth centuries. These were, as might be guessed, not the industrial revolution, or the discoveries of modern science, or the movements of peoples, or even the development of the European state system. They were, instead, five conceptions of reality with their corresponding ethical systems; they were, to be more explicit, five religions[104]—Catholicism, authoritarianism, democracy, communism, and liberalism, and their warfare constitutes the true history of Europe in the nineteenth century, the history of its religious and moral soul. Obviously, the true faith is liberalism, which conceives of reality as struggle and life as an end in itself, to be increased and enriched without measure, while the opposition faiths are false because based on misconceptions of reality. Catholicism Croce regards as the "most direct and logical negation of the liberal idea,"[105] since it places the aim of life outside of life, in heaven, which alone it considers ultimately real. At the same time Catholicism was the least of the enemies, since it was intellectually bankrupt and had been so since the days of the Counter Reformation, when the body had been saved at the expense of the soul. In the face of liberal attacks Catholicism could only revive the study of medieval scholasticism. Authoritarianism likewise viewed the world as a process of shepherding mankind and protecting it from the wolves and the weather, but its paternalism was now worn thin, and its strength was based only on its ownership of modern state organization, which it had founded.[106]

Catholicism and authoritarianism were the conservative faiths, guardians of ancient traditions. Democracy and communism were new and radical. Democracy, indeed, was outwardly similar to liberalism, especially in its advocacy of liberty, equality, and popular sovereignty. But democracy was revolutionary rather than progressive, materialistic rather than idealistic. Democracy advocated equality of fact and therefore government of the masses by themselves, whereas liberalism understood that equality meant only the humanity common to man and therefore recognized the necessity of a ruling class. Nor did liberalism oppose communism, because the latter advocated socialization of the instruments of production. Private enterprise was with liberalism a purely empirical formula; should it ever hinder, rather than foster, the production of goods, liberalism would be the first to abandon it. Liberalism opposed communism because communism was materialistic, because it regarded economic activity as basic and the other forms of activity as mere derivatives of this, because it considered history a struggle between economic classes and liberalism a mere screen for the business interests of the bourgeoisie, and because it accepted other such nonsense. A society organized in terms of communistic materialism is deprived of its liberty, loses its capacity for creativeness and self-direction, and becomes a perpetual dictatorship, an army for the ends of the dictator or a crew of slaves who erect astonishing pyramids.[107]

Not surprisingly the soul struggle of Europe culminates in the triumph of the religion of liberty in the years 1870–1914. In the course of the century liberalism formulated the basic doctrines on which it still lives—a non-Jacobin notion of liberty, a nonviolent idea of politics, and especially a civilized nonmilitary idea of the function of peoples. It brought to virtual completion the second great revolution in modern history, the substitution of liberal regimes for absolute monarchies, a process begun in seventeenth-century England and become European with the French Revolution, and it began the reorganization of Europe on the basis of national self-determination. By adopting the better elements of democracy and extending the franchise it freed Europe from the tutelage of aristocracies and created a more varied and flexible ruling class of its own. By separating church and state and by secularizing education it circumscribed the activity of Catholicism and could now calmly await the gradual extinction of that faith. With its formula of laissez faire it promoted an amazing expansion of industry; and when economic conditions had changed and the expectation of an automatic solution of the social problem through free trade had proved illusory, liberalism adopted state intervention. After transforming communism into socialism, as is shown by the formation of marginal revolutionary parties, it made a convert of socialism, as evidenced in the policy of social legislation—old age pensions and the like.[108] Above all, liberalism won for itself the civilized public opinion of Europe, which was permeated with

a living and general consciousness of progress, not only as a concept of historical interpretation, but as a certainty that the royal road had been entered upon at last, that the human race now had acquired the mastership over things and, what was more important, over itself, and that it would not again abandon or lose this road but would follow it forever.[109]

Yet at the very moment of its triumph liberalism lost its way. The liberal synthesis began to disintegrate, and Europe had to endure the holocaust of world war. Again Croce's explanation is the revival of Romanticism, but here he makes a clearer distinction. He marks off theoretical from practical Romanticism. The former he considers a profound reaction to the superficial rationalism of the Enlightenment, a movement of thought which, finding its greatest exponent in Hegel, "grasped life in its active and combative sense, and thus prepared the theoretical premises of Liberalism,"[110] as, for illustration, in the elaboration of historicism. Practical Romanticism, on the other hand, was a malady, best exemplified in Byron—a restless anarchical unhappiness which arose among men whenever they were unable to live up to the strenuous religion of liberty and instead took refuge in a sentimental Catholicism, or in erotic love, or in racial mysticism, or in a politics which longed for the restoration of medieval society. Practical Romanticism was the *mal du siècle*, and its resurgence is identical with the decline of liberalism.[111]

The immediate impetus to this resurgence was provided by the unification of German power (1871) and the renewed prestige it gave to authoritarianism; but the real genesis lies much deeper than this: in the gradual cessation of that theoretical activity—historicist and idealist—which had made the practical achievements of nineteenth-century liberalism possible. After 1870 the place of history-philosophy was taken by a science which concerned itself solely with forces, which it treated deterministically in order to take measurements and find laws. Mankind became richer in facts but poorer in values, master of ever more efficient techniques but less aware of the meaning and worth of human life. The Kants and the Hegels of an earlier age were replaced with physicists, sociologists, and psychologists, who could produce techniques but not what is above or at the basis of every technique. So liberalism gradually lost consciousness of its values. Its practical activity came to be divorced from any serious theoretical activity. Hence the growing emphasis after 1870 on the politics of sheer force, on the justification of war in and for itself, on pros-

perity, on sports, on speed become a passion, and mechanism become a process of *Entseelung;* hence the increasing emphasis, in
short, on action for action's sake. This conception Croce refers
to as activism, in his mind a very ugly form of practical Romanticism, a nihilism which is the very antithesis of liberalism.[112]

> For if liberty is deprived of its moral soul, if it is detached from the past and
> its venerable tradition, if the continuous creation of new forms that it demands is
> deprived of the objective value of this creation, if the struggles that it accepts and
> the wars and the sacrifice and the heroism are deprived of the purity of the end,
> if the internal discipline to which it spontaneously submits is replaced by exter-
> nal direction and commands—then nothing remains but action for action's
> sake, innovation for the sake of innovation, and fighting for the fight's sake; war
> and slaughter and death-dealing and suffering death are things to be sought for
> and desired for themselves, and obedience too, but the obedience that is cus-
> tomary in war; and the upshot is activism. This is, accordingly, in this transla-
> tion and reduction and mournful parody that it achieves of an ethical ideal,
> a substantial perversion of the love of liberty, a devil-worship taking the place
> of that of God, and yet still a religion, the celebration of a black mass, but still
> a mass.[113]

That activism assumed the catastrophic form of world-war is
largely ascribable to the failure of nineteenth-century liberalism
to extend the principle of liberty to international relations. Liberalism should have created a free European union, and this was not
an impossibility until the establishment of German hegemony on
the continent. The peace of Europe had thenceforth to be maintained by alliances and armament, in an empirical and not a constitutional fashion; and it is useless to argue the question of war
guilt, since it is a question rather of a common error that demanded common expiation. This is not to deny that the war had a
moral issue, which was rightly proclaimed by the Allies as the
defense of liberalism, the freeing of the remaining subject nationalities, and the establishment of a permanent European union.
The threat of an authoritarian world-hegemony was a threat to
liberal civilization itself, as was proved by the failure of German
propaganda, which was unable to set up a counterideal capable
of gaining the support of the civilized world. Nonetheless, the
German accusation of hypocrisy was rightly taken, for the statesmen of the Entente used the liberal ideal as a camouflage for their

material interests, and the activistic state of mind was common to all participants—the English and the Americans as well as the Germans.[114]

The post-war differs from the pre-war world only in the greater prevalence of activism, as is to be seen in the rise of Fascism. No doubt the western world will undergo a couple of centuries or so of despotism and barbarism, but all that is nothing but the swing-back of the dialectical pendulum, brought about by the inevitable internal contradictions within nineteenth-century liberalism itself. And if the liberals are unduly disheartened by the process, that is because they do not understand that liberty is necessarily associated with no particular economic order, such as laissez-faire capitalism, and no particular political form, such as universal suffrage, and that Fascism is not a new faith but an absence of all faith and therefore cannot be the ultimate victor. The crisis through which we are passing can only mean the creation of the conditions for a more intense liberty.[115] For liberty

is the sole ideal that has the solidity once owned by Catholicism and the fluidity which this was never able to have, the only one that can always face the future and never claim to determine it in any particular and contingent form, the only one that can resist criticism and represent for human society the point around which, in its frequent upheavals, equilibrium is perpetually restored. So that when the question is asked whether liberty will enjoy what is known as a future, the answer is that it has something better still, it has eternity.[116]

The way forward lies in the restoration of that systematic theoretical activity whose decline is at the bottom of our troubles. No doubt Croce feels that in his own historical idealism the distant future already possesses the basis of a new and greater liberal synthesis.

NOTES

1. G. A. Borgese, *Goliath, the march of Fascism* (New York, 1937), pp. 295–98.

2. E. Troeltsch, *Der Historismus und seine Probleme. Erstes Buch: Das logische Problem der Geschichtsphilosophie. Gesammelte Schriften*, III (Tübingen, 1922), 619.

3. A. Carlini, "Benedetto Croce," *Enciclopedia italiana di scienze, lettere ed arti*, XII, 4–5; W. A. Drake, *Contemporary European writers* (New York, 1928), pp. 43–46; W Durant, *The story of philosophy: the lives and opinions of the greater philosophers* (New York, 1926), p. 509; Borgese, pp. 299–302.

4. Durant, p. 516.

5. Giuseppe Natoli, quoted in Durant, p. 509.

6. Borgese, p. 196.

7. H. W. Carr, " 'Time' and 'history' in contemporary philosophy; with special reference to Bergson and Croce," *Proceedings of the British Academy, 1917–18*, pp. 334–46, 348–49; Troeltsch, p. 618.

8. "Benedetto Croce," *New international encyclopedia* (2d ed.), VI, 281.

9. *An autobiography*, trans. R. G. Collingwood (Oxford, 1928), pp. 5–18; R. Piccoli, *Benedetto Croce: an introduction to his philosophy* (New York, 1922), pp. 3–15; Durant, pp. 507–9.

10. Piccoli, pp. 3–15; Durant, pp. 507–12.

11. Piccoli, pp. 3–15; *Aesthetic as science of expression and general linguistic*, trans. D. Ainslie (London, 1909), p. xiii.

12. Piccoli, pp. 3–15; Durant, pp. 507–9.

13. Piccoli, pp. 3–15; *Autobiography*, pp. 78–99.

14. Bari, 1912.

15. Bari, 1916.

16. Bari, 1918.

17. Bari, 1914.

18. Carlini, pp. 4–5; Piccoli, pp. 3–15, 28–42; *Autobiography*, pp. 26–77.

19. Piccoli, pp. 16–28; Troeltsch, p. 619.

20. Drake, pp. 43–51.

21. Piccoli, pp. 28–42; Troeltsch, p. 619; *A history of Italy, 1871–1915*, trans. C. M. Ady (Oxford, 1929), pp. 237–45; Drake, pp. 43–46.

22. *La storia come pensiero e come azione* (2d rev. ed.; Bari, 1938), pp. 51–65.

23. Quoted by B. Croce, "Giovanni Battista Vico," *Encyclopedia of the social sciences*, XV, 250.

24. A. Lion, *The pedigree of Fascism: a popular essay on the western philosophy of politics* (London, 1927), pp. 166–68.

25. *Autobiography*, p. 82.

26. *Italy*, pp. 145–62; Borgese, pp. 196–99.

27. Bari, 1900. Translated by C. M. Meredith as *Historical materialism and the economics of Karl Marx* (London, 1914).

28. Durant, pp. 509–12; *Historical materialism*, pp. 3–14, 11–20, 77–80; *Italy*, pp. 145–62; Piccoli, pp. 71–84.

29. Piccoli, pp. 87–98; Carlini, pp. 4–5; *Autobiography*, pp. 78–99.

30. Borgese, pp. 196–99, 295–98.

31. Palermo, 1902. For the English translation see n. 11.

32. *Italy*, p. 245.

33. 3d rev. ed.; Bari, 1917. Translated by D. Ainslie as *Logic as the science of the pure concept* (London, 1917).

34. 3d rev. ed.; Bari, 1923. Translated by D. Ainslie as *Philosophy of the practical: economic and ethic* (London, 1913).

35. Bari, 1917. Translated by D. Ainslie as *History, its theory and practice* (New York, 1923). Reviewed *AHR*, XXVIII (1922–23), 288–90.

36. Bari, 1911. Translated by R. G. Collingwood as the *Philosophy of Giambattista Vico* (London, 1913).

37. Bari, 1907. Translated by D. Ainslie as *What is living and what is dead in the philosophy of Hegel* (London, 1915).

38. Bari, 1921.

39. Borgese, pp. 196–99, 259–98.

40. Lion, p. 216.

41. *Italy*, pp. 237–55.

42. Borgese, pp. 295–302.

43. Piccoli, p. 15; Carlini, pp. 4–5; Borgese, pp. 295–304.

44. Bari, 1928. For translation see n. 21. Reviewed *AHR*, XXXIV (1928–29), 595–97; *EHR*, XLV (1930), 137–39.

45. 3d rev. ed.; Bari, 1932. Translated by H. Furst as *History of Europe in the nineteenth century*. Reviewed *EHR*, LI (1936), 145–47.

46. See n. 22. Reviewed *AHR*, XLIV (1938–39), 860–61. Translated by Sylvia Sprigge as *History as the story of liberty* (New York, 1941).

47. H. W. Carr, *The philosophy of Benedetto Croce: the problem of art and history* (London, 1927), pp. 189–209.

48. G. Calogero, "On the so-called identity of history and philosophy," *Philosophy and history: essays presented to Ernst Cassirer*, ed. R. Klibansky and H. J. Paton (Oxford, 1936), pp. 43–44.

49. *History, its theory and practice*, p. 14.

50. Carr, *Philosophy of Benedetto Croce*, pp. 189–209.

51. *Ibid.*, pp. 189–209.

52. Carr, " 'Time' and 'history,' " *loc. cit.*, pp. 334–46; Carr, *Philosophy of Benedetto Croce*, pp. 189–209; M. Mandelbaum, *The problem of historical knowledge: an answer to relativism* (New York, 1938), p. 47; Troeltsch, pp. 620–22.

53. Carr, *Philosophy of Benedetto Croce*, pp. 1–13; Piccoli, pp. 99–129.

54. *History, its theory and practice*, p. 108; *La storia come pensiero e come azione*, pp. 19–24.

55. *Logic as the science of the pure concept*, p. 338; Carr, *Philosophy of Benedetto Croce*, pp. 189–209; Carr, " 'Time' and 'history,' " *loc. cit.*, pp. 334–46; Lion, pp. 184–85.

56. *Logic as the science of the pure concept*, p. 332.

57. Piccoli, pp. 116–29, 158–68; Troeltsch, p. 622; *La storia come pensiero e come azione*, pp. 19–24.

58. *La storia come pensiero e come azione*, pp. 295–303; Piccoli, pp. 207–24.

59. *La storia come pensiero e come azione*, pp. 184–93; *History, its theory and practice*, p. 76.

60. Piccoli, pp. 99–115.

61. Carr, *Philosophy of Benedetto Croce*, pp. 189–209; Calogero, p. 36; *History, its theory and practice*, pp. 117, 151; Piccoli, pp. 159–68.

62. Durant, p. 512.

63. Quoted by Calogero, p. 35.

64. Piccoli, pp. 15, 141–68, 258–88, 295–304; Calogero, p. 36; *Autobiography*, pp. 101–7; Lion, p. 172; Mandelbaum, pp. 43–46; *History, its theory and practice*, p. 60; Carr, *Philosophy of Benedetto Croce*, pp. 189–209.

65. *La storia come pensiero e come azione*, pp. 143–49; *History, its theory and practice*, pp. 61–62, 77; Carr, *Philosophy of Benedetto Croce*, pp. 189–209.

66. *La storia come pensiero e come azione*, p. 137.

67. *History, its theory and practice*, pp. 68–69; *La storia come pensiero e come azione*, pp. 5–9, 136–43.

68. *La storia come pensiero e come azione*, pp. 32–37, 175–83, 198–210; Piccoli, pp. 173–87.

69. *History, its theory and practice*, p. 86; *La storia come pensiero e come azione*, pp. 9–13, 75–92.

70. *History of Italy*, p. 20.

71. Carr, *Philosophy of Benedetto Croce*, pp. 180–209; Piccoli, pp. 141–68; 253–58; *La storia come pensiero e come azione*, pp. 75–92, 128–35; Mandelbaum, p. 52.

72. Troeltsch, pp. 623, 628–29.

73. *La storia come pensiero e come azione*, pp. 1–5, 105–12; Piccoli, pp. 253–58; *History, its theory and practice*, pp. 17, 136.

74. *History, its theory and practice*, p. 136.

75. *Ibid.*, pp. 138–39.

76. *La storia come pensiero e come azione*, p. 109.

77. *History, its theory and practice*, pp. 17, 25, 140; *La storia come pensiero e come azione*, pp. 5–9, 105–12, 150–55, 295–303; Mandelbaum, pp. 50–53; Calogero, p. 36; Piccoli, pp. 253–58.

78. Carr, " 'Time' and 'history,' " *loc cit.*, p. 347.

79. *La storia come pensiero e come azione*, pp. 37–42, 128–35; Piccoli, pp. 159–68.

80. B. Croce to C. A. Beard, June 24, 1933, quoted by C. A. Beard, "Written history as an act of faith," *AHR*, XXXIX (1933–34), 230–31.

81. *La storia come pensiero e come azione*, pp. 14–18, 24–27, 210–15; *History, its theory and practice*, p. 73.

82. *La storia come pensiero e come azione*, pp. 214–15.

83. *Ibid.*, pp. 14–18.

84. *Ibid.*, pp. 92–104, 261–68.

85. Piccoli, pp. 188–206; *History, its theory and practice*, p. 84; *La storia come pensiero e come azione*, pp. 157–66, 274–77.

86. *History, its theory and practice*, p. 85; *La storia come pensiero e come azione*, pp. 157–66.

87. "The roots of liberty," *Freedom: its meaning*, ed. R. N. Anshen (New York, 1940), p. 36.

88. *La storia come pensiero e come azione*, pp. 37–42, 157–66; *History, its theory and practice*, pp. 87–88.

89. *History, its theory and practice*, pp. 48, 91; Mandelbaum, pp. 55–56; Carr, *Philosophy of Benedetto Croce*, pp. 189–209; Piccoli, pp. 295–304; Calogero, p. 41.

90. *La storia come pensiero e come azione*, pp. 37–42, 253–59; Lion, p. 185; *History, its theory and practice*, p. 85; Piccoli, pp. 289–95; Troeltsch, p. 627; Mandelbaum, p. 57.

91. *La storia come pensiero e come azione*, pp. 46–50, 223–31, 242–47; "The roots of liberty," *loc. cit.*, p. 24.

92. "The roots of liberty," *loc. cit.*, p. 24, pp. 29–31; *La storia come pensiero e come azione*, pp. 46–50, 175–83, 242–47; Lion, p. 186.

93. *La storia come pensiero e come azione*, pp. 171–75.

94. *Ibid.*, p. 198.

95. *Ibid.*, p. 4.

96. *History, its theory and practice*, p. 12; *La storia come pensiero e come azione*, pp. 1–5, 30–32; Lion, p. 175.

97. *La storia come pensiero e come azione*, pp. 175–93.

98. *History of Italy*, pp. 26–105, 214–36, 256–69.

99. *Ibid.*, pp. 1–20, 26–105.

100. *Ibid.*, pp. 162–213, 256–88.

101. *Ibid.*, pp. 1–25, 106–44, 245–55.

102. *Ibid.*, pp. 126–44, 237–45.

103. *Ibid.*, pp. 145–62, 237–69.

104. *History of Europe*, p. 19.

105. *Ibid.*, p. 20.

106. *Ibid.*, pp. 20–41.

107. *Ibid.*, pp. 20–41.

108. *Ibid.*, pp. 97–103, 135, 273–76, 286–94, 297–315.

109. *Ibid.*, pp. 243–44.

110. *Ibid.*, p. 43.

111. *Ibid.*, pp. 42, 54–55, 260–64.

112. *Ibid.*, pp. 246–47, 253–59, 264, 317–19, 340–46.

113. *Ibid.*, p. 342.

114. *Ibid.*, pp. 325–30, 345, 347–51.

115. *Ibid.*, pp. 280–81, 351–52; *La storia come pensiero e come azione*, pp. 46–50, 223–31, 238–42; "The roots of liberty," *loc. cit.*, pp. 25, 37–39.

116. *History of Europe*, p. 358.

V

HANS DELBRÜCK (1848–1929)

RICHARD H. BAUER*

URING the third quarter of the nineteenth century German historiography was largely dominated by an influential group of political historians. Led by such eminent historians as Dahlmann, Droysen, Sybel, and Treitschke, whose patriotic and nationalistic sentiments had been profoundly stirred by the contemporary political developments of Europe, they vigorously advocated the unification of Germany under the leadership of Prussia. Hence they were sometimes called the *kleindeutsch* historians. Moreover, they favored the establishment of a constitutional monarchy resting on a national foundation. In general, they considered themselves as belonging to the school of historians founded by Leopold von Ranke. Some of them, as a matter of fact, had received their historical training from him. All accepted both his methodology and his interpretation of history. They agreed with him that history should confine itself primarily to political matters; that it should emphasize the role of the state as the supreme cultural and political achievement of mankind; and, finally, that it should particularly stress the relations of the states to one another and the effect of these relations on their internal policies. Unlike Ranke, who insisted upon treating all states on a basis of equality and without partiality, they gave preference and special consideration to their own state. In other words, his approach to history was largely universal; theirs was definitely nationalistic. Basically, however, they differed from him in degree rather than in substance.[1]

As one of the last important representatives of the political

* Assistant professor of European history, Mary Washington College.

historians, the name of Hans Delbrück should be mentioned. Long after their influence had declined, he continued to emphasize political history and to defend it against all attacks. His interesting career and noteworthy achievements deserve careful examination.

Hans Delbrück was born of a distinguished family of Prussian officials on November 11, 1848, in Bergen on the island of Rügen. Among his ancestors were noted jurists, theologians, and university professors.[2] One of his great-uncles, Johann Friedrich Gottlob Delbrück (1768–1830), had served as tutor of two Prussian kings, Frederick William IV and William I. During the nineteenth century several of his relatives achieved distinction as Prussian statesmen. His father, Berthold Delbrück, was a judge of the district court in Bergen and was later promoted to the court of appeals in Greifswald. His mother was a highly gifted woman, the daughter of Dr. Leopold von Henning, who had been a professor of philosophy at the University of Berlin and an enthusiastic disciple of Hegel. Undoubtedly, young Delbrück's devotion to Hegel can be traced to his maternal grandfather.

He received his preparatory training at the *Gymnasium* in Greifswald. Protestant in its outlook and dominated intellectually by the local university, this institution gave him an excellent humanistic education. It was here that he met Max Lenz,[3] with whom he established a lifelong friendship. He continued his higher education at the universities of Heidelberg, Greifswald, and Bonn. Deeply interested in history, he attended the lectures of such prominent historians as Noorden, Schäfer, and Sybel, from whom he gained an insight into Ranke's methodology and approach to history. They also imbued him with their political ideals and objectives. According to his own testimony, he was particularly grateful to Noorden, an intimate friend of the family, for advice and guidance.[4]

In the meantime his career as a university student was briefly interrupted by two events. Keenly interested in the political developments of Germany, he gave enthusiastic support to Bismarck's plan for the unification of Germany under the leader-

ship of Prussia. He was profoundly stirred by patriotic sentiments and eagerly awaited the opportunity to serve Prussia.
When he realized that war with France was inevitable, he enlisted in the army and as a lieutenant of the reserves took part in
the battle of Gravelotte and the siege of Metz. Moreover, for a
short period he tutored Crown Prince Gustav of Sweden.

Like most doctoral candidates of this period, he published his
dissertation, *Über die Glaubwürdigkeit Lamberts von Hersfeld*, on a
medieval topic. Since this thesis contained the main characteristics of his later writings, it proved to be a most revealing contribution. After carefully examining and evaluating the writings
of Lambert von Hersfeld, a German monk and chronicler of the
eleventh century, whose *Annales* and other works heretofore had
been generally accepted by reputable historians, Delbrück concluded that numerous passages were totally unreliable. With remarkable insight and clarity of expression, he proved that Lambert von Hersfeld was an untrustworthy source of information. In
doing so he did not hesitate to challenge the conclusions of Giesebrecht, who was considered an authority on medieval German
history. In short, the dissertation reflected his independent spirit,
his sharp critical faculties, his ability to present historical material in a clear and logical fashion, and his fearlessness in challenging accepted beliefs and traditions. Nothing gave him more
satisfaction than the opportunity to destroy historical legends.

In 1874 Delbrück was appointed tutor of Prince Waldemar,
one of the younger sons of Crown Prince Frederick, He held this
position for five years until the premature death of Prince Waldemar in 1879. As tutor he often accompanied the royal family to
various parts of Europe, thereby increasing his geographic knowledge and understanding of other countries. He became intimately acquainted with the crown prince and crown princess,
for both of whom he had the deepest respect and admiration.
Not only was he frequently consulted by them in matters pertaining to the education of Prince Waldemar, but he was given many
opportunities to discuss problems of general interest with them.
In all his relations with the royal family he never acted the part

of a courtier or flatterer but always remained true to his nature. He never hesitated to express his sincere and honest convictions.

His experiences as tutor were extremely profitable. In the first place, they enabled him to gain a better insight into the contemporary political scene. It was his firm belief that every historian should concern himself with current affairs and should never lose sight of the present. In meeting various higher officials of the government he made many valuable political observations. Moreover, his contacts with the crown princess, a gifted and intelligent daughter of Queen Victoria of England, stimulated his interest in English history. As a result he wrote several essays dealing with the development of English political parties and the nature of the English monarchy.[5] Finally, it was during this period that he decided to make military history his particular field of specialization.

It is rather difficult to explain the circumstances which finally led him to concentrate on military history—all the more so because he himself could give no satisfactory explanation. Perhaps his experiences during the Franco-German War, or perhaps his associations with army leaders at court, were partly responsible for his growing interest in military matters. According to his own version, he gradually discovered that such topics as the organization of the army and its relations to the state had a peculiar fascination for him.[6] He became deeply interested in analyzing the campaigns and strategy of famous military leaders. While attending military exercises in Wittenberg in the spring of 1874, a copy of Rüstow's *History of infantry* fell into his hands. This book influenced him profoundly and stimulated him to do further research. Most important in strengthening his decision to write military history was the request he received in 1877 from Countess Hedwig Brühl to complete the unfinished biography of her illustrious grandfather, Neidhardt von Gneisenau, a work that had been begun by Georg Heinrich Pertz, the noted historian. In accepting this request he realized that a comprehensive understanding of the campaigns of the War of Liberation was essential for evaluating the work of Gneisenau. He therefore made a thorough study of Clausewitz, whose complete works had been presented to him by the crown prince, and consulted leading military experts, including such authorities as Field-Marshal Count Blumenthal, General von Gottberg, General von Winterfeld, and others.

With his appointment in 1881 as Privatdozent to the University of Berlin, he finally realized his ambition to become a professor of history. He began his long and distinguished career at that institution by offering a series of lectures on "The war of 1866." These were shortly followed by others on "The war of 1870," "The general history of the art of war from the Persian wars to the present," and "The main battles of Frederick the Great and Napoleon." As a teacher he was unusually successful. From the very beginning he attracted many students to his classes and as his popularity increased, the largest auditorium of the university was assigned to him.[7] His genial personality, combined with an ability to organize and present his material in a clear and stimulating manner, largely explained his success. He knew how to make past historical scenes live in the minds of his students. With rare humor and irony he exploded many historical legends.

Unfortunately, his promotion at Berlin was very slow. His independent attitude in military and political matters antagonized influential army and state officials. His new viewpoints on the strategy of Frederick the Great and Napoleon gave rise to a bitter controversy that lasted over a decade. Some of his opponents in the army tried to silence him by demanding that the university drop all courses in military history. Unsuccessful in this attempt, they managed to place obstacles in the way of his promotion. That explains why he had to wait until 1897, shortly after Treitschke's retirement from the faculty, for his promotion to the rank of professor. In that same year he was asked by Dr. Friedrich Althoff, the Prussian minister of education, to offer a course in world-history. The magnitude of the assignment did not frighten him. As a matter of fact, he believed that the offering of such a course was not only justified but imperative, especially in view of the glaring lack of general historical knowledge displayed by the average student of history. Using his knowledge of military history as a framework, he soon prepared a long series of lectures on world-history. From 1896 to 1920 his course on world-history, offered in cycles of four semesters each, proved to be one of the most popular courses in history at the University of Berlin.

Unlike the typical German professor, he did not believe in removing himself from the realities of life by secluding himself behind the cloistered walls of a university. Following in the footsteps of Treitschke and Sybel, he remained in close touch with all political developments.[8] As a member of the Prussian legislature from 1882 to 1885 and as a member of the Reichstag from 1884 to 1890, he gained valuable political experience. In fact, he considered this experience as an indispensable preparation for his professional work as a historian. He was no parliamentarian of the stature of Richter, Bebel, or Windthorst. He preferred to play the role of observer to that of active participant. Nominally belonging to the Free Conservative party, which had given loyal support to the policies and program of Bismarck, he was really no "party man" at all. He was too independent to give blind obedience to any party program or leadership. Party discipline irked him. He liked to think of himself as standing above all parties and classes. Hence, he judged all measures independently on their own merits, no matter what party had proposed them. At times he even supported measures sponsored by left-wing parties. When the crown princess once asked him to state his political affiliations and beliefs, he smilingly replied: "I am a conservative social democrat."[9]

Delbrück, to be sure, was a conservative. But his conservatism was not class-conscious like that of the Prussian military nobility, which sought to achieve an aristocratic self-administration by opposing the omnipotence of the bureaucracy.[10] On the contrary, his conservatism was rooted in the traditions of the bureaucracy, with which administrative group his family had been identified for generations. He accepted the monarchy as a reasonable institution and favored the administration of government by a group of educated officials. He did not object to the privileged economic position of the landed aristocracy, since he felt that its welfare was essential to the morale and strength of the Prussian corps of army officers. Unlike the aristocratic conservatives, however, he viewed the state as an organization of theoretically equal individuals and not as a society of classes. Since the masses are not able to govern themselves, he believed that it was imperative for the monarch in collaboration with the bureaucracy to govern reasonably and justly. With such views as the foregoing dominating his thinking, it is easy to explain his independent and nonpartisan political attitude.

In addition to his parliamentary experience he soon found other outlets for his historical and political interests. From 1881 to 1894 he served as editor of the *Staatsarchiv*, a semiannual publication.[11] Founded in 1861 and edited for the first ten years of its existence by L. K. Aegidi and Alfred Klauhold, it was published under the auspices of the Institute of Foreign Politics of Hamburg, the Institute of Foreign Public Law and International Law of Berlin, and the German foreign office. Each issue contained a collection of important official and diplomatic documents made public during the six months preceding publication. From 1886 to 1893 he was also editor of Schulthess' *Europäischer Geschichtskalender*.[12] Founded in 1860 and published annually, it reviewed the leading events of the preceding year, particularly those of Germany, in chronological order. It included many excerpts from newspapers, speeches, and official documents. Delbrück's main task consisted in writing the concluding chapter, or summary, in which he interpreted with his usual clarity the political and international developments of the past year.

His appointment in 1883 to the editorial board of the *Preussische Jahrbücher* really marked the beginning of his most important work as a publicist. Founded by Rudolf Haym in 1858 to serve as an official organ of the political historians, the *Preussische Jahrbücher* had advocated German unification under the leadership of Prussia and after 1871 had become a vigorous supporter of imperial orthodoxy. Until 1890 Delbrück served as coeditor with Treitschke, but thereafter he assumed sole responsibility for almost thirty years. Under his leadership the *Preussische Jahrbücher* became one of the most influential political journals of Germany and an important molder of public opinion. In its columns he sought to bind history and politics closely together, the one enriching and stimulating the other. Never succeeding in gaining a large circulation, because of the unusually high quality of its articles, it was consistently read by a small group of influential men, the élite of Germany. Among its subscribers were prominent government officials, army officers, educators, and historians. Its articles were frequently quoted in other publications.

With the expiration of his term of office in the Reichstag in 1890 Delbrück withdrew from active participation in politics. His withdrawal, however, was not caused by any diminution of interest in political affairs. On the contrary, by releasing him from the uncomfortable restraints of party discipline, it gave him more time for a calm and dispassionate evaluation of the political scene. Nothing pleased him more than to interpret political developments in the light of history. Unlike many other historians, whose political fervor had rapidly cooled after the unification of Germany, he retained his strong political inclinations until the end. In every issue of the *Preussische Jahrbücher* he commented on current domestic and international affairs. Independent and courageous in his outlook, he never hesitated to express his own views, regardless of the consequences.

Like most German intellectuals of the Wilhelminian period, he became an ardent admirer of the imperial government established by Bismarck.[13] He warmly defended it against all attacks by maintaining that it would lead Germany to great heights as a nation. Perhaps his optimistic view of German political institutions can be traced to his intimate and pleasant associations with some of the higher officials of the government. In general, he was too far removed from the provinces to observe some of the disagreeable features of the bureaucracy. To his credit, however, he never permitted his unbounded confidence in the German political system to interfere with his right to criticize the policies of the government. Thus he fearlessly denounced Bismarck's un-

reasonable persecution of the Catholics and socialists and repeatedly condemned the oppression of the Polish and Danish minor-
ities as morally unjustified and politically unwise.

Prior to 1914 he also viewed the course of Germany's foreign
relations much too favorably. In this respect he was no more optimistic than the majority of his countrymen. With rare exceptions, he never fully grasped the extent to which the Emperor
William II's foreign policies were endangering Germany's international position. For example, the seriousness of the Russian
threat never dawned upon him until the spring of 1914, shortly
after he had received a letter from Professor Paul Mitrofanov,
one of his former students.[14] He staunchly supported the acquisition of colonies on the ground that they would offer Germany an
outlet for her surplus of educated young people, for whom it was
becoming increasingly difficult to establish a career at home. If
Britain would only adopt a more sympathetic attitude toward
Germany's desire for more colonies, he cheerfully predicted that
the German demands for a larger navy would gradually subside,
thereby removing the main source of friction between the two
nations.

While supporting Germany's colonial aspirations, he constantly urged the government to exercise some degree of moderation in
international affairs. He opposed the chauvinistic demands of
the Pan-Germans, whom he considered a real menace, since they
might plunge Germany into war at an inopportune time. During the Boer War, while many German leaders were outspoken
in their sympathies for the Boers, he came to the defense of Great
Britain. When the tension with England reached alarming proportions, he urged the German government to negotiate a naval
agreement. In facing a hostile public opinion he favored the acceptance of Winston Churchill's proposal of a "naval holiday" as
a preliminary step toward a better understanding between England and Germany.

More than any other period of his life, the war of 1914 revealed
his remarkable courage and lofty patriotism. He deplored the invasion of Belgium, which he characterized as a political blunder

of the most disastrous proportions, since it had hastened the entry of England into the conflict. Military strategy, he emphasized, should always be subordinated to higher political aims. When news of the military reverses on the Marne reached the German people, he advocated the negotiation of a reasonable peace settlement with the Allies, by which Germany would renounce her territorial ambitions in Europe for colonial concessions elsewhere. His proposals, of course, angered the militarists, annexationists, and other superpatriots. Led by the Fatherland party, which was generously supported by Ludendorff and Tirpitz, they bitterly assailed him for his lack of patriotism, and for the remainder of the war made life miserable for him. Unlike the other famous political historians, who had died while being admired by a grateful nation, he had to suffer unjustified abuse during his declining years.

Undaunted by the attacks that were directed at him, he quietly sought to gain a hearing for his views. With this objective in mind he helped in the founding of the *Mittwochgesellschaft* ("Wednesday Club"), which consisted of a small group of influential men from various walks of life.[15] Meeting regularly every Wednesday evening to discuss timely political and international problems, the group as a whole hoped to induce the government to enter into peace negotiations with the Allies. This organization tried to counteract the influence of the Fatherland party. Included in its membership were Count Hatzfeld and Count Hutten-Czapki; Adolf von Harnack, Wilhelm Kahl, and Max Sering, from the University of Berlin; Karl Helfferich and Paul von Schwabach, from the financial world; Schiffer, Krause, Friedberg, and Lusensky, who were representatives of the National Liberal party and members of the Reichstag; Schlutius, a representative of the Center party; August Stein, representative of the *Frankfurter Zeitung;* and high-ranking government officials. Prince Max of Baden, who later became a member, reported in his memoirs that Delbrück was the recognized leader of the group, to whom all members looked for inspiration and enlightenment. Unfortunately, the main objective of the *Mitt-*

wochgesellschaft was never realized. After the war it continued to discuss various problems confronting the Weimar Republic.

The collapse of the Empire overwhelmed Delbrück with unspeakable grief. Thanks to his natural optimism and sense of reality, however, he quickly adapted himself to the new political situation—certainly no easy task for a man who had reached the proverbial biblical age of threescore and ten. Without sacrificing his deep-rooted affections for the old imperial government, he gave loyal support to the Weimar Republic. In 1919 he insisted that "anyone who loves the German people must serve the Republic with German faithfulness."[16] With the approval of the new government he and several other prominent historians, including Count Montgelas and Professor Mendelssohn-Bartholdy, were commissioned to make formal reply to the Allied charge that Germany had been solely responsible for the war.[17] The result of their work was the publication of the German White Book, which contained new evidence to disprove Germany's guilt. Like many other German historians who had taken offense at the inclusion of Article 231 into the Treaty of Versailles, which specifically designated Germany as the nation responsible for the war, he became involved in the *Kriegsschuldfrage*, or war-guilt question. He was among the first historians to emphasize the importance of studying pre-war diplomacy as indispensable for an understanding of the fundamental causes of the war. During the next few years he contributed many articles on the origin of the war to the *Berliner Monatshefte*, in which he usually stressed the role of France and Russia in precipitating the conflict. He dealt rather sharply with Poincaré's foreign policy.

In 1919 he resigned from his position as editor of the *Preussische Jahrbücher*, with which he had been associated for thirty-six years. Two years later he retired from active teaching at the University of Berlin. But the septuagenarian had no intention of spending his remaining years in idleness. Relieved of his heavy responsibilities as editor and professor, he now found time for other projects. Following the example of Ranke, he decided to write a world-history based on the lectures he had delivered at the University of Berlin. "There's no better way to spend your last days," he remarked to a friend.[18]

Meanwhile he engaged in a series of bitter controversies with Ludendorff, Tirpitz, Kautsky, and Harden. He boldly accused Ludendorff and Tirpitz of having destroyed the Empire by their senseless strategy. He attacked Kautsky for having exaggerated the incompetence of the imperial government and the blunders of William II, thereby giving the outside world the impression that Germany had started the war. Nor did he have any kind words for Maximilian Harden, the brilliant editor of *Die Zukunft*, whose testimony on the origins of the war before a special committee of the Reichstag he considered as totally unreliable and worthless.

On his eightieth birthday (November 11, 1928) he was signally honored by many of his friends and former students. They presented him with a *Festschrift*, entitled *Am Webstuhl der Zeit*, which contained some interesting articles on a variety of historical topics contributed by Emil Daniels, General Wilhelm Groener, Major-General Ernst Buchfink, Paul Rohrbach, Paul Rühlmann, Friedrich Meinecke, and others.[19] On this occasion President Paul von Hindenburg paid tribute to him by presenting him with a shield of honor. Six months later, shortly after completing another article on the Treaty of Versailles, he was attacked by a severe case of grippe. He died on July 14, 1929, widely mourned by his numerous friends in Germany and elsewhere.

Delbrück's many writings can be divided into two groups. Some of them are primarily political; others are primarily historical. The line of demarcation between these two groups, however, is rather artificial, since Delbrück ordinarily used the historical approach in writing his political articles and unduly emphasized the political factor in his historical works.

Undoubtedly his most important political writings appeared regularly in the *Preussische Jahrbücher* under the title of "Politische Korrespondenz," in which he summarized and interpreted the current political and international situation. Always written in a clear and stimulating manner, these summaries contain intimate pictures of leading men and events. To the *Preussische Jahrbücher*

Delbrück also contributed innumerable articles of a more scholarly character on a most amazing variety of topics, including biographical sketches of important political leaders, criticisms of military strategy, arguments for social legislation, condemnations of the Prussian oppression of the Poles and Danes, and discussions of constitutional questions.[20] Collections of the more important of these articles appear in the following volumes: *Historische und politische Aufsätze;*[21] *Erinnerungen, Aufsätze und Reden;*[22] *Krieg und Politik*, which appeared in three volumes;[23] and *Vor und nach dem Weltkrieg.*[24]

By no means are Delbrück's political works confined to shorter essays and articles. Several of his books and pamphlets are definitely political in their scope. In his *Regierung und Volkswille,*[25] which contains a series of lectures on the German constitution delivered by him at the University of Berlin during the summer of 1913, he expounded his views on the leading features of the German government. In general, this volume gives the reader an unusually favorable and optimistic picture of imperial Germany. He maintained that the constitution embraced the best features of a democracy and an autocracy without incorporating any of their glowing defects. Like the constitution of the ancient Roman Republic, he argued that it united the principles of authority and democratic self-determination by bringing the Prussian nobility into a working agreement with the democratically elected Reichstag. He summarized its merits as follows:

Without closing my eyes to the inner defects which cling to our system of government, I must say that I see in it a much higher and better form of political organization than in any other modern state; but, be it well understood, only inasmuch as both phases of the government (i.e., the hereditary authority plus the national assembly) are recognized and exercise their right. The bills which are proposed by the representatives of the people, the control which the people exercise, the necessity of justifying oneself before the representative body, of treating with it, of dealing with this, then with that, faction, of making compromises, of concentrating the people, at least a majority of them, on one point —that constitutes the peculiarity of our strength and gives us the secure feeling that our nation is destined to a great future. . . . . If one should suppress the Reichstag, or exanimate it by a violent change of the electoral law, one would bring the German Empire to destruction just as surely as if the Reichstag should win the powers of a so-called parliamentary government. If both government and parliament work together, they can reach the highest aims, or at least more than do the states which are always called upon to follow now this, nor that, party; that is, to pursue politics not from the standpoint of the whole, but of a part of the whole.[26]

In a revised edition of the book, which appeared in 1920, Delbrück stated that the war of 1914 had vindicated his former opinions concerning the inherent strength of the empire.

Not because of any lack of parliamentary system of government did we go down to defeat, not because we had been more militaristic in the past than our opponents, but because the militarism of our opponents was able to win and ours was not. . . . . Our curse was not that we had a monarchical government for leadership, but that this monarchical government was not strong enough to counteract the chauvinistic currents of public opinion and to lead the people against its will into the right path.[27]

Undoubtedly this book exaggerated the merits of the old imperial government and underestimated its shortcomings. While it offered nothing new to the student of political theory, it was an important contribution to political psychology, since it represented the views of the ruling classes in their defense of the Prussian hegemony and the privileges of the officer class. According to Professor W. Y. Elliott,

the psychology of a very large part of the German people is reflected in these strictures of Herr Delbrück on parliamentarism and democracy. . . . . The book is full of the most interesting personal anecdotes of political parties in the Old Germany and of illustrations taken from the author's other works, chiefly his *Geschichte der Kriegskunst im Rahmen der politischen Geschichte.*[28]

Professor Elliott observed that Delbrück, as a specialist in military history, tended "to see political problems only in terms of an efficient military machine with which to assure national power."[29]

No other political writing of Delbrück aroused such bitter controversy and widespread interest as *Bismarcks Erbe.*[30] Hastily written after the opening of the war of 1914, it urged the German government to make a reasonable peace settlement with the Allies at the earliest possible moment; it also attacked the annexationist designs of the Pan-Germans. By negotiating such a treaty,

Delbrück boldly asserted, the German government would follow the admonitions of Bismarck, whose "main objective was to preserve peace under all conditions and whose teaching was to avoid a preventive war at all costs."[31] Germany, he insisted, should renounce her territorial ambitions in Europe for colonial concessions elsewhere. He favored the acquisition of colonies, not primarily for economic reasons or for the sake of prestige, but for the opportunities they might provide for Germany's surplus of educated young men. What Germany really needed, in his opinion, was an India, where talented and trained young Germans might go to establish successful careers for themselves. He bemoaned the fact that

thousands of our young men of thirty and over, who have attained the full powers of manhood and whose extensive knowledge and specialized training have prepared them for larger fields of activity, are often to be found idle or partially employed among us, all of them waiting to obtain some poorly paid position. Following the example of England in India, we must send them as technicians, merchants, planters, physicians, overseers, officers, and officials to the colonies, in order that they might govern the large masses of backward races.[32]

Since Delbrück considered the African colonial possessions of Germany to be both economically unprofitable and climatically unsuited for colonization, he eagerly looked forward to the day when the Turks would grant exclusive privileges to German technicians, scientists, physicians, and other professional groups to aid in the rejuvenation of modernization of their country. Both Turkey and Germany, he predicted, would derive lasting benefits from such collaboration. Here is what he wrote in *Bismarcks Erbe:*

Since Africa, or any other exotic territory for that matter, will not satisfy our needs, there fortunately remains for us another type of colonization and another field for colonial activity, both of which have been opened to us and placed at our disposal by the war. Namely, there remains Turkey, whose possessions in Europe, Asia Minor, Syria, and Mesopotamia include the oldest and most fertile cultural areas of mankind. At present this country is striving to achieve closer contacts with European civilization, from which course it cannot depart, especially if it emerges successfully from the war. For this work it requires the services of European instructors, whom at present it cannot find in any other country save in Germany.[33]

Bismarcks Erbe, of course, aroused the anger of the Pan-Germans, who loudly demanded the annexation of Belgium and other conquered territories, without which, they insisted, Germany could never feel secure against attack. In *Wider den Kleinglauben*,[34] one of his more important political pamphlets, he denounced their annexationist designs. He was convinced that the annexation of Belgium and other regions, if anything, would embroil Germany in endless wars, because

the various nations would consider themselves threatened by our preponderance of power. Since the feeling of independence is the most cherished treasure of all peoples—in fact, their very breath of life—the ultimate realization of our demands for annexation would result in a renewal of the war within a short time. Instead of enjoying the blessings of lasting peace, we would stumble into one conflict after another, without having Austria-Hungary, Bulgaria, and Turkey on our side. . . . . It is possible for us to become a great power without Belgium, as the future will teach us; but we cannot hope to become one if we proceed to annex Belgium, since our possession of that country would arouse the hostility of the entire world against us. . . . . . Anyone who has faith in German strength knows that we can dispense with Belgium; and anyone who has a correct insight into the world-situation realizes that we must dispense with it. . . . .[35]

In order to defend the exiled emperor and the old regime against the attacks of Kautsky and Harden, Delbrück published a short pamphlet entitled *Kautsky und Harden*.[36] In this pamphlet he took occasion to assail Kautsky's book on the origins of the war, *Wie der Weltkrieg entstand*,[37] in which the author quoted freely from German pre-war diplomatic documents to expose the glaring deficiencies of the imperial government. The conclusions of the socialist leader, according to Delbrück, are untenable, since they are based on a wholly subjective interpretation of the documents. Not only does Kautsky deliberately distort the facts, but "he doesn't even make the slightest attempt to give an objective interpretation."[38] Delbrück added that Kautsky had shown poor taste in giving such widespread publicity to the emperor's marginal notes, which appeared on various diplomatic documents, while the latter was still alive. In a similar vein he denounced Harden's accusations against the old regime. In view of the fact that Harden had supported the Pan-Germans before and during the war, Delbrück felt that it was rather unbecoming of the journalist to condemn the old imperial government.

Shortly after Delbrück had been sharply reprimanded in Ludendorff's *Kriegführung und Politik*[39] for his criticisms of the diplomatic and military conduct of the war, he quickly wrote a scathing reply in self-defense. In *Ludendorffs Selbstporträt*[40] he refused to retract any of his former accusations and ridiculed Ludendorff's belated attempts to justify the military strategy of the war. Moreover, he reviewed the field-marshal's political and strategical blunders at great length, explaining how they finally led to the collapse of the Empire. The greatest blunder of all, he contended, was Ludendorff's continued refusal to negotiate a satisfactory treaty of peace with the Allies at a time when Germany enjoyed undoubted strategic advantages. He vehemently denied the charge that Germany had been "stabbed in the back" by subversive elements at home. He concluded by insisting that

just as two great men, Bismarck and Moltke, had created the Empire, so two others, Ludendorff and Tirpitz, have destroyed it. The senseless construction of dreadnaughts by Tirpitz and his refusal to negotiate a satisfactory naval agreement with England had forced the British to join our enemies. By converting a defensive war into one of conquest, Ludendorff committed a serious blunder.[41]

Unfortunately, Delbrück's lack of moderation in his attacks on Ludendorff seriously weakened the effectiveness of his arguments. "It would have been much better," according to Professor Johannes Ziekursch, a noted German historian, "if Delbrück had expressed himself with the greatest moderation. The bitterness of his words did not tend to strengthen his case in various influential circles."[42] Ziekursch also pointed out that Delbrück overemphasized the political role of Ludendorff, thereby leading the reader to believe that the army virtually dictated all the political policies of Germany. Obviously, this was not the case, since it had been "the intentional policy of the government to keep the officers' corps from close contacts with the political, economic, and social forces of the nation."[43]

Delbrück's views on the origin of the war are briefly summarized in *Der Stand der Kriegsschuldfrage*.[44] In this pamphlet, which the *Historische Zeitschrift* described as "a remarkably clear presentation of the war-guilt question," he endeavored to prove that Germany had not instigated the conflict.[45] After pointing out the responsibility of Russia, France, and other countries he frankly admitted that the imperial government had made three serious mistakes:

> The real political mistakes made by Germany were, first of all, the construction of large battleships which unnecessarily aroused the suspicion of the English, thereby driving them into the camp of the enemy; second, the underestimation of the magnitude and imminence of the danger of war by the emperor and the diplomats; and, third, the German plan of war, which did not take the tremendous moral and political consequences of the invasion of neutral territory sufficiently into consideration.[46]

Delbrück's numerous political writings are important for two reasons. Besides illustrating the varied interests and journalistic activities of a typical political historian, they shed considerable light on the Wilhelminian period. Indeed, his political observations are almost indispensable for an understanding of recent German history. "They are personal and contemporary documents of the greatest interest," wrote Dr. Friedrich Luckwaldt, "since they offer a delightful and worth-while review of the years immediately preceding and following the war."[47] In general, they are rather subjective, often reflecting his political prejudices, but they are much less so than the writings of Treitschke and his contemporaries. At least Delbrück tried to be reasonably objective, as his calm and restrained style will testify.

Far more important than his political writings were his contributions to military history. More than anything else, these contributions explain his reputation as a historian. They are the result of a lifelong interest and specialization in military history. In his biography, *Das Leben des Feldmarschalls Grafen Neidhardt von Gneisenau*,[48] he made a penetrating study of the military strategy of the Napoleonic era. This book contains numerous letters of Gneisenau and constitutes a valuable addition to the literature of the Prussian reform period. By 1920 it had passed through four editions. The *Historische Zeitschrift* hailed the appearance of this biography as "one of the best publications in the field of modern history. Delbrück's careful and objective analysis and description of the military events, particularly his treatment of the campaigns of 1813, deserve highest commendation."[49]

Following the publication of this biography Delbrück wrote many articles on the military strategy of ancient, medieval, and modern times, most of which were devoted to an analysis and comparison of the military strategy of Frederick the Great and Napoleon. These articles formed the basis of his most important book, *Geschichte der Kriegskunst im Rahmen der politischen Geschichte*.[50]

As a military historian he made three noteworthy contributions. First, he exploded many legends dealing with the size of armies. For example, he contended that the Persian army which confronted the Greeks at Plataea never consisted of a million men, as various Greek writers had estimated, but merely of some 15,000 to 25,000 soldiers. Nor did the army by which Charlemagne destroyed the Saxons amount to more than 10,000 men. The size of the crusading armies, often exaggerated by medieval writers, never exceeded several thousand knights. Delbrück likewise sought to destroy the legend that the discovery of gunpowder had been chiefly responsible for the decline of knighthood. To use one of his many illustrations, he pointed out that the army of Charles the Bold, which was equipped with firearms and artillery, was signally defeated by Swiss footmen who lacked such equipment.

A second contribution of Delbrück as a military historian was his interesting observation that all military strategy could be divided into two kinds—*Ermattungsstrategie*, or strategy of exhaustion, and *Vernichtungsstrategie*, or the strategy of annihilation—each of which employed different methods in dealing with the enemy.[51] The purpose of *Ermattungsstrategie* was to weaken the enemy gradually by a series of maneuvers without necessarily destroying his forces, thereby compelling him to sue for peace. The object of the *Vernichtungsstrategie* was to strike at the enemy directly in order to destroy his forces. Heretofore it had not been customary to distinguish between these two kinds of strategy. As a matter of fact, all strategy had been considered variations of the *Vernichtungsstrategie*. Delbrück characterized the strategy of the eighteenth century, particularly that of Frederick the Great, as *Ermattungsstrategie*. The strategy of Napoleon and the nineteenth century he described as *Vernichtungsstrategie*.

Unfortunately, the formulation of the aforementioned types of strategy was not accepted by the Prussian military leaders, with whom he subsequently engaged in a literary feud. Led by Theodor von Bernhardi and Conrad von der Goltz, various officials of the army maintained that the *Vernichtungsstrategie* was the only recognized form of strategy.[52] They denied that the strategy of Frederick the Great differed radically from that of Napoleon. In fact, they were inclined to think of Frederick as a forerunner of Napoleon in strategical matters. Finally, they accused Delbrück of belittling Frederick by calling him an adherent of the *Ermattungsstrategie*.[53]

Delbrück, however, refused to make any concessions to his critics, and tried to strengthen his position by insisting that Clausewitz, the famous German military authority, had indicated the existence of the two types of strategy in one of his later writings. After fortifying himself with additional evidence he stood virtually alone in defending his views against the leaders of the Prussian army. Although his theories were never accepted by the military authorities, he at least emerged as the victor of the literary feud itself. He succeeded in silencing his enemies.

He made his third and greatest contribution as a military historian by weaving military history into the general pattern of world-history. In order to appreciate the significance of this contribution, it need only be recalled that heretofore the historian had treated military affairs as isolated events. He was satisfied to give the date of the battle, the size of the contending armies, and the number of troops killed or wounded. He made no attempts to fit military events into the general picture. Even the more technical descriptions of battles and campaigns by military experts were often unsatisfactory in this respect. Delbrück, therefore, made a distinct contribution to history when he succeeded in integrating military and general history.[54]

In his *Geschichte der Kriegskunst im Rahmen der politischen Geschichte* he surveyed the development of the art of war from ancient Greece to modern times. Basing his conclusions on a profound knowledge of military science, he reconstructed the chief battles and military campaigns of history. In doing so he ruthlessly destroyed military legends and smashed military heroes. But at the same time he carefully analyzed the important battles and campaigns by describing the organization and leadership of each contending army, the equipment of the soldiers, the nature of the weapons, the topographical and climatic factors, the problem of supplying armies with food and material, the natural resources of the opposing states, and the relations of the army to the state and its political institutions. While omitting no details, he always pointed out their relationship to other important factors. In other words, he adopted the methods of Clausewitz of criticizing military events and developments. He thereby gave a new meaning and deeper understanding to military history.

In a lengthy review of the third volume of the *Geschichte der Kriegskunst*, which analyzes the military developments of the middle ages, Professor T. F. Tout, a distinguished English historian, admirably summarized Delbrück's contribution to the history of the art of war as follows:

It [the third volume] is a wonderful evidence of Delbrück's vigour, industry, and breadth of vision. His book contains much that is interesting and important. There are many sound particular observations; there are excellent and spirited accounts of many individual battles, and there are so many shrewd statements as to the general features of medieval warfare that no student of the Middle Ages can fail to derive great advantages from its study. Professor Delbrück always tries to test the accounts of battles and campaigns by the touchstone of military possibility, and his habit of regarding medieval problems from a modern soldier's point of view saves him from the characteristic defects of that of the mere student, and gives a certain freshness and individuality to his whole work. Besides being something of a practical soldier, he is a widely read historian. Setting before himself the ideal of uniting military knowledge with military criticism, he has undertaken a task of great boldness and complexity, and often with some approach to success. . . . . As a professor, even more as a writer, he

has given a real impulse to the detailed study of medieval military history. . . . .
I have illustrated already the arbitrary way in which some fights are singled out
for treatment while others of equal significance are ignored. . . . . But when all
has been said against it, we must still thank the author for imparting to it a
quality that is eminently stimulating and human. Its very defects are provoca-
tive of thought and suggestive of inquiry.[55]

With all of Delbrück's predilection for military affairs, it is
rather difficult to think of him as a general or staff officer
charged with the practical execution of military maneuvers. It
is much easier to imagine him playing the role of a military theorist like Clausewitz, with whose interests and type of reasoning
he had much in common. His stimulating and original observations reflect thinking of the highest order. Moreover, his formulation of the two forms of strategy proved to have great military
significance. With the phenomenal growth in the size of the
European armies at the close of the nineteenth century, various
military authorities began to question the future possibility of
crushing the enemy's forces in a few short engagements. Some
of them were inclined to agree with Delbrück that future wars
would last much longer than previous ones. The elder Moltke
spoke of the possibility of a new "Seven Years' War" or even a
"Thirty Years' War." Under these circumstances might it not
have been advisable for the general staff to have adopted the
Ermattungsstrategie, as advocated by Delbrück, in future conflicts?
The general staff, however, rejected the adoption of this type of
strategy in favor of the famous Schlieffen plan, which was based
on a strategy of annihilation. The general course of the war of
1914, which witnessed the collapse of the Schlieffen plan, amply
justified the correctness of Delbrück's observations.

Second only in importance to his military contributions was
his *Weltgeschichte*.[56] Published in five volumes, it is largely a
compilation of his lectures on world-history which he had delivered at the University of Berlin for many years. Since these
lectures were based on his researches in military history, his
Weltgeschichte might be considered a by-product of his *Geschichte
der Kriegskunst*. Not only does the book retain the style and char-

acteristics of the lecture method, but it devotes many sections to the more important military campaigns and battles of history. Tremendous as was the task of writing a history of world-civilization, his work was facilitated by two factors. In addition to having taught world-history for a generation, he had the added advantage of having begun his studies in this field when there was no superabundance of monographic literature on the various periods of history.

In harmony with his opinion that one of the main functions of history is to explain the present, he attempted to bring the past into intimate relations with the present and sought to rediscover the present in the past. He conceived of world-history as the history of all peoples who have made lasting contributions to modern European civilization, Hence he excluded the ancient civilizations of America, India, and China and cast aside everything which he deemed unimportant. In general, his selection of material was largely determined by his own interests and conception of history. According to his own testimony, he borrowed heavily from Ranke's *Weltgeschichte*. In the classification and arrangement of his material he followed the traditional organization of world-history. Beginning with the history of ancient Egypt, Mesopotamia, Palestine, Greece, and Rome, he traced the growth of civilization to the close of the nineteenth century. Ancient history, he believed, ended with Diocletian, by which time the Roman Empire had fulfilled its historic mission. He concluded the middle ages with a discussion of Dante and began modern history with a study of the Renaissance and humanism, both of which he considered as forerunners of the Reformation.

Aside from the subjective selection and presentation of his material, his *Weltgeschichte* has several serious shortcomings. Underlying economic and social forces are often neglected and underestimated. Like other historians of the Ranke school, he devoted too much space to international relations and military affairs. In reviewing his treatment of ancient history in the *Historische Zeitschrift*, Professor Matthias Gelzer observed that fully six pages are required to describe the battle of Marathon and only eight to discuss the importance of Hellenism! "The reader will find absolutely nothing on the intellectual influence of Hellenism on the Roman Empire or anything on the gradual orientalization of Hellenism itself."[57] Gelzer also pointed out that the analysis of the internal organization of the Roman Empire is too brief and sketchy.[58] Perhaps the chief defect of the book is that too many of its conclusions are no longer tenable in the light of recent research. With all of its shortcomings, however, the *Weltgeschichte* remains a clear and stimulating review of world-history. It stands as a tribute to Delbrück's comprehensive knowledge of history and to his indefatigable industry.[59]

A further analysis of his historical works will show that they bear a close resemblance to the writings of Sybel and Treitschke, except that his style is much more moderate in tone. Hence it is obvious that he established no new school or philosophy of history but merely continued to write as an exponent of political history. Nevertheless, he was no blind imitator of Sybel and Treitschke, since he developed some independent views concerning the nature of history. In acknowledging his indebtedness to the aforementioned historians, he confessed that he owed much more to Hegel and Ranke, for both of whom he had the warmest admiration. In his introduction to his *Weltgeschichte* he remarked that "after Goethe, German intellectual life of the nineteenth century reached its zenith in Hegel and Ranke."[60] He observed that these two famous men had more in common than they themselves had realized, in spite of Ranke's emphatic denial to the contrary.

Strangely enough, he accepted Hegel's idealistic philosophy long after it had been discarded by the majority of historians. What appealed to Delbrück was not so much Hegel's philosophy of history as his idealistic explanations concerning historical developments and the nature of the state. Thus he conceived of world-history as the revelation of the Spirit in the events, institutions, and movements of mankind. Like Hegel, he regarded the state not merely as an institution but as a spiritual organism having a will and personality of its own.

In reality man first becomes man as a member of the state; he is thereby elevated above himself. The state, therefore, exists on a higher level than does the individual; so much so, in fact, that the individual must sacrifice himself to it. This is a moral law, which mankind has recognized at all times and among all peoples. This law is empirical proof to show that there are higher objectives than the individual. The transcendental nature of man is documented in the existence of the state. The so-called "altruism" merely recognizes individuals. But why should one individual sacrifice himself for another? Obviously, there must be something transcendental, some purposes that are higher than individuals, in order that one might demand of the latter to sacrifice their very existence voluntarily. But by no means is the individual worthless or without rights on that account. While it is true that he is under the state in one sense, in still another he is above the state. Is it not the abundance of individuals that makes the state purposeful? The rights of the state and those of the individuals form a polar antithesis. Both of them make demands and both carry these demands to the absolute.[61]

It is not surprising, therefore, that Delbrück devoted so much space to the state in his writings. He was also willing to concede that historical developments might take place according to a certain Hegelian rhythm of thesis, antithesis, and synthesis. He sometimes ascribed the activities of mankind to the interaction and interplay of various antitheses, the most important of which he listed as the individual and the community, state versus state, state and church, state and society, and personality and the mass. For example, in ancient history he emphasized the struggle between aristocracy and democracy and occasionally the conflict between aristocracy and plutocracy; the more important developments of the middle ages he attributed primarily to the tension between church and state and between priest and knight; and, finally, he believed that the course of modern history was largely determined by the interaction of many groups and institutions, such as the nobility, bourgeoisie, peasants, nationalism, Protestantism, and others. But he would never admit the existence of any laws of history.

In the last analysis, however, he mainly looked to Ranke for inspiration, whose writings and methodology he accepted as criteria by which to judge historical scholarship. In his seminar at the University of Berlin he never failed to emphasize Ranke's concepts of history, which sought to confine the historian to political history. In both his lectures and books he limited himself to a political discussion of such topics as the rise and decline of states, the relations of various states to one another, and the impact of their foreign relations on their internal political structure. Like Ranke, he urged his students to view historical periods objectively and to base their conclusions on a critical evaluation of all documents.

But in some respects he differed from Ranke. Motivated by a strong feeling of patriotism, he was inclined to interpret history from a nationalistic viewpoint. In theory he tried to be impartial in his treatment of other states, but in practice his writings displayed a definite bias in favor of his own. His nationalism, however, was much more subdued and controlled than that of Sybel and Treitschke. Moreover, by indicating the relationships of wars and military affairs to various political factors, he gave a broader interpretation to military history than Ranke. Most important of all, in his methodology he was not merely satisfied in establishing the authenticity of historical documents, but he was much more interested in trying to prove or disprove the plausibility of the actions and scenes described in them. To this second type of criticism he applied the word *Sachkritik* to distinguish it from *Quellenkritik*, or criticism of the sources. By subjecting military actions described in trustworthy Greek documents to his *Sachkritik*, he succeeded in proving that many of them were gross exaggerations and distortions of the actual happenings.

While historians in increasing numbers were attracted by the newer interpretations of history, he clung tenaciously to political history. He was not impressed or influenced by any passing fads and fancies. He bitterly lamented the fact that so many of the new historical theories had been evolved by individuals without adequate historical background and training:

Scientists, jurists, sociologists, economists, and so-called "philosophers" have attempted to master history in order to tell the historian how to interpret history. But they lack the first and most essential prerequisite: knowledge of historical events. How can anyone dare to set up the correct theories without knowing the basic facts and without a preliminary evaluation of these facts?[62]

Delbrück contended that many of the critics of political history have no clear conception of its scope and functions. In his opinion the distinction between political and cultural history is, after all, rather artificial, since the state is not only the supreme cultural achievement of mankind but serves as the channel by which the civilization of the past is handed down to future generations. He insisted that cultural progress was inconceivable without the state. He was firmly convinced that political history furnished the best framework within which to interpret the economic, social, and cultural developments of mankind. May not another generation of historians prove him to have been correct?

In his defense of political history, however, he often underestimated the economic and social factors. At times he ignored them completely. He refused to accept Rostovtzeff's brilliant economic interpretation of the decline of the Roman Empire. He had little patience with historians who ascribed everything to economic motives. He vigorously denounced the Marxian interpretation of history. He expressed his opinion of Karl Marx as follows: "As a demagogue he was a hero; as a thinker he was a sophist; and as a scholar he was a charlatan."[63] In a lengthy article on the Marxian interpretation of history he tried to point out the fallacies in the Marxian concepts of "the class struggle," "the proletariat," "the iron law of wages," and others.[64] Unfortunately, this article revealed a none too comprehensive knowledge of basic economic principles. Delbrück's tendency to minimize the nonpolitical factors of history undoubtedly constituted his chief weakness as a historian.

If he established no new school of history or left any noteworthy successors to carry on his work, he at least must be regarded as the last distinguished representative of the political historians. As his friend Friedrich Meinecke stated shortly after his death, "he is the last of the select group of political historians who had engaged in political journalism from the days of Dahlmann to Treitschke and whose scholarly writings reflected a deep interest in the affairs of the present."[65] As a brilliant professor of history and gifted editor of the *Preussische Jahrbücher*, he will be remembered primarily for his researches in military history and his many valuable political observations. But he will also be remembered for his love of truth and justice, his unfailing courage, his integrity of character, and his firm belief in intellectual freedom. Obviously, there would be no room for him in the Germany of Adolf Hitler.

NOTES

1. Georg von Below, *Die deutsche Geschichtsschreibung von den Befreiungskriegen bis zu unsern Tagen* (Munich and Berlin, 1924), pp. 38–63.

2. A few of his more important relatives were: Rudolf von Delbrück (1817–1903), Prussian minister of state and later president of the imperial chancellery under Bismarck; Clemens von Delbrück (1856–1921), Prussian minister of commerce and later secretary of the interior of the German Empire; Berthold Delbrück (1842–1922), a noted philologist; Max Delbrück (1850–1919), a brother, who distinguished himself as a chemist.

3. A distinguished German historian (1850–1932), known especially for his writings on Bismarck and other historical essays.

4. See autobiographical sketch in *Die Glaubwürdigkeit Lamberts von Hersfeld* (Bonn, 1873), p. 78.

5. Consult *Deutsches biographisches Jahrbuch* (Stuttgart and Berlin, 1917–20).

6. *Geschichte der Kriegskunst im Rahmen der politischen Geschichte* (Berlin, 1900), I, vii.

7. Roy S. MacElwee in his introduction to Delbrück's *Government and the will of the people* (New York, 1923), p. vii. See n. 25 below.

8. Eugen Schiffer, "Delbrück als Politiker," *Preussische Jahrbücher*, CCXVIII (1929), 290 f.

9. *Ibid.*, p. 291.

10. Arthur Rosenberg, "Hans Delbrück, der Kritiker der Kriegsgeschichte," *Die Gesellschaft*, VI (1921), 245.

11. *Das Staatsarchiv: Sammlung der offiziellen Aktenstücke zur Aussenpolitik der Gegenwart* (Leipzig, 1861–1919).

12. Munich, 1881–94.

13. The best summary of his views on the imperial constitution are to be found in *Regierung und Volkswille* (Berlin, 1913).

14. This letter is published in *Krieg und Politik* (Berlin, 1918), I, 6–16.

15. This organization is described at length by Paul Rühlmann in an article, "Delbrücks Mittwochabend," in Emil Daniels, *Am Webstuhl der Zeit* (Berlin, 1929), pp. 73 f.

16. Walter Simons, "Dauer im Wechsel," in Daniels, pp. 132 f.

17. Max Montgelas, "Hans Delbrück," *Berliner Monatshefte*, VII (1929), 730.

18. *Berliner Monatshefte*, VII (1929), 77.

19. The full title of the book is: Emil Daniels und Paul Rühlmann, *Am Webstuhl der Zeit: eine Erinnerungsausgabe. Hans Delbrück dem Achtzigjährigen von Freunden und Schülern dargebracht* (Berlin, 1928).

20. The reader's attention is called to Delbrück's article, "Die gute alte Zeit," which appeared in his *Erinnerungen, Aufsätze und Reden* (see n. 23 below). Caricaturing the human frailty of idealizing the past, it aroused widespread discussion and controversy. Another one of his more widely quoted articles, "The role of numbers in history," has been published in English as a separate pamphlet (London, 1913).

21. Berlin, 1887.

22. Berlin, 1905.

23. Berlin, 1919.

24. Berlin, 1926.

25. Berlin, 1914. A revised edition of this book (Berlin, 1920) has been translated into English by Roy S. MacElwee, a former student of Delbrück, under the title of *Government and the will of the people* (New York, 1923).

26. *Government and the will of the people*, p. 148.

27. *Ibid.*, pp. 179 f.

28. *Political science quarterly*, XL (1925), 144–46.

29. *Ibid.*, p. 145.

30. Berlin, 1915.

31. *Ibid.*, pp. 212 f.

32. *Ibid.*, pp. 193 f.

33. *Ibid.*, pp. 206 f.

34. Berlin, 1917.

35. *Ibid.*, p. 23.

36. Berlin, 1920.

37. Berlin, 1919.

38. *Kautsky und Harden*, p. 6.

39. Berlin, 1922.

40. Berlin, 1922.

41. *Ibid.*, p. 64.

42. *HZ*, CXXX (1924), 527 f.

43. *Ibid.*, p. 528.

44. Berlin, 1925.

45. *HZ*, CXXXII (1925), 570 f.

46. *Der Stand der Kriegsschuldfrage*, p. 32.

47. *HZ*, CXXXVIII (1928), 90 f.

48. Berlin, 1882.

49. *HZ*, LI (1885), 135.

50. In four volumes (Berlin, 1900–1920). In 1928 a fifth volume was added in collaboration with Emil Daniels. Still later a sixth and seventh volume, published in 1932 and 1936, respectively, were written by Emil Daniels and Otto Haintz.

51. Konrad Lehmann, "Ermattungsstrategie-oder Nicht?" in *HZ*, CLI (1934), 48–86.

52. Friedrich von Bernhardi, *Denkwürdigkeiten aus meinem Leben* (Berlin, 1927), pp. 143 f.

53. Theodor von Bernhardi's *Delbrück, Friedrich der Grosse und Clausewitz* (Berlin, 1892) contains the chief criticisms of Delbrück's views on strategy.

54. Arthur Rosenberg, "Hans Delbrück, der Kritiker der Kriegsgeschichte," *loc. cit.*, p. 249.

55. *EHR*, XXII (1907), 344–48.

56. Berlin, 1924–28. A revised edition of this work appears under the title: Hans Delbrück und Konrad Molinski, *Die Weltgeschichte für Alle* (4 vols.; Berlin, 1929–33).

57. *HZ*, CXXXII (1925), 109.

58. *Ibid.*, p. 110.

59. A lengthy summary of Delbrück's *Weltgeschichte*, written by S. Mette, appears in *Archiv für Politik und Geschichte*, X (1928), 78–85.

60. I, 10.

61. *Ibid.*, p. 16.

62. *Ibid.*, p. 27.

63. *Ibid.*, p. 10.

64. *Preussische Jahrbücher*, CLVII (1920), 157–80.

65. *HZ*, CXL (1929), 703.

VI

SIR CHARLES FIRTH (1857–1936)

ELEANOR SMITH GODFREY*

I T IS ill gleaning after Gardiner."[1] Such was the saying that went the rounds of historical circles soon after the death of Samuel Rawson Gardiner. It is no reflection on Gardiner's greatness, however, to point out that one historian at least has gleaned from English history of the seventeenth century a considerable harvest "after Gardiner." That one is Sir Charles Harding Firth, whose achievements are worthy of serious consideration.

Firth's reputation has been based primarily on his studies of Cromwell and the interregnum. His own background admirably fitted him for a sympathetic understanding of Puritanism, for his family, of the industrial middle class, was not only nonconformist but evangelical.[2] His grandfather, Thomas Firth, began as a workingman who became dissatisfied and set up for himself in Sheffield making steel.[3] Soon he had built a thriving and profitable business. Firth's father, the third son and only educated member of the family,[4] was apprenticed to an architect but deserted that calling to join his father's firm. His choice was undoubtedly a wise one from a financial point of view, for when he died (1869) he left an estate of £150,000, every penny of which, Firth tells us, came from "honest steel-making."[5]

On week days Firth's father traveled for the firm. On Sundays he attended to his duties as church warden. But Firth relates that his father had a wandering eye:

* Mrs. James L. Godfrey, Chapel Hill, N.C., sometime Cleo Hearon fellow in history.

He observed a schoolmistress sitting with her girls in church and her somewhat austere beauty charmed his eyes. He was a prompt man, as I am myself.
They were married in April, 1856, and I was born on March 16, 1857.[6]

From such a family background may be traced many of Firth's
lifelong traits—simplicity, directness, tenacity in his convictions,
and, behind a genial spirit, a deep strain of Puritanism. He was
always very conscious of his background and the region from
which he came. "Dark and true and tender is the North."[7]

Firth's father had come to the United States the year before his
marriage to the schoolmistress (his second marriage).

He was driven to this desperate course [Firth writes] by the Crimean war.
Unable any longer to sell steel to the Russians he determined to sell it to the
Yankees. The ultimate result of this judicious step was a trade which ran into
many millions [of pounds]. . . . .[8]

After the outbreak of the American Civil War representatives
from the United States came to Sheffield to buy munitions. Their
conversation and that of the children which they occasionally
brought with them resulted in some of the young Charles's most
vivid impressions. He tells us that his great interest in the American Civil War was the beginning of his political education.[9] It
was probably also the beginning of his interest in military history.

If we may believe his own testimony, Firth learned the first
principles of sound scholarship while a student at Clifton College
(1870–75). He said of William Thomas Dunn, one of his masters
there:

[I owe to him] a greater debt than to any other man. He converted me from
a lazy boy into a hard working one. . . . . He taught me to aim at accuracy and
thoroughness in all I wrote and to undertake cheerfully any labour needed to
attain them.[10]

Although trained in the classics at Clifton, Firth went up to New
College, Oxford, in 1875 to read history. The next year he migrated to Balliol as Brackenbury scholar.[11] There J. Franck
Bright was his tutor; but Bishop Stubbs, then regius professor of
modern history, influenced him more. In later years Firth spoke
of Stubbs as "Oxford's greatest historian."[12] Although he complained in later years of the absence at Oxford of systematic train-

ing in method, such as German and French universities gave,[13] the example of Stubbs undoubtedly taught him much about historical criticism and method. His interests and efforts were rewarded when in 1877 he won the Stanhope prize for an essay on the Marquess Wellesley.[14]

Upon taking his degree, Firth went to Germany for a short time to improve his knowledge of the language, but he seems not to have studied in a German university. In 1880, soon after his return, he married Frances Ashington, the daughter of a vicar in Lincolnshire. For a short time the young historian lectured at Firth College, Sheffield,[15] an institution founded by his uncle, Mark Firth, the second head of the steel firm. Then he gave some thought to a political career but abandoned that idea.[16] Finally, in 1883, in spite of warnings that the climate in the valley of the Thames was bad for his asthma, he went to Oxford to live for the rest of his life. Firth taught but seven years of the first twenty years of his residence at Oxford. He received an appointment in 1886 as history tutor in Pembroke College, but resigned it in 1893 because the college was unable to establish a scholarship in history. The remainder of the time his private income enabled him to devote his full energy to historical research. Firth himself remarks that by the early eighties he had settled down to "the steady jog-trot of the professional historian."[17]

Deliberately Firth became a specialist and disposed of many of his books, except those relating to the seventeenth century. The choice of this period for specialization he attributes to this reading of John Forster's *The grand remonstrance*, *The arrest of the five members*, and *Sir John Eliot*.[18] It is interesting that Firth did not mention as an influence in his choice Samuel Rawson Gardiner, who had published four volumes of his great work before Firth took his degree.[19] There is no doubt, however, that Firth greatly admired Gardiner and soon looked up to him as master.

Shortly after coming to Oxford, Firth began to be active in historical work of every nature. He was one of a group of historians whose meetings in 1885 lead to the founding of the *English historical review*.[20] Although never an editor, he was for many years a regular reviewer, and particularly before the turn of the century there was scarcely a single volume without at least one contribution from his pen. Reviews of documentary material, including the government calendars of various state papers, form nearly two-thirds of the total number.[21] So great was Firth's knowledge of his chosen field that he was always able to point out what new information each publication added, what material had been used in its preparation and what neglected, and finally what still remained to be done on the same subject.[22]

In the same year as the founding of the review Firth made his first important publication—a new and handsome edition of the well-known *Memoirs of the life of Colonel Hutchinson*.[23] The following year he published a similar edition of the Duchess of Newcastle's life of her husband.[24] The notes are full and well chosen; the introductions extremely useful. Both volumes give ample evidence that Firth was doing careful, accurate work and also that he was well along in his truly extensive reading in the pamphlet and newspaper literature of the period. His later editions show the same high standards. If anything, *The memoirs of Edmund Ludlow*[25] are edited too elaborately. Firth himself felt so,[26] and yet Ludlow's bias was so pronounced that it was necessary to correct it with voluminous references to other materials. The *Journal of Joachim Hane*[27] and the *Narrative of General Venables with an appendix of papers relating to the expedition to the West Indies and the conquest of Jamaica*,[28] though edited with characteristic thoroughness, are particularly important.

In his editions it was Firth's consistent policy to give full reference to an amazing amount of other relevant material for corroboration and amplification. In his introductions he undertakes a discussion of the manuscript itself, the life and personality of the author, his trustworthiness, and the general value of the work. Firth was fortunate in beginning his historical labors with editing of this type, for in later years he believed it to be the most valuable training a young historian could have.[29]

Some of Firth's most interesting editorial contributions were made in the literary field. His edition of Dr. Johnson's *Life of*

Milton,[30] published in 1891, proves that his interest in literary subjects dates from early in his career. In the introduction he combines the critical method of a historian with the appreciation of the lover of good literature. The same approach made his introduction to Bunyan's *Pilgrim's progress*[31] one of the best ever written on that subject. This introduction, together with other essays, has been published in *Essays historical and literary*,[32] one of Firth's most interesting volumes.

In the nineties, with the publication of the *Clarke papers*,[33] Firth produced his most important editions from a scholar's point of view. The papers themselves were of first-rate importance and up to that time had been entirely unknown. Sir William Clarke had been assistant to the New Model army in 1646, secretary of the army council, and later (1651–60) secretary to General Monck in Scotland. His papers had long lain in Worcester College, Oxford, unnoticed by scholars. Once his attention was called to them by the librarian of the college, Firth perceived their value and used them to great advantage. From them he derived also most of the documents in the two volumes entitled *Scotland and the Commonwealth* and *Scotland and the Protectorate*.[34] The condition of the manuscripts was such that a great deal of work was required to make them intelligible. Firth's editing was most valuable,[35] and in the *Clarke papers* the biographical notes are especially helpful.

By the time the *Clarke papers* appeared, Firth had become thoroughly familiar with the personnel of both the army and parliament through his work on the *Dictionary of national biography*, for which he wrote 229 articles.[36] Firth was one of the historians working on the *Dictionary* who blocked out a special preserve—his was the Civil War and the Protectorate—which he worked at consistently, gathering material for later articles while working on the one at hand. In consequence, an enormous amount of research often went into comparatively short articles. With the mind of an organizer, Firth was well fitted for such a task, and in return he benefited greatly from the training in careful, methodical, continuous work. Despite errors that inevitably crept into a work of such magnitude,[37] he soon earned a reputation for great accuracy.

The biographical notice of Cromwell, the fourth longest in the *Dictionary*, was particularly distinguished. It gave Firth a reputation for insight as well as for accuracy. In it he demonstrated his ability to overcome the special difficulties inherent in a biographical dictionary by writing an article in which the wealth of detail necessary for such a project did not cloud the clear picture of the man's personality. The success of the article provided the encouragement for expanding it into a full-length biography of Cromwell, written for the "Heroes of the nations" series.[38] Although Firth modestly expected it to be overshadowed by Gardiner's beautifully illustrated biography of the Protector, published the year before, or by John Morley's published the same year, it enjoyed instantaneous success and has continued to be one of the best-known biographies of Cromwell.

The narrative follows the article in the *Dictionary* rather closely, in spite of the fact that it is based upon much additional research, including careful use of the Clarke papers. By the time Firth wrote this book the facts of Cromwell's life had been fairly well established, owing in large part to his own industry in connection with the *Dictionary* article and a number of others dealing with Cromwellian subjects.[39] The popular nature of the series, however, forced him to omit many details and much general discussion which might have gone into a longer biography.[40]

On the whole, Firth's attitude toward Cromwell is very sympathetic, much more so than Gardiner's.[41] His attitude is best summed up in the following quotation:

> Either as a soldier or as a statesman Cromwell was far greater than any Englishman of his time, and he was both soldier and statesman in one. We must look to Caesar or Napoleon to find a parallel for this union of high political and military ability in one man. Cromwell was not as great a man as Caesar or Napoleon, and he played his part on a smaller stage, but he "bestrode the narrow world" of Puritan England "like a colossus."[42]

Firth has been taken to task for two lenient judgment of Cromwell's domestic policy;[43] yet he censored much in Cromwell's policy and pointed out his inconsistencies. On the whole, the critical balance is held fairly even. Gardiner, who is perhaps best qualified to stand in judgment, remarked that up to the dissolution of the Long Parliament the narrative is accurate, fair, and altogether admirably done.[44] On the difficult question of the Protector's relations with his parliaments, however, Gardiner considered that Firth did not quite grasp the essentials of the problem.[45] Firth believed, rightly according to Gardiner, that Cromwell's difficulties were inherently political and constitutional and were not the result of the recalcitrance of the army. What he did not sufficiently emphasize, Gardiner thought, was that in his quarrels with parliament Cromwell was fighting against the sovereignty of a single house, operating without check. Firth puts his emphasis, however, on the theory that Cromwell's difficulties arose mainly from his attempt to preserve the interests of the "people of God" (the Puritan party). In this connection he points out that Cromwell always put the interests of the "people of God" before the interest of the Commonwealth as a whole. He writes:

> England might have acquiesced in this [Cromwell's] temporary dictatorship in the hope of a gradual return to constitutional government. What it could not accept was the permanent limitation of the sovereignty of the people in the interest of the Puritan minority whom Cromwell termed the people of God. Yet it was at this object that all the constitutional settlements of the Protectorate aimed. It was in the interest of this minority that the Instrument of Government restricted the power of Parliament and made the Protector the guardian of the constitution. It was in their interest that the Petition and Advice reestablished a House of Lords. That House, as Thurloe said, was intended "to preserve the good interest against the uncertainty of the Commons House," for, as another Cromwellian confessed "the spirit of the Commons had little affinity with or respect to the Cause of God."[46]

There is nothing essentially contradictory in the interpretations of Firth and Gardiner. The matter is one of emphasis and relative importance, and it seems to the writer that Firth has grasped the more essential point. In spite of this disagreement on emphasis, Gardiner gives Firth credit for knowing more about the subject that any of his critics and for presenting a true picture of events with only a few minor errors of fact. Certainly the book merits the general acclaim it has received, and it seems likely to remain the standard life of Cromwell.[47]

In 1900, the year in which this biography appeared, Firth was appointed to deliver the Ford Lectures at Oxford. The content of these lectures he published in 1902 in a monograph entitled *Cromwell's army*.[48] Perhaps the most notable of all his works, this book has been called "easily the best book on an army in the English language."[49] This high praise is well deserved. For his material Firth went not only to the Clarke papers but to the huge mass of Commonwealth exchequer papers, the first scholar to make use of those uncalendared bundles. There he found a wealth of detail elucidating every side of the army. The information which he put together concerning the structure and internal organization of the army was absolutely new and very important for any true understanding of the Civil War.

Firth's researches brought out one fact in particular—the relatively high pay which even common soldiers received. The chapter on discipline is especially good. It presents a stirring picture of the energy of Cromwell and his best officers, as they went about their task of converting a rabble into one of the most self-restrained soldieries in the entire history of the world. Although the subjects of religion and politics in the army had been treated before, Firth filled out the accepted story with many specific instances. All in all, the reader gets a graphic picture of the life of the average soldier in the army: how he was fed, housed, and equipped, and what he thought of the army, his superiors, and politics in general. The proportion and choice of detail is excellent. The only notable omission is the lack of a description of the civilian bodies associated with the army. Firth realized this deficiency but felt that the collection of the material necessary for such an account would be an insuperable task.[50] While regrettable, the omission is not so serious as to impair the usefulness or the value of the book. Well organized, well written, unquestioned in accuracy, and without noticeable bias, the work is one of which any historian might well be proud.

In 1902 Gardiner, who had long been Firth's personal friend, died just as he was nearing the end of his great project.[51] It was his wish that Firth should complete it for him. Indeed, there was no other so well suited. Firth accordingly took over Gardiner's notes and six years later published *The last years of the Protectorate*.[52] In a truly remarkable way these volumes continue Gardiner's plan of organization, manner of presentation, and style of writing.[53] Firth's organization, however, is better than Gardiner's. There are fewer digressions in Firth's narrative, although his fondness for military and naval history induced him to remain longer than was necessary on the northern wars and relations with Sweden.[54]

There is little to choose betwen the two as to accuracy and method. It is probably true that Firth was superior to his predecessor in the critical evaluation of sources,[55] but one must remember that he had the advantage of the older man's pioneer work through an uncharted wilderness of documents. Perhaps the most noticeable feature in Firth's two volumes from the point of view of scholarship is the fact that, in spite of a fairly large amount of new material which he used, the findings do not reverse a single accepted interpretation or add anything substantially new. The principal value in the work, beyond the mere fact of confirmation, is the large amount of detail which the general scale of the work permitted Firth to include.

The second volume, ending with the death of the Protector, brought a great disappointment to those who had been awaiting a final estimate of the character and influence of Cromwell. Firth buried the hero of the tale with scarcely a word of comment. Although this has been deplored,[56] it must in fairness be pointed out that it was simply another example of the faithfulness with which he carried out Gardiner's plan. Working in the tradition of Ranke, Gardiner aimed to present the facts as they appeared to him without comment, letting them tell their own story and leaving final judgments to the reader. If only one would read the entire work, Gardiner thought, one would understand not only what was but how it came to be. Firth, who knew Gardiner's method well,[57] carefully followed it. It is regrettable, however, that one so ably equipped to pronounce a general estimate of the Protector and his work passed by this opportunity.

In another way Firth also disappointed his readers. The two volumes of *The last years of the Protectorate* carry the narrative down only as far as the death of Cromwell (September 3, 1658). The preface states that Firth intended to complete the story down to the Restoration, as Gardiner had planned, but with emphasis upon social and economic history under both the Protector and his son.[58] These last volumes, if completed, would have changed somewhat the comparison between the two historians.[59] Firth was admittedly weaker in his treatment of foreign affairs, a fact hardly offset by his better grasp of military matters. A study of social and economic history, for which his extensive knowledge of literature, newspapers, and all kinds of pamphlet material especially fitted him, would have weighed heavily in the scale.

That these volumes were never completed may in part be attributed to the fact that, while working on them, Firth was appointed regius professor of modern history at Oxford, succeeding F. York Powell.[60] From then until his resignation in 1926 he felt the pressure of regular teaching duties and other responsibilities of the chair. The appointment may be taken as a rough turning-point in his career, for from that time his literary output declined considerably.

The only monograph which Firth completed after his appointment was *The house of lords during the Civil War*,[61] evidently prompted by the contemporary political crisis over the power of the house of lords. The first part of the book contains material on the history of the peerage under the first two Stuarts. A large part of this information can also be found in Gardiner's works, though Firth's narrative is much fuller and more pointed. The last part, concerning the house of lords during the interregnum, was completely new. It is especially good for quotations showing current political theories. In an effort to avoid a polemical manner Firth refrains from comment and nowhere draws any historical comparisons. Yet the comparison is implied both by the timeliness of the book and even more by passages which inevitably suggest to the reader that the issues in 1647 were much the same as those in 1910.[62] Firth also draws the conclusion that after the experiments with a single chamber all political parties became so disillusioned that by 1660 even the radical republicans became convinced of the need for a second chamber.[63]

Whether or not Firth sympathized with the lords during the political crisis, he undoubtedly hoped that his book would be useful in clarifying opinion. He always held that history is a branch of learning which should be studied not only for its own sake but because it is useful to men in daily life, " 'the end and scope of all history being,' as Sir Walter Raleigh says, 'to teach us by example of time past such widsom as may guide our desires and actions.' "[64] Although interest in the book fell off with the passing of the political crisis, it is still a very useful volume.

The only other work of importance which Firth completed after his appointment as regius professor was the three-volume *Acts and ordinances of the interregnum*,[65] which he edited with R. S. Rait. The compilation was useful in itself but was made much more so by the addition of many previously unpublished documents and a lengthy introduction discussing the acts which survived the Restoration and the manner in which parliament took over the function of independent legislation.

Although the number of books which Firth published declined after he received the regius professorship, he continued to publish a large number of articles, frequently on literary topics. His writings on ballads and broadsides belong to this period. A series of articles in the *Transactions of the Royal Historical Society*[66] form a complete history of ballads from the reign of Henry VII through that of Charles I. Most of the ballads discussed have some social, economic, or political significance. Firth shows how they illustrate the history of the period and can be of use to the historian as a rough measure of popular sentiment. The chapter on ballads which he contributed to *Shakespeare's England*[67] is thought to be one of the best in the book. In addition to these, Firth published two separate collections—one of naval songs and ballads, the other of Elizabethan ballads relating to America.[68]

Another group of articles present critical studies of historians and writers of memoirs—for example, the brilliant analysis of Clarendon's *History of the rebellion*.[69] Not content with the Macray edition[70] or the preliminary analysis of Ranke,[71] Firth went back to the original manuscripts and decided for himself on the bais of marginal notes, handwriting and ink differences, and internal evidence when each section of the finished *History* was written. Next he sought out the motives back of the writing of each section. The original *History*, he shows, was written in the author's first exile in 1646–48 from mixed motives, possibly at the king's suggestion and for his vindication. It was not intended for publication. The autobiography, written between 1668 and 1670 in his second exile, was intended as a vindication of his own career meant for circulation among the family and close friends. Finally, Firth shows that about 1672 Clarendon combined the two into the finished *History* by deleting parallel passages and writing additional connecting passages. Firth then investigates the sources at Clarendon's disposal when he wrote each part, the nearness of the writing to the events, the extent of the author's personal knowledge of events, and the incorporation of material gathered by him from other persons. In the end he is able to establish the amount of reliability to be placed upon different segments of the finished *History*. The artistic merits of the different versions also receive some attention.

The same general type of analysis, though on a large scale, is exhibited in Firth's one-volume *Commentary on Macaulay's history of England*,[72] published by Godfrey Davies after Firth's death. Although concerned mostly with literary style and method, this volume also analyzes Macaulay's reliability as a historian. The essays on Milton's *History of Britain* and Sir Walter Raleigh's *History of the world* indicate the extent of his interest in historical and literary criticism.[73]

Firth's duties as regius professor would not have occupied such a large share of his time had he not put great deal of energy into projects for university reform. A firm and convinced believer in the validity of scientific historical methods, he wished to introduce at Oxford "a proper professional training for the study of history," by which he meant "a technical training . . . . in the methods of investigation, in the use of original authorities and in these auxiliary sciences which the Germans call 'Hilfswissenschaften.' "[74] At the time there was very little interest at Oxford in research methods. What Stubbs called "the class-getting system of teaching" was then the only one in use.[75] By this he meant the system still prevalent whereby the student is required to absorb through formal lectures and specific requirements certain information which is to be handed back in written examinations. In his inaugural address Firth denounced this system in no uncompromising terms. It might be adequate, he thought, for undergraduate instruction, but it certainly should be supplemented in advanced work by some acquaintance with the materials and methods of history. He wished to place the responsibility for advanced training in method, leading toward the degree of Bachelor of Letters, in the hands of the university professors, while the college tutors managed the undergraduate instruction. He rightly foresaw, however, that the B. Litt. would attract only foreign students, unless in the appointment of tutors preference were given those with advanced training.

Unfortunately, Firth's tactlessness aroused general indignation. The tutors resented the implication that the training they had received was not completely adequate.[76] Firth's unwillingness to compromise alienated many who did not agree with his emphasis upon research technique. Yet, undaunted by opposition, he continued to pour forth a volley of speeches and pamphlets whenever the occasion presented itself. The program was not a new one, for both Stubbs and York Powell had proposed something similar.[77] By acting slowly and tactfully he could perhaps have accomplished more. As it was, it was not until the tenure of his successor that the reforms he desired were accomplished.

Firth's own advanced classes were very poorly attended.[78] A former student has described his formal lectures as full of meat but, with some exceptions, not very stimulating.[79] In seminars, small classes, and private consultations, however, Firth was at his best. There the effect of his total personality came into play. To personal relationships he brought kindliness and a delightful sense of humor.[80] In appearance he has been described as short, thickset, and in later years inclined to corpulence. His head was most distinguished: "white hair, carefully combed, a short white beard, cut square, ruddy cheeks and small but piercing blue eyes."[81] In daily life he has been described as "simple, even austere in his habits."[82] He scorned artificialities in both dress and speech. In politics he changed from liberal to conservative; in religion he was strongly Protestant without adhering strictly to any one church.

Firth was very much interested in his students and gave freely of his time and advice. Although strict in his standards, he believed in giving all the encouragement he could. Many American scholars, other than those who studied with him, sought out his advice. In the end his influence toward higher standards of research was perhaps greater as a result of his personal advice than through all his printed pamphlets and lectures.

The teaching of English literature concerned Firth almost as much as the teaching of history. He watched closely the creation and development of the School of English Language and Literature. For a time he lectured and took pupils there, but perhaps his greatest contribution, characteristically, was his work in establishing high standards for research degrees.[83]

Outside the university Firth was equally busy. For four years (1913–17) he was president of the Royal Historical Society, and for two different periods (1906–10, 1918–20) president of the Historical Association. From 1910 to 1919 he was the leading figure on the royal commission on public records. Three volumes of reports bear witness to his industry. In 1913 he also served on an admiralty commission for study of Nelson's tactics at Trafalgar.[84] He was rewarded for these and other labors in 1922, when he was knighted.

Twice in his life Firth planned monumental works. While working on the continuation of Gardiner, he conceived the idea of bridging the gap between Gardiner and Macaulay by a work on the same scale.[85] For some time he worked on the Restoration period, but all that was ever written out were the two chapters in the *Cambridge modern history*.[86] After Firth's retirement in 1926 he undertook another project, a regimental history, on a large scale, of Cromwell's army. Several articles on the subject appeared in periodicals,[87] and a first draft was completed. Although Firth died, in February, 1936, before he could revise it sufficiently for publication, Godfrey Davies, who assisted him with it, has recently completed and published it.[88]

From all that has been said of Firth's writings and of his efforts at Oxford it is clear that he put great emphasis upon critical method. His knowledge of the bibliography of the seventeenth century was remarkable, especially in the field of primary materials. Some idea of the extent of this knowledge may be gained from his reviews, the footnotes and introductions to his editions, and his bibliographical notices. His students testify, moreover, that his knowledge was even greater than might be inferred from his printed works.[89]

For his own writings Firth relied largely on manuscript materials of the usual kind—letters, journals, official and state papers —but he overlooked little, however insignificant, that might be of assistance. He showed discretion in handling his material, moreover; and his knowledge of ballads, literature, and newspapers was always used with great care. With all his sources Firth was extremely critical. His method is amply illustrated by the type of analysis he used in the discussion of Clarendon's *History of the rebellion*. We may be certain that the same carefulness exemplified there lay behind all his printed works. In no other way could he have been able to keep the quality of his work so uniformly high. Yet, though he was as scientific with his use of material as any historian of his day, he was able to dispense with many of the impedimenta of modern research—elaborate notes and card files with cross-references.[90] His retentive memory, his large private library, and the freedom from distractions which his private income made possible during his early years were largely responsible for this. He was careful, however, in his published works to furnish adequate bibliographies and footnotes.

Although Firth put most of his emphasis upon the selection and criticism of material, he was not unaware that the writing of history was a special problem. In his inaugural address he adopted the attitude, now fairly prevalent but not so common in his day, that history is both a science and an art.[91] More specifically, in the commentary on Macaulay, he stated that "the art of telling a story is an essential qualification for the writing of history."[92] Both Froude and Macaulay received his praise for their narrative power and stylistic brilliance.

Firth's publications demonstrate his ability to organize his material well. There is a solid architectural quality about his work. He was inclined to use a topical arrangement whenever possible, even in biography, although he also proves his ability to tell a story. As has been pointed out, he was better able than Gardiner to handle the proportion in a work on a large scale.

In spite of his admiration for Froude and Macaulay, Firth's own style was singularly straightforward, without any tricks of rhetoric. In his early writings it was so simple as to be austere. The "no flowers by request" tone of the *Dictionary of national biography* undoubtedly influenced him to keep his sentences terse. In maturity his style benefited greatly from his wide reading of literature. His writing kept its simplicity, its lucidity, and its straightforward manner, but there was added to it more grace and more individual flavor. Firth also developed a felicity for quotation which stood him in good stead. His skill in organization supplied a firm foundation for a clear narrative. Some have remarked that Firth's style is much like Gardiner's,[93] and indeed it is hard to discover a difference at times. Firth's later writings seem to have a smoothness and a flavor, however, which mark them as superior to the rather monotonous style of Gardiner.[94]

Although Firth's talents and style made him superb in the handling of detail, he was not overly concerned with general ideas. Gardiner, who has himself been taken to task for not supplying more general comments and criticisms,[95] finds Firth guilty of the same omission. In reviewing *Cromwell and the rule of the Puritans* he remarks: "One would like to find Mr. Firth looking a little more backwards and forwards and placing the movements he describes in a wider setting."[96] It is regrettable that Firth did not attempt more generalization, for when he does he achieves work which Gardiner rightly calls the "salt of history," as, for example, in the chapter on Ireland in the biography of Cromwell. His judgment was of a very high order, both in discriminating between the essential and the nonessential and in deciding the truth in a given situation.

That he did not comment more is partly attributable to the fact that he followed so faithfully the "scientific" method of letting the facts speak for themselves and also partly to his own natural interest in the concrete and the individual. Firth was at his best when dealing with personalities. His thumbnail sketches in the notes to various memoirs are often worthy of quotation. He always gave personal details; it was typical that his essay on Wellesley was the only one of those submitted for the Stanhope prize to describe the Marquess' appearance.[97]

Firth's interest in the concrete perhaps has something to do with the fact that he never subscribed to any "school" of history. If anything, his interest in personality caused him to lean slightly to the "great-man" thesis, although he brings out so well the influence of circumstances upon Cromwell's actions that it is scarcely fair to put his works in that category. More than many historians of his day, Firth realized the importance of social and economic factors in history;[98] yet his published works do not greatly reflect this attitude.

Perhaps the main influence that kept Firth from subscribing to any specialized school of thought was his belief in the unity of history—"l'histoire intégrale." He expressed it thus: "The unity of history is not only in its continuity, but in its integrity; it implies regarding the past as a whole, and therefore studying every side of your chosen portion of it, as well as looking before and after it."[99] He deplored the modern tendency to cut history into little strips and fragments.[100] It is true that he believed in specialization, but to him that did not mean such a narrowing of interest as it means to many. He belied that a historian should confine his major interest to one period, since it was no longer possible for one man to sit down and write the history of the world. But a very wide and varied background might be necessary for writing about one small period. For example, in order to understand English political thought of the seventeenth century, one should know something of Greek political thought and also of contemporary European political thought.[101] Thus he saw each period as a microcosm of the world, reflecting ideas and trends from all others.

Firth's own interest ranged widely, as we have seen, through military history, social and economic history, ballads, literature, and portraits. America especially interested him, although he wrote very little about it. His fund of information came from a lifelong devotion to a field of study which he believed to be very useful to mankind.

Firth realized that the point of view in history was continually changing, that each age asked new questions of history and changed the relative importance of facts. Yet he was not discouraged thereby from continuing his work. He recognized the importance of an accumulation of facts toward which each historian could contribute. Taken altogether, this mass of facts would form a solid basis upon which interpretations could be built. The "jog-trot of the professional historian" was therefore not to be despised.

Firth's own record proves just what may be accomplished by steady, continuous work. He propounded no brilliant theses which might attract future generations of students to confirm or refute. He wrote no monumental works of great magnitude such as Gardiner's, no work of stylistic brilliance such as Froude's or Macaulay's. Such works as he did leave, however, both editions and original writings, are solid contributions to history which seem likely to survive and be used for a long time. Their amount is certainly not negligible, as the Firth bibliography testifies. Yet when one remembers his skill of organization, his ability for prolonged investigation, and his freedom from teaching in the early years, one cannot help wishing that he had undertaken a larger project. As was suggested in the beginning, Firth has gleaned a considerable harvest "after Gardiner"—one that will keep him in the ranks of illustrious historians for many years— and yet it is to be regretted that he did not go on to fresher fields.

NOTES

1. W. C. Abbott, *AHR*, XV (1909–10), 851.

2. G. N. Clark, "Sir Charles Firth," *EHR*, LI (1936), 257.

3. S. E. Morison, "Sir Charles Firth and Master Hugh Peter with a Hugh Peter bibliography," *Harvard graduates magazine*, XXXIX (1930–31), 124.

4. *Ibid.*

5. *Ibid.* All the quotations from this article and nearly all the information were derived from a long letter from Firth to Morison dated June 19, 1929.

6. *Ibid.*, p. 122.

7. Clark, *loc. cit.*, p. 258.

8. Morison, *loc. cit.*, p. 122.

9. *Ibid.*

10. Godfrey Davies, "Charles Harding Firth," *Proceedings of the British Academy*, XXII (1936), 380. This article was reprinted as a separate leaflet under the same title (London, n.d.).

11. Clark, *loc. cit.*, p. 257.

12. *A plea for the historical teaching of history* (Oxford, 1904), p. 32. Cited hereafter as "*A plea.*"

13. *Ibid.*, p. 5.

14. *The Marquess Wellesley* (Oxford, 1877).

15. Davies, *loc. cit.*, pp. 380–81. Firth College became the University of Sheffield in 1905.

16. *Ibid.*

17. Clark, *loc. cit.*, p. 257.

18. Davies, *loc. cit.*, p. 381.

19. Clark (*loc. cit.*, p. 257) feels that Gardiner's early works did influence Firth's choice of a period. Although Davies implies the contrary (*loc. cit.*, p. 381) he does give ample testimony of the long and close friendship between the two (*ibid.*, p. 390).

20. Clark, *loc. cit.*, p. 258.

21. See *Bibliography of the writings of Sir Charles Firth* (Oxford, 1928) (hereafter cited as "*Bibliography*") for a list of the reviews.

22. For typical examples of Firth's reviews see *EHR*, XXII (1907), 175–77; XXIII (1908), 155–56; XXV (1910), 776–77.

23. 2 vols.; London, 1885.

24. *The life of William Cavendish, Duke of Newcastle, to which is added the true relation of my birth, breeding and life by Margaret, Duchess of Newcastle* (London, 1886).

25. 2 vols.; Oxford, 1894.

26. Davies, *loc. cit.*, p. 384.

27. Oxford, 1896.

28. "Publications of the Camden Society," N.S., Vol. LX (1900).

29. Davies, *loc. cit.*, p. 382.

30. Oxford, 1891.

31. London, 1898.

32. Oxford, 1938. Godfrey Davies collected and edited these essays after Firth's death. All but one, that on Clarendon, had been published before.

33. "Camden Society," N.S., Vols. XLIX (1891), LIV (1894), LX (1899), LXII (1901).

34. *Scotland and the Commonwealth; Scotland and the Protectorate* (Edinburgh: "Publications of the Scottish History Society," Vols. XVIII [1895], XXXI [1899]).

35. A. S. P. Woodhouse has recently re-edited portions of the Clarke manuscripts: *Puritanism and liberty; being the army debates (1647–9) from the Clarke manuscripts with supplementary documents* (London, 1938). His edition is better than Firth's in that he is much more scrupulous about recording every deviation of his text from the original and every rearrangement. Woodhouse has also taken more pains to supply missing words and phrases; he adopts some of Firth's emendations and rejects others (*Puritanism and liberty*, p. 12). In tribute to Firth's editing, however, he writes: "I can only . . . . record my constant debt to—for it would be impertinence to praise—his editorial labours: his many valuable emendations, and, where he has not ventured to mend, his luminous footnotes on the argument" (*ibid.*, p. 13).

36. The names of those about whom Firth wrote biographical sketches are listed in the *Bibliography*, pp. 7–9.

37. A review of Vols. XXIX–XXXIII of the *DNB* in *EHR*, VIII (1892), 181, notes two small inaccuracies in Firth's articles.

38. *Oliver Cromwell and the rule of the Puritans in England* (New York and London, 1900).

39. For a list of these articles with locations see *Bibliography*, p. 10.

40. The nature of the series also forced him to eliminate footnotes, but most of the references can be checked from the article in the *DNB*.

41. Review by Firth of Gardiner's biography of Cromwell, *EHR*, XV (1900), 175.

42. *Oliver Cromwell*, p. 467.

43. *Athenaeum*, II (1900), 78.

44. *EHR*, XV (1900), 803.

45. *Ibid.*, pp. 804–5.

46. *Oliver Cromwell*, pp. 484–85.

47. W. C. Abbott in his *Bibliography of Oliver Cromwell* (Cambridge, 1929, p. 332) calls it "accurate, comprehensive, valuable; one of the best biographies if not the best."

48. London, 1902.

49. Davies, *loc. cit.*, p. 385.

50. *Ibid.*, p. 386.

51. Gardiner wished to carry his narrative down to the Restoration but died when his *History of the Commonwealth and Protectorate* (London, 1902), was complete only down to 1656.

52. 2 vols.; London, 1908.

53. Reviewed *Nation*, XC (1910), 375; *EHR*, XXV (1910), 177–81; *AHR*, XV (1910), 851–53.

54. *Last years of the Protectorate*, Vol. I, chap. x.

55. E.g., he detected that Clough's narrative describing John Hampden's last hours was spurious, though Gardiner had accepted it as genuine. Gardiner accepted Firth's judgment in his revised edition. Cf. Gardiner, *History of the great civil war*, I (1886), 178–79, and *ibid.*, I (new ed., 1893), 152–53. W. C. Abbott remarks of Firth's *Last years of the Protectorate* that "it is in fact such a model of method in its way that no reviewer is likely to detect any errors if such exist, and it is not probable that the severest analysis would find any of importance" (*AHR*, XV [1910], 851).

56. *Athenaeum*, I (1910), 118.

57. Firth not only knew Gardiner's methods but defended them against such critics as Roland G. Usher, whose *Critical study of the historical method of Samuel Rawson Gardiner* ("Washington University studies," III, Part II [October, 1915], 5–159) attacks him with great vigor. Some of the conclusions in the foregoing paragraph are from Usher's study. Firth's defense of Gardiner against an anonymous critic who quotes Usher is to be found in the *Times literary supplement*, XIX (1919), 515, 591, 630, 650, 674, 695, 714, 768.

58. *Last years of the Protectorate*, I, xix.

59. For a detailed comparison see Davies, *loc. cit.*, pp. 390–92.

60. The part of the continuation dealing with social and economic life had been written out as lectures to be delivered at Harvard when Firth received his appointment. Clark (*loc. cit.*, p. 260) says the lectures still exist in typewritten form.

61. London, 1910.

62. E.g., Firth points out that the rift between the two houses came to a head when the lords began to block legislation which the commons thought desirable for the good of the Commonwealth. See *ibid.*, chap. vi, especially pp. 214–15.

63. *Ibid.*, p. 296.

64. *A plea*, p. 8.

65. London, 1911.

66. 3d ser., II (1908), 21–50; III (1909), 51–124; V (1911), 21–61; VI (1912), 19–64.

67. Oxford, 1916, chap. xxix. This chapter is reprinted as the leading article in the *Essays historical and literary*.

68. *Naval songs and ballads* ("Publications of the Navy Records Society," Vol. XXXIII [London, 1908]); *An American garland; being a collection of ballads relating to America, 1563–1759* (Oxford, 1915).

69. See *Bibliography*, sec. III, "Critical studies of historians and writers of memoirs," pp. 3–4.

70. Earl of Clarendon, *History of the rebellion and the civil wars in England*, re-edited by W. Dunn Macray (6 vols.; Oxford, 1888).

71. *History of England principally in the 17th century* (Oxford, 1875), VI, 3–29.

72. London, 1938. Davies explains in the preface (p. iv) that the manuscript was prepared about 1915 and therefore represents the state of historical knowledge at that time.

73. *Essays historical and literary*, pp. 34–60, 61–102. Both essays are reprinted from the *Proceedings of the British Academy*.

74. *A plea*, p. 5. This was the inaugural address.

75. *Ibid.*, p. 32. Help on this controversy came from personal conversations with Professor Marshall M. Knappen, of Michigan State College.

76. Firth said: "I cannot infer from anything I have seen that the possession of a proper professional training for the study of history is one of the requisites held necessary for teaching it" (*ibid.*, p. 30). He explained this statement in the preface (p. 5) when the speech was printed.

77. Clarke, *loc. cit.*, p. 260. See also *A plea*, p. 32.

78. *Modern history at Oxford, 1841–1918* (Oxford, 1920), p. 49.

79. From a letter from Professor Elmer A. Beller, of Princeton University, to the author, dated September 24, 1940; corroborated by Davies, *loc. cit.*, p. 388.

80. Mr. Beller in the letter mentioned (n. 79) tells of meeting Firth in an Oxford bookstore looking over the detective stories. Noting Mr. Beller's surprise, Firth said with a chuckle that he had read all the serious books.

81. Mr. Beller's letter.

82. Davies, *loc. cit.*, p. 399.

83. Davies, *loc. cit.*, pp. 393–95, gives a fuller account of Firth's activities in connection with the English school and also in connection with the Honour School of Medieval and Modern Languages, the Honour School of Geography, and the Taylorian Institute. See *Bibliography*, p. 36, for his pamphlets on these projects.

84. *Bibliography*, pp. 6, 33–34, gives a list of publications in connection with these commission activities.

85. Davies, *loc. cit.*, p. 386.

86. "Anarchy and the Restoration (1659–60)," *Cambridge modern history*, Vol. IV (1906), chap. xix, pp. 539–59; "The Stewart restoration (1660–7)," *ibid.*, Vol. V (1908), chap. v, pp. 92–115.

87. "Cromwell's regiments," *Journal of the Society of Army Historical Research*, VI (1927), 16–23, 141–46, 222–28; "Colonel James Berry's regiment," *ibid.*, II (1923), 70–3.

88. C. H. Firth and Godfrey Davies, *The regimental history of Cromwell's army* (2 vols.; Oxford, 1940).

89. Clark, *loc. cit.*, p. 261. Mr. Beller also remarks several times on Firth's "enormous knowledge."

90. Clark, *loc. cit.*, p. 259.

91. *A plea*, p. 89.

92. *Commentary on Macaulay*, p. 25.

93. A review in the *Nation* (XC [1910], 375) states: "It would be well nigh impossible for the most careful student to tell, either from manner or style, where one author leaves off and the other begins." Cf. also *EHR*, XXV (1910), 117; *ARH*, XV (1910), 851–53; *Athenaeum*, I (1910), 118–19.

94. Firth did not like to have Gardiner's work compared unfavorably with his own, even in the matter of style (Clark, *loc. cit.*, p. 261).

95. See above, n. 56.

96. *EHR*, XV (1900), 803–4.

97. Davies, *loc. cit.*, p. 380. Firth's interest in the appearance of historical characters made him one of the best informed of the trustees of the National Portrait Gallery (1908–29).

98. Clark, *loc. cit.*, p. 261; Davies, *loc. cit.*, p. 391.

99. *A plea*, p. 14.

100. Clark, *loc. cit.*, p. 261.

101. *A plea*, p. 15–16.

VII

ÉLIE HALÉVY (1870–1937)

CATHERINE HAUGH SMITH*

THE writings of Élie Halévy are not so widely known to the general public of America and England as they should be, but their influence on English historians and through them on more popular written histories is immense. Halévy was the first historian to give due weight to the influence of nonconformity on English social evolution in the nineteenth century, and his particular thesis was that everything was apparently ripe for a social revolution in England during the Napoleonic period and that there was no police to prevent it, or indeed, anything to account for the passivity of the working class in the face of extreme suffering except the evangelical revival. He wrote:

> If we would understand the gulf which separates the history of modern England from the contemporary history of the other European nations . . . . we must . . . . be always on the alert to detect the silent influences exercised over the nation by these independent Churches of the lower middle class, an influence which their very number and diversity renders it most difficult to define. These Free Churches created an atmosphere in which the two mighty watchwords, revolution and reaction, were emptied of all their significance; for, on the one hand, the idea of a Church was not identified with that of a single Church which claimed the support of the State, and, on the other hand, when the people protested against the abuses in the secular administration, they did not revolt at the same time against all spiritual discipline.[1]

The basic idea in Halévy's interpretation of English history in the nineteenth century, the real theme of his whole work, was due in part, perhaps, to his belonging to a family in which the tradition of French Protestantism and French liberalism were united.

* Mrs. Theodore H. Smith, Pelham Manor, N.Y.

Élie Halévy was a child of the Third French Republic, for he was born on September 6, 1870, in Étretat, where his mother had fled from Paris before the final advance of the German army. His father, Ludovic Halévy, was the nephew of Berthelot, a famous Jewish composer of opera and was, himself, a scholar, an author, and a well-known liberal. Artists, musicians, liberals, and scholars frequented his home, and from early years Élie came in contact with those ideas which were later to become the dominant interest in his life. It was in his father's home that he first met Taine, whose influence on him is recognized by all. From his father he inherited St. Simonian traditions; and from his mother, a Protestant of wide learning and high moral character, he inherited his austere mind. Halévy's philosophical interest always had a "moral cast and a moral purpose and was always connected with a profound interest in the inner springs and motives of actual contemporary life."[2]

As a young man Halévy's interest was not in history but in philosophy, and while he was a student at the Lycée Condorcet he won the first prize in philosophy. He continued to pursue his philosophical studies after he entered the École Normale in 1890, and during his second year he worked on a parallel study of Pascal and Spinoza and also concentrated on an analysis of the dialogues of Plato. He continued these studies after he passed his agrégation in 1892, and as the result he published his first book, *La théorie platonicienne des sciences*.[3] Halévy retained this interest in Platonic and Stoic philosophy throughout his life; and, indeed, it might be said that this interest gave an additional point and purpose to all his studies, for it was his philosophical interest which led him to the historical field. "He only became a historian because he was a philosopher," wrote Ernest Barker after his death, "and because he sought to find in the study of history a solution of some of the problems which had been raised by the study of philosophy."[4] Léon Brunschwicg, a philosopher like Halévy and one of his oldest friends, wrote of him in this connection: "If what Plato had at heart was, above all, to transcend, for the salvation of his city, the opposition between purely speculative criticism and purely empirical politics, then the work of Èlie Halévy may be explained by his fidelity to the inspiration of Plato."[5]

When Halévy became a candidate for his doctorate at the École Normale he offered, along with a Latin thesis, a study which later became part of his first important book, *La formation du radicalisme philosophique en Angleterre*.[6] This work (Vol. I dealing with the youth of Bentham, 1776–89; Vol. II, the evolution of the utilitarian doctrine from 1789 to 1814; Vol. III, philosophical radicalism) immediately attracted the attention of scholars in France and England. It is not surprising that the first of Halévy's major works dealt with English philosophy, for he had acquired a great interest in England from his mother and father.

Halévy's exposition showed generally that the philosophical radicals introduced no fundamentally new ideas, that their contribution was of a different sort. He showed that they reduced current ideas to statements which were clear and precise and which appeared plausible and workable. As a result, they were able, by an "unusual combination of incisive theoretical expression, semi-popular propaganda and practical political activity," to promote free trade, the simplification of civil and criminal law and judicial procedure, and the democratization of parliamentary government. He showed that philosophical radicalism owed much to French thought, by tracing in a most interesting fashion how the ideas of Locke developed in France into clear, consistent systems and came back in their French form to inspire Bentham and his successors. Halévy also clearly established the connection between the philosophy of Bentham and the theories of the classical economists; in a masterly fashion he showed how the thought of Bentham influenced the economies of Ricardo, James Mill, and McCulloch. One of the most striking impressions left by these volumes is how much of our thought on modern social problems, regardless of the school of thought with which we identify ourselves, still follows the lines laid down by, and still accepts, the presuppositions of the philosophical radicals.

Shortly after Halévy had completed the course at the École Normale in 1892 he was invited, at the age of twenty-two, by Émile Boutmy to lecture at the École des Sciences Politiques. He eagerly accepted this offer and continued this connection throughout his life. For some time before Halévy's appointment a successful course had been offered at the École on the evolution of political ideas in Germany, and Boutmy wished to add a parallel course on England, a course which he felt Halévy was admirably suited to give. After 1900 Halévy gave two courses at the school in alternate years, lecturing one year on England and the other year on socialism. In addition to his teaching, he became interested, along with his friend Xavier Léon, in the organization of the *Révue de metaphysique et de morale*, an interest he retained throughout his life and for which he worked unceasingly. At the time of his death in 1937 he was editor of this journal.

As the result of his interest in England and his courses at the École des Sciences Politiques, Halévy began, toward the close of the nineteenth century, his visits to England. For forty years he spent part of each year in England, where he made a host of friends among historians and officials, and he became a familiar figure at the British Museum. He met and came to know intimately Bertrand Russell, Graham Wallas, the Webbs, Sidney Ball, G. M. Trevelyan, and many others. To quote Professor Barker:

> He knew England and Englishmen at first hand as perhaps no other foreign student has ever done; he knew intimately, and by regular study in the British Museum, the documents and sources of English history (such as he could not readily procure in Paris) from beginning of the nineteenth century down to the present.[7]

After 1901 he was always accompanied by his wife, who was his colleague and who loved England no less than he and shared his English friendships.

This growing interest in England and his continued interest in the philosophical radicals are what probably influenced Halévy to commence what was to become his magnum opus, *Histoire du peuple anglais aux XIXe siècle*.[8] Since he never ceased trying to determine what was the social background and what were the causes of the social development which explained the vogue of utilitarianism, it might be said that it was the desire to answer these questions that caused Halévy's work, after the publication of *La formation du radicalisme philosophique en Angleterre*, to become definitely and primarily historical. The difficulties involved in writing a history of the English people in the nineteenth century might have caused a historian of less patience and capacity for hard work to hesitate before commencing such an undertaking. Halévy, himself, was conscious of the enormity of his task; and in his preface to Volume I he justified his undertaking on two counts: in the first place, he considered the monographs already written, which dealt with particular aspects of English history in the nineteenth century, to be insufficient; and, in the second place, he felt that, in order to justify the labors of specialists, attempts must be made from time to time to utilize their researches for more general accounts. He wrote:

> Perhaps by the very fact of employing this synthetic method, I shall avoid a fault common among writers of monographs. Man inevitably generalizes even when he is at pains to avoid generalization. The historian, who deliberately sets himself to study Society under one aspect alone, unconsciously comes to consider this aspect as possessing a special importance above the others, and even as being the key to their explanation. And he will thus come to teach according to the special class of phenomena which he studies, either a political or a religious or an economic philosophy of history. The method here followed, precisely because its object is less narrowly limited, is better able to guard against excessive simplifications and to make us realize the complexity and variety of the strands, which, woven together, compose the facts of history.[9]

Volume I of this great work, which was published in 1912, deals with England in 1815 and is considered by most authorities to be the outstanding volume of the series. Indeed, it is usually acclaimed his greatest achievement. Anyone who reads the volume as a whole will understand how it differs from previous English histories. A great historian once declared that history is past politics, but Halévy has done much more than give us an accurate description of political events and an analysis of the characters and motives of the statesmen who were directly responsible for these events. Graham Wallas, in his introduction to the English translation of this volume, stated:

Both of these elements, set out with meticulous care, and drawn from independent analyses of contemporary sources, are found in M. Halévy's volume. But the outstanding importance of his work lies in the fact that he has accepted a more difficult task. He has tried to explain why statesmen found it possible in one year to pass laws and carry through executive policies which were impossible in another year, and even why it was that statesmen found themselves in different years desiring to pass different measures. So far the only interpretation of history in that sense had been based upon an analysis of economic forces— the growth of new forms of industry and finance, the extension of overseas trade, the commercial rivalry of nations, the appearance of economic "class consciousness," and the like—and a deduction from that analysis of the resulting legislation. M. Halévy—and it is this which constitutes the essential originality of his work—denies that economic changes, or the personal characters of statesmen, or even the forms of political constitutions are the only, or, in the case of England, even the most important factors in national evolution.[10]

Halévy wrote:

If the materialistic interpretation of history is to be trusted, if economic facts explain the course taken by the human race in its progress, the England of the nineteenth century was surely, above all other countries, destined to revolution, both politically and religiously.[11]

Then, after stating that "in no other country in Europe have social changes been accomplished with such a marked and gradual continuity" as in England, he wrote:

The source of such continuity and the comparative stability is, as we have seen, not to be found in the economic organization of the country. We have seen also, that it cannot be found in the political institutions of England, which were essentially unstable and wanting in order. To find it we must pass on to another category of social phenomena—to beliefs, emotions and opinions, as well as to the institutions and sects in which these beliefs, emotions and opinions take a form suitable for scientific inquiry.[12]

Thus, in his study of "beliefs, emotions and opinions" he came to realize the immense importance of English nonconformity in the development of English national life in the nineteenth century. Nonconformity, he felt, was the fundamental ingredient which not only could reconcile itself with Benthamism (its apparent enemy, but yet its ally, for both had the same fundamental stoicism) but could also reconcile the antinomies of Benthamism itself and the conflicts or divergencies of English society. This was the factor which held England together: "Le methodisme est le veritable antidote du jacobinisme, et que l'organization libre des Eglises est, dans le pays qu'il gouverne, le véritable principe d'ordre."

This interpretation, new and challenging, was not accepted with equal enthusiasm by all historians. J. H. Clapham wrote: "No praise could be too high for the knowledge, candour, and perfect taste of the section dealing with religion," and: "As a general sketch of economic England in 1815 it would be most difficult, I think, impossible, to find anything better than we have here offered."[13] On the other hand, C. E. Freyer wrote:

The common place view that English political institutions make for stability he [Halévy] rejects entirely: in the sphere of economics he sees in distribution, based upon contract, only provocation to anarchy; whilst toward the Established Church he betrays the prejudice of the philosophical radicals. How then, if not through these, is the non-revolutionary character of English society in the nineteenth century to be explained? M. Halévy answers: by religious nonconformity, nonconformity evincing itself subjectively in the mental attitude induced by evangelicalism and objectively in the institution of Dissent, or the freedom of religious association. . . . . The view is novel, almost startling. Admit it and we shall have to rewrite one of the most important chapters of English history. Probably many critics will disregard the theory entirely, especially those for whom the canon of the nineteenth century is already determined.[14]

However, by the time the next volume of the series appeared, almost all historians had come to understand and accept the great contribution which Halévy had made to the interpretation of nineteenth-century English social history.

Between the publication of the first (1912) and of the second and third volumes (1923) the war of 1914 intervened. Volume II deals with the period from Waterloo to the eve of the Reform Bill of 1832, while Volume III commences with the crisis of the Reform Bill and carries the narrative to the beginning of Peel's ministry in 1841. The same high level of scholarship which characterized the work of the first volume is evident in the second and third volumes; yet these later volumes do not compare in sheer brilliance with the first. Halévy, himself, is obviously conscious of the fact that in these volumes he might be accused of writing merely of "past politics," and he feels the necessity of explaining his plan. He states, in the preface to Volume II, that because of the rapidity of action he can do no more than relate the events.

Only at a later period, when the democratic and revolutionary movement seemed to have been finally defeated by the triumph of the pacifist and middle-class school of free trade, and when England, having attained at least a temporary equilibrium, ceased for a quarter of a century to have any history in the strict sense of the term, shall we be free to interrupt our narrative and return to description.[15]

That the war had left its mark on Halévy there can be no doubt. He, himself, told Graham Wallas how, when he returned to his home after the war and took up again the sheets which recorded (in Vol. II) his conscientious but comparatively uninterested researches into the controversies of 1816–19 as to the resumption of the gold standard and the rate of exchange of paper money, he found that the old facts had suddenly acquired a new and menacing vividness.[16] In addition to acquiring new interests, the war caused him to revise certain traditional judgments. In his honest fashion he asked himself: "Has the spectacle of the present troubled my vision of the past, or, on the contrary, as I believe, has it enabled me to see the past more clearly as it really was?"[17] For example, on the subject of the two great English statesmen, Canning and Peel, Halévy confessed that ten years earlier he would have been tempted, without doubt, to have pardoned Canning for his dangerous decisions, which constantly led him to the brink of war; perhaps he would have in this attempt used a very plausible phraseology to explain how "war is often progress, movement and life." In 1923 he thought otherwise.

In the interval I have learned what war means. . . . . I prefer to a Canning—possibly more liberal, perhaps, at least in his speeches, but certainly more bellicose—a Robert Peel, who was proud to call himself a Conservative but who was a far more resolute friend of peace.[18]

This hatred of war influenced very greatly and visibly the personal orientation of Halévy and even the publication of his works. After 1923 Halévy changed his original plan and turned his attention to the writing and publishing of two volumes dealing with the period immeditely preceding the war of 1914. Although the war had not shaken his determination to finish and publish Volumes II and III of the original undertaking, it had shifted his center of interest; also, for the purpose of his lectures at the École des Sciences Politiques he had collected a mass of material on the period of English history from 1895 to 1914, which he was eager to use. Professor Barker, in his appreciation of Halévy at the time of his death, wrote:

> The interruption was an inevitable aftermath of the war, which turned his thoughts irresistibly back to the twenty years which preceded its outbreak; and it was an even more inevitable result of his own practical and moral temper, which engaged his attention upon the deep issues of contemporary life. . . . . The *Épilogue* was bound to come: it was all the more bound to come because the Frenchman in Halévy (and he was, above all, French) was naturally drawn to instruct his countrymen on the causes and the motives which had drawn England and France together and associated their destinies.[19]

These two volumes were termed an *Épilogue;* Volume I (Vol. IV in the series), published in 1926, deals with the imperialists in power and covers the period from 1895 to 1906, while Volume II, published in 1930, takes as its theme, "Towards social democracy and towards war," 1905–14. Halévy called these two volumes an epilogue because he felt that the year 1895—about the time Gladstone disappeared from political life—marked the close of the nineteenth century. He felt that the period between 1895 and 1914 did not belong to the British nineteenth century; it was, at most, the epilogue of that century, as it was the prologue of the twentieth century.

Halévy was conscious of the difficulty of the task he had set himself. He wrote:

> I shall not plead against or in favour of any government. In 1914 the aims respectively pursued by the different governments and which each regarded as legitimate proved incompatible with the maintenance of peace. Moreover, the aims of the German government proved irreconcilable with the aims pursued by all the great nations, and in that sense Germany "deserved" the alliance which was formed against her. I do not intend to discuss in its usual form the question of the "moral" responsibility of the war. I hope the day has already gone by for the literature of war propaganda, and equally for that propaganda against war, which is a form of war propaganda.[20]

The detachment with which Halévy treated this controversial period is admired by all. J. H. Clapham, in reviewing the volumes, wrote that Halévy had "no perceptible bias" and that "his appreciations of the currents in English public opinion seem extraordinarily just—'seem,' because in these contemporary matters few reviewers would dare so to endorse their own opinions as to write 'are.' "[21] Perhaps the *Épilogue* was appreciated even more in France than in England. Charles Seignobos hailed it as the most satisfactory contemporary history of any state which had been written, and Robert Dreyfus wrote of its second volume as indubitably "le chef d'œuvre du grand historien."[22] Although Halévy's interest had shifted to the period immediately preceding the war of 1914, he was still absorbed in social problems. The sections dealing with religion and education, the labor movement, and the birth of the Labour party are by far the best in these volumes. Here was a general field in which he was at home and to which he could make a real contribution.

In 1929 the University of Oxford, which had previously (1926) conferred upon him an honorary doctorate, invited Halévy to deliver a course of Rhodes Memorial Lectures. Halévy regarded this invitation as a singular honor not only to himself but to his country as well. At the beginning of his first lecture he made this characteristic speech:

But it is not only on my own behalf that I wish to express my gratitude to you, it is also on behalf of my native country, France. The first Rhodes Memorial Lecturer was a Canadian statesman, one of the leading figures of the British Commonwealth of nations. The second was an eminent American scientist, who belonged, if not to the Commonwealth, at all events to what might be called the Commonwealth of the English speaking nations. But you have now remembered that this is the century of the League of Nations. You have thought it might be well if you looked for a third lecturer outside the circle of the English speaking world . . . . and finally, having taken this decision, you have invited a Frenchman to come; for which, again, I thank you. Your purpose has been to give the *Entente* its true interpretation, not as a passing diplomatic contrivance, not founded, let us hope, upon fear of a common enemy but upon the more positive qualities of charity, hope, and faith. Charity towards mankind as a whole, Hope in the future welfare of the human race, Faith in the possibility of furthering, through co-operation between nations, the cause of knowledge and culture, of everything that the eighteenth century, the most Anglo-French in history, called by a fine name "enlightenment"—*Les Lumières*.[23]

The lectures covered the period of the war and were published in 1930 under the title *The world crisis of 1914–1918*. This volume preceded by two years the publication of the second volume of his *Épilogue*, but it is nonetheless "his last testament in the field of European history."[24] In a sense, this was an epilogue to his own *Épilogue*, and it rounded out and put the finishing touches to the volumes which had covered the previous twenty years. Halévy approached his task in a philosophical spirit. He determined to disregard the suggestions made retrospectively as to what such and such sovereign, prime minister, or foreign secretary might have said or not said, done or not done, at such and such an hour to prevent the war. He said:

> The object of my study is the earthquake itself. I shall attempt to define the collective forces, the collective feelings and movements of public opinion, which, in the early years of the twentieth century, made for strife. I say "strife," not "war," because the world crisis of 1914–18 was not only war, the war of 1914— but revolution, the revolution of 1917. . . . . All great convulsions in the history of the world, and more particularly in modern Europe, have been at the same time wars and revolutions.[25]

His first lecture he called, "Towards revolution"; his second, "Towards war"; his third, "War and revolution." At the end of his third lecture Halévy pointed out forcefully what "his method of approach" had been:

> I have looked not in the acts of individual statesmen, but in collective anonymous forces, against which individual statesmen were powerless. . . . . It means, rather, if you understand me well, a shifting of responsibility for the evils under which mankind labours, from the statesmen to us, the common people, ourselves. The wisdom or folly of our statesmen is merely the reflection of our own wisdom or folly.[26]

This "method of approach," as Halévy called the interpretation of events, was a fundmental factor in his philosophy and was apparent in all his writings. He never subscribed to the "great personality" theory, but throughout his writings he emphasized the importance of the common man, the responsibility of the individual.

After 1932 Halévy turned back to his original undertaking and continued to work on the Victorian era until his death at Sucy-en-Brie (Seine-et-Oise) on August 21, 1937. One hopes that another and posthumous volume of the *History of the English people* will be edited from his notes and papers.

The death of Halévy was regarded as a calamity by the historical world, and as a result there was such an outpouring of appreciation and praise by his friends and colleagues in the various learned journals and periodicals in France and England that the École des Sciences Politiques had these spontaneous tributes collected into a memorial volume to honor their beloved teacher and distinguished writer. In reading these tributes, written shortly after his death, by friends and colleagues who had known him over a course of a great many years, one is impressed with the constant repetition of certain adjectives in eulogizing this great man. All emphasize his great modesty, his sincerity and simplicity, his diligence and patience, his impartiality and complete independence of judgment.

Halévy was a prodigious worker. His power of concentration, his thoroughness and patience, and his orderly mind were known to, and admired by, all his friends. One of his earlier friends wrote: "He followed rules spontaneously, this, for example, which astonished me when he told me of it, that he would never read anything outside the course of his studies, simply to amuse and distract himself, except on a Sunday evening."[27] This devotion to work, this determination to complete any task he commenced, remained his guiding principle regardless of how much sacrifice it entailed. Shortly after the League of Nations was organized, Halévy was asked to become a member of the secretariat, a position which he would have found most congenial because of his almost passionate interest in peace and his belief that the only hope for better international understanding lay in such an organization. Yet he felt that a work once commenced should be finished, and so he declined the offer in order that he might complete his *History of the English people in the nineteenth century*.[28] In addition to his teaching, research, and writing and his editorial duties with the *Révue de metaphysique et de morale*, he became, in 1928, an active member of the commission for the publication of the French diplomatic documents on the origin of the war of 1914. This work was of great interest to him, and he applied to it the same high standard of impartial scholarship that is characteristic of all his work.

Halévy's wide and extensive use of source material is obvious to all who read his books. He made extensive use of the press, reports of speeches, pamphlets, and official documents, and he made such good use of the out-of-the-way sources and was so generous in printing his extracts that this, in itself, is of great value to a historical student. Probably no Englishman has had a wider knowledge of the sources of nineteenth-century English history and thought. It has been said that Halévy is the only man who has ever been through the vast mass of Bentham's manuscripts in the library of University College, London. In writing his history Halévy followed the admirable custom of giving full references to his authorities. Graham Wallas, in his introduction to the English translation of Volume I of the *History of the English people in the nineteenth century*, wrote that he could imagine nothing more delightful for a special student of any period or section of English nineteenth-century history than to acquire the habit of looking up Halévy's references. The first volume of the *History of the English people* includes an excellent classified bibliography. It was his intension to prepare a similar bibliography for each of the following volumes, but he abandoned this idea before the publication of the second and third volumes. He realized that either he would have to incorporate into the subsequent bibliographies the whole, or almost the whole, of the first, which would have inconveniently increased the size of the books, or he would have to content himself with a mere supplement to the first bibliography. He therefore decided to enlarge, considerably, the footnotes of the subsequent volumes until they constituted a species of scattered bibliography. It was his hope that some day, after he had completed his great work, he might offer to the public a general bibliography of the history of the English people in the nineteenth century.

Halévy did not have an unusual gift of style, but he wrote clearly and forcefully. He expressed his views with the same simplicity which characterized him: "He laboured simply to understand and to set down simply his understanding."[29] There is no passage that more clearly illustrates this characteristic of his writing than the last words of Volume V of his *History of the English people*. Where many a historian has described with dramatic phrases England's final step into the war in 1914, Halévy wrote, in utter simplicity, the following:

> Next morning the Prime Minister without troubling to consult the Cabinet and confident of the silent support of the entire country authorized Sir Edward Grey to send Sir Edward Goschen a telegram calling upon the German government to pledge itself before midnight to respect the neutrality of Belgium. What could the German government reply? The invasion of Belgium had already begun. Night fell. England entered the war.[30]

Halévy cannot be said to belong to any "school" of history. He rejected frequently and emphatically the materialistic conception of history; yet he was aware of the importance of economic forces. "The basis of history," he wrote, "is idealistic, not materialistic."[31] Politically, he is properly classified as a liberal, a liberal in the nineteenth-century meaning of the term. He had no sympathy with socialism, and many of his shorter works and articles deal with this subject. In *The world crisis* he stated:

> The doctrine of Karl Marx has always struck me as unfair, because it directs the hatred of the multitude against the particular class of capitalists, the captains of industry whose activity has been the most positively beneficial, to the exclusion of many more parasitic forms of capitalism.[32]

Yet Halévy cannot be said to belong to the "political school" either. If it can be said that he had a bias, it was his emphasis on the part Nonconformity played in the development of English history. He thought not only that this was true of the nineteenth century but that it was the key to an understanding of the twentieth century as well. One of his friends, writing at the time of his death, describes a correspondence he had had some years before with Halévy in which the latter ended by triumphantly pointing to the significant fact that the leader of the Labour party (then J. Ramsay MacDonald) was no intellectual rationalist but a nonconformist at the head of a still predominately nonconformist party.[33] This was a typical argument to have with Halévy, because he knew historically more about England than almost any Englishman, and he was always intensely interested in relating this historical knowlege to current English politics. No doubt his interest in liberalism and nonconformity was due in part to the influence of his father and mother (he was especially close to his Protestant mother, who lived almost as long as he), but one has the feeling, after reading his works, that his conclusions as to the importance of nonconformity on English social development in the nineteenth century are the result of his patient research and study rather than the result of his inheritance. He set himself the task of analyzing and evaluating the forces that determined the trend of the nineteenth century. That he succeeded in his undertaking is conceded by all; his works will be enduring witnesses of his success. His interpretation of English thought and life in the early nineteenth century is regarded as definitive, while his volumes on the period preceding the war of 1914 and his volume on England during the war are recognized as a definite contribution to the understanding of the period. It is remarkable that what is likely to become for a generation the standard history of nineteenth-century England was written by a Frenchman. It is a great contribution that French scholarship has made to England, and it is one that English scholars will long remember and acclaim.

NOTES

1. *A history of the English people in the nineteenth century*, trans. E. I. Watkin (New York, 1926), II, vi. Permission to quote from this work has kindly been granted by the publishers, Harcourt, Brace & Co.

2. Ernest Barker, "Élie Halévy," *EHR*, LIII (1938), 79.

3. Paris, 1896.

4. Barker, *loc. cit.*, p. 80.

5. L. Brunschvicg, "Le philosophe," *Élie Halévy* (Paris: École Libre des Sciences Politiques, n.d.), p. 20.

6. Paris, 1900–1903. These volumes were translated into English by Mary Morris (London, 1928). An excellent bibliography of the writings of Bentham and the works on him, prepared by C. W. Everett, was included in this edition.

7. Barker, *loc. cit.*, p. 81.

8. Paris, 1912–30. Vol. I was translated into English by E. I. Watkin and D. A. Barker; Vols. II–V, by E. I. Watkin (New York, 1924–34).

9. *Ibid.*, I, ix.

10. *Ibid.*, pp. v, vi.

11. *Ibid.*, p. 334.

12. *Ibid.*, p. 335.

13. *EHR*, XXVIII (1913), 176.

14. *AHR*, XVIII (1913), 367.

15. *History of the English people*, II, vii.

16. *Ibid.*, I, x.

17. *Ibid.*, II, ix.

18. *Ibid.*, p. x.

19. Barker, *loc. cit.*, p. 85.

20. *History of the English people*, IV, xi.

21. *EHR*, XLII (1927), 444.

22. R. Dreyfus, "L'ami," *Élie Halévy*, p. 39.

23. *The world crisis of 1914–1918: an interpretation*, being the Rhodes Memorial Lectures delivered in 1929 (Oxford, 1930), pp. 3–4.

24. Barker, *loc. cit.*, p. 85.

25. *The world crisis*, p. 7.

26. *Ibid.*, p. 55.

27. Quoted in Barker, *loc. cit.*, p. 81.

28. André Siegfried, "Souvenirs personnels," *Élie Halévy*, p. 14.

29. Barker, *loc. cit.*, p. 87.

30. V, 665.

31. *The world crisis*, p. 30.

32. *Ibid.*, p. 9.

33. *New statesman and nation*, N.S., XIV (1937), 330.

VIII

GABRIEL HANOTAUX (1853——)

VESTA SWEITZER VETTER*

GABRIEL HANOTAUX (Albert Auguste Gabriel) was born at Beaurevoir in Brittany on November 19, 1853. His rather discursive memoirs, continuing through one book and a number of periodical articles,[1] give an interesting, if rambling, picture of his boyhood and youth. His paternal ancestors were primarily of peasant stock interspersed with an occasional artisan, such as his great-grandfather, who was a carpenter. His father, a more intellectual type, rebelled against the bucolic life and became a notary, with a small legal office. Hanotaux's mother was a Martin, from a family in business. The most outstanding relative on this side, as far as Hanotaux was concerned, was his mother's great-uncle, Henri Martin, the historian, who served as inspiration to the young student, and, on occasion, rendered practical service in arranging meetings with influential people and opening official doors.

Young Gabriel grew up happily with an older brother and a sister in a family with a modest but adequate income, plenty of hard work, and few conveniences. As a youth, his health was none too good, and many vacations were spent on family farms, where he learned to love the soil. His interest in the needs of farmers can definitely be traced in the commercial treaties negotiated while he was foreign minister, and he later boasted that he had never disposed of his share of the family property which he inherited.[2]

The old man looking back on his youth remembered many impressions which aroused an interest in history. His father was

* Mrs. Carl H. Vetter, Berkeley, Calif.; sometime fellow in history.

a studious man who particularly enjoyed reading historical works, and there were always uncles and great-uncles at hand with stirring tales of battles and famous events. The Hanotaux children played frequently in the near-by ruins of the Chateau de Luxemburg, where Jeanne d'Arc had been imprisoned.[3]

"The frontier where I was born and the times in which I have lived" are the two factors which Gabriel Hanotaux himself considered to be the determinants of his life and work.[4] Living on the northeastern border of France, he experienced the full impact of the invasion and occupation by the Germans in 1870–71. The Franco-German War began when he was sixteen, and his father died in November of that year, as the Germans were marching into the city in which he lived.[5] In May, 1871, before the smoke of the Commune had cleared away, the young adolescent was sent to Paris to study.

Although Hanotaux had early announced his intention of becoming a professor of history,[6] much to his father's disgust, it was not until he was about twenty-five that he really found himself. At the age of six he attended the village school, and at nine he entered the *lycée* at Saint-Quentin, where his brother had preceded him and where the family later moved. According to his father's wishes, both he and his brother studied to become notaries. In May, 1871, he went to Paris, where he failed to pass the Sorbonne examinations. After a summer in the country he entered the École de Droit in Paris and become a licentiate in law before he attained his majority.

Law never really interested him, however, and he was increasingly attracted toward history. The fear of examinations caused by his earlier failure at the Sorbonne might have slowed up his formal education, but his excellence as a student counterbalanced this. He began by reading history at the École des Hautes Études.[7] Here, his knowledge of the Picard dialect enabled him to make an unusual study of one of the sources of the Fourth Crusade, which brought him to the notice of the already prominent historian, Gabriel Monod, who published the article in the newly founded *Revue historique*.[8] The publication of this monograph caused a flutter in historical circles. Henri Martin evinced an interest as his young relative gained prominence, and he introduced him to Jules Quicherat, who was at that time director of the École des Chartes. The latter encouraged Hanotaux's entrance in 1879 into that famous French institution specializing in methods of medieval history which has trained so many French historians.[9]

Gabriel Hanotaux always spoke of the École des Chartes with affection and respect. He learned method there and made contacts with such men as Quicherat, Montaiglon, Gautier, Léopold Delisle, Gaston Paris, Boislisle, and Giry. His diploma was granted on the basis of a thesis on the origins of intendants in France,[10] a subject in the field of institutions which he selected because he was not greatly interested in medieval history.[11]

Hanotaux chose Richelieu as his principal interest as early as 1878 and was prepared to devote the rest of his life to research in that field. He proposed to enter the teaching profession, despite his father's contempt for that way of earning his living. "Professor! don't think of it," his father told him. "A professor! He is only an underteacher who has made good. And you would shut yourself up for life in a *lycée* to teach classes . . . . when you could be a notary!"[12] Hanotaux's experience in this field, however, was limited by events to a little teaching in a Parisian private school, undertaken while he was still a student, to eke out his meager allowance,[13] and the more interesting experimental work of conducting a "conference" (the subject was not considered worthy of the designation "course") on the sources of modern history at the École des Hautes Études.[14]

Although Hanotaux enjoyed teaching, his life lay along other paths. Most of the young historians of his day were politicians, and politics appealed to him. At an early age he had shocked his father by his radical republican ideas;[15] and although he soon lost his radicalism, he remained a devoted Republican all his life. The assiduity of his work in the archives of the foreign office brought him to the notice of Waddington, the foreign minister, who was Henri Martin's colleague from the department of Aisne in the National Assembly. After refusing, because of bad health, a diplomatic assignment which would have involved his leaving France, Hanotaux accepted a position as "attaché without pay" to the foreign office.[16] This in February, 1880, became "attaché with pay" on the archives staff, and he was soon given an increase in salary because of an article on Greece.[17]

Gambetta, one of his political heroes, encouraged Hanotaux in his growing desire to make history alive by presenting it in an interesting manner and by bringing the lessons of the past to bear on the decisions of the present. When the former became prime minister he appointed the young historian co-chief of the office assisting the cabinet in foreign affairs, a position which he assumed again under Challemel-Lacour and Ferry. In 1885, after a few minor missions, he became counselor of the French embassy in Constantinople; and in the following year, as chargé d'affaires, he was French delegate at the conference charged with regulating the Bulgarian question.

That same year he was elected to the chamber of deputies at a special election but served only one term, being beaten by a royalist in 1889. He returned at once to the foreign office as a functionary in charge of the countries held under French protectorates. In 1890 he was a member of the French delegation to the conference relative to the delineation of the spheres of influence in Africa, and two years later he assumed the direction of consulates and commercial affairs. This steady progress was crowned in 1894 by the offer of the portfolio of foreign affairs, a position which Hanotaux accepted and held for four years, with the exception of a short interval in the beginning of 1896. As foreign minister he was particularly interested in the development of the Franco-Russian alliance and the expansion of French interest in the countries bordering on the Mediterranean, especially Africa. After the fall of the ministry in June, 1898, Hanotaux renounced politics to devote himself to the writing of historical works.

Although he later spoke with scorn of those who liked the security of government positions[18] and claimed that the "taste for retreat, for silence, for intellectual independence" caused him to abandon public life,[19] this was hardly the whole truth. As the years went by, Hanotaux had identified himself completely with that section of the Republican party which disliked factionalism and believed, above all, in getting things done. In order to accomplish its ends, this group manifested a tendency to split more and more from the Left and draw closer and closer to the Right through the policies of "appeasement" and "rallying." The high point of this policy was reached in the nineties in the series of ministries under Dupuy, Ribot, and Méline (1894–98), which came to a sudden end amid the violent controversies of the Dreyfus case. The coming into power of the more radical republicans put an end willy-nilly to the political careers of their predecessors. The fact that Hanotaux stood as candidate for the senate in the Aisne in 1904, where he was badly defeated, indicated that public life still had its attractions. For the remainder of his life, however, he was restricted to serving as delegate on occasional missions and making innumerable public speeches.

Hanotaux had not neglected history even in the midst of his diplomatic labors. The concentration upon the restoration of France after the Franco-German War was general, and most of the young historians studying in Paris in the seventies were ardent patriots. They were affected by the current belief that superior German intellectual methods and scientific techniques had won the war. *Ergo*, they studied German historical method assiduously, hoping to demonstrate to the intellectual world that they could be as scientific as their conquerors and in that way do their part in helping their country.

Hanotaux was not the least of these, and for his own research he proposed to concentrate on the period of Richelieu. When he entered political life he inevitably had less time for study. He did not abandon history, however; he simply enlarged his conception and technique to include his new activities. In fact, he came to consider his writings and his political career as inseparable parts of one whole, and he felt that his contribution to French life as a writer of history was just as significant as his contribution to the development of the French colonial empire and the restoration of French influence in the concert of the European powers.

This combination of historian and politician was not unusual in France. Guizot, the minister of Louis Philippe, and Thiers, the first president of the Third Republic, were notable historians in their day who occupied the highest state positions. Henri Martin, always a model for Hanotaux, played a significant part in the political events of his time, and nearly all living French historians took sides publicly in the agitation of the Dreyfus case. Hanotaux, however, was more conscious and specific in his approach than were his contemporaries.

The role which he assigned to historians was no mean one. "Sciences, arts, techniques, all the productions of human activity flowed into history,"[20] he thought. But more than that, history is the "mistress of princes and of peoples; she works without cessation to distinguish good from evil; she passes the acts of man through the sieve and separates the bad from the good grain. She judges and is the tribunal where sits the conscience of future generations."[21] In consequence of this,

when a man decides to write history, no matter how feeble and slender the subject he selects, he becomes the instrument of Destiny; as he is responsible for his narrative and his judgment, so he is responsible for their consequences. According to the fashion in which he exposes the affairs of the past, the affairs of the future will go well or ill.[22]

Thus, history became for him not merely an exposé of the past but a way of life for the future. His ideal was not the scholar, publishing pedantic works which no one would read, but the man of action,[23] even the prophet.[24] Underlying all his writings is his conviction that history is definitely a moral force.[25]

Although his conception seems very grandiose indeed, the inevitable result of this kind of thinking is a very personal sort of history written around its author's own experiences and interpretations. That, in the case of Hanotaux, these should be concentrated on his country was natural, for the significant events of his impressionable adolescent years centered around the

Franco-German War. "I have seen frightful things," he wrote many years later, "and the most frightful of all is defeat."[26]

Thus nationalism dominated all of his historical writings. He became interested in the causes of the greatness of France in the past and concerned himself with trying to analyze and interpret those causes in a manner which might help those who were trying to rebuild the nation. By revealing the past glories of their country to the French people, particularly the youth, he hoped he was inspiring his countrymen to renewed efforts at restoring those glories and perhaps even increasing them.[27]

Love of one's country, to him, was a most commendable quality; but when that country was France, devotion was inevitable,[28] for it was a country "so worthy of being loved."[29] It possessed nearly everything to make men happy. "To speak of France, what an undertaking!"[30] and it was to this that Hanotaux devoted his life and his vision.[31] He was a sentimental nationalist. France, "so lovely,"[32] was to him almost a living person, beautifully proportioned, smiling, full of grace, hard working, vivacious, ardent, yet restrained, reasonable, the good sister of all those in trouble, loving and seeking to be loved.[33] He admitted generously that France was not the largest or strongest power in the world, but balanced his admission by his claim that the moderation of French riches was more desirable and more permanent.[34] French thrift, he insisted, was due not to miserliness but to a desire to save for investment, and thus was a potent factor in spreading French civilization throughout the world[35]—an end much to be desired. Above all, he admired French spirit and morale.

His works can be divided into two parts. As a young man, he published a number of scholarly works such as might be expected to come from the pen of any well-trained historian of promise. These include a few monographs on various subjects of the middle ages; his dissertation on intendants; the collections published as a result of his association with the commission on diplomatic archives;[36] and his studies on Richelieu. After 1900 his works are less erudite and cover various phases of contemporary French life.

The earlier works on medieval topics can be ignored here, for they were the product of his student days. Hanotaux was always a little proud of them; but, while they indicated merit, they were written before his ideas matured and play only an introductory part in his development as a historian.

The other writings in this earlier period were concentrated around the subject of Richelieu or were the by-products of his research in that field. Unquestionably Hanotaux's claim as a scholarly historian rests primarily on these works, which include a large number of articles and the famous *Histoire du cardinal de Richelieu,* of which four volumes have appeared. His interest in the past glories of France had, to a considerable extent, determined his selection of the seventeenth century—France's *grand siècle*—as his special field of interest.[37]

His conception of his task was immense.

My idea was to write a history of the great century. But the history of a century is the accumulated knowledge of all that the men of this century have done during the hundred years it has lasted, of all the meeting and crossing of the passions, the acts, the illusions, the disillusions throughout its course; I say that the history of a century includes the knowledge of the centuries which have followed in order to judge its accomplishments. It is, then, a world, it is the universe, it is mankind! To know all, that is the program![38]

Limitation was necessary, however, and he decided to concentrate on Richelieu in particular because he felt that that statesman gathered up and perfected the work of Sully and Henry IV and prepared the way for the culminating magnificence of Louis XIV.

Hanotaux considered that Richelieu's great work was the unification of the kingdom. The cardinal, to him, "set the seal on French unity, consecrated religious tolerance, and established the rules of a language destined to serve the spokesman of nations in making more precise, formulas of justice and treaties of peace."[39] The adequate portrayal of these contributions meant a tremendous undertaking. It involved a knowledge of the work of Richelieu's predecessors and successors; an understanding of developing French institutions and all the complex relationships between royalty, nobility, bourgeoisie, and common people; a clarification of the religious problem and its entanglements with the political and economic situation; and a study of foreign affairs, including all the complications of the Thirty Years' War. It was a task which, indeed, required a lifetime.

The personality of Richelieu interested Hanotaux. In the introduction to the first volume, published in 1893, fifteen years after he began his research, the historian states his conviction that he has added to the accuracy of the portrait of Richelieu the statesman.

> I have found in Richelieu a genius, accessible, with a psychology rather simple and easy to decipher. . . . . I have seen a French statesman, in the practical and positive sense, with a glance cold and certain, and a rough hand. I have added his name with no effort to the series of our great political figures, to Philip the Handsome, Charles V, Louis XI, and the men of the Revolution. What distinguished him is his clarity, his logic, the measure of his energy, and, it is necessary to add, his marvelous agility. This thin and delicate man maintained himself in power for so long a period only by *tours de force* in which he demonstrated his great patience and his adroitness. . . . .
>
> There was in him a priest, believing, as did all the world in his day. But there was, above all, a man of action. . . . . He retained always . . . . something of the cavalier, which shows clearly in his face with its pointed beard. He had his romances. . . . . But his real passion, the flame which devoured and consumed his entire life was his ambition. He wished power, he wished to keep it until his death; once minister, his ambitions identified themselves with the well-being of the state, he consecrated himself to a great work: the achievement of French unity by the definite establishment of the absolute authority of the king and by the ruin of the Spanish royal house. This man lived only for that.[40]

Hanotaux proposed to recount the "drama" of the life of this man in detail. The early volumes are undoubtedly the best. The first is excellent in plan and treatment, describing the background and early life of Richelieu and the geography, the institutions, and the people of France in 1614. With the concluding summary the stage is carefully and completely set for the incidents presenting themselves when Richelieu achieved supreme power. Hanotaux never again reached the standard set by this book.

The second volume, published in 1896, treats of the early political problems confronting Richelieu and his method of handling them. By its nature, this volume is not as perfect in outline as its predecessor. It was at this point that active political work interrupted Hanotaux's concentration upon his cardinal, and the third volume was not published until thirty-seven years later (1933). It was written with the collaboration of the Duc de La Force, as was the fourth volume, which appeared in 1935; together they complete the story of the internal unification of France.

These four volumes are far from fulfilling the original plan of Hanotaux. They do not represent a complete story of Richelieu's career chronologically. Moreover, while foreign affairs are not ignored, the emphasis is definitely on the internal situation. The latter volumes are not as heavily documented as the earlier, and they are of less significance in the field of historical writing.

After he abandoned active public life, contemporary events absorbed more and more of his time, and Hanotaux never returned single-heartedly to the study of the seventeenth century.

To join the past to the present, such was the work of the time and the situation in which destiny had placed me. It was not a question of enclosing myself in the seventeenth and eighteenth centuries, or even in the nineteenth, which was passing; it was necessary to consider the totality of the work of the nation and of the world.[41]

The breadth of his interest soon defied specialization.

Hanotaux's works on his own period are prolific and cover nearly all aspects of contemporary life. By their nature they are personal books, the expression of his own beliefs on current topics, often arising from his practical experience. Because that experience had come primarily in the field of politics, his political writings constitute his major contribution.

Politically, as we have seen, he was a conservative republican. He believed in democracy, but he felt that the masses needed rulers. He admired most those prime ministers who tried hardest to overcome the party quarrels which so complicated the early life of the Third Republic and to accomplish a definite program. Thus Gambetta,[42] Jules Ferry,[43] Jules Méline,[44] and Poincaré[45] became his political heroes. He supported the moderate and conservative republican groups in the crises besetting the Third Republic, opposing General Boulanger, whose supporters wished to make him dictator,[46] blaming the Panama financial scandals on a weak government and an uncontrolled press[47] and supporting the position of the Méline cabinet which considered the Dreyfus case closed.[48] The maintenance of order and a vigorous government policy seemed vitally necessary to Hanotaux, and such a program always won his support. Unity, frequently absent from French politics, seemed to him the most admirable and desirable trait.[49]

He wrote innumerable articles on political questions, but the best expression of his ideas and his methods can be found in his interesting and readable four-volume *Histoire de la France contemporaine* (1903–8), which treats of events from 1870 to 1878, and from his *Histoire politique de 1804 à 1926*, included in the *Histoire de la nation française* (1929). The first of these is, by its nature and concept, more scholarly than the second and ranks second to *Richelieu* as a contribution to historical writing. It covers a less ambitious field than that earlier work, and Hanotaux had the advantage of having lived through the events of the period about which he was writing. This study comes closer to fulfilling Hanotaux's original conception; but it is, of necessity, despite its basis on actual documents, a source rather than a definitive treatment. No student of the founding of the Third Republic can afford to ignore it, but it is colored by the views and experiences of its author.

Admittedly a popular history,[50] Hanotaux maintained that it was based upon accurate historical methods. He proposed to "present to democracy a sufficient quantity of precise information, of documents which were checked, and proceedings which were verified."[51] While he strove to be impartial, he averred his republicanism;[52] had he been strictly accurate, he would have added "conservative" republican.

The four volumes portray in an interesting manner the events incidental to the firm establishment of the Third Republic. They present a touching picture of the tragic events of the war and the Commune and an eloquent analysis of the struggles to bring to an end the German occupation. Thiers is treated with great sympathy. The general lack of bitterness toward the Right may be explained not only by Hanotaux's "impartiality" but by his own political position.[53] Incidentally, this is the only title of Hanotaux's that has been translated into English,[54] but the translation shows evidence of haste and is not too well done.

Hanotaux's career in the foreign office developed as a result of his interest in foreign affairs, and he definitely believed that it was necessary to study international relationships in order to arrive at a proper understanding of history.[55] Specifically he was interested in the restoration of France as a great power in Europe, which he believed could best be accomplished by close association with the Mediterranean countries. His book on the diplomacy of the years 1907–11[56] adequately illustrates his ideas. It is true that France had played no insignificant part in world-history from the time of the Crusades, but Hanotaux regularly extolled this influence to the point of gross exaggeration.[57]

As an ardent nationalist, it was natural that he should hate Germany, and he disliked everything about not only that nation but the northern countries and their Teutonic background in general. Materialism, diabolical sophism, the worship of brute force, he felt, were the attributes of their philosophers and their rulers,[58] and he would have none of them. He rebelled not only against their politics and philosophy but against their historical method. His *Histoire de la nation française* disavowed the significance of German influences in the life and culture of medieval France.[59] Moreover, the entire conception of the fifteen volumes aimed at discarding German historical method and setting up a new kind of history, more vital and more true, he believed, than the stodgy German method of documentation alone.

Hanotaux was an Anglophobe as well; he thought the English just as bad as the Germans,[60] and his anti-English policy in the foreign office was not insignificant as a contributing factor in the development of the Fashoda incident in 1898, which nearly led to serious trouble between France and England.

On the other hand, he revered the Latin tradition and Mediterranean culture. He never tired of comparing the clear sunny weather and brilliant coloring of the south with the gloomy fogs of the north. Latin reasonableness and the generally gentler way of life (his description) he always contrasted with the brutality and ferocity of the Teutonic countries.[61] The religion of the south—Catholicism—appealed to him,[62] as did the Latin language.[63] His collection of sketches in La paix latine[64] was the result of his travels in the Mediterranean area. He always emphasized the inheritance which France had received, sometimes carrying it to rather ridiculous extremes.[65]

The high spot of his writings on international relations can be found in his works on the war of 1914, which include a dozen books and many periodical articles, of which the outstanding is the set of fifteen volumes of his Histoire illustrée de la guerre de 1914 (1915–23), "the passionate subject of his supreme efforts as a patriot."[66] To him, the Allied victory, due primarily to France[67] with a little help from the United States,[68] represented the defeat of brute force, the triumph of good over evil. During the war he constituted himself an ardent agent of French propaganda, writing constantly, both to keep up French morale and to interest the United States in the conflict. The only hope for the future of the world lay, for him, in the complete and total crushing of Germany. Once the war was ended, he continued his polemical writing against that country, and there was no more vigorous supporter of the French policy of keeping Germany down.

Hanotaux had had extensive and close contact with the colonies during his office-holding days, and he believed wholeheartedly in the development of the French colonial empire not only because it was of benefit to France but because he felt that it helped the countries where French influence spread. There was nothing mercenary in his attitude, for he was contemptuous of those who spoke in terms of money and wanted to know only how much the colonies cost and what they were worth.[69] For him, France had a world-task to perform: spreading the benefits of French language, customs, laws, and civilization as far as possible and creating new Frances wherever opportunities presented themselves.[70] He felt that this was a vital part of French tradition, a special role which Providence had assigned to France since the days of Julius Caesar.[71] As he personified France, he personified her colonies. "For peace, for war, internally, externally, for the present, for the future, colonies are to people as children are to families. A nation without a colony is a sterile power: all the praise and all the applause of history will go always to colonizing countries."[72]

He begrudged the loss of the French colonial empire in the eighteenth century, particularly in America, and always maintained a deep interest in the entire western hemisphere. He boasted of the strong French traditions which still persisted in sections of both Canada and the United States; and South America, he thought, possessed a close sympathy with France because of her Latin traditions.[73] Hanotaux was one of the moving figures and first president of the Comité France-Amérique established in 1909 to promote a cordial relationahip between France and the Americas, particularly through educational means.[74]

In keeping with his ambition of inspiring the French people with descriptions of their glories, Hanotaux presented his ideas in books. *L'affaire de Madagascar*[75] and *Fachoda*,[76] covered events with which he had had actual experience. But these were not enough. Publication of the impressive *Histoire des colonies françaises et de l'expansion de la France dans le monde*,[77] in six volumes, began in 1929 under his editorship, and the general introduction to this series gives us the best exposition of his ideas on colonial development.

Although Hanotaux was at his best in the fields of political and international relations, he came increasingly to feel that history concerned more than politics. He felt that earliest origins should be considered, as well as soil, climate, and the customs of daily life.[78] Religion and human passions were also vitally important.[79] In fact, it was really necessary to consider the ensemble of national and worldly accomplishment,[80] for only in that way could a complete picture of an age and a country be rendered.

This interest led to the publication of his *Énergie française*, in 1903, and *La fleur des histoires françaises*, in 1911, both comprising sketches of various phases of French life from notes taken on his travels in the late nineties in the course of his research for his studies of Richelieu. The culmination of this idea came with the publication of the fifteen volumes of the *Histoire de la nation française*, for which he acted as editor, wrote the general introduction, and contributed the volume on nineteenth-century history. Although Hanotaux had conceived the idea and planned the collaboration in 1914, the war postponed publication until the twenties.

The study of geography always appealed to him, and he felt that French geography, particularly her location as a "crossroad" of European travel, had played an important part in the development of French history.[81]

The rise of interest in economic and social history did not leave him untouched. On one occasion he even stated that political history is nothing other than economics,[82] but this is little more than lip service, for he never penetrated more deeply than generalization. In nearly all of his works he devoted sections to the life and customs of the time of which he writes. These are interesting and often valuable, but they are descriptions of local and national life rather than analyses of social and economic forces.

In his economic ideas he represented, as he did in politics, the best of the middle class. The bourgeoisie, he felt, were "the most enlightened and most sensitive part of the nation."[83] His youthful experiences as a witness of the last agonies of the Commune colored his ideas for life; the chief crime of the Communards to him lay in their platform of decentralization and their disruption of French unity in the face of the German occupation rather than in their social ideas.[84] He disliked socialism in all its forms[85] and Marxism in particular, for not only was the latter based on materialism, with which Hanotaux had little sympathy, but it bore the stigma of a German origin.

Hanotaux did not dislike the masses; on the contrary, he had great faith in them, but, as we have seen, he felt they needed rulers and control. These rulers should devote themselves to the welfare of all the people,[86] and society should do its utmost to create equality of opportunity.[87] He believed profoundly in the sanctity of private property, but he did not like parasites;[88] he felt that work was necessary to all,[89] and that all work was honorable. His book *Du choix d'une carrière* (1902), in which he describes the great variety of occupations possible in France, was addressed to French youth. Laws tending to ameliorate the condition of the working class won his support as a parliamentarian and as a writer, for he felt that the laborer ought to receive a fair wage[90] and that no one ought to go hungry.[91]

In the field of education Hanotaux's ideas were modern. He believed in making it less formal and more vocational. Character, rather than an accumulation of useless knowledge, should be the aim of education; and life was a better teacher than books. "To know is a little thing; to will, to act, that is what matters. To give man this character, this certainty of judgment, and this power of decision which are everything in life, what is the best teacher? Books? No. Life itself."[92]

Religion and philosophy were closely associated for Hanotaux. His mother had followed the current bourgeois practice of being a good but not ardent Catholic.[93] Like most students of his time, he himself ignored the church after making his first communion and went through the gamut of all the nonreligious fashions which prevailed.[94] As a middle-aged man, however, he became affected by the religious revival in France and adopted an increasingly spiritual approach.

Catholicism was in keeping with his general philosophy. Its unity, language, and Mediterranean inheritance all appealed to him. France, of course, was also traditionally Catholic, the "eldest daughter of the church." He wrote no special book on religion; his *Jeanne d'Arc*[95] comes closest to it and was a vital factor in his religious development. Despite his interest in Catholicism, he was never intolerant and always definitely liberal in his religious views.

All this had an effect upon his historical writing in so far as his ideas on causation were concerned. He claimed that it was the enigma in history which attracted him,[96] but he made little contribution to its solution. His thinking in this direction was obscure and never carefully developed. He was essentially an idealist rather than a materialist in his philosophy; beyond that there was nothing concrete. The "soul" of what he was studying always interested him, whether he was working on a person,[97] an institution,[98] or a country.[99]

A few lines might be devoted to a consideration of *Jeanne d' Arc*, published in 1911, as a step in Hanotaux's development as a historian. He spent considerable time on this work, both in collecting material and in preparing it for the press. Its illustrations and format are admirable; that is more than can be said for the contents, for it represents some of its author's most ambiguous thinking and his most ambitious claims for his country and for the subject of his selection.

The problem of the source of Jeanne's inspiration interested him, and he proclaimed her as a combination of the human and divine approaching each other "in a mysterious collaboration to work in a common cause, the safety of France."[100] Her accomplishments were nothing short of marvelous! She saved France and the monarchy. She established the principle of freedom of belief and preserved the thought and culture of antiquity, of Catholicism, and of the Mediterranean countries (against the encroachments of Germanic Burgundy and England). She prevented the spread of the Reformation to France and prepared the way not only for the absolutist kings but for the Revolution. She was

the "angel" of the Renaissance, the messenger of the new order, the "annunciatrix" of a freer and better humanity; her virtue, her patriotism, her religion, can be designated as purity, courage, and sacrifice. This is the teaching she leaves us. We are only at the dawn of the days which will see her mission accomplished without limit.[101]

It is no wonder that one reviewer felt Hanotaux was heading toward the clouds;[102] and it is needless to say that this book, while popular in certain circles, added little to its author's prestige as a scientific historian.

Although he frequently wrote about individuals, and even went so far as to state that "explaining an epoch through its heroes is a task to which one can worthily devote one's entire life,"[103] and, again, that "without heroes there is no progress and no history,"[104] he had little of the concept of heroes as the determining factors of historical movements. He made those statements when he was writing about individuals; when he wrote more generally, it was to the people as a whole, he felt, that France owed her greatness.[105] He attributed more to Providence than to anything else. For example, he stated definitely that Jeanne d'Arc was sent by divine intervention to save France[106] and that Poincairé's leadership during the war of 1914 was the gift of Providence.[107] Frequently he was more vague, as when he stated that a country had the historians,[108] the generals, and the rulers that it deserved.[109] This can scarcely be called profound thinking.

Science interested Hanotaux, and he thought it important; but he felt that as a philosophical basis of life it was insufficient and inadequate.[110] History to him possessed the attributes of science in its methods of research and criticism of facts, in its attempt first to analyze and then to synthesize.[111] But "as a daughter of action, history reached heights that science did not know."[112]

Art in all its phases also interested Hanotaux. He was fond of architecture[113] and constantly extolled the French language and literature. He was particular about his books, choosing, when he had the opportunity, the type and paper and deciding the format himself.[114] He preferred to have his works illustrated and, when that was possible, selected the illustrators and subjects with great care.[115] His *Jeanne d'Arc, Histoire des colonies françaises, Histoire illustrée de la guerre de 1914*, and *Histoire de la nation française* are all profusely, interestingly, and even beautifully illustrated.

He felt that history was an art, because the story gave pleasure and aroused emotion. It attempted to attain beauty by an animated recital of events, harmony of proportions, clearness of deductions, descriptions of persons, and the illusion of life.[116] History should be well written, more than a literal copy of details, and selective like art, indicating significance by throwing important things into relief.[117]

But history is not an art alone; rather art is the instrument of history. The historian is a story-teller, but his stories are true.[118] Truth must always be the first law of history, he thought,[119] and he believed that he followed it implicitly. It is difficult, however, for a man with a thesis to be sure that he is following the truth, particularly when his thesis is based on patriotism acquired in adolescence through the unhappy experience of his country's conquest by a foreign power. He wanted to tell the truth, and he tried by the best means in his power, but the odds were against him.

The development of his historical thought naturally affected his historical method. Early in his career he made a great contribution to French historical writing by sharing with Albert Sorel, historian of the French Revolution, the privilege of being the first of the students allowed to enter and use the archives of the French foreign office.[120] Hanotaux considered this opening of the archives to be a "veritable revolution in the history of France."[121] It was an accomplishment befitting the Third Republic, giving the reality of the facts of the past back to the French people. In March, 1880, he became the secretary of the commission newly created to consider the means of communicating these documents to the public, and when the first volume of the analytical inventory appeared in 1882, his name was on the title-page. In 1888 he published the *Recueil des instructions données par les rois de France à leurs ambassadeurs près du Saint-Siège*, another task assigned to him by the commission on diplomatic archives. He worked with this group for more than fifty-five years. His volume of *Maximes d'état et fragments politiques du cardinal de Richelieu*, published in 1880, won universal praise as a work of scholarship.

It is not surprising, however, that this work of erudition, limiting itself to the publication of texts, did not suffice for him. He stated again and again that documents were the basis of all historical writing[122] but added that this did not mean the confusion of documentation with history; rather, it was the anatomical construction or skeleton of historical writing.[123] As a statesman himself, he knew how much was left out of written documents, and he believed that a dependence on them alone might easily result in false interpretation.[124] Dates, he thought, were insignificant except to establish a relationship between events.[125]

Hanotaux was conscientious by nature and had spared no pains to perfect his education, even taking a course at the Paris Conservatoire des Acteurs to get rid of his Picard accent and learn to speak pure French.[126] He knew Latin, Greek, German, English, and Italian but, like most of his countrymen, never cited a reference to a foreign book if a French translation existed. He knew the French archives and libraries intimately and studied occasionally in foreign countries. His studies on Richelieu are heavily documented, but the very concept of his later works meant the elimination of footnotes. His *L'énergie française*, he almost boasts, "has nothing scientific about it. Neither figures, nor tables, nor statistics; it says only what has appeared to me to be amiable in a country so worthy of being loved."[127]

The necessity of making an income from his historical writings was a problem which Hanotaux had to face from the beginning. He began writing historical sketches for newspapers early in his career, and his most common procedure was to write a series of articles on the subject on which he was working and later collect them in a book. Thus, a not inconsiderable part of his research on Richelieu, much of his work on Jeanne d'Arc, and most of the essential portions of his writings on contemporary events and historical criticism appeared first in current periodicals.[128] Gambetta's newspaper, the *République française*, was his earliest medium, but that gave way to others, particularly the *Revue des deux mondes*, for which he wrote during most of his active life.

As his interests broadened, he found his individual efforts at writing inadequate to cover the vast field of his curiosity and the message which he wished to give to all Frenchmen. He wrote voluminously and prolifically; but as he tried conscientiously to have some basis of research or experience at the foundation of all of his works, he could not do as much as he desired. To achieve his ends, he used secretaries and collaborators. He secured the help of the scholarly Duc de la Force for his third and fourth volumes on Richelieu and of Lieutenant-Colonel Fabry for his studies of the generals of the war of 1914.[129] Even these methods proved inadequate, and Hanotaux conceived the idea of compilations, whereby a large subject could be covered by dividing it into a number of volumes and the exigencies of research satisfied by assigning each volume or subject to an expert in that particular field. He used this method most successfully in the fifteen volumes of his *Histoire de la nation française*, which he felt developed "the complete meaning of his life as a historian."[130] He selected his collaborators with care and supervised their work closely. He demanded expert knowledge, but he also insisted upon a clear, interesting presentation and a good style.[131] Above all, he required that the men he chose agree with his ideals. The result of this is evident if the series is compared with the compilations of Ernest Lavisse.[132] The latter's work is more scholarly, but it is less readable, more valuable to the historian than to the general reader, and less broad in its scope. Lavisse was more interested in history for its own sake; Hanotaux considered his series a "task of national piety."[133]

History as a subject appealed to him. He discussed it frequently in all his works and devoted several books to the presentation of his ideas.[134] He considered that the greatest historians had lived in Greece and Rome.[135] His own debt to many modern historians he admitted; Fustel de Coulanges came closest, of all the nineteenth-century writers, to his ideal.[136] Contemporary historical writers of other countries were ignored.

Hanotaux's style is almost always interesting, often eloquent, and occasionally brilliant. His picture of Richelieu, already quoted,[137] is typical of his best work. The vigor and picturesqueness of his language is particularly effective for the kind of popular writing at which he aimed. He wrote appealingly and persuasively, particularly when he was discussing his work or his country.

> The professor raises future generations and transmits to them the gains of the past; the writer and the philosopher apply themselves to the soul, nourishing the sacred flame of the idea, and exhaust themselves, seeking, in the shadows of the future, the beacon toward which humanity should direct its route.[138]

. . . .

> [France] is a living person: her body is slender and well proportioned, her bearing supple, her face lights with a smile in which there is ecstasy; her glance is straight, high, and far. As the fairies in the tales of Perrault, she has, despite her age, the privilege of being always young. Through her smiling optimism, through the limpid vivacity of her thought, through the light which emanates from her, she radiates upon humanity.[139]

One is almost convinced.

Hanotaux could write with delicacy as well as with ardor. He used figures of speech effectively, and his wide vocabulary aided him in description in which he was particularly adept. "Sky, soil, water, fauna, and flora,—all these co-operate, harmonize, and adapt themselves to play the magnificent symphonies of nature which are the traditional renown of our provinces."[140] A munitions factory is described with as much sensitiveness and color as that used in depicting a French rural scene,[141] and the man who first developed water power was "the poet who baptized the new industrial force" which he called "white oil."[142] While his style was often flamboyant, it could be concise, even epigrammatic. "Do you understand what the expression 'My property' [Mon bien] means to [the peasant]? Work, honor, dignity, profit, savings, independence. . . . . His property is liberty itself."[143]

As he grew older, he became more discursive and rambling, and the number of books he wrote and the breadth of the subjects he selected were conducive to repetition.

In appearance he was the scholar rather than the politician. He was tall and distinguished, with a high forehead, curly hair, and fine hands. His health, which was bad during his youth, left him always a little delicate. His mother, a good manager of the modest sum left her by her husband, came to Paris to live with her children while they went to school. She continued to make her home with the historian, exercising a considerable influence upon his life until her death at a ripe old age. She was a practical sort of person, never experiencing a thrill over the political honors accorded to her son and refusing to visit him at the foreign office during the four years he was in charge. She did attend his reception by the Academy, however, the only satisfaction his public career ever afforded her.[144] Hanotaux did not marry until late in life.

The historian was pleasant and unassuming in his manners, appealing personally to all who met him. He enjoyed society moderately but was naturally of a retiring disposition and had no great social ambitions. He was on familiar terms with most of the outstanding people of his day. Journeys on foot and bicycle were, with hunting, his favorite sports.[145]

Hanotaux was always particular about his personal surroundings. He was a bibliophile with a collection which reached over a third of a million books and included many notable items. He also collected autographs, documents, and reproductions of the Annunciation.[146] He tells us that when he was working on a book like *Richelieu* or *Jeanne d'Arc* he tried to surround himself with physical mementos of the life of the period he was studying.

Great honor was accorded to Hanotaux in France. Just before Gambetta's death, that statesman procured the young historian's nomination to the Legion of Honor for the first volume of the inventory of the foreign-office archives. The early volumes of *Richelieu* won for him, in 1896, the Gobert Prize, the highest honor bestowed by the French Academy, and his election into that institution itself the following year. Hanotaux was proud to identify himself with that group for the remainder of his life.

The unquestionable attainment of his earlier works assured reviewing-space for all his later productions. Because of the definitely personal nature of their ideas, however, the character of the review depended upon whether or not the reviewer's opinions coincided with those of the author. Thus the more scholarly reviews, such as the *Revue historique* and the *Revue des questions historiques*, were restrained and even skeptical, while the *Revue des deux mondes* was always full of praise and respect. The only significant article on Hanotaux's work is a very favorable one by Imbart de la Tour, a historian of the medieval period.[147]

In summary, Hanotaux's early contributions to history stand unchallenged. His later works are important for the vigor, eloquence, and breadth of their ideas rather than for their originality or profundity. Some of them will long be read for the picture they give of French life and for their point of view, for they represent a close association with the conservative intellectual group of his time. They are more important, perhaps, as source material than as definitive historical writing.

Advancing age did not put a stop to Hanotaux's activity. Despite frequent reiteration of an optimistic view of the future of France, there was an undercurrent of fear present in all his writings. He protested a little too much. This fear came into the open with the outbreak of the war with Germany in September, 1939, when he was nearly eighty-six years old. His polemical writings against his old *bête noire*, published regularly in the *Illustration*, urging an economic federation of Europe and the moral supremacy of the pope as the only possible safeguards against the menace of Naziism, were stopped in the spring of 1940 only by the new German occupation of France.

NOTES

1. *Mon temps* (Paris, 1935); "Mon temps," *Revue des deux mondes*, 8th period XXXIII (May 15–June 15, 1936), 315–48, 539–72, 811–41; XXXIV (July 1, 1936), 83–107; XXXVIII (Apr. 15, 1937), 774–800; XXXIX (May 1–May 15, 1937), 52–83, 334–70.

2. *Mon temps*, p. 77.

3. *Sur les chemins de l'histoire* (Paris, 1924), I, ii.

4. *Ibid.*, p. xiii.

5. *Ibid.*, p. v.

6. *Mon temps*, p. 138.

7. "Mon temps," *loc. cit.*, XXXIII (May 15, 1936), 332.

8. "Les Vénitiens ont-ils trahi la Chrétienté en 1202?" *RH*, IV (1877), 74. Reprinted in *Sur les chemins de l'histoire*, Vol. I.

9. *Mon temps*, pp. 232–36.

10. Published as *Origines de l'institution des intendants des provinces, d'après les documents inédits* (Paris, 1884).

11. *Mon temps*, pp. 336–37.

12. *Ibid.*, p. 38.

13. *Ibid.*, pp. 332–35.

14. *Ibid.*, p. 341.

15. *Ibid.*, p. 138.

16. "Mon temps," *loc. cit.*, XXXIII (May 15, 1936), 326–28.

17. *Ibid.*, pp. 346–47.

18. *La fleur des histoires françaises* (Paris, 1911), pp. 270–71.

19. *Mon temps*, p. 297.

20. *De l'histoire et des historiens* (Paris, 1919), p. 8.

21. *Ibid.*, p. 10.

22. *Ibid.*, p. 42.

23. *Ibid.*, pp. 39–41; *L'énergie française* (Paris, 1903), p. 329.

24. *Sur les chemins de l'histoire*, II, 239, 248–49; *Histoire et historiens*, p. 11.

25. I.e., *Histoire du cardinal de Richelieu* (3d ed.; Paris, 1899), I, vii; *Histoire de la nation française* (Paris, 1929), I, 11.

26. *Sur les chemins de l'histoire*, I, vi.

27. "Mon temps," *loc. cit.*, XXXIII (May 15–June 15, 1936), 315–16, 337–38, 822; XXXIV (July 1, 1936), 106; *Sur les chemins de l'histoire*, I, viii, xi–xiii; *Histoire de la France contemporaine* (Paris, 1903–8), I, viii; *La fleur des histoires françaises*, pp. i, 280; *L'énergie française*, p. 329; "Défense de l'histoire," *Revue des deux mondes*, 8th period, V (Oct. 15, 1931), 772–73.

28. *La fleur des histoires françaises*, pp. 93–94.

29. *L'énergie française*, p. 5.

30. *Ibid.*, p. 6.

31. In the introduction to his *Histoire de la France contemporaine* (I, vii) he states that all the works he has begun or published have but one object: France.

32. His dedication of *L'énergie française*, title-page, also pp. 33, 199.

33. *Ibid.*, p. 199; *La fleur des histoires françaises*, pp. 312–13.

34. *La fleur des histoires françaises*, pp. 310–11.

35. *Ibid.*, p. 281; *L'énergie française*, p. 150.

36. See below, p. 186.

37. *Histoire du cardinal de Richelieu*, I, viii; *Mon temps*, pp. 312–13, 317; "Mon temps," *loc. cit.*, XXXIII (May 15, 1936), 331–33; *La fleur des histoires françaises*, p. 187.

38. *Mon temps*, p. 312.

39. "Mon temps," *loc. cit.*, XXXVIII (Apr. 15, 1937), 782–83.

40. *Histoire du cardinal de Richelieu*, I, vi–vii.

41. "Mon temps," *loc. cit.*, XXXVIII (Apr. 15, 1937), 777–78.

42. *Ibid.*, XXXIII (June 15, 1936), 838; "Gambetta," *ibid.*, 6th period, XX (Nov. 1, 1920), 5–23.

43. "Mon temps," *ibid.*, 8th period, XXXIX (May 15, 1937), 348–49.

44. "Jules Méline," *ibid.*, 7th period, XXXI (Jan. 15, 1926), 440–53.

45. *Raymond Poincaré* (Paris, 1934), pp. 59–60, 85, and *passim*.

46. *Histoire de la nation française* (Paris, 1929), V, 642–48.

47. *Ibid.*, p. 631.

48. *Ibid.*, p. 641.

49. *Joffre* (Paris, n.d.), p. 72.

50. *Histoire de la France contemporaine*, I, ix.

51. *Ibid.*

52. *Ibid.*

53. See above, pp. 170–71.

54. *Contemporary France* (4 vols., London, 1903–9).

55. *Histoire et historiens*, pp. 82–83.

56. *Études diplomatiques: la politique de l'équilibre, 1907–1911* (Paris, 1912).

57. See particularly his introduction to the *Histoire des colonies françaises et de l'expansion de la France dans la monde* (Paris, 1929), Vol. I, *passim;* and *Jeanne d'Arc* (Paris, 1911), *passim.*

58. *Sur les chemins de l'histoire*, I, 342.

59. In the introduction he boasts that the first volume on literature (Vol. VI of the series) proved that the *chansons de geste* were Latin and not German in tradition (p. xv) and that the volume on the Frankish invasion put Teutonic influence in its "proper" light (pp. 1, li).

60. *Sur les chemins de l'histoire*, I, 343.

61. E.g., in *L'énergie française*, pp. 72–74.

62. *Ibid.*, p. 73.

63. *Ibid.*, p. 74.

64. Paris, 1903.

65. As, e.g., when he claimed that it was the Mediterranean tradition which won the war of 1914 for France and the Allies (*Histoire et historiens*, preface).

66. *Sur les chemins de l'histoire*, I, xxv.

67. *Poincaré*, pp. 20–21.

68. *Le secours américain en France* (Paris, 1915).

69. *L'énergie française*, pp. 292–95.

70. *La fleur des histoires françaises*, p. 128.

71. *Histoire des colonies françaises*, I, xlviii.

72. *Sur les chemins de l'histoire*, I, 296.

73. *La politique de l'équilibre*, p. 239.

74. *Ibid.*, pp. 240–41. For a general summary of his interest in North America see his *La France vivant en Amérique du Nord* (Paris, 1913).

75. Paris, 1896.

76. Paris, 1909.

77. 6 vols.; Paris, 1929–33.

78. "Mon temps," *loc. cit.*, 8th period, XXXIII (May 15, 1936), 315; *Histoire de la nation française*, I, ii.

79. *Mon temps*, p. 317.

80. "Mon temps," *loc. cit.*, 8th period, XXXIX (Apr. 15, 1937), 778.

81. *La fleur des histoires françaises*, pp. 30, 47, 63; *L'énergie française*, p. 6. The first two volumes of the *Histoire de la nation française* treat of geography.

82. *Histoire et historiens*, p. 27; see also *Histoire de la France contemporaine*, III, 474.

83. *Histoire de la France contemporaine*, III, 76.

84. *Mon temps*, p. 182; *Histoire de la France contemporaine*, I, 157–59.

85. See his *La démocratie et le travail* (Paris, 1910), for his ideas on socialism.

86. *Poincaré*, pp. 89–90.

87. *La fleur des histoires françaises*, p. 292.

88. *Ibid.*, p. 270.

89. *Ibid.*, pp. 269–70, 293, 295; *L'énergie française*, p. 30.

90. *La fleur des histoires françaises*, p. 293.

91. *Ibid.*, p. 295.

92. *Du choix d'une carrière*, p. 6 and *passim*.

93. *Mon temps*, p. 64.

94. *Ibid.*, p. 292.

95. Paris, 1911.

96. *Mon temps*, p. 231.

97. Such as Richelieu, Jeanne d'Arc, Poincaré, etc.

98. "L'esprit de l'Académie," *Les quarante, 1635–1935: trois siècles de l'Académie française* (Paris, 1935), p. 33.

99. *L'énergie française*, p. 331; *Mon temps*, p. 340; *La fleur des histoires françaises, passim*. See also his description of France in 1614 in the last chapter of his *Histoire du cardinal de Richelieu*, Vol. I.

100. *Jeanne d'Arc*, p. 38.

101. *Ibid.*, pp. 420–21.

102. Charles Petit-Dutailler, *RH*, CX (May, 1912), 83.

103. *Mon temps*, p. 317.

104. *Histoire et historiens*, p. 35.

105. *La fleur des histoires françaises*, p. 269; *Histoire de la France contemporaine*, I, ix; *Joffre*, p. 6.

106. *Histoire des colonies*, I, xxvi.

107. *Poincaré*, pp. 26, 65.

108. *Histoire et historiens*, p. 48.

109. *Joffre*, p. 5.

110. See his article on "Monsieur Taine et Monsieur Pasteur," *Sur les chemins de l'histoire*, Vol. II, *passim*.

111. *Histoire et historiens*, p. 23.

112. *Ibid.*, p. 43.

113. *L'énergie française*, pp. 77–80.

114. *Histoire et historiens*, preface; "Mon temps," *loc. cit.*, 8th period, XXXIX (May 1, 1937), 72.

115. *Jeanne d'Arc*, pp. ix–xi; *Histoire de la nation française*, Vol. I, introduction.

116. *Histoire et historiens*, pp. 13–14.

117. *La fleur des histoires françaises*, p. iii; *Histoire et historiens*, pp. 18–19.

118. *Histoire et historiens*, preface.

119. *Ibid.*, pp. 22, 43; *Sur les chemins de l'histoire*, I, 4.

120. *Mon temps*, p. 328; *Sur les chemins de l'histoire*, II, 294; "Mon temps," *loc. cit.*, 8th period, XXXIII (May 15, 1936), 318–19.

121. "Mon temps," *loc. cit.*, 8th period, XXXVIII (Apr. 15, 1937), 782.

122. *Histoire et historiens*, p. 24; *Sur les chemins de l'histoire*, II, 240.

123. *Histoire et historiens*, p. 24.

124. *Histoire de la France contemporaine*, III, 61–62; *Histoire des colonies françaises*, I, xx.

125. *Histoire et historiens*, p. 31.

126. *Mon temps*, pp. 258–59.

127. *L'énergie française*, p. 5.

128. E.g., *La politique de l'équilibre* was originally published in the *Revue hébdomadaire*, 1907–12; *Histoire et historiens*, in the *Revue des deux mondes*, 1914; etc.

129. I.e., *Joffre*.

130. *Sur les chemins de l'histoire*, I, xv.

131. *Histoire de la nation française*, I, ix.

132. Ernest Lavisse, *Histoire de France depuis les origines jusqu'à la Révolution* (Paris, 1900–1911) and *Histoire de France contemporaine depuis la révolution jusqu'à la paix de 1919* (Paris, 1920–22).

133. *Histoire de la nation française*, I, ii.

134. *Histoire et historiens; Sur les chemins de l'histoire* (2 vols.); *Henri Martin, sa vie— ses œuvres—son temps, 1810–1883* (Paris, 1885); see also "Défense de l'histoire," *loc. cit.*, pp. 768–73.

135. *Histoire et historiens, passim.*

136. "Fustel de Coulanges," *Revue des deux mondes*, 7th period, XIV (Mar. 1, 1923), 34–56.

137. See above, p. 176.

138. *La fleur des histoires françaises*, p. 280.

139. *Ibid.*, p. 285.

140. *Ibid.*, p. 47.

141. *L'énergie française*, pp. 153–61.

142. *Ibid.*, p. 172.

143. "Mon temps," *loc. cit.*, 8th period, XXXIII (June 15, 1936), 812.

144. *Mon temps*, pp. 62–63.

145. *Ibid.*, p. 282.

146. "Mon temps," *loc. cit.*, 8th period, XXXIX (May 1, 1937), 68, 72–73.

147. Imbart de la Tour, "L'œuvre historique de M. Hanotaux," *Revue des deux mondes*, 7th period, XXIII (Sept. 1, 1924), 166–86.

IX

VASILY OSSIPOVICH KLYUCHEVSKY
(1841–1911)

ALBERT PARRY*

VASILY OSSIPOVICH KLYUCHEVSKY was born in 1841, in the province of Penza, on the eastern outskirts of the central Russian plateau.[1] The locale is significant. It may, in part, account for the originality and consistency with which the future historian was to treat geographic factors in Russia's development through centuries. The woods and fields of Klyuchevsky's birthplace were deeply cut by streams flowing toward the Oka, the Volga, and the Don. Once upon a time these currents made these forests the outpost of an early eastward drive of Russian colonizers. To this day the population of the Penza region is highly mixed: one finds here the conquering Great Russians cheek by jowl with the conquered Tatars and such half-assimilated Finnish tribes as Mordvinians and Meshcheryaks. Not in vain Klyuchevsky, growing to manhood in this frontierland, was to view the entire Russian history primarily as a series of colonizations and assimilations.

Klyuchevsky's father was a poor priest in a rural district. Young Vasily was also to be a clergyman. In the provincial theological seminary to which he was sent he soon gained the praise of his masters and fellows. His brilliance and industry promised a career in the higher reaches of the church hierarchy. But the youth was interested in his country's history. Night after night he devoured old tomes of Karamsin's history of Russia "by feeble candle light, as his poverty precluded any better."[2] By his late teens he had already resolved to become a historian, not a priest.

* Chicago, Ill.; sometime fellow in history.

196

History was a thing of life, of forward motion, of broad meaning; theology was not—especially as practiced under Russian Ortho-doxy. The Crimean War had just ended, exposing his country's inner ills. A new and liberal tsar was on the throne; the times were stirring, opinions daring. Klyuchevsky's decision to re-nounce his clerical career was made "under the influence of the growing radical movement."[3] But so tenacious, so narrow, was theology that it would not easily let go those who once entered its field. Klyuchevsky had to seek a special permission of the local bishop before he could leave the seminary for a university. This was granted after considerable difficulty.

He entered the University of Moscow in 1861. According to Milyukov, it was this notable year of the serfs' emancipation that inspired Klyuchevsky's "decision to study the history of the so-cial classes in Russia in the light of Russian economic develop-ment."[4] Klyuchevsky himself admitted that the impressions of reforms then introduced by Alexander II "had a strong influence not only on his feelings as a citizen but on his purely scientific in-terests."[5] Nevertheless, it may be of value to look beyond the 1860's for the origin of this decision and these interests. The fact that Klyuchevsky came from a long line of poverty-stricken priests and himself barely missed a clergyman's mane helped to mold him as a historian of socioeconomic forces. His critical at-titude toward Russia's nobles and bureaucrats, his concern with the sorry fate of peasants, his general view of the empire's history as a story of classes—all this may partly be explained by the fact that his own class of clerics was sharply defined and roughly used by the tsars, boyars, and noblemen and that economically and socially the mass of the Russian clergy was closer to the soil and its burdens than to the court and its privileges, appearances not-withstanding.

There were other traces of a village rectory discernible in Kly-uchevsky the historian. The skill with which the young research-er handled endless stacks of documents couched in the old Slavic of Muscovy may be traced back to the ancient speech and writ-ings of the Russian Orthodox church which formed part of his early surroundings as a child and the interrupted training as a theologian. He utilized this background in the very choice of a topic for his Master's thesis: *Ancient Russian saints' life-stories as a historical source.*[6] In later years it was frequently remarked that by his manner of dress and speech, by his entire appearance, Klyuchevsky seemed to be a most astonishing reincarnation of a petty clergyman of the seventeenth century.

It may have been the young student's origin, as well as his ability, that attracted Professor Solovyev's attention. For nearly three decades, up to his death in 1879, Solovyev published a volume a year of his monumental history of Russia. Spiritual forces in Russian history were Sergey Solovyev's main concern. A priest's son might best of all understand the master and carry on his work. And so, beginning with his third year at the University of Moscow, young Klyuchevsky was Solovyev's favorite pupil. The more important results of his own researches Klyuchevsky began to publish in the early 1880's. Thus, in a sense, the student took up the standard where the master left off—but in a manner far less ponderous and surely more discerning.

This is not to say that Klyuchevsky failed in any way to acknowledge his debt to Solovyev. On the contrary, he felt that this Russian admirer of Guizot was profoundly right in stressing the "lawfulness" and "inevitability" of historic phenomena, their natural and necessary connection with one another, their organic chain. Yet, unlike Solovyev, Klyuchevsky did not permit himself to be crushed by the sheer weight of the data. Whereas the old savant in his persistent search for spiritual and factual continuity often degenerated into a mere reteller of events and recounter of documents, the younger man kept an ever sharp eye on the main outline of Russia's evolution, seeking for premises, interpreting, and drawing conclusions where his master had omitted to do so. Klyuchevsky did his own research, but he also used the data gathered by Solovyev, crossing the latter's *t*'s and dotting the *i*'s. Later, somewhat too generously, he was to say that every Russian historian should start with whatever Solovyev had ended in saying on the subject in question, for Solovyev, "like a lighthouse, will for a long time continue to serve as a guide even for those who differ with him in regard to conclusions."[7]

It was in the approach, as well as in the conclusions, that Klyuchevsky differed with his mentor. Although Solovyev, too, had at times ued a sociologist's yardstick, the use was altogether too occasional and vague. Klyuchevsky's socioeconomic point of view was far more consistent and clear, and its application full-bodied and only in spots somewhat verbose. He started with this method early and never retreated. His doctoral dissertation on *The duma of boyars in ancient Russia* had a significant subtitle: "An experiment in history of a state institution in connection with history of society."[8] He clarified this thought by declaring in his introduction to the monograph that political institutions are built of social sticks and stones and that a historian of Russia's ancient establishments should have as his task the study of the origin and significance of those social classes whose representat tives made up such state institutions as the boyars' duma.

In 1883 Klyuchevsky became a professor in the University of Moscow, lecturing on Russian history in its chronological sequence. But his preoccupation with the past of his native land as a history of its social strata soon brought him to the point where, in the fall of 1886, he delivered a course entitled "History of classes in Russia." We hear an echo of Solovyev's teaching of "connected history" in Klyuchevsky's thesis of "historic succession of social divisions" reduced to the formula: "The base of each succeeding division is in the consequences issuing from the division immediately preceding."[9] Even more important, and certainly more original, was Klyuchevsky's insistence that economic inequality had much to do with this story of Russia's classes:

Difference in economic status of individuals conditioned the variance of contractual relations between such individuals and the princes during the *udel* [appanage] centuries. By the variation in the [economic] status, created by such contractual relations, the assessment of persons with state duties in the Moscow state was defined. Out of the unequal appraisal of importance of these duties to the state there developed an inequality of rights, and this served as the base of society's division into classes.[10]

Purely economic problems of the past, as the surest key to an understanding of man's present, had early claimed the young scholar's attention. In 1884 he published an essay on the Russian ruble of earlier (sixteenth to eighteenth) centuries in its relation to the ruble of his own time. To this day it is considered one of Klyuchevsky's weightiest contributions to Russian historical literature. In 1885 appeared Klyuchevsky's reply to *Die Leibeigenschaft in Russland*, a book on the origin of Russian serfdom by J. Engelmann, a professor at Dorpat. In this essay Klyuchevsky, with great force and considerable originality, proved that serfdom was caused by debt rather than by any arbitrary order from above.[11]

Not that Klyuchevsky disregarded the history of the state as told in its decrees. In fact, he often said that a good practical way of learning the history of a given society is to trace the development of its laws. In the academic year, 1884–85, while giving a special course in terminology of Russian history, he used a number of ancient codes of law as laboratory material for his students.[12] But especially rich in the use of such sources—as sources of data and not as causes in themselves—is his *Course of Russian history*.

The *Course*, regularly delivered by Klyuchevsky for three decades until his death in 1911, published in numerous editions and translated into the German and English, remains his magnum opus. It is this work, more than any other, that made his reputation among historians and laymen, at home as well as abroad.

The sociological approach in the *Course* is reflected in the several introductory lectures devoted to the theoretical discussion of history as a social science. Klyuchevsky defines history as (1) a process, a motion in time, and (2) a study of the process. The process is nothing but a cavalcade through centuries of various unions of people that make up society. The three basic historic forces which build man's community are (1) the individual and his personality, (2) human society, and (3) the nature of a given country.[13] He thus marries sociology to geography and presents their child as history.

Klyuchevsky is on surer grounds when in his *Course* he dwells upon economic factors in Russia's evolution. While tracing the complex growth of what he regards as two chief elements in his fatherland's being—the state and the nationality—he again and again builds the political and ethnographic structure on a foundation of economic forces. It is in conformity with these standards that he divides Russian history into four periods: (1) the Dnieper period, from the eighth to the thirteenth century, of towns and trade; (2) the Upper Volga period, from the thirteenth to the middle of the fifteenth century, of petty principalities (*udel*-ducal) and free agriculture; (3) the Great Muscovy period, from the middle of the fifteenth century to the second decade of the seventeenth, of tsars and boyars, of military landownership; and (4) the All-Russian period, from the beginning of the seventeenth century to the middle of the nineteenth, of emperors and noblemen, of peasants and factories, with the main emphasis on serfdom.[14] The whole is shown as the Russians' colonizing spread. The huge canvas is one not of a blind drive but of the highly logical development of a struggle for social prestige closely coupled with trade advantage.

Thus, the Dnieper period of Rus, until the Mongols swept it off the face of the southern steppes, is pictured by Klyuchevsky as an era of growth of strategic settlements along the trade routes to the Black Sea and Constantinople. Quite plausible, as explained by our historian, is the economic reason for the Varangians' coming to serve and rule here: they came to safeguard, for a price, this trade route to Byzantium. Princes and their warriors were at first free lances on a salary and thus closer to the merchant class (nay, at times part of it) than they ever were in the centuries to follow.

These succeeding centuries are traced by Klyuchevsky mainly from the peasant's standpoint, again in socioeconomic terms. It was the peasant, as yet nominally free, who carried on his back the burden of "collecting" Russian lands for the state. The chief process to be watched here is the gradual loss of the peasant's freedom. The rulers deprived him of his fields and of the fruit of his labor, handing these over to noblemen in payment for the latter's services to the state. In a sense the nobles also had no freedom, being obliged to serve. Such a society could have no truly representative institutions. Klyuchevsky, indeed, shows that the *zemsky sobor* of ancient Russia was a far cry from the estates-general of western Europe. He explodes the fiction of the free and elected character of the *sobor*, demonstrating that the deputies were picked and appointed by the tsars, not elected by their peers, and that upon coming to Moscow they merely carried out the tsars' wishes.

With the dawn of the seventeenth century begins the process of Russia's Westernization. Here Klyuchevsky is clearly indebted to Solovyev, who refused to regard Peter the Great as a sudden phenomenon but pointed out that the great reforms were preceded by spade work of the very first Romanovs. Klyuchevsky, however, goes farther back than his teacher. He freely hints that the entire course of early Russian history made for Peter's appearance and work. Peter continued the age-old work of the preceding dynasty. The early princely dynasty, the Ryurikovichi, first "collected" Russia, then fought off the Eastern invaders. Already Ivan the Terrible had to face and fight the West increasingly more than the East. The first Romanovs inherited the problem and handed it down to Peter. Because of the stupendous task before him, Peter had to build an entirely new military machine. This required money—much of it. To obtain money Peter was compelled to overhaul the administratiove apparatus as a tax-gathering medium. In the process he inevitably reformed much else, to his own amazement. Klyuchevsky writes that Peter did not set out to be a reformer, that only late in his life did he realize the extent of his accomplishments, that many of his reforms were rather superficial, for they did not strike at the base of Russia's economic edifice—at serfdom, which, on the contrary, Peter aggravated in many ways.

Klyuchevsky is particularly indignant with Peter's successors, for they complicated the already hopeless muddle of serfdom by relieving the noblemen of the duties they owed the state in exchange for the serfs the state had given them. Especially from the time of Catherine II (argues the historian) is Russia's history one of serfdom, that deepest, meanest, most harmful social and economic evil. From that time—that is, the 1760's—until 1861, almost nothing was done to solve the awful problem. Klyuchevsky betrays something close to disgust with the stagnation of the one hundred years in question. In this we may see partial explanation of the fact that, while lovingly and patiently probing into the empire's more distant past, he hardly touches the nineteenth century.

Because Klyuchevsky concerned himself with economic factors, he was, on occasion, crudely mistaken — if not for a Marxist, then at least for one who somewhat unwittingly exerted Marxist influences.

Thus Peter Struve once remarked that he imbibed Marxism first from *Das Kapital* and later from Klyuchevsky's writings.[15] But Struve was destined to forsake the faith, to travel as far to the Right as reactionary monarchism; apparently, in his unwitting role as a teacher of Marxism, Klyuchevsky was not a success. That grand old man of Russian Marxism, George V. Plekhanov, sneeringly quoted from *The duma of boyars* Klyuchevsky's definition of capital as "tools of work" and wrote: "Our researchers have rather peculiar concepts as to capitalism."[16] If a moderate socialist of Plekhanov's type would not consider the professor a Marxist, even less so would communists. Marxian-sounding notes may be scattered through Klyuchevsky's writings, and Russia's "learned Marxists readily use them," but always with the reservation that Klyuchevsky was "very far withdrawn from the materialistic conception of history."[17] Klyuchevsky's other definition of capital as "a combination of labor and nature" possessed in varying forms by all classes is "of unaccustomed and wild sound to a Marxist's ear."[18] When, in 1921–22, the Soviet state publishing house brought out the hitherto unpublished Volume V of Klyuchevsky's *Course*, one of the late professor's pupils, the extreme Marxist Pokrovsky, protested bitterly. He called the work "archaic," guilty of dismissing "objective economic con-

ditions" while describing the failure of serfdom reform under
Nicholas I, and generally full of "childish explanations." He
chided the state publishing house for issuing the book without
"the necessary commentaries by some Marxian."[19] In 1930 the
official historical journal of the Soviets branded Klyuchevsky as a
chauvinistic nationalist, a selfish Great Russian totally indifferent
to the fate and sufferings of the other races inhabiting the former
empire. Klyuchevsky was scolded for his rejection of monism,
"that is, rejection of Marxism"; above all, he was accused of
serving as "the flag of a whole school," of endowing and hearten-
ing with his views "the bourgeois historiography of our times."[20]
More particularly, Klyuchevsky was "a delegate of traders'
groups, of the kulak strata of the bourgeoisie."[21]

Yet, we cannot say that orthodox Marxists always mourned or
despised Klyuchevsky as a doomed heathen. They did try to convert him while he lived. A certain Ghizetti, a friend of the professor, persisted in supplying him with popular digests of Marx,
although another friend attempted to tell the missionary that his
labor was surely in vain, that Klyuchevsky, were he of a mind to
do so, would read the great Karl in the original but not in popu-
larizations, that the professor had never read Marx and would
hardly be disposed to tackle him at anyone's prompting.[22]

It would, indeed, be lost work to look through Klyuchevsky's
pages for anything approaching Marxian terminology. Each
time he subscribed to what seemed like a Marxian postulate, he
appended thereto a lengthy exception of a most non-Marxian nature. Thus, while declaring that in Russian history economic
factors often gave birth to political consequences—a statement
most pleasing to Marxists—he insisted that on other occasions in
Russia, and at all times in western Europe, economic phenomena
were but a result of political events—a statement which horri-
fied his Marxist readers. He wrote: "The initial political division into rulers and the ruled led to an economic inequality."[23]
He gave this illustration: A region already well-developed economically, possessing a set society with a set division of labor and
profits, is invaded and conquered by a strange tribe or nation.

The invasion is, of course, a political event. The invaders settle down in the conquered region, composing a class of their own, dislocating the socioeconomic relationship of the area, causing a new setup of economic factors, with themselves as the predominant profit-garnering element.[24] But Plekhanov argued that in this interpretation Klyuchevsky was only seemingly right, but actually wrong; that the invasion itself was an economic factor because both the invaders and the aborigines possessed unequal economic structures of their own, and it was this economic inequality that led to the conquest.[25] In other words, the invasion, a political event, was merely a reflection and a consequence of the economic fact that the inhabitants of the region of Klyuchevsky's illustration possessed certain goods and productive abilities coveted by the dwellers of a region whence the invading wave came.

Most unorthodox, from the Marxist viewpoint, would also be such statements of Klyuchevsky's as that many rebellions of the Russian masses in the seventeenth century, the Razin movement among others, were "uprisings of the ruled against their rulers, but not of the lower classes against the upper," that "it is very difficult to discern in these riots a social trend."[26] His view that Peter's economic reforms were not of economic origin but came from Russia's national, political need of a new military machine is also non-Marxian. A Marxist would insist that the military machine was so desperately needed at the time precisely because Russia's economic interests were at stake, and that, if the tsar himself was not aware of this, a good historian should be. An orthodox Marxist would further be grieved by Klyuchevsky's view of the wars waged by Peter's successors in the eighteenth and nineteenth centuries not as conflicts of aggression and conquest —in short, of imperialism—but as holy campaigns "of political liberation of other nationalities, kinsmen of the Russian people through religion or blood."[27]

Actually, then, Klyuchevsky was a stranger to radicalism, to internationalism. At times he puzzled even liberals but gladdened the hearts of conservatives. There is his faint sneer at the impractical education of Alexander I by Laharpe, that "very

liberal and garrulous French booklet."[28] Speransky's fine project
of a constitution for Alexander's empire is called good inten-
tioned but woefully artificial and therefore unsuitable. The conservatives' scheme of serf emancipation—the so-called "Arakcheyev plan"—is frankly preferred by the historian to a project
by Mordvinov representing the liberals of Alexander I's era. According to the Arakcheyev plan, the state was to buy peasants
and land from those nobles who would want to sell. The nobles
were to receive good prices; the peasants were to gain their freedom. But the liberals' plan was for the peasants to buy their own
freedom, with their own money, and with no aid from the state.
It was their personal liberty, but no land, that they were to purchase. Klyuchevsky scorned Mordvinov's plan as "bourgeois and
idyllic," as placing a premium upon individual thrift among peasants, for "only labor and thrift could bring freedom." He praised
the scheme of the conservatives because it promised mutual advantage: "One side [the serfs] would have obtained freedom
without losing land, the other [the nobles] would have obtained
capital without losing labor supply."[29]

Thus it is no wonder that on occasion the conservatives of the
Russia of 1881–1911 hailed Klyuchevsky as their own. On a
higher plane "he was doubtless a conservative" if only because
"Russia for him began not with Peter, not even with the era of
Moscow's ascendancy, but centuries earlier," because "in her
progression he was not reluctant to mention the cultural work of
the Pechora cloister, of the Sergius-town, of the Novgorod and
Pskov freemen, and of the Moscow princes with their boyars
duma and their policy of unifying Russian lands."[30] On a lower
level, the conservatives of his time counted Klyuchevsky as their
own because he now and then derided the Germans and their
role in the post-Petrine Russia, because he hinted that the un-
suitability of Speransky's project was conditioned by its being
"built of the elements of a political system arising in the West."[31]
So safe did he seem to the reactionaries that in the 1890's Klyuchevsky was entrusted with the task of teaching Russian history
to the Grand Duke George.

On whose side, then, was Klyuchevsky? Sir Bernard Pares, a pupil of the great master, writes of Klyuchevsky: "The thing that I have always felt about him was that with his vision and his entire justice of mind, he was absolutely independent and unidentifiable with any school."[32] It was true that (to cite an outstanding example) in the quarrel between the Westernizers and the Slavophils he seemed to take both sides at once, praising the scientific approach of the former and the emotional beauty of the latter, and so appeared to be wholly impartial and schoolless. Milyukov felt that Klyuchevsky represented a synthesis of both these schools.[33] Kiesewetter, however, held that the master was equidistant from the starting-points of both; the quarrel was of the 1840's and to Klyuchevsky seemed "no more than an already vanished phase of our intellectual life."[34] Yet, sharper-eyed observers than either Milyukov or Kiesewetter could and did show that Klyuchevsky, while praising both schools, was actually nearer to the Westernizers than to the Slavophils. For was he not, in his praise of the latter's emotionalism, paying them a left-handed compliment? Was he not himself a scientist, to whom the Westernizers' scientific approach would ever prove of more value?[35] That the conservatives erred in claiming Klyuchevsky for their own ranks, that the liberals had more right to such a claim, is borne out by the fact that in 1905, when called by the bureaucrats to a state conference at Peterhof, he amazed and angered them by advocating, in the presence of Nicholas II, a democratic representation instead of a limited one by classes. "God save us," he said, "from such a state of affairs where in the people's mind there would arise the dark ghost of a class tsar."[36] Later, he was a member of the Constitutional-Democratic party; yet he "naturally stood nearer to the democratic-populist than the constitutional-liberal movement within our intelligentsia."[37]

But, above all, there was the evidence of the historian's own writing and lecturing—that is, if, disregarding occasional winks or lapses to the Right or Left, we seek his most consistent motif. And this motif was not Klyuchevsky's criticism of the West and its ways, not his extolling of national virtues of the Great Russians, or, on the other hand, what seemed like a flirtation with the Marxists, but his negative attitude toward the nobility with their "overwhelming and unjust predominance over the other classes,"[38] the nobility that existed mentally at the expense of the West and physically at the expense of "the unpaid labor of the Russian serfs."[39] If at times Klyuchevsky appeared to be antagonistic toward the West, it was but an antagonism toward indiscriminate borrowing of things Western, toward their poor digestion and application by the overenthusiastic Westernizers among the Russians. Whatever utterance he made in regard to capitalism was, on the whole, favorable. He was, thus, a typical liberal of the nineteenth century, of the era characteristic for its welding-together of altruism and patriotism, of democracy and healthy skepticism.

Klyuchevsky's popularity with Russian intellectuals of his time can, in sum, be explained by this liberalism first of all, the liberalism which was, in the main, fairly clear to his contemporaries despite the occasional but unimportant setbacks and contradictions within his speech and text. For the Russian listener and reader of 1881–1911 was of liberal tendencies.

In addition to the idea and the approach, there were Klyuchevsky's technique and style, peculiarly endearing him to the young (or young-thinking) people of his period.

He was easy on his audience. In the course of his lectures he seldom paused to elaborate upon his sources, to explain in detail their dates, titles, and other earmarks. There is hardly a footnote in the volumes of his published lectures, and very few in the special monographs he wrote. This lack seemed a virtue to many of his pupils and colleagues. "Not always did he mention his sources," a fellow-historian recalled fondly. "I do not know a researcher more sparing in his quotations, more foreign to the heaping of them after the German manner in the lower story of the book pages."[40] Nevertheless, we must not doubt the most prodigious amount of research done by Klyuchevsky in primary sources almost to the exclusion of secondary, or the fact that at all times he remembered or kept in his notes the exact dates and pages of the documents or ancient tomes whence came his statistics, dates, anecdotes, and other illustrations. It is enough to glance through the back pages of the posthumous editions of his *Course*, where some of these private notes are reproduced, to realize the painstaking labors with which he prefaced the actual delivery of his lectures and the writing of his books. In 1913, after following for six years Klyuchevsky's old trail in the mountainlike archives dating back to seventeenth-century Muscovy, a former student of his wrote that he had recognized many a document as the base of this or that of the professor's lectures, that he had stood in awe, and only then had begun "to comprehend the extraordinary erudition and amazing industry of the late teacher who in such a superior manner familiarized himself with this enormous material, yet so modestly appraised his own work."[41] But was it modesty alone? Was it not also an attempt, conscious or not, to popularize his work by stripping it of forbidding-looking and forbidding sounding paraphernalia of footnotes and bibliographies?

This tendency toward popularization becomes apparent when we consider Klyuchevsky's style. Among Russian historians there has never been a style like his; for its freshness and lucidity, its literary excellence and pithy aptness, it is unsurpassed. He never told a historical anecdote for its own sake but made each story serve a major point of exposition or theory. His examples were varied, concise, vivid, and logically connected with one another. Most of his stories, similies, and aphorisms bore the air of spontaneity; yet most were carefully and thoughtfully prepared beforehand. Especially deliberate was his use of archaic words: he felt the quaintness of Russia's old language, and was well aware of nuances distinguishing one century from another; sparing in the use of the ancient word or phrase, he could and did, with a single shade of speech, convey the spirit of a whole epoch, Thus, saying *reshpekt* ("respect," "honor") in the eighteenth-century fashion instead of his own contemporary *uvazheniye*, he immediately conjured up the atmosphere of Catherine's time. He coined his own descriptions of men and moods bygone that at once brought dead eras to life. Depicting Russian society of the late eighteenth century, he could not verily give its more apt characterization than mention, in passing, its "unbuttoned speech and jumping thoughts."[42] He defined Paul's mental state through the long years of waiting for his throne as "spiritual fever."[43] Nor was he averse to playing with sounds, with results so happy, as when he dubbed Osterman "a Mephistopheles from Westphalia."[44]

He was a master of simile. He compared Patriarch Nikon to "a sail which only in a storm is its real self, but in still weather flaps from a mast like a useless rag."[45] He summarized Alexander I as "a beautiful flower, but of the hothouse variety which lacked perhaps time, perhaps ability, to acclimatize itself to the Russian soil: it grew and bloomed splendidly while clear weather lasted, but, as soon as northern storms and our Russian rains of the autumn came, it withered and declined."[46]

He realized that many went out of their way to hear or read him for the sheer enjoyment of it. Quietly he let it be known that he was not exactly pleased. "It is a great misfortune," he once remarked while describing a tsar's education, "when students assume toward their teacher an attitude of spectators toward an actor, when his lectures become their amusement, be it though an aesthetic amusement."[47] That he wanted to humanize history and its teaching was true, but he had no desire of playing to the grandstand. His irony was at times biting, but chiefly mild, sometimes tinged with sadness, and always shrewd, for he coupled it with a steady understanding of these pitiful humans, these frail beings even when they happened to be heroes, whose history he was telling. Although he did not overestimate the leaders' or villains' role in history, although the greatest of them appear but mere bubbles on the broad social stream of his narrative, their thumbnail portraits, as sketched by him, are like lightning flashes illuminating the whole wide scene in a trice.

As Solovyev had designated him his pupil, so Klyuchevsky wished to leave behind serious continuators of his own work. Paradoxically, while giving a great deal of time and attention to composers, novelists, and artists who sought guidance from him in their search for historical themes and data, he was not over-generous to young historians who wished to specialize under him. His idea seemed to be that, while those laymen were totally help-less and really needed his aid, the young historians could help themselves. To the latter, his favorite command was: "Sam dok-hodi," or "Reach it yourself." Thus, ingeniously, firmly, he tried to inspire the young historians to independent work rather than take them to their goal by the hand.[48]

Did he succeed? In the year of his death it was said that he did, that he was "leaving behind a whole school of men who study in detail certain angles of that past" which Klyuchevsky had presented as a great, harmonious canvas "of the progressive march of Russian civics."[49] Among his pupils there were: Mat-vei K. Lyubavsky, author of monographs on the old Russo-Lithuanian state; Yury G. Gautier, known for his researches in the economic and social life of Muscovy; M. M. Bogoslovsky, spe-cializing in Peter's reforms in provinces; Kiesewetter, "recreating the past of Russian towns of the eighteenth century."[50]

And yet, polite opposition to Klyuchevsky's theories arose among some of his pupils even while he lived. The main point of difference was the evaluation of the role of the Russian state: the opposition within the master's school felt that the master was unwarrantedly scornful of the state. Led by Alexander Presnya-kov, the opposition was most articulate in St. Petersburg, the imperial capital which, by its very character, was a city of offi-cialdom and jurists worshiping the state, in contrast to Klyu-chevsky's Moscow, a relaxed city of anti-state tendencies. Some observers hold that only the war of 1914 and the Revolution pre-vented this group of pro-state historians from crystallizing into a significant school of its own.[51]

A few of them managed to continue with their researches and writing in exile in western Europe. Frightened by the excesses of the Revolution into extreme mysticism and general conservatism, they now criticize Klyuchevsky for his alleged failure to examine "the spiritual past" of the Russian people. They even recommend forsaking Klyuchevsky and going back to Solovyev, his spiritually minded teacher of long-faded decades. They claim that "an educated reader . . . . will not learn from Klyuchevsky's school the life-springs and life-aims of Russia." In a Dostoyevskyian mood they gloomily chant that "the Revolution was the crisis of Russian conscience even more so than of the Russian state," and thus Klyuchevsky and his followers hold no answer for a true-blue soul-scratching Russian in exile.[52] The anti-Soviet Russians of Paris and Berlin, of New York and Harbin, are bitter about Klyuchevsky "for painting only the darker sides of our past," and so "it is only consistent that by now . . . . those courses of Klyuchevsky's have lost part of their charm, and his old admirers are ashamed of their enthusiasm."[53]

Within Soviet Russia itself, as we have seen, Klyuchevsky's fame and school at first fared as badly as they did among the exiles. He was a patriot in the outmoded sense, dangerously near to acquitting the nationalistic imperialism of the tsars and of the merchants. For this he was condemned by the official historians of the new Soviet republic, or at best forgotten a bare half-dozen or dozen years after his death. By 1930 it seemed that never again would he emerge to his full stature as a revered master—indeed, not unless the old middle class of traders and manufacturers was once more resurrected to guide Russia's fates.

And yet, certain changes in Soviet concepts were becoming apparent even as Pokrovsky and other orthodox Marxists castigated Klyuchevsky's memory. Nationalism was officially reasserting itself among the new rulers of Russia, for, from the very beginning, whether they knew it or not, "although preaching a doctrine of internationalism, they were psychologically, without exception, egregious nationalists," their heads turned "by the fact that under their leadership, even though in a backward country, a proletarian revolution had actually occurred."[54] Klyuchevsky's nationalism was not so egregious; yet nationalism it was. To quote a former pupil, now in anti-Soviet exile:

He knew and cared little for life outside Russia; his knowledge of languages was bad; by nature he was thoroughly Russian; he was fond of the Russian life, the Russian past, and Russian peculiarities; he loved that in which Russian life differed from the Western.[55]

How close is this nationalism to the brand displayed by present-day Russia! How parallel are some of the characteristic features of Klyuchevsky's nationalism to those shown by the dictator of today's Muscovy! And, in fact, Stalin's advent symbolizes the emergence of a new wave of anti-Westernism in the Russian people. Not the extreme kind of the Slavophils' anti-Westernism, it is, nonetheless, a strong scorn of certain trends prevalent in Western civilization. And yet, paradoxically, like Klyuchevsky's, this new Soviet nationalism admires certain other things of the West—without subscribing to them in the wholehearted fashion of the old-time Westernizers or the latter-day Pokrovskians.

Only Pokrovsky's death in 1932 saved that Westernizing historian of the Soviets from demotion and exile, if not execution. A few brief years following his funeral a campaign of devastating criticism was opened against Pokrovsky's writings and memory. There was Pokrovsky's disapproval of a number of things marking the personality and reign of Peter the Great—the very Peter whom Stalin now respected as his own prototype. Klyuchevsky, on the other hand, although criticizing Peter, did so without Pokrovsky's vehemence; Klyuchevsky, on the whole, considered the great tsar an honest, sincere, self-denying man. There was also Pokrovsky's passionate denunciation of the tsarist wars of conquest in the eighteenth and nineteenth centuries as rank manifestations of shameless imperialism. Far more pleasing to Stalin's Moscow was Klyuchevsky's explanation of the same wars as part of a wide campaign to free kinsmen from foreign yoke.

And so, in the late 1930's, a new Soviet edition of Klyuchevsky's *Course* appeared in Moscow, and schools are now encouraged to use it as a foremost textbook. To be sure, there are footnotes of sufficient warning that the late master was not a Marxist. Yet, his reinstatement in Soviet favor is helped by the fact that the master, although a middle-class man of a middle-class philosophy, was undoubtedly a pioneer in considering the economic roots of man's history and was certainly so in decrying the socioeconomic and political predominance of old Russia's useless nobles.

Thus have the rulers of today's Russia and of her mind recognized the great scholar's achievements, if only in part. Thus they are using his contribution for whatever value they see therein for their own ends.

But such, after all, is the fate of many another historian, East or West—fate not always of his own choosing.

NOTES

1. Paul Milyukov, "Klyuchevsky," *Encyclopaedia of the social sciences*, VIII (New York, 1932), 577; Alexander Kiesewetter, "Klyuchevsky and his *Course of Russian history*," SR, I (1923), 510; Anatole G. Mazour, *An outline of modern Russian historiography* (Berkeley, California, 1939), p. 44. In their fullest detail, facts of Klyuchevsky's biography are to be found in Matvey K. Lyubavsky, "Vasily Ossipovich Klyuchevsky," *V. O. Klyuchevsky, kharakteristiki i vospominaniya* [Appraisals and reminiscences] (Moscow, 1912), pp. 5–25. Professor Lyubavsky also edited Book I of *Chteniya v imperatorskom obshchestve istorii i drevnostey rossiyskikh* [Lectures before the Imperial Society of Russian History and Antiquities] (Moscow University) for 1914, which was dedicated to Klyuchevsky's memory and contains much biographical data. At the close of the last-named volume, pp. 442–73 are devoted to bibliography of Klyuchevsky's work.

2. Kiesewetter, *loc. cit.*, p. 510.

3. Milyukov, *loc. cit.*, p. 577.

4. *Ibid.*

5. Kiesewetter, *loc. cit.*, p. 510.

6. *Drevnerusskiya zhitiya svyatykh, kak istorichesky istochnik* (Moscow, 1871).

7. A. Lappo-Danilevsky, "Pamyati V. O. Klyuchevskago" [In memoriam], *Vestnik Yevropy* [Herald of Europe] (St. Petersburg), August, 1911, p. 338. Cf. the same author's "Istoricheskiye vzglyady V. O. Klyuchevskago" [Klyuchevsky's views on history], *Kharakteristiki i vospominaniya*, pp. 100–101.

8. *Boyarskaya duma drevney Rusi* (Moscow, 1883).

9. *Istoriya sosloviy v Rossii* [History of classes in Russia] (Moscow, 1913), p. 214.

10. *Ibid.*

11. Both essays, on the ruble and on serfdom, are reprinted in *Opyty i issledovaniya, pervy sbornik statey* [Experiments and researches, first collection of essays] (Petrograd, 1918), pp. 107–83, 184–267.

12. S. Tkhorzhevsky, "V. O. Klyuchevsky, kak sotsiolog i politichesky myslitel" [Klyuchevsky as a sociologist and political thinker], *Dela i dni* [Affairs and days], II (St. Petersburg, 1921), 165.

13. *Kurs russkoy istorii* (5th ed.), I (Moscow, 1914), 2–11.

14. *Ibid.*, pp. 26–28.

15. S. Piontkovsky, "Velikorusskaya burzhuaznaya istoriografiya poslednego desyatiletiya" [Great-Russian bourgeois historiography of the last decade], *Istorik-marksist* [The Marxian historian], XVIII–XIX (Moscow, 1930), 175.

16. G. V. Plekhanov, *Istoriya russkoy obshchestvennoy mysli* [History of Russian social thought] (Moscow, 1914), I, 57, n. 4.

17. Tkhorzhevsky, *loc. cit.*, p. 157.

18. *Ibid.*

19. M. N. Pokrovsky, "O pyatom tome 'Istorii' Klyuchevskogo" [About the fifth volume of Klyuchevsky's *History*], *Pechat i revolyutsiya* [The press and the revolution] (Moscow), April–May, 1923, pp. 101–4.

20. S. Piontkovsky, "Velikoderzhavniye tendentsii v istoriografii Rossii" [Great-power tendencies in Russian historiography], *Istorik-marksist*, XVII (Moscow, 1930) 21–26.

21. Piontkovsky, "Velikorusskaya burzhuaznaya istoriografiya . . . . ," *loc. cit.* p. 160.

22. Tkhorzhevsky, *loc. cit.*, p. 158.

23. *Istoriya sosloviy*, p. 214.

24. *Ibid.*, pp. 15–17; also *Boyarskaya duma*, pp. 5–6.

25. Plekhanov, I, 16–18.

26. *Kurs*, V (St. Petersburg, 1921), 116.

27. *Ibid.*, pp. 150–51, 159.

28. *Ibid.*, p. 165. Klyuchevsky used the Russian word *knizhka*, which has a sharper bite to it than its literal translation, "booklet." The sense in which this word was used in this instance is "a dilettante" rather than anything else.

29. *Ibid.*, pp. 196–97.

30. Maxim Kovalevsky, "Vasily Ossipovich Klyuchevsky," *Vestnik Yevropy*, June, 1911, p. 406.

31. *Kurs*, V, 187.

32. Sir Bernard Pares to Albert Parry, May 13, 1937.

33. Milyukov, *loc. cit.*, p. 577.

34. Kiesewetter, *loc. cit.*, p. 511.

35. Tkhorzhevsky, *loc. cit.*, p. 175.

36. P. Milyukov, "V. O. Klyuchevsky," *Kharakteristiki i vospominaniya*, pp. 214–15.

37. *Ibid.*, p. 212. As Milyukov was the leader of the Constitutional-Democratic party, we must accept his word that Klyuchevsky was in that party's ranks despite Basil Maklakov ("Klyuchevsky," *SR*, XIII [1935], 325): "He did not join any political party and could not have done so."

38. *Kurs*, V, 154.

39. *Ibid.*, p. 134.

40. Kovalevsky, *loc. cit.*, p. 407.

41. A. Yushkov's introduction to *Istoriya sosloviy*, pp. xv–xvi.

42. *Kurs*, V, 125.

43. *Ibid.*, p. 134.

44. *Ibid.* (2d ed.), IV (Moscow, 1915), 336.

45. *Ibid.*, III (Moscow, 1912), 386.

46. *Ibid.*, V, 171. An able treatment of Klyuchevsky's style is in A. Amfiteatrov, "V. O. Klyuchevsky, kak khudozhnik slova" [Klyuchevsky as an artist of word], *Grani* [Frontiers], I (Berlin, 1922), 175–97.

47. *Kurs*, V, 167. But Basil Maklakov (*loc. cit.*, p. 321) wrote: "Klyuchevsky was not a lecturer, but an 'actor' . . . . a wonderful actor." On Klyuchevsky as lecturer also see A. Belov, "V. O. Klyuchevsky, kak lektor," *Istorichesky vestnik* [Historical herald], CXXIV (St. Petersburg, 1911), 986–90.

48. Yury Gautier, "V. O. Klyuchevsky kak rukovoditel nachinayushchikh uchenykh" [Klyuchevsky as mentor of beginning savants], *Kharakteristiki i vospominaniya*, pp. 177–82.

49. Kovalevsky, *loc. cit.*, p. 409.

50. *Ibid.*, p. 410. For an appraisal, in English, of Lyubavsky, Bogoslovsky, and a few other pupils of the master see Mazour, *passim.*

51. G. Fedotov, "Rossiya Klyuchevskago" [Klyuchevsky's Russia], *Sovremenniya zapiski* [Contemporary annals], L (Paris, 1932), 360–62.

52. *Ibid.*, pp. 361–62.

53. Maklakov, *loc. cit.*, p. 327.

54. Max Eastman, *Stalin's Russia and the crisis in socialism* (New York, 1940), p. 98.

55. Maklakov, *loc. cit.*, pp. 325–26.

X

KARL GOTTHARD LAMPRECHT
(1856–1915)

ANNIE M. POPPER[*]

KARL GOTTHARD LAMPRECHT was born in 1856 in Jessen, a small town near historic Wittenberg in the province of Saxony. His mother was of German and Wendish descent. She was a devoted wife and mother upon whom, however, the deeper conceptions of the world and of religion did not dawn until after Karl, her youngest son, had reached the age of manhood.

His father, of Kur-Saxon stock, was a Lutheran minister in Jessen, with the reputation of being an expert in biblical interpretation. He was a man of truly Christian spirit but was averse to all doctrinal discussions and controversies. He even refused to help clarify his son's conceptions when the latter found himself troubled with religious doubts. All the comfort he ever gave his son was to say that he considered all religious doubts as happy symptoms of the development of a stronger personality out of which they would also clarify themselves.[1]

Perhaps the example of his father's religious liberalism, combined with a truly pious spirit, later encouraged Lamprecht to pursue his historical and psychological studies regardless of the conclusions he might reach. There actually was a time when he was denounced as an atheist, though later even opponents declared this accusation unwarranted.[2] Moreover, Alfred Doren, an intimate friend of Lamprecht, recorded that in his "biblical faith"[3] Lamprecht found comfort again and again in the storms of his life. Like his father, Lamprecht avoided talking about con-

* Associate professor of history, Florida State College for Women.

troversial theological questions, and similarly he shunned partisan politics.[4]

Lamprecht seems to have resembled his father in more than one way. Like him, he became a man highly above the average, endowed with a versatile mind, a vivid imagination, tenacity of purpose, and an indestructible optimism. In his *Kindheitserinnerungen* he tells us how impressed he was by some of the strange tricks his imagination played upon his boyish mind, how he loved to watch nature closely and collect many of its treasures. He also speaks of his ever present urge to explore the country beyond the limits known to him. All these traits we find again in the man and his writings, but particularly the last one. Never was he satisfied with the knowledge gained; it merely served him as a gateway to new fields of exploration.

At the age of ten he entered the *Gymnasium* in Wittenberg. Three years later he was sent to the *Gymnasium* in Pforta (Schulpforta), famous for its discipline and thorough humanistic training. During his five years of education in Schulpforta, Lamprecht, like other great men before him, such as Ranke, received impressions which greatly influenced his later life. He once confessed that the seed for his principal work, his *Deutsche Geschichte*, had been planted in Schulpforta, where Rector Herbst, a historian, had opened his mind to the mutual relationship between individuals and their times.[5]

Lamprecht received his university training in Göttingen, Leipzig, and Munich (1874–79), where he studied history, political science, economics, and the history of art. Among his professors were J. Weizsäcker, E. Bernheim, E. V. Noorden, W. Arndt, and W. Roscher. Of these men, Bernheim and Roscher, the latter the head of the historical school of economics, fascinated him most. The influence of Roscher can be detected in Lamprecht's Ph.D. dissertation: *Beiträge zur Geschichte des französischen Wirtschaftslebens im elften Jahrhundert.*[6] Based on primary sources, it was intended by its author to be a contribution to *Kulturgeschichte*, thus foreshadowing the main interest of his later life.

The early death of his father, in 1879, obliged Lamprecht to earn his living. He therefore became a tutor in a well-known banker's family in Cologne and at the same time did his required year of practice teaching at the Friedrich Wilhelm Gymnasium. In 1881 he habilitated himself in Bonn, where he became professor extraordinarius in 1885. Five years later he accepted a call as professor in Marburg, and in 1891 he became a professor at the University of Leipzig, where he remained active to the end of his life in 1915.[7]

Lamprecht owed his freedom from financial cares in Bonn to the civic spirit of Gustav von Mevissen, leader of the Rhenish National-Liberal party. Mevissen, wishing to promote the intellectual life of his country by furnishing the means for historical research, engaged Lamprecht to work for him on Rhenish history for a period of three years. One of the early results of Lamprecht's activities was the publication of the *Westdeutsche Zeitschrift für Geschichte und Kunst*,[8] to which he contributed numerous articles. The following year he founded the Gesellschaft für Rheinische Geschichtskunde, which became the very center for thorough research in Rhenish history and for the collection and publication of valuable primary sources.

As in Bonn, so throughout his later career, Lamprecht not only collaborated with existing learned societies, journals, etc., but also became the inspirer and even founder of various new ones. In Leipzig the Sächsische Kommission für Geschichte, which became the model for similar commissions in other parts of Germany, owed its origin to Lamprecht and enjoyed his active support from 1896 until his death. He also became editor of various collective works, such as Heeren-Uckert's *Geschichte der europäischen Staaten*, *Leipziger Studien aus dem Gebiet der Geschichte*, and various others.[9]

His organizing activities, much frowned upon by his opponents, found a large field at the University of Leipzig. There, in 1909, he became the founder of the independent Institut für Kultur- und Universalgeschichte, which was to breathe his very spirit and to remain his favorite creation. Later it was mainly he who inspired the founding of the Friedrich August Stiftung for

the establishment of various institutions for research in intellectual sciences, though in matters of organization his suggestions
were rejected by his colleagues.

In view of the active part Lamprecht had been taking in the
agitation for a reform of the German universities, it goes without
saying that he tried to introduce various innovations when he
held the annual office of rector, 1910–11.[10] However, most of his
suggestions were strongly opposed by his colleagues.[11]

Lamprecht's capacity for work was astonishing. He was a
prolific writer. His main work, the *Deutsche Geschichte*, finally
comprised twenty-one volumes.[12] Not counting these or his collected works, Kötzschke lists one hundred and eighty of his writings.[13]

As early as 1885, while still in Bonn, Lamprecht published his
Deutsches Wirtschaftsleben im Mittelalter.[14] It was a voluminous
work on the development of the material culture of the countryside (*plattes Land*) of the Moselle region which was to serve as a
preliminary study for his *Deutsche Geschichte*. Perhaps stimulated
originally by Nitzsch's stress on economic factors in the shaping
of constitutional developments in medieval Germany and France,
Lamprecht's own investigations led him beyond Nitzsch. Lamprecht used his economic findings in his own way, to show the
interdependency of seemingly unrelated phases of development
in the history of his country. Winter praised this as a great
achievement on the part of Lamprecht, attained by new means,
namely, by applying the statistical method to his historical materials.[15] Instead of using each document only for the sake of its
individual information, Lamprecht compared a great many
documents on related events and transactions in order to arrive
at the laws that might have governed them. Winter's enthusiasm
for Lamprecht's *Deutsches Wirtschaftsleben im Mittelalter* apparently
was not entirely shared by Lamprecht's professional colleagues.
. Particularly, the soundness of his theories about landlords was
questioned. Certain parts of his work, they said, showed signs
of hurried composition and too hasty conclusions. Schmoller, by
no means blind then to Lamprecht's weaknesses and still less so

later, admits that when reviewing the book in 1888 he had re-marked, in all sincerity, that it had raised Lamprecht to the ranks of the older German agrarian historians, such as Hanssen, Maurer, Nitzsch, Arnold, Inama (Sternegg), Meitzen, and Schroeder.[16]

Although genuinely interested in economic questions, Lam-precht did not fail to turn with like eagerness to the investigation of the intellectual and spiritual forces in life and particularly to those of the imagination. An early fruit of such studies was *Die Initialornamentik des 8.–13. Jahrhunderts*.[17] To him the science of history (in the broadest sense of the word) was the science of the psychic changes[18] of the communities of man.[19]

With this conception of history forcing itself upon his mind more and more, Lamprecht wrote his *Deutsche Geschichte*, fully ex-pecting sharp criticisms from the historians of the influential "political school." However, not until after the publication of the fourth and fifth volumes of his great work in 1891 and 1894 was a controversy opened that was to become most heated in the period from 1896 to 1900 and was not to abate entirely for nearly twenty years.

From a historiographical standpoint Lamprecht's publications during those stormy years are most revealing of all. Their great number makes it impossible, within the frame of this essay, to go into a detailed critical analysis of his views as they formed and transformed themselves during the progress of his work and the crossfire of the literary guns.[20] For our purposes it seems best to limit our attention to a selected few of his articles and to some passages in certain volumes of his *Deutsche Geschichte*. From the be-ginning of the controversy Lamprecht maintained that the dif-ferences between his historical approach and that of his oppo-nents were indicative of still existing "contrasts" between the newer tendencies in the science of history and the older, between the collectivistic school of historians and the individualistic.[21] In fact, Lamprecht believed his time to have practically reached the turning-point in a movement the faint beginnings of which he ascribed to Herder, the originator of the concept of *Volksseele*.[22]

Lamprecht hoped that his *Deutsche Geschichte* might help to strengthen the existing tendencies in that direction.[23]

Seen through Lamprecht's eyes, the main diversities between the newer school and the older may be reduced to a few essential points. Investigations of the older school are hemmed in by Ranke's "ideas," with their roots in metaphysics; those of the younger school can pursue freely the inductive method. The older school is prevailingly artistically descriptive and directed teleologically; the younger, genetic and causal. The former restricts its studies mainly to the leading individuals and their actions as reflected in the life of the state; the latter extends them to conditions as reflected in all phases of life of a given human group. The one is concerned with what is unique in history, the other with what is typical; thus one leads to political history (hero history) and the other to *Kulturgeschichte*. Since the latter is mainly concerned with what is typical, it stands for a more scientific method; indeed, Lamprecht, as Comte had done before him, maintains that it alone can raise history to the rank of a genuine science.[24]

Lamprecht was convinced that history should be re-written ever so often in order to reflect the prevailing *Zeitgeist*. In his own time he sensed a tendency not to content itself any longer with research for the sake of research. There appeared to be a demand for higher criteria for purposes of an analysis and an eventual synthesis of the uncountable phenomena of life.[25] Besides, like Buckle before him, Lamprecht was deeply impressed by the great progress the natural sciences had accomplished with their exact methods. He, too, felt that history had fallen behind and should be raised to a genuine science by a study of the laws behind it. To Lamprecht it seemed a psychological necessity that the intellectual sciences should follow the lead of the natural sciences.

The thought of raising history to the rank of a science winds itself like a red thread through practically all of Lamprecht's discussions of historical theories and methods.[26] It is true, he emphasized again and again, that historical writing as such, because of its very nature, would always remain a piece of art,[27] but he maintained that this was equally true of any description of scientific phenomena.[28] Sciences, according to Lamprecht, are systems of judgments.[29] Like so many others in his day, he believed that the sciences focused their attention exclusively on what was typical, regular, determined by law. This assumption became of great significance for his historical thought.

Working scientifically means to determine not what is singular but what is general, not to ascertain in things what separates them but what connects them; it means to grasp the endless world of the singular—for what exists in nature and history is singular—in general concepts and thus classifying, master it. This concept of science holds for history as well as for any other science.[30]

Lamprecht maintained that the "political" historical school could not fulfil the scientific prerequisite of a comparative method to detect what was "typical" in the historical phenomena because of the peculiar individualistic origin of their "ideas" and the important role as historical forces which they were ascribing to them as disciples of Ranke.[31] Thus Lamprecht became the champion of *Kulturgeschichte*, as contrasted with "political history."[32] Since the days of Voltaire the term *Kulturgeschichte* has been interpreted in many different ways.[33] Lamprecht defined it as follows:

Kulturgeschichte therefore is the comparative history of the factors of socio-psychic development; and its relation to the histories of language, economics, art, etc., is the same as that of other comparative sciences to those subordinated to them. It too, therefore, operates—of course with application to its peculiar material—with the specific methods of the comparative sciences: with inductive synthesis, comparisons, generalizations.[34]

Lamprecht emphasized that his history-of-civilization method was not determined by any particular Weltanschauung.[35] He did not think it a contradiction to this statement, however, to presuppose the application of the principle of causation to all phenomena of history.[36] In fact, he considered this the very strength of his system—if "system" it may be called.

Allegedly, Lamprecht had arrived at his history-of-civilization method purely empirically. While studying the source materials of German history, as well as those of church history of the tenth century, he was struck by the psychic distance, i.e., the difference between the psychic attitudes of men of those days and of his own. On the other hand, he was impressed by the great similarity of psychic tendencies in the two fields. Such a psychic homogeneity he discovered also in the realms of art, literature, manners, etc. In other words, he found a common dominant for that particular period. Thus he arrived empirically at a concept of *Kulturperiode* as an all-prevailing sociopsychic condition of a particular period, as a diapason that diffuses all psychic expressions and hence all historical phenomena.[37]

The concept of cultural periods itself was not new. Lamprecht remarked that it might be traced as far back as the end of the eighteenth century and that applications of it in historical writings might be found at least since the middle of the nineteenth century.[38] He frankly stated that he had adopted the term "age of individualism" for the corresponding period in German history from Jacob Burckhardt's *Kultur der Renaissance* and that a precedence for periodization had been established, too, by political economists. But he justly claimed originality for his finding of a uniform principle of orientation for all periods.[39] It was his pride that his *Deutsche Geschichte* was the first practical application of the so-called *kulturhistorische Methode*, for in it he had disposed almost of the entire subject material from the viewpoint of those sociopsychically determined cultural periods.[40]

As indicated above,[41] to ascertain the characteristics of a cultural period Lamprecht endeavored to study various forms of expression of the human soul. He gave special attention to sociopsychic utterances of man's intellect, will, and feeling as reflected in language and sciences, in economic life, in law and morals, and in arts.[42]

Lamprecht stated that theoretically an analysis of all component sociopsychic factors of a cultural period would have to be made to arrive at sound conclusions. But this would obviously take more than a lifetime. In practice, at least for the present, this was made unnecessary by what he considered the legitimate device of applying the laws of physiological and psychic relations to the phenomena of history.[43] Just as according to Cuvier, we can determine the character of a whole skeleton from an examination of but a few of its parts, it would be possible in the field of human psychogenesis to gain not an entirely perfect, but nevertheless a first, view of the total course of the historical life of a period by a study of merely a selected few of the countless relations of its psychic phenomena.[44] Experience had taught Lamprecht to start an analysis of the psychic factors in the field of art.[45] The plastic arts, because of their three-dimensional nature, had proved even more revealing to him than paintings. When the "diapason" for a given period of art had been ascertained he would search for a similar dominant in the other realms of human imagination. The outcome of his investigations was, according to his own statement, that all the factors involved could easily be subsumed under the specific periods realized through a study of the evolution of art. They appeared to form a psychic unit.[46] After further research Lamprecht finally convinced himself of the existence of five main cultural periods in German history, each governed by its peculiar "diapason":[47]

1. Symbolism: early historical days
2. "Typism": early middle ages
3. Conventionalism: late middle ages
4. Individualism: modern times
5. Subjectivism: more recent days, approximately since the eighteenth century[48]

Correspondingly, he found the following economic stages in German history:

1. Primitive economy: *occupatorische Wirtschaft*
2. Natural economy, collectivistic: the community of the mark
3. Natural economy, individualistic: landlordism
4. Money economy, collectivistic: guilds, etc.
5. Money economy, individualistic: capitalism

He deliberately chose connotations for the great cultural periods broad enough to serve as highest concepts to which all psychic developments of human communities of a given period could be subordinated—hence all historic phenomena.[49]

A study of the history of other nations led Lamprecht to find evidence of cultural periods similar to those listed above for Germany. He maintained that they could be proved, too, by the application of the logic of statistics based on calculations of probability and the law of great numbers. While the periods therefore did not partake of the nature of an absolute law, they were of "the eminent heuristic value of any statistic rule."[50]

Lamprecht admitted that some psychic factors appeared to be stronger in one cultural period than in another and that it was impossible to separate the periods with any chronologic preciseness.

As the underlying principle common to all sociopsychic, as well as to all individual-psychic, life, Lamprecht detected a tendency toward an increasing psychic intensity, expressing itself in a growing differentiation in every field of psychic development, in a movement from a stage of bondage of the soul to greater and greater freedom. Thus, money economy was a more intensive form of economic life than the natural economy of the preceding period. Painting in the age of individualism was more intensive than in that of conventionalism.

Lamprecht tried to prove the correctness of his findings by the application of the principle of the creative synthesis, by Wundt's law of psychic resultants, about as follows: A chord is not just the sum of the individual tones of which it is composed but is something qualitatively new. Similarly, if a majority of people feels, conceives, and wills the same, their common feelings, concepts, and volitions are not identical with the mere sum of the individual factors involved. Owing to an immanent psychic causality, there has been created an element of a qualitatively different nature which finds expression as public opinion, patriotism, etc. If, therefore, numerous sociopsychic factors exist side by side, each with a continuous effect—as they do in any normal course of historical development—these must keep the surplus of psychic energy increasing; hence the historical life must be evolving into every increasing intensity (psychic differentiation).[51]

Thus Lamprecht believed he had found the causal connection between his cultural periods. To confirm this theory he cited two

other laws taken from the realm of individual psychology and applied by him to the sociopsychic phenomena.[52]

In the first place, no concept (*Vorstellung*) can entirely disappear; it must
continue to be effective. Therefore, the living concepts of one generation can
never become extinguished; they must, consciously or unconsciously, influence
succeeding generations.

In the second place, all psychic life is change, acquiring of new contents, in
the case of the individual as well as the group. The new contents cannot gain
exclusive mastery because of the persistence of the old. The necessary result
is a synthesis of the old and the new.[53]

The psychic processes that eventually bring a new cultural period into being have been described by Lamprecht at great
length.[54] He based his "psychic mechanic of transitions" mainly
on Lipp's psychology. Lamprecht distinguished, as in cases of
individuals, the following psychic phenomena of transition in the
normal course of human communities: strong new stimuli, coming from without or from within,[55] penetrate the psychic life of
contemporaries, or at least of their leading portion,[56] and cause a
sort of a psychic storm during which the old dominant is destroyed; a new naturalism is gained, which is finally replaced by
the victorious new dominant in an unprecedented climax of
idealism; this stage is followed by a rationalization of the dominant, ending in a period of decadence until new stimuli appear
and start the whole series of processes anew.[57]

Lamprecht explained that not every single psychic phenomenon of one period of transition in German history would be found
in the others, and still less so in those of other countries. Great
similarities, but not identities, were to be expected. The same was
true of the great cultural periods themselves. Their applicability
to the course of any normal national history could be considered
as having been empirically proved.[58] Yet the boundary lines
might have to be changed here and there after further investigation. Moreover, only a universal history, i.e., a comparison of
the cultural developments of a greater number of nations—in
principle, of all great communities—could ascertain whether certain factors, now considered typical, were not, in reality, merely
characteristic of Germany or the Germanic nations.[59] He frankly

admitted that, seen from this angle, his cultural periods had only tentative validity. However, before they could be determined with any claim to finality many a problem would have to be solved that had hardly been touched yet. Among others, he mentioned questions regarding the psychic scope (*Seelenweite*) and the rules, if not laws, behind the transmissions of cultures in the various forms of renaissances (revival of past cultures) and of receptions (influences of one contemporary culture upon another).[60] Practically nothing could be said, as yet, about the factors determining national decadence. For the present he gave a rather interesting warning against mistaking temporary nervous and psychopathic symptoms for signs of national decline, for they might reveal themselves later as nothing but psychic growing-pains.[61]

While in principle it would take generations to do the necessary comparative research work to arrive at a universal history, in practice he hoped he might accomplish this task himself, in a tentative form, with the aid of his history of civilization method, i.e., with the short cuts already discussed. At one time he was even optimistic enough to think it possible, theoretically at least, that after the necessary research of generations historians might be able to take the last step and arrive at a history of mankind which he considered as the ultimate end of the science of history. Later, however, he saw obstacles that seemed insurmountable even to him, and he confessed his belief that the last origin of historical development would probably forever remain unfathomable to the human mind.[62]

Let us pause here and restate briefly Lamprecht's fundamental viewpoints as discernible from his writings and, within the necessary limits, from our presentation above. Lamprecht assigned to history a task similar to that which Comte and Wundt ascribed to philosophy.[63] It is not surprising, therefore, that Lamprecht's philosophy of history and his Weltanschauung coalesced. They might be expressed as follows: Mind and nature are one.[64] History is human psychogenesis. The sociopsychic forces are stronger than the individual ones; hence they determine the course of history to a greater extent. Among all psychic stimuli, the economic ones seem to play not an exclusive but a most prominent role. All historic phenomena are subject to causality—at least they appear so to the human mind. They are in a constant evolutionary flux.[65] All being is at the bottom a becoming, the ultimate origin of which is beyond the scope of history; in fact, beyond the reach of the human mind, it will remain "God's Secret."

A summary of Lamprecht's essential views on historical methodology, like that just given of his philosophical thought, might be useful here. He proposed to raise history to the level of a science. The historian should approach his materials without any preconceived metaphysical concepts. For the ascertainment of any laws that might govern the historical forces he recommended his history-of-civilization method. The latter emphasized factors typical rather than individual, applied biological and psychological laws to the sociopsychic phenomena of history, and purported to follow closely the scientific devices of induction, isolation, comparison, analogy, classification, statistics, and hypothesis.

Innovations of Lamprecht, or at least partly such, were: his isolation of the artistic elements as a starting-point for an analysis of a cultural period of a nation, the choice of a uniform principle —the growing sociopsychic intensity—for the distinction of cultural periods, the contention of their inwardly determined chronological order, the claim of their general validity, not to speak of the application of his scheme to his voluminous *Deutsche Geschichte*.

While even most of his antagonists have given Lamprecht credit on some score, it seems no exaggeration to say that almost every one of his propounded views has been weighed and found wanting by one historian or another. Because of limits of space only a few particularly relevant criticisms will be added to those already made or mentioned in passing. Bernheim attacks the narrow definitions of science with which Lamprecht justifies his one-sided collectivism.[66] What Lamprecht sometimes characterizes as individual, as irrational, and therefore as an object of artistic but not of scientific perception[67] is, for Bernheim, the very factor ("the differentiating plus") which determines a development.[68] He admits that the latter is unpredictable, but he refers to the fact that after it has come into being it can be explained by regressive analysis on the basis of the laws of psychic and physical causation involved.[69]

Worth mentioning also are observations made by Eulenburg, one of Lamprecht's most objective and, at the same time, penetrating critics. He remarks that the history of the Jews shows that artistic ability does not always hold pace with that in other fields. Even so, he does not actually object to Lamprecht's starting with an examination of the elements of arts in order to facilitate an analysis of the cultural factors involved. What he criticizes most is Lamprecht's shifting from this original basis when he justifies the choice of his point of departure with the contention that the very flowers[70] of a civilization should be taken as criteria for its nature.[71] Eulenburg points out that expressions of the human imagination thus become a standard of values with Lamprecht and are ranked above those of the intellect. It means that in the last analysis he answers the question, "How can a scientific universal history be established?" with an aesthetic evaluation.[72]

Like other critics, Eulenburg rejects Lamprecht's analogies between the psychic attitudes of the individual and those of the group (nation).[73] He takes the stand that there is an essential difference between the individual soul, tied to a biological unit which fulfils certain physical and psychic functions, and the "social soul," not connected with a real substratum, neither with the nation nor with any other. According to him, it is merely an auxiliary concept, artificially created, and therefore without a sociopsychic development. Nor is the nation a biological unit, sharply separated from other nations as one individual is from another. Similarly, he judges Lamprecht's analogy between the stages of development of an individual and the various cultural periods of a nation as untenable, as a comparison between two incommensurable factors—between the individual that has a reality and the cultural periods that have none—are but concepts.

Hence Eulenburg holds that a proof for a succession of cultural periods determined by necessity has not been produced. In fact, Eulenburg ends with the contention that the law of increasing psychic differentiation (Lamprecht's sociopsychic mechanic) is, in reality, not a specific psychic law but a general biological one, in accordance with Spencer's principle of the "change from an incoherent homogeneity to a coherent heterogeneity."[74]

So far we have directed our attention to Lamprecht's theories rather than to his practices in historical research and writing. Only a few comments on these will be necessary, since various reviews of individual volumes of Lamprecht's *Deutsche Geschichte* are available.[75] These contain both high praises and severe criticisms, the latter coming chiefly from German scholars.[76]

It may be said that Lamprecht did not—and perhaps could not—come up to modern standards of historical research because of the immense range of the task he had set for himself. It was because of this circumstance that he avowedly availed himself, for the time being, of secondary sources on a larger scale than otherwise justifiable. However, he often used them without sufficient discrimination, which caused specialists in the field to discover numerous mistakes taken over from unreliable sources.

As mentioned before, Lamprecht also became guilty of applying analogies and drawing conclusions without a proper basis for them;[77] of ignoring certain factors as irrelevant that did not fit into his history-of-civilization scheme; and of insufficient restraint of his imagination in cases of missing links.[78]

Lenz's accusations of plagiarism were disproved by Lamprecht. The latter might have saved himself some insinuations of this kind if he had used more footnotes with references to specific authorities and had not restricted himself to such a great extent to rather general bibliographical acknowledgments.

When Lamprecht plagiarized, he did it unwittingly, perhaps as a result of careless note-taking, as Schmoller suggests, or because he assimilated thoughts of others so readily and later presented them as his own, unconscious of their real origin.

Spiess criticizes Lamprecht for giving broad space to some cultural phases—economics and arts—but comparatively little to others—religion, morals, and sciences. He proves his point with a reference to the striking lack of balance in the first volume of Lamprecht's *Zur jüngsten deutschen Vergangenheit*.[79] Yet it would be an error to assume this weakness to be evident throughout his voluminous work to any such extent. We know that Lamprecht himself regretted that no more preliminary studies of moral forces had been available. To religion he ascribed great importance in German history well into the modern period, but he believed it to have lost some of its driving-power in the twentieth century.

When the shortcomings alluded to above, and others, were revealed in often lengthy reviews Lamprecht usually made light of them. When his opponents had used insulting language he would occasionally answer in like coin. He repeated again and again that all criticisms of detail missed the real issue, that because of the scope of his task his work was more of the nature of a first draft and should not be expected to have been written with the exactness of a little monograph.

Nevertheless, there was little excuse for as many inaccuracies regarding facts, dates, etc., as have been found, for instance, in Lamprecht's account of the peasant revolt of 1525, in his *Deutsche Geschichte*, Volume V.[80] Also, his style showed signs of too hurried composition. Certain passages ought to have been polished, and numerous clumsy and vague terms might have been avoided. On the whole, though, his language was rather fluent and powerful. Lamprecht availed himself amply of rhetorical aids, such as contrasts, satires, etc. His *Deutsche Geschichte* was not written in the usual scholarly form, and he was therefore sharply criticized. Yet he succeeded in rousing the historical interest of the educated middle class,[81] and no work of his critics ever reached the large number of readers that were fascinated by Lamprecht's *Deutsche Geschichte* and his historical articles. Contemporary historians, such as Lenz and Bernheim, began to speak in all seriousness of a Lamprecht "danger."

Although Lamprecht did not found a school and deservedly

received many criticisms during his lifetime and later, he seems entitled to a place in German historiography. The broad historical interest he succeeded in kindling among his devoted students, many of whom have made a name for themselves and show his influence in their writings, has often been attested even by his enemies. As a merit, too, it may be considered that Lamprecht's writings were largely the expression of the age in which he lived. With some exaggeration,[82] it is true, Kuhnert remarks of him: "We value him because he has turned the full illuminating power of our own time upon the past and has thereby restored to history its soul."[83]

To us, most credit seems due to Lamprecht for having deliberately caused a controversy among historians which roused many of them from a tendency toward self-complacency and decadence to a careful re-examination of their own historical tenets. Although many of Lamprecht's views have been rejected, the cultural factors of history, as well as mass phenomena, have received far more attention ever since than they would have been accorded—at least in Germany—without him.[84] In the last analysis, his merit rests perhaps less with his writings as such than with their challenging force.

NOTES

1. Most of the remarks on Lamprecht's childhood and his early environment are based on his *Kindheitserinnerungen* (Gotha, 1918).

2. O. Hintze, "Über individualistische und kollektivistische Geschichtsauffassung," *HZ*, N.F., XLII (1897), 62.

3. Alfred Doren, "Karl Lamprechts Geschichtstheorie und die Kunstgeschichte," *Zeitschrift für ästhetische und allgemeine Kunstwissenschaft*, XI (1916), 386; cf. Rudolph Kötzschke, "Karl Lamprecht," *Deutsches bibliographisches Jahrbuch, 1914–1916*, p. 148.

4. It is easy, though, to detect passages in his writings and speeches betraying his Lutheran background and his nationalism and cultural imperialism nourished by the significant developments in Germany of which he was an eager eyewitness from 1866 to 1915.

5. As the first-fruit of his historical outlook, some notes may be considered which he wrote as early as 1878, without any intention of publication at that time: "Über Individualität und Verständnis für dieselbe im deutschen Mittelalter," printed in his *Deutsche Geschichte* (1st and 2d eds.; Berlin, 1909), pp. 3–48.

6. Leipzig, 1878. Ten years later it was translated into French, which seems to speak well for the dissertation.

7. Lamprecht visited the United States in 1904 and gave lectures in St. Louis and New York which were published under the title *Moderne Geschichtswissenschaft* (Freiburg, 1905; English trans., *What is history?* [New York, 1905]). His impressions of the visit were recorded in *Americana: Reiseeindrücke, Betrachtungen, geschichtliche Gesamtansicht* (Freiburg, 1906).

8. Trier, 1882. This was a joint undertaking with another author (Hettner), who had already planned it; Lamprecht was an editor from 1882 to 1891.

9. See Rudolf Kötzschke, "Verzeichnis der Schriften Karl Lamprechts," *Berichte über die Verhandlungen der Königlich Sächsischen Gesellschaft der Wissenschaften zu Leipzig, Philologisch Historische Klasse*, LXVII (1915), 105–19.

10. See, e.g., his article "Zur Fortbildung unserer Universitäten," *Internationale Wochenschrift für Wissenschaft, Kunst und Technik*, Dec. 4, 1909.

11. During his rectorate he and President Butler of Columbia University tried to bring about the establishment of an American-German exchange professorship at the University of Leipzig, such as there was already at the University of Berlin. Unfortunately, their efforts had only temporary success. (*Rektoratserinnerungen*, ed. Dr. Arthur Köhler [Gotha, 1917]).

12. *Deutsche Geschichte* (12 vols. in 16 parts; Berlin, 1891–1901); *Deutsche Geschichte zur jüngsten deutschen Vergangenheit* (2 vols. in 3 parts; Berlin, 1905–11); *Deutsche Geschichte der jüngsten Vergangenheit und Gegenwart* (2 vols.; Berlin, 1912–13). Before Lamprecht's death a third edition of most volumes was published, a fourth of some, and a fifth of the first.

13. This is the most complete bibliography of Lamprecht's writings available (Kötzschke, *loc. cit.*, pp. 139–49).

14. 3 vols.; Leipzig, 1885–86.

15. Georg Winter, "Die Begründung einer sozial-statistischen Methode in der deutschen Geschichtschreibung durch Karl Lamprecht," *Zeitschrift für deutsche Kulturgeschichte*, N.F., I (1894), 196–219.

16. Gustav von Schmoller, "Zur Würdigung von Karl Lamprecht," *Schmollers Jahrbuch für Gesetzgebung, Verwaltung u. Volkswirtschaft im Deutschen Reiche*, XL (1916), 1113. Schmoller was for years an intimate friend of Lamprecht, but later they became estranged; this obituary is impartial enough.

17. Leipzig, 1882.

18. This included economic factors, for Lamprecht thought any economic activity as much determined psychologically as any other "mental" activity (*Alte und neue Richtungen in der Geschichtswissenschaft* [Berlin, 1896], pp. 11, 17.

19. *Die kulturhistorische Methode* (Berlin, 1900), p. 15.

20. A bibliography of the polemical and methodological literature that had already appeared in connection with his *Deutsche Geschichte* by 1901 is to be found in the first volume of that work (2d ed., and 3d rev. ed.). It lists over a hundred contributions, including some from foreign publications.

21. "Was ist Kulturgeschichte?" *Deutsche Zeitschrift für Geschichtswissenschaft*, N.F., I (1896–97), 77. The writer feels justified in speaking henceforth of a collectivistic and an individualistic "school," though Lamprecht frequently uses the term *alte und neue Richtungen* ("old and new tendencies").

22. However, Bernheim and Lamprecht were the first German historians to consciously distinguish between individualistic and collectivistic historical writing. See Paul Barth, *Die Philosophie der Geschichte als Soziologie* (Leipzig, 1915), I, 502.

23. Vol. I (2d. rev. ed., 1894), p. viii.

24. Auguste Comte has been considered the founder of so-called "French positivism" through his work *Cours de philosophie positive*, the fourth volume of which (1839) contained the foundations of a scientific sociology and at the same time the fundamentals of his philosophy of history.

Bernheim regrets that Comte's thoughts for a long time became known to a wider public, particularly in Germany, only indirectly and frequently in a somewhat distorted reproduction, as, for instance, in Henry Thomas Buckle's *History of Civilization in England*. Moreover, Comte's views were spread through so many writers that, as in the case of those of Hegel, they were frequently adopted with no consciousness of their origin. See Ernst Bernheim, *Lehrbuch der historischen Methode und der Geschichtsphilosophie* (5th and 6th newly rev. and enl. ed.; Leipzig, 1908).

Perhaps this was true also with Lamprecht, who vigorously denied any dependence whatsoever on Comte and, as proof of this contention, published his private notes of the year 1878 (see above, n. 5).

Writers do not agree to this day whether Lamprecht was a positivist or not. Thus Rachfahl, Bernheim, and Spiess take the affirmative; Kötzschke, Doren, and Kuhnert, the negative. However, while Rachfahl speaks of positivism as "disguised materialism," Bernheim maintains that "Lamprecht is no more a materialist than Comte."

25. Hintze, *loc. cit.*, pp. 60–67, charges that the craving for a historical synthesis was in Lamprecht's own personality. Perhaps so, but this does not alter the fact that such a tendency was characteristic of his time. Alfred Doren (*loc. cit.*, p. 385) remarks as follows: "The aesthetic convention at Berlin, 1913, has revealed, perhaps surprisingly to many, how very deeply rooted a longing there is in the historically orientated sciences of art for critical methodological self-reflection on their own field of work and its limits . . . . , the demand for simplification, synthesis, methodological clarification, pressing toward the last principles was distinctly discernible with the historians [of art] too. . . . ."

26. *Zwei Streitschriften den Herren H. Oncken, H. Delbrück, M. Lenz zugeeignet* (Berlin, 1897), p. 37; "Die historische Methode des Herrn von Below," *Beigabe zur HZ*, LXXXII (1899), 48; *Die kulturhistorische Methode*, pp. 27–30, 38. In the article mentioned last, Lamprecht suggests for the study of the cultural periods (see p. 19) the founding of a "historical ethnology," i.e., of a discipline taking the same place in its relation to historical writing as ethnography does to ethnology.

27. *Die kulturhistorische Methode*, pp. 6, 25, 29.

28. *Ibid.*, pp. 8, 29.

29. "Die historische Methode des Herrn von Below," *loc. cit.*, p. 15.

30. *Zwei Streitschriften den Herren H. Oncken, H. Delbrück, M. Lenz zugeeignet*, p. 37.

31. *Die kulturhistorische Methode*, pp. 21–25. It should be noted here that in the course of time Lamprecht considerably modified both his interpretation and his evaluation of Ranke's historical concepts. One is tempted to consider Lamprecht as the very personification of evolutionism; his philosophy of history never became static. Toward the end of his life he seems to have stood much closer to Ranke, perhaps

closer than he himself realized (Emil J. Spiess, *Die Geschichtsphilosophie von Karl Lamprecht* [Erlangen, 1921], p. 17).

32. "Was ist Kulturgeschichte?" *loc. cit.*, p. 142.

33. Georg Steinhausen, "An den Leser," *Archiv für Kulturgeschichte*, VIII (1910), 1; Walter Goetz, "Geschichte und Kulturgeschichte," *ibid.*, p. 6.

34. "Was ist Kulturgeschichte?" *loc. cit.*, p. 145.

35. *Alle und neue Richtungen*, p. 8.

36. Lamprecht is occasionally guilty of a rather loose use of terms, such as "laws," "causality," etc. They occur with different meanings in his various writings. In one of his pamphlets he protested vigorously against the assumption that he had used the term "causality" in the sense of "absolute causality." He wished it to be understood that what he meant was "subjective causality," which was a necessity of our thinking due to the peculiar structure of our mind (psyche). ("Die historische Methode des Herrn von Below," *loc. cit.*, pp. 21–22).

37. *Die kulturhistorische Methode*, p. 26.

38. *Ibid.*, p. 31.

39. For details see *ibid.*, p. 21.

40. In the preface to the third edition of Vol. I of his *Deutsche Geschichte* (1902) Lamprecht makes the illuminating statement that he would now permit himself to indicate also in the outward appearance of the book (by respective subtitles) the sequence of those periods of psychic developments of the nation on the assumption of which he had already based the very first edition (1891). He had made one great exception to this, however. Although he had early acknowledged the principle that economic factors were psychic, the need of an enormous amount of preliminary work prevented him from applying it systematically until he wrote the supplementary Vol. II, *Zur jüngsten deutschen Vergangenheit* (1st ed.; Berlin, 1903). Lamprecht saw the "soul" of economic life in sensations of wants and the will to satisfy them. Cf. *Einführung in das historische Denken* (Leipzig, 1912), p. 105.

41. See above, p. 224.

42. "Was ist Kulturgeschichte?" *loc. cit.*, p. 118; cf. Spiess, pp. 146, 185.

43. Lamprecht based his law of psychic relations on Wundt's law of historical relations (Spiess, pp. 63–65).

For years Wundt was Lamprecht's main authority as to psychological theories. Later he was also influenced by those of Theodor Lipps. But when Lamprecht applied their principles, he frequently did this in such a sweeping fashion that the philosophers themselves could not follow him. "But as a psychologist," writes Wundt, "he went his own ways. . . . . The psychology in which he lived simply was not one which seeks to explain connections between psychic phenomena through an analysis of them but it was the intuitive psychology of the artist . . . ." (Wilhelm Wundt und Max Klinger, *Karl Lamprecht* [Leipzig: S. Hirzel, 1915], p. 17). See also Adolf Kuhnert, *Der Streit um die geschichtswissenschaftlichen Theorien Karl Lamprechts*, inaugural dissertation, Universität Erlangen (Gütersloh, 1906), p. 13.

44. *Einführung in das historische Denken*, p. 70.

45. *Ibid.*, p. 127.

46. *Ibid.*, pp. 71–72, 127–30; see above, p. 224.

47. "Was ist Kulturgeschichte?" *loc. cit.*, p. 129; *Einführung in das historische Denken*, p. 310. A brief survey of their evidence in German history may be found in *Moderne Geschichtswissenschaft*, pp. 22–50.

48. At the end of the nineteenth century Lamprecht became conscious of the dawning of a second period of subjectivism (*Deutsche Geschichte der jüngsten Vergangenheit und Gegenwart*, I, iv). A table of the characteristics of each period is given by Spiess, pp. 166–67.

49. Above, p. 221; see also *Die kulturhistorische Methode*, pp. 28–29.

50. "Was ist Kulturgeschichte?" *loc. cit.*, pp. 133–35.

51. *Ibid.*, pp. 94, 114–32.

52. According to Lamprecht, the law of psychic resultants applies to the socio-psychic factors gained from the past (*das Gewordene*), just as it does to those of the present (*Das im Werden Begriffene*). Thus Lamprecht claimed to have ascertained sociopsychic causality for those factors, too, and to have proved that all so-called "conditions" (*Zustände*), apart from the natural factors, such as climate, etc. (and even they were not absolutely static), were psychic mass phenomena, hence creative forces, mightier than the strongest influence of any individual historical personality. This served him at the same time as another argument in favor of the collectivistic historical method ("Was ist Kulturgeschichte?" *loc. cit.*, pp. 109–15; also *Zwei Streitschriften den Herren H. Oncken, H. Delbrück, M. Lenz zugeeignet.*, pp. 50–51).

53. *Die kulturhistorische Methode*, p. 28.

54. *Moderne Geschichtswissenschaft*, pp. 76, 80–88; *Einführung in das historische Denken*, pp. 42–46, 146–49.

55. Lamprecht held that they appeared very frequently in connection with economic and social life (*ibid.*, pp. 46, 145). For an illustration see n. 56.

56. "Was ist Kulturgeschichte?" *loc. cit.*, pp. 138.

57. One of Lamprecht's illustrations in German history: from 1750 to 1870, first period of subjectivism; since about 1850, owing to new and strong stimuli largely connected with the economic and social life, elements of disintegration; this stage of "*Reizsamkeit*" ("neurosis") leading to new naturalism in the seventies and eighties. During the nineties slight indications of the newly arising idealism, ripening into full evidence in the first decades of the twentieth century. This psychic scheme Lamprecht used as the foundation for his *Deutsche Geschichte der jüngsten Vergangenheit und Gegenwart*. See also *Einführung in das historische Denken*, pp. 42–51; for the development of historical concepts ("historical sense") during the periods of subjectivism see *ibid.*, pp. 42–45.

58. See above, p. 225.

59. *Moderne Geschichtswissenschaft*, pp. 87–88.

60. *Einführung in das historische Denken*, pp. 160–62.

61. As an example in the past he mentions Germany's periods of sentimentality and of *Sturm und Drang* (*ibid.*, pp. 138–39).

62. "Was ist Kulturgeschichte?" *loc. cit.*, p. 137; Doren, "Karl Lamprechts Geschichtstheorie und die Kunstgeschichte," *loc. cit.*, p. 78.

63. The task of joining the last generalizations of all sciences into a well-ordered harmonious whole (Spiess, p. 85).

64. Cf. Spiess, p. 51. Kuhnert (p. 12) draws attention to similarity with Herder's thought.

65. "And how much time has entered into eternity since man's first attempts, with hesitating steps, to pass from stimulus and association to the beginnings of that tremendously complicated process which enters into the simplest conclusions of our thinking today" (*Moderne Geschichtswissenschaft*, p. 120).

66. Many passages in Lamprecht's articles undoubtedly confirm the weakness referred to by Bernheim, while others do not convey this impression. In theory Lamprecht overstressed his point in order to show the difference between the individualistic and collectivistic tendencies and to bring about a shift of emphasis. He pronounced himself to be neither a pure individualist nor a pure collectivist but a universalist, i.e., one who combines the methods of the two. He maintained that the universalist did not underestimate the importance of the genius but considered also "the many," who, because of the power of their historical effects, after all domineered over the genius. The moral value of the latter should, in principle, not be estimated differently from that of any other person ("Der Ausgang des geschichtswissenschaftlichen Kampfes," *Die Zukunft*, XX [July 31, 1897], p. 207; "Ältere und neuere Richtungen in der Geschichtsschreibung," *Deutsche Zeitschrift für Geschichtswissenschaft*, N.F., II [1897–98], p. 125; cf. *Moderne Geschichtswissenschaft*, pp. 117–18.

67. "Die historische Methode des Herrn von Below," *loc. cit.*, p. 17.

68. Bernheim, pp. 115–17, 154.

69. Like Wundt and Bernheim, Lamprecht himself emphasizes that in history no results can ever be predicted, because like causes do not necessarily have like results according to the law of contrasts. ("Was ist Kulturgeschichte?" *loc. cit.*, pp. 14–95).

70. *Moderne Geschichtswissenschaft*, p. 119. It might be mentioned that Lamprecht thought that an examination of the flowers of a civilization would enable the historian to distinguish also its roots.

71. For further inconsistencies involved see Franz Eulenburg, "Neuere Geschichtsphilosophie," *Archiv für Sozialwissenschaft*, N.F., XXV (1907), 135.

72. *Ibid.*, pp. 334–35. Eulenburg draws attention to two earlier attempts of using aesthetic standards, the one for philosophy by Zorschammer (*Imagination as fundamental principle of the world process*) and the other for history by Moritz Carrière (*Art in connection with the development of civilization*).

73. Lamprecht considered a nation the most regular of human communities. As one of the exceptions he named the United States, because her nationhood began with people already possessed of a high civilization (*Moderne Geschichtswissenschaft*, pp. 87–88; *Die kulturhistorische Methode*, p. 27). Since nations do not live in isolation and Lamprecht himself attached importance to their mutual influence, it is difficult to conceive of a "normal nation." See also Bernheim, p. 116.

74. *Loc. cit.*, pp. 320, 332–37; for relations between Lamprecht's thought and Spencer's see also Spiess, p. 39.

75. They may be found in the leading periodicals, magazines, etc., professional and popular, of Germany as well as of English- and French-speaking countries. For English-speaking readers who have no access to the German literature on Lamprecht, the following references to *AHR* may prove useful: E. W. Dow, "Features of the new history apropos of Lamprecht's *Deutsche Geschichte*," III (1898), 431–48; reviews of individual volumes by W. E. Dodd, VII (1902), 789–91; IX (1904), 394–97; and Camillo von Klenze, XII (1907), 633–36.

76. For a long time he was more appreciated abroad than among scholars in Germany. He received honorary degrees from Columbia University in New York (1904), St. Andrews University in Edinburgh (1911), and the University in Kristiania (1911).

77. See above, p. 230.

78. Spiess, p. 21.

79. *Ibid.*, p. 173.

80. Max Lenz published an unusually detailed review of this volume in *HZ,* N.F., XLI (1896), 358–447, but it was far from impartial, for Lenz was one of Lamprecht's bitterest opponents and wrote the article with the avowed aim of ruining Lamprecht's reputation as a historian.

81. Schmoller, *loc. cit.*, pp. 1124–27, 1137, admits that the great success of Lamprecht's *Deutsche Geschichte* rested, after all, primarily on its intrinsic merits. Of Vol. V, Schmoller writes: "I do not feel competent to judge the greater part of its contents . . . . but I wish to emphasize how much I admire this volume. There is not another German economist or historian who could write it. The amount of his knowledge of art and literature is amazing."

82. Even so, there is some truth in Kuhnert's statement, and it may partly explain the unusual appeal Lamprecht's writings had to the public at large.

83. P. 50; cf. Schmoller, *loc. cit.*, p. 1137.

84. Cf. Bernheim, p. 717; see also Walter Götz "Geschichte und Kulturgeschichte," *Archiv für Kulturgeschichte*, VIII (1910), pp. 4–5.

XI

ERNEST LAVISSE (1842–1922)

DONALD F. LACH*

ERNEST LAVISSE was born in the small northern French village of Nouvion en Thiérache in December, 1842. In his later years he recalled most clearly his summers at home: the green fields and sloping hills stretching far around the town and encompassing it in the quiet noises of the countryside. He recalled the thrifty farmers, their industrious wives, and the lonely chapel bell which called them home at the first long shadows of evening.[1] His memories were not of domestic hardship. The father, a small merchant, managed to provide well and to give his oldest son the advantages of education which he himself had never had. Of his mother, Lavisse remembered but little, except that she was a sturdy peasant by origin and that she always remained a little in awe of the son whom she had borne and could not understand. In recalling his father Lavisse recollected best the kind modulation but firmness of his tone. It was a voice which brooked no disobedience but rewarded with kindly encouragement.

His father's teachings were supplemented by the historical recollections of his grandmother. He sat on her knee while she told of Napoleon's campaigns and of "Brother Theodore," who never returned from Russia; and then he shivered as she described the horrors brought to France by the Cossacks and by invasion.[2] She vaguely remembered Robespierre and had even heard tell of Danton, and she believed they were wicked men, not brave and gentle like the emperor.

From his grandmother's history lessons he rapidly moved on to the village school, where Father Matton taught all subjects.

* Research assistant in history, University of Chicago.

There he read, learned to write and to figure. Six times nine was torture until it was learned; nine times six was even worse. Father Matton was kind but strict, even excessively so. The child liked especially the saints' holidays and religious pageants, but he definitely could not understand the logic of the Old Testament, although he enjoyed the many battles, and the story of Samson was always an attraction.

Then shortly after his tenth birthday he was required to put aside his friends and playmates at Nouvion and go off to Laon, where the ambitious father felt his son might receive more adequate instruction in the *collège*.[3] Despite his first fears, Lavisse later recognized these as his happiest days. Many of his teachers he only vaguely remembered, while insignificant incidents remained in his memory as milestones. These years of apprenticeship gave him the necessary techniques for further study. Here he learned Latin and Greek, the teaching of which he later defended. Not only did he study foreign tongues, but for the first time he learned to be at home in his own. For practice in style he described the beautiful forest of Nouvion, using the masters as background for his work. He learned to appreciate Lamartine and to take pride in the intellectual heritage of his country. The "battle stage" in his historical studies was extinguished here, never to be revived again.

After three years' stay at the *collège* Lavisse left for Paris, in October, 1855, where he entered the Lycée Charlemagne.[4] At this institution he had men as teachers who were prominent figures in the life of Paris, and certain of the students were sons of eminent Frenchmen, among whom Albert Duruy was outstanding. History was a *specialité* to both Duruy and Lavisse. The latter chose for himself the field of history, since it was a pleasure for him "to see men act and to hear them speak and to watch life move along." Michelet was his great master. The introduction to Michelet's *Universal history* appealed to the young student as "a poem of humanity." He admired in Michelet "the gift of reliving life with the vision of a poet and of expressing in the words of a poet the feelings of sorrow, hate, and love."

With his mind made up, young Lavisse left the *lycée*, in November, 1862, and enrolled in the École Normale Supérieure. After three years' study at this institution, he was appointed as a fellow in history and at the same time renewed his connections with Albert Duruy. In the Latin quarter he met certain radical students like Gambetta and Clemenceau, and he himself became a Romantic in literature and a Republican in politics. This strain of radicalism did not last long. By the end-years of the sixties he was once more a good Bonapartist. He had used to good advantage his friendship with Albert Duruy, the son of Victor Duruy, Napoleon III's minister of education. In 1868 Lavisse was recalled from Nancy, where the year before he had accepted a position, to assume the post of secretary to Victor Duruy.[5]

Through his connections with Duruy he became interested in the minister's designs for revamping the French educational system. Shortly thereafter, however, he was appointed as private tutor to the Prince Imperial, the future Napoleon IV, even as Michelet had tutored the son of Louis Philippe. His teaching days were cut short by the war of 1870, but he maintained a steady stream of correspondence with the prince until 1878, meanwhile remaining an active and even a belligerent Bonapartist.[6] He chided the *Journal de l'Aisne*, his departmental newspaper, for expressing Republican sympathies and did not hesitate to advance by devious means the cause of his erstwhile student.

Not only did the war of 1870 throw Lavisse out of a job, but it created in him a realization that there must be some basis for German victory. Fitting action to the thought, he left for Germany to study with Waitz and other Germans of the Ranke school. From 1873 to 1875 he observed carefully the diverse features of the German educational system in Berlin and concluded that it was from these splendid organizations that Germany derived amazing technical and intellectual progress. He also wrote articles for the *Revue des deux mondes* on such contemporary topics as the Reichstag, the German worker's movement, and the Hohenzollern family.[7]

His more profound researches were in the medieval and early

modern history of Brandenburg and Prussia. After his doctoral
dissertation, entitled *La marche de Brandenbourg sous la dynastie
ascanienne*,[8] he published his *Études sur l'histoire de Prusse*,[9] which
continue the story after the Ascanian dynasty. In these works
Lavisse does not attempt to contribute anything to the data of
Brandenburg-Prussian history; he presents, rather, the thesis that
the Prussian state owes its basic formation to the border peoples
who have colonized it. He stresses the importance of the early
Slavic infiltrations from the east and the conquests of the knights
of the Teutonic order in Prussia. In the turmoil of the Thirty
Years' War, Lavisse asserts that other foreign groups, especially
Bohemians, were forced to seek refuge in Brandenburg. He contends that the general depopulation occasioned by this war was
met by the Great Elector through importation of Dutch engineers
and scientists. In maintaining his thesis Lavisse naturally plays
up the importance of the French Huguenot refugees who emi-
grated to Brandenburg after the revocation of the Edict of Nantes
(1685). He argues that it was not until the time of Frederick II
that deliberate governmental steps were taken to supplement the
population by the encouragement of immigration. Lavisse contends that from this mosaic of foreign peoples the Prussian state
received its laborers, artisans, scholars, and scientists who formed
the backbone of its rise to power and distinction.

In his lengthy comments on these works, Ernst Berner, the
German historian, wrote:

The emigration of the Protestants who had been driven from their homeland,
especially the French, certainly contributed much profit and many blessings
to the Prussian people, and the colonization of west Prussia through the efforts
of Frederick the Great remains one of the outstanding feats of his career; but
despite these considerations . . . . it is impossible to see in them the founders of
the Prussian state. Within the series of wise measures taken by the Hohen-
zollerns colonizing activity has rightly a place of honor, but to try to understand
the history of the Prussian state on this basis alone results in a complete misin-
terpretation of history. Ingrafted branches on the tree of a great state Lavisse
sees as the roots of the tree itself.[10]

Upon returning from Germany, Lavisse taught at the Lycée
Henri IV until 1878, when he was appointed professor at the

École Normale. One of the most famous of his students, Charles Seignobos, writes of this period:

> I was in the first class when Lavisse arrived at the École Normale, as the *maître de conférences* of history. He had no experience in teaching and had only a very meager command of historical data; but he had courage, intelligence, and a love for history and education. He told us of everything he had studied and to what a degree he had penetrated it. He never tried to impress us . . . . with his erudition; on the contrary, he always remained the virtuous master and historian, and scientific investigator. He always pointed out to us his sources and his working tools.[11]

Hardly was the young professor established in his new post than he launched out vigorously against the French system of education. On the public platform and in the contemporary periodicals he urged much-needed reforms in elementary, secondary, and advanced schools. He not only made recommendations, but he acted. He wrote histories of France for school children from a purely patriotic-nationalistic point of view in which he begged the children not to forget the huge indemnity imposed upon the fatherland by Germany and also to remember that the Alsatians and Lorrainers loved France but were forced to live under German rule.[12] In the universities he advocated the adoption of Ranke's system of historical research. He was willing always to take the best of Germany for the good of France.

With his reforms in education only in the first stages, Lavisse was called in 1883 to act as assistant to Fustel de Coulanges at the Sorbonne. From this vantage position he was able to crusade even more advantageously for reform. The anticlerical attitude of Jules Ferry and the Republican government won Lavisse over to their camp, so that he became as rabid a Republican as he had been a Bonapartist. With the winning of free and compulsory primary education in 1882 Lavisse was able to concentrate his attention more on the secondary schools.

When he went to the Sorbonne there was no organization in that great institution for initiating the advanced student of history into the mysteries of scientific research. His first point of attack had to be made on the government and especially on the Committee for Reform in Education. To these people he had to justify the study of history from a practical point of view. In this attempt Lavisse conveniently outlined his reasons for studying history:

The principal purpose in the teaching of history is to aid the intellectual and moral education of the students.

The teaching of history develops the intellect by exercising the memory, by cultivating the imagination, by creating an ability to discern, appreciate, and evaluate facts, persons, ideas, periods, and countries, and by placing intellectual data, literature, and art in their proper places from the social and political perspective.

The teaching of history helps moral education, but it is necessary to say in what ways and to what degrees. . . . .

It is not always true that the virtuous are rewarded or the guilty always punished; unhappily, evil and violence often succeeded. It is no more true that the destinies of a nation can be justified and explained solely by its virtues and vices: there also enter the elements of the energy and wealth of the country.

The design to make history serve as a sort of moral sermon is laudable, but a teacher must always be sincere above all else. . . . . That is to say, he is not to doubt that historical instruction may be and ought to be used as a stronghold of moral consciousness.

From the very first he is a searcher after truth; he makes every effort to uncover it; and he proclaims it without reserve. The professor is an impartial judge of facts and of doctrines; his personal beliefs and his patriotism do not influence his judgment, which must be absolute. All historical instruction thus practiced is a moral object lesson. . . . .

The professor of history then has the right to be a moralist; in fact, it is his duty. He will shun dogmatism, declamation, and evangelism, but he will pause before the good men whom he will encounter. He will expound at length on the charity of a Saint Vincent de Paul. He will minimize the details of Louis XIV's campaigns and expend the time necessary to delight in the persons of Corneille, Molière, Turenne, and Vauban.[13]

Professor Lavisse carried the fight for reform still further. He upheld classical education, for he claimed that the "youth of a generation should study the adolescent period of humanity" before approaching more mature contemporary problems. Into the Sorbonne he introduced the German seminar, having as some of his first students such eminent scholars as Langlois and Seignobos. Besides the introduction of the seminar, he insisted that less attention be paid to chronology and political history and that more stress be laid on proper research methods and on other technical phases of historical activity. He insisted that his students should be well grounded in the arts and literature and that they should have an understanding of contemporary social and political problems as well as a profound knowledge of their respective fields of specialization.[14]

In the spring of 1886 Lavisse journeyed again to Berlin, after being away from the German capital for over nine years.[15] While in Germany he worked at the archives in Berlin and Königsberg. Meanwhile he published a series of articles under the general title *Études sur l'histoire de l'Allemagne*.[16] These essays deal with medieval Germany and are noteworthy contributions because of the skilful manner in which the machinations of church and state are interwoven. In 1887 he published a book of essays dealing with nineteenth-century Germany, entitled *Essais sur l'Allemagne impériale*. These were followed by a comparative study of the backgrounds and lives of the three German emperors of 1888: Wilhelm I, Frederick III, and Wilhelm II.[17]

In the early nineties Lavisse produced his famous biography, *La jeunesse du grand Frédéric*,[18] which is still generally acknowledged as a historical classic. The clear delineation of the character of the young Frederick, the love for illuminating details and anecdotes, coupled with incomparable simplicity and directness of style, served to enhance the beauty of Lavisse' biographical masterpiece. Even the German scholars were forced to admit that he shed new light on Frederick and especially on the relations between father and son. Only one major criticism could be offered, namely, that his reliance on memoir accounts was too evident.[19] The French scholars hailed the *Youth of Frederick* as a classic of French historical literature.[20] This work, probably more than any of his others, won for him in 1892 election to the French Academy.

In 1893 he continued his biographical study of Frederick by publishing *Le grand Frédéric avant l'avènement*.[21] This work is not comparable in organization or style to its predecessor. The author in his preface states that if the work makes any real contribution to Frederican studies it is largely because of the minute detail with which the prince's life is surveyed. Probably the most important contribution from the point of view of foreign observers is the carefully edited letters preserved in the appendixes. These were found in the French archives of foreign affairs and were written by contemporary Frenchmen living in Berlin. They cover the period from 1732 to 1740.

In 1888 Lavisse had succeeded Henri Wallon as professor of modern history at the Sorbonne. In the nineties he reached the pinnacle of his triumph as a public lecturer. One of his American students, Othon Guerlac, later of Cornell University, recorded the following remembrances of Lavisse's lectures:

Those who studied in Paris in the last decade of the last century may remember an unsightly brick structure temporarily erected in the inner court of the Sorbonne. It served as a shelter for public lectures while the main wing of the old building was being demolished and the masons were tearing down the historic amphitheater to which, for eighty years, some of the most renowned orators from Guizot to Brunetière, had attracted vast throngs.

At the door of this provisional shack one could see, every Thursday morning, at half-past nine, an eager crowd waiting for the opening. Then they would climb up the narrow stairs leading to the amphitheater, and, in an instant, the whole room would be full. Down in front, a few benches were occupied by registered students, while the rest of the hall was filled by the usual public of Sorbonne public lectures: old gentlemen, mature ladies, pretty young girls, serious-looking and spectacled old school teachers, Russians, Englishmen, Americans, Swiss, Swedes, even Frenchmen—all ages, all nationalities. At ten o'clock sharp the doors were shut. Coming from a little side office, the lecturer would appear, preceded by the traditional glass of water and three pieces of sugar on a tray. He was a man in the fifties, tall, vigorous, with a big head slightly inclined, a gray beard, sharp blue eyes, a strong, sonorous, well-modulated voice. With his commanding stature, the rosette in his button-hole, his somewhat abrupt delivery, he reminded one of a colonel in citizen's clothes more than of a professor. At the beginning of every year he would explain to his public two rules that were special to his course: the doors were closed after the beginning of every lecture, so that no one could, in the midst of it, come in or go out. This was to discourage idle curiosity, which has a way of entering anywhere simply because there is a door open. Likewise, applause was discountenanced as foolish and insulting to the speaker, for this was not an operatic performance but a university lecture by Ernest Lavisse, professor of modern history.[22]

Many of his other students record with what quiet dignity he unceremoniously began to talk. He did not launch into great flights of eloquence, but he soberly described the varied careers of Louis XIV or Colbert. His audiences at the Sorbonne were well aware of his scholarly interest in the era of the Sun King, for not only his lectures but also his articles in the contemporary periodicals betrayed his field of concentration.

Despite his unquestioned scholarly abilities, Lavisse had not that type of mind interested in delving into a minutiae of detail to seek for a solitary fact or idea.[23] He did not despise such work, for he encouraged and aided his students in every way possible to perceive the unsolved historical problems and to employ the scientific method in their solution. Such problems, however, held little personal appeal for him. He visualized history not from the point of view of specialized topics but as an integrated picture in which the layman, as well as the scholar, might indulge.

His great work in universal history, the *Histoire générale du 4e siècle à nos jours*,[24] was produced in editorial collaboration with Alfred Rambaud. He did, however, little of the actual work connected with this endeavor, for he was too preoccupied with his regular work and with the *Revue de Paris*, the editorship of which he had assumed in 1894.[25]

At the dawn of the new century he began to edit the massive *Histoire de France depuis les origines jusqu' à la Révolution*,[26] which was to gain for him a place of pre-eminence as a historian of his own country. This work was a survey of French history from the most ancient times to the Revolution of 1789. Various experts in the different periods of French history wrote sections. For himself, Lavisse retained the era of Louis XIV. At last his many lectures and articles were compiled in a single manuscript which appeared in 1906. The American historian, James Westfall Thompson, stated definitely that no man was so capable of writing an adequate study of the era of Louis XIV and that no other historian could have done an adequate job so well and with so much beauty.[27]

The one thing Lavisse set out to do, and a thing which he accomplished successfully, was to "debunk" the standard accounts of the era of Louis XIV which took seriously the versions of Vol-

taire and Michelet. Lavisse deprived the Sun King of many of
his rays by showing him in his later years as a weak and stubborn
old man who refused to acknowledge that his day was past.
Louis XIV was reduced from "the state" to the man.

He divided the work on the era of Louis XIV between two
volumes of the *Histoire de France*. The first of these two, Volume
VII, was divided into two parts. In these parts he attacks the era
of Louis XIV primarily from the point of view of institutional development. The first book, on the period from 1643 to 1661, remains one of the most concise and understandable histories of the
Fronde. In the simple and direct style characteristic of his works,
Lavisse analyzes the Fronde in the following words:

> France was torn apart by persons with no high ideals, no benevolent senti-
> ments, except for certain high-minded parlementarians and members of the
> middle class. Nothing is sadder or more scandalous in our history than these
> four years of war. . . . . The history of the Fronde reveals the immaturity of the
> state and the country. It discloses a dreadful inability to work and act together,
> to find the means and ideals to oppose the power of the king. Finally, the young
> king's observation and comprehension of the Fronde explains in part the politi-
> cal ideals and opinions of Louis XIV.[28]

As Lavisse recognized the influence of the Fronde in Louis
XIV's development, so also did he observe the effects of Richelieu's policies on the young king. Especially did he stress the
evolution of government interest toward such institutions as
finance, commerce, agriculture, industry, the press, laws, police,
justice, religion, and the various strata of society, not to mention
his outstanding analysis of the effects of autocratic government
in intellectual development. Volume VII, Part II, concluded
with an analysis of foreign policy from 1661 to 1685 and a general
survey of the period.

The epoch from 1685 to Louis's death in 1715 was done with
the collaboration of Ṣaint-Léger, Sagnac, and Rebelliau. Lavisse wrote only the last book of this Volume VIII, in which he
studied Louis in relation to the court. This chapter gives the
reader the feeling that he is visiting an art gallery in which he
finds word pictures of such characters as the Duke de Bourgogne,

the Duke de Chartres, and Madame de Maintenon. The other writers in this volume concern themselves primarily with internal politics and diplomacy, although an adequate survey of institutions is also given.

When Lavisse was not occupied with his work in teaching and research, he studied further the groundwork of French education. When the École Normale was joined to the University of Paris in 1904, he accepted the post as director of the new organization. These early days of the twentieth century saw Lavisse at the prime point in his career—at the point where he engaged in active living, where he confronted problems of administration and settled student quarrels. It was in this pre-war period that he most enjoyed returning to Nouvion each spring to give a little talk to the graduating class of the local school and to gossip about "old times" with the white-haired men he had known as schoolboys. Each year he also spoke to the *collège* at Laon, which had since become one of the outstanding *lycées* of northern France. Gradually the rugged fighter of earlier days assumed the calm security of a life well spent, and the mellow philosophy of three score and ten found its way in 1912 into a little volume of *Souvenirs*. Here the historian had, of necessity, to give way to the aged artist, who paints in glowing colors, and with no attempt at objectivity, the triumphs and discouragements of boyhood and youth.

Hardly had his pen formed the last hopeful words of these memories when reality in the guise of war drove sweet remembrances from the old man's mind. Once again the ancient hatreds and prejudices were revived. In Lavisse no thought remained of quiet meditation and mellow contemplation. War, as in 1870, directed his attention once more to the people across the Rhine who again had invaded his beloved France. Even the quiet countryside of Nouvion was forced to play host to the enemy. Two great swords he had to fight with: the sword of an enviable reputation as an objective historian of Germany and the agile pen of an experienced journalist.

No magazine in France issued more propaganda than the *Re-*

vue de Paris, and no historian distorted history more than Ernest Lavisse.[29] Perhaps his position was understandable in that the Germans had burned his home at Nouvion and indirectly killed his brother, who died, as contemporary accounts say, of a "trench disease."[30]

In the years of war Lavisse wrote no fewer than fourteen propaganda articles for the *Revue de Paris.*[31] In these he argued that public opinion should be manipulated for nationalistic purposes. He damned the Germans for rape and pillage and for their ideas on the "necessity for war." In March, 1914, he had organized, with the aid of General Pau, the Ligue Française, which favored country over party, intensive exploitation of colonies, and hostility toward Germany. At the same time he argued that wars in a general sense are harmful but that the war of 1914 would be beneficial since it would spell the end of German militarism.[32] His denunciations of Germany included a terrific outburst against a system of education which creates "efficient bandits"—against that selfsame system which he was so instrumental in giving to France.

At the conclusion of peace he was chosen chairman of the committee investigating territorial questions[33]— he who, with Charles Pfister, had written a pamphlet on Alsace-Lorraine during the war denouncing all German claims as lies. He did not confine his activities to investigation of territorial claims, for he spoke to the German delegates at the Paris Peace Conference with all the venom of four years' hate:

> You are here before your judges, to answer for the greatest crime in history. You are going to lie, for you are congenital liars. But, beware, lying is awkward when you know that those who are listening to you and are looking at you know that you are lying.[34]

It is hard to reconcile the tender sentiments of 1912 with this vicious hate of 1919. It is less difficult to understand that by 1921–22 war clouds had cleared, and Lavisse was able to publish perhaps the greatest monument to modern French history, the *Histoire de France contemporaine depuis la Révolution jusqu' à la paix de 1919.*[35] In writing his conclusion to these ten great volumes he expressed with unforgettable simplicity the faith and hope he felt in the future of France and the republican form of government.

Let me recapitulate: From 1800 to 1814, the parliamentary régime; from 1814 to 1830—except for the Hundred Days—a divine-right kingdom; from 1830 to 1848, a constitutional kingdom; from 1852 to 1870, the Second Empire, which endured longer than any preceding form of government. Since then, we have had a republic for more than half a century.

It remains to be said that a republican government is never a perfectly harmonious government. A republic must be extremely tolerant. We are told that liberty of the press and of assemblage, that the free right to protest and demonstrate against the acts of the government, are fertile seedbeds of trouble. But I fancy that no one of us expects to live an absolutely untroubled life. Liberty has this beneficent quality: popular passions wear themselves out, so to speak, in experiments. The leaders of the most violent factions are sobered by sharing the responsibilities of the government. They are flattered by the honors of office. Public debates are better than secret conventicles, where men conspire to do violent deeds. Imprudent speakers and writers involuntarily disclose the hidden purposes that animate them. They enlighten public opinion, which is, after all, the supreme and final judge.[36]

Hope was always a characteristic element in Lavisse's more philosophic works. Although he recognized the difficulties of the present moment, he was always optimistic enough to believe that humanity and France, despite the awful interlude of the war, would emerge, by natural bounty and by human strength, into the full sunlight of prosperity. His thoughts did not include the human race as a whole, for he lived and died a nationalistic liberal of the nineteenth century who felt that man's destiny must be worked out on national lines established by war and tradition.

Although he was a product of nineteenth-century liberalism and a firm believer, in his later years, in the virtues of a nationalistic-republican-capitalistic system, his later historical writings were definitely tinged with that flavor to which the name "new history" has been ascribed. He used all the technical means at his command not to ferret out the details of political and diplomatic history but rather to give meaning to epochs by describing customs, manners, commerce, religion, literature, art, and science.[37] He was not a conscious follower of the theory of economic determinism, but he gathered about himself a group of men who were fully aware of the importance of that theory.

His writings were models of Rankean technique written with that simple and grand style peculiar to masters of French. He went back to the sources but contented himself with picking out the summits of interest, leaving the valleys to be explored by those students and followers of his who possessed such patience and time. His works were usually arranged with deference to chronology, but from time to time he found a topical arrangement more suitable. His writings were always narrative, with philosophic bits interspersed. His only limits were geography, for he confined himself to the study of Prussia, Germany, and France, although he did limit his most intensive researches to the middle ages on one side and the eighteenth century on the other. The most characteristic feature of his writings was the sunny optimism he always felt for the future. He never studied a period for itself but endeavored always to connect it with the present. He was a greater editor than a scholar.[38] In this role he gave to history three monumental works.[39] He gave further to France that technique known as "scientific history." His influence in educational reforms was great and has been of lasting consequence.

In August, 1922, his wish of seventy years was granted, for he returned then to Nouvion, and he was buried in his native soil with all the honors due a distinguished member of the French Academy. Nowhere does he express his outlook on life more clearly than in the closing sentences of his *Souvenirs:*

Oh, I see very well all the imperfections of men and of things. I have known, and I know many hours of fear and anxiety; but, never, have I despaired and I shall never give up to despair. The feelings of my youth, intact and strong, command in me hope. I am hoping.[40]

NOTES

1. *Souvenirs* (Paris, 1912), pp. 1–8.
2. *Ibid.*, pp. 103–6.
3. Cf. *ibid.*, pp. 129–78, for a complete account of his life at the *collège* of Laon.
4. Cf. *ibid.*, pp. 179–230.
5. *Un ministre, Victor Duruy* (Paris, 1895).
6. Cf. Charles L. d'Espinay de Briort, "Une correspondance inédite: le prince impérial et Ernest Lavisse, 1871–79," *Revue des deux mondes*, 8th period, L (1929), 55–91.

7. See in the *Revue des deux mondes:* "Les élections au parlement d'Allemagne," 3d period, II (1874), 158–77; "Une visite au parlement de l'empire d'Allemagne," 2d period, CVIII (1873), 187–206; "Les partis socialistes et l'agitation ouvrière en Allemagne," 2d period, CVII (1873), 442–64; "La crise économique en Allemagne," 3d period, XVIII (1876), 373–402; "Les prédécesseurs des Hohenzollerns, d'après un historien allemand," 3d period, XII (1875), 407–31; "Un livre français et un livre allemand sur l'Allemagne," 3d period, XXI (1877), 924–39.

8. Paris, 1875.

9. Paris, 1879; reviewed by Karl Lohmeyer, *HZ*, LIX (1875), 318–20.

10. Ernst Berner, "Neuere französische Forschungen zur preussischen Geschichte," *Forschungen zur brandenburgischen und preussischen Geschichte*, II (1889), 316.

11. C. Seignobos, "Ernest Lavisse," *Revue universitaire*, XXXI (1922), Part II, 260.

12. See his *Histoire de France: cours élémentaire* (Paris, 1875), p. 175. In 1926 his *cours moyen* went through its twenty-fifth edition and the year before his *cours supérieur* went through its second edition. The *cours élémentaire* has also gone through more than one edition, for it was republished in 1925. Lavisse also edited patriotic readings for classes in civic training: *Les récits de Pierre Laloi* (Paris, 1925) and "Tu seras soldat," *Histoire d'un soldat français* (Paris, 1916). See Carlton J. H. Hayes, *France, a nation of patriots* (New York, 1930), pp. 350–51, 363–64, 374.

13. "Du rôle de l'enseignement historique dans l'education," *À propos de nos écoles* (Paris, 1895), pp. 77–78.

14. Cf. his speech given before the Faculté des Lettres of the Sorbonne on Nov. 3, 1885, as recorded in his *Études et étudiants* (Paris, 1890), p. 114.

15. See "Notes prises dans une excursion en Allemagne," *Revue des deux mondes*, 3d period, LXXV (1886), 903–21.

16. Includes the following articles in the *Revue des deux mondes:* "Les préliminaires de l'histoire d'Allemagne," 3d period, LXX (1885), 390–417; "La foi et la morale des Francs," 3d period, LXXIV (1886), 365–97; "L'Entrée en scène de la papauté," 3d period, LXXVIII (1886), 842–81; "La conquête de la Germanie par l'église romaine," 3d period, LXXX (1887), 878–902; "La fondation du Saint-Empire," 3d period, LXXXVII (1888), 357–93.

17. *Trois empereurs d'Allemagne* (Paris, 1888).

18. Paris, 1891.

19. This opinion was expressed in *Jahresberichte für Geschichtswissenschaft*, 1891, sec. 62, Part II, p. 21.

20. Cf. Gabriel Monod's appreciation in *RH*, XLVI (1891), pp. 90–92.

21. Paris, 1893.

22. Othon Guerlac, "Ernest Lavisse, French historian and educator," *South Atlantic quarterly*, XXII (1923), 23–24.

23. On this interesting part of Lavisse's historical outlook see especially C. V. Langlois, "Ernest Lavisse," *Revue de France*, V (1922), 472: "M. Lavisse, who was a great historian in every sense of the word, was not a scholar."

24. 12 vols.; Paris, 1893–1901.

25. Cf. Charles Pfister, "Ernest Lavisse," *RH*, CXLI (1922), 317.

26. 9 vols.; Paris, 1900–11. Condensed version in one volume *Histoire de France illustrée depuis les origines jusqu'a la Révolution* (Paris, 1911).

27. *AHR*, XII (1907), 130–33.

28. *Histoire de France*, VII, Part I, 44.

29. Although this accusation is grave, ample evidence of such distortions may be found in his articles in the *Revue de Paris* for the war period. Such articles as "La Prusse" were mere compilations of excerpts from his earlier works proving the "brutality of the Germans." From these partial truths he drew his conclusions. In 1923 Georges Demartial, French political writer and "revisionist," first published a denunciation of Lavisse's war activities in his *La guerre de 1917: comment on mobilisa les consciences* (Paris, 1923). This denunciation is repeated in H. E. Barnes, *The history of historical writing* (Norman, Okla., 1937), p. 278.

30. Pfister, *loc. cit.*, p. 318.

31. "La guerre," XXI (November, 1914), 1–9; "L'état d'esprit qu'il faut," XXII (January, 1915), 5–12; "La Prusse," XXII (February, 1915), 673–93; "Trois idées allemands," XXII (May, 1915), 225–35; "Bonne année," XXIII (January, 1916), 5–14; "Un sincère témoignage sur la guerre," XXIII (April, 1916), 673–80; "La direction de l'opinion publique," XXIII (July, 1916), 5–10; "Si la guerre est bienfaisante?" XXIII (October, 1916), 669–76; "Lettre à une normalienne," XXIV (December, 1917), 779–90; "Seconde lettre à une normalienne," XXV (January, 1918), 65–75; "Comme dans un rêve," XXV (November, 1918), 449–52; "Réflexions pendant la guerre," XXV (December, 1918), 702–8; "Réflexions pendant la guerre II," XXVI (January, 1919), 225–34; "Réflexions pendant la guerre III," XXVI (June, 1919), 449–62.

32. See his *German theory and practice of war* (Paris, 1915).

33. J. T. Shotwell, *At the Paris Peace Conference* (New York, 1937), p. 14.

34. Quoted in Barnes, p. 278.

35. 10 vols.; Paris, 1920–22.

36. These conclusions of the *Histoire contemporaine* were also published under the title "Raisons de confiance en l'avenir," in *Revue de Paris*, XXIX (May, 1922), 225–41. The English translation was published in the *Living age*, CCCXIV (July 15, 1922), 137. Charles Andler wrote an appreciation of the work entitled "La dernière œuvre d'Ernest Lavisse," *Revue de Paris*, XXX (January, 1923), 303–40.

37. This is admirably illustrated in his little *Vue générale de l'histoire politique de l'Europe* (Paris, 1890).

38. Phillip Sagnac, "Ernest Lavisse," *Encyclopaedia of the social sciences*, IX, 199–200.

39. In addition to the three *Histoires*, he edited *La vie politique à l'étranger* (Paris, 1889–91), *Album historique* (Paris, 1897–1907), and *Le monde contemporain, 1870–1900* (Paris, 1905).

40. *Souvenirs*, p. 287.

XII

SIR RICHARD LODGE (1855–1936)

JOHN H. DAVIS*

WHEN Sir Richard Lodge, full of years and of honors, addressed the Royal Historical Society, of which he had just been elected president, upon the subject "Thomas Frederick Tout: a retrospect of twin academic careers," he closed with an unexpected note of humility in comparing his accomplishments with those of his predecessor:

It was inevitable that two men starting from very much the same point, with similar interests, aims, and occupations, should regard themselves as having run a race against each other for over half a century. And over the long course he had won. I may have gained certain advantages at the outset, but he had superior grit and staying power. He kept his gaze more firmly fixed upon the finishing post, whereas I had allowed my eyes and even my steps to wander too often by the way. He accomplished solid and lasting work, mine so far has been scantier and more fugitive. . . . . He overcame all obstacles, he lived a gallant life, he was in many ways a great man, and he will go down to posterity as a great teacher and a great historian.[1]

The statement gives a clue to the speaker's career, and the final sentence might well have been used as his own epitaph, for Lodge has been justly called "a signal and outstanding example of the combination of the scholar and the man of action."

Brief though it was, the address, which was far more autobiographical than biographical, revealed its author as a remarkable man who twice did not hesitate to break with what seemed to be a successful career for the greater glory of history. And few who heard it expected their septuagenarian president to live to produce works which rivaled, if they did not surpass, the sum total of his previous productions in quantity as well as in quality.

* Professor of history, Southwestern College, Memphis, Tenn.

Indeed, the life of Sir Richard holds an interest which his writings do not invariably display, and in that time-honored dichotomy of "life and work" one is tempted to dwell upon the former at the expense of the latter.[2] If further justification for this were needed, it might be found in the following reasons: his long career formed a connecting link between the age of Stubbs, Creighton, and Freeman and the organized research of today; he was intimately associated with the development of historical study in three important universities and a messenger of the gospel of history to Scotland; finally, an understanding of his activities makes clearer the trends of his writing and explains the long gap in his productivity.

Family influence played an indirect and minor role in making a historian of Lodge, although he guided his sister Eleanor's footsteps in pursuit of the muse. It must have been, nevertheless, an unusual family which could produce in one generation four such outstanding scholars as Sir Oliver, the scientist, spiritualist, and one-time principal of Birmingham University; Alfred, a famous mathematician; and two historians, Sir Richard and Eleanor Constance, vice-principal of Lady Margaret Hall, Oxford, and later principal of Westfield College, London.

A remote ancestor of the Lodges migrated to Ireland from Yorkshire in the time of Charles II, and the family remained there until the beginning of the nineteenth century, when Richard's grandfather, the Reverend Oliver Lodge, returned to England and finally settled in Cambridgeshire. As he was the husband of three wives and the father of twenty-five children, it was natural that the family should scatter; so Lodge's father, another Oliver, settled and then married in Penkhull, Staffordshire, in the eighteen-forties. Here, as agent for the sale of blue clay to the neighboring potteries, he did a flourishing business, which later necessitated a move to Wolstanton, but business remained a family affair, with the children frequently taking a hand in clerical tasks.

Richard, the fourth son, was born at Penkhull on June 20, 1855, and grew up in the smoky atmosphere of the "five towns" under the stern Victorian discipline of his business-like father. Literary tastes were instilled by the mother's side of the family. Partly because of the father's belief in rigorous treatment and partly because of family connections with the school, Richard was sent to Christ's Hospital, an ancient foundation of Edward VI in Newgate Street, London. For nine years he wore the traditional blue coat and yellow stockings of the school.[3] Here he attained his enormous height of six feet, four inches, which so distinguished his physical appearance and which was characteristic of his family. The parental philosophy (that support would be freely forthcoming for sons who adhered to the family business but that anyone who wished to pursue the career of learning must help himself) led Richard to seek the Brackenbury historical scholarship at Balliol College, Oxford. This launched his historical career.

The long interval of years which elapsed from the day he entered Oxford as a shy, angular schoolboy in ill-fitting, borrowed clothing until he was returned to Oxford to be laid to rest in Holywell cemetery with dignitaries from several universities and learned societies in attendance, may conveniently be divided into three periods—geographically, Oxford, Scotland, and Harpenden; or, occupationally, undergraduate and don, professor and man of action, and researcher and scholar.

Oxford left an indelible impress on Lodge. Friends, ideas, and affections of his Oxford days remained with him through life; and he became, as it were, an amalgam of the spirit of his two colleges, Balliol and Brasenose. He made his first assault on the Brackenbury in 1873 and always retained a vivid memory of that ordeal: the portrait-lined hall, the self-assured, gowned undergraduates, and the two awkward and timid London schoolboys, himself and Tout, writing furiously.[4] He failed in the first attempt but secured an unexpected exhibition which enabled him to enter Balliol the following autumn, and he succeeded on the third try. Oxford in the seventies was an exciting place. Ruskin was leading his "diggers" (of whom Lodge was to be one) to work on the Ferry-Hincksey road. Balliol, enjoying its golden age under the mastership of Benjamin Jowett, was the nursery of many outstanding men of the next generation. Observe the historians alone: slightly senior to Lodge were Richard Prothero, Herbert Warren, C. H. Simpkinson; his own year was a veritable *annus mirabilis,* for among his contemporaries were W. P. Ker, R. Lane Poole, Horace Round, T. F. Tout, Arnold Toynbee, and F. C. Montague; and C. H. Firth was one year junior.[5]

At the time, Balliol had no regular fellow of history. Lodge and some of his friends took their first essays to J. Franck Bright, of University College. In mid-career, however, he came under the instruction of the great Stubbs, thanks to the bargaining-power of Benjamin Jowett, who, in obtaining the services of the regius professor as chaplain of the college, required that he teach four selected undergraduates in history.[6] As an undergraduate, Lodge won all the available history laurels: the Stanhope prize (1875), with an essay on Cardinal Beaufort, and in the next year the Lothian, on the subject "The causes of the failure of parliamentary institutions in Spain and France." Then came the expected "first" in a class which included G. E. Buckle and Arthur Hassall. He had just resumed his interrupted study of the classics when Brasenose College "startled Oxford" by announcing a fellowship in both ancient and modern history. Lodge, one of thirteen applicants, entered the contest and won.

Later he confessed a regret that he had not followed Jowett's advice to continue with "greats" (Latin, Greek, and philosophy) or to proceed with advanced study; but, weary of examinations and "satiated with success," after a brief stay at the University of Vienna he plunged, as he said,

into the absorptive life of college lecturer, tutor, librarian, vice-principal, as promotion came to me. I also took to a number of other occupations, including the game of golf which left me sadly little time for the serious study of history. . . . . It is true that like Tout I wrote text books, but unlike him I did little else.[7]

Little else, if one is to except his wide interest in games, the boat club, Vincent's; his editorship of the nascent *Oxford magazine*

(1883); his famous Sunday breakfasts—all of which endeared him to the undergraduates and made the attractive don and his charming wife outstanding in the life of the college.[8] His influence, however, was felt beyond its walls. He, A. L. Smith, and Arthur Johnson were the leading members of the Association of History Tutors, which did so much to formulate the program of the school of modern history (recently divorced from law) and to complete the system of intercollegiate lectures, or "lecture pool," inaugurated by Mandell Creighton in the sixties. This "history ring," or "gang" (as their opponents dubbed them), became so powerful that on many occasions it did not hesitate to thwart the plans and ignore the lectures of successive regius professors.[9] Meanwhile Lodge's own lectures were crowded, and his ability as examiner and tutor was acknowledged by all; but a growing sense of dissatisfaction haunted him. "I was beset," he wrote, "by the thought that I was dissipating my energies and that I was getting into a groove from which there was no obvious exit except a complete change of scene."

Many old Balliol friends in Scotland urged him northward, and so, when a Royal Commission finally forced the establishment of chairs of history in the Scottish universities (1894), he applied first for Edinburgh; but when Prothero was chosen, he transferred his candidature to Glasgow and was successful.[10] The Scottish phase had begun.

The subject of his inaugural lecture at Glasgow was "The study of history in a Scottish university." As champion of a newcomer to the curriculum, especially one which was forced from the outside, Lodge felt "impelled . . . . to advertise the wares which I have to submit for your approval or consumption." He developed three propositions: that history deserves to be studied, that it should be studied in universities, and that it had especial claim to the attention of a Scottish university. He based his apologia upon the experience of other universities; upon the thesis of Sir John Seeley that history offers excellent training in morals and citizenship; upon the necessity of observing the continuity of history; and upon the idea that practical discipline of the reasoning faculties is provided by "the sifting of evidences, the comparison of authorities, and the judicial decision between conflicting views." It is impossible to judge a structure from a few bricks, but to quote *obiter dicta* from the address may reveal some of Lodge's ideas on history. "It is true," he said, "no success has attended the attempt to formulate general laws of history, or to find a scientific basis for the actions of states so that men can prophesy the future from the past"; or, "Nothing is more misleading than a partial or a pedantic knowledge of history," which is able to supply arguments for the most opposite political views. He held that "it is not the business of a professor . . . . to make proselytes to any particular view: it is his business to supply knowledge rather than convictions; to furnish his students with the means of forming their own judgements, and not to force down their throats his own opinions." Or again, "Few things are more likely to contribute to the stability and prosperity of a democratic state than the training of its members by an intelligent study of history." After sketching his own plans and praising the work of Scottish historians and historical societies, he concluded:

If any exertions on my part can create or extend an interest in the study of history in general; still more, if they can induce any student to devote himself to historial research, and especially to the history of his own country . . . . I shall feel that the modest hopes with which I commence my teaching in this university will have been more than fulfilled.[11]

The stay in Glasgow proved brief. Even before he journeyed to Scotland a siege of illness necessitated a long vacation abroad. Since he suffered most of his life from bronchial asthma, the murky, foggy atmosphere of the west proved too severe for him. When Prothero resigned at Edinburgh in 1899, Lodge gained that appointment.

In both Glasgow and Edinburgh the professor lectured five days a week to an "ordinary class" during the short Scottish term (October to April) on a general survey of British history which broadened out to include England's European relations.

Less frequently he met smaller "honours classes." Here he specialized on his favorite topics: the eighteenth century, the British Empire, or the importance of sea power. These courses were designed less for research than to furnish lucid outlines of a period; to show the chain of cause and effect; and to enable a student to master other periods by independent work. The numbers in his ordinary classes grew rapidly: in Glasgow from an original nineteen to over fifty, while in Edinburgh, especially after the new Arts Ordinance (1908) placed history on an equality with older subjects, the number of students increased from fifty to well over two hundred.[12]

In Scotland the friendly don developed gradually into the more isolated and austere Scottish professor. In his new surroundings the old links with the students—the coachings, the breakfasts, and playing-fields—were gone. His method of lecturing also underwent a change. At Oxford he spoke rapidly, often from notes, and moved about on the dais; but in Scotland his tempo slowed, he became less dependent upon notes, more formal and formidable. Students spoke of him as "the most competent and masculine lecturer I have heard," or "the finest lecturer of my time, the perfection of form, charm, delivery."

In Edinburgh, since history was already firmly established, Lodge chose as his inaugural subject, "How should history be studied?"[13] In this lecture he compared two views of history: one history as a means of general education, the other history as training in research (he called them the "approach" of Oxford and of Paris). He maintained that an ideal school should secure the benefits of both by combining with a broad general knowledge the minute study of one particular field. For he held that the student, "by tracing his knowledge back to original sources and subjecting them to the most minute examination" would gain an insight and surety of judgment unattainable in any other way. And he voiced violent disagreement with an American professor who had told him: "Don't bother yourself with all that grubbing among mouldy records, leave that to the Stubbses and Freemans, they are the hewers of wood and the drawers of water for us whose business is to expound the lessons of history to the world."

In the Scottish years Lodge developed into a great administrator, a civic figure, active in national and local politics but more especially in various forms of social and educational betterment. At Edinburgh he became assessor of the *senatus* on the university court and dean of the faculty of arts, and many expected that he would be made principal—but, as he later told a friend, his colleagues thought he had too much power already. Under his guidance the department expanded enormously, both in numbers, and in the range of subjects offered.

Always a believer in the close connection between history and politics, he plunged, soon after his arrival in Edinburgh, into the activities of the Liberal League. These "imperialistic" Liberals, under the leadership of Rosebery, Haldane, and Grey, condemned the "labby and flabby" wing of the party at the time of the Boer War. As president of the eastern Scottish branch, Lodge presided at numerous meetings, made many speeches, and formed an enduring friendship with Lord Rosebery. Seeley's influence may have led him into politics, but the Balliol of Jowett, Green, and Toynbee taught him to believe that every man was bound to give some social service to the community. He wanted to prove to himself "whether a university professor . . . . was altogether the feckless and rather incompetent person in practical life which he was often perhaps justifiably considered to be." Thus he took a leading part in organizing and directing such social services as the University Settlement, the Charity Organization Society, and the Distress Committee. A natural leader of men, these organizations brought out his fighting qualities, whether with the government in behalf of the unemployed or against refractory workers. He was also drafted by his old pupil, Lord Askwith, to act as arbitrator during the era of strikes which preceded the war, an employment which sometimes found reflection in his books.[14]

The war of 1914 only increased Lodge's activities and burdens. In addition to his other work he was made secretary of the Scottish Committee of the Prince of Wales' Fund for Relief of Distress. With two sons in the army he went abroad himself on two occasions to lecture to troops, and in the final year of the war death took three of his seven children. Honors, as well as sorrows, came to him, for during the Edinburgh years he was knighted (1917), made honorary fellow of Brasenose, and received honorary degrees from Glasgow, Manchester, and Edinburgh.[15] But old qualms of discontent again assailed him. "Extraneous activities" were making him neglect the study of history, "which at the outset," he said, "I had taken as my life's work."

> I trusted too long to past accumulations of knowledge, and it was necessary to replenish the store. This could not be done if I stayed in Edinburgh. . . . . So after thirty one years of service in Scotland and seventy years of life I quitted Edinburgh and migrated to the neighborhood of the Public Record Office and the British Museum in the hope of rejuvenating myself by becoming once more a student of history.[15a]

With this valiant statement he retired into activity. How well he succeeded during the Harpenden period will be seen from the discussion of his work.

His historical writing falls into two uneven divisions. During the forty-five years of teaching in Oxford and in Scotland the register of his writings is relatively small. Indeed, in Dr. Horn's unpublished bibliography titles from the years 1878 to 1923, including books, reviews, and articles, take up only three pages; whereas seven are required to enumerate the work of his last twelve years. Another sharp difference is that, whereas the books of the earlier period are entirely textbooks, the latter work represents more specialization and research.

In England the final quarter of the last century and the early years of the present one were a veritable "age of text books," ranging from simple manuals, designed to meet the need of the new historical instruction in schools and universities, to the elaborately planned series, such as the Cambridge histories, the Oman, or the Hunt and Poole multiple-volumed histories of England, which were designed to embody the latest results of "scientific" scholarship. Lodge and most of his well-known contemporaries in the field of history took an active part in laying this solid foundation of political texts. On this proclivity of the English for texts, the French reviewer of Lodge's *Richelieu* remarked: "Le petit livre ... fait honneur à la collection qu'il a inaugurée et qui vient de s'ajouter à toutes celles que le gout de vulgarisation historique a suscitée chez nos voisins, nos précurseurs dans un genre qui convient particulièrement à leur esprit positif et *matter of fact*."[16]

During his years of teaching he produced: "a pioneer work," *The history of modern Europe, 1453–1878*,[17] more familiarly known as *The student's modern Europe; Richelieu*,[18] in the "Foreign statesman series"; *The close of the middle ages, 1273–1494*,[19] in the Rivington series "Periods of European history"; and *The history of England from the Restoration to the death of William III, 1660–1702*,[20] for the "Political history of England" series. In addition to these books he contributed chapters on eastern diplomacy to the *Cambridge modern history:* "The European powers and the eastern question," "The extinction of Poland, 1788–1797," and "Austria, Poland, and Turkey";[21] three articles for the ninth edition of the *Encyclopaedia Britannica*, on the Hanseatic League and on medieval and modern Spain; numerous articles for the three volumes of *Palgrave's dictionary of political economy;* a translation of two chapters of Bluntschli's *Theory of the state;* and about an average of one review a year for the *English historical review*, many of which were on successive volumes of the famous French *Recueil des instructions données aux ambassadeurs et ministres de France, depuis les traités de Westphalie jusqu'à la Revolution française*, though occasionally the work reviewed reflected the subject of the book he was engaged upon at the time.

This condensed bibliography of the early period indicates interest in an extensive range of subjects, a gradually increasing concentration on more limited but more amply treated periods, and a definite fondness for political and diplomatic history. The author also showed a progressive improvement in the manipulation of subject matter. Trained at the hands of Stubbs, an intimate friend and disciple of Creighton, a lifelong admirer of

Ranke, "whom," he said, "I was brought up to regard as perhaps the greatest all round historian of the nineteenth century," his work naturally reflects their characteristics—their sober, cautious, analytical style. One reviewer expressed it in these words:

> Professor Lodge is of the school of Ranke rather than Macaulay. His volume has none of the premeditated brilliance of the great Whig historian. It is free from that "stamping emphasis" of which Lord Morley once complained. But the style fits the subject, being concise yet supple; it is laudably free from needless rhetoric, being set rather in the scientific key.[22]

Another spoke of his books as "without ornament, but judicious and compact."

It would be a work of supererogation to attempt to enumerate the many changes and discoveries made by research since the publication of these texts. At the time they were written they incorporated the results of the best available secondary work. They have been through many editions and are still useful. To condemn them as severely political, tending to be compendiums of names and facts presented in an almost chronological order, is merely to call them typical of the "new history," the vulgarizations of their time. James Harvey Robinson, prophet and propagandist of the succeeding brand of "new history," which has emphasized economic, social, and intellectual developments at the expense of the political, took this ironic thrust at the type of writing represented by Lodge and his generation in the following short notice of Lodge's *Close of the middle ages:*

> Professor Lodge has added . . . . another somewhat dreary sketch of political events to the somewhat juiceless series known as "Periods of European history." . . . . His chronicle is but slightly more philosophic than one of the ninth century, and he shows that extreme partiality for proper names which one finds in the Catalog of the Ships or in an Icelandic Saga. To judge from the index, Professor Lodge has found occasion to mention within the modest compass of his volume upwards of a thousand proper names. Obviously if the capture of the fortresses of Elna and Girona, "both after an obstinate resistance" by Philip le Hardi, and the fact that Giovanni, the third son of Sixtus IV's brother married the daughter of Federigo de Montefeltro—if all events of similar importance must at least be mentioned in a small volume covering over two centuries of European experience, no wonder that there is no room to say anything of

European progress except in a most perfunctory chapter upon the Renaissance at the end of the volume, entirely uncorrelated with the rest of the book. Those familiar with Professor Lodge's gloomy *Modern Europe* will find that his conception of the functions of an historian have been in no way modified by the current discussions in France and Germany as to the proper scope of general history, nor by the recent contributions to economic history.[23]

This assault, though containing elements of truth, is unfair. Lodge knew, as well as any, that each generation must re-write its texts and had himself expressed that idea ten years before in his Glasgow inaugural:

History is a progressive and not a stationary subject. The books which satisfied and instructed one generation have to be re-written, altered, and added to, the next. There is a constant bringing to light of new evidence . . . . which compels students to reopen what seem to be settled questions and to reconsider verdicts which appeared final and conclusive. . . . . The process is both necessary and stimulating; without it history would still be instructive, but it would be lifeless and dull; to borrow a simile from a Scottish game, it would be like playing golf forever on a course that contained no hazards, no bad lies. It would be exercise, but it would be a poor game.[24]

Indeed, in his review of G. N. Clark's *The later Stuarts*, which superseded his own best text, Lodge graciously pointed out the shift in emphasis and Professor Clark's successful blending of economic and social history into the political narrative, explaining that his own "rather perfunctory chapter on literature and kindred topics" was added to a volume "somewhat ostentatiously called the 'Political history of England' " because of an afterthought on the part of the editor.[25]

Great Britain and Prussia in the eighteenth century,[26] the Ford Lectures delivered at Oxford in the spring of 1922, marked a turning-point in Sir Richard's career. He said:

The preparation of the Ford lectures . . . . reawakened old enthusiasms, and convinced me that I must free myself from other business and establish a closer connection with the Record Office and the British Museum. So at last I cut the Gordian knot, by resigning my chair and came south in the hope of becoming once more an historian rather than a factotum.[27]

Its preparation was somewhat hasty. As its author was too engrossed in manifold activities during the preceding years to keep *au courant* of contemporary literature on the subject, the book has been criticized for shortcomings in documentation and for certain dubious conclusions,[28] but it inaugurated the long line of articles and studies on the eighteenth century which did much to throw light on that period of which Carlyle declared "not dismal swamp under coverlet of London fog could be uglier."

The bibliography of the final years (1924–36) may be summarized as follows: one full-length book (his best), *Studies in eighteenth century diplomacy, 1740–1748;*[29] two volumes of diplomatic correspondence, edited with introductions and explanatory notes, *The private correspondence of Chesterfield and Newcastle, 1744–46*[30] and *The private correspondence of Sir Benjamin Keene, K.B.*;[31] chapters in four books of collected essays or lectures;[32] two articles for the *Dictionary of national biography* (on Sir William Turner and Sir James Henry Ramsay); five documented articles and twenty reviews for the *English historical review;* eight articles or addresses for the *Transactions of the Royal Historical Society;* and five articles, forty-five reviews, and almost as many short notices for *History*—a formidable total.

Some of the articles were based directly upon archival research; others were simplifications of his own findings which often took the form of "historical revisions" or lectures to learned societies. With two exceptions—a lecture on Sir Robert Peel and his first presidential address to the Royal Historical Society on Machiavelli's *Il principe*[33]—they were devoted to the early eighteenth century and dealt primarily with three fields: the War of the Austrian Succession, Anglo-French relations prior to that war, and some aspects of England's relations with Spain and Portugal. On the first of these, in addition to the *Studies*, Lodge wrote four well-documented articles for the *English historical review*, which give a fairly complete picture of England's diplomatic maneuvers at the Russian court between 1739 and 1748; undoubtedly he intended to collect them later into a volume. These were: "The first Anglo-Russian treaty, 1739–1742"; "The Treaty of Abo and the Swedish succession," "Russia, Prussia and Great Britain, 1742–1744"; and, in two instalments, "Lord Hyndford's embassy to Russia, 1744–1749."[34] Within the same field were: "An episode of Anglo-Russian relations during the War of the Austrian Succession"; "The mission of Henry Legge to Berlin, 1748"; and two simplifications, "The continental policy of Great Britain, 1740–1760" and "The maritime powers in the eighteenth century."[35]

The two other periods were covered much less technically. On Anglo-French relations prior to 1740 one should mention: "English foreign policy, 1660–1715," "English neutrality in the War of the Polish Succession," "The Treaty of Seville, 1729," "The Anglo-French alliance, 1716–1731," and "Sir Robert Walpole"; on Spain and Portugal, two addresses to the Royal Historical Society, "Sir Benjamin Keene, K.B.: a study in Anglo-Spanish relations" and "The English factory at Lisbon: some chapters in its history," and two historical revisions, "The Spanish succession" and "The Methuen treaties of 1703."[36]

The devotion to one period and to one type of writing called forth occasional apologies from Sir Richard:

> But a shoemaker must stick to his last, and I own that I myself take such pleasure in fitting together the jig-saw puzzle of diplomatic relations I find myself impelled to assume . . . . a similar enthusiasm on the part of listeners and readers. I have tried to remember that diplomacy is carried on by human beings and not by labelled machines.[37]

This delight in constructing coherent pictures from scattered diplomatic correspondence, this almost personal interest in the "humbler agents of diplomacy," gave to his later work a freshness and immediacy lacking in the textbooks. Not that it was without a certain tediousness, for diplomatic history is a field of which Professor Temperley truly said: "Some parts are as technical and difficult as chess or mathematics and cannot be treated artistically at all." But Lodge's work was clear, and clarity was his aim.[38]

No English historian since the days of the "industrious" Archdeacon Coxe read such "acres of despatches" or soaked himself more thoroughly in the papers of the politicians of the mid-eighteenth century. He utilized the letters of Newcastle, Carteret, Hyndford, Chesterfield, Bedford, Sandwich, Keene, and many others—whether from the Record Office, the British Museum, private collections, or printed versions—for a work which Professor Muret called "si probe, si consciencieusement documenti, et si utile."

The approach was somewhat unique. Even on the brief period which Sir Richard considered pre-eminently his own he never produced a comprehensive magnum opus, one in which an attempt was made to weave together all the complex threads of diplomacy into a single pattern. Instead, he attempted to throw light upon certain important negotiations, certain selected diplomatic landmarks. This method, described as "quelque peu arbitraire," allowed him to avoid the dangers of overaccumulation (as in the work of J. F. Chance) or the accusations of being incomplete. In this detailed work his "researches among the trees enriched his presentation of the wood." In the *Studies in eighteenth century diplomacy*, which is typical,[39] he demonstrated the vital position of the Dutch, the predominant part England and France played in the War of the Austrian Succession, and the way in which their diplomacy conditioned the actions of the other powers. He rescued from obscurity and neglect politicians and diplomatists like Lord Cartaret and Lord Sandwich (whose papers at Hinchingbrooke he was permitted to use); and from the Duke of Newcastle he scraped the mud of previous detractors. He clarified the policies of the "professor in politics," the Marquis D'Argenson, and of St. Severin, pointing out incidentally the mistakes of older historians of the period, like Arneth, Broglie, and Droysen. Finally he gave a much clearer insight into the *concilabulum* than many constitutional historians, for as a background to the diplomatic negotiations at Hanau, Worms, Breda, and Aix-la-Chapelle he revealed the intrigues of the shifting groups within the inner circle of cabinet ministers.[40]

Most of the detailed work will survive and form an incentive for further study of the period. Its sins are rather of omission than of commission. A conspicuous flaw pointed out by Pierre Muret in his study "L'histoire diplomatique du milieu du XVIIIe siècle d'après les travaux de Sir Richard Lodge" is his failure to give adequate consideration to the pressure of public opinion, or of the royal will, in influencing the decisions of cabinet members in regard to foreign policy. Some contend that Lodge's work is too nationalistic, too much an English counterpart to that of J. G. Droysen;[41] but this criticism applies rather to the Ford Lectures than to the *Studies*, and even here the "nationalism" consists rather in the employment of English sources than in a chauvinistic defense of English policy. More unfortunate, from the student's point of view, is the fact that Sir Richard, who had such a thorough knowledge of the English documentation, never saw fit or took the time to produce an "étude d'ensemble" of his sources or to include a bibliography of any sort in his later work. Instead, one must scan footnotes which include explanatory material on the text, supplementary quotations, pungent critical remarks on historians, as well as bibliographical information and standard documentary references, some of which are far too abbreviated.[42]

In addition to articles of pure research, Sir Richard wrote many summaries. Some were prefatory sketches to a situation he was about to describe in detail; some were historical revisions; some appeared as reviews of books or of documents. These historical *coups d'œil* furnished students and others who might have been intimidated by his technical work on opportunity to observe his conclusions with less effort. Take, for example, the article "The Treaty of Seville, 1729"; in it he devoted thirty of his forty-three pages to a sketch of the succession problems and of the conflicting commercial interests which confronted each of the major powers in the early eighteenth century. In discussing the "Polwarth papers" he reviewed at length the relations of England with the northern powers; in "Sir Benjamin Keene," with Spain; in the "English factory at Lisbon," with Portugal—all before approaching the real subject of his discourse.[43] Some simplifications oversimplified. In the articles in *History*—for example, on "The continental policy of Great Britain, 1740–1760" and "The maritime powers in the eighteenth century"—he attempted to differentiate between Whigs and Tories on the basis of foreign policy (the former, "interventionists"; the latter, "isolationists"), in contrast to the caution and the qualifications with which other recent historians have applied party tags during the mid-century.

"Although a reviewer is bound, in the exercise of his trade, to lay stress upon what he considers the defects of a book, he is equally bound to point out its merits."[44] This was Lodge's reviewing creed. It was an occupation which interested him, which he enjoyed, and at which he excelled. As he approached his eighties the trips from Harpenden to the Record Office and the Museum became increasingly difficult, but he could sit in his garden and do reviewing "with a promptness not usual with scholars" (as the editor of the *English historical review* remarked). What a number of them he produced! In his seventy-sixth year, for example, he turned out fourteen reviews and short notices for *History* and three for the *English historical review*. It is impossible to analyze all and difficult to make generalizations applicable to all. He was perhaps at his best on foreign documentary publications or foreign books. Over a period of years he followed such series as the *Recueil des instructions données aux ambassadeurs et ministres de France*, or the *Politische correspondenz* of Frederick II. In reviewing these collections he presented with great clarity the general story, any new discoveries, and any suggested revisions of interpretation provided by the documents. In considering the work of foreign historians or of solid scholarship he usually subordinated any tendency to discover peccadilloes to the larger purpose of explaining important findings.[45] But he could be scathingly critical, as when he tore apart the editing of the Polwarth manuscripts in an address to the Royal Historical Society.[46] He had a passion for correct dates and correct genealogies, and time and again he was annoyed by the work of amateur historians, "whose blemishes might have been easily got rid of if some expert had been induced to revise the proofs,"[47] while his lifelong career as an examiner often made him mention new discoveries in the form of possible examination questions. Special *bêtes noires* were errors on details of the Spanish Succession, confusion in such dual personalities as the ruler of Austria and the Holy Roman Empire or of England and Hanover, oblique allusions to contemporary political conditions, and the lack of footnote references or their consignment to the rear of chapters or books in any serious work of scholarship. "Pemmican" history and the "contemporary craze for journalism in history and biography" also came in for condemnation.

Indefatigable to the end, from his suburban retreat Sir Richard descended almost daily upon London to do research in the archives, to assist in the work of his old school, to take part in historical meetings. He had a passion for organization, and one friend remarked that he should have been the governor of an Indian province rather than a historian. He helped to found the Historical Association (1906) and later to develop several of its branches. In addition to his presidency of the Royal Historical Society, he was active on the committee of the Institute of Historical Research and a keen organizer of those "academic jaunts," the Anglo-French and the Anglo-American historical conferences.[48] At the same time he maintained an interest in the accomplishments of old pupils and younger scholars. "He worked at my edition [of Chesterfield's letters] as hard as I did myself and seemed to grudge no labor in teaching me the things I ought to have known," said Professor Dobrée. But years crept on apace. The old passion for lecturing, even on a pleasure cruise, brought on a collapse in 1935; and, though he recovered, it was the prelude to the end. He died August 2, 1936, with a book at his bedside for review and with a card asking that certain books be laid out for him at the British Museum.

NOTES

1. *Cornhill magazine*, N.S., LXVIII (1930), 126.

2. I wish to acknowledge my great indebtedness to Miss Margaret Lodge for her extraordinary kindness in sending me the typescript copy of her very interesting unpublished biography of her father. I am dependent on it for many unacknowledged facts and quotations. I must also express my gratitude to Dr. D. B. Horn for his valuable assistance, his unpublished bibliography, and other inaccessible material; to Sir Francis Wylie for his help; and to many other English and American scholars who took time to answer requests for information.

3. Mr. G. L. O. Flecker, headmaster of Christ's Hospital, wrote a letter to the *Times*, Aug. 6, 1936, enumerating Lodge's many activities in behalf of his old school. He was almoner twice and later president of the council.

4. *Cornhill*, N.S., LXVIII (1930), 117. For this examination Lodge spent three weeks cramming Hallam's *Middle ages*, Robertson's *Charles V*, Macaulay's *Essays*, and the *Institutes* of Justinian.

5. *The collected papers of Thomas Frederick Tout* (3 vols.; Manchester, 1935), I, 3. Charles E. Mallet, *History of the University of Oxford* (3 vols.; London, 1924–28), III, 457.

6. *Cornhill*, N.S., LXVIII (1930), 119. Sir Charles Oman (*On the writing of history* [London, 1939], pp. 221–35) gives an interesting account of the development of the Oxford history school. Lodge frequently mentioned Stubbs's influence—e.g., *History*, XVI (1931), 188, where in a book review he condemned the study of contemporary history and remarked: "I am fortified by the recollection that my eminent teacher, Dr. Stubbs, always maintained that recent history was wholly unsuited for educational purposes."

7. *Cornhill*, N.S., LXVIII (1930), 121.

8. Mallet, III, 461; *Oxford magazine*, LV (October, 1936), 81. Lodge is described at the time by a younger Brasenose colleague, F. J. Wylie, in an obituary notice in the college magazine, as follows:

"Lodge too, was a lovable man. He might easily have been formidable, with his great height, somewhat truculent moustache, and eyes that looked so very straight at you. 'Sometimes when Lodge looks at me,' a fellow of the college once said to me, 'I have an uneasy feeling that he wants to kick me.' And he *could* look like that on occasions. But he couldn't go on being formidable, he had too much humor, and too much kindliness. Anything brusque was on the surface, a thin cover to a warm humanity. His manliness, his broad judgement, his dislike of anything affected or pretentious, whether in behavior or in writing—these fitted him well for the business of a Brasenose don, and it was as that that he spent what must have been among the happiest and most satisfying years of his life."

9. Oman, pp. 221–35. The Creightons interested Lodge in the Association for the Education of Women, and after 1882 he took two women pupils a year.

10. In his article "History in Scottish universities: reminiscences of a professor" (*University of Edinburgh journal*, IV [1931], 97–109) Lodge enumerated the problems, associates, pupils, departmental changes, etc., of his long residence in Glasgow and Edinburgh. His chief competitors at Edinburgh were P. H. Brown and G. W. Prothero. At Glasgow he won over Oscar Browning, H. A. L. Fisher, and W. J. Ashley.

Sir Charles Firth ("Dates and anniversaries," *History*, N.S., XVI [1931], 97) gives this anecdote: "I remember being asked in 1894, when a professorship of history was vacant at Glasgow, which of the numerous candidates was likely to be appointed. I said, 'Lodge.' My friend replied, 'Well, he is the right man for the place. He has more lectures concealed about his person than any man in Oxford.' "

11. *The study of history in a Scottish university; an inaugural lecture delivered on October 22nd, 1894* (Glasgow, 1894).

12. See *University of Edinburgh Journal*, IV (1931), 101–6, for departmental struggles and changes at Edinburgh during Lodge's tenure. Some research was possible in Scottish history, but it was more difficult in his field. Dr. D. B. Horn writes: "If an exceptional student wished to continue work on history after graduation Lodge was always ready to give generous advice and assistance, but post-graduate work in

European history meant months or years reading at the P.R.O. and B.M. Few Scottish students could afford to do this. . . . . When the Institute of Historical Research was founded in London, Lodge did everything in his power to encourage post-graduate students to work there and shortly before he retired he arranged for the University to pay the fees of students from Edinburgh who went to the Institute."

13. *How should history be studied?* (Edinburgh, 1901).

14. E.g., in *Great Britain and Prussia in the eighteenth century: being the Ford Lectures delivered in the University of Oxford* (Oxford, 1923), p. 36, he speaks of Lord Hyndford's acting "very much as a conciliator in a modern industrial dispute." In *Studies in eighteenth century diplomacy, 1740-1748* (London, 1930), p. 47, he says of the Convention of Turin that it "reads more like a labour agreement than a political convention."

15. See *Times*, Feb. 13, 1917, for an account of the knighthood. Two other historians, Julian Corbett and Paul Vinagradoff, were knighted at the same time. Lodge's honorary degrees were: LL.D., Glasgow (1905); Litt.D., Manchester (1912); LL.D., Edinburgh (1926).

15a. *University of Edinburgh journal*, IV (1931), 109.

16. G. Fagniez, *RH*, LXIII (1897), 379.

17. London, 1885. This became a standard text in schools and colleges in Great Britain for over forty years and went through many editions. Revised in 1927 under the title *History of Europe, 1789-1920*, the section from 1871 to 1920 was written by Lodge's "brilliant pupil," D. B. Horn. His own section remained virtually unaltered, and he took no cognizance of changes in information and interpretation. In the preface of the new edition he tells of writing the original text at the request of Mr. Strachan-Davidson, of his desire to exploit his new-found knowledge, of the unpleasant task of curtailing the proofs and cutting out all the "purple passages."

18. London, 1896. T. Kükelhaus (*HZ*, LXXIX [1897], 325-27) speaks of it as "die beste moderne Biographie Richelieus." G. Fagniez (*loc. cit.*, pp. 379-81) is more critical. He carefully notes Lodge's contributions but points out the need of revision. Short notice in *AHR*, III (1898), 384-85.

19. London, 1901. J. H. Robinson (*AHR*, VII [1902], 396) is critical; J. P. Whitney (*EHR*, XVII [1902], 819-20) is complimentary. In the *Guide to historical literature* (New York, 1931) R. A. Newhall says of the series: "After the lapse of a generation these books are probably the most useful handbooks of political history in English" (p. 68). Other contributors to the series were: C. Oman, T. F. Tout, A. H. Johnson, H. O. Wakeman, A. Hassall, H. M. Stephens, W. A. Phillips—all prolific textbook-writers.

20. London, 1910. Critically reviewed by W. C. Abbott in *AHR*, XV (1910), 853-55. Other analytical reviews: *EHR*, XXVI (1911), 791-94; *RH*, CVI (1911), 146-47; *Scottish historical review*, VIII (1911), 203-4.

21. Also contributed chaps. xi and xvii to *Cambridge modern history*, VIII (Cambridge, 1904), 306-37, 521-52; and chap. xii to *ibid.*, V (Cambridge, 1908), 338-71.

22. *Scottish historical review*, VIII (1911), 203. When Lodge addressed the newly formed Glasgow Historical Society on the subject of grest historians he particularly praised Thucydides, Tacitus, Gibbon, Macaulay, and Robertson (*ibid.*, I, 224).

23. *AHR*, VII (1902), 396. For an interesting modern defense of the political approach see Miss Violet Barbour's review of G. N. Clark, *The later Stuarts, 1660–1714* (Oxford, 1934), in *AHR*, XL (1935), 728–31.

24. *The study of history in a Scottish university* (Glasgow, 1894), p. 17.

25. *EHR*, L (1935), 717–19. Several reviewers had censured Lodge for this "inadequate postscript."

26. Oxford, 1923.

27. *Cornhill*, N.S., LXVIII (1930), 123. His return for the lectures was a personal triumph. He had a large audience, which included old associates and friends, and so impressed the undergraduates that they broke tradition in applauding the performance. He gave the same lectures on the following days at Westfield College for his sister Eleanor.

28. W. L. Dorn, "Frederick the Great and Lord Bute," *JMH*, I (1929), 529–61, defends Bute against Lodge's strictures. In his *Competition for empire, 1740–1763* (New York, 1940) Dorn contends that Sir Richard interpteted Frederick's actions of 1756 too much in the light of the *Politische Correspondenz;* see especially chaps. iv, vii, and viii and his able bibliographical essay. Reviews of *Great Britain and Prussia: AHR*, XXIX (1924), 325–26, by B. E. Schmitt; *EHR*, XXXIX (1924), 292–93, by Basil Williams; and *RH*, CXLVII (1924), 250–52, by A. Waddington.

29. London, 1930.

30. Camden series, Royal Historical Society, 1930.

31. Cambridge, 1933.

32. "Sir Robert Peel," *Political principles of some notable prime ministers of the nineteenth century*, ed. F. J. C. Hearnshaw (London, 1926), pp. 43–104; "The Anglo-French alliance, 1716–1731," *Studies in Anglo-French history during the eighteenth, nineteenth and twentieth centuries*, ed. A. Coville and H. Temperley (Cambridge, 1935), pp. 3–18; "Sir Robert Walpole," *From Anne to Victoria*, ed. B. Dobrée (London, 1937), pp. 108–29; and "The Methuen treaties of 1703," *Chapters in Anglo-Portuguese relations*, ed. E. Prestage (London, 1934).

33. *Transactions of the Royal Historical Society*, 4th ser. (London, 1918———), XIII, 1–16. This lecture derived from his Oxford teaching and from his admiration of Ranke.

34. *EHR*, XLIII (1928), 354–75, 540–71; XLV (1930), 579–611; XLVI (1931), 48–76, 387–422.

35. *Trans. Roy. Hist. Soc.*, 4th ser., IX, 63–83; XIV, 141–73; *History*, N.S., XVI (1932), 298–304; XV (1930), 246–51 (hirtorical revision No. 55).

36. *History*, N.S., XV (1931), 276–307; *Trans. Roy. Hist. Soc.*, 4th ser., XIV, 141–73; XVI, 1–43; *Studies in Anglo-French History*, pp. 3–18; *From Anne to Victoria*, pp. 108–29; *Trans. Roy. Hist. Soc.*, 4th ser., XV, 243–69; XVI, 211–47; *History*, N.S., XII (1928), 333–38; XVIII (1933), 33–35 (historical revisions Nos. 44 and 65).

37. *Trans. Roy. Hist. Soc.*, 4th ser., XVI, 43. In *ibid.*, XIV, 1, he says: "I have written a good deal about diplomacy during the war of the Austrian succession in defiance of Carlyle who calls it 'an unintelligible huge English and Foreign delirium . . . . a universal rookery of diplomatists whose loud cackle and cawing is now as if gone mad to us; their work fallen putrescent and avoidable, dead to all creatures.' "

38. In reviewing an epigrammatic historian, Lodge remarked: "But it may be doubted whether his frequent allusive and enigmatic sentences, reminiscent of Lord Acton in his occasional moods of suggestive obscurity, are really suited to diplomatic history, which requires above all things clarity" (*History*, N.S., XV [1931], 299).

39. The chapter headings indicate his topical method: (chap. i) the so-called "Treaty of Hanau," 1743; (chap. ii) the Treaty of Worms, September 13, 1743; (chap. iii) D'Argenson's relations with Germany and Sardinia; (chap. iv) D'Argenson and the Dutch; (chap. v) Breda and Lisbon, August, 1746—January, 1747; (chap. vi) Sandwich and Macanaz at Breda, January–May, 1747; (chap. viii) Between Breda and Aix-la-Chapelle; (chap. viii) the Treaty of Aix-la-Chapelle. In his books Lodge followed the chapter heading with an analytical table of contents, or outline. For a complete analysis of the *Studies* see P. Muret, "L'histoire diplomatique du milieu de XVIIIe siècle d'apres les travaux de Sir Richard Lodge," *Revue d'histoire moderne*, VII (1932), 77–83. He says: "Ils constituent certainment la contribution la plus étendue et beaucoup la plus critique que nous possedons aujourd'hui sur cette periode si confuse." On the early part of the war, especially on the Bavarian phase, his book is superseded by Fritz Wagner, *Kaiser Karl VII und die Grossen Mächte* (Stuttgart, 1938). Favorable reviews of the *Studies:* P. Vaucher in *History*, N.S., XV (1931), 371–73; W. F. Reddaway in *EHR*, XLV (1930), 653–55; G. Pagès in *RH*, CLXXIII (1934), 384–85; C. Perkins in *AHR*, XXVI (1931), 805–7.

Of the *Studies*, Lodge's friend and pupil, C. R. L. Fletcher, wrote: "I feel it is the best thing you have ever done. You have really made state papers tell their own story, so consecutively, so humanly, so unlike the style in which nearly every other 'scientific historian' makes them tell it. Gardiner and Ranke will, when you meet in Valhalla, hold out a hand of welcome to you as one of their own true breed" (Miss Lodge's manuscript).

40. In the *Studies*, as in the introduction to the *Private correspondence of Chesterfield and Newcastle*, one gains a clearer insight into the workings of the "inner cabinet," or "closet," than from the recently published posthumous article of E. R. Turner on that subject (*AHR*, XLV [1940], 761–76). Lodge was so convinced of the need for an understanding of foreign policy that he took Professor Namier severely to task for his "conspicuous omission" in this respect and for his resultant unfairness to Newcastle in his interesting review of *England in the age of the American revolution*, Vol. 1 (London, 1930), in *History*, N.S., XVI (1931), 172–76.

41. W. L. Dorn, *Competition for empire*, p. 401. In the preface of his book, Lodge contends that he was struggling against this very thing. "I was impressed by the danger that the retrospect of the past might be colored by the hostility aroused during the conflict. Against this danger—already conspicuous in the course of the war—and against the degradation of history to be the handmaid of political passion I could, at any rate, offer a passive protest."

42. For illustration: In *Great Britain and Prussia* the first four chapters contain thirteen explanatory notes, sixty references to published documents (mostly Frederick II's *Politische Correspondenz*), and sixty-three references to manuscript sources—nearly all bare references with no comment. In the later *Studies* notes are much fuller; e.g., chap. i contains thirty-three notes, of which only two are simple explana-

tions and only four are bare references to books or documents. The remaining twenty-seven contain ten references to published and twenty-four to unpublished sources and include three discussions of books or historians, as well as one German, six French, and seventeen English quotations. Nearly all contain explanatory remarks of some kind.

43. *Trans. Roy. Hist. Soc.*, 4th ser., XV, 243–69; XVI, 1–43, 211–47. There was a good deal of repetition, especially on Anglo-French relations, prior to 1740.

44. *History*, N.S., XVI (1932), 356.

45. See reviews of P. Vaucher, *Robert Walpole et la politique de Fleury* (Paris, 1924), in *EHR*, XL (1925), 438–41; of P. Geyl, *Willem IV en England tot 1748* (The Hague, 1924), in *ibid.*, pp. 616–21; or of J. F. Chance, *The alliance of Hanover* (London, 1923), in *ibid.*, XXXIX (1924), 293–97.

46. "The Polwarth papers and the Historical Manuscripts Commission," *Trans. Roy. Hist. Soc.*, 4th ser., XV, 1–43. He attacked the editor for translating French documents, for an inadequate introduction, and for a poor index. His enthusiasm for published documents led him to defend the "excerpt method" followed by the Royal Historical Society in editing the *British diplomatic instructions* (*EHR*, XLIII [1928], 433–38), in contrast to Professor Temperley's outspoken condemnation (*ibid.*, XLI [1926], 603–4).

47. *History*, N.S., XII (1928), 335; XVIII (1933), 55.

48. He visited Canada and the United States in 1924, for the Richmond meeting of the American Historical Association.

XIII

ERICH MARCKS (1861–1938)

GORDON M. STEWART*

WHEN Erich Marcks came to this country in 1913 to lecture on history at Cornell University he was told by an American colleague to be thoroughly German in his presentation of the subject. He was not to speak down to his students but to make them aware of their cultural deficiencies by showing them those aspects of the historical nature of personality, society, and the state which were typically German in their age and complexity. The assignment was a happy one. Marcks said later that he had never before rejoiced so completely in being a German. These were not the sentiments of a narrow patriot. He was sincerely interested in American life and was generous in his praise for our schools. He could not, however, avoid feeling that he was the product of a high civilization bringing light to a promising but immature new world.[1]

A review of Marcks's career down to the time when he came to America shows him to have been admirably well fitted to represent those elements in German scholarship which the world prior to 1914 had learned to admire. His training in method had been in the rigorous tradition of classical studies. When he began to write and teach he joined the group of historians who, after the war of 1870–71, had returned to Ranke's ideal of objective history written from a broad, supernatural point of view. Thus, his first works were on the French wars of religion. Although later studies dealt with German subjects, they were considered notable for their lack of bias. His published works revealed him as a master of a rich and flowing style. Finally, he was endowed with

* Chicago, Ill.

279

a genuine enthusiasm for history, which made him an engaging and stimulating lecturer.

As he spoke to his American students of Germany's development in the nineteenth century, Marcks made no effort to conceal his pride in her military power and in the leadership of Bismarck. The army, he explained, owed its importance in Germany's constitutional framework to the country's geographical position in Europe.[2] These remarks, he noticed, were met with friendly incredulity. Prussian militarism and the ideals of the Bismarckian state were hardly part of the Cornell tradition. But this was to be expected, and it added something to the joy of teaching in a foreign country to be able to talk about matters which were generally taken for granted at home.

The pleasure which Marcks took in justifying the old Reich before a critical audience was to return to him in an unexpected way. When the German monarchy fell in 1918 and the republic was formed at Weimar, the nation's leadership throughout most of the preceding century appeared to have been discredited. Bismarck's policy of building the state around a powerful and militaristic Prussia was no longer accepted generally as a model of political wisdom. Particularist, liberal, and pacifist writers found a wide market for their attacks on the old regime. To defend the great chancellor's policy against such criticism was to adopt the program of the "political historians," of whom Treitschke, Häusser, and Sybel were the greatest. This was the task which Marcks set for himself in 1920. He brought it to completion with the publication of *Der Aufstieg des Reiches*,[3] a book which glorified the Bismarckian empire. Thus it was that within his lifetime he had been an exponent of the two dominant schools of nineteenth-century German historiography, the school of Ranke and that of the "political historians." The study of his development reveals a gradual but steady shift from the former to the latter.

There was a serenity and balance to Marcks's early life which gave tone to his whole career. He was born in 1861, the year before William I called Bismarck to Berlin. His father was a successful architect; his mother, a descendant of the Huguenots who had settled in Germany.[4] As he grew up in Magdeburg he was introduced to the world of classical culture at the *Gymnasium*.[5] This led him into the study of ancient history, which he pursued at the universities of Strassburg, Bonn, and Berlin under Heinrich Nissen and Theodor Mommsen. His thesis for the Ph.D. degree, based on a study of Greek and Latin sources, was an evaluation of the classical accounts of Drusus' tribunate and the civil war of 91–89 B.C.[6] He graduated *summa cum laude* in 1884.

In addition to his work in ancient history, Marcks studied under Jacob Sturms and Hermann Baumgarten.[7] It was through the influence of these men that he developed an interest in modern history. He was especially impressed with the teaching of Baumgarten, who, though he had been a strident publicist in the days of unification, had returned to the ideals of Ranke.

Shortly after receiving his degree Marcks entered the field of Reformation history. An inherited interest in the fate of the Huguenot party took him to London and Paris to study the materials on the French wars of religion. In a letter dated Easter, 1886, he gave a charming account of his experiences in France.[8] He told of his dislike for the dusty archives, the noisy streets, and the cold, damp weather. The miserable little stove in his room was quite unequal to the task of keeping him warm. But what a change when spring came and the gay crowds thronged the Champs Élysées! The superintendent of the archives had the good sense to declare a six-day holiday during Easter week, and so, with Baedeker in hand, Marcks set out for the Huguenot towns of Orléans and La Rochelle. His enthusiasm for history, dampened, perhaps, by the arduous work and bad weather of Paris, flamed anew when he visited the buildings which had once housed the characters of his study. Standing in the Gothic hall at Amboise, he could picture Francis II and Mary Stuart trembling before the threatening Huguenots and nobles. From the documents in Paris he had reconstructed an hour-by-hour account of the conspiracy. Now he could complete the picture of the event which he had formed in his mind.

In view of what he saw in the provinces, Marcks was forced to revise his estimate of the French. They were not, he decided, the frivolous, nervous, and overcivilized race pictured by most of his compatriots who knew only the capital. Their clean towns and solid farms showed them to be honest and unaffected folk.[9]

In his study of the wars of religion Marcks became involved in the general problems of French diplomacy during that period. Finding that the meeting between Catherine de Medici and the Spanish representatives at Bayonne had never been treated satisfactorily, he interrupted his work and produced a three-hundred-page monograph on the subject, *Die Zusammenkunft von Bayonne*.[10] In it he traced the origins of the meeting, gave an analysis of Catherine's motives, and offered the thesis that its influence in French affairs had been obliterated by April, 1566. His zeal was rewarded by a very favorable review from the pen of Theodor Schott.[11] In France a somewhat less friendly view was taken of the work.[12] The author's conclusions were considered well reasoned and plausible, but it was felt that he had failed to offer sufficient evidence in their support.

Three years later, at the age of thirty-one, Marcks published the first volume of a biography of Gaspard de Coligny.[13] That he considered himself to be a full-fledged historian can be seen in the boldness of his plan. Along with the life of the Protestant hero, he set out to include a history of the Huguenot party "organically conceived."[14] Moreover, he rejected the timid practice of biographers who simply recounted the external history of their subject. His work was to be a deep introspective study.[15]

The first part of the volume deals with Coligny's life down to the year 1559. The second part, almost two-thirds, is devoted to a description of French society and a history of Calvinism. This division of the material met with enthusiastic approval in Germany.[16] In France the objection was raised that the method of including a general survey of society in a biography disrupted its unity and deprived it of any logical limits. Why, it was asked, does the author neglect the intellectual history of the Crusades and church history in the days of the early popes?[17]

While engaged in research and writing, Marcks had begun his

career as a teacher. In 1887 Heinrich von Treitschke sponsored his application for the position of lecturer in modern history at Berlin.[18] Six years later he was called to Freiburg as Privat-dozent, the advancement coming partly because of the success of his *Coligny*. In 1894 he moved on to Leipzig.[19]

In his formal acceptance of the post at Freiburg, Marcks addressed the university on the subject of Philip II. The reception given this address and others on subjects related to his work encouraged him to cultivate the form of the historical essay. When, some years later, a collection of these was published under the title *Männer und Zeiten* it proved to be his greatest popular success.[20]

Marcks next wrote a small work called *Königin Elisabeth von England*.[21] Although somewhat longer than his essays, it, too, was intended for the general public. Accordingly, he employed a new technique in composition. After months of intensive study he wrote the whole book in eleven days.[22] The result was a broad and lively account molded into a firm unity. Without limiting himself in the choice of subject matter, he had solved the problem of synthesis.

The ten years which Marcks had spent studying and writing about the age of the Reformation had been a period of rapid development. Endowed at the outset with unusual talents— Mommsen had valued him highly as a student of ancient history[23] —he had applied himself industriously to the problem of mastering historical material and presenting it. His proved ability as a historian was recognized when he was asked to write a life of William I for the *Deutsche allgemeine Biographie*.

The request came while his work in the field of the Reformation was still unfinished; yet he welcomed the chance to move into nineteenth-century German history. His interest in the period had been developing since childhood. The great events of 1866 and 1870 had been among his earliest memories.[24] As a student he had known and admired the publicist-historians Baumgarten and Treitschke. When he began teaching, his closest friends on the faculty at Berlin—Koser, Schmoller, Meinecke,

Hintze, and Naudé—were all students of Prussian history.[25] Finally, he had grown up with the name of Bismarck ringing in his ears.[26] He had caught a glimpse of the "sad but mighty" face of the chancellor at the funeral of William I.[27] Two years later he pushed through the crowd at the Stettiner Bahnhof and watched the old gentleman as he sat talking in a coach. Never had he seen such grandeur in nature or in man.[28] An interview with Bismarck in 1893 impressed him with the tragedy of the passing of such a figure from national life.[29] In the years that followed, Marcks could not avoid a feeling of uneasiness about the course of German affairs.[30] He became convinced that the country needed to capture and preserve the memory of its great leaders as a guarantee for the future.[31] Thus the biography of William I gave him the opportunity to perform what he considered to be a patriotic act.

The directors of the Bavarian Historical Commission had originally called upon Heinrich von Sybel to produce the account of the emperor's life. When Sybel died in 1895 they turned to Marcks. It was the article for the *Deutsche allgemeine Biographie* which formed the basis for his *Kaiser Wilhelm I*.[32] His research was restricted to a survey of the published sources,[33] much of his material coming from Sybel's *Begründung des deutschen Reiches durch Wilhelm I*.[34] For this reason he presented the account without footnotes. It made, nonetheless, a great impression. A French reviewer pointed to the author's psychological insight and his loyalty to the tradition of Ranke.[35] Munroe Smith, an American biographer of Bismarck, was especially impressed with the frank treatment of the less favorable side of William's character.[36] In Germany the modification of Sybel's account of the origins of the war of 1870 was looked upon as a marvel of objectivity and candor.[37] It can be said to have been his most successful book up to this time.

Marcks once wrote that every day which passed after Bismarck's death proved over again how great was the need for a biography of the chancellor.[38] In order to fill this need he had begun collecting materials for such a work around the turn of the century. In the spring of 1901 an official of the foreign office introduced him to Prince Herbert Bismarck.[39] The prince gave him invaluable help in his work: collecting documents, making available the family papers at Schönhausen and Friedrichsruh, and sending for information from numerous other sources. Other members of the family and friends of the chancellor were equally co-operative in supplying material for the biography. Because the documents took years to master, it was not until 1909 that the first volume appeared.

In his introduction Marcks stated that again his aim had been to write a well-rounded biography.[40] By this he meant that the materials had been integrated and related so as to present a portrait rather than a simple narrative. In no other work did he succeed so well in realizing this ideal.[41] Although the volume ends with Bismarck's entry into public life in 1848, Marcks's profound analysis of his formative years illuminates all his later life.

While compiling and writing his great biography Marcks had moved from Leipzig to Heidelberg, and finally to Hamburg, where, in 1907, he became one of the first appointees of the Scientific Foundation. These were his happiest and most successful days as a teacher. His lectures are said to have been "models of clarity and elegance."[42] It was his practice to read from a prepared text, but in such a way as not to lose contact with his auditors.[43] His voice was controlled; his delivery appropriate to the material.[44] Much as he admired the fire and passion of Treitschke, he remained true to himself, infusing his polished sentences with that warmth of feeling which is to be found in all of his works. Each lecture had a beginning and end; many of them were considered memorable for their unity and force.

The age of the Counter Reformation was his favorite topic.[45] The four-hour lecture which he devoted to this period has, fortunately, been printed.[46] It begins with a brilliant description of the two opposing forces of the age—Calvinism and Catholicism. Calvin and Geneva are given as symbols of the first; Loyola and Trent, as symbols of the second. A survey of the international scene is followed by discussions of the internal affairs of Spain,

France, the Low Countries, and England. Here the narration of the actual course of events begins. The unfolding of the struggle is interspersed with character sketches in the style of Ranke. Cultural, economic, and social developments are introduced into the account. As the lecture draws to a close, the material takes on a new form. The political forces active in Europe have replaced religion as the center of interest. The sweeping syntheses which appear at the beginning of the lecture are repeated at the end, but with special regard for the new state system. Religion and politics are thus balanced almost perfectly, and through the study of their mutual interplay the diverse aspects of the age are molded into a unified whole.

The students who chose to work under Marcks found him to be a master craftsman, more concerned with the development of their talents and interests than with the founding of a new school of history. The variety of subjects in the *Festschrift* dedicated to him on his sixtieth birthday bears witness to this.[47] They found, moreover, that he made it a point to be accessible to them and to cultivate them as his friends. Many of them came to know the hospitality of his home. Throughout the latter part of his career he spent hours answering letters from his former students, giving advice and encouragement and keeping alive that feeling of loyalty and friendliness which it was his genius to inspire.[48]

Marcks was extremely conscientious in upholding the standard of history. A good scholarly book called forth his warmest praise.[49] He could be appreciative of sincere and honest work of the second rank, although he was outspoken in pointing to its shortcomings.[50] When he felt called upon to deal with an author whom he considered unqualified to handle the subject under review, Marcks was most direct in his criticism. "I know," he wrote of Guilland's *L'Allemagne nouvelle et ses historiens*, "that my demands are high, but historiography requires that one who undertakes to generalize about such difficult and intricate things must have a sound knowledge of facts, not just a nodding acquaintance with them."[51]

It appears that Marcks rarely became involved in academic

quarrels. His was an irenic disposition. This was fortunate, for he grew up in a world famous for its bitter disputes. Baumgarten and Treitschke had been at each other's throats over the question of the latter's disregard for truth in writing his great history. Mommsen had stood out against Bismarck after the unification of Germany had swept most of the historians into the chancellor's camp. In writing about these disputes Marcks displayed a high degree of tact and good will.[52] It was perhaps this quality, along with his ability as a teacher and author, which won for him the position he held in academic circles. Years ago Guy Stanton Ford wrote that "no other living German historian with the possible exception of Professor Schmoller is so universally respected by his colleagues, to whatever school they may belong."[53] There is no reason to believe that this opinion changed in later years.

Marcks was apparently as fortunate in his private life as he was in his career as a historian. His wife, the former Friederike von Sellin, bore him three sons and a daughter. Their home was far more than a mere adjunct to the university. A lively interest in contemporary painting led them to cultivate the artists Leopold von Kalckreuth and Ludwig von Hoffmann, in addition to the many friends they had in the academic world.[54]

An interest in world-affairs led Marcks to contribute to the public discussion of the issues facing Germany in a number of speeches and articles. The statesman, he believed, must be left to make decisions in specific instances. As a historian, he sought merely to "connect the past with the present and illuminate the one with the other."[55]

He expressed the uneasiness which he felt about the course of German development in an address entitled *England and Germany, their relations in the great crises of European history, 1500–1900*, which he gave in London in 1900 and which was subsequently printed both in German and English. In the introduction to the German edition he spoke of a "lack of moderation in our public discussion."[56] The strained relations with England caused him concern, for he believed that "a certain historical and intellectual, and perhaps also political community," existed between the two countries.[57] These views did not, by any means, lead him into a liberal or pacifist position. He was proud of the "decidedly monarchical"[58] constitution of Germany and saw imperialism as the path of glory and strength to be followed in the future.[59] He knew the dangers involved in challenging the position of England in the world; and, though he hoped for a peaceful issue in the coming competition for lands and markets, he advised his countrymen to give full support to the army and navy.[60]

After the outbreak of the war of 1914 Marcks charged England with having entered the conflict in cold blood.[61] Russia, Germany, Austria, and France had legitimate historical reasons for war. The issue would be decided by earnest and serious fighting, but it would not involve the terrible hate which Germany felt for England. Her entry into the war was a crime committed in the name of selfishness and pride. She was close to Germany in race, institutions, cultural heritage, and religion. How could such action be explained? There was but one answer: the war on England's part was attempted fratricide.

Marcks believed that the war was the final stage in Germany's growth.[62] In 1866 Prussia had become dominant in Germany; in 1870 Germany had become a European power; and in the war of 1914 she would become a world-power.

The sacrifices demanded of his countrymen, and perhaps the loss of his eldest son during the first months of fighting, convinced Marcks that merely to understand the nature of the conflict was not enough. It was, of course, necessary to "connect the past with the present," and he sought to do this by speaking in public and writing for the periodical press. He was certain, however, that in turning to the past one could find inspiration as well as understanding. Germany, in her life and death struggle, must be led and encouraged by the memory of her greatest leader, Otto von Bismarck. The long, contemplative biography which he had begun would not be finished for years and could hardly be expected to command a very wide audience. Marcks decided, therefore, to write a "report" (*Bericht*) of Bismarck's life.[63] After years of study he was steeped in the materials relating to the chancellor's career. Thus it was that he was able to complete his famous "report" in six weeks, almost entirely from memory.[64] It was entitled *Otto von Bismarck, ein Lebensbild*, and was published in 1915.

In some respects the "report" is the most remarkable book he ever wrote. The flamboyant and leisurely style of his earlier and later works is nowhere in evidence. It is an outpouring of information. The sentences are short; the paragraphs, tightly knit. Yet there is a satisfying completeness about it. Although the narration of the chancellor's career moves on at a headlong pace, it is supported by a simple but adequate outline of the history of the period. It apparently gave Marcks great satisfaction to be able to create a truly popular work about Bismarck. He is said to have regarded it as the best book he ever wrote.[65]

The war stimulated Marcks. Hard as it was to witness the terrible loss of life and the growth of prejudice and hate, he was, in a way, prepared for it. The peace which brought defeat, revolution, and privation found him, at first, unprepared. A new world had sprung up around him. In presenting his views he was prone to refer to himself as a member of the older generation, as a man who had not changed with the times.[66] "I am a historian," he said, "who in his personal feelings is accustomed to live in the days of Bismarck, that is, in the glorious heights of our past."[67] The great biography, which was from his point of view a confession of faith, lay unfinished, for it required a sympathetic audience. Writing about it to a friend, he said: "My deepest emotions have not changed. Can they find expression in a changed world?"[68]

Although Marcks's longing for pre-war Germany was doubly strong, since he was both a monarchist and a creative writer who identified himself with the period, this did not lead him into the camp of the pessimists. In the darkest days of the breakdown, when the productive machinery of the country was crippled and France threatened invasion, he counseled patience and, above all, elasticity.[69] Recovery, he believed, would be slow.[70] The disloyalty of the workers, political particularism, and pacifism, "the most baneful of all social forces,"[71] stood in the way. There were, however, more encouraging elements in the picture which were not to be overlooked. The political structure bequeathed by Bismarck was still intact. Economically the nation was unified as never before. The rising generation impressed one with its keenness.[72] Finally, no nation with a past as great as Germany's could be thoroughly disheartened. Even in her darkest hours Germany had reason to be proud of her record.[73]

Turning to the past, Marcks dwelt on the days of the Great Elector, Frederick II, the War of Liberation, and Bismarck. Prussia and Germany, he declared, owed their greatness to a successful foreign policy.[74] If the nation would rise again, it must look abroad for its opportunities. These were not far to seek. England's grip on the continent would relax, for her chief interest was in her empire and the unsolved social problems at home.[75] France, "the real Napoleon of the twentieth century,"[76] would split the entente by her policy of ruthless aggression.[77] If Germany could but find a ruler to embody the unified will of the nation, she could again assume her rightful position in the affairs of Europe and the world.[78]

It was with such thoughts in mind that Marcks began his last great work, *Der Aufstieg des Reiches*, in 1920. The very title suggests its pertinency to the times. In it he hoped to trace the history of Germany from 1807 to 1890.[79] Although the material was by no means new to him, he went about his task with painstaking care. After his retirement in 1928 he worked under severe pressure. His strength was declining, and he was forced to disregard bodily pain in order to continue his research and writing.[80] As it was, he was unable to carry the main body of the account past the year 1871. His treatment of the period 1871 to 1878 was handled in a single chapter, and the remainder of Bismarck's official career was omitted.

The book which cost Marcks the enjoyment of a restful old age has been called his greatest contribution to historical literature.[81] If anything could fill the gap left by his unfinished biography of Bismarck, it is probably the second volume of *Der Auf-*

stieg, which covers the period from 1862 to 1871. Bismarck holds the center of the stage throughout the whole account. The treatment is not that of the biography, since the personal side of the chancellor's career is almost entirely omitted. Yet one may safely say that the two books, taken together, present the complete Bismarck. The period of formation, described intimately, is balanced by an account of the period of greatest activity, treated as history.

The question naturally arises why Marcks did not simply continue the biography. It has already been suggested that he found it difficult to express his deepest feelings in the uncongenial atmosphere of the Weimar Republic; and that, as a monarchist, he turned to history to defend the unification of the nation under the Prussian crown. It may well be that the most compelling reason for leaving the biography and starting work on *Der Aufstieg* was his concern for the future. The "political historians" had hoped to inspire and direct action by writing the nation's history at a time when they looked forward to a fundamental change in the constitution. It is the writer's opinion that Marcks accepted their program and ideals after 1918 because he considered the republic unsatisfactory and ephemeral and hoped for the establishment of a more unified state.

The publication of Heinrich Ritter von Srbik's *Deutsche Einheit* in 1935 naturally invited comparison between the two books. Srbik wrote from the *gesamtdeutsch* point of view, making out a better case for Austria than is customary in the writing of German history. The reviewers seem to agree that Marcks differed from Srbik more in approach than in spirit.[82] He was fair to the Austrians; but since he regarded the Bismarckian empire as fully justified in its time, his choice of materials was naturally different from that of the Austrian historian.

Except for two lines in the introduction which state that the Third Reich is carrying on the traditions of the past, there is nothing in *Der Aufsteig* to suggest that it was completed in the time of Hitler.[83] Marcks bore somewhat the same relation to Nazi historiography as Hindenburg did to the dictatorship. He accepted the idea of authoritarianism, but he was not certain that the National Socialists were the right people to lead Germany. In 1932 he penned a fulsome sentence describing them as

the raging and unstemmed current; the offspring of all the political, cultural, economic, and social maladjustment which has bedeviled Germany during the last decade; growing at a mad pace in reaction against these conditions; motivated by patriotic feeling and social bewilderment; fed and strengthened by privation and wrong; increased by a fighting enthusiasm for Germanism, fatherland, and unity; enlarged beyond bounds by the fall of the middle class; pushed on to the extreme by anger and scorn, by radical will to reform and naïve utopianism; a movement of noble passion, but not without dregs, full of youthful drive, sacrifice, and hope; noble and wild forces shoulder to shoulder; a wonderful organization of the masses, ready to give and ready to act, but undisciplined and, from the point of view of the state, dangerous.[84]

Hitler he regarded as a pure-minded agitator and a gifted party politician, unqualified to lead the nation in such a time of stress.[85] The formation of the *junker* cabinet under Franz von Papen greatly pleased him, for he believed that the dynamic forces of National Socialism could, under strong leadership, be brought into the service of the nation.[86]

This was Marck's last printed statement before the Nazis came into power. There is reason to believe that after January, 1933, he accepted Hitler as the true leader of Germany.[87]

In the fall of 1938 Marcks died. With the exception of the biography of William I, not one of his major works was completed. He left the study of Coligny's life to begin his *Wilhelm I.* and *Bismarck.* The latter was dropped after the war when he undertook the writing of *Der Aufstieg.* In each case the new work that he took up bore a distinct relation to his view of the world around him. The general trend of his development suggests two elements in his character which may be mentioned in partial explanation of the fact that he wrote history appropriate to the times. One was an increasing patriotism. As long as he lived, he remained loyal to the Germany he had known in his youth. As he saw conditions change, he felt compelled to do what he could to maintain the old order of society and, after 1918, to bring Germany back to the position of a great power in Europe. The other was a profound artistic sense. In his historical writings Marcks expressed his innermost feelings. As these became clarified under the pressure of a changing world, he shifted from one subject to the next in order to give them adequate expression. In reviewing his career one is impressed with the fact that, although his greatest works are unfinished, he fulfilled himself to a remarkable degree in his writings.

The academic career which he began in Berlin took him to Freiburg, Leipzig, Heidelberg, Hamburg, Munich, and finally back to Berlin. In addition to writing and teaching, he served from time to time as an editor and was a member of several commissions and boards.[88] The ultimate importance of his busy and productive life cannot be estimated. An analysis of his method and thought may, however, throw some light on the matter.

The foundation stones upon which good history rests are the documents. Marcks was thoroughly trained in their use. As some of his books are without footnotes, it is impossible to know in every instance what sources he used. It is said, however, that he never considered his ability as a writer to be an excuse for poor workmanship. In all his books, according to those competent to judge, the evidence of careful research is to be found.[89]

The limitations of his sources are usually indicated. When he made use of noncontemporary documents their nature and degree of reliability was frankly stated. If an apocryphal story was worth telling, he told it as a story, not as a fact. When conjecture could suggest what might have occurred, he gave his opinion but made clear that no historical material could be found to bear him out.

The greatest feat that he performed in finding and marshaling information was in the writing of his *Bismarck*. Every imaginable type of material was used: stories, legends, newspapers, letters, and records. The truly amazing element in his work is not the amount of the material but the way in which it was used. At no time does the reader feel that the order, emphasis, or tone of the text is dictated by the sources.

In writing, Marcks generally adhered to the narrative form of arrangement. Periodization is based upon what seem to be the epochs in the development of the subject. One chapter may deal with a period of two years, another with twenty. The narrative, from time to time, is dropped in order to introduce explanatory material or to summarize and interpret an intricate course of events. In his scholarly works he never sacrificed completeness for the sake of simplicity; nor did he, on the other hand, forget the reader who is finding his way through the material for the first time.

In determining the emphasis to be placed on the various aspects of the subject, Marcks used a technique as a biographer which differed considerably from that which he employed as a historian. In *Bismarck*, *Coligny*, and *Wilhelm I.* he attempted to do four things: to give a sound account of the subject's life, to penetrate into his psychology, to relate him to the period in which he lived, and to show his historical importance.

The narrative is the form around which the other elements of the biography are grouped, but it is not of first importance. Facts are included more for their significance in the interpretation of the character than because they were considered of some consequence at the time they occurred. Sometimes, indeed, there is almost a scarcity of factual material. In the case of *Bismarck*, Marcks assumed a fairly complete knowledge of the period on the part of the reader and felt free to allude to episodes and stories without recounting them. Something is doubtless lost to one whose store of information is inadequate; yet the effect of familiarity, the very boldness of such a procedure, lends great vitality to the portrait.

His chief interest as a biographer was in presenting a psychological study of motivation. That he was considered highly successful in this has already been indicated. Certainly he was far from timid in what he attempted. "I demand of the biographer," he wrote, "that he have the courage to go beyond the external and visual aspects of his subject and present completely and without restraint the vivid picture of the personality which has come to him intuitively."[90]

The best illustration of Marcks's method is in the famous description of Bismarck's religious conversion. This was not an easy task. One need only recall the widely varying interpretations of Luther's early life to realize the extreme difficulty an author encounters in presenting this most elusive element in man's emotional and intellectual constitution. In the case of Luther one can choose between the certainty of the believer in spiritual determinism, the unction of the institutionalist, the analysis of the intellectual historian, and the findings of the psychologist. Marcks shunned any of these approaches in his treatment of Bismarck and chose to present a warm introspective study. First, the spiritual difficulties of the young Junker are described in detail: his restlessness and lack of adjustment; his loneliness after a number of unsuccessful love affairs; his interest in Spinozistic rationalism and his feeling of its inadequacy as a philosophy of life. Thus the stage is set for the entrance of Blankenburg and Maria von Thadden, who were to introduce him to pietism. So delicate and penetrating is the account of Bismarck's relations with these earnest people that one almost feels transplanted into the dreamy world of Wilhelm Meister. For a time the masterful young aristocrat gives way to the romantic German. The experience was a profound one. In presenting it in its full intensity and beauty, Marcks has shed light on all of Bismarck's subsequent career. That the chancellor was a man of faith can be discovered in any account of his life, but the quality of his religious experience has never been so ably described.

Although Marcks was invariably impressed with the uniqueness of a great personality, he did not neglect the less distinguished persons who lived close to the giants of history whom he chose to study. There is breadth and fulness in all of his works. Brilliant portraits abound in the *Coligny* and *Elisabeth*. The intellectual and spiritual struggles of Bismarck's contemporaries are introduced to balance the section dealing with his own inner life. Indeed, the claim has been made that the biography is a significant contribution to the history of romanticism.[91]

The historical importance of the subject is suggested by references to the past and the future and to the political framework of the contemporary world. The biographer never completely eclipses the historian. The continuity of historical development in time and the interplay of forces across the face of Europe are never forgotten. Marcks mastered the history of a period as a prerequisite to writing biography.

The range of materials which he included in his history follows the pattern set by Ranke and Treitschke. Political and intellectual phenomena, supported by numerous biographical studies, make up the bulk of his history. The emphasis which he placed on the various elements in society was dictated by three considerations. First, the state was looked upon as the highest form of social organization, and therefore his whole account is built around political history. Second, the period itself determined, to some extent, the relative importance of the other elements included. In the age of religious wars the church looms large in the account; later it assumes a position of less importance. Never, however, does he reflect the characteristics of a period in perfect balance. This is because of his third criterion, an organic and generic conception of society. As in the case of his biographical works, in which the child and the schoolboy are treated in the light of the author's understanding of the man, so, in his history, the various forces at work in any one period are seen in the perspective of their later development.

There is no evidence in any of Marcks's scholarly works that he skimmed over or slighted material simply because it was difficult to grasp or hard to explain. Indeed, from the point of view of content alone, Marcks is heavy reading. Yet, the presentation of intricate phases of diplomatic, constitutional, military, and theological history is rarely pedantic. In describing either the defense of St. Quentin in 1557 or the theology of Calvin, he does not struggle along with the obvious help of secondary sources. He is sure-footed, free, and opinionated. His reasoning is forceful, and his summaries clear. For pure elegance of thought and exposition his complicated passages are by far the most enjoyable.

Karl Alexander von Müller has called Marcks the greatest

artist of his generation of German historians.[92] It is true that in his works he strove for fine effects and a polished style. His sentences, except in the "report" of Bismarck's life which he wrote during the war, bear the mark of the older German academic idiom. They are often massive, full of ideas packed into a succession of clauses. His paragraphs would do as chapters in a novel, some of them running for five or six large pages. Yet, if the framework is heavy, the content is, at times, lively. The epigram and the well-turned phrase appear frequently, especially in his later works. There is sly humor in his description of the town of Kassel, in which he listed its characteristics as, "poetry and humility, purity and narrowness."[93] Flashes of this sort stand in sharp relief, for the general tone of Marcks's text is mellow and serious. It is impossible here to quote at sufficient length to give the impression one gains from reading *Der Aufstieg*. The paragraphs, huge as they are, have an organic unity. It is not uncommon for them to begin with a long recitation of facts and then gradually to gain in freedom as the interpretative passages are introduced. By a skilful selection and arrangement of details Marcks is able to command the reader's attention at the outset and, indeed, to create a degree of suspense regarding his comments on the material. The full richness of his prose is displayed, however, in the purely interpretative sections. Working within the frame of reference which he has carefully constructed, he is able to use a suggestive and allusional style and to attain a striking intensity and warmth.

At times he was obviously carried away with his subject. It was then that he employed extravagant phrases which recall the great period of romantic literature in Germany. Hegel, for instance, "carried his banner from Heidelberg to Berlin";[94] the music of Schubert and Weber expressed the "restless yearning of the German heart."[95] Philip II "embodied the tragedy of his warm-blooded southern people," and his influence was "more a power of death than of life."[96]

Certain words, high in emotional content, appear often in his works. They were not chosen merely for effect. Marcks confessed that he could not write on some subjects with a feeling of inner coldness.[97] The question naturally arises whether he was able to combine his warmth of feeling with accuracy and reliability. The answer, in part, is that his works show careful research and a high degree of professional integrity. In this matter he followed his old teacher Herman Baumgarten, who was noted for his "passionate sense of justice."[98] A conservative, a Protestant, a monarchist, and a Prussian partisan, he described the limitations of William I without hesitation and praised the achievements of Philip II, Friedrich Ebert, and Stresemann. In reading *Der Aufstieg des Reiches* one is impressed with the fact that Marcks is more than just in treating characters with whom he disagreed fundamentally. His deep feeling for Germany made it impossible for him to hate or scorn any part of it. The two negative acts which combined to make the Bismarckian empire possible—the frustration of the hopes of 1848 and the exclusion of Austria from Germany—are treated with firm loyalty to the victorious parties but with deep sympathy for the defeated.

In the field of biography Marcks's bias is perfectly evident. He admired Bismarck intensely. As a historian he tried to be frank about his subject's shortcomings. There are certain aspects of the chancellor's career, however, which he treated lightly because they did not seem to represent the true Bismarck. Eberhard Gothien pointed with keenness to Marcks's description of the Aachen period as an illustration of this type of writing.[99] On the other hand, his defense of Bismarck in the matter of the Ems dispatch comes close to special pleading. One feels that his practice of writing introspective and highly interpretative biographies led him of necessity into a type of distortion.

Marcks did not base his writings upon a systematic philosophy of history. He rejected the title of *Geschichtsphilosoph* emphatically and claimed that he was merely a historian who interpreted the past on the basis of documents.[100] As an artist, he disliked theorizing. At one time, indeed, he refused to talk about the nature of history because, he said, too many of his colleagues had become entangled in the problem of analysis.[101] Although he felt a certain sympathy for those who sought evidence of supernatural forces acting in human affairs, he was certain that the discipline of history had nothing to do with such explanations.[102]

It is possible, nonetheless, to discover a number of ideas about the nature of history which he developed in the course of his studies and used in explaining the past. They occur most frequently in his essays, in which he achieved a level of abstraction not common to his more scholarly works. For the sake of clarity they will be presented in a simple and straightforward form, which must, of necessity, do violence to the author's fine shadings of emphasis and meaning.

In the first place, Marcks believed that the future could be regarded as undetermined. Man is free, but he is free only within certain bounds. Geographic and economic factors limit his activity. The great deeds of history cannot, however, be explained in purely materialist terms. For an understanding of them, one must grasp the nature of the state and its rulers.

Marcks treated the state as an animate being. The characteristics of the national state are those of the race, and the race is closely rooted to the soil. The life of the state is like the life of the individual. Some states are vigorous; some are inert. Some have the enthusiasm of youth; others, the timid hesitancy of old age. A tired state wants peace; a restless one demands war. It is in an aggressive foreign policy that the state expresses its personality and brings to itself the greatest blessings of internal progress. The very essence of the state is the will to power. Because he believed this, Marcks feared any form of weakness. The liberals of 1848 carried their policy beyond the limits of patriotism and endangered the future of the state. Thus it was right that they should fail. Labor politics, pacifism, and communism are diseases which must be cured in order that expansion and healthy progress may continue. When war comes, the individual, in sacrificing his life for the state, loses his small individuality and passes into a higher union with the totality. The state, then, has a mystical quality, not unlike the church.

In times of stress men lay hold of the spiritual powers of the state, and in doing so they find within themselves the moral strength of the great leaders of the past. Frederick II was not far from the battlefields of Saxony in 1813, and Bismarck stood close to men during the last years of the war of 1914. Such leaders are able to influence and guide the future, for in their days of greatest activity they embodied the state itself. Marcks believed that they themselves were conscious of this and that the highest interests of the state became identified with their own interests.[103] He did not mean that they saw into the future or served some remote goal. The Hohenzollern rulers who were obsessed with greed for power showed great statesmanship, for their interests were those of the state. Those who wished to rule in peace were statesmen of the second rank.

Since the leader and the state do, in fact, become identified, it is not possible to understand the former by viewing him simply as a man. In his biography Marcks dealt with the day-to-day life of Bismarck. He insisted, however, that the true meaning of the Iron Chancellor is not to be grasped by visiting him at Friedrichsruh and seeing what he ate and drank and how he read his newspaper during a conversation. The heroic statue which dominates the port of Hamburg shows his real significance. The details of his features are indistinguishable; the man recedes; and the massive bulk of the leader, the symbol, alone remains.[104]

The race must cherish and preserve the memory of its great, for in their lives the direction of the future has been given. Marcks believed in the power of ideas. A good part of *Coligny* and *Der Aufstieg* is given over to intellectual history. The greatest ideas, however, are those which carry the strength of the nation's leaders into the life of the people. Goethe and Bismarck are, for Germany, the supreme guides. Similar in some respects, but essentially antagonistic, they represent the two basic components of the nation's glorious future.[105]

Marcks had a low opinion of the "scientific" type of analysis in the study of social phenomena. "True reality," he wrote, "more real than any types we may construct, is still the individual. Woe unto that concept of human things which forgets this."[106] Whether actually he has freed himself from types and categories may be questioned. His books are studded with brilliant character sketches. Movements are understood in terms of their leaders, and nations epitomized by their rulers. It is not a far cry from the classifications of the sociologist to the use of representative men. One feels, at times, that history is a play in which the symbolic significance of the characters is of more importance than their given parts. Roon is the embodiment of traditional aristocratic Prussianism; Wellington and Hindenburg are the great conservatives who carry the ways of the past into a changing world; and David Hansemann is the smart, aggressive, middle-class capitalist. Junkerdom, conservatism, and liberalism are not referred to as movements so often as they are introduced in the persons of their leaders. It must, in justice, be pointed out that, although Marcks did not escape a type of implicit classification, he did avoid the mistake of transferring categories uncritically from one discipline to another. His categories are the creations of his own mind and carry the full force of his thought and imagination.

The very personal nature of Marcks's history is, perhaps, its best guarantee for survival in the future. Its scientific value is, of course, high. Much of the research which he did will not have to be done over again for a long time. Even his *Wilhelm I.*, which was written before the opening of the archives, is said to be unequaled to the present day. Yet it is true that eventually more accurate history will be written. When that time comes Marcks will be read for his fine imaginative insight and for the ideas and feelings which he expressed at a given stage in Germany history.

In writing about Friedrich Schlosser, a liberal historian of the first half of the nineteenth century, Marcks made the comment that he approached the discipline of history with preconceived ideas.[107] On the basis of the Kantian categorical imperatives Schlosser damned the rulers and aristocrats of the preceding generation to the inferno of his works. In reading of such a feat, one cannot avoid the feeling that, although history should be more than an uncritical and universal damnation, the old liberal did exhibit a certain crude dignity in performing his task. His personal convictions in the realm of ethics and philosophy rendered him independent of the standards set by the world. It is exactly this element of independence which is lacking in Marcks's treatment of nineteenth-century German history. He regarded Bismarck as the greatest teacher historians could have. "If we do not learn from him," he wrote, "we are hopeless."[108] To judge the chancellor in the light of historical knowledge would be presumptuous. To Marcks's way of thinking, it appeared far more seemly to judge history in the light of a knowledge of Bismarck. It would be foolish to claim that there is not much to be learned from the great German statesman. There is, however, much which must be repudiated. In omitting to do the latter, Marcks displayed the one great weakness in his history. As an artist he was able to re-create the past as few have done it. As a diligent historian he based his works on sound and extensive research. Had he been able to free himself sufficiently from the past to render an independent and unique judgment of it, his works might well have ranked with the greatest in historical literature.

NOTES

1. *Männer und Zeiten* (5th ed., Leipzig, 1918), I, 407–35.
2. *Ibid.*, p. 425.
3. 2 vols.; Stuttgart and Berlin, 1936.
4. Arnold Oskar Meyer, "Erich Marcks Nachruf," *Forschungen zur brandenburgischen und preussischen Geschichte*, LI (1939), 168.
5. K. Stählin, "Erich Marcks zum Gedächtnis," *HZ*, CLX (1939), 496.
6. *Die Überlieferung des Bundesgenossenkreiges 91–89 v. Chr.* (Marburg, 1884).
7. Stählin, *loc. cit.*, p. 496.
8. *Männer und Zeiten* (3d ed.; Leipzig, 1912), I, 85–93.
9. *Ibid.*, p. 88.
10. Strassburg, 1889.
11. *HZ*, LXIV (1890), 306.
12. *RH*, XLI (1889), 418.
13. *Gaspard von Coligny* (Stuttgart, 1892)
14. *Ibid.*, p. vi.
15. *Ibid.*, p. v.
16. *HZ*, LXXV (1896), 522.
17. *RH*, LII (1893), 391.
18. Stählin, *loc. cit.*, p. 497.
19. *Ibid.*

20. 1st ed.; Leipzig, 1911.
21. Bielfeld and Leipzig, 1897.
22. Meyer, *loc. cit.*, p. 172.
23. *Ibid.*, p. 169.
24. Stählin, *loc. cit.*, p. 502.
25. *Ibid.*
26. *Männer und Zeiten* (1912), II, 34.
27. *Ibid.*, pp. 34–35.
28. *Ibid.*, p. 35.
29. *Ibid.*, p. 52.
30. *Geschichte und Gegenwart* (Berlin and Leipzig, 1925), p. 148.
31. *Männer und Zeiten* (1912), II, 28.
32. Leipzig, 1897.
33. Stählin, *loc. cit.*, p. 505.
34. Munich and Leipzig, 1889.
35. *RH*, LXXI (1899), 394.
36. *AHR*, III (1898), 725.
37. *HZ*, LXXXII (1899), 316.
38. *Bismarck eine Biographie.* Vol. I, *Bismarcks Jugend 1815–1848* (Stuttgart and Berlin, 1909), p. vii. A second volume has appeared posthumously but could not be obtained for the preparation of this article: *Bismarck und die deutsche Revolution 1848–1851* (Stuttgart, 1940).
39. *Ibid.*, p. x.
40. *Ibid.*, p. viii.
41. Cf. *AHR*, XVI (1910), 127; *EHR*, XXV (1910), 622; *HZ*, CIV (1910), 322.
42. *AHR*, XLIV (1939), 479.
43. Meyer, *loc. cit.*, p. 172.
44. Stählin, *loc. cit.*, p. 496.
45. Meyer, *loc. cit.*, p. 172.
46. "Die Gegenreformation in Westeuropa," *Propyläen Weltgeschichte* (Berlin, 1930), V, 217–314. For another excellent example of his pedagogical skill see also "Bismarck und die Bismarck-Literatur des letzten Jahres," *Deutsche Rundschau*, LXXXXIX (1899), 37–66, 240–80.
47. *Vom staatlichen Werden und Wesen* (Stuttgart, 1921).
48. Stählin, *loc. cit.*, p. 531.
49. See review of Paul Herre, *Papstum und Papstwahl im Zeitalter Philips II.* (Leipzig, 1907), in *HZ*, CIV (1910), 151.
50. See review of Baron Alphonse de Ruble, *Le traité de Cateau-Cambrésis* (Paris, 1899), in *HZ*, LXIV (1890), 303.
51. *Männer und Zeiten* (1912), I, 320.
52. Cf. Marck's introduction to Hermann Baumgarten, *Historische und politische Aufsätze und Reden* (Strassburg, 1894). See also *Männer und Zeiten* (1912), I, 305–13.
53. *AHR*, XVII (1912), 834.
54. Karl Alexander von Müller, *Zwölf Historikerprofile* (Stuttgart and Berlin, 1935), p. 18.
55. *England and Germany, their relations in the great crises of European history, 1500–1900.* London, Edinburgh, and Oxford, 1920), pp. 5–6. This essay, along with others

dealing with British foreign policy since the time of Elizabeth, has recently been re-printed in *Englands Machtpolitik: Vorträge und Studien* (Stuttgart, 1939).

56. *Ibid.*, p. 6.
57. *Ibid.*, p. 4.
58. *Ibid.*, p. 42.
59. *Männer und Zeiten* (1912), II, 313.
60. *Ibid.*, p. 282.
61. *Ibid.* (1918), II, 293.
62. *Ibid.*, p. 289.
63. *Otto von Bismarck, ein Lebensbild* (Stuttgart, 1915), p. vii.
64. *Ibid.*
65. Stählin, *loc. cit.*, p. 513.
66. *Geschichte und Gegenwart*, p. 3.
67. *Ibid.*, p. 83.
68. Stählin, *loc. cit.*, pp. 512–13.
69. *Geschichte und Gegenwart*, p. 167.
70. *Ibid.*, p. 87.
71. *Ibid.*, p. 99.
72. *Ibid.*, p. 101–2.
73. *Ibid.*, p. 107.
74. *Ibid.*, p. 111.
75. *Ibid.*, p. 112.
76. *Ibid.*, p. 79.
77. *Ibid.*, p. 163.
78. Erich Marcks and Karl Alexander von Müller (eds.), *Meister der Politik* (Stuttgart and Berlin, 1923), I, vi.
79. Müller, p. 20.
80. Stählin, *loc. cit.*, p. 529.
81. Meyer, *loc. cit.*, p. 168.
82. *Historisches Jahrbuch*, LVIII (1938), 463; *Historische Vierteljahrschrift*, XXXI (1939), 787; *JMH*, IX (1937), 523.
83. *JMH*, IX (1937), 523.
84. Erich Marcks and Ernst von Eisenhart Rothe, *Paul von Hindenburg als Mensch, Staatsmann, Feldherr* (Berlin, 1932), p. 65.
85. *Ibid.*, p. 69.
86. *Ibid.*, p. 73.
87. Stählin, *loc. cit.*, p. 526.
88. Marcks founded the *Heidelberger Abhandlungen zur mittleren und neuen Geschichte*. He edited: *Deutsche Zeitschrift für Geschichtswissenschaft; Leipziger Studien aus dem Gebiet der Geschichte; Karl August, Darstellungen und Briefe zur Geschichte des weimarischen Fürstenhauses und Landes* (Berlin, 1915——); *Meister der Politik* (with K. A. von Müller) (3 vols.; Stuttgart and Berlin, 1923–24). He was a member of the historical commissions of Saxony and Baden and of the Berlin Academy of Science, secretary of the historical class of the Bavarian Academy of Science, president of the Munich Historical Commission, and Prussian historiographer.
89. Meyer, *loc. cit.*, p. 170.
90. *Coligny*, p. v.

91. Meyer, *loc. cit.*, p. 174.
92. Müller, p. 17.
93. *Der Aufstieg des Reiches*, I, 112.
94. *Ibid.*, p. 117.
95. *Ibid.*, p. 115.
96. *Männer und Zeiten* (1912), I, 22.
97. *Der Aufstieg des Reiches*, I, xvi.
98. Meyer, *loc. cit.*, p. 169.
99. *HZ*, CIV (1910), 329.
100. *Geschichte und Gegenwart*, p. 111.
101. *Männer und Zeiten* (1912), I, 3.
102. *Ibid.*, p. 161.
103. *Ibid.*, p. 172.
104. *Paul von Hindenburg*, p. 75.
105. *Männer und Zeiten* (1912), II, 28.
106. *Ibid.*
107. "Ludwig Häusser und die politische Geschichtschreibung in Heidelberg," *Heidelberger Professoren aus dem 19. Jahrhundert* (Heidelberg, 1903), I, 292.
108. *Männer und Zeiten* (1912), II, 34.

XIV

ALBERT MATHIEZ (1874–1932)

FRANCES ACOMB*

ALBERT MATHIEZ was born of peasant stock on January 10, 1874, at La Bruyère in Haute-Saône. If he left memoirs they have not been published and the more personal and private aspect of his life has yet to be reconstructed by some diligent researcher. Friends and associates have, however, furnished us with some record of his career and some testimony regarding his personality and his interests.[1] The record begins with adulthood. Mathiez, after attending a series of provincial *lycées*, entered the École Normale Supérieure in 1894 and left it as *agrégé* in 1897. Following a short interlude in the provinces, he was admitted to the Fondation Thiers, remaining there from 1900 until 1902. At this time he became a student of Alphonse Aulard and under Aulard's direction wrote the theses for which in 1904 he received the degree of *docteur ès lettres* from the Sorbonne. The major thesis was *La théophilanthropie et le culte décadaire, 1796–1801; essai sur l'histoire religieuse de la Révolution;*[2] the minor one, *Les origines des cultes révolutionnaires (1789–1792).*[3] Mathiez then became a teacher in the Lycée Voltaire, where he remained until 1911, with two short interruptions during which he was substitute instructor (*suppléant*) on the faculties of Caen and Nancy, respectively. Meantime he had broken with Aulard and founded the Société des Études Robespierristes, becoming editor of its journal, a new organ, the *Annales révolutionnaires.* In 1924, by amalgamation with the *Revue historique de la Révolution française*, it became the *Annales historiques de la Révolution française.*

* Dorothy Bridgman Atkinson Fellow (1941–42), American Association of University Women.

This journal was, in its earlier years, almost a single-handed enterprise, and Mathiez himself always remained one of the principal contributors, as well as editor. In 1911, in consequence of his now growing reputation, Mathiez was appointed to the faculty of the University of Besançon, where he remained until the close of the year 1919. He was not drafted for service during the war, it is said, because he had lost the sight of one eye.[4] His interest in scholarly output was not diminished by the war; indeed, it was stimulated. The *Annales* and the Société des Études Robespierristes were suspended for a while, but in 1916 they were revived. A vigorous critic of the war dictatorship, although not an opponent of the war, Mathiez only narrowly escaped the censorship.[5] This activity as critic, coupled with his defense of Bolshevism, is generally believed to have been the reason why, when Aulard resigned from his chair at the Sorbonne in 1924, Mathiez was passed over in favor of Philippe Sagnac.[6] To Mathiez it was always a cross that so much of his life had to be spent in the provinces and that he could work in the great Parisian archives only during the vacations.[7] But he was to receive his reward. Professor at the University of Dijon from 1919, he was, in 1926, called to the Sorbonne as *suppléant* for M. Sagnac, who was to be absent in Egypt. When Sagnac returned, Mathiez was retained as assistant lecturer (*chargé de cours*). He had little more than five years in Paris. Suddenly, on February 25, 1932, in the course of delivering a lecture, he was stricken and died.

Not long afterward there appeared in *La Révolution française*, organ of the late Alphonse Aulard and of the Société de l'Histoire de la Révolution Française, the following curious eulogy, spoken at the annual assembly of the society by Pierre Caron, its general secretary. Caron said:

Another name upon our lists is to be marked with the obituary cross—that of Albert Mathiez, assistant lecturer at the Sorbonne, deceased February 25th last. In truth, actually estranged from us since 1908 because of incidents it would be out of place to recall today, he had ceased to be a colleague to become simply a subscriber, and I might omit any allusion to the sudden stroke which carried him off under the dramatic circumstances of which you are aware. But I am loath to maintain a silence which could be attributed to a lack of serenity. Death must efface personal injuries. Questionable as have been and remain certain of the theses which he defended with so much ardor, the man who has just gone from us played for thirty years, in the realm of our studies, a role of the first rank, the importance of which only prejudice could deny. We give to the memory of Albert Mathiez the homage due to that of a relentless worker, a great inspirer [*remueur*] of ideas and of minds, entirely devoted to his self-assigned mission of revisionist [*animateur*], and fallen while acquitting himself of it.[8]

Here, in these few words, one senses the peculiar bitterness of the schism which for upward of twenty years divided French scholars of the Revolution, a bitterness which was in no small part due to the personality of Mathiez himself. There was apparently no trace of urbanity in his spirit. It is evident not only from his writings, which are generally polemical in tone, but from the testimony of both foe and friend, that he neither asked nor gave quarter. From one academic post to another, a fearsome reputation preceded him. After he had arrived and had become known, the greater part of this evaporated. There were, according to Louis Gottschalk, two Mathiez—the one brusque and aggressive, the other genial and friendly.[9] Yet his friends would seem to have been disciples rather than persons chosen without reference to their opinions. To his students, writes Georges Lefebvre, he was a master, not only because of the trouble he took with them, but because of his vigor and enthusiasm: "He not only awoke minds; he enlisted wills and called forth vocations."[10] His work was, in a very complete sense, his life; and he could not easily separate professional differences from personal ones. Was he ever guilty of the converse fault, that is, did he ever elevate a personal hostility into a professional one? There is no shadow of accusation that this was ever the case in his relations with his equals or his inferiors, but it is possible to suppose that his quarrel with Aulard had some personal motivation. Aulard was originally his master and virtually the official revolutionary historian to the Third Republic. Mathiez was ambitious; and Georges Lefebvre, who was closely associated with Mathiez professionally, suggests that the feud may in part be laid to Mathiez' ambition.[11] Mathiez himself said, not that he was jealous of Aulard, but that

Aulard was jealous of *him*. But the dispute arose in the first instance, he insisted, for scientific reasons,[12] and very likely this is
true. For it is hardly to be conceived that Mathiez, from the very
outset, envisaged a great battle with his teacher as the likeliest
way to fame. It seems more probable that he discovered only
gradually that neither his interpretations nor his ambition would
brook subordination to Aulard, of whom he had formerly been the
admirer.

What were the "scientific reasons" which were the original
cause of the break between the two? It has been pointed out by
M. Lefebvre that Mathiez' initial interest in religious history was
inspired by Aulard.[13] But, although Aulard praised the "irre-
proachable documentation" and the "personal and original"
gifts shown by Mathiez in the presentation of his doctoral
theses,[14] he was unable to accept Mathiez' interpretation. It was
Aulard's opinion that the revolutionary cults were simply expedi-
ents of revolutionary defense, whereas Mathiez held that they
were related profoundly to the whole thought of the revolutionaries on the role of religion in society. Other elements of difference in religious history appeared[15] about the same time that
Mathiez came under the influence of Jean Jaurès.[16] One could
not do better than to let Mathiez speak for himself here. He
wrote:

It is true that in this period of beginnings, the idea of associating the historical movement with the class struggle was not, with me, a dominant conception
to which I subordinated other explanations. But already, as you notice, the
social conflict was attracting me. . . . . But I should like you to be convinced,
my dear friend, that I do not adhere to systematic views on philosophy and on
the world. I have a horror of abstract constructions. It is because the former
explanations (political or religious, etc.) of the revolutionary crisis did not satisfy my mind that I abandoned, completed, rectified them. It would be a mistake to catalogue me in a classification, in a herbarium. I am a devotee of life
[*J'ai le culte de la vie*], and I love to picture to myself its complexity in the mass
and in detail. . . . . Nothing systematic, but as complete a description as possible in order to show the concatenation of facts and situations which dominate
men and parties and involve them in spite of themselves. If I had the time and
space, I would explain to you why history such as Aulard understood it is a
polemical history for the profit of a party and why I rose little by little, while

freeing myself from his influence, to a more objective view of things. . . . . Thus I embarrassed the republican defense politics of Aulard and of his Radical friends, who, systematically, did not wish to draw attention to the primordial role of the bourgeoisie and to the misery of the people, who played the role of dupe. In other words, I departed early from the apologetical theses of the master as soon as I perceived whither they led.[17]

Mathiez has here indicated what an extended reading of his works would only confirm in regard to the salient points of his notions on the subject matter of history and its interpretation. He has so frequently been thought of as a Marxist that it is worth inquiring just in how far this is true. Certainly he found the conception of the class struggle profoundly illuminating. He carried his belief in economic motivation to the point of entertaining a low opinion of human nature, at least in its political manifestations—Robespierre and a few others excepted. But these ideas were merely tools, not dogma. Mathiez did, in fact, at one time (as we shall see in a later connection) almost abandon the thesis of the class struggle for that of nationalism. He might upon occasion invert the Marxian order by showing that economic results had political causes, as he did, for example, when he analyzed the crisis of the spring of 1792.[18] Despite his assertion, quoted above, that men are influenced by circumstances against their wills, he elsewhere had disowned determinism: "I do not believe in Destiny, in the existence of an irresistible force of things which drags men along and dominates them, blind instruments for unknown ends."[19] Certainly Mathiez always wrote as if his characters must be judged responsible for their acts. The two statements seem, at first sight, difficult to reconcile; but probably the truth is that it appeared to Mathiez, as it does to many people, that sometimes men are free and sometimes they are not. For the distinctly accidental, also, he found a place. The death of the dauphin was a "fortuitous event"; yet Mathiez said that it postponed the Restoration for twenty years.[20]

In his own words, Mathiez did not have a "systematic" approach. He adopted the notion of the class struggle. Likewise he had earlier adopted Durkheim's definition of religion as any body of beliefs and practices which are obligatory for all members of a group[21] and made it the basis of his doctoral theses. But apparently he took no other ideas from sociological theory; indeed, he distrusted sociology as an adjunct to history.[22] His approach is quite aptly summarized in his words: "J'ai le culte de la vie." This is probably what J. M. Thompson, the English historian and biographer of Robespierre, implies in his appraisal of Mathiez: "Mathiez remains a 'pure' historian of a distinguished and unusual kind, one who reverenced facts as facts, and understood men as men."[23] If in regard to individuals Mathiez allowed his prejudices to obstruct the subtlety of his valuation, his characters are, nonetheless, human beings.

Although Mathiez will be best remembered for having done the most to supply a social and economic basis for the political superstructure of French Revolutionary history, nevertheless he was not primarily a social or economic historian. He was not, for instance, a historian of institutions per se. Lefebvre complains that Mathiez devoted too little attention to the feudal and agrarian problem and that in his study of opinion he did not pay sufficient attention to the mentality of the popular classes. Furthermore, he was not an economist.[24] Certainly he did not write economic history as such, divorced from the political milieu. Mathiez' major interest was the history of parliamentary parties and opinion. Lefebvre sees in this a survival of the influence of Aulard,[25] but such a judgment seems somehow inadequate. And if Mathiez inherited anything here from Aulard, the legacy was not complete, for Mathiez, unlike Aulard, was not much interested in constitutional history. One could not say that he denied the significance of constitutional history, for it finds a place in his writing, but his interest in it was distinctly minor. In the fact that Mathiez' synthesis was political, the primary influence would seem to have been not Aulard but Rousseau—the Rousseau of the *Contrat social*, wherein political society becomes the ultimate good and finds its justification in the semimystical concept of the general will. There is a good deal of the general will in Mathiez, for, cynic though he was, the notion of the transcendental transformation of personal into public interest was to him of real and passionate concern, the very core of the democratic way of life. This is primarily why he attacked Danton and glorified Robespierre. The rehabilitation of Danton, he wrote, "is not only an outrage to the truth but the indication of a policy which is equivocal and dangerous for democracy."[26] Of Robespierre, he said: "We love him for the teachings of his life and for the symbol of his death."[27] A rather curious declaration this, wherein Mathiez, anticlerical and unbeliever, resorted to a kind of figure of the incarnation to express his almost religious conviction.

It cannot be denied that Mathiez used history as a text from which to preach an ideal—a social-democratic ideal. During the period of the war of 1914 and its aftermath, Mathiez' idealism so affected his scholarship as to lead him into certain aberrations of historical judgment. In a lecture entitled "Pourquoi nous sommes Robespierristes," delivered in 1920 and published in *Robespierre terroriste*, Mathiez declared that the death of Robespierre left such a breach in the ranks of the Revolutionary leadership that the republic was shaken to its foundations.[28] But in neither *La Révolution française*[29] nor *La réaction thermidorienne*,[29a] both written subsequently to the *Robespierre terroriste*, did Mathiez imply any such complete adherence to the great-man theory of historical causation. In these other works there can be discerned, rather, the interpretation that what really shook the republic to its foundations was not the death of Robespierre but the break at that time within the Committee of Public Safety and the consequent collapse of its dictatorship.[30] That is, the death of Robespierre was more properly effect than cause. Again, in order to excoriate the exceptional regime that was imposed upon France from 1914 to 1918, Mathiez painted an idyllic picture of the Terror of 1793. He did not argue that war should not involve a degree of "regimentation"; quite the contrary. What he did contend was that, since France in 1914 was united and republican, there was no excuse for censorship and the general suspension of civil liberties. The revolutionaries of 1793, said Mathiez, never organized a preventive censorship, never delivered civilians up to military justice, never closed the rostrum of the Convention or of the clubs.[31]

Well, one may answer, the tribunals were no doubt civil tribunals; but what of that in view of the Law of Suspects? And as for opinion, it was doubtless legally free, if one dared to express it! In another place, again with the object of attacking the internal policy of the French government during the war of 1914, Mathiez wrote:

Far from being a cause of weakness, liberty was for Revolutionary France the instrument of salvation. The divisions, the factions, even the risings, are only surface incidents. Feuillants, Girondins, Montagnards, Dantonists, Robespierrists, succeeded each other in power. But it was the patriot people who judged their differences. . . . . Never did it exercise such an influence in public affairs; never was it to such a degree a sovereign people, master of its destinies.[32]

The reader may well wonder whether he is reading Mathiez or Michelet. How far this democratic mysticism, which, indeed, is latent in all Mathiez' work, has carried him away from the thesis of the class struggle as reflected in the party history of the national assemblies is here strikingly evident. It is true that Mathiez had not at this time set forth all his evidence for the existence of the class struggle, but it can hardly be maintained that he had not yet made up his mind that it really did exist and that the conflict of the parties was of fundamental importance.

But if, under the influence of emotion engendered by wartime conditions, Mathiez was guilty of diverging from his own more sober judgments in order to plead a case, he ought not to be too harshly judged. Others have done as much and more. And, furthermore, if Mathiez quite consistently preached an ideal of social democracy, he had too high a regard for the sacredness of historical facts to write history in the interest of a particular party. This is how he himself put it:

If history is past politics, that is no reason . . . . why it should become the humble servant of the politics or rather of the politicians of the present. It has a reason for existence only if it says in complete independence what it believes to be the truth. . . . . I do not write in order to catechize, to recruit adherents for this or that party, but to instruct and inform. I should be lowered in my own eyes if I concerned myself, in taking up my pen, with how politicians of the day, in France and abroad, will use my writings. That these men of action —red, black, or white—should concern themselves with exploiting my books to the profit of their cause is a vexation [ennui] that I must endure with patience.[33]

Now if Mathiez believed that the past is not the servant of the present—that is, in historical writing—what did he hold to be the uses of the present in historical interpretation? Here, again, he was explicit:

My whole effort has consisted in withdrawing myself as much as possible from our present ways of thinking and judging in order to find again those of the men of the eighteenth century. . . . . The historian ought not to interrogate the past with the formulas of the present. His task is more modest but more difficult. It consists in rediscovering the formulas under which the eternal problems of humanity are posed at different epochs and in showing what varied solutions they have received.[34]

Again: "The fundamental problems are always the same, but their aspect changes, and their solutions depend on those multiple factors which can be grouped under the general denomination of 'spirit of the age.' "[35] Mathiez quite successfully lived up to his theory of the universal problem and the particular solution. For example, he insisted that, contrary to the prevailing practice among liberal historians, the religious conceptions of the revolutionaries could not be read in the light of the modern ideal of the completely neutral state, for such an ideal was then unknown, it being deemed that some form of religion was an essential bulwark of the state. Yet Mathiez was extremely sensitive, as a historian, to present events. They were always suggesting analogies that became the basis of his work. M. Lefebvre indicates a probable relationship between the failure of the Radical party, in the first decade of the twentieth century, to institute social reforms and Mathiez' disparagement of Danton.[36] He also points out the coincidence between the war of 1914 and Mathiez' studies on the economic foundations of the Terror, on the status of foreigners in France during the Revolution, and on the organization of the Revolutionary army.[37]

Mathiez' interest did not stray much beyond the confines of the Revolution and its immediate antecedents. The number of his publications outside that field is almost negligible. But from the summoning of the estates-general to the coup d'état of 18 Brumaire, there was no period in which he had not done spade-work and contributed to its reinterpretation. His last book, *Le Di-*

rectoire,[38] did not extend in time beyond September 4, 1797, but he had planned to carry his work to the advent of Napoleon. Mathiez' interest in the post-Thermidorian period led him to make a characteristic observation, apropos of the fact that historians have often revolted from this period in disgust. "The historian," he remarked, "has no right to choose from what is to be the object of his studies, to accept what pleases him, to reject what is repugnant to him. . . . . Reality is a whole."[39] His devotion to synthesis was only equaled by his power of achieving it. Mathiez' work as historian has a remarkable unity. None of the threads he had once picked up were ever dropped, and he ended his career as he had begun it, with the policies of the Directory. Furthermore, he never really reversed his essential judgments. There is a development in his interpretation, but it is one of expansion rather than of change. In part, this consistency was probably due to method, to the fact that Mathiez was not in the habit of running after theories; but no doubt it was primarily the consequence of a strong inner consistency of viewpoint and personality and of an early intellectual maturity.

In spite of what has just been said about the unity of Mathiez' work, it can rather easily be divided into successive, if overlapping, phases.[40] His principal doctoral thesis, the reader may be reminded, was *La théophilanthropie et le culte décadaire*, the minor one a suggestive sketch entitled *Les origines des cultes révolutionnaires*. The idea set forth in these books has already been stated. It is, in brief, that there was a close relation between the Revolutionary cults and the view of their propagators, anti-Christian though they were, that society must have a religious sanction. Mathiez' first interest in Robespierre arose out of the study of the part played by him in connection with the de-Christianizing campaign and the festival of the Supreme Being. There followed a battery of articles dealing with various aspects of religious history. A number of these were collected into two books, entitled, respectively, *Contributions à l'histoire religieuse de la Révolution française*[41] and *La Révolution et l'église; études critiques et documentaires*.[42] These Mathiez followed with a significant work entitled *Rome et le clergé français sous la Constituante,*[43] which successfully maintained that the break with Rome was at least as much the fault of the papacy as of the Constituent Assembly. In the same year Mathiez also published a short study, *Les conséquences religieuses de la journée du 10 août 1792: la déportation des prêtres et la sécularisation de l'état civil,*[44] in which he held that the legislation of this moment of the Revolution was probably not intended to secure the separation of church and state, although, in fact, it constituted a step in this direction. It might be added here, in connection with Mathiez' reading of the religious history of the Revolution, that the real separation between the church (i.e., the constitutional church) and the state dated, he insisted, from the beginning of the campaign of violent de-Christianization in the fall of 1793, rather than from the date of the legal and financial separation in the fall of 1794, after Thermidor.

From religious history Mathiez passed to the task of destroying Danton's reputation and recreating Robespierre's. This involved extended studies in parliamentary corruption and foreign policy, especially under the Convention. As usual, Mathiez published his work first in the form of short articles. Some of these were collected into two volumes, entitled *Études Robespierristes: La corruption parlementaire sous la terreur* and *La conspiration de l'étranger.*[45] Then came *Danton et la paix,*[46] a new study devoted to Danton's intrigues with foreign governments, and *Un procès de corruption sous la terreur; l'affaire de la Compagnie des Indes,*[47] an exposé of a case of graft in which the documents are published and practically allowed to speak for themselves. *Robespierre terroriste*[48] was again in part a reprinting of hitherto published articles but contained also Robespierre's notebook and his notes on the Dantonists, critically edited. *Autour de Robespierre*[49] was a collection chiefly of articles published between 1910 and 1924 and bearing on the policies of Robespierre and his relations with the Committee of Public Safety, the Committee of General Security, and the Convention in the last months before the events of 9 Thermidor. *Autour de Danton*[50] was, on the other hand, a study published completely and for the first time in 1926, covering Danton's entire

career. But it was not a biography. Mathiez never wrote a real
biography of either Danton or Robespierre. *Girondins et Montagnards*[51] was Mathiez' last volume on the history of parliamentary
struggles under the Convention. The outcome of what he himself referred to as "this great lawsuit,"[52] that is, Robespierre
versus Danton, has undoubtedly been that Danton's reputation
has been rather badly damaged, and Robespierre's enhanced.
But it is generally agreed that Mathiez' prejudices led him
to judgments in this matter beyond what his evidence would
warrant.

The judgment on Robespierre is closely related to a third line
of investigation that Mathiez began pursuing in the course of the
war of 1914, namely, the origin and development of the policy of
the "maximum." Some of this work was published in *La victoire
en l'an II*,[53] but the culmination of Mathiez' research and writing
along this line was *La vie chère et le mouvement social sous la terreur*.[54]
A brief summary of the argument of this book will not, perhaps,
be out of place. Under the old regime, said Mathiez, the state
pursued a policy of intervention in the interest of the consumer.
Toward the end of the period there were experiments in laissez
faire, but they were not popular. Economic liberalism had cap-
tured only the thinking élite and the capitalist classes. The great
majority of the *cahiers* demanded a policy of intervention and
regulation, but the bourgeois Constituent Assembly nevertheless adopted a free-trade policy. Since the year 1789 produced a
good harvest, there was acquiescence. But when times were bad
again, in 1792, there was a widespread and profound, if unor-
ganized, class movement in favor of regulation. Some slight concession in the direction of price-fixing was made following the
August revolution, but it was soon withdrawn. The year 1793
witnessed a continuation of the economic crisis, intensified by invasion and the provincial revolts which were themselves a class
movement centering in the bourgeois departmental administrations. Now Montagnards, as well as Girondins, were free-traders;
but to save the Revolutionary republic the Montagnards, after the
fall of the Gironde, entered into an alliance with the Hébertists,

the demagogues of the sans-culottes, who demanded the maximum and the Terror to enforce it. The Revolutionary Tribunal was made competent for all cases of fraud and illicit profits. Mathiez did not attempt to estimate how great a proportion of the total number of executions was decreed for economic reasons directly, although he gave examples of such cases. Nor did he insist that the maximum was the only reason for the Terror, for, although the severity of the maximum was somewhat relaxed after the fall of the Hébertists, the severity of the Terror increased. What Mathiez did demonstrate was that there was a definite relationship between the instigation of the Terror of 1793–94 and the admission into the government of the popular and terrorist faction and that the Terror was an integral part of the policy of the maximum demanded by that faction. This is perhaps the most notable single contribution made by Mathiez to the history of the Revolution.

It will have been observed that the work of Mathiez is like a mosaic, built up out of small pieces of research. But one does not have to read through all the fragments to reconstruct the picture, for Mathiez did partly succeed in writing one continuous narrative of the Revolution. In 1922 he published the first volume of *La Révolution française*, entitled *La chute de la royauté (1787–92)*. The second volume, *La Gironde et la Montagne*, appeared in 1924; and the third, *La terreur*, in 1927. *La Révolution française* was designed for the general reader as well as the student, and this fact, beside the limited space allotted by the publishers, precluded documentation, a restriction which Mathiez deplored. In *La réaction thermidorienne*, which Mathiez intended to be a continuation of the synthesis, he reverted to the more detailed type of study, thoroughly footnoted. *Le Directoire, du 11 brumaire an IV au 18 fructidor an V*, edited by Jacques Godechot from Mathiez' notes, is the last volume of the synthesis and is on the same extended scale as *La réaction thermidorienne*.

Pre-eminently a research historian, Mathiez ransacked the archives—those of Paris especially, since he wrote about the Revolution from the viewpoint of Paris. In addition, he examined the contemporary journals (the *Moniteur* being the chief source for parliamentary proceedings), memoirs, and correspondence, and for the study of public opinion he used pamphlets extensively. In fact, there is apparently no type of source which escaped his scrutiny. His synthesis of the Revolution is not a summary of the monographic studies of the subject, though it is hardly permissible to doubt that Mathiez, whose listed book reviews total around six hundred, had an unrivaled knowledge of that sort of literature. His footnote references to secondary works are generally given either because such works contain source material or because Mathiez is examining the opinions therein expressed. His method of dealing with the documents has not been without criticism. M. Lefebvre, for example, hovers between rebuke and admiration. Mathiez, he says, was likely to apologize for the *témoinage unique* (reliance upon which is, of course, against one of the canons) simply because it is often the only available evidence, but, on the other hand, the boldness of his imagination in the interpretation of the documents was, M. Lefebvre implies, a quality of the first order.[55]

Mathiez distinguished scholarship from history. The one, he said, searches for and criticizes the evidence; the other reconstructs and expounds. That is, one might say, history is the more creative and is akin to literature. In writing *La Révolution française* Mathiez said he was attempting to perform the function of the historian.[56] Perhaps he would have agreed that in a rather considerable portion of his work he does hardly more than the scholar's task. This reflection may be illustrated by reference to Mathiez' practice of publishing archival material along with a more or less extensive commentary demonstrating some particular contention, with the result that the reader is somethat in doubt whether to classify the production as book (or article) or as documents. *Un procès de corruption sous la terreur* is one example of this sort of hybrid; another is *Le club des Cordeliers pendant la crise de Varennes et la massacre du Champ de Mars*,[57] a study not hitherto mentioned.

Probably Mathiez did not intend to give a great emphasis to

literary construction as one of those attributes of history which distinguish it from scholarship. Yet it is none the less true that *La Révolution française*, which is prefaced with the explicit statement of Mathiez' determination herein to transcend scholarship and to write history and which is the most broadly "reconstructive" of all his works, is likewise the most finished from a literary viewpoint. Here there is the same terse and often mordant vocabulary which distinguishes his other writing, but displayed with a greater economy of language. Antitheses, of which Mathiez was fond, are carefully worked out and effectively employed. The narrative is extremely detailed, without, however, any sacrifice of smoothness of style and without any obscuring of interpretation. Indeed, Mathiez manages to impart a distinctly dramatic quality to the presentation of both issues and situations. Although he wrote always with clarity—and, above all, with vigor—he wrote too much, one may infer, to take such pains habitually.

With all his passion for archival research and his not infrequent exposition of bits of evidence uncovered thereby, Mathiez was not primarily interested in the systematic publication of documents. This task he left to others. His editorial activity consisted chiefly in the publication of the *Annales révolutionnaires* and its successor the *Annales historiques de la Révolution française*. Besides this, there was the new edition of Jean Jaurès' *Histoire socialiste de la Révolution française*.[58] Finally, with Léon Cahen, he prepared a small elementary source book of French laws and treaties entitled *Les lois françaises de 1815 à nos jours*.[59]

The eulogy of Mathiez by Pierre Caron quoted earlier in this essay indicates something of the effect of Mathiez' influence in France upon studies of the Revolution, despite the mutual antipathies of the schools. The quality of his contributions has been widely recognized abroad. Translations of *La Révolution française* exist in English, Russian, and Norwegian.[60] Perhaps nowhere outside of France has his work been more generally appreciated than in the United States, where the younger historians of the French Revolution well-nigh universally acknowledge their indebtedness.[61] Mathiez is still, as it were, a contemporaneous influence. The interpretations which he set forth are alive in a very immediate sense; they have not yet had time to become venerable and classic.

NOTES

1. For biographical material see the *Annales historiques de la Révolution française*, Vol. IX (1932), especially the following articles: Henri Calvet, "Albert Mathiez, professeur en Sorbonne," pp. 264–70; Louis Gottschalk, "L'influence d'Albert Mathiez sur les études historiques aux États-Unis," pp. 224–29; letter of Mathiez to Louis Gottschalk, Nov. 23, 1930, pp. 218–20; Georges Lefebvre, "Albert Mathiez," pp. 98–102, and "L'œuvre historique d'Albert Mathiez," pp. 193–210; Georges Michon, "Albert Mathiez et les événements de 1914–1920," pp. 247–51; Albert Troux, "Albert Mathiez à Nancy (1908–09) et à Besançon (1911–1920)," pp. 240–46; and Hermann Wendel, "Albert Mathiez vu par un 'Dantoniste' allemand," pp. 235–39. See also J. M. Thompson, "Albert Mathiez," *EHR*, XLVII (1932), 617–21.

2. Paris, 1903.

3. Paris, 1904.

4. Troux, *loc. cit.*, p. 243. I have not seen any other reference to this disability.

5. *Ibid.*, p. 244.

6. Michon, *loc. cit.*, p. 250; Thompson, *loc. cit.*, p. 619. In an article, "Le Bolchévisme et le Jacobinisme" (*Scientia*, XXVII [1920], 52–65), Mathiez held that the analogy between the Bolshevist and Jacobin phases of the Russian and the French revolutions, respectively, was very close. This article exists also as a separate publication under the same title (Paris, 1920).

7. *Autour de Danton* (Paris, 1926), p. 7.

8. *La Révolution française*, LXXXV (1932), 98.

9. Gottschalk, *loc. cit.*, p. 228.

10. Lefebvre, "Albert Mathiez," *loc. cit.*, p. 99.

11. Lefebvre, "L'œuvre historique d'Albert Mathiez," *loc. cit.*, p. 198.

12. Mathiez to L. Gottschalk, Nov. 23, 1930, *loc. cit.*, pp. 218–19.

13. Lefebvre, "Albert Mathiez," *loc. cit.*, p. 99.

14. Thompson, *loc. cit.*, p. 617.

15. Mathiez to L. Gottschalk, Nov. 23, 1930, *loc. cit.*, pp. 218–19.

16. Lefebvre, "L'œuvre historique d'Albert Mathiez," *loc. cit.*, p. 198. In a review of his own edition of Jaurès' *Histoire socialiste de la Révolution française* Mathiez later wrote: "For myself, who have had the honor to append my name [as editor] to the reprinting of his work, I humbly declare that I have drawn from it not only the stimulation without which my researches would have been impossible but many suggestions which served me as governing ideas [*lignes directrices*]" (*Ann. hist.*, II [1925], 76). Mathiez admired particularly Jaurès' analysis of class interests in the earlier stages of the revolution (*Annales révolutionnaires*, XIV [1922], 256).

17. Mathiez to L. Gottschalk, Nov. 23, 1930, *loc. cit.*, pp. 219–20.

18. *La vie chère et le mouvement social sous la terreur* (Paris, 1927), p. 56.

19. *Rome et le clergé français sous la Constituante; la constitution civile du clergé, l'affaire d'Avignon* (Paris, 1911), p. 1.

20. *La réaction thermidorienne* (Paris, 1929), p. 271.

21. *Les origines des cultes révolutionnaires*, p. 11.

22. Lefebvre, "L'œuvre historique d'Albert Mathiez," *loc. cit.*, p. 196.

23. Thompson, *loc. cit.*, p. 621.

24. Lefebvre, "L'œuvre historique d'Albert Mathiez," *loc. cit.*, pp. 208–9.

25. *Ibid.*, pp. 195–96.

26. Wendel, *loc. cit.*, p. 236.

27. *Robespierre terroriste* (Paris, [1921]), p. 188.

28. *Ibid.*, pp. 169–70.

29. 3 vols.; Paris, 1922–27. References in this essay will be to the excellent translation by Catherine A. Phillips entitled *The French revolution* (New York, 1929).

29a. See above, n. 20.

30. *The French revolution*, Book III, chap. xiv; *La réaction thermidorienne*, pp. 2–20.

31. *Robespierre terroriste*, p. 6.

32. *La victoire en l'an II, esquisses historiques sur la défense nationale* (Paris, 1916), p. 279.

33. *La réaction thermidorienne*, pp. vii–viii.

34. *La Révolution et l'église; études critiques et documentaires* (Paris, 1910), p. viii.

35. *La Révolution et les étrangers; cosmopolitisme et défense nationale* (Paris, [1918]), p. 1.

36. Lefebvre, "L'œuvre historique d'Albert Mathiez," *loc. cit.*, p. 199.

37. Lefebvre, "Albert Mathiez," *loc. cit.*, pp. 99–100.

38. *Le Directoire, du 11 brumaire an IV au 18 fructidor an V*, publié, d'après les manuscrits de l'auteur, par Jacques Godechot (Paris, 1934).

39. *La réaction thermidorienne*, p. 4.

40. This has been pointed out by M. Lefebvre in "Albert Mathiez," *loc. cit.*, pp. 99–100.

41. Paris, 1907. Preface by Gabriel Monod.

42. See above, n. 34.

43. See above, n. 19.

44. Paris, 1911.

45. 2 vols.; Paris, 1917–18.

46. Paris, [1919].

47. Paris, 1920.

48. See above, n. 27.

49. Paris, 1926. Translated into English as *The fall of Robespierre and other essays* (New York, 1927).

50. See above, n. 7.

51. [Paris], 1930.

52. *Robespierre terroriste*, p. 169.

53. See above, n. 32.

54. See above, n. 18.

55. Lefebvre, "L'œuvre historique d'Albert Mathiez," *loc. cit.*, pp. 201–2.

56. See Mathiez' preface to *La Révolution française*.

57. Paris, 1910. A *Supplément* was published in 1913.

58. 8 vols.; Paris, 1922–24. See above, n. 16.

59. Paris, 1906. The second edition (Paris, 1919) was entitled *Les lois françaises de 1815 à 1914*. A third edition with the same title as the second was published in 1927.

60. Ricardo R. Caillet-Bois, *Bibliografía de Albert Mathiez* (Buenos Aires, 1932), p. 17. Reprinted from the *Boletin del Instituto de Investigaciones Históricas* [de la Facultad de Filosofía y Letras], XIV (1932), 268–453. This useful compilation purports to be a complete bibliography of Mathiez' writings. Its principal divisions are books, articles (about 475), and reviews (about 600).

61. See Gottschalk, *loc. cit.*, pp. 224–29; also his article. "The importance of Albert Mathiez," *Nation*, CXXVII (July–December, 1928), 619–21. For an English estimate of the significance of Mathiez' work see J. N. Thompson, *loc. cit.*, pp. 617–21. For German estimates see, respectively, Hermann Wendel, *loc. cit.*, pp. 235–39, and Hedwig Hintze, "Die französische Revolution, neue Forschungen und Darstellungen," *HZ*, CXLIII (1930), 298–319. An Italian appreciation is that of Corrado Barbagallo, "Albert Mathiez," *Ann. hist.*, IX, 221–23. The best of the French critiques is contained in the two excellent articles by Georges Lefebvre, *loc. cit.*, pp. 98–102 and 193–210.

XV

PAUL NIKOLAYEVICH MILYUKOV
(1859——)

ROGERS P. CHURCHILL*

IN ENFORCED retirement at Montpellier in unoccupied France, after the agony of the summer of 1940, an octogenarian Russian historian has found his world tumbled down around him. This was not the first such experience, for the October (N.S., November) Revolution of 1917 had uprooted his life, forcing him into the emigration with those who left their native Russia for the rest of time. After a brief period of wandering, this Russian scholar settled in Paris and created a new, influential life. It is hardly likely that time and circumstance will enable him, even with his skill and knowledge, to put the pieces together again; so a career is closing and an opinion upon it can now be appropriately formed.

Paul Nikolayevich Milyukov was born in Moscow on January 28, 1859, the son of a prominent architect and sculptor.[1] Raised in comfortable physical surroundings, after an uneventful childhood the boy gained his secondary education in the First Moscow Gymnasium, where he manifested an early interest in classical literature and philosophy, reading the great works in Greek and Latin. Upon graduation he participated briefly (in 1877) in the Russo-Turkish war, serving with medical units, before he entered the University of Moscow, in the historical-philosophical faculty. Here he continued his study of philosophy and, later on, comparative philology and some archeology. Gradually, however, he turned toward the study of history, coming under the influence of the renowned professors M. M. Kovalevsky and P. G. Vino-

* Instructor in history, Brooklyn College.

gradov. In the latter's seminar Milyukov "had the opportunity of becoming acquainted with the views of contemporary Western science on the tasks and methods of historical research."[2] He also began to read for the first time the books of the protagonists of economic materialism and the opinions of Karl Marx, which stimulated his interest in economic forces in history and in radical thought, although he became neither an economic determinist nor a revolutionary socialist.

Milyukov attended the university in those years when the revolutionary, terrorist movements attained their fullest intensity. He had become involved in the sympathetic activities of the students and was arrested by the government for participation in a meeting. A short jail sentence prevented him from entering upon his "fourth course"; so Milyukov traveled abroad, studying Italian painting and sculpture. He returned the following year to complete his studies, graduated in 1882, and promptly plunged into advanced courses of Russian history. In this intensive study he came under the instruction of Professor Vasily O. Klyuchevsky, whose knowledge and methods made a profound impression on Milyukov. A vigorous Moscow school of historians, under the inspiration of Klyuchevsky and Vinogradov, was vitally interested in the study of the internal history of the country, particularly in the development of Russian institutions, social questions, and economic influences; and the rich quantity of archival material in Moscow facilitated both teaching and research. The members of this school strove to avoid the adoption of any special point of view, to describe the Russian past in concrete terms based upon facts, yet evidencing a marked tendency to look beyond social and political events to find their dependence on economic factors.[3] Milyukov once wrote that his teacher Klyuchevsky considered "general schemes and interpretation . . . . more important than the accumulation of factual material";[4] and this was essentially true of the Moscow group in general, Milyukov included. In this atmosphere, under inspiring instruction, Milyukov finished his studies for the Master's degree in 1885.

Milyukov now commenced his amazingly versatile career as a

historian, politician, and publicist, of which a description would
form a separate biographical study. As a teacher of history, his
first positions were in a pedagogical school for women and as a
Privatdozent in the University of Moscow. At the same time he
set about preparing his Master's thesis for publication and
launched the first of the articles and lengthy book reviews which
were to come from his prolific pen.[5] Soon he became involved
in the recrudescence of revolutionary activity, and a government
suspicious of his political reliability engaged him in tasks farther
removed from Moscow. With other scholars in 1893 Milyukov
assisted in the labors of a commission for home study among the
poorer classes of society; he participated in historical conferences
in provincial cities and gave a series of memorable lectures in
Nizhny Novgorod.[6] After two years of exile in Ryazan, Milyukov
was permitted to accept an offer to teach in the University of
Sofia, and in consequence of this experience he was afterward
reputed to be an authority on Balkan politics. Because of a social
indignity on the name day of Nicholas II, an implacable government forced his dismissal from this position in 1899, whereupon
Milyukov soon returned to St. Petersburg and busied himself in
the editorial direction of the prosperous periodical *Mir Bozhi*
[World of God] and *Russkoye bogatstvo* [Russian wealth].

Hereafter a university teaching-post in Russia was no longer
open to Milyukov; so he continued with his historical composi-
tions, at the same time persisting in his associations with student
movements and radical, political activity. He was intimately connected with the publication from Stuttgart of the *Osvobozhdeniye*
[Liberation] in 1902; but the exasperated political authorities
kept after him, occasionally jailing him, until he took a favorable
opportunity to go abroad. Milyukov spent much time studying
and traveling in Europe, besides coming to the United States,
where he spoke in several cities and gave a course of lectures at
the University of Chicago under the auspices of the Crane Foundation in the summer of 1903. During a return appearance at
this university, where he met with an appreciative reception, although some of his peculiar viewpoints attracted newspaper

notoriety, the Russian Revolution of 1905 broke out, and Milyukov abruptly stopped his lectures to hasten home, there to join
in the political turmoil.[7]

For many years to come, Milyukov followed his political
career and activities as a publicist, with only slight historical
productivity. In May, 1905, he became president of the groups
of professional people who combined to form the Union of Unions. Steadily increasing his leadership over the liberal, opposi-
tionary elements, Milyukov emerged as an outstanding champion
of full democratic forms for the government of Russia. He was an
organizer and then the president of the Constitutional Democratic (Kadet) party and became the editor of its newspaper
Ryech [Speech]. Although he was not a member of the first two
dumas, he was elected to the third and fourth, wherein he became an outspoken leader of the liberal opposition, while he controlled the Kadet party with an authoritarian hand. His ready
speech gained him a reputation as an orator. In the third duma
he spoke on seventy-three occasions, and thirty-seven more
times before the fourth duma disappeared.[8] These addresses were
invariably well prepared, but many members often filed out
rather than listen to another precisely developed professor's lecture.

Throughout the war period Milyukov ardently supported full
participation with the Allies, and so strongly championed Russian claims upon the Straits that he won the soubriquet "Mil-
yukov-Dardanelsky."[9] He was largely instrumental in forming
the Progressive bloc which gave a duma majority to the liberal
and moderate parties who strove to bolster the government.[10]
In the hesitation and confusion after the abdication of Nicholas
II, fearing a revolutionary catastrophe which would destroy all
connection "with the political symbols of the past,"[11] Milyukov
labored with indefatigable perseverance for the establishment of
a provisional government. In this government he became minister for foreign affairs, but quarrels with the Soviets over divergent policies undermined his position, until on May 3, 1917,
pressed by some of his colleagues, he resigned.[12] Hereafter his in-

fluence waned. With the rapid leftward course of the revolution Milyukov lost hope, and the seizure of power by the Bolsheviks started him on his travels.

After some wandering Milyukov made his way to Kiev, which in 1918 was occupied by German forces. There some nebulous relations with the Germans yielded no results and formed an incident in his life about which he had little to say afterward.[13] As a member of a delegation seeking foreign aid against the Bolsheviks, Milyukov was unceremoniously turned away in Paris by Clemenceau on the charge that he was a Germanophile.[14] So he went on to London, where, by 1920, he was editing and writing for the English-language periodical *New Russia*. By the end of the year Milyukov removed to Paris, which thenceforward became his home. Early in 1921 Milyukov became the editor of the best-known *émigré* Russian newspaper *Poslyedniya Novosti* [Last News] and a leader among the liberal and radical bourgeois opponents of Bolshevism. He delighted in revealing the shortcomings and enduring difficulties of the new rulers; yet the Communists survived until Milyukov's attitude mellowed and his criticisms softened as the Soviet government manifested a growing inclination to protect the Russian national interests which he had cherished.[15]

In new, comfortable surroundings Milyukov returned to more formal historical writing,[16] while his talents and activity won him a pre-eminent position in the Russian emigration. In the early days of March, 1929, many celebrations in honor of his seventy years were held in Paris, Prague, Berlin, Warsaw, Riga, and Sofia. At banquets exuberantly laudatory addresses were delivered, with greetings and testimonials sent to him from all over the world.[17] Ten years later he experienced another personal tribute, when a bound volume of testimonials (which included an engrossed letter from the University of Chicago) was presented at a festive gathering in Paris. Shortly afterward, although he had clearly perceived the approach of a new war in Europe and warned of its coming, catastrophe overwhelmed Milyukov again and completely disrupted his life.[18]

Despite his long career and numerous publications, Milyukov's most valuable historical contributions came in his younger years. Aside from a few notes and book reviews, his first substantial study was his revised Master's thesis (not the frail product associated with the American degree), entitled *Gosudarstvennoye khozyaystvo Rossii v pervoy chetverti XVII stolyetiya i reforma Petra Velikago* [The state economy of Russia in the first quarter of the eighteenth century and the reforms of Peter the Great].[19] This was the first study in Russian of the reforms of Peter from an economic viewpoint, coming as the fruit of many years of labor in an enormous quantity of hitherto unused archival material. The long book won for Milyukov a lasting reputation as an economic and financial historian. Besides the new information, a cleaner interpretation of known facts changed the earlier opinions of this period of Russian history. Especially noteworthy has been the description of the "administrative havoc" occasioned by Peter's violent changes and the destructive policies toward manufacturing in consequence of the artificial nature of some of the reforms.[20] The entire reign of Peter forever remained a favorite subject with Milyukov, to which he frequently returned in later lectures and writings.

Quickly following came another, slighter book on a subject closely related in the field of economic history, *Sporniye voprosy finansovoy istorii Moskovskago gosudarstva* [Debatable questions of the financial history of the Muscovite state].[21] This book was undertaken on commission from the Academy of Science as an extended review and criticism of a work by A. S. Lappo-Danilevsky on taxation and kindred subjects in old Muscovy. Milyukov's response went into such critical detail, disclosing much fresh information, that it constituted an independent contribution which cleared up many misty and perplexing questions of the economic and financial life in the pre-Petrine state.

In his next important study, *Glavniya techeniya russkoy istoricheskoy mysli* [Main currents of Russian historical thought],[22] Milyukov engaged in the congenial task of an entirely new presentation of the development of Russian historical writing in accordance with the changing philosophical concepts of the historians and the times in which they wrote. The accomplishment was greater than a mere catalogue of names and writings. Milyukov attempted to illustrate the relationship between the growth of Russian historiography and the quality of the contemporaneous philosophical thought which consciously sometimes, but unconsciously at other times, colored the views and influenced the methods of Russian historians. The only completed volume of this work carried out this purpose, from the earliest foreigners and Russian primitives of the eighteenth century, through Karamzin and his successors, to Chaadayev and Ivan Kireyevsky, who reflected the influence of Schelling in Russian historical writing. Milyukov affirmed that the real beginning of genuine historical writing came with the works of the foreigners and early native writers, destroying completely the fable of Karamzin as the father of Russian history.[23] Although the historians and their products are carefully described and put in their places with new interpretations well supported by solid argumentation, the thoroughness in which the fundamental philosophical concepts of the thought of their times are described constitutes the unique contribution of this brilliant historiography. "In the literature on Russian historiography this work by P. N. Milyukov occupies, to the present time, a prime place and serves as an indispensable book for every man who wishes to study the development of Russian historical thought."[24] While, despite encouragement, Milyukov never continued this work, he did later write other, briefer articles on Russian historiography and the outlook of Russian historians, the most recent and accessible of which is his introductory chapter to the composite *Histoire de Russie*, the best sketch in any non-Russian language.[25]

Meanwhile Milyukov's greatest historical accomplishment, his *Ocherki po istorii russkoy kultury* [Studies in the history of Russian culture], was being published serially in the periodical *Mir Bozhi* before being collected into three volumes.[26] It is not a political history, nor does it have a chronological framework. It is the first, and still the only, substantial synthesis of the decisive developments in all phases of the life of the Russian people nearly through the nineteenth century. In its uncommonly broad scope the author has included not only economic and social history but also the development of the political institutions of the state, the history of religious and intellectual movements, and the appearance of moral and aesthetic concepts.[27] It is a history of civilization and of society, in keeping with the trend of the times to get away from a factual study of events. Milyukov envisaged his work in the French sense of an "histoire de la civilization," embracing all the elements in the life of the mass rather than in the German form of a "Kulturgeschichte," more narrowly limited to the intellectual and artistic accomplishments of the people.[28]

In this large undertaking Milyukov pleaded the necessity of making a severe selection of the most essential portions of the vast amount of available material, much of which was accessible only to specialists and some of which was the gleaning of his own research. Of all the particular studies of Russian history already written by others, only a meager part could aid in composing a history of Russian civilization, while there remained to be discovered and used other evidence on untouched topics. Therefore, Milyukov admitted that there would be inequalities and complete gaps in places throughout his history, but he hoped to succeed in presenting the most essential components of the cultural historical process in a simple manner which would allow the knowledge and conclusions to become popular and generally known. He anticipated criticism that some of his judgments would appear audacious, his method of presentation too popular, and the whole venture premature in the existing state of knowledge. This only encouraged Milyukov to believe, however, that the popular need for such a book was all the greater, that the deficiencies in it might turn other historians from cultivating their own small fields to work in the entire domain, and that the popularization of this learning for the Russian people was not the same thing as its vulgarization.[29]

In the introduction to this work Milyukov revealed something of his conception of history as it had then come to be. He was an adherent of what he described as the "organic school," which was characterized by its scientific method, its use of statistics, and its unceasing search to discover and to comprehend the causes and the meaning of historical events. Then came the effort to present the conclusions of this study as a comprehensive, intelligible whole, to be of genuine practical utility, and not solely as an object of mere curiosity or a collection of stories about past times.[30] He was excited over the ascendant sociological approach to history and an adept in its terminology. In these early pages he somewhat consciously devoted space to this viewpoint and attitude, turning the subject around and about without any precise conclusions crystallizing his discussion. He did not believe in the necessity of a philosophy of history, because that idea was only one of the remains of an older conception of history which had been discarded. Likewise, he argued a while over the presence of laws in history, but the complexity of historical phenomena seemed to discredit the presence of special laws while not preventing the idea of a scheme or pattern of some sort.[31] In his cultural history the view of the uniqueness of the Russian historical past, influencing the entire development of the growth of the country, is strongly expressed. Even after Peter's violent efforts at Europeanization, the Russian historical process remained an organic growth, assimilating the foreign innovations but not losing its national basis. Milyukov was certain that this, and later, revolutionary periods only interrupted, without breaking, the normal evolution in national development. The accidental features of any particular time would not distort the fundamental characteristics of the cultural development of Russia over the longer ages in harmony with its unique and persisting sources of influence.[32]

The first volume described the material civilization of Russia. The original settlement of the land is shown, and then the growth of this population and its shifting movements are followed through the centuries. The differences in the character of the people settled in the northern, central, and southern regions of the country are set forth; and the role they played in the filling-up of the Russian land, as well as the colonization of Siberia, is explained. Several chapters narrate the economic conditions and customs of the people, the original exploitation of the native riches, and the slow transfer to an agrarian culture, with the decline of trade with Byzantium and Hanseatic towns. Later on, there came the building-up of a home, hand industry, which Peter and his successors supplemented by a factory system, until toward the close of the nineteenth century modern capitalism arose, fostered by an interested government. The nature of the development of the Russian government and the close connection of the administration with the military tasks and tax revenues are carefully shown throughout the Muscovite era and in Peter's impulsive reign. The imposition of a European bureaucratic autocracy and the growth of local administration never fully satisfied Russian conditions, and Milyukov increasingly criticized its failures to reform itself the nearer he came toward contemporary times. At the end of this volume the author again returned to studying the population in its social and class structure. He described the persisting inadequacy of the landed aristocracy as a self-sufficient group; the thin numbers and weakness of urban classes as Russian cities grew; the growth of serfdom, with its attendant economic and social problems; and the consequent agrarian politics, which led to emancipation but which did not settle the future of the commune or solve the bitter material conditions of a multiplying peasantry.

The importance of the church in the cultural development of Russia is decisively stated in the opening paragraphs of Milyukov's next volume. In clean-cut literary expression, revealing something of his sociological approach, the author handled the variable opinions on the role of the church in a wholly realistic manner. He analyzed these divergencies, rejected those parts with which he was unable to agree, but salvaged and reconciled the rest, which was pertinent in evaluating the contributions of religion.

The cultural influence of the church and religion absolutely predominated in the historical life of the Russian people, as it always does with all peoples who find themselves in a similar stage of development. Nevertheless, there was, and there still persists, a widespread opinion that this prevailing influence of the church was the national peculiarity of the Russian people. There were two divergent views regarding this peculiarity. Out of this uniqueness the one group deduced all the virtues of Russian life, while the other was inclined to attribute to it all the shortcomings. The progenitors of Slavophilism believed that submission to the will of God, love and humility, kindliness to neighbors, and spiritual contemplation, which constituted the very substance of Christian ethics, were natural, in the highest degree, to Russian character. This complete harmony of the Christian and national virtues assured the great future of the Russian people. The generation of intellectuals of the eighteen-nineties tried to revive this attitude, and they gained an unanticipated influence among the youth of a later time, who grew up under the impressions of war and the catastrophe by which Russia was overwhelmed.

The other view was entirely antipathetic to this one. It found its clearest formulation in the expressions of Chaadayev. If Russia straggled on behind Europe, if its past was woebegone and its future obscure, if it risked remaining congealed for ages in its Chinese immobility, then this was the fault of corrupted Byzantium. From this poisoned well Russia took the great concept of Christianity, whose living strength was sapped at its root by Byzantine formalism. The influence of the Byzantine church on Russian culture was indeed actually great, but it was a destructive influence.

Both these contrary views agree in the recognition of the immense cultural importance of a renowned religious form. We shall not analyze this view in its essense; but, whatever our opinion may be, one thing is indisputable: that to exert the fulness of its influence on life, the loftiest, the most perfect religious principle must permeate that life more or less fully and consciously. Even the Slavophiles themselves (in the person of one of the wisest of their representatives, most competent in religious questions, Khomyakov), recognized that to represent ancient Russia as truly Christian amounted to an excessive idealization of the Russian past. According to Khomyakov's just opinion, old Russia accepted only the external form, the ritual, of the Christian religion, but not its spirit or substance. Therefore, this religion could exercise neither as beneficent nor as retarding an influence on the development of the Russian nation as the Slavophiles and Chaadayev supposed. In our time Khomyakov's view has become generally accepted and is to be met with in the textbooks on the history of the church.

So then, to consider the Russian nation as truly Christian without further inquiry would be to exaggerate greatly the degree of its assimilation of genuine Christianity. An equal exaggeration of the influence of religion would be to reproach it for Russian backwardness. There were other, organic reasons for this lagging, the effect of which was extended to the religion itself. Religion was not only unable to build up the Russian psychic mind, but, on the contrary, it even suffered from the primitiveness of this mentality. In the face of the most diverse opinions on the Byzantine form of religion accepted by Russia, it is impossible to deny that in its source this religiousness represented something incomparably superior to what the Russian people of that early time could have assimilated.[33]

After some consideration of the primitive religion of the old tribes Milyukov carried Christian Russia from its conversion to Eastern Christianity through the nationalization of faith and church to the condition of religion in his own time. He was fascinated by the prolific development of schisms and their angry quarrels in Muscovite times, and he pursued the fortunes of the dissenters and the growth of their sects over all persecution.

Besides the spiritual culture, a substantial part of this volume is concerned with the schools and the content of Russian education. The schools of pre-Petrine times, mostly church sustained and staffed, had a fabulous body of myths which passed for knowledge; these furnished the author an obviously welcome opportunity to give humorous and satirical descriptions. The educational improvement, both in the number of schools and the quality of learning, is recognized, even statistically, in modern times; but Milyukov often castigated the illiberal policies of ministers of public instruction and circumstantially portrayed the distrust of a small intelligentsia class by the uneducated, suspicious masses—a gulf into which he himself later fell during his political career. Much of this appears in the delayed and less well-known third volume, which is especially concerned with the intellectual culture of Russia, its nationalism, and the formation of public opinion. Milyukov has represented the enduring conflict between the archaic ideology of old Muscovy and the intrusive western-European thought from the seventeenth century onward, and also the encounters of the modern, Westernized intelligentsia with a government that was often imbued with the spirit of the past. Milyukov clearly revealed himself as a Westerner who believed that Russia, despite much legitimate feeling for its native traditions, must adapt itself to Western civilization, since its strength insured its triumph anyhow.

Alone among his writings Milyukov revised and enlarged this one in numerous subsequent editions. The character of the study was not altered until the appearance of the "Jubilee edition," for the changes consisted of new sources of statistical data tucked into the existing text and many improvements in language in order to make the presentation more precise or to ease the effort of the reader. Reasonably long forewords began to appear with the third edition, in which the author carried on vigorous polemics with confreres who had ventured to criticize an interpretation, or conclusion. With Peter B. Struve he disputed the role played by native peasant industry in the eighteenth and nineteenth centuries and argued several "general sociological questions" dear to his heart at the time.[34] When Professor Tugan-Baranovsky declared that the development of a strong industry under Peter was the natural and inevitable result of the economic and social conditions of Russia, then Milyukov tore this view to pieces—at least to his own satisfaction—while defending his own interpretation that the Petrine industrialization was unnatural and artificially forced.[35] After the celebrations of 1929 Milyukov harkened to the pleas of his admirers and practically re-wrote this work in the next eight years. This "Jubilee edition" is double the length of the old version. The first volume has not yet been completed, but the published first part is an entirely new book which is an amazing accomplishment dealing with prehistoric times. The second volume has now two parts, and these carry the subjects of the older editions through the remaining years of the nineteenth century, with much fresh material down into the Soviet period. Only the third volume remains substantially the same, without noteworthy extensions. This new edition, despite its superiority, remains less known than the old work, which itself was without a peer.[36]

Before long Milyukov published a group of eight lectures or essays relating to another of his favorite themes, *Iz istorii russkoy intelligentsii: sbornik statey i etyudov* [From the history of the Russian intelligentsia: a collection of articles and studies].[37] These vignettes are as overflows, in detail, from the cultural history, and supplementary to it. The binding thread through these essays is

an analysis of the character of the Russian spirit and its development, as well as of some of the men responsible for this, from S. T.
Aksakov, through the theoreticians of the mid-nineteenth century, to the last, forlorn giants of Slavophilism. An introductory
study, not fully in keeping with this substance, analyzed the first
attempt to limit the power of the Russian autocracy made by the
"intellectuals" of 1730 during the crisis when Empress Anne came
to the throne. The princes Galitzyn and Dolgoruki, as members
of the supreme council, played the leading parts in this first constitutional movement attempted by the early liberals. After paying tribute to the thoughtfulness and lasting influence of the old
Slavophile, S. T. Aksakov, the author has inserted four essays on
the idealists of the middle of the last century, in which he contrasted, with a deft, half-humorous touch, their struggles with
their love affairs and the seriousness of their philosophical problems. Milyukov illustrated the chief error of these idealists as ly-
ing in the abstract quality of their idealism. They repeated the
same tendency in their love-making. To one of them, N. V.
Stankevich, love was, "before everything, the cosmic force which
had given life to the world and all that lives in it"; love was "a
pretty vision of the soul."[38] Well, in due course these soulful idealists had their love affairs; and their terrible struggles to preserve
the quality of their idealism, unblemished by the passion of any
violent love, tormented both their thinking and their loving.
While they finally succeeded in attaining lovely ideals, they never
became ideal lovers, although they did eventually marry.

Of especial interest to historians should be the essay on the
course of medieval European history taught by Professor Granovsky at the University of Moscow. This course Milyukov was enabled to reconstruct from the voluminous notes taken by, and
circulated among, the students, with all the "usual student errors."[39] Granovsky had a most important career in improving the
quality of history taught in Russian universities. Originally he
was no specialist in medieval history, and he labored mightily to
present a sound treatment. He had a genuine love of his subject
and a way with students that gave him a memorable reputation.

On the basis of the copious notes, containing a list of the fifty-two lessons (which the professor never quite covered), Milyukov analyzed the course and showed its relation to the thought of those times.

The gem of the collection, however, is the essay on the disintegration of Slavophilism by the close of the nineteenth century. This was a topic on which Milyukov was accounted an outstanding, critical authority. In this tightly constructed study (a lecture once read in the Moscow Historical Museum) the decline of Slavophilism is shown through the analysis of the ideas in the masterpieces of the last three giants of the movement—N. I. Danilevsky, Konstantin Leontyev, and Vladimir S. Solovyev, the philosopher. Already threatened by the ascendancy of western European ideas, these great thinkers, each in his own way, labored to restore the old Slavophile concepts of the national uniqueness of Russia and Russian ways. So bitter in his dislike for the influx of novel Western ideas did Leontyev become that he recommended that "Russia must be kept frozen lest it become putrid,"[40] while Solovyev declared that the universal church could only resurrect Europe and the world through an alliance of the tsar and the pope.[41] Yet, despite his devastating criticism of these last, reactionary or philosophical Slavophiles, there is a trace of wistful, romantic sentiment in Milyukov's writing when he explained that this revival of Slavophilism was doomed from the outset and that, if it was not yet quite dead, "it was disappearing before our eyes."[42]

With this book Milyukov's purely historical writing ended until his years in western Europe. While he still wrote much more, this production is a mixture, sometimes unequal, of politics and history. To this category belongs Milyukov's best-known book in English, *Russia and its crisis*, which criticized the internal economic and political disruption of the country on the eve of the Revolution of 1905.[43] His strictures on the faulty, oppressive policies of the Russian autocracy are vigorous with excessive partisan zeal; but there is enough of substantial information in the chapters to make the book significantly valuable, and the lengthy chap-

ter on "The crisis and the urgency of reform" remains an outstanding, penetrating description from an advanced liberal outlook. The readability of this work is impaired by poor organization, an awkward transliteration of Russian names, and the author's pardonable unfamiliarity with the English language; but
the last chapter partly redeems the earlier diffuseness in its skilful
summary.

After his return to Russia, Milyukov became involved in the
constitutional movement and contributed a plethora of brief articles to Kadet newspapers. Many of these sketches were collected
in two stout volumes before their composition was hindered by
his entrance into the third duma.[44] These articles cover such vital
matters as the first constitutional concessions by the autocracy,
the immediate formation of political parties, the political position
at the turn of the year 1905–6, the electoral campaigns, the ses-
sions and dismissals of the first and second dumas. Besides being
shrewd commentaries on current politics, many of these articles
have much learned historical background and should not have
been so neglected by later historians in writing about these formidable years. With Milyukov's participation in the third and
fourth dumas he had less time for writing. He contributed articles to the *Ryech*, but these were never collected; and there was an
occasional address or lecture delivered abroad, but only one little-
known book critical of Izvolsky's foreign policies, particularly his
mishandling of Balkan affairs and his slighting of Bulgaria, whose
qualities Milyukov was still championing.[45]

During the war and the period of the bourgeois revolution
Milyukov's political activity reached its zenith, but with the
seizure of power by the Bolsheviks he fled from Petrograd and
forthwith began to compose his *Istoriya vtoroy russkoy revolyutsii*
[History of the second Russian revolution].[46] The author deliberately entitled his labor a "history" because it included much
more than his own participation and recollections. He recalled
that he was a professional historian, accustomed to objectivity
and disinclined to warp facts. Although he likewise recognized
that he was writing too soon after the events for his pages to be un-

impassioned, he cultivated this stricter form, thereby depriving himself of certain privileges of a writer of memoirs in order to fulfil more closely the duties of a historian.[47] The manuscript of the three volumes was completed between November, 1917, and August, 1918, but most of it was lost in his flight from Kiev; and it was not reconstructed until the end of 1920, while a contemplated fourth volume never has appeared.[48]

Admittedly, these volumes are not successfully impartial history; yet they contain some of the most vigorous thinking of a participant in tremendous events who possessed a knowledge of many of them for which no neutral source ever existed. In the occasional footnotes there is sometimes a reference to printed material in periodicals little known, short-lived, and seldom preserved. Other times citations indicate an individual's statements told orally to Milyukov at later meetings in the south of Russia or in the emigration in western Europe after the struggle was over. In the later volumes there are a few more references to periodical articles and the first books that were already appearing in the Russian *émigré* colonies, and once there is a dissection of a later, more colorful story in place of an earlier, little known version which Milyukov formerly had used.[49] For the most part, however, these volumes are full of the recollections and experiences of the participant author, who made an effort to portray them with care and precision, even writing his narrative severely in the third person. Although he failed to remain the cool historian, much information not elsewhere available is generously scattered through the books.

Many of these ideas Milyukov sought to popularize on a lecture tour in the United States. These miscellaneous lectures were brought together in book form; but they lack a uniform theme, and the language is too often faulty. The lectures certainly did not tell the whole story of the failure by the liberals to establish a democratic government in Russia, while the hope was then still existent that Bolshevism was only a temporary phase in the unrolling of "the great and complicated revolutionary process" which had sometimes in other countries required decades to reach its constructive fruition.[50] The story of the revolution and the further development of the struggle against the Bolsheviks formed the substance of another large publication a few years afterward, *Rossiya na perelomye; bolshevistsky period russkoy revolyutsii* [Russia at the abyss; the Bolshevik period of the Russian Revolution].[51] The events here described occurred after the period of Milyukov's personal participation was over, so that his information came from other sources, many of which are indicated in bibliographical footnotes scattered through the two volumes. His interpretations, somewhat softened by passing time, still were so bitter that this work retains the characteristics of a protagonist of a defeated cause rather than the objectivity of a distinguished historian, despite the quantity of data and shrewd criticism it undeniably has.

Some Russian *émigré* historians, with a few others, entered upon a collaboration which culminated in the appearance of an outstanding, extensive general *Histoire de Russie*.[52] In this project Milyukov assumed a position of leadership, founded upon the esteem of his high historical reputation and his valuable political experience. To this undertaking he contributed a number of chapters on his favorite historical subjects, including the excellent introductory chapter on Russian historians and historiogaphy and those on the early Romanovs, the reign of Peter the Great, and the rise of the revolutionary movement and ideologies after the middle of the nineteenth century, which are certainly among the best in the book. He was likewise responsible for the chapters on the reign of Nicholas II, which is treated from the viewpoint of the liberal opposition—although he no longer ascribed to it all the wisdom he did in the years before the revolutions of 1917. Also modified, but still not impartially historical, is his attitude toward the Soviet regime. He believed that the failure of collective agriculture (by 1932) and the inability to find an internal market for the products of a disproportionately expanded industry ought to indicate the end of the Stalinist period of the revolution. With satisfaction he attested that the international nature of the movement had weakened before a revival of Russian nationalism; yet he now admitted that there was no longer any hope of resuming the course of Russian history engulfed by the October Revolution.[53] The chapters from the other associates regularly maintain the high level of this publication.

Paul Milyukov has already an established position in the ranks of important Russian historians. He was a descendant of the Moscow school of historians which emphasized research on the internal development of Russian life. He was one of the first to stress the value of the study of the material side of this historical process, but he thought it was entirely too one-sided to attribute the whole growth of the Russian people to economic causation. In time he became the eldest representative of this Moscow school; yet he broadened his interests beyond those of its founders.[54] He brought to his own writings the viewpoint of a pronounced Westerner and liberal. He represented Russian history as an organic process, possessing unique elements which could be influenced by foreign assimilations but which were never lastingly disrupted by them. Russian historians like himself were never reluctant to admit foreign influences, although they took pains to show how these imported models were adapted to the conditions of Russian life.[55] He possessed a fine, sometimes even a brilliant, mind, combined with an extraordinary capacity for work. His interpretation of historical material was courageous and occasionally original, which others might question, although Milyukov was then prone to defend it. At the same time he was outspokenly critical of the doctrines advanced by others, and he poked derision at the Eurasian conception of Russian history long before he accorded it a grudging, partial acceptance.[56]

Russian historical literature was rarely equipped with precise documentation or resplendent, critical bibliographies. Milyukov's own writings usually were not exceptions. He did share the Russian fondness for marshaling statistics to buttress an argument, and he made generous use of them without always revealing where they were obtained.[57] His footnotes are illustrations or amplifications of the text more often than they are references to authority or suggestions for further reading. In his great cultural history of Russia he specifically declared his decision not to encumber the pages with citations, although in considerable measure he listed at the close of most of the chapters those books and articles which had been of chief value in their composition.[58] Here are included the sources of those viewpoints which the author adopted or with which he quarreled, all held together with a brief commentary seldom possessed of critical importance. In his earlier years he went through vast quantities of archival material, which he often quoted and sometimes described in his books, but not often did he identify its location in the precise manner of Western historians.

The truly historical reputation of Milyukov must rest chiefly on the works of his younger years, before he turned to a political career, and on the cultural history which he rewrote late in life. His numerous writings on current happenings are done with the point of view of a trained historian dominant over that of a memoir-writer or apologist, although these habits are undeniably present. While Milyukov was a better historian of the past than he was of his own turbulent times, nevertheless these writings contain much stuff and knowledge not to be found elsewhere. Even as these contributions stand, they are no less impartial or bigger failures than the output of the advocates of opposing factions.[59] There has not been any too clear an evaluation of Milyukov's historical position by English-speaking historians, since so few of his books have been translated, while the two volumes originally written in that language suffer from the author's imperfect command of it and because they treated disputatious, contemporary problems. The sometimes cloying adulation of his admirers during the celebrations honoring Milyukov in 1929 is well-motivated but excessive praise; in Berlin the university professor Karl Stählin made his comparisons of Milyukov with Ranke.[60] At the other extreme stands the charge that Milyukov as a historian was an "unprincipled eclectic" and that his *History of the second Russian revolution* was clearly a work of "historical falsification."[61] No one of his detractors so vigorously impugned his personal character and motives, or so scornfully and often tellingly criticized his political actions, as Leon Trotsky, himself in great need of charitable handling.[62]

The likelihood is slight that Milyukov wrote much "definitive" history; he was himself keenly aware of the gaps in his cultural history, the most valuable of all his writing. He hoped that these deficiencies would spur other historians to do the research required to make them good.[63] No one knows, meanwhile, how much material may have been destroyed or how much cultivated historical skill has been neglected. Milyukov's contributions will have to suffice for the present, for, as one of the capable, cultured historians of Russia slips from view, no worthy successor peeps above the plain.

NOTES

1. The incidents in Milyukov's life can be found in S. A. Smirnov, N. D. Avksent-yev, M. A. Aldanov, I. P. Demidov, G. B. Sliozberg, and A. F. Stupnitsky (eds.), *P. N. Milyukov:sbornik materialov po chestvovaniyu ego semidesyatilyetiya, 1859–1929: yubileyny sbornik* [P. N. Milyukov: a collection of materials in honor of his seventy years, 1859–1929: Jubilee collection] (Paris, 1929), pp. 1–19 (hereafter cited as *Milyukov: sbornik . . . . ego semidesyatilyetiya*); *Bolshaya entsiklopediya* [The great encyclopedia] (St. Petersburg, 1909), XXII, 12; *Bolshaya sovietskaya entsiklopediya* [The great Soviet encyclopedia] (Moscow, 1938), XXXIX, 417–18; *Encyclopaedia Britannica* (12th ed.; New York, 1922), XXXI, 947 (this sketch by Paul Vinogradov is superior to the lesser accounts in the 13th and 14th eds.); *Le mouvement intellectuel russe*, preface by the translator J. W. Bienstock (Paris, 1918), pp. 1–4. Milyukov had also begun the publication of chapters of his memoirs, "Rokoviye gody" [Fateful years], *Russkiya zapiski* [Russian annals] (Paris, 1938–39), Vols. IV–XXI. These cover the period from immediately preceding the Revolution of 1905 through the first duma, ending with the Vyborg manifesto. For other details I am indebted to Professor Samuel N. Harper, of the University of Chicago, and Professor Michael M. Karpovich, of Harvard University, who have been acquainted with Milyukov for many years.

2. *Milyukov: sbornik . . . . ego semidesyatilyetiya*, p. 2.

3. "The chief currents of Russian historical thought," *Annual report of the American Historical Association, 1904* (Washington, 1905), p. 114; P. N. Milyukov, Ch. Seignobos, L. Eisenmann, with the collaboration of Camena d'Almeida, G. Danilov, P. Gronsky, A. Kizevetter, V. Myakotin, B. S. Mirkin-Getsevich, and L. Niederle, *Histoire de Russie* (3 vols.; Paris, 1932), Vol. I, *Des origines à la mort de Pierre le grand*, pp. 25–26; V. I. Picheta, *Vvedeniye v russkuyu istoriyu. (Istochniki i istoriografiya.)* [Introduction to Russian history. (Sources and historiography.)] (Moscow, 1922), pp. 151–52. The rival St. Petersburg school, of which the historian Bestuzhev-Ryumin was the leading exponent, pursued the narrower purpose of "critical study of sources" (*Annual report, AHA, 1904*, p. 114).

4. "Klyuchevsky," *Encyclopaedia of the social sciences* (15 vols.; New York, 1930–35), VIII, 577.

5. Between 1886 and 1894 most of Milyukov's articles and reviews appeared in *Russkaya mysl* [Russian thought], *Istorichesky vyestnik* [Historical messenger], *Istoriches-*

koye obozryeniye [Historical review], *Russky arkhiv* [Russian archive], *Russkaya starina* [Russian antiquity], and *Kievskaya starina* [Kievan antiquity]. In 1889 his first publication in a foreign-language periodical appeared: "Insigne énigmatique sur la monnaie des grand-ducs de Kieff," *Annales de la Société Française de Numismatique*. He also contributed regular articles on literature in Russia to the *Athenaeum* of London, 1889–96. See *Milyukov: sbornik . . . . ego semidesyatilyetiya*, pp. 313–16.

6. In the Paris celebration in Milyukov's honor on Mar. 2, 1929, I. P. Demidov paid glowing tribute to Milyukov as a lecturer. He recalled with appropriate nostalgia the effect on the audience of these lectures on "Social currents from the time of Catherine II" (*Milyukov: sbornik . . . . ego semidesyatilyetiya*, pp. 154–55).

7. The substance of these Chicago lectures made Milyukov's book, *Russia and its crisis* (Chicago, 1905).

8. *Milyukov: sbornik . . . . ego semidesyatilyetiya*, pp. 352–58. His most famous duma speech of Nov. 1/14, 1916, in denunciation of the "dark forces" in the government and around the throne, may be conveniently read in Frank A. Golder (ed.), *Documents of Russian history, 1914–1917* (New York, 1927), pp. 154–66.

9. *Bolshaya sovietskaya entsiklopediya*, XXXIX, 417.

10. *Russia to-day and to-morrow* (New York, 1922), p. 19; Bernard Pares, *The fall of the Russian monarchy: a study of the evidence* (New York, 1939), p. 261; Basil Maklakov, "On the fall of tsardom," *SR*, XVII (1939), 75–76, 87, 92; Maklakov's views are developed in greater detail in his memoirs, *Vlast i obshchestvennost na zakatye staroy Rossii* [The state power and public forces during the decline of old Russia] (3 vols.; Paris, 1936), and the many circumstantial comments in V. I. Gurko (ed. J. E. Wallace Sterling, Xenia Joukoff Eudin, and H. H. Fisher; trans. Laura Matveev), *Features and figures of the past: government and opinion in the reign of Nicholas II* (Stanford University, Calif., 1939).

11. *Milyukov: sbornik . . . . ego semidesyatilyetiya*, p. 15.

12. Pares, p. 478; O. H. Gankin and H. H. Fisher (eds.), *The Bolsheviks and the world war: the origin of the Third International* (Stanford University, Calif., 1940), pp. 587–90; see Milyukov's own version in his *Istoriya vtoroy russkoy revolyutsii* [History of the second Russian revolution] (3 vols.; Sofia, 1921–23), I, 109–16.

13. *Encyclopaedia Britannica* (12th ed.), XXXI, 947; *Bolshaya sovietskaya entsiklopediya*, XXXIX, 418.

14. *Milyukov: sbornik . . . . ego semidesyatilyetiya*, p. 17.

15. Communist rebuttal asserts that Milyukov edited his paper in a spirit of "democratic unification" which was a cloak for counterrevolutionary forces of bourgeois, menshevik, socialist revolutionary, and Trotskyist persuasions (*Bolshaya sovietskaya entsiklopediya*, XXXIX, 418). Milyukov's more resigned attitude is seen in *Histoire de Russie*, III, 1382.

16. In addition to books, described later on, Milyukov sent articles on current political problems to learned journals and contributed sketches on incidents and individuals prominent in Russian history to the *Encyclopaedia Britannica* and the *Encyclopaedia of the social sciences*. He also traveled and lectured frequently in western Europe, besides coming twice more to the United States, in 1921–22 and 1928.

17. In honor of this occasion a collection of twenty-five historical articles, some of which are of considerable merit, was assembled into a presentation volume by the Prague editorial committee, consisting of B. A. Evreinov, A. A. Kizevetter, N. D.

Lossky, Jan Slavik, and E. F. Shmurlo: *Sbornik statey, posvyashchennykh Pavlu Niko-layevichu Milyukovu. 1859–1929* [Collection of articles, dedicated to Paul Nikolayevich Milyukov, 1859–1929] (Prague, 1929). Full details of the festivities, with the addresses, are in the other presentation volume cited above, in n. 1.

18. Milyukov so steadfastly opposed the policies of National Socialism that his newspaper was proscribed in Germany after 1936. He advocated the firm bridling of the menace of German aggression (" 'Indivisible menace' and the two blocs in Europe," *SR*, XV [1937], 587). He dreaded that the 'few hours of inadvertent concession at Munich" would compel democratic Europe "to pay a heavy price for the deficiency of its representatives at a most critical moment" ("Edward Beneš," *SR*, XVII [1939], 322).

19. St. Petersburg, 1892; 2d ed., 1905.

20. *Milyukov: sbornik . . . . ego semidesyatilyetiya*, pp. 3–4, 40–41, 82; A. G. Mazour, "Modern Russian historiography," *JMH*, IX (1937), 192.

21. St. Petersburg, 1892.

22. Moscow, 1897; 2d ed., St. Petersburg, 1898; 3d ed., St. Petersburg, 1913.

23. See V. Myakotin in *Milyukov: sbornik . . . . ego semidesyatilyetiya*, p. 44; Mazour, *loc. cit.*, p. 192.

24. S. Smirnov in *Milyukov: sbornik . . . . ego semidesyatilyetiya*, pp. 5–6.

25. See above, n. 3. Beginning in 1895, Milyukov contributed to the famous *Entsiklopedichesky slovar F. A. Brokgauza i I. A. Efrona* [Encyclopedic dictionary of F. A. Brockhaus and I. A. Efron]. One article is "Sources of Russian history and Russian historians," Vol. XXVIII (St. Petersburg, 1899), Book 55, pp. 430–36.

26. Vol. I, *Naseleniye, ekonomichesky, gosudarstvny i soslovny stroy* [The population, the economic, political, and class structure]; Vol. II, *Tserkov i shkola (vyera, tvorchestvo, obrazovaniye)* [Church and school (faith, creative genius, education)]; Vol. III, *Natsionalizm i obshchestvennoye mnyeniye* [Nationalism and public opinion] (St. Petersburg, 1896, 1897, 1901–3). In all, there were seven editions to 1918 of Vol. I, four editions to 1905 of Vol. II, and three printings to 1909 of Vol. III. The re-written and enlarged "Yubileynoye izdaniye" [Jubilee edition] (3 vols.), in several parts, still unfinished, was published in Paris (1930–37). There is a German edition, somewhat abridged, of the first two volumes: *Skizzen russischer Kulturgeschichte* (Leipzig, 1898, 1901). Only the first volume was translated into French: *Essais sur l'histoire de la civilization russe* (Paris, 1901). All volumes were published in Czech: *Obrazy z dějin ruské vzdělanosti* (Prague, 1910). There is forthcoming an authorized abridged version in English of the second volume of the "Jubilee edition" on religion, literature, and art: *Outline of Russian culture*, ed., Michael M. Karpovich (Philadelphia: University of Pennsylvania Press).

27. *Milyukov: sbornik . . . . ego semidesyatilyetiya*, pp. 45, 83; *Ocherki po istorii russkoy kultury*, p. 18.

28. *Ocherki po istorii russkoy kultury*, pp. 2–3.

29. *Ibid.*, pp. 18–19.

30. *Ibid.*, p. 2; *Annual report, AHA, 1904*, p. 111; *Milyukov: sbornik . . . . ego semidesyatilyetiya*, p. 41.

31. *Ocherki po istorii russkoy kultury*, I, 6–8.

32. *Ibid.*, p. 18; Picheta, pp. 152–53; review by N. Hans, *SR*, XI (1933), 466.

33. *Ocherki po istorii russkoy kultury* (Jubilee edition, Paris, 1931), II, 10–11.

34. *Ibid.*, I, 277–86, 290–93.

35. *Ibid.*, pp. 288–90.

36. This opinion does not overlook the existence of M. N. Pokrovsky's *Ocherk istorii russkoy kultury* [Study of the history of Russian culture] (2 vols.; Petrograd, 1923); see also Hans, *loc. cit.*, p. 463.

37. St. Petersburg, 1902. Only the French translation by J. W. Bienstock, *Le mouvement intellectuel russe* (Paris, 1918), was available to me.

38. *Le mouvement intellectuel russe*, p. 124.

39. *Ibid.*, p. 305.

40. *Ibid.*, p. 409.

41. *Ibid.*, p. 426. In a rejoinder Solovyev disputed Milyukov's assertions and denied that he was a Slavophile at all. See his "Zamechaniya na lektsiyu P. N. Milyukova" [Remarks on P. N. Milyukov's lecture], *Sobraniye sochinenii V. S. Solovyeva* [Collected works of V. S. Solovyev] (8 vols.; St. Petersburg, 1901–3), V, 458–62.

42. *Le mouvement intellectuel russe*, pp. 378, 439.

43. See above, n. 7. Reviewed by C. E. Fryer in *AHR*, XI (1906), 678–79.

44. *God borby: publisisticheskaya khronika, 1905–1906* [Year of struggle: a journalistic chronicle, 1905–6] (St. Petersburg, 1907); *Vtoraya duma: publisisticheskaya khronika, 1907* [The second duma: a journalistic chronicle, 1907] (St. Petersburg, 1908).

45. See Milyukov's address, *Constitutional government for Russia* (New York, 1908); his testimonial, "Kharakhteristiki i vospominaniya" [Characteristics and reminiscences], in the memorial *Sbornik "V. O. Klyuchevsky"* [Collection "V. O. Klyuchevsky"] (Moscow, 1912); two lectures in 1916 at Cambridge University in James D. Duff (ed.), *Russian realities and problems* (Cambridge, 1917), and *Balkansky krizis i politika A. P. Izvolskago* [The Balkan crisis and the policy of A. P. Izvolsky] (St. Petersburg, 1910).

46. Vol. I, *Protivoryechiya revolyutsii* [Inconsistencies of the revolution]; Vol. II, *Borba burzhuaznoy i sotsialisticheskoy revolyutsii: Kornilov ili Lenin?* [Struggle of the bourgeois and socialist revolution: Kornilov or Lenin?]; Vol. III, *Agoniya vlasti* [The agony of power] (Sofia, 1921–23). The only translation is of the first volume into Bulgarian, ed. M. Arnautov, *Istoriyata na vtorata ruska revolyutsiya* (Sofia, 1921).

47. *Istoriya vtoroy russkoy revolyutsii*, I, 3–4; III, 308.

48. *Ibid.*, I, 3; III, 107, 152, 308. An edition of the first volume actually was published in Kiev in 1918, almost all copies of which were destroyed when the city was seized by Petlura's troops (*ibid.*, I, 3; *Milyukov: sbornik . . . . ego semidesyatilyetiya*, p. 335).

49. *Istoriya vtoroy russkoy revolyutsii*, III, 241–42.

50. *Russia to-day and to-morrow*, pp. viii, 31–32, 39–40. Reviewed by S. A. Korff, in *AHR*, XXVIII (1922), 126–27.

51. Vol. I, *Proiskhozhdeniye i ukryepleniye bolshevistskoy diktatury* [The origin and strengthening of the Bolshevik dictatorship]; Vol. II, *Antibolshevistskoye dvizheniye* [The anti-Bolshevik movement] (Paris, 1927). A third volume, in preparation in 1930, has not appeared. There is a German translation, fairly complete, by E. Janowski, *Russlands Zusammenbruch* (2 vols.; Stuttgart and Berlin, 1925–26).

52. Vol. I, *Des origines à la mort de Pierre le grand;* Vol. II, *Les successeurs de Pierre le grand; de l'autocratie appuyée sur la noblesse à l'autocratie bureaucratique;* Vol. III, *Réformes, réaction, révolutions, 1855–1932* (Paris, 1932). Also above, n. 3.

53. *Ibid.*, III, 1382.

54. *Milyukov: sbornik* . . . . *ego semidesyatilyetiya*, p. 41; Picheta, pp. 151–52; *Ocherki po istorii russkoy kultury*, I, 2.

55. Picheta, pp. 152–53; *Histoire de Russie*, I, xvi; Hans, *loc. cit.*, p. 466.

56. *Histoire de Russie*, I, 30–31; A. G. Mazour, *An outline of modern Russian historiography* (Berkeley, Calif., 1939), pp. 103–4. See also Milyukov's article contributed to the celebration of T. G. Masaryk's eightieth birthday, "Eurasianism and Europeanism in Russian history," *Der russische Gedanke*, I (Bonn, 1930), 225–36.

57. As an exception, full references are given in Milyukov's early study, *Gosudarstvennoye khozyaystvo Rossii v pervoy chetverti XVIII stolyetiya i reforma Petra Velikago.*

58. *Ocherki po istorii russkoy kultury*, I, 18.

59. Mazour, *An outline of modern Russian historiography*, p. 106; Pares, pp. 19, 39; *SR*, VII (1929), 768; *Milyukov: sbornik* . . . . *ego semidesyatilyetiya*, p. 47.

60. *Milyukov: sbornik* . . . . *ego semidesyatilyetiya*, pp. 92–95.

61. *Bolshaya sovietskaya entsiklopediya*, XXXIX, 417–18. For another Bolshevik opinion—lengthily stated, yet without historical merit—see O. A. Lidak, "P. N. Milyukov kak istorik" [P. N. Milyukov as a historian], in M. N. Pokrovsky (ed.), *Russkaya istoriya v klassovom osveshchenii* [Russian history from the point of view of class struggle] (2 vols.; Moscow, 1927–30), II, 123–214.

62. L. Trotsky, *The history of the Russian revolution* (3 vols.; New York, 1932), wherein the attacks on character are liberally sprinkled through the first volume, and on political activity throughout the second.

63. *Ocherki po istorii russkoy kultury*, I, 18–19.

XVI

MIKHAIL NIKOLAYEVICH POKROVSKY
(1868–1932)

THOMAS R. HALL*

W ITH the victory of the October (N.S., November, 1917), Revolution in Russia the doctrine of Marxian socialism became the official philosophy of a great state. An organized campaign was immediately inaugurated to overthrow theories of government, education, and science which leaders of the Russian Communist party considered "bourgeois" and reactionary. The effects of this campaign were especially significant in the field of historical studies. It was considered imperative to uproot and discard a philosophy of history which was dangerous to the revolution and to replace it with one more suitable to a socialist state. Soviet historians likewise faced the task of opening and arranging archives and documentary collections which had been neglected under the former government, as well as that of organizing historical work on a scale far wider than had existed before the revolution. The successes achieved on what came to be known as the "historical front" were largely the result of the scholarly work and organizing ability of a single individual. Mikhail Nikolayevich Pokrovsky, for a decade and a half the guiding genius of Soviet historians, has placed the ineradicable imprint of his personality on a generation of scholars.[1] Although after his death his philosophy was officially discarded and his disciples called from their allegiance, his work has preserved his commanding position in Soviet scholarship. To him, more than to any other man, must be charged the failures and successes of Soviet historical research.

* State director, Illinois Historical Records Survey, Chicago, Ill.

Pokrovsky was born in Moscow in 1868. Following the accepted course of sons of good bourgeois families, he entered one of the best classical Gymnasiums of his home city, afterward matriculating in the historical-philological faculty of the University of Moscow. Here he came under the influence of Klyuchevsky and Vinogradov, two of the leading lights in Russian historical study during the last of the nineteenth and the early twentieth centuries. At the university he was exposed to the "national history" of Klyuchevsky and the first feeble influence of economic interpretation, which was such a great factor in his later career.[2]

As the result of some temperamental difficulty with Klyuchevsky, he abandoned his university work after graduation in 1891. For several years he taught in the secondary schools of Moscow, beginning in 1895 his lectures in history at the Pedagogical Institute in that city.[3] This work was continued until the suspicion of the police forced the young professor to discontinue his educational career.

Marxian doctrines had been seeping through the Russian censorship since the early eighties. The necessity of combating the police led writers on political and economic subjects who wished to discuss Russian problems from the viewpoint of Marxian philosophy to adopt the subterfuge known as "legal Marxism." This was Marxism shorn of its revolutionary dialectic. Russian history, particularly its latest phase, was subjected to intensive analysis. The influence of the growing capitalism on society and the state led to increasing emphasis on the importance of the economic factors of civilization. In such works Marxism was often "stood on its head"; the critique of capitalism became its apology, and Marx was made to glorify the new life instead of condemning it.[4]

Pokrovsky fell under the influence of this new current of thought. By the late nineties he had come to view history from the Marxian standpoint, although he was not yet formally enrolled in any party. However, under the pressure of the times his thinking was beginning to assume a revolutionary character. In 1903 the police forbade him to deliver public lectures; in 1904 he contributed his first article, "Idealism and the laws of history," to the Bolshevik newspaper, *Pravda* [Truth].[5] The events of 1905 brought the historian into active revolutionary work. In the atmosphere of great events he entered the Bolshevik ranks, helping to organize the uprising in Moscow at the end of that year.[6] After avoiding the police for several years Pokrovsky went abroad in 1907, as a delegate to the London congress of the Social-Democratic party and remained in exile for the next decade. Most of this period was spent in France in political and historical work. While lecturing in the party school at Capri, he joined Bogdanov and other dissatisfied Bolsheviks in forming the "Forward [Vpered] Group." These Leftwingers favored a boycott of the third duma and opposed the participation of the Bolsheviks in legal working-class organizations. In the spring of 1911, however, he broke away and rejoined the orthodox followers of Lenin.[7]

The events of 1917 opened the last and most productive phase of Pokrovsky's career. In August of that year he returned to Moscow and entered active party work, later representing the new Soviet state at the Brest-Litovsk peace negotiations. As a result of this experience he deviated from the party line, taking the Left view that to sign the peace treaty with Germany would be a tragic mistake; however, this was his last departure from the policies of Lenin, and he returned to the official party position within a short time.[8] Other high government posts were conferred upon him in rapid succession. Although he was not of the inner circle of the Communist party, Lenin's respect was sufficient to assure his position and guarantee his advancement.[9] In May, 1918, he was made a member of the commissariat of education, a position he held until his death. Workers' faculties (*Rabfaki*) were developed by Pokrovsky in 1920 to enable factory workers to prepare themselves for university work. Many of the great learned institutions of the Soviet Union were organized by this historian. The Institute of History, the Society of Marxist Historians, and the Institute of Red Professors of History were developed by Pokrovsky to give the new regime a foothold on the "historical front."

Many of the leading historical publications of the U.S.S.R. were edited by this indefatigable worker. *Istorik-Marksist* [The Marxist historian], *Borba klassov* [The class struggle], and *Krasny arkhiv* [Red archive] were among the most important journals under his direction. Pokrovsky's work on *Krasny archiv* was particularly significant in connection with the reorganization of the Russian archives. Shortly after the October Revolution Pokrovsky made his first examination of the secret records of the foreign office. In 1920 he was appointed head of the archival organization (*Centrarkhiv*), occupying this position until his death. With V. V. Adoratsky he directed the reorganization of the archives and the publication of the great collections of documents issued by the Soviet government.[10]

For fifteen years, until his death in 1932, Pokrovsky administered important departments and edited numerous learned journals and documentary collections; yet he found time to present his conception of Russian history in several books and scores of articles. These divide themselves into two classes: theoretical-philosophical studies and historical narratives of a more extended and general character. The former are articles and reviews which appeared from time to time in Marxist journals.[11] His more extended works were produced during his exile and after the success of the revolution.[12] They stamp Pokrovsky as one of the greatest Marxist historians of modern times—a writer whose works, though uneven, are of the greatest significance in modern Russian historiography. His philosophical concepts, although scorned by Soviet scholars in recent years, broke new ground in the study of Russian history.[13] It was Pokrovsky's task to overthrow the philosophy in which an older generation of historians had been nurtured, replacing it with one more suitable to a young, dynamic, and revolutionary people. We shall now examine the philosophy of history which molded a whole generation of Soviet historians and which, until 1934, formed the theoretical basis for their research and writings.

For Pokrovsky history is a revolutionary weapon. Through it, all the past can be revealed in its complexity; the richness of the future, if not foretold, then at least anticipated. History is utilitarian.[14] A man studies the series of regular changes through which his kind have gone in order more fully to understand his own conditions of life, examining the rise and fall of social orders in the past. This study will reveal the general laws governing social change, which may then be utilized in shaping the future course of society. This future society we can never know completely; only the tendencies can be foreseen and preparation made to avoid the mistakes of the past.[15]

Human events are in an eternal course of development. As the face of the earth has changed, so have the social systems of its human inhabitants. Only those whose interests are served thereby, those who wish the masses of the people to think that the rich and powerful will always rule, deny the development of society.[16] None but the Marxian interpretation of human life can break the influence of this selfish, bourgeois interpretation and place before the enslaved both the picture of their misery and the means of crushing the oppressor. Marxism does this through its emphasis on the struggle for the satisfaction of human needs, which is the basis of all human activity, and the resulting class warfare, the key to the understanding of any social order.[17]

Each ruling class, feudal or bourgeois, must guard its dominant position, which it does, in part, through the history it allows to be written. Every historical work must be understood as a product of the class struggle.[18] If subordinate social classes can be led to think that they are equal partners with their rulers or that their rulers occupy their post by right, the position of the higher class is more secure. The bourgeois historian cannot admit the possibility of the warfare of classes; to do so would be a recognition of the doom of his class. Marxist historians, on the contrary, must emphasize class conflict as a major historical fact, for only in this way can they destroy the belief of the bourgeoisie that its parliaments, literature, and science represent the interests of all the people.[19]

All literature and science, and especially history, has a class character. Every historical production of the middle or landown-

ing classes is permeated with the point of view of the class from
which its author came. This is not limited to simple suppression
of fact; it is much broader, including a belief in the fundamental
correctness of the way of life of that particular class and the ideology proceeding from it. Many are completely sincere in their
adherence to such principles and simply cannot conceive of any
other interpretation.[20]

In the opinion of Pokrovsky, Russian history affords many illustrations of this class interpretation of events. The story that
Rurik and his cohorts were invited by the primitive Slavs to come
from Scandinavia to preserve order in their country is, in his opinion, a fabrication which served the interests of the ruling class. At
the beginning of the twelfth century, according to Pokrovsky,
Kiev experienced a social revolution evoked by high interest rates
and monopolies. The remnants of the upper classes of that city,
to forestall their complete destruction, decided to call the popular
Prince Vladimir Monomakh from Pereyaslavl to rule over them.
In order to increase the prestige of the ruler, and at the same time
assist his own class, Sylvester, the monkish chronicler, one of the
prince's adherents, drew an analogy between the coming of Monomakh to Kiev and Rurik to Rus. Since the latter prince had
come to his new territory to preserve order, so must the former
have done.[21] This is an excellent example of Pokrovsky's class
interpretation of history. Only a mind sharpened by its search
for class factors could see in bold outline such details in an event
so obscured by lapse of time.

Later writers of Russian history, in like manner, have reflected
the viewpoint of their class. Thus Karamzin, the first great Russian historian of the nineteenth century, represents the interests
of the conservative, serf-owning nobles.[22] It was in their interest
to present the Russian state as a static body, fixed for all time and
existing unchanged. In this way the pressure of the bourgeoisie
and serfs for greater freedom might be lessened. Increasing bur-
geois influence (the development of society toward eventual
communism cannot be halted) brought in its wake a bourgeois
reinterpretation of the development of the Russian nation. These

newcomers placed particular emphasis on the state, since it was through this organ that they controlled the proletariat and peasantry, carried on their struggles with the middle-class rulers of foreign nations, or sought new markets for their goods. Solovyev[23] and Klyuchevsky[24] present Russian history as the history of the formation of the state machinery, "the principal and essential part of the historical process." The state, as reflected in their work, stood above classes and was the arbiter of the people's destiny.[25]

The Marxist historian must fight these tendencies. He is the guardian of the new regime on the cultural front; it is his duty to struggle against the influence of bourgeois history and, at the same time, to reinterpret the history of Russia and the world according to the concepts of Karl Marx. Every proletarian historian must be on his guard lest he be deceived by bourgeois writers of the past. Their "sincere and convinced tone" is dangerous. Naïve Marxists may believe that in those works they can find the facts as they were; what they really find is the reflection of facts through the bourgeois mind.[26]

Pokrovsky belongs to the destructive phase of the revolution. His historical writings helped break the hold of the past on the younger generation in which the party placed its trust. For this reason much of his writing, including his synthetic history, is polemical and bitter in tone. Ridicule and sarcasm were ready weapons to be used against all who refused to accept the Communist theory of society.[27] The economic base of society became almost the sole motivating cause in human life. Personality was a factor not to be considered; the history of an epoch could be derived from the record of grain prices and production.[28] He has devoted so much attention to the revolutionary periods of Russian history that other significant phases have been neglected. Culture and learning are scarcely mentioned by the historian, who devoted himself to the study of the economic background of Russian life.

Within the last three years Pokrovsky's work has been subjected to severe criticism by Soviet scholars. They accuse him of for-

getting that proletarian science is objective, that it seeks reality
and the "logic of the historical process." So great was his emphasis on the element of struggle that he made Soviet historical science subjective, unable to see the world as it really is, differing
little in this respect from bourgeois science, which from fear of the
revolution has become a "systematic falsification."[29] Pokrovsky
has carried the Marxian philosophy to its logical extreme as a
revolutionary doctrine. The element of struggle has been mag-
nified out of all proportion because the author was actively par-
ticipating in a great revolution which drew its inspiration from
those doctrines which form the basis of his philosophy of history.

Although Pokrovsky offers himself as a victim to the "fetishism
of documents," it is extremely difficult to make an adequate survey of his source materials. Footnotes are scarce or completely
lacking in all his narrative accounts and articles.[30] An examination of the source references in the chapter on the Revolution of
1905 to be found in the *Brief history* will serve as an illustration.[31]
There are in this chapter twelve references to material used. Nine
of these cite secondary works; Lenin is referred to twice; a volume of memoirs (unnamed) is the final citation. Documentary
sources are entirely missing from this important discussion of the
revolutionary movement. In several cases the secondary work is
quoted but no page reference is given.[32]

In his discussion of the working-class movement during the last
part of the nineteenth century the historian uses more source material. Official instructions and reports, petitions to government
departments, and reports of factory inspectors are frequently
quoted. These are taken from the originals verbatim and set off
by quotation marks. Yet not one of them can be identified; the
author did not see fit to include the titles of the materials from
which his quotations were taken.[33]

The volumes produced before the revolution are scarcely better. In an extended discussion of the reign of Peter the Great the
writer has given thirty references to material used in its preparation. Ten of these cite documentary collections; eight are references to monographical studies; and secondary works make up

the remaining twelve. Some effort was made in this case to give volume and page references, although the reader can never be certain that Pokrovsky will permit a check.[34]

It is difficult to tell exactly what types of sources Pokrovsky has used. Where documents were cited they appear to have been taken from printed collections; however, with full access to the archives since the revolution, it is more than probable that he has made extensive use of unprinted material. The lack of proper references makes a check impossible, but it is clear that secondary works have been referred to frequently. These have been given generally as corroborative evidence, without any effort to discuss their value or to refute their conclusions; and little effort has been made to disprove the conclusions of other historians in particular cases.[35]

Considerable use has been made of statistics in providing a background for events in Russia. Wage scales, commodity prices, and production figures form the basis for a discussion of the rise of the working-class movement and socialism.[36] No source of any kind is given for these facts, so that it is impossible to know whether they are quoted from private or public records, although the latter is more probable. In view of the unreliability of Russian statistics, the utter lack of source references is a grievous drawback. Little or no attempt has been made to present this material in an attractive form. The figures are lumped together, often occupying several pages, and present a formidable obstacle to a smoothly flowing style.

Only to a limited degree can Pokrovsky's larger works be considered as chronological presentations. His account of the history of Russia begins with the earliest period of the Slavs and closes with the revolution, but within this framework there is more use of the topical than the chronological method. One example of this treatment must suffice. The author prepared a chapter in his *Brief history* entitled "The serf-owners' state."[37] This was essentially an examination of Russia in the first part of the nineteenth century; yet here, for the first time in the volume, is presented the complete account of the Pugachev rebellion of fifty years before.

The reader of the volume must follow long and complicated discussions, aided only by the chronological tables in the appendix, which bring some order into the *Brief history*.[38] Without them it is difficult for anyone other than the specialist to connect the various phases of Russian history as set forth by Pokrovsky.

This great Marxian's interpretation of the history of his nation was conditioned both by his own intellectual development and the pressure of external events. His most important contribution (and in some respects his most faulty) was the theory of the influence of commercial capital on the development of the Russian state and people. Commercial capital he defines as the accumulations of wealth derived from trade. It does not control the production of goods; it merely buys the product from the makers and sells it elsewhere. Industrial capital, on the other hand, controls the production of commodities. The former is prevalent in societies based on land tenure, whose manufacturing is in the hands of the manor or the independent artisan. When the latter form develops, the production of commodities becomes more highly specialized; a new class which works for wages, the proletariat, arises; and the competition to dispose of goods thus created becomes sharper.[39] Commercial capital is the prime motivating force in Russian history before the middle of the nineteenth century, to the exclusion of the landowning nobility. The latter part of the century sees the rise of industrial capitalism, imported from the west under the aegis of the bourgeoisie, which now begins to play an important part in the Russian state. Russian history from this time on is a struggle between the two forms, culminating in the victory of industrial capital in February, 1917, and the overthrow of all capital by its nemesis, the proletariat, in October.[40] The reforms carried through by Alexander II in the sixties were the result of a compromise between the two types of capital. Revolution itself was the result of their conflict and the fluctuation in grain prices.[41]

It is not difficult to see that such an interpretation can develop into a mechanistic causal relationship, whereby every phenomenon is considered the effect of one fundamental cause.[42] "Economic materialism," as elaborated by Pokrovsky, is basically mechanical in nature, excluding individuals from consideration and neglecting all possible factors in the historical process other than that one which the author has chosen to emphasize.[43]

Peter I has been almost entirely ignored by the author. The ruler whose reign is supposed to mark a definite era in Russian life has been reduced by the historian to the status of agent of commercial capitalism.[44] He, whom "fawning historians have called the Great," has been lowered from his role as the reformer to the creature of forces beyond his power to understand. Even in this role he is pictured as primarily the destroyer, his innovations resulting in havoc, discord, and suffering.[45]

The "age of Alexander III" was the result not of his personality but of "objective conditions," fluctuating grain prices, increasing peasant poverty, and the development of industrial capitalism.[46] Nothing so well illustrates the essentially mechanistic character of Pokrovsky's thought as this similar estimate of two greatly dissimilar characters. There is no effort to discover the multiplicity of factors which are the motivating forces in the historical process, no attempt to discover the relative effect of various personalities on the development of Russia.

This extreme emphasis on impersonal forces has called forth bitter criticism from later Soviet writers. Marx, they say, presented men as living individuals, playing a definite part in the movement of history. Pokrovsky has made them automatons, without real importance in the scheme of things. History through Pokrovsky has become a "sociological scheme," an abstraction, nothing but "socio-economic formations." History is no longer a science —Pokrovsky has liquidated it and set up economic fatalism in its stead.[47] It is interesting to see this new emphasis on personality and its place in the study of history. The first phase of the revolution, as reflected in Pokrovsky, is passing. The work of demolition having been completed, the new structure must be erected. On the historical front this is a new, a more complete record, no longer emphasizing unduly certain revolutionary aspects of Russian and world-history but seeking an organized presentation on the basis of Marxist philosophy as officially interpreted.[48]

This new interpretation places due emphasis on the U.S.S.R. and its national achievements, another departure from the school of Pokrovsky. Pokrovsky himself was no nationalist. He savagely attacked the theory that the Russian tsars were the enlightened guides of backward peoples; in every way he assailed the Romanovs and their part in Russian history.[49] Their crimes against the people are set forth in great detail; every defeat met by them is retold in biting words.[50] The historian admits no pride of race or nation; his sole interest is the welfare of the working class of Russia and the world. For that purpose alone is Marxist history written. The achievements of the U.S.S.R. are merely the victories of the vanguard of the world-proletariat, to be duplicated by it as the revolution broadens itself and embraces all working and colonial peoples.

An examination of Pokrovsky's work brings to light certain general principles which must be weighed when assessing his importance as a historian. The first is the simplicity of his philosophy. It is essentially utilitarian. History is a weapon of revolution, and everything interfering with that purpose must be avoided or suppressed.

History is the affair of social classes. Where the proletariat has been victorious it must re-write history from its point of view. The study of a class to which little attention was paid formerly is a valuable contribution to knowledge; it ceases to be such when distortion of history as a whole results from exaggerated emphasis on its class features. One of Pokrovsky's greatest services has been the inspiration to a careful study of the history of the Russian working class. Unfortunately, such a basis of interpretation as commercial capital has led to a rather dry and lifeless history; "antihistorism" is the term applied by Soviet critics.[51]

The Marxist, since he is certain of his ground, need not suspend judgment. This Pokrovsky never does. As a result, the impartial reader finds much to criticize, and the opponent much to ridicule. But the carping of bourgeois critics need never worry the Marxist. It is this type of intellectual snobbery that is so distasteful to non-Marxists and which has so limited the usefulness of the Marxist analysis.[52]

Pokrovsky did not consider historical writing to be a literary exercise. His writing, like his history, is eminently practical. The result is a rather pedestrian account, often difficult to understand and at times even ungrammatical. Brilliance of language is to be found only in denunciatory passages; Pokrovsky is a master of harsh and biting terms and delights to open the vials of his wrath on his opponents and the enemies of his class. The result is picturesque, but it does not conduce to tempered judgment.

To the non-Marxist, Pokrovsky's faults are many and serious; yet none can deny the great service he has performed for Russian history. His documentary publications alone have earned him a high place and are, perhaps, his greatest contribution to historical studies. His emphasis on the economic phase of history, while undoubtedly extreme, has resulted in intensified study of certain sections of the Russian people whose history was little known. The revolutionary movement was a vital part of his adult life; he believed that he understood it from the theoretical and practical standpoints, so that his writings on its course are of vital importance to all students. Lastly, his work as an administrator and organizer, though much of it is now under fire, has enabled great successes to be achieved in the study of history in the U.S.S.R.

Mikhail Nikolayevich Pokrovsky was a pioneer. His work as a historian was, in fact, secondary to his work as a professional revolutionary. Even the most bitter critics must pay high honor to his sincerity and singleness of purpose though they continually condemn his "mistakes." Russian historiography and literature are infinitely richer because Pokrovsky spent his life in this work.

NOTES

1. A recent review of a volume attacking Pokrovsky's historical views has lamented the slowness of Soviet historians to proceed with the "liquidation" of his "school." See A. Bochkarev and others, "Protiv istoricheskoy kontseptsii M. N. Pokrovskogo: sbornik statey." [Against the historical conceptions of M. N. Pokrovsky: a collection of articles], Part I, ed. Academician B. Grekov, S. Bushuyev, V.

Lebedev, A. Sidorov, A. Shestakov, and Em. Yaroslavsky (Academy of Sciences of the U.S.S.R., 1939), *Istorichesky zhurnal* [Historical journal], No. 8 (August, 1939), pp. 133–42.

2. Pokrovsky states that in historical technique Vinogradov had great influence upon him; see *Istoricheskaya nauka i borba klassov* (*istoriograficheskiye ocherki, kriticheskiye stati i zametki*) [Historical science and the class struggle (historiographical sketches, critical articles, and notes)] (Moscow, 1933), II, 304 (hereafter cited as "*Istoricheskaya nauka*").

3. Otto Hoetzsch, "M. N. Pokrovskij," *Zeitschrift für osteuropäische Geschichte*, VI (1932), 535–52. For further details of Pokrovsky's early career see P. Milyukov, "Velichiye i padeniye M. N. Pokrovskogo" [Grandeur and downfall of M. N. Pokrovsky], *Sovremenniya zapiski* [Contemporary annals], LXIV (1937), 368–87.

4. For a Communist interpretation of legal Marxism and its effect on Pokrovsky see *Protiv istoricheskoy kontseptsii M. N. Pokrovskogo*, pp. 11–15.

5. *History of Russia from the earliest times to the rise of commercial capitalism*, trans. and ed. J. D. Clarkson and M. R. M. Griffiths (New York, 1931), p. 15. This article is reprinted in *Istoricheskaya nauka*, II, 5–13. For Pokrovsky's views of his earlier political opinions see *ibid.*, pp. 297–300.

6. *Brief history of Russia*, trans. D. S. Mirsky (New York, 1933), I, 7. Pokrovsky was a member of the editorial board of every Bolshevik newspaper published in Moscow during the Revolution of 1905. In 1906 and 1907 he lectured to groups of workers on socialism, his talks being advertised as discussions on the "theory of music" (*Istoricheskaya nauka*, II, 300–301).

7. *Brief history*, I, 7. See also N. Popov, *Outline history of the Communist party of the Soviet Union* (New York, 1934), I, 242–44. A. Bogdanov (A. A. Malinovsky), a well-known Social-Democratic economist and philosopher, left the Bolshevik faction of the party after the Revolution of 1905. He did much to develop the concepts of "commercial capital" and "industrial capital" as motivating forces in Russian history. For an account of the influence of Bogdanov and certain German historians on Pokrovsky see P. Drozdov, "Resheniye partii i pravitelstva ob uchebnikakh po istorii i zadachi sovietskikh istorikov" [The decision of the party and government concerning history texts and problems of Soviet historians], in *Istorik-Marksist* [The Marxist historian], No. 1 (53) (1936), 9–22.

8. "Up to the last days of his life he remained a steady supporter of the general line of the party" (*Brief history*, I, 8).

9. Hoetzsch, *loc. cit.*, pp. 535–52.

10. *Ibid.*, pp. 535–52. Among the documentary collections edited by Pokrovsky are *Pugachevshchina* [Material on Pugachev] (Moscow, 1926–31); *Vosstaniye Dekabristov, materialy po istorii Dekabristov* [The uprising of the Decembrists: materials on the history of the Decembrists] (Moscow, 1925———); *Mezhdunarodniye otnosheniya v epokhu imperializma; dokumenty iz arkhivov tsarskogo i vremennogo pravitelstv 1878–1917* [International relations in the epoch of imperialism; documents from the archives of the tsarist and provisional governments, 1878–1917] (Moscow, 1931———), German trans.: *Die internationalen Beziehungen im Zeitalter des Imperialismus; Dokumente aus den Archiven der zarischen und der provisorischen Regierung* (Berlin, 1931———).

11. Many of these have been collected and published in book form. Among them are *Istoricheskaya nauka i borba klassov* (see above, n. 2); *Imperialisticheskaya voyna:*

sbornik statey 1915–1927 [The imperialist war: a collection of articles, 1915–27] (Moscow, 1934); *Borba klassov i russkaya istoricheskaya literatura* [The class struggle and Russian historical literature] (Leningrad, 1927); and *Diplomatiya i voyny tsarskoy Rossii v XIX stoletii* [The diplomacy and wars of tsarist Russia in the nineteenth century] (Moscow, 1923).

12. *Russkaya istoriya v samom szhatom ocherke* [A short sketch of Russian history] (Moscow, 1925——). This volume was written in the early twenties and translated into English by D. S. Mirsky, as *Brief history of Russia*. *Russkaya istoriya s drevneishikh vremen* [Russian history from the earliest times] (4 vols.; Moscow, 1923–25), his most pretentious work, was first published in St. Petersburg shortly before the war of 1914. The first part has been translated into English. A volume of Pokrovsky's lectures on the revolution has been published under the title *Ocherki russkogo revolyutsionnogo dvizheniya XIX–XX v.v.* [Sketches of the Russian revolutionary movement in the nineteenth and twentieth centuries] (Moscow, 1924). An attempt at a complete bibliography of Pokrovsky's writings is to be found in *Istorik-Marksist*, September, 1928, pp. 215–31.

Few reviews of Pokrovsky's works have appeared in the learned journals of the western world. For a brief résumé of the historian's career see Otto Hoetzsch, "M. N. Pokrovski," *Osteuropa*, VII (1931–32), 456–57. A more detailed study of Pokrovsky's life by the same author with reference to his important works has been cited above, in n. 3. A. F. Dobbie-Bateman explored his career briefly in his article "Michael Pokrovsky," *SR*, XI (1932), 187–89. The translation of his *History of Russia from the earliest times* by Clarkson and Griffiths was reviewed by Samuel H. Cross in *JMH*, IV (1932), 282–85. Bernadotte E. Schmitt examined the German edition of the documentary collection on the origins of the war of 1914 (see above, n. 10), ed. Pokrovsky, in *Foreign affairs*, XIII (1934), 133–53.

13. Pokrovsky's theories have been described officially as "anti-Marxist, anti-Leninist, essentially liquidationist, anti-scientific," and serving as a cover for the "Trotskyite-Bukharinist retainers of Fascism" (*Protiv istoricheskoy kontseptsii M. N. Pokrovskogo*, p. 3).

14. "History is the *concrete* investigation of concrete social questions" (*Istoricheskaya nauka*, II, 395).

15. *Brief history*, I, 24; *Istoricheskaya nauka*, II, 284–93, *passim*. " 'The Revolution teaches not only politicians. It also teaches historians and teaches [them] because every real historian, not only the one who collects facts (often not knowing why and for what) but also he who meditates on facts, is a politician. And all politically alive, dialectically thinking persons will always study history as Marx, Engels, and Lenin studied it. . . . . They will study history in general, in its full extent, as our great teachers studied it" (*Istoricheskaya nauka*, II, 387).

16. "The fairy tale about the world having been created all at one time and remaining unchanged ever since has been destroyed by the study of the earth's past and that of its animals and plants, by the sciences of geology and paleontology. The other fairy tale which says that human society has always been, and will consequently always be, as it is today, is being destroyed by history and archeology. Man changes and will go on changing, like everything else. One social order grows up, another falls to pieces, and in its place a new one is evolved, and so on. We can neither foresee nor imagine an end to these changes, but if we observe them over a

space of several decades or centuries, we shall find that there is a certain order in them and discover the laws to which they are subject" (*Brief history*, I, 24).

17. *Ibid.*, p. 27.

18. *Istoricheskaya nauka*, I, 12–13.

19. *Ibid.*, p. 12.

20. *Brief history*, I, 236. Ideology is the reflection of actuality in the eyes of people through the prism of their interests, chiefly class interests (*Istoricheskaya nauka*, I, 10).

21. *Istoricheskaya nauka*, I, 13–18.

22. N. M. Karamzin, *Istoriya gosudarstva rossiyskogo* [History of the Russian state] (St. Petersburg, 1816–29). "The history of the State in the hands of Karamzin thus became the history of its sovereigns. The State had no history of its own. This has deprived Karamzin's work of all significance, even for bourgeois historians. . . . . The question of how the Russian State came into existence, and what was its evolution, never occurred to Karamzin" (*Brief history*, I, 238).

23. S. M. Solovyev, *Istoriya Rossii s drevneishikh vremen* [History of Russia from the earliest time] (29 vols.; St. Petersburg, 1897). Solovyev was, in the opinion of Pokrovsky, the greatest Russian historian of the nineteenth century (*Istoricheskaya nauka*, I, 52).

24. V. P. Klyuchevsky, *A history of Russia*, trans. C. J. Hogarth (5 vols.; London, 1911–31). Pokrovsky considers Klyuchevsky to have been an eclectic, combining portions of P. L. Lavrov's theory of the critically thinking personality, B. Chicherin's belief that the state was the principal creative factor in Russian social and economic life, and the elementary, pre-Marxian materialism of Shchapov (*Istoricheskaya nauka*, I, 63–64).

25. *Brief history*, I, 236–37.

26. *Ibid.*, p. 236. "Pokrovsky did brilliant work in destroying conservative, bourgeois, and petit-bourgeois historical conceptions" (N. Bukharin, "Nuzhna li nam marksistskaya istoricheskaya nauka?" [Do we need Marxist historical science?], *Izvestiya*, Jan. 27, 1936).

27. On occasion, however, he did recommend certain volumes by bourgeois historians as being of great value to Marxist students. See, e.g., *Istoricheskaya nauka*, II, 105–8.

28. *Brief history*, I, 201.

29. Bukharin, *loc. cit.* It is interesting to note that on one occasion Pokrovsky laid especial emphasis on the influence of political conditions on the economic development of peoples and nations (*Istoricheskaya nauka*, II, 266–83).

30. This is not true of the documentary collections of which he was editor. These are equipped with the necessary references, cross-references, and explanations in footnote form.

31. *Brief history*, II, 143–218.

32. *Ibid.*, pp. 159, 179.

33. *Ibid.*, I, 200–235.

34. *Russkaya istoriya s drevneishikh vremen*, II, 269–326. Since Clarkson and Griffiths have omitted all references to Russian sources, their translation, *Russian history, from the earliest times to the rise of commercial capitalism*, could not be used.

35. As has been pointed out above, Pokrovsky has attempted to disprove the interpretations of older historians *in toto*. Perhaps for this reason he did not deem it necessary to discuss their conclusions in detail.

36. *Brief history*, I, 200–235. This is a good example of Pokrovsky's use of statistics.

37. *Ibid.*, pp. 118–42.

38. These tables were inserted at the suggestion of Lenin, who realized that the lack of form handicapped the work. See his letter to Pokrovsky in *ibid.*, p. 5. Milyukov (*loc. cit.*, pp. 368–87) shows the weakness of the *Brief history* as a textbook.

39. *Brief history*, I, 37–50. However, Pokrovsky defends himself by citing Lenin's conception of the importance of commercial capitalism in the development of the early Muscovite state (*Istoricheskaya nauka*, II, 276).

40. Drozdov, *loc. cit.*, pp. 9–22.

41. *Ibid.*

42. In the opinion of one *émigré* scholar, the unsuccessful Revolution of 1905 had considerable effect on the development of Pokrovsky's "historical automatism" (E. F. Maximovich, *Doctrine marxiste-léniniste appliquée à l'étude concrète de l'histoire* [Prague, 1938], p. 248).

43. "Having established some fact in economics, M. N. Pokrovsky habitually explains all the phenomena of the social life of a given period by it alone, not understanding dialectically the relationship between the foundation and the superstructure and absolutely ignoring a number of other factors which do not fit into his scheme" (Drozdov, *loc. cit.*, pp. 9–22).

44. *Brief history*, I, 97–101.

45. *History of Russia*, p. 283. Karl Radek has denounced Pokrovsky's treatment of Peter, to whom the historian left "only cruelty and syphilis" ("Nedostatki istoricheskogo fronta i oshibki shkoly Pokrovskogo" [Weaknesses of the historical front and errors of the Pokrovsky school], *Borba klassov*, No. 3 [1936], 135).

46. *Brief history*, I, 235.

47. F. Rotshtein, "Marks-Istorik" [Marx as historian], *Pravda* [Truth], May 18, 1937. The criticism of Pokrovsky which has developed in recent years is the result of efforts to make the study of history in the Soviet Union more thorough and more systematic. After an examination of the question by Stalin, a decree was issued on May 16, 1934, over the signatures of Stalin and Molotov, president of the council of peoples' commissars of the U.S.S.R., ordering a revision of method. Teaching by means of "sociological epochs" was to be abolished, and a carefully organized chronological history was to be introduced and new textbooks written for this purpose. Since that date a bitter and never ending struggle has been carried on against the remnants of the Pokrovsky school, and the new methods have been introduced. See Drozdov, *loc. cit.*, pp. 9–22. For later developments see "O prepodavanii grazhdanskoy istorii v shkolakh SSSR (postanovleniye SNK Soyuza SSR i TSK VKP [b])" [Concerning the teaching of civil history in the schools of the U.S.S.R. (a decree of the Council of Peoples' Commissars of the U.S.S.R. and the Central Committee of the All-Russian Communist party [Bolshevik])], *Istorik-Marksist*, No. 3 (37) (1934), pp. 83–84; Ya. Bocharov, "Zadachi prepodavaniya istorii" [Problems in the teach-

ing of history], *ibid.*, pp. 84–92, and "Na fronte istoricheskoy nauki: v Sovnarkome Soyuza SSR i TsK VKP (b)" [On the front of historical science: in the Council of Peoples' Commissars and the Central Committee of the All-Russian Communist party (Bolshevik)], *ibid.*, No. 1 (53) (1936), pp. 3–8.

48. According to one of Pokrovsky's critics, among the problems faced by the new Marxist historiography were "the bourgeois-landowners' conception of the Russian historical process," the theory that the autocracy was created by the Russian people for their own safety, and the belief that Russian historical development was the complete opposite of that of western Europe. Pokrovsky destroyed this conception of Russian history (Drozdov, *loc. cit.*, pp. 9–22).

49. Maximovich, pp. 251–52.

50. Thus, the historian excuses the surprise attack made by the Japanese on Port Arthur in 1904 (*Brief history*, II, 94–95; *History of Russia*, p. xii).

51. N. Bukharin, *loc. cit.*

52. Maximovich (pp. 245–48) points out that the Soviet critics of Pokrovsky are governed by the same essentially unscientific principles to which they objected in the master.

XVII

JOHN HOLLAND ROSE (1855——)

E. WILSON LYON*

THE writings of John Holland Rose cover nearly half a century and reflect the transition from the literary to the more scientific documentary approach in British historiography. His researches first revealed the value of the British archives for the Napoleonic era and led to a new conception of British policy in the period.

Rose was born at Bedford in 1855. Like most of his colleagues, he received little formal historical training in school and university. His educational background was the standard classical course of his day, but he was not a typical Anglican product of public school and college.[1] His parents were congregationalists of modest means, and he attended the Modern Grammar School in his native town. From Bedford he went to the new Owens College, Manchester, where he distinguished himself by winning the Latin prose essay prize. At the end of his course in Owens College he won a scholarship at Christ's College, Cambridge, receiving a second class in the classical tripos.

The university extension movement was becoming a significant feature of English education, and Rose secured a position as lecturer with the Cambridge University Lecturers' Syndicate, from which he later transferred to the London Society for the Extension of University Teaching. He remained in this work until 1911, when he was called to Cambridge. In the meantime, he had developed a deep interest in history and had performed some of his greatest services for historical scholarship. He was fortified for

* President of Pomona College.

these laborious years by a robust constitution and a happy home. In 1880 he married Laura Haddon, with whom he has had the good fortune to spend over sixty years of married life.

Rose found himself handicapped as a popular lecturer by lack of adequate textbooks in European history. It is not surprising, then, that his earliest publications were chiefly manuals growing out of his needs in instructing workingmen. The first work from his pen, *A century of continental history, 1780–1880*,[2] needs no particular notice. A second text, *The Revolutionary and Napoleonic era, 1789–1815*,[3] marked a significant step in his career and determined the course of his studies for many years to come. It achieved immediate success and is still in print. The book had been preceded by the author's first scholarly article, an excellent bit of research on economic history in the Napoleonic period.[4]

The Revolutionary and Napoleonic era made no claim to original scholarship but based its case on a summary and interpretation of recent continental writing. Rose relied greatly on Aulard, Sorel, and Vandal, but he had also read the new flood of memoirs on the Napoleonic period. In addition to these French authorities, he endeavored "to enter into the general spirit of the age by studying the chief histories, memoirs and biographies relating to other European lands."[5] Some use was made of the Public Record Office. These sources, as well as the author's inclinations, led to the presentation of the era as an age in the diplomatic history of Europe rather than as an episode in the history of the French people. Rose felt that the drama of the French Revolution had obscured its relation to the revolution in other countries, and he aimed "to explain the influence of French ideas and policy on Europe." He turned away in distaste from the party squabbles of the Revolution, and it is not unfair to say that he never really penetrated the significance of much that happened in the decade before Napoleon. This part of his book soon fell so far behind the newer scholarship that it was no longer a safe guide. A few illustrations from the latest edition will suffice: Taine's calculations are accepted for the payments due from peasants; the Girondins are pictured as moderates; Danton is exonerated from all charges of corruption; and Robespierre is held primarily responsible for the Terror.[6]

Although much of the book has been superseded by later research, it is invaluble for an understanding of Rose's career as a historian. Its poor proportions—two hundred and fifty-two pages on Napoleon, compared to one hundred and eighteen for the decade 1789–99—revealed the author's increasing occupation with the Corsican. The emphasis upon international relations foreshadowed Rose's growing love for diplomatic history.

Rose turned aside briefly from continental affairs to a consideration of economic and political problems produced in England by the industrial revolution. His work as an extension lecturer stimulated his interest in the origins of the radical movement and its development in the nineteenth century. In a sympathetic account of the unlicensed journals,[7] he concluded that these papers were largely responsible for the popular reception of the six points of the Charter in 1837. At this time Rose undertook the editorship of a series of popular volumes, "The Victorian era series," which presented "the great movements and developments of the age in politics, economics, religion, industry, literature, science, and art, and of the life work of its typical influential men." The editor himself contributed a volume on *The rise of democracy*.[8] The little book was an engaging, objective account of the early radicals, the Chartist movement, the three reform bills, and the ebb and flow of public opinion in Great Britain. It was especially commendable in its judicious treatment of contemporary questions.

These studies, however, were but a temporary digression from the larger field which he was destined to make peculiarly his own. Preparation of *The Revolutionary and Napoleonic era* revealed that little scholarly work on the period had been done in England. It was an amazing fact that the archives of Napoleon's greatest enemy had been among the least explored. Rose set himself to this task, and a number of scholarly articles in the *English historical review* resulted.[9] These essays, though significant themselves, were preliminary studies for a major work.

The appearance of Rose's *Life of Napoleon I* in 1901 was an outstanding event in English historical scholarship. For the first time British readers were given a scholarly, adequately documented life of the emperor. As in *The Revolutionary and Napoleonic era*, Rose made full use of the best European scholarship, drawing heavily from the works of Aulard, Chuquet, Houssaye, Sorel, and Vandal in France; Beer, Delbrück, Fournier, Lehmann, Oncken, and Wertheimer in Germany and Austria; and Lumbroso in Italy.

> But [he added] I should not have ventured on this great undertaking, had I not been able to contribute something new to Napoleonic literature. During a study of this period for an earlier volume published in the "Cambridge historical series," I ascertained the great value of the British Records for the years 1795–1815. . . . . I have striven to embody the results of this search in the present volumes so far as was compatible with the limits of space and with the narrative form at which in my judgment history ought always to aim.[10]

Such scholarship had its reward. Rose's *Life of Napoleon I* attained immediate success and is still a standard work after nearly forty years. It remains today, as in 1901, the best full-length, scholarly life of the great conqueror yet written in our language.

A recent book on historiography suggests that a biography should "vividly recreate a character," present "a full, careful, unbiased record of his acts and experiences," and "indicate the place of the hero in history."[11] It is in the first of these objectives that the *Life of Napoleon I* is open to the greatest criticism. We do not sense the drama of the meteoric rise and fall of the emperor, for the man is lost in the political and military events of the times. Rose would answer that his book was so planned:

> While not neglecting the personal details of the great man's life, I have dwelt mainly on his public career. . . . . He once said to M. Gallois: "Je n'aime pas beaucoup les femmes, ni le jeu—enfin rien: *je suis tout à fait un être politique.*" In dealing with him as a warrior and statesman, and in sparing my readers details as to his bolting his food, sleeping at concerts, and indulging in amours where for him there was no glamour of romance, I am laying stress on what interested him most—in a word, I am taking him at his best.[12]

Rose did, however, present a full and, on the whole, fair picture of Napoleon's life and his place in history. The emperor's greatness is accepted, and the book is generally sympathetic to him. The author does not claim a solution for all the questions of the period and admits that "Napoleon is often unfathomable."[13] Great admiration is shown for Napoleon's military prowess, but details of his campaigns are often criticized—even the famous first Italian campaign in which Rose feels that Napoleon made mistakes and owed a good deal of his success to the blunders of his opponents.[14] Rose denies that the main losses of the Russian campaign were due to an exceptionally hard winter and states that the bulk of Napoleon's losses came before the first snowstorm.[15] At Leipzig "the plain truth is that he was out-generalled by the allies."[16] On the other hand, "it was not chance but science" that gave him successes early in the 1814 campaign.[17] Like many modern writers Rose was even more impressed with Napoleon as a statesman than as a warrior. Although he gave little credence to the legendary account of Brumaire, he considered "the triumph of Napoleon in the three years subsequent to his return from Egypt as the most stupendous recorded in the history of civilized peoples."[18]

Rose dismisses tales of Napoleon's decline in mental and physical vigor and ascribes his fall to the character of the man and to the circumstances of an age that presented no first-rate rival on the continent before 1812. Napoleon thus developed a complete contempt for his enemies. "A dogma of personal infallibility" settled upon him and led "the greatest political genius of the age," for want of moderation, to unite Europe against him.[19]

The *Life of Napoleon I* revealed the author's growing interest and skill in diplomatic history. In all matters concerning the relations of the continental nations he offered a fresh and objective point of view. From the Record Office he was able to present a more favorable view of British foreign policy than had hitherto prevailed in scholarly works. In the crucial rupture of the Peace of Amiens, Rose vindicates Great Britain, though he admits her responsibility in retaining Malta and believes that Napoleon desired to avoid war until the autumn of 1804, when his dispositions in the east would have been secure.[20] Napoleon's provocations,

and not Pitt's gold, are held responsible for the formation of the
Third Coalition.[21] Tilsit appeared as an attempt to force peace
from England rather than a plan to dominate the continent.
"Neither Napoleon nor Alexander was deaf to generous aspirations. They both desired peace, so that their empires might ex-
pand and consolidate."[22] Rose admitted his inability to determine whether the attempted domination of Europe that led to
Napoleon's ruin was prompted by ambition or by a belief that such
control was necessary to destroy England.[23] The book concludes
with a charming chapter on St. Helena and a warm defense of
Sir Hudson Lowe, whom he had already championed in an earlier essay.[24]

Despite its appreciation of Napoleon, the work reflects a pro-
British bias.[25] The use of certain phrases reminds the reader that
the author is a patriotic Englishman steeped in nineteenth-century tradition. Yet Rose was more objective than most British
historians of his generation, and most of his conclusions are quite
fair to Napoleon. Rose criticized his own country frequently,
characterizing British diplomacy in 1801–3, in 1806–7, and in
1809 as "the laughing stock of Europe." He convicted the British
government of complicity in the Cadoudal conspiracy.[26]

Every age re-writes the past, and it would be surprising if ours
were content with Rose's approach to Napoleon. Except in certain details there is not likely to be serious quarrel with his handling of diplomacy and military campaigns; yet Professor
Bruun's discussion of the Napoleonic army opens the way to a
reconsideration of the causes of Napoleon's eventual military
failures.[27] Although Rose's first scholarly article dealt with economic policy, his treatment of this phase of the Napoleonic era
appears insufficient today. Internal affairs in France were given
scant consideration, but contemporaries of Hitler and Mussolini
would like to know more about the methods employed by the
first great dictator of modern history. We also desire light on intellectual and cultural questions, which Rose scarcely considered at all.

After the publication of the *Life of Napoleon I* Rose attained recognition as an authority in the field and was invited to contribute to the *Cambridge modern history*. He prepared the chapters on "Bonaparte and the conquest of Italy," "The Egyptian expedition," and "The Second Coalition" in the volume on the French Revolution and the chapters on "The Napoleonic empire at its height, 1807–9," and "The continental system, 1809–14" in the volume on Napoleon.[28] These studies afforded an opportunity to test the conclusions of the earlier work. Compression of Napoleon's personal activities was required, but some topics could be treated at greater length than heretofore. In tone, and particularly in style, these chapters reveal a deeper scholarship and a broader outlook on the part of the author. The Italian campaign is handled in masterly fashion. Napoleon's genius is shown to have been abetted by the quarrels of Sardinians and Austrians and by Britain's withholding subsidies in a vain hope of peace. The Egyptian campaign is portrayed as the first stage in the commercial and colonial struggle which was to be so different from the war begun against the revolutionaries in 1793. The chapter on "The Second Coalition" is a masterpiece of diplomatic writing, and decidedly Rose's best contribution to the *Cambridge modern history*. No better analysis of international relations between Campo Formio and Napoleon's return from Egypt has ever been written. The chapter on "The Napoleonic empire at its height, 1807–9" is exceptionally good on the Prussian revival after Tilsit. British policy during the "continental system" is warmly defended.

Many years later the Cambridge University Press undertook a co-operative work on British foreign policy since the American Revolution. A unique opportunity was thus afforded Rose to write the kind of history at which he excelled in the period of his greatest interest. His chapters on "The struggle with Revolutionary France, 1792–1802" and "The contest with Napoleon, 1802–1812"[29] provide a synthesis of British foreign policy detailed enough to be convincing, yet brief enough to keep the main thread of events constantly in view. He succeeds in showing great continuity in British policy throughout the period.

Pitt and Grenville did not object to the French republic but to its aggressions and propaganda. War was not inevitable in 1793; and "pedantic insistence [in Paris] on the imprescriptible laws of nature, and rigid adherence [in London] to the text of treaties complicated a question which, with good will and tactfulness, might have been settled in a month."[30] The peace proposals of 1795, 1798, 1805, and 1814 show a marked similarity.[31] In all the crises after 1792 British policy turned on questions of naval strategy; the real issues in 1793, 1797, 1803, and 1806 were not the Scheldt, Gibraltar, Malta, and Sicily but French control of the Netherlands and the Mediterranean.[32] Rose considers that Pitt missed a real chance to pacify Europe in 1795–97, but he had "no knowledge of continental nations and their politics."[33]

Other British shortcomings are frankly admitted. England was unprepared for the struggle, "her warfare tentative, her blunders colossal."[34] No apology is offered for the weak diplomacy of Cornwallis and Addington in the Treaty of Amiens.[35] The affair of the Spanish treasure ships in 1804 was handled in "a way detrimental to British prestige."[36] Britain had tried unsuccessfully for twenty-six months to form a Third Coalition when Napoleon, by his annexation of Genoa, brought it about in nine weeks.[37] Prussia is blamed for the failure of Pitt's plans in 1805–6: "Who could have foreseen the surrender of Frederick William to Napoleon, his mean acceptance of Hanover at the Emperor's hands and the sequel—Jena, with the countless humiliations that followed."[38] Canning's evidence in 1807 on Napoleon's and Alexander's secret agreement concerning Denmark was not definite, and Rose questions the wisdom of seizing her fleet and shocking the conscience of the world.[39] Although the plans of the British ministers were often artificial, their repeated efforts made possible the final combination against Napoleon. This service was particularly notable in 1812, when Great Britain made peace with Sweden and secured a cessation of Russo-Turkish hostilities. Russia was thus relieved of hostilities on both her flanks.[40]

Rose's labors in the Napoleonic field were indefatigable, and for over a decade after the appearance of his *Life of Napoleon I* specialized studies in the field flowed from his pen. He performed a distinct service to critical scholarship by publishing the dispatches in the British archives relating to the Third Coalition.[41] As a by-product of the biography he presented a volume of essays[42] on subjects that did not fit well into the larger study. Some of the chapters were reprints of earlier articles; but those on "Wordsworth, Schiller, Fichte and the idealist revolt against Napoleon," "Pitt's plans for the settlement of Europe," "Egypt during the first British occupation," and "Austria and the downfall of Napoleon" appeared for the first time. The volume also contained ten appendixes of documents on aspects of the Napoleonic era ranging from "Nelson in the Mediterranean, 1796–98" to "Letters of Major Gorrequer from St. Helena." Of the new essays, that on Pitt was most significant and original. "Austria and the downfall of Napoleon" made recent research in the Austrian archives available for English readers. In collaboration with A. M. Broadley, Rose prepared a biography of Dumouriez, emphasizing his role in the defense of England against Napoleon.[43] The volume gave a somewhat too flattering portrait of Dumouriez and concluded with a lengthy memoir, said to have been his plan for the defense of the country. Rose also contributed a lively and penetrating introductory essay on "Pictorial satire as a factor in Napoleonic history" for a work on caricature of the era.[44]

During these years Rose popularized his great knowledge of Napoleon with articles in the reviews.[45] The essays may be commended as examples of interesting popularization without sacrifice of scholarship. He combated the legend then popular in Europe that Napoleon was "a beneficent ruler anxious to give peace to the world, but constantly thwarted by greedy England." Readers were reminded that even in politics and war Napoleon's originality had been greatly exaggerated. Rose summarized the effects of the Napoleonic activity in Italy in a brilliant article marked by a light touch and sound judgment. Years later he analyzed in similar happy vein Napoleon's influence upon Europe.[46]

Rose's reputation as a Napoleonic scholar secured for him wide recognition in the United States, and in 1912 he visited this country to deliver the Lowell Lectures in Boston. The lectures may be regarded as a reply to the criticism that his *Life of Napoleon I* gave an inadequate portrait of the man, for he chose as his subject *The personality of Napoleon*.[47] After the biography this is the best of Rose's books on the Corsican. The reflections of a scholar are presented in a charming and very human manner. We see Napoleon as man, Jacobin, warrior, law-giver, Emperor, thinker, world-ruler, and exile. There is a sense of dramatic unity lacking in the biography. The book does not add to our knowledge, but it admirably synthesizes existing information.

Study of the Revolutionary and Napoleonic era brought Rose more and more in contact with the career of the younger Pitt. Simultaneously with his later studies on Napoleon he began the publication of scholarly articles on the great prime minister. The first of these articles, using quotations from the correspondence of Pitt and Eden, threw new light on the actual negotiation of one of the most significant commercial treaties of modern history.[48] Another notable article gave a scholarly account, based on hitherto unused documents, of Pitt's skilful handling of the Dutch crisis in 1787–88.[49] A number of other publications revealed Rose's increasing occupation with Pitt.[50] It was apparent that he had undertaken an ambitious work on the English champion against Napoleon.

The first decade of Pitt's administration is an inspiring period for a patriotic Briton, and Rose turned to it with enthusiasm. His *William Pitt and national revival*[51] was designed as the first part of an extended biography. A defeated nation, bereft of her greatest American colonies, in 1783 called a schoolboy to lead her, and a decade later she faced the French Revolution rich and strong. It is the purpose of the volume to show how this was achieved. Domestic issues are treated skilfully. Rose thinks that Pitt's reorganization of British financial life may well have saved the nation from a revolution comparable to that in France. He pays tribute to Pitt's parliamentary ability and is generally sympathetic to him in the conflict with Fox. Pitt is defended in his desertion of parliamentary reform and for voting against Warren Hastings in the great impeachment. On imperial questions Pitt proved a worthy son of Chatham, and his reorganization of the government of India and Canada were measures of splendid statesmanship.

Rose's treatment of foreign affairs was the best that had appeared on the period. Under Pitt, England recovered the place in Europe which she had lost as a result of the American Revolution. Pitt sought at once to end the dangerous isolation, first negotiating the commercial treaty with France. He was able to intervene effectively in the Dutch crisis and to emerge from it with the Netherlands and Prussia as his allies. Although balked by Catherine II when his policy seemed ahead of public opinion, he secured a victory over Spain in the Nootka Sound affair. By 1790 the nation had "emerged from defeat, isolation, and discredit which bordered on bankruptcy, until she soared aloft to a position of prestige in the diplomatic and mercantile spheres which earned the envy of her formerly triumphant rivals."[52]

The second phase in Pitt's career was inaugurated by the French Revolution. Hitherto Pitt had been in his element— parliamentary government and reconstruction at home and abroad. By training and inclination he was ill prepared for the contest with Revolutionary France and the dreary negotiation with treacherous allies which opposition to the Revolution entailed. In a second volume, *William Pitt and the Great War*,[53] Rose admits the colossal blunders that marked Britain's prosecution of the war, but he champions Pitt's plan for the eventual settlement of Europe. He successfully exonerates Pitt in the Quiberon disaster and properly places the blame on the French royalist leaders. Subsequent research has further strengthened Rose's view that Pitt was unjustified in the laws and measures he invoked to suppress the English Jacobins, who did not constitute a serious danger to the state. Pitt's resignation when the king refused to sanction Catholic emancipation is characterized as a more honorable action than the conscience of the age dictated.

The policies of Addington that led to the Peace of Amiens are roundly criticized, and Pitt's opposition to his ministry is praised. The tragedy of Pitt's final years is attributed to the deficiencies of his allies rather than to the failures of Britain. Military historians have dissented from Rose's conclusions, holding that his defense of Pitt showed little appreciation of strategy.[54]

Of the two volumes,[55] the earlier is superior, largely because the period lends itself better to biographical treatment. Pitt does not appear as a very vivid character, for he was too much a man of business. Because of more restricted interest in its subject, the book never enjoyed the wide popular reception given the biography of Napoleon. Both volumes, however, represent a distinct advance in style and scholarship over Rose's previous work. There are fewer mixed metaphors and grandiose figures of speech than in the *Life of Napoleon I*, and the biography of Pitt is also much more a work of research. Except in his treatment of British foreign policy, Rose had relied in his *Life of Napoleon I* upon memoirs and continental authorities. In the case of Pitt, available manuscript and printed material in Great Britain was utilized. Although admirers of Fox thought their idol had been handled too harshly and other critics considered Pitt's motives less generous than Rose interprets them, the main contentions of the work have been generally accepted. After nearly thirty years it remains the best life of Pitt ever written.

It is surprising that the biographer of Napoleon and Pitt should have been so late in receiving adequate recognition from the British universities. In 1911 Cambridge tardily appointed him reader in modern history, a university position involving teaching duties of the type prevalent in the United States. Five years later he became a fellow of his old college, Christ's. In Cambridge Rose speedily acquired a deserved reputation as a popular lecturer. His lectures were imaginative and descriptive, portraying the sweep of history rather than interpretation of details. They were interesting, "clear and incisive."[56] His personal relations with students were unusually warm. One of them said that he "never knew him to be angry or even ruffled."

By 1914 Rose had reached a turning-point in his scholarly interest. A volume of essays and correspondence relating to *Pitt and Napoleon*[57] indicated that the law of diminishing returns had been reached in their period. Rose turned briefly to the Seven Years' War and produced two scholarly articles defending Britain from the charge of deserting Frederick the Great.[58] But just prior to the war of 1914 the eighteenth century seemed far away, and Rose had already begun the study of contemporary diplomacy when the outbreak of hostilities fixed his attention on current problems.

It must not be thought that Rose was a novice in the field of recent history. In 1906 he had published the first notable manual in our language on the period since 1870. *The development of the European nations*,[59] as it was called, enjoyed a wide public in the years before 1914. The title was hardly appropriate, since it treated the European states rather than the nations. The book was primarily an account of European diplomacy. The first volume dealt chiefly with the Franco-German War and the Near Eastern crisis of 1875–78. The second concerned Europe's relations to the larger world of Africa and Asia. The Central Asian disputes, Britain in Egypt and in the Sudan, and the partitions of Africa were described unusually fully. The book portrayed sound judgment and freedom from prejudice to a most commendable degree, but as a well-rounded account of the latest age it left much to be desired. The amazing industrial and commercial development of the period was largely ignored. Little attention was given to forces that shaped nationalism, especially cultural and sentimental factors. It remained a good account of international relations until the opening of archives after 1918 completely revolutionized our knowledge of European diplomacy since 1870. This pioneer work made its way through "thickets all but untrodden." It is difficult for a later generation to appreciate how fully the author achieved his aim of enabling his successors "to know what to seek and what to avoid."

Upon the outbreak of war Rose did what he could to assist the British cause. He lectured at Cambridge several terms and also to the soldiers in France. His writings of the period have no permanent value, but they afford a valuable portrait of a historian in war time. Two sets of his lectures were published in book form. *The origins of the war*,[60] which treated European diplomacy from 1871 to 1914, was, of course, a tract for the times. The deliberate war guilt which it charged to the Kaiser and the German government soon became an exploded thesis. *Nationality in modern history*,[61] less a product of the war, traced the evolution of national feeling in Europe since the French Revolution. Rose felt that nationality had been a beneficent force until 1885, after which it had altered its character. He proved a poor prophet on nationality, for a decade before the war he had predicted its decline and, with it, the end of conscript armies.[62] Despite the evidence around him, he retained his faith in the ultimate triumph of internationalism and looked forward to an era of peace and good will among nations.[63]

The patriot usually triumphed over the historian in the numerous articles Rose contributed to reviews during the war. German policy was compared to that of Napoleon. The Kaiser, like Napoleon, underestimated his rivals; both had extensive plans at Britain's expense in the Near East.[64] German colonial ambitions were said to have prepared the upper class in Germany "to fight Great Britain for South Africa, East Africa, and Egypt at the first favorable opportunity."[65] As the war progressed, Rose rejected all proposals of a compromise peace, insisting that the struggle should be continued until Germany was completely defeated. Then she should receive a reasonable peace, such as that imposed on France in 1815.[66] His ideas on the peace often show the historian victorious over the nationalist. Danzig should be left to Germany. "The good sense of the Poles will discern," he wrote, "the impossibility of possessing that port and thereby cutting the German race in half. A good commercial treaty guaranteeing to them full trade privileges, ought, surely, to satisfy all but the Chauvinists."[67] He foresaw difficulties between Italy and the Southern Slavs and urged that Austria not be excluded from an outlet to the Adriatic.[68] France should receive Alsace-Lorraine and the Saar, but her demand for the left bank of the Rhine should be rejected as "incompatible with her national solidarity, her military security, and, above all, with that peaceful development which the free nations of the West alike desire."[69] Rose was lecturing at Cambridge on "Schemes of universal peace" when the armistice was signed.[70]

He had reached an age when most men contemplate retirement, but for one of his industry and enthusiasm there could be no cessation of work as long as his health continued good. He was, in fact, on the threshold of a new and most congenial phase of his career. Still ahead lay significant contributions to scholarship. Lord Rothermere decided to found a chair of naval history at Cambridge in honor of his son, Vere Harmsworth, who lost his life in the war. On November 27, 1918, he wrote the acting vice-chancellor, offering £20,000 as an endowment, under certain provisions:

> One of the conditions governing this offer is that such chair is to be for all time described in all official statutes, documents, lists, etc., of the University as the Vere Harmsworth Chair of Naval History.
> The other condition is that the first appointment to the chair is to be made by me. It is my intention to offer the appointment to Dr. Holland Rose. Failing his acceptance, the appointment will be left to the University authorities.[71]

Rothermere had met Rose during the war and had been greatly impressed with him. The university accepted the gift, and it was announced in the spring of 1919 that Rose had received the appointment. That autumn he began his duties with a series of lectures on British naval history from 1755 to 1854.[72]

Rose brought to naval history a fresh point of view, the product of a lifetime's study of war and diplomacy.[73] As he saw it, naval historians had hitherto specialized in accounts of battles, and general historians had neglected the navy's role in national life. Naval history should

> launch out into wider realms; it will treat of economics, so far as that science influences the clash of interests at sea, the consequent growth of navies and the causes of maritime conflicts. Naval history will describe the chief geographical

discoveries, especially the marine explorations of naval officers. . . . . The naval historian will also show how the discoveries and settlements of the new lands induced new rivalries and influenced the policy of competing nations.[74]

Naval history, properly written, could be of incalculable benefit to the nation. A review of naval administrations would indicate where economies might be effected and where they would impair efficiency. Particular attention should be given to the coordination of naval and military operations. The war of 1939 with Germany proved again the truth of Rose's warning that Great Britain had begun all her great wars with an inadequate supply of small naval craft.[75]

The first published research of the new professor treated an episode chiefly remembered for its connection with the career of Napoleon Bonaparte—the siege of Toulon in 1793.[76] The failure of the British fleet to hold the naval base which had opened its gates to Lord Hood's squadron was a serious blow to the allied campaign against Jacobin France. The causes of the disaster were attributed to lack of co-operation by Britain's allies and inadequate support from home. Lord Hood was not to blame for his inability to hold the city. The defense of the city was an amphibious operation requiring large bodies of troops, which never arrived. When the French, under Bonaparte, erected batteries on the heights of La Grasse the fleet was engaged in an unequal combat which necessitated its withdrawal. Rose believes that the success of this conflict between land and sea power convinced Bonaparte of the supremacy of the former.[77] This study of the campaign was based on new material, much of which was published in an extended appendix. The volume was a good example of naval history, as the author defined it in his inaugural lecture. The work was followed by the publication of a collection of essays, most of which dealt with problems or episodes of naval warfare.[78]

New academic distinctions came to Rose. Both Cambridge and the University of Manchester, of which Owens College had become a part, had conferred D.Litt. degrees upon him early in the century. In 1922 the Institute of International Education, in New York, invited him to lecture in a score of American colleges and universities. Two of them, Amherst and Nebraska, honored him with the LL.D. degree. Rose enjoyed the trip immensely and was much pleased at the attention everywhere showered upon him. The tour began at Johns Hopkins and ended at Clark University. Meanwhile, Rose had made his first visit to the Middle West, which interested him tremendously. It was a matter of great pride to him that he drew a full house on one occasion at the University of Chicago when Einstein and William Jennings Bryan were lecturing on the campus at the same hour. Despite the heat, his stay at Nebraska, where he remained for the summer session, was one of the features of the tour. At Oberlin, 1,200 people heard him give the Phi Beta Kappa address. In Amherst he participated in the centennial celebration by speaking on the state of public education in Great Britain.[79] Rose refrained from the criticisms and provincial advice that his visiting countrymen often heap upon the good-natured American. It is not surprising, then, that he could testify to "the warmth of welcome which a Briton will everywhere receive if he delivers his message without stiffness, pedantry, or affectation."[80]

Rose's work as a naval historian deepened the scholarly interest in the British Empire which he had already shown in his earlier writings. He considered the war with Napoleon a commercial and imperial struggle, describing the rupture in 1803 as the most significant event of the century from the viewpoint of racial expansion.[81] Full attention had been given to developments in Australia and Canada during Pitt's first ministry.[82] The second volume of *The development of European nations* was primarily a study of imperialism after 1870.

The war of 1914 had vindicated the political vitality of the British Empire and proved its spiritual unity. Rose believed the time had come to write its history on a broader scale than had been attempted hitherto, and upon his return from America he embarked upon the project. *The Cambridge history of the British Empire*,[83] which resulted, at once took its place with the other great Cambridge histories, upon which it had been modeled. Rose was

senior editor; his fellow-editors were A. P. Newton, Rhodes professor of imperial history in the University of London, and E. A.
Benians, fellow and senior tutor of St. John's College, Cambridge.
The vast enterprise involved the co-operation of scholars in Great
Britain, the United States, and the British Dominions; for example, thirty-three authors are represented in the volume on Canada. The great number of contributions from the dominions indicated that these countries had come of age in scholarship as well
as in politics.

Praise was universal when the first volume, *The old Empire to
1783*, appeared in 1929. The subsequent volumes on Canada,
Australia, New Zealand, and South Africa were even more enthusiastically received. The later volumes naturally broke newer
ground and presented the results of more original scholarship.
They also performed the great service of synthesizing the history
of these regions for the first time. The editorial work in the entire series was unusually good. Overlapping, so great a problem
in co-operative works, was reduced to a minimum. The organization, as in the other Cambridge histories, made the volumes
very usable. The bibliographies were an outstanding aid to the
further study of imperial history.

In addition to his labor as senior editor, Rose contributed
chapters or sections to four volumes: "The spirit of adventure,"
"National security and expansion, 1580–1660," and "Sea power
and expansion, 1660–1763" in Volume I; "The conflict with
Revolutionary France, 1793–1802" and "The struggle with Napoleon, 1803–1815" in Volume II; "The struggle for supremacy
in America, 1682–1748" in Volume VI; and "Captain Cook" in
Volume VII, Part II. The essays were dignified by a lucid style
and objective scholarship. The section on the Tudor adven-
turers, though a fine piece of writing, presented little new material, except on naval construction. Rose's most original contributions were his accounts of the wars against Louis XIV in the
West Indies and Canada. The combination of new material and
stimulating suggestions on these campaigns makes Rose's work
the best brief account of the seventeenth-century Anglo-French

conflict for North America. The long chapters on the French Revolutionary and Napoleonic era devote so much space to diplomacy and naval warfare that other imperial questions are often slighted. The most valuable sections portray the economic importance of the West Indies. Rose believed Britain's salvation lay in her sole control of tropical products and that "in the last resort Napoleon was beaten by cotton and dyes, by sugar and coffee."

The *Cambridge history of the British Empire* was more than a scholarly enterprise to Rose, for his deep love of the Empire invested the work with a spiritual quality. He believed in the Empire as a force for good in the world, attributing to it a mission of peace and civilization. Not long after Rose's graduation from Cambridge, Sir John Seeley had delivered his famous lectures on *The expansion of England*. Rose remained true to this faith in imperialism, and he had no patience with the post-war cynics who complacently discussed the dissolution of the Empire. Such weak souls were unworthy of their heritage. He realized that difficulties lay ahead, but he believed England would surmount them, as in the past. His concern for the future is shown in a letter he wrote soon after the foundation of a studentship at Cambridge in 1932 for study of the recent history of the Empire: "I have long been working to this end, and hope the Studentship may train up a succession of men who will benefit the Empire. Certainly, we need all the thought and training possible if we are to win through."

Rose's magnificent enthusiasm for history was never more apparent than during the years just prior to his retirement. In 1931 he began a new course of lectures on the Mediterranean in the ancient world with all the joy of a young instructor. "I believe this subject has never been tackled before," he wrote, "and I find it immensely interesting. It has been a refreshing return to my beloved classical times." The lectures, upon publication,[84] were especially commended for originality in the treatment of Roman policy in the Mediterranean. As one critic noted, Rose brought "the outlook of one who sees the sea first and has not been march-

ing for years along the dusty roads at the heels of Roman legion-
naires." [85] While lecturing on the Mediterranean in classical
times, Rose began the preparation of a course on "Man's struggle with the sea" from the earliest days through the Napoleonic
era. "Does not that stir your blood?" he wrote exuberently.
Upon his retirement in 1933 he prepared these last lectures for
the press and they appeared in an attractively illustrated volume.[86] The author roved the seas in a dozen chapters, sailing
with captains, great and small, from Odysseus to the last of the
Atlantic slavers. No ancient mariner "in tiny craft against watery
wastes haunted by deathly terrors" found greater adventure on
his travels than Rose experienced in presenting this panorama of
maritime progress. *Man and the sea* was a unique presentation of
much learning in a most appealing form—the kind of book that
only a lifetime of reading and reflection can produce.

Retirement at the age of seventy-eight made no change in
Rose's devotion to research and writing. Not until 1939 did failing health force him to cease work. In addition to his work on the
Cambridge history of the British Empire, one scholarly paper and a
fine popular article came from his pen after *Man and the sea*. The
former, communicated to the British Academy, showed that the
role of the weather in the defeat of the Spanish Armada had been
overemphasized.[87] In fact, the wind had favored Spain off
Cornwall, again off Portland and the Isle of Wight, and particularly north of Scotland. Lack of "weatherly ships and absence of
an experienced commander" were important causes of the failure. In 1938, much disturbed by the hostile attitude of Fascist
Italy, he tried to reason with his old Italian friends regarding the
Mediterranean.[88] Philip II, Louis XIV, and Napoleon, he stated, had all tried unsuccessfully to monopolize that sea, but Britain
since 1815 had not used her ascendancy in a way to hinder the
development of other nations. Rose reminded Italy that the
Mediterranean was vital to the interests of countries like Australia and that her claims to monopoly there were impossible
and based on unrealities. This appeal to Italy reflected the
strange world in which Rose's career drew to a close. It was his

fate to witness a dissipation of the great victory of 1918 and to see the Empire once again fighting for its very existence. Yet to the historian of Napoleon the world of Hitler, with its many parallels should not have been something new under the sun.

In a field as ephemeral as history the long life of Rose's best books has been most impressive. The *Life of Napoleon I* and the two volumes on Pitt have enjoyed careers of nearly forty and thirty years, respectively. The former must be read in the light of much later research, but it still remains an important work. The volumes on Pitt are Rose's greatest work of scholarship, and they eclipse anything else in the field. Rose's contributions to the *Cambridge modern history* continue valuable, and his chapters in the *Cambridge history of British foreign policy* constitute an invaluable summary of the years 1792–1802. The *Cambridge history of the British Empire* should be indispensable for at least a generation.

Rose's influence on historical scholarship must be sought primarily in his writings. He came to Cambridge too late to gather the large group of graduate students which a professor of his distinction would normally attract. This was a real loss to learning, for he was tremendously interested in his students and gave more time to graduate students than any other Cambridge professor of the post-war era. As a teacher he was open minded, warmhearted, and very approachable.

Rose's use of the British archives helped to revolutionize the writing of diplomatic history in Great Britain. Like most scholars of his generation, he seemed at times to worship documents for their own sake. Some of the documents he published in the *English historical review*, for instance, were not worth such attention.[89] Despite his years in the British archives, Rose did not go the last mile and consult the archives of other countries. It remained for men like his younger Cambridge colleagues, Temperley and Webster, to explore the continental archives along with those of Great Britain. Rose's use of materials, however, was marked by sound judgment and remarkable factual accuracy.

His style, often grandiloquent in earlier writings, acquired restraint and dignity with the years. All his writings show the influence of his classical education. Although he lacked the artistry of G. M. Trevelyan, who makes readers *feel* the grandeur of his theme, Rose's work possessed the essential qualities of good history. It was extremely lucid and exceptionally well organized— attributes which secured wide audiences for his biographies and made his textbooks outstanding successes. But none of his works possessed the literary and interpretative qualities of a classic. Despite his great learning, he never produced anything on Napoleon comparable to the little biography written by H. A. L. Fisher.

His works were analytic and imaginative but did not advance a general philosophy of history. History meant more to him than past politics, but he would hardly have considered it a social science. His chief interest was *state* policy. Even when he talked of nations, he was unconsciously thinking of states. Napoleon and Pitt appealed to him primarily as rulers, only incidentally as individuals. When he dealt with economic history, as he did in several able articles, he emphasized the political aspect of that science. As a military historian he was generally first rate, sometimes superb. To naval history he brought new viewpoints and a wide background which gave scope and vitality to his writings in the field. His forte was diplomatic history, and this part of his work will endure longest.[90]

NOTES

1. Biographical information from *Who's Who*, 1899–1940.
2. London, 1889; numerous subsequent editions.
3. Cambridge, 1894; 7th ed. 1935.
4. "Napoleon and English commerce," *EHR*, VIII (1893), 704–25.
5. *Revolutionary and Napoleonic era*, pp. v–vi.
6. *Ibid.*, pp. 19, 63, 86–88.
7. "The unstamped press, 1815–36," *EHR*, XII (1897), 711–26.
8. London, 1897.
9. The following may be listed as the more important from this period: "Canning and Denmark in 1807," XI (1896), 82–92; "The dispatches of Colonel Graham on the Italian campaign of 1796–97," XIV (1899), 111–24, 321–31; "The secret articles of the Treaty of Amiens," XV (1900), 331–35; "Sir Hudson Lowe and the beginnings of the campaign in 1815," XVI (1901), 517–27; "A British agent at Tilsit," XVI, 712–18; "France and the First Coalition before the campaign of 1796," XVIII (1903), 281–302. Other articles include: "The ice incident at Austerlitz," XVII (1902), 537–38; "The political reactions of Bonaparte's eastern expedi-

tion," XLIV (1929), 48–58. Also "Canning and Spanish patriots in 1808," *AHR*, XII (1906–7), 39–52; "Napoleon and sea power," *Cambridge historical journal*, I (1924), 138–57; "British West Indian commerce as a factor in the Napoleonic war," *ibid.*, III (1929), 34–46.

10. 2 vols.; London, 1901; 11th ed., 1935. References in this essay are to the edition of 1916.

11. Allan Nevins, *The gateway to history* (Boston, 1938), p. 335.

12. *Life of Napoleon I*, I, ix–x.

13. *Ibid.*, I, 466.

14. *Ibid.*, I, 106, 127.

15. *Ibid.*, II, 241.

16. *Ibid.*, II, 337.

17. *Ibid.*, II, 362–66.

18. *Ibid.*, I, 301.

19. *Ibid.*, II, 238, 304, 471, 528.

20. *Ibid.*, I, 385–90.

21. *Ibid.*, II, 11.

22. *Ibid.*, II, 127.

23. *Ibid.*, II, 98.

24. *Ibid.*, II, 497–529; "The detention of Napoleon at St. Helena," *Historical essays*, first published in 1902 in commemoration of the jubilee of the Owens College, Manchester (Manchester, 1907).

25. Reviewed by T. A. Dodge, *AHR*, VIII (1902–3), 565–69.

26. *Life of Napoleon I*, I, 416.

27. Geoffrey Bruun, *Europe and the French imperium* (New York, 1937), pp. 69–73.

28. *Cambridge modern history*, VIII (Cambridge, 1904), 553–93, 594–619, 633–64; IX (Cambridge, 1906), 294–340, 361–89.

29. A. W. Ward and G. P. Gooch (eds.), *Cambridge history of British foreign policy, 1783–1919*, I (Cambridge, 1922), 216–391.

30. *Ibid.*, pp. 236.

31. *Ibid.*, p. 337.

32. *Ibid.*, p. 355.

33. *Ibid.*, pp. 216–18; "France and the First Coalition before the campaign of 1796," *EHR*, XVIII (1903), 287–302.

34. *Cambridge history of British foreign policy*, I, 266.

35. *Ibid.*, p. 307.

36. *Ibid.*, p. 334.

37. *Ibid.*, p. 340.

38. *Ibid.*, p. 346.

39. *Ibid.*, p. 364. This is a reversal of Rose's earlier position: "If we put ourselves in the place of Canning,—we shall, I think hesitate to censure him." "Canning and the secret intelligence from Tilsit (July 16–23, 1807)," *Transactions of the Royal Historical Society*, NS., XX (1906), 72.

40. *Cambridge history of British foreign policy*, I, 382–91.

41. *Select despatches from the British foreign office archives relating to the formation of the Third Coalition against France, 1804–1805*, ed. John Holland Rose, Litt.D. (London: Royal Historical Society, 1904).

42. *Napoleonic studies* (London, 1904).

43. *Dumouriez and the defence of England against Napoleon* (London, 1909).

44. A. M. Broadley, *Napoleon in caricature, 1795–1821* (2 vols.; London, 1911).

45. "The limitations of Napoleon's genius," *CR*, LXXXIX (1906), 549–61; "Napoleon the Great and Italy," *ibid.*, XCVI (1909), 417–29; "Napoleon's last campaign in Germany," *Edinburgh review*, CCXVIII (1913), 298–312. To this list may be added a later article, "Napoleon I and modern Europe," *ibid.*, CCXXXV (1922), 302–14.

46. Rose also edited *Napoleon's last voyages; being the diaries of Sir Thomas Ussher and John R. Glover* (London, 1906) and the *Memoirs of Madame Campan* (2 vols.; London, 1917).

47. Boston, 1912.

48. "The Franco-British commercial treaty of 1786," *EHR*, XXIII (1908), 709–24.

49. "Great Britain and the Dutch question, 1787–88," *AHR*, XIV (1908–9), 262–83. In this connection one should also consult "The missions of William Grenville to The Hague and Versailles in 1787," *EHR*, XXIV (1909), 278–95.

50. "Pitt and the campaign of 1793 in Flanders," *EHR*, XXIV (1909), 744–49; "The Duke of Richmond on the conduct of the war in 1793," *ibid.*, XXV (1910), 554–55; "Papers relating to the Irish rebellion of 1798," *ibid.*, pp. 748–52; "Burke, Windham, and Pitt," XXVII (1912), 700–716; XXVIII (1913), 86–105; "The rout of a coalition," *Nineteenth century*, XCV (1924), 451–58.

51. London, 1911. Reviewed by E. D. Adams, *AHR*, XVII (1911–12), 134–36, and H. E. Egerton, *EHR*, XXVI (1911), 589–92.

52. *William Pitt and national revival*, p. 536.

53. London, 1911.

54. C. T. Atkinson's review, *EHR*, XXVIII (1913), 583–84.

55. Published in one volume as *The life of William Pitt* (London, 1923) and best known under this title. *A short life of William Pitt* (London, 1925), though an abridgment, used some materials not consulted for the original work.

56. *Cambridge magazine*, Oct. 16, 1915.

57. London, 1912; new ed., 1930.

58. "Frederick the Great and England, 1756–63," *EHR*, XXIX (1914), 79–93, 257–75.

59. 2 vols.; London, 1905; 6th ed., 1922.

60. London, 1915.

61. London, 1916. Rose employed the term "nationality" in the sense we use the word "nationalism" today. To him "nationalism" denoted "the intolerant and "aggressive instinct which has of late developed in Germany and the Balkan States."

62. "Nationality and militarism," *International quarterly*, IX (1904), 170–85.

63. "The war and nationality," *Scientia*, XVIII (1915), 24–34; *Nationality in modern history*, pp. 200–202.

64. "1815 and 1915," *CR*, CV (1915), 12–18; "The imitation of Napoleon I by the Germans," *CR*, CVIII (1915), 471–80.

65. "British and German policy," *Fortnightly review*, CIII (1915), 371–81.

66. "The folly of early offers of peace," *ibid.*, pp. 693–704; "The national idea," *CR*, CIX (1916), 331–37.

67. "Polish problem: past and present," *CR*, CX (1916), 716.

68. "The future of Europe," *Scientia*, XIX (1916), 294.

69. "France and the Rhine frontier," *Nineteenth century*, LXXXI (1917), 297.

70. *Cambridge magazine*, Oct. 26, 1918.

71. *Ibid.*, Dec. 7, 1918.

72. *Ibid.*, May 31 and Oct. 25, 1919.

73. For information on the later phase of his career I am greatly indebted to Professor Gerald S. Graham, Queen's University, a former graduate student under Rose and an intimate friend of the family. Professor Graham kindly allowed me to see a number of personal letters covering the years 1929–37. He also read this essay and made a number of valuable suggestions.

74. *Naval history and national history* (Cambridge, 1919), p. 10. The inaugural lecture delivered to the University of Cambridge on Trafalgar Day, 1919.

75. "A plea for the further study of naval history," *Fortnightly review*, CXIV (1920), 807–17.

76. *Lord Hood and the defence of Toulon* (Cambridge, 1922).

77. *Ibid.*, p. 41.

78. *The indecisiveness of modern war and other essays* (London, 1927).

79. "The problem of education in England today," *Amherst graduates' quarterly*, X (1921), 309–18.

80. "Impressions of American universities," *CR*, CXX (1921), 644–51.

81. *Life of Napoleon I*, I, 396.

82. *William Pitt and national revival*, pp. 432–54.

83. 8 vols.; Cambridge, 1929———. Space was distributed as follows: Vol. I, *The old Empire, from the beginnings to 1783;* Vol. II, *The growth of the new Empire, 1783–1870;* Vol. III, *The Empire Commonwealth, 1870–1921;* Vol. IV, *British India, 1497–1858;* Vol. V, *The Indian Empire, 1858–1918;* Vol. VI, *Canada and Newfoundland;* Vol. VII, Part I, *Australia,* Part II, *New Zealand;* and Vol. VIII, *South Africa.* Volume III has yet to appear. Volumes IV and V were edited by H. H. Dodwell and also form part of the *Cambridge history of India.*

84. *The Mediterranean in the ancient world* (Cambridge, 1933).

85. Review by Olwen Brogan, *History*, XVIII (1933–34), 154–56; see also the review by W. W. Hyde, *AHR*, XXXIX (1933–34), 358–59.

86. *Man and the sea: stages in maritime and human progress* (Cambridge, 1935).

87. *Was the failure of the Spanish Armada due to storms?* (Oxford, 1937), reprinted from *Proceedings of the British Academy*, Vol. XXII.

88. "Struggles for the Mediterranean," *CR*, CLIII (1938), 419–26.

89. "The action at Vallegio, 30 May 1796," XIII (1898), 741; "The French expedition at the Cape, 1803," XV (1900), 129–32; "The funeral of Napoleon and his last papers," XVII (1902), 311–16; "A document relating to the continental system," XVIII (1903), 122–24; "A report on the battles of Jena-Auerstadt and the surrender at Prenzlau," XIX (1904), 550–53; "A protest of Talleyrand against his expulsion from England," XXI (1906), 330–32; "Documents relating to the rupture with France in 1793," XXVII (1912), 117–23, 324–30; "The Comte d'Artois and Pitt in December 1789," XXX (1915), 322–24; "Lord Elgin's report on Levantine affairs and Malta, 1803," XXXVI (1921), 234–36; "A French memoir on Pitt's naval operations of 1757–58," XXVIII (1913), 748–51.

90. I am indebted to Professor Geoffrey Bruun, of New York University, who kindly read my manuscript and made several suggestions.

XVIII

FRANCESCO RUFFINI (1863–1934)

S. WILLIAM HALPERIN*

FRANCESCO RUFFINI was many things. He was a distinguished historian and canonist whose writings are held in the highest esteem by scholars the world over. He was an inspiring teacher and a fecund stimulator of scholarly interest in unexplored areas of investigation. He was an ardent patriot whose love of country balked at no sacrifice. He was a genuine liberal to whom all tyranny was anathema. He was a loyal friend. Above all, he was true to his innermost convictions, ready to do battle for them even in the most disheartening circumstances. Ruffini, the man, has received no finer tribute than these words of Benedetto Croce:

> That which really unites human beings is something deeper than . . . . agreement in the matter of ideas: it is agreement in their attitude toward life. And here Francesco Ruffini was a teacher, and a prop and comfort to his friends. The latter admired in him the simplicity of resoluteness toward that which is duty: a resoluteness which almost excluded the moment of perplexity, which almost left no room for the very virtue of courage, because he did not even suspect that he could do otherwise than that which, in following the path of honor, he was doing.[1]

Ruffini was born in Lessolo, in the Piedmontese section of Italy, on April 10, 1863. His family had neither noble lineage nor wealth, but some of its members had distinguished themselves as scholars, as civil servants, and in the liberal professions. The premature death of the head of the household forced heavy responsibilities upon Ruffini's mother. She acquired a small farm and sought to make it pay for the education of her children. To see

* Assistant professor of modern history, University of Chicago.

their sons secure a university training was a widespread ambition among even the most modest families of provincial Piedmont. It was at the *collegio civico* of Ivrea that Ruffini completed his classical studies. Armed with a scholarship, he entered the University of Turin in 1882. His proclivities were decidedly literary; but yielding, perhaps, to practical considerations and pressure from home, he matriculated in the school of jurisprudence.[2]

His favorite professors, those who most deeply and permanently influenced his intellectual development, were Giuseppe Carle and Cesare Nani. From Carle he gained an insight into the processes governing the evolution of those interlocking and interacting ideas which, in turn, fashioned the course of legal history. From Carle he also learned to appreciate the national traditions behind movements of thought and to perceive the ideological and spiritual roots as well as the imposing but superficial externals of political and juridical institutions. Nani's analytical mind, his rigorous adherence to the niceties of historical method, and his careful and exact researches left a lasting impression on Ruffini.[3]

Shortly after the completion of his work at the university he decided in favor of an academic career. He chose the field of ecclesiastical law. Because it was just beginning to be cultivated methodically and in a thoroughly secular spirit in Italy, it offered many unexplored areas. But since his own country lacked, as yet, a scientific tradition in this branch of study, Ruffini went to Germany in 1889 to secure more advanced training. He attended the courses of Professor Emil Friedberg at the University of Leipzig and came away an enthusiastic disciple of that celebrated scholar. Upon his return to Italy he taught ecclesiastical law at the universities of Pavia and Genoa and then, in 1899, was invited to occupy the chair of legal history at the University of Turin. Finally, in 1908, he was transferred, at his own request, to the chair of ecclesiastical law in the same institution.[4] This post he retained for twenty-three years.

In 1900 Ruffini married Ada Avondo, who belonged to a wealthy and aristocratic Piedmontese family. But this union ended tragically. The birth of a son, Edoardo, was for the mother the beginning of a long illness that proved incurable. Her death in 1910 was a stunning blow to Ruffini. However, his child, the self-effacing devotion of his sister-in-law, Giulia Avondo, and the historical researches which were claiming more and more of his attention afforded him some solace.[5]

Academic honors were showered upon him. For a number of years he was president of the Accademia delle Scienze di Torino and vice-president of the Deputazione di Storia Patria per le antiche Provincie. He presided over the faculty of the University of Turin from 1904 to 1907 and was rector of the institution from 1910 to 1913. But these time-consuming professional activities and the innumerable hours lavished upon his studies failed to keep him out of the political arena. Here, from the outset, he wielded all the influence he could muster to promote the liberal cause. He had the greatest respect for those who sincerely professed a given faith; but he was, and remained to the end of his life, an uncompromising foe of every species of intolerance and fanaticism.[6] He fervently believed that the preservation of religious and political liberty was vital to the highest interests of the nation and humanity. His creed was epitomized in the word "freedom."

His first major opportunity in the field of practical politics came in 1906, when he served as departmental chief under Boselli, who was then minister of public instruction. It was not, however, until the outbreak of the European war in the summer of 1914 that he came into his own as a public figure. He strongly supported the interventionist policy of Salandra, on whose recommendation he was named a senator of the kingdom on December 30, 1914. Throughout the years of Italy's participation in the struggle against the Central Powers he gave unstintingly of himself to the national cause. He became, almost overnight, an impassioned propagandist whose every nerve was strained to awaken in others the kind of patriotism which was electrifying him. The scientific habit and outlook were momentarily abandoned. He now presented himself to his compatriots as an apostle preaching the gospel of self-sacrifice and faith in Italy's high destiny. To those who persisted in their opposition to the war he recalled the farsighted boldness of Cavour[7] and the high-minded teachings of Mazzini.[8] Following the disaster of Caporetto, he endeavored to remind his gloom-ridden countrymen of the deplorable situation in which Piedmont-Sardinia found herself after the battle of Novara and of the remarkable recovery she achieved thereafter under Victor Emmanuel II.[9] He extolled the martyrdom of Cesare Battisti, who sensed that Italy needed heroism and the spirit of self-sacrifice above all else and who foresaw that only struggle—not inglorious passivity or pusillanimous bargaining—could bring a fulfilment of her legitimate aspirations.[10]

Speeches and tracts were not all he contributed to the war effort. In 1915 he organized a committee in Turin to aid the national military effort. The work of this committee called for the expenditure of large sums, and when financial difficulties were encountered he sacrificed all his possessions to take care of the deficit.[11] When Boselli formed his national union cabinet in June, 1916, Ruffini was appointed minister of public instruction. His ministerial career proved short lived, however, ending with the fall of the Boselli government in October, 1917. His last important activity during this period was his participation in the work of the interparliamentary committee which sought to promote complete concord between the Allies.[12]

The immediate aftermath of the war found him preoccupied with a number of things, among them the Wilsonian program and the projected League of Nations, of which he was a fervent champion,[13] the problems and prospects of political Zionism,[14] and the repercussions of the recently concluded hostilities on existing political and constitutional arrangements.[15] He continued active, during these first post-war years, in the ranks of the liberal party. Notable in this connection is the speech he delivered in the senate on December 8, 1919. With characteristic courage and vision, he summoned the liberal elements of the country to do what they could to prevent the nation from falling under the sway of the extremist parties. Imbued, as always, with optimism, tolerance, and humanitarianism, he believed the liberal state capable of absorbing and fructifying all the interests and energies of those who dwelt within its borders.[16]

After the advent of Fascism, Ruffini continued to be a staunch champion of personal and political liberty, and his refusal to take the oath demanded of all professors by Mussolini cost him his post at the University of Turin in 1931. His son, who had been teaching Italian legal history at the University of Perugia, was dismissed for the same reason. The closing years of his life witnessed a steady withdrawal from politics and public office, even from the Committee on Intellectual Co-operation, established by the League of Nations, to which he had given much of his time and energy from 1923 to 1927.[17] He surrendered himself entirely to his studies, and it was while he was busily at work on them that he was fatally stricken. He died on March 29, 1934, and was buried in his native province without official honors, without speeches, with the very same simplicity which throughout the long and fruitful life had been the hallmark of the man.

But simplicity was not his only engaging trait, as the author of this essay discovered when he met Ruffini in the summer of 1932. He was a charming and gracious host, delightfully informal and affable. What stood out most of all, however, was his extreme gentleness. The ensuing conversation touched upon many things of common interest, and the present writer came away with the feeling that he had met not only a great scholar but a lovable man. What he saw and felt on this occasion has been affirmed and re-affirmed by all those who knew Ruffini well—friends, colleagues, and students.

The death of Francesco Ruffini robbed his country of one of its outstanding jurists.[18] It was he, together with Professor Francesco Scaduto, of the University of Rome,[19] who restored the study of canon law in Italy. The first scientific elaboration of Italian ecclesiastical law was due in large part to him. His translation of Friedberg's classic treatise[20] helped to diffuse among Italians a systematic knowledge of the constitutional and administrative law of the church.[21] His own writings in this field are legion. They deal with a wide assortment of topics and vary markedly in length and scope, but the scholarship which produced them is uniformly sound. The best known of all, perhaps, is his *Corso di diritto ecclesiastico*,[22] which quickly established itself as a standard treatment. His early essays deal, for the most part, with the role of canon law in the development of Italian private law. He subsequently devoted considerable attention to the study of ecclesiastical institutions viewed in their historical evolution and in the light of prevailing juridical norms. Not to be overlooked are his contributions to the expanding literature in the field of public law. He trained a number of Italy's leading canonists of today, including Mario Falco and Arturo Carlo Jemolo. Such was Ruffini the jurist.

Ruffini's career as a historian, which extends over a period of more than forty years, began with the publication of his justly esteemed and famous *Lineamenti storici delle relazioni fra lo stato e la chiesa in Italia*.[23] This succinct and pithy outline was a direct outgrowth of his interest in the development of Italian ecclesisatical law. By far the greater part of it deals with the situation in the various sections of the peninsula prior to unification. Despite its brevity, it is an indispensable manual. It filled a serious lacuna, for of general histories of the relations between church and state in Italy there was then a dearth. It performed still another important service: it pointed the way to further studies of a comparable type.

Ruffini's interest in problems of ecclesiastical policy and the relations of church and state soon crystallized into a sustained preoccupation with the vicissitudes of toleration in Italy and the rest of Europe. Out of this preoccupation was born the idea of surveying briefly the history of religious liberty. The task proved a much bigger one than he had anticipated, and it was not until 1900 that it was completed. The study was published shortly thereafter under the title: *La libertà religiosa: storia dell'idea*.[24] After a few introductory pages on the ancient and medieval periods it traces the slow and painful progress of the idea of religious liberty, considered both in its theoretical formulations and as the subject of legislative enactment, from the sixteenth century to the close of the eighteenth. The writings of philosophers, theologians, political theorists, jurists, essayists, dramatists, and statesmen who at one time or another concerned themselves with the problem of religious toleration are analyzed and appraised, as are also the texts of governmental pronouncements which constitute land-marks in the history of this great theme.

The historian of religious liberty was led, before long, to ad-dress himself to a closely related subject: the genesis of Cavour's very liberal views on ecclesiastical policy. The appearance, in 1908, of the celebrated "Le origini elvetiche della formula del conte di Cavour: 'Libera chiesa in libero stato,' "[25] inaugurated a long series of studies on the great Piedmontese. The predominant and, indeed, decisive role played by Swiss liberal Protestantism in the development of Cavour's politico-religious thought is ably and convincingly set forth. During his youth the future statesman spent much time in Geneva, and it was there that he first came under the influence of ideas which were at complete variance with those which prevailed in his own country after 1815. What Cavour saw and learned in Switzerland enabled him to view with keener understanding the liberal Catholicism which raised its head in France during the period of the July Monarchy. His at-titude toward this movement forms the subject of a suggestive essay which Ruffini published in the *Stampa* of Turin on August 9, 1910.[26]

In Switzerland, while he was investigating the origins of the famous Cavourian formula, Ruffini stumbled upon something which was to absorb his energies for years to come: a sheaf of unpublished and hitherto unknown documents that turned out to be letters written by Cavour between 1828 and 1845—from his eighteenth to his thirty-fifth year—to his Geneva cousin, Adèle de Sellon, and her husband, Baron Paul Emile Maurice. Before chancing upon this treasure of information, without which his two-volume *La giovinezza del conte di Cavour: saggi storici secondo lettere e documenti inediti*[27] could not have been written, Ruffini had not had the faintest intention of working on a life of Cavour. But previous inclinations and plans now counted for nought. "This," he himself tells us, "was the beginning of everything. The saying, 'Opportunity makes the thief,' may very well be applied to me with this variation: opportunity, or, better, the document, made the biographer."[28] The letters which Ruffini was thus privileged to see are invaluable for the light they shed on the personality and intimate life of the young Cavour. In them are mirrored his thoughts, his feelings, certain of his idiosyncrasies. Ruffini supplemented their contents with material drawn from letters in the Cavourian archives at Santena, from those parts of the count's diary which had escaped the attention of Berti, and from other unpublished documents in sundry private and public archives, including those of Vienna, to produce his great work on the youth of Cavour. The formative years of the statesman are here painstakingly and sympathetically reconstructed. The portraiture is full and rich, revealing its subject's warmth, his precocious intellectual development, the range and depth of his interests. The world in which he matured comes to life: his family; the people who in one way or another influenced his mental and emotional growth; the theories and doctrines which attracted his attention; the places he visited; the events, in Italy and abroad, which he pondered. The story possesses a remarkable unity. When Cavour was only sixteen Charles Albert wrote a letter containing the following passage about the lad, who was then serving as one of his pages: "Le petit Camille Cavour a fait le Jacobin et je l'ai mis à ma porte; pleurs, lamentations de toute la famille." The entire history of Cavour's youth, Ruffini remarks, is epitomized in the prince's words: "incoercible manifestations of political and religious liberalism; indignation and opposition on the part of his large family, especially those of its members who were blindly devoted to the old regime; suspicion and persecution on the part of the government."[29]

The intimate picture of the youthful Cavour which had emerged from the pages of *La giovinezza del conte di Cavour* was further enriched by Ruffini's *Camillo di Cavour e Mélanie Waldor (secondo lettere e documenti inediti)*.[30] Written with admirable tact, and based in part on unpublished letters from the Cavourian archives in Santena, it recounts the brief liaison between the twenty-eight-year-old count and a French woman fourteen years his senior. She had been, for a time, the mistress of Alexandre Dumas, *père*, and was herself a writer of some reputation. This erotic interlude ran a course that was not at all extraordinary, but its few vicissitudes, however commonplace, throw invaluable light upon certain aspects of the young man's psychology. The correspondence between the lovers reveals, among other things, the "invincibly realistic, positive, *raisonneur*" foundation of his character. He was, to be sure, an "idealist"; but he had, as Ruffini insists, a profound and sustained abhorrence for "sentimentality" of any kind.[31]

The war years halted Ruffini's researches, but the very morrow of the armistice found him directing his attention to a totally different chapter of the Cavourian saga: the great statesman's relations with two of his bitterest political adversaries—Angelo Brofferio, the Piedmontese writer and politician, and Francesco Domenico Guerrazzi, the famous Tuscan patriot. In 1920 he published three articles on various phases of this theme in successive issues of the *Nuova antologia*.[32] They are substantial and exceedingly valuable essays. Ruffini analyzes the reasons for the aversion which Brofferio and Guerrazzi felt for Cavour, an aversion that was personal as well as political. Especially telling are the unflattering sections devoted to Brofferio, whose dogged and deviously manifested hostility evoked reprisals in kind from his doughty opponent. For ten long years Brofferio and Cavour fought one another in parliament and in the press. The struggle went on without interruption and with increasing bitterness until the count's death. There can be little doubt that Brofferio was Cavour's "vero castigo di Dio." Guerrazzi was likewise a persistent and vigorous foe; but he, unlike Brofferio, enjoyed the admiration and respect of his distinguished adversary. The crescendo of the Cavour-Guerrazzi feud was reached in May, 1860, when the two men clashed in parliament over the question of ratifying the treaty with France.

Ever since 1915, when Italy entered the war, there had been an upsurge of interest in the perennial Roman question. The already formidable literature on the subject had undergone tremendous accretions, and to many it seemed that a new phase of the thorny issue was in the offing. Ruffini, whose interest in the problem was of long standing, had followed closely its most recent vicissitudes. In an effort to elucidate some of these he wrote a series of articles which appeared in 1921 and once again in successive issues of the *Nuova antologia*.[33] These essays, which attracted considerable attention and lent further impetus to the already spirited nation-wide discussion of certain issues connected with the Italo-papal feud, are of capital importance for the student of the Roman question. They contain much valuable information, abound in trenchant analyses, and skilfully take the reader through the intricacies of their complex theme.

Shortly after the completion of these articles, Ruffini turned his attention to Alessandro Manzoni. Many things about the great Lombard writer had for long interested him—above all, the religious values from which much of his inspiration was derived. It was this intriguing aspect of the man that Ruffini now resolved to explore. The projected study was conceived on a vast scale. It was to deal with every phase of Manzoni's religious life. The ensuing investigations quickly converged on the writer's addiction to Jansenist ideas. His relations with Jansenism, to be sure, had attracted the attention of scholars long before Ruffini turned to them, but so far no exhaustive elucidation of the subject had appeared. Pushing far beyond the limits reached even by his most enterprising predecessors, Ruffini came to the conclusion that Manzoni had found in Jansenism the deep spiritual satisfaction that he craved and which he had vainly sought elsewhere. The first important fruit of his researches was an article calling attention to the period of Manzoni's life which centered around the year 1817.[34] This period, according to Ruffini, witnessed a serious spiritual crisis, in the course of which Manzoni turned resolutely to Grégoire, the head of French Jansenism, and manifested a sharp aversion for Lamennais, who at the time was still one of ultramontanism's most applauded spokesmen. To a further elaboration and documentation of Manzonian Jansenism, Ruffini devoted several years of patient and minute research. In the course of his investigations he came upon unpublished sources which proved of crucial importance. Heralded by the publication of two suggestive articles,[35] the two-volume *La vita religiosa di Alessandro Manzoni*[36] finally made its appearance. It is a highly absorbing and trenchant study. Ruffini manages to penetrate into the innermost intimacy of Manzoni's religious convictions. He exhibits, in all their fulness, his powers of analysis, his resourcefulness in piecing together scattered bits of evidence, his insight and subtlety in assaying the nuances of feeling and belief. The usefulness of the work is appreciably enhanced by several learned digressions, such as those, for example, on the history of the Jansenist movement, Pascal, and the religious life of France during the Restoration.

A few years before the completion of *La vita religiosa di Alessandro Manzoni* Ruffini began work on a comparable study of Cavour's religious ideas and experiences. Here he was on familiar terrain and finally at grips with a subject which he had long before tentatively outlined but thereafter repeatedly put aside as other preoccupations bobbed up to monopolize his attention. Unfortunately, the task, so tardily undertaken, was never finished. Death intervened in the midst of his labors,[37] and only a few precious fragments of what was to have been a large and comprehensive work have been published.

There were impressive elements of similarity in the religious experiences of Manzoni and Cavour which could hardly have failed to make this newest project all the more meaningful and inviting. Both men went through an acute religious crisis in their youth, and both of them very early in their lives were exposed to Jansenist ideas. In Manzoni these ideas took root, but not in Cavour. The Jansenist element in the latter's background became the first preoccupation of Ruffini. *I giansenisti piemontesi e la conversione della madre di Cavour*[38] constitutes a fundamental and, in many respects, original contribution. Piedmontese Jansenism was merely a reflection of its French parent, and as Ruffini points out, was kept alive by a small coterie which included Tardy, an ecclesiastic who was an intimate friend of the Cavour family. Tardy turned out to be for Cavour's mother what Degola, the well-known Jansenist leader, was for the wife of Manzoni. As a matter of fact, Tardy followed Degola's catechistic methods in bringing the good lady, who was a rigid Calvinist, into the Catholic fold. The conversion took place at Santena on October 21, 1811. Until his death in 1821 Tardy remained the spiritual adviser of the Cavour household, and it was he who served as the first confessor of young Camillo.

Of much greater moment in the evolution of Cavour's religious attitudes was the acute *crise de conscience* which began when he was little more than eighteen and which carried him from the orthodox and traditional Catholicism of his paternal ancestors to a militant rationalism and anticlericalism. First set forth briefly in an article dealing with Cavour's intellectual development,[39] it forms the subject of the trenchant second chapter of the posthumously published *Ultimi studi sul conte di Cavour*.[40] The significance, in this connection, of his sojourn in Geneva, where, for the first time, he breathed the pure air of reason, and of his careful perusal of the writings of Constant, Guizot, and Jouffroy is brilliantly elucidated and convincingly documented. A fitting introduction to this essay is provided in the first chapter, which is entitled "La devozione infantile del conte di Cavour." Based in part on unpublished documents from the archives at Santena, it underlines some of little Camillo's salient traits. That the youngster, when barely out of the infantile stage, showed an interest in religious ceremonies is noteworthy; but even more so is the fact that a bit later, when he was in his early teens, he evidenced a certain amount of independence and an "incipient rationalism."[41] The remaining chapters of the volume are reprints of earlier articles.

The youthful Cavour for a time came under the sway of Socinian ideas. This fact, coupled with the long-standing desire to return to a subject originally encountered when he was working on his history of religious liberty, led Ruffini during the closing years of his life to direct some of his inexhaustible energies into still another channel of investigation. These researches embraced the history of Socinianism from its origins to the time when Cavour came into contact with it in Geneva. Death interrupted this project, too, but the results achieved were nevertheless imposing. They were incorporated in a series of erudite essays on the Italian Reformers and the checkered fortunes of the Socinian movement. Among the more important contributions are *Francesco Stancaro: contributo alla storia della riforma in Italia*[42] and *Metodisti e sociniani nella Ginevra della restaurazione*.[43] Also deserving of honorable mention are some of the articles published between 1928 and 1933.[44] One of the noteworthy by-products of Ruffini's preoccupation with the religious problems and experiences of certain sixteenth-century Italians is the essay on the ecclesiastical policy of Emmanuel Philibert.[45]

More than those of any other historian, Ruffini's researches have given impetus in his own country to studies on the Italian Reformers and on the influence of specific Socinian and Jansenist doctrines.[46] From the very beginning of his academic career he deplored the dearth of scholarly interest in religious history. As his own work in this field progressed, he helped increasingly to focus attention on the contributions of Italians to the ferment of ideas which accompanied the great religious upheaval of the sixteenth century. As we have seen, Manzoni's relations with Jansenism had attracted the attention of scholars long before the appearance of Ruffini's study on the subject. But its publication caused this interest to bound forward powerfully. The conclusions advanced in *La vita religiosa di Alessandro Manzoni* evoked in academic circles a lively and sustained controversy which provided still another fillip to the progress of Manzonian studies.

The majority of Ruffini's historical writings bear the stamp of painstaking and exhaustive research. The documentation is uniformly careful and copious. There is a pronounced reliance on primary sources, both printed and manuscript. The latter variety made possible, as we have seen, the studies on Cavour and Manzoni, but a host of other writings are based entirely on published material. Not inconsiderable is Ruffini's indebtedness to the works of other scholars, and he is candid in acknowledging it. He tells us, in the preface to *La libertà religiosa*, that to do justice to a subject of this kind, a large modern library was essential. But Turin, where the study was completed, did not possess one. And so, because he was unable to procure some of the primary material he needed, he had to rely on references to it in the writings of other historians.[47] In the introduction to *La giovinezza del conte di Cavour* he pays his respects to the documentary publications of such predecessors as Chiala and Berti.[48] The opening pages of *La vita religiosa di Alessandro Manzoni* contain an appreciative allusion to the contributions of a small but indefatigable group of Manzonian scholars who for some time had been investigating the emotional and religious experiences of the great Lombard.[49]

Ruffini maintains throughout a high standard of factual accuracy, thanks to his rigorously orthodox methods of establishing or verifying a given point. He was adept at handling critically historical evidence. His works bear witness to his skill in analyzing, collating, and appraising documentary material. They show, too, his deftness in establishing the settings in which individually important documents appear in their truest and fullest light. This penchant for panoramic backgrounds is one of the salient traits of the man as a historian. He knew how to extract the maximum from the data at his command. When the evidence was fragmentary he did not seek to bridge the hiatus by making rash deductions. When it was conflicting his acumen and analytical powers were generally equal to the situation. He was a resourceful investigator. He worked with tremendous enthusiasm, and when he was thrilled by a discovery he hid the fact from no one. He was patient and assiduously persistent even in the face of recurring and sometimes painful distractions. His early Cavourian researches were carried on at a time when his wife's illness was a source of constant preoccupation. The last and very productive decade of his life was spent among men who had turned their backs on his lifelong ideals. The studies on Manzoni, the religion of Cavour, and Socinianism had to compete for his attention with a political situation which finally brought dismissal from his professorial post.

Although Ruffini had little difficulty in mastering and in organizing effectively the material he worked with, he was wont to minimize his own role in accounting for the finished product. Thus he relates that he intended originally to make the history of religious liberty the subject of a lecture. When the manuscript began to grow, he decided to make a sizable pamphlet out of it. But the pamphlet soon got out of hand and gave every indication of swelling into a robust tome. In the end, it appeared as a volume of 542 pages. And so, Ruffini concludes retrospectively, the book emerged almost against his will; the process was like the downward course of a snowball that ended as an avalanche.[50] He fails to add, however, that he did an excellent job of controlling and directing this avalanche, thanks to a skilful combination of the chronological and topical approaches.

No less candid is his version of how he wrote *La giovinezza del conte di Cavour*. "The material dominated me, not I the material," he avers. "I proceeded like someone who discovers a vein of precious metal and who follows it in all its twists and turns, without giving thought to where it would end."[51] This statement must not be taken too seriously, for it springs from the author's excessive modesty. Actually, although important documents are reproduced in their entirety and the main thread of the story is thus continually encountered in the words of the protagonists themselves, the contents of these documents are carefully fitted into an elaborate pattern, the informing principle of which is the steady intellectual and emotional growth of Cavour. In each of the *saggi storici* announced in the subtitle, the data bearing on one particular period of Cavour's early life is skilfully integrated about a person, idea, or event that influenced the young man, with the result that each of these periods is invested with a distinctive character. An equally effective manipulation of material is evident in the essays that make up *Camillo di Cavour e Mélanie Waldor*, although here the principal problem confronting the author was that of making the most of rather exiguous data. The way in which this problem is handled affords the reader a typical illustration of Ruffini's technical competence.

His skill in organizing a vast amount of material is perhaps nowhere better demonstrated than in *La vita religiosa di Alessandro Manzoni*, although here, too, he is quite self-effacing in explaining how the work was written. The whole thing, he declares, sprang "automatically" from a theological dispute between the great writer and Alexis Billiet, a learned ecclesiastic who later became the Archbishop of Chambéry and a cardinal. The subject thus presented itself to him *sub specie controversiae;* and so this initial dispute had to remain the foundation of the study. The entire treatment does revolve, as a matter of fact, about it. Occupying the pivotal position is an unpublished letter in which allusion is made to the Manzoni-Billiet discussion: a letter of September 23, 1819, from Manzoni's mother to his spiritual adviser, Monsignor Luigi Tosi. The crucial passage of this document provides a principal clue to Manzoni's views on the basic question of grace. With this passage serving as the point of departure, the analysis is developed with the aid of material drawn from other letters, the testimony of unimpeachable witnesses, and Manzoni's writings. That a high degree of unity and thematic effectiveness is thus achieved is due to the author's resourcefulness in making the most of this particular technique.

Ruffini's works are more than readable; they possess a genuine literary quality—thanks to a style that combines fluency, verve, and elegance. It is a sensitive style, too, and yet not lacking in vigor. The author's flair for the well-turned phrase is evident, as is also his penchant for interpretation. His writings abound in considered observations of a general nature about specific periods, developments, and persons. That most of these generalizations will stand the test of time and new evidence is more than likely. The character and amount of the data and the acumen in analysis upon which they rest vouch, as much as anything can, for their soundness. The polemical note is not lacking, for much of Ruffini's work is definitely *à thèse*. In *La libertà religiosa* he was anxious to prove that modern toleration derived its "first and most fecund source" from the Socinian movement. A good part of his work on Cavour pulsates with the desire to explode certain traditional but grievously mistaken conceptions of the man which sprang from one-sided preoccupation with the period of his greatness and facile acceptance of judgments pronounced by certain of his contemporaries. *La vita religiosa di Alessandro Manzoni* was written to prove that the theological and moral doctrines of the French Jansenists and of their followers in Italy constitute the basis of the great Lombard's religious outlook and that he retained faith in those doctrines until the end of his life. Everything that could be adduced in favor of the central thesis is brought into the picture. And that this was by no means an easy task will be appreciated by those who know how energetically and stubbornly Manzoni at all times sought to keep secret his most intimate religious beliefs.

Ruffini tried always to combine comprehensiveness of treatment with depth of investigation, and he generally succeeded. But he found it necessary to sacrifice the former for the sake of the latter in one conspicuous instance: his history of religious liberty. Confronted with the task of covering a tremendous period and many countries, he saw fit to exclude several significant topics. These lacunae did not fail to evoke a certain amount of adverse criticism.

Religious values and problems in their manifold manifestations always intrigued Ruffini. The canonist constantly impinged upon the historian, and in this fact lies one of the keys to an understanding of what he was attempting. Indeed, we are told, on excellent authority, that *la religiosità*, "studied in its external and internal life, in its juridical and historical forms, analyzed in great individual consciences, constituted the keenest spiritual interest of his scientific activity."[52] This religiosity, according to Ruffini, was essentially liberty and conscience. As such, compulsion of any kind was repugnant to it. Moreover, it was the duty of the state, in dealing with ecclesiastical matters, to safeguard the manifestations of this religiosity within the limits imposed by its sovereign interests. This conception of religiosity and of ecclesiastical policy, affirmed by Ruffini from the first days of his career, affected profoundly the direction of his historical investigations.[53]

Ruffini reacted rather sharply against the excessive provincialism of Italian historiography. But his own cosmopolitanism of outlook never became a fetish and was not allowed to warp his perspective. Nevertheless, both *La giovinezza del conte di Cavour* and *La vita religiosa di Alessandro Manzoni* have been criticized in some quarters because, so it is alleged, too much attention is paid in them to non-Italian influences and not enough to what was transpiring in the peninsula. These critics freely admit the charge of provincialism, but they contend that Ruffini goes to the opposite extreme of "Europeanism."[54] To which there is only one rejoinder: Ruffini's "Europeanism," far from vitiating the soundness of his judgment, helped him to do justice to Cavour and Manzoni, who were so much under the influence of extra-Italian ideas.

To his researches Ruffini brought an unfailing sympathy for the men and women whose experiences he recounts. More than that, he tended to become identified with the protagonists of his principal works, Cavour and Manzoni, and particularly with the kind of political and religious liberalism which they personify—this, despite his rejection of Cavourian separatism[55] and his failure to concur in Manzoni's religious opinions.[56] Indeed, as one who knew him intimately puts it, "there was in the impassioned and persistent historical investigations of Ruffini a personal and almost autobiographical note, which consisted in affirming, through the minds of the two supreme exponents of the ideals which animated our Risorgimento, his own political and religious conscience."[57] His liberalism tinges, in varying degree, the products of his labors. To this his history of religious liberty, his analysis of Cavour's ideas, and his discussion of Manzoni's heterodox proclivities bear ample witness.

Though the bent of his mind was decidedly philosophical, Ruffini made no attempt to reduce historical phenomena and processes to a few laws or universally applicable principles. He did not seek to unearth the eternal or underlying truths of history. His treatment of the subjects that monopolized his attention reflects no particular view as to the dynamics of all major historical trends. And it would be rash, indeed, to make his unwavering interest in religiosity the springboard for deductions along this line. He did have, however, very positive ideas about the functions and duties of history and the historian. He believed that historical research should not be content merely to enrich our knowledge of the past. It should seek, he felt, not only to inform but to educate. Its supreme purpose should be to aid in developing the public mind.[58]

The direction of Ruffini's investigations led him to take a particular interest in the educative value of biography. The lives and careers of great men, he averred, are replete with inspirational value; and the more one knew about them, the more could one love and be inspired by them. Indeed, one had to know their frailties as well as their strength, What he has to say, in this connection, about his work on Cavour, is enlightening. When dealing with historical figures like the great Piedmontese, the biographer, Ruffini contends, must record every detail, however minute or unflattering. Nothing which pertains to such men can be considered "too petty or insignificant or superfluous; because genius . . . . has the faculty of transmuting into historical gold everything . . . . it has touched."[59] On another occasion, he remarks:

There are some who took offense when I sought to clarify those . . . . profound and decisive factors in the psychology of the count which were his youthful amours and errors; and they reproached me for having crossed the threshold of that intimate sacrarium to whose inviolability he and . . . . the women who loved him had a right. . . . . I must say, once and for all, that I have an absolutely different conception of the rights of history. I believe that only someone who has lived and died in obscurity can claim eternal obscurity. But with respect to those who still dominate, from beyond the grave, our present thought and life by virtue of the omnipotence of their genius, the least we can demand is to know what they were like.[60]

It might be said, he continues, that

to attempt to bring these great makers of our history as close as possible to our common human denominator is almost to lessen . . . . the educative efficacy of their example. As if . . . . one could really love that artificial semidivinity which a very recent patriotic mythology would like to attribute to great historical figures and not, on the contrary, their eternal and common humanity.

And, Ruffini concludes, there is no better way to illustrate this "eternal and common humanity" of great men than to show "whom, how, and with what success they loved, and by whom, how, and with what success they were loved."[61] All of which did not prevent one obtuse reviewer of Ruffini's *Camillo di Cavour e Mélanie Waldor* from remarking: "Our modest opinion is this: when dealing with Cavour, it is well to study that which honors him and conceal his weaknesses."[62]

Ruffini's contributions to historical scholarship are many and highly significant. His *Lineamenti storici delle relazioni fra lo stato e la chiesa in Italia* has remained a fundamental work. *La libertà religiosa* placed him in the front rank of Italy's historians and won him considerable recognition in other countries as well. Despite some serious omissions, it is, in the words of J. B. Bury, an "illuminating contribution to the history of liberty."[63] It provides perhaps the fullest elucidation we possess of the significance of Socinus in the annals of toleration. Ruffini has given us a new and revealing picture of the youthful Cavour. His contributions in this field are of paramount importance. They have made indubitably clear the enormous significance of Cavour's early life for an understanding of the celebrated contriver of Italian unity. Ruffini himself remarks:

By studying well the youth of Count Cavour, one manages to comprehend thoroughly his later heroic work. Indeed, this is perhaps the only way to do so. Because to him is applicable, and to no one more so, the beautiful dictum of Alfred de Vigny: Qu'est ce qu'une grande vie? Une pensée de la jeunesse réalisée par l'âge mûr."[64]

Ruffini does not overstate the case, for the mentality and attitudes of the man who so suddenly skyrocketed to fame after 1848 were the result not of overnight improvisation but of many years of preparation and ripening—years when he was, to use his own melancholy words, "un obscur citoyen piémontais." Only in the light of this fact does the effulgent figure of the statesman become truly intelligible. Ruffini has effectively disposed of the charge, first made by Brofferio[65] and repeated by others since, that Cavour had no knowledge of literature and philosophy; and he has also made it clear that those who saw and admired in the great Piedmontese only the gifted politician or the resourceful diplomatist were seeing and admiring only one aspect of the man.[66] Indeed, he has relegated to a well-deserved limbo the long prevalent but grossly mistaken conception of Cavour as a man whose interests were exclusively political, economic, and diplomatic in character.[67] In its place he has given us a Cavour who from his earliest years manifested a keen and sustained interest in matters of the spirit and the intellect. Ruffini has done more than anyone else to explore and clarify the part played by Jansenism in the spiritual life of Manzoni. He has enriched our understanding of the significance of Jansenist ideas in the intellectual and religious history of Italy during the early decades of the nineteenth century. He has made fundamental contributions to our knowledge of the Italian Reformers and of the vicissitudes of the Socinian movement. It is therefore not surprising that at the time of his death he was universally recognized as a foremost Cavourian scholar, an outstanding authority on Manzoni, and an unsurpassed student of religious history. In a brief but pithy summary of his contributions to historical scholarship a number of his fellow-workers in this field called him "a historian of the highest importance."[68] Posterity is not likely to alter this judgment.

NOTES

1. Benedetto Croce, "Francesco Ruffini," *Critica*, XXXII (1934), 230.

2. Gioele Solari, "La vita e l'opera scientifica di Francesco Ruffini (1863–1934)," *Rivista internazionale di filosofia del diritto*, XV (1935), 191.

3. *Ibid.*, p. 192.

4. *Ibid.*, pp. 192–93, 194, 195; Mario Falco, "Francesco Ruffini," *Rivista di diritto civile*, XXVI (1934), 390.

5. Solari, *loc. cit.*, pp. 195–96.

6. Mario Falco, "Francesco Ruffini," *Rivista di diritto privato*, IV (1934), 206.

7. *L'insegnamento di Cavour* (Milan, 1916).

8. *L'insegnamento di Mazzini* (Milan, 1917).

9. *Vittorio Emanuele II* (Milan, 1918).

10. *Cesare Battisti* (Milan, 1918).

11. Solari, *loc. cit.*, p. 197; Mario Falco, "Francesco Ruffini," *Rivista di diritto civile*, XXVI (1934), 391.

12. Solari, *loc. cit.*, p. 198.

13. *Il presidente Wilson* (Milan, 1919).

14. *Sionismo e società delle nazioni* (Bologna, 1919).

15. *Guerra e riforme costituzionali* (Turin, 1920).

16. Solari, *loc. cit.*, pp. 198, 199.

17. As a member of this committee, Ruffini had prepared a report on the protection of scientific works which was destined to serve as the point of departure for all subsequent legislation on this matter.

18. Cf. the estimate of Ruffini as a jurist in Falco, "Francesco Ruffini," *Rivista di diritto privato*, IV (1934), 202–3; Arturo Carlo Jemolo, "Francesco Ruffini," *Archivio giuridico*, CXII (1934), 111–12.

19. Scaduto was the author of *Diritto ecclesiastico vigente in Italia* (2 vols.; Turin, 1892–94).

20. *Trattato del diritto ecclesiastico cattolico ed evangelico del Friedberg* (Turin, 1893).

21. On the importance of this translation see Solari, *loc. cit.*, p. 194.

22. Turin, 1924.

23. Turin, 1891.

24. Turin, 1901.

25. It is one of the essays in *Festschrift Emil Friedberg zum siebzigsten Geburtstage* (Leipzig, 1908).

26. This article is entitled "Il cattolicismo liberale (1844)."

27. Turin, 1912.

28. I, 18. This and subsequent references are to the second (1937–38) edition of this work.

29. *Ibid.*, I, 48.

30. Turin, 1914.

31. P. 152.

32. "L'antipatia del Brofferio e del Guerrazzi per il conte di Cavour," CCXCII (1920), 193–208; "Il Brofferio ed il Guerrazzi all'opposizione contro il conte di Cavour," *ibid.*, pp. 302–20; "La rottura del Brofferio e del Guerrazzi con il conte di Cavour," CCXCIII (1920), 19–33.

33. "Il potere temporale negli scopi di guerra degli ex-imperi centrali," CCXCV (1921), 289–301; "Progetti e propositi germanici per risolvere la questione romana," CCXCVI (1921), 24–40; "Sovranità temporale, congressi della pace e società delle nazioni," *ibid.*, pp. 118–130; "La questione romana e l'ora presente," *ibid.*, pp. 193–206.

34. "Il 'masso' del natale manzoniano e il giansenismo," *Rivista d'Italia*, XXVIII (1925), 143–62.

35. "Manzoni e Lamennais," *Cultura*, IX (1930), 255–67; "Il 'miracolo' nella fede, nella vita e nell'arte di Alessandro Manzoni," *ibid.*, pp. 665–78.

36. Bari, 1931.

37. Jemolo, *loc. cit.*, p. 110.

38. Turin, 1929. This study is one of a series published under the auspices of the Academy of Sciences of Turin.

39. "La cultura filosofica del conte di Cavour," *Cultura*, X (1931), 214–29.

40. Bari, 1936.

41. P. 11.

42. Rome, 1935. This monograph was originally published in Buonaiuti's *Ricerche religiose* in 1932–33.

43. Florence, 1936. The publication of this essay two years after Ruffini's death was supervised by Adolfo Omodeo, the noted Italian historian who also edited the *Ultimi studi sul conte di Cavour.*

44. E.g., "Il giureconsulto chierese Matteo Gribaldi Mofa e Calvino," *Rivista di storia del diritto italiano*, I (1928), 207–69, 417–32; "Matteo Gribaldi Mofa, Antonio Govea e lo studio generale di Mondovì," *Studi pubblicati dall regia università di Torino nel IV centenario della nascita di Emanuele Filiberto* (Turin, 1928), pp. 279–96; "La 'cabale italique' nella Ginevra del seicento," *Cultura*, X (1931), 786–808; "La Polonia del Cinquecento e le origini del socinianismo," *ibid.*, XI (1932), 248–59; "Voltaire e Rousseau contro i sociniani di Ginevra," *ibid.*, XII (1933), 83–116; "Carlo Alberto e il socinianismo ginevrino," *Atti dell'accademia delle scienze di Torino*, LXVIII (1933), 407–66.

45. "La politica ecclesiastica di Emanuele Filiberto," *Emanuele Filiberto*, ed., Costanzo Rinaudo (Turin, 1928), pp. 395–426.

46. Croce, *loc. cit.*, p. 229.

47. Pp. viii–ix.

48. I, 37–39.

49. I, xii.

50. *La libertà religiosa*, p. viii.

51. I, 21.

52. Solari, *loc. cit.*, p. 206.

53. *Ibid.*, p. 207.

54. See in this connection the review of *La vita religiosa di Alessandro Manzoni* by W. Maturi in the *Nuova rivista storica*, XV (1931), 328–29.

55. For a discussion of Ruffini's views on separatism see S. William Halperin, *The separation of church and state in Italian thought from Cavour to Mussolini* (Chicago, 1937), pp. 67–68.

56. *La vita religiosa di Alessandro Manzoni*, I, xv.

57. Solari, *loc. cit.*, p. 221.

58. *Ibid.*, p. 207.

59. *La giovinezza del conte di Cavour*, I, 43.

60. *Camillo di Cavour e Mélanie Waldor*, pp. 168–69.

61. *Ibid.*, pp. 170, 171.

62. *Risorgimento italiano*, VII (1914), 474.

63. See Bury's preface to the English edition (London, 1912) of *La libertà religiosa*.

64. *La giovinezza del conte di Cavour*, I, 12.

65. *Storia del parlamento subalpino* (Milan, 1866), I, 146.

66. See in this connection Ruffini's remarks in *Camillo di Cavour e Mélanie Waldor*, pp. 21–22.

67. See the illuminating observations on this point in *Ultimi studi sul conte di Cavour*, pp. 22–23.

68. See the appreciation of Ruffini by the editors of the *Nuova rivista storica*, XVIII (1934), 270.

XIX

GUSTAV VON SCHMOLLER (1838–1917)

PAULINE RELYEA ANDERSON*

GUSTAV VON SCHMOLLER did not write history merely for the satisfaction of re-creating the past. As a historian, he has made notable contributions in a field which he wished to make the basis for a realistic approach to the study of economics and politics. The founder of the younger historical school of economics, Schmoller used history as his method, not his goal. Since Schmoller early repudiated the classical economic theory of Adam Smith and Ricardo and despised the "abstract" rationalism of the Austrian school, as well as the neo-Hegelianism of Rodbertus and Marx, he turned to a method which would place man and values as the focus of economic study. Schmoller did not give up the aim of the economist of the nineteenth century—that of arriving, like the natural scientist, at laws of economic activity; he merely wished history to enlarge the field of observation from which theoretical economic assumptions could be tested and, as he argued, more validly stated than with a minimum of observation and a maximum of logic. It is clear that history written under the auspices of economics had many of its problems and materials set. Possibly without consciously weighing the need for and value of intensive study of internal history, Schmoller turned from the first to social, economic, administrative, and institutional life, making here the innovations which his predecessors in historical research had made in the study of foreign policy and political institutions.

Another powerful factor was at work in dictating Schmoller's

* Mrs. Eugene N. Anderson, Washington, D.C.

415

emphasis upon history and in determining the nature and materials of his research—his burning interest in politics. This interest led him to demand of himself and of his profession co-operation in a program of social reform.[1] Only a thorough history of each question, he thought, could lay the foundation for practicable suggestions of reform, could teach the country to understand its social problems, and could indicate the goals which should be pursued. No one may doubt that the importance in the Bismarckian Reich of the tariff question occasioned Schmoller's essay on mercantilism (1883) and, later, his extensive treatment of tariff history in the publications of the Verein für Sozialpolitik and in his *Grundriss der Volkswirtschaftslehre*. Similarly, the problems connected with *Gewerbeordnung* led to his investigation of the guild system, as did inner colonization to the essay "Die preussische Einwanderung und ländliche Kolonisation des 17. und 18. Jahrhunderts."[2] This interest of Schmoller in that which should be (*Seinsollen*) unifies his work and hence any essay about him. It led him to reject rationalism and idealism for realism and historism; to accept as subjects for research those set by the problems of his own age; and, finally, to organize his own and the knowledge of his contemporaries for use as a guide to the state in its measures of reform.

Schmoller was not alone in his interest in history, for the rush of new life lent to the age a desire to understand the course of its own development. It was the same with economics: new interest in material things aroused new interest in economic processes. Nor was Schmoller alone in his turn from intellectualism, idealism, and romanticism toward naturalism and realism. Every state in the western world was struggling to decide between individualism and state-ism, democracy and autocracy; and reliance on state power increased as imperialism increased. The century, like Schmoller, worked many virgin fields of knowledge and, like him, sought to bring the fruits together in a new synthesis. Life in Germany exercised, in addition, its specific influence upon thought: here idealism was stronger than elsewhere, democracy weaker, techniques of historical research at a high level, and historical feeling rapidly developing. These vital influences molded Schmoller, who, in turn, left his mark upon his time.[3]

The southern German family and environment of Gustav Schmoller contributed to his interests.[4] Schmoller was born in Heilbronn in 1838. On the father's side his family had served the state of Württemberg since the seventeenth century; and the father (1791–1865), too, after being severely wounded in the Wars of Liberation, had settled in Heilbronn as a bureaucrat. The son mentions nothing else striking of his father except that he fascinated his children with stories of his youth in the campaigns against Napoleon. The mother's family, although originally in business, consisted of professional men, and the maternal grandfather and great-grandfather of Schmoller were famous botanists. Schmoller said of his grandfather's influence upon him, "In his greenhouses, among his collections, and in his library I first learned what science was";[5] and he spent many pleasant summer hours in the Gärtner household in Calw. Since Schmoller learned little at the *Gymnasium* in Heilbronn, where, he says, he had only one good teacher and where he conceived a lifelong distrust of philologists, his active mind remained all the more open to the stirring historical events of which his father told, to natural history, and to the scientific method which he was learning in Calw.

After 1847, the date of the marriage of Schmoller's sister Marie with Gustav Rümelin, Schmoller grew up in close contact with the man whom he admired above all others.[6] From this man, who rose from a secondary-school teacher to be minister of education of Württemberg in the fifties and later professor at Tübingen, who sat in the parliament of Frankfurt in 1848, and who was one of thirty chosen to offer the crown to Frederick William IV, Schmoller took his taste for politics, economics, psychology, statistics, and pedagogy. Through Rümelin he acquired, as early as 1848, his devotion to the Prussian state; he learned to prefer the *kleindeutsch* solution of the German problem; and with Rümelin he awaited the developments of 1870–71 as the beginning of a new era for Württemberg and Germany. When, in later years,

Schmoller strengthened his admiration of Prussia, of the Hohen-zollerns, and of Germany by a thorough knowledge of their history, he brought to fruition the impetus which Rümelin had given him.

Before entering upon his university career Schmoller joined his father's staff for a year and a half, every morning receiving instruction from his father in administrative law and in finance, before entering upon office work. "I learned to know my country and its people and carried on business with peasants and renters of the royal lands, with handicraftsmen and taxpayers. Before I even went to the university I understood the entire mechanism of administration, both in its executive and legal phases. I already had a clear idea of the relationship between all economic development and administration," said Schmoller later.[7] This experience matured Schmoller's judgment and taught him to raise pertinent questions touching economic and administrative problems. It taught him what to admire and what to disparage in estimating the effectiveness of a bureaucracy. It undoubtedly gave him a permanent bias in favor of bureaucratic supremacy, with the result that history never showed him a better regime than that controlled by a well-trained bureaucracy. It likewise prescribed his university course; but it showed him, as well, that if he were to find solutions for the new problems of the social and economic life of a great state in the making, he could not be satisfied with a relearning of old formulas.

At Tübingen, Schmoller did not have much economics, and the greatest single influence among his professors remained the liberal Max Duncker, under whom he studied history and through whom he came in contact with the work of Ranke, Droysen, Nitzsch, and Gneist. These men deepened his love of history; but on his own initiative he must also have been studying the work of Roscher and Knies, who had employed history to develop an empirical method of study for economics. By 1860, in a prize essay-dissertation, "Darstellung der in Deutschland zur Zeit der Reformation herrschenden nationalökonomischen Ansichten," Schmoller indicated why he needed history and the historical point of view for his work:

> The subject of national economy is the life of man and the way in which this acts in the ever widening circle of the individual, the family, the community, the nation, finally of all humanity in its thousand fold relations and connections; it is not the whole life, it is only one aspect of it—the relation of man to production, possession, and consumption of worldly goods; but in this sphere it is the whole of man with his freedom and his necessity which acts and which, with his activities, forms the subject of science. If man were compelled only by necessity, we could rightfully call our science a mathematical one, and we should only need to seek for the natural laws involved; then we should have an eternally valid theory. But since this is not so, we must place economics among the social sciences, which cannot be separated from space, time, and nationality, and whose foundations we must seek, not alone, but primarily in history.[8]

In this essay Schmoller made a beginning of freeing economics from the dogma of the English and French philosophy of utilitarianism.[9] At twenty-two Schmoller saw what he wished to do and —in the large, at least—how he wished to do it.

Schmoller early made himself acquainted with the main currents of modern thought. It has been said that in the controversy over method with Carl Menger, the Austrian economist, he failed to triumph because he was inferior to Menger in ability to think logically;[10] and his proficiency in abstract thinking has been questioned. Yet Schmoller had read widely in philosophy and had thought through several systems, weighing their value to him as an economist and social reformer.[11] As the essays collected in the *Literaturgeschichte* show, he had read Fichte, Kant, and Hegel with care, had sought to understand each in relation to his period, and had appraised the applicability of the philosophy of each to the late nineteenth century. He rejected Kantian ethics as wrongly based in pure reason, maintaining that what ought to be (*Seinsollen*) could grow only out of what had been. Since man, he thought, could reflect upon his past, he had developed a conscience, which in turn set up standards and so influenced the course of history; but at all times such standards were in relation to the culture which produced them. Thus Schmoller threw aside

the categorical imperative and rationalism for a realistic, histori-
cal-cultural understanding of ethical values.

Fichte had a deeper appeal for Schmoller as a philosopher
who argued concretely, could see economic facts clearly, wished
knowledge to be placed in the service of the age, and thought in
terms of general welfare. He criticized severely Fichte's socialism,
which, he thought, like the socialism of his own day, set up a
machine in place of the historical, living organism; but he found
it superior to English and French socialism because it was closer
to German character and culture. In short, he praised in Fichte
the practical elements which constituted his divergence from pure
idealism, while disagreeing with Fichte's separation of *Recht* and
Sitte. For Schmoller the culture determined formal right and
spiritual-moral values, and law based upon pure reason could
never succeed.

All life, even economic [he wrote], permeated by moral considerations, will
grow more and more from the relationships, connections, and opposing ten-
sions, organs, and institutions of free cultural life and will make, especially in
economic life, more difficult and less seldom any divergence from that which
is truly right and good.[12]

Hegel likewise found little favor with Schmoller, for his theory
of history was to Schmoller a construct based on a priori reasoning. More exact than earlier theory, Schmoller thought it still
not exact enough. Thus Schmoller, who had already repudiated
the English classical economic theory, turned against German
idealism as a fruitless method for approaching contemporary
problems, both because it was unhistorical and because, as
Schmoller wrote in an essay on Schiller, "the materialistic, egoistic ethics [*Sittenlehre*] of the French and the subjectivity and
sensualism of the English became translated in German idealistic
philosophy into the cult of individualism."[13]

Schmoller did not lack acquaintance with positivism and naturalism. It is often said that he owed most to Spencer and Comte,
and he knew John Stuart Mill and Wundt, who is frequently
called the "German Spencer." From Comte, Spencer, Mill, and
Wundt, Schmoller gained the ability to use the empirical method,

to think in terms of society, to analyze causality from many aspects, to compare cultures, to consider psychology and its influence upon cultural development, to make use of anthropology, prehistory and ethnography; and he strengthened his interest in naturalism and natural laws as applied to human culture. Schmoller's *Grundriss* is written entirely in Spencer's spirit, although not every section is worked out in an identical way.[14] In this connection it should not be forgotten that positivism, with its aim of raising social disciplines to a science by means of "laws," appealed to Schmoller's love of science. Lastly, it may be pointed out that emphasis upon change belongs to a period of swift cultural transition, such as that in which Schmoller, as well as Comte, Spencer, and Mill, lived. Schmoller did not imitate them; at some points his experience touched theirs, as did that of Lorenz von Stein, Schäffle, Wagner, and others, for all of whom economic life had become something in flux, no longer explicable by reference to timeless laws.

Schmoller is commonly connected even more closely with Roscher, Knies, and Hildebrand, his predecessors in the use of the historical method in economics. Informed analyses seem thoroughly to justify not pressing these connections too far,[15] for Schmoller knew the philosophical and methodological shortcomings of these men as well as their contributions. The nineteenth century saw the development of separate disciplines and of experimental methodology; and Schmoller had a long line of useful predecessors and contemporaries—among them Hanssen and Hildebrand, who first began detailed investigations of individual institutions or periods; J. G. Hoffmann and Ernst Engel, who used statistics extensively; List, who used the comparative method of study and who first countered "international" with "national" economy; Knies, who introduced ethics into economics; and Mommsen, Niebuhr, Ranke, Savigny, and Dahlmann, whose historical work and method were necessary preliminaries. Schmoller made use of all, but he sought a synthesis different from any and laid out a way of his own. In his review of Roscher's *Geschichte der Nationalökonomik*, in 1875, Schmoller pointed

out that the work was a transitional one between the school of
Adam Smith and Schmoller's young historical group. His own
plans went far ahead of this work.

After the success of his first essay Schmoller published further,
in 1862, "Systematische Darstellung des Ergebnisses der zu Zoll-
vereinszwecken im Jahre 1861 in Württemberg stattgehabten Ge-
werbeaufnahme," and in the same year an anonymous work, *Der
französische Handelsvertrag und seine Gegner: ein Wort der Verständi-
gung von einem Süddeutschen.* Although the free-trade liberalism of
the latter work made it impossible for Schmoller to hope for a
career in protectionist Württemberg, both indicated his interest
in, and knowledge of, contemporary conditions. In 1863 appeared "Die Lehre vom Einkommen in ihrem Zusammenhang
mit den Grundprinzipien der Steuerlehre," wherein Schmoller
tried to deal anew with the relationship between state and individual.[16]

His early publications helped to secure for Schmoller a post as
professor extraordinarius of political science in Halle (1864). Here
Schmoller spent the sixties, at last in close contact with the Prussian state and in a liberal group. He went frequently to Berlin,
where he came in touch with Treitschke, Erdmannsdörffer,
Droysen, Hermann Grimm, Dilthey, and others. During this
period he developed in at least four important directions: he did
his first extensive work in Prussian administrative, social, and
economic history; he began to deal with the question of the worker and to consider the matter of socialism; he published the first
of his historical-economic monographs, *Zur Geschichte der deutschen
Kleingewerbe im 19. Jahrhundert;* and he was maturing the views
which led to the plan for the Verein für Sozialpolitik, founded in
the autumn of 1872 to further co-operative research into contemporary economic and social problems.[17] The constitutional struggle of Bismarck in the sixties showed Schmoller the importance
of administrative forces, thus strengthening his interest in the history of the Prussian bureaucracy and sending him to the archives
for new materials. At the same time, he realized that the extent
of new social and economic problems in the Second Reich would

call for vast knowledge, and he determined to place academic resources at the service of the government and the public.

In the early seventies Schmoller left Halle for the new German University of Strassburg. The years of his stay at Strassburg (1872–82) were among the most fruitful for Schmoller in purely historical research and writing. To this period belong the foundation of the Verein, the assumption of the editorship of the *Jahrbuch für Gesetzgebung, Verwaltungs- und Gewerberecht*, which has always been known as *Schmollers Jahrbuch*, the investigations into the history of Strassburg, and the famous controversy with Treitschke, in which conservatism and social liberalism stated their irreconcilable cases. The Verein für Sozialpolitik had its best days in the seventies, when Bismarck and even industrialists like Baron von Stumm looked favorably upon the "socialists of the chair" and heed was paid to the meetings and publications of the Verein.

In embarking on researches in the history of Strassburg, Schmoller performed an important service to historical effort. He opened local archives and placed his seminarists at work in them. He secured the co-operation of local officials and, in time, grants of city money for the work of publication of documents. He demonstrated how such detailed local history could be used as a test case for the study of wider economic changes. This latter aspect appears in the most important work, *Das strassburger Tücher- und Weberzunft: Urkunden und Darstellungen nebst Regesten und Glossar: ein Beitrag zur Geschichte der deutschen Weberei und des deutschen Gewerberechts vom 13. bis 17. Jahrhundert*,[18] in which Schmoller discussed almost all the problems of the economic-political town life of the middle ages on the basis of this concrete study. Delving into local history was in line with Schmoller's desire to understand the problems of his milieu by thorough acquaintance with their historical background. But the Strassburg researches served another end as well: they brought about gradually a change of emphasis in Schmoller's historical interest. He turned from Prussian history under Frederick William I to the general history of Prussian economic development. This purpose appears in the introduction to his essay, "Die russische Compagnie in Berlin," written at the end of 1882.[19] The change is significant for Schmoller's entire future work.

Since Schmoller had shifted his historical emphasis, his call in 1882 to succeed Adolf Held, secretary of the Verein, at the University of Berlin did not lead to the resumption, on the former scale, of the historical work begun at Halle and partly interrupted by the stay at Strassburg. In other ways as well, the Berlin post marked the beginning of a new life for Schmoller. Through Althoff, Prussian minister of education, Schmoller frequently gave advice in educational and cultural matters. In 1884, he became a member of the Prussian council of state; in 1887, of the Preussische Akademie der Wissenschaften; and subsequently, of a variety of German and foreign academies. He was made official historian of Brandenburg (1887) and associate editor of the reorganized *Forschungen zur brandenburgischen und preussischen Geschichte*, whose inspiration he soon became. In 1887 the Akademie der Wissenschaften accepted his memorandum for the publication of the *Acta Borussica, Denkmäler der preussischen Staatsverwaltung im 18. Jahrhundert*, and in the next year work on these volumes began under Schmoller's direction. In 1899 Schmoller became a member of the upper house of the Prussian legislature (*Herrenhaus*) for the University of Berlin, and he held appointments to several commissions of investigation. Since he was already assisting with the publication of the monographs put out by the Verein, was writing for and editing *Schmollers Jahrbuch*, was connected with *Die staats- und sozialwissenschaftlichen Forschungen*, and was contributing articles and reviews to former publishers, Schmoller led an exhausting life. His daily contact with privy councilors and statesmen enhanced his tendency to aloofness from all except a small circle of family and friends. The eager student and scholar had become a man of affairs.[20]

Schmoller continued in Berlin during the remainder of his life. He gave up the last of his seminars in 1912 and died in 1917. As was the case with earlier participation in administrative work, he gained in stature for his scientific work by contact with public

figures and problems.[21] Few academic men have had his opportunities for participation in public life. He saw how he could be
useful to those who sought his advice, and hence what kind of
academic knowledge was needed and at what points. This made
him valuable as a teacher of future bureaucrats. He had occasion
to observe more precisely the importance of the administrative
unit and the necessity of attempting to keep it above party and
class interest. He gained new belief in the state and in society, as
against individual interest. To this public life in Prussia is due
some part of the wisdom and courage of the *Grundriss*, the general
work in economics upon which Schmoller spent his scientific effort during most of the Berlin years. To do this task he left his
Prussian history a torso, but he completed the expression of an
even deeper interest. He wrote in the preface to Volume II:

However incomplete my *Grundriss* may remain, however little it may satisfy
the theoretical economist or the individual historian, the effort at a general
synthesis is not superfluous and not unfruitful. It had to be undertaken by an
economic historian, one who has always considered it a false charge aganst himself that he was striving for description, not for a general understanding of the
laws of economic life. Only with such a representation created from the whole
can one serve the greater purpose of all scientific understanding. I do not pride
myself too much on my work when I say that I have written it in the service of
the leading economic ideas and trends of our time and of the ideals which rule
my life. Without coming too close to other fields, I believe I may say that it is
clear that a *Grundriss* of economic theory has been written by a scholar who is as
much an historian of constitutional, administrative, and economic life as an
economist, who has followed the process of psychological and social development as well as economic and who, with the far greater means of present-day
economic history, has attacked the work which Roscher began fifty years ago.[22]

Fundamental to an understanding of Gustav Schmoller is a
knowledge of the philosophy of history and of the political and
social values that he held. Although he had rejected German
idealism and English laissez-faireism in favor of an empirical
method of system-building, he had formulated, early in his
career, his own views of history and of contemporary problems.

Schmoller's theory of change and progressive development had
its roots in his own life and in the age in which he lived. All about
Schmoller events had happened and were happening so quickly,

and the change effected was so fundmental, that there could be no question of static systems, whether political, social, or economic. One of the basic appreciations of the historian—the feeling for process—was present in Schmoller from the start of his career. His first problem was to show the forces at work in conditioning the cultural process; and when once he had concluded that these were both spiritual and material, he sought to explain their connection. This led him to the natural-science concept of the integral causal relationship of all happening. It was the age, too, which showed him the complexity of causality. But the course of development proved more interesting to Schmoller than the why. Rejecting pure Darwinism, he held to the primacy of moral forces ("sittliche Kräfte"). Although he saw the struggle for existence and in the *Grundriss* dealt with the fall of empires, culture continued, he thought, to advance to new high points; struggle was natural and healthful, for weaker peoples fell and new forces took up the advance. Further, he assumed a general line of advance for all humanity, with moral forces slowly effecting a rise of economic, social, and political levels. That different peoples had had differing lengths of cultural existence he took as proof of the fact that they were not merely fulfilling a process of nature. "The time of flower of every people and state," he wrote in the *Grundriss*, "is at once one of great internal spiritual-moral, technical, and organizational progress and then one of power-superiority or power-improvement in relation to foreign countries, whereby directly and indirectly wealth is increased." He recognized that the rhythm of economic life differed from the rhythms of other institutions, but he could not explain this.[23] Nor did he try to give an exhaustive picture of the connections between various forms of spiritual life and their relationship to institutions. He frankly left to the future the working-out of these things. In the meantime, in spite of the "cutthroat spirit of gain, social indifference, and the burdening of our social and political life with all manner of trials," he wrote in concluding the *Grundriss:*

The time will come when all good and normally developed men will know how to reconcile a decent desire for gain and the search for individuality, self-assertion, egoism, with a sense of complete justice and of community of feeling. Let us hope that the way will not be so long as was that which led from the brutality of men of force to the culture of the men of today.[24]

Schmoller's belief that cultural change was leading to new and better cultural levels rested on his idea of justice (*Gerechtigkeit*).[25] The ideal of justice is native to man, Schmoller thought, and determines his action. It is the means by which he approaches the ideal, although he never reaches this goal. The setting-up of the ideal is complicated, and, again, it is dependent on the stage of the cultural development; yet it has never failed to break through the darkest ages and to resume the forming of the ideal "good." Thus the "ideal" became for Schmoller a part of history. Especially important to social and economic progress is what he called "verteilende Gerechtigkeit." This form of justice demands that men be given rights and goods in proportion to their ability and activity on behalf of the whole of society. Men are not equal, according to Schmoller, and do not, as of right, merit an equal share in society's goods and privileges. Society divides men into groups, classes, and ranks according to their activities and accords each group what seems just; the *Volksgefühl* has always granted more to those whose abilities and achievements have been beyond the average. Class struggles, with their bases in economic equality, have always resulted from this division of goods as new groups demanded recognition of their importance. Difficult as it is, however, to solve the problem of their demands, justice will give to each his due and will, even more importantly, give to the whole that which is due it—in time. Meanwhile, struggle must continue, but it will become milder as justice advances over the earth. "As no penal code and no judge is absolutely just," wrote Schmoller, "so no existing division of income and property is entirely just. But every succeeding epoch of human history has won a greater degree of justice in this field as well."[26]

Because Schmoller believed so thoroughly in the future, he could make plans for reform. Only in the measure that serious men gave their effort to further the "spiritual forces" could these be strengthened among the masses and progress furthered.

Throughout his essay on justice, as well as in all his political writings, it is the commonweal which Schmoller considers. He is prepared to devote his own energies to this common good. Unlike some of his contemporaries, Schmoller does not see history working itself out as a natural process; man can assist in the progress of culture by raising the level and broadening the base of spiritual understanding. On this ground rested all Schmoller's work in the Verein and in his own and other journals, designed, as they were, to inform the citizen about his problems and to point the way to just solutions.

The specific content of Schmoller's justice and the nature of the injustices which he judged as problems are not far to seek. The highest cultural institution for Schmoller was the state, and its preservation was the prime necessity. The achievements of Prussia and Germany under Bismarck had given him great respect for political power, while the economic development of the Second Reich had seemed to prove that a strong state could guarantee progress in this field as well. The state easily appeared superior to the individual and as easily became for Schmoller the vehicle for reform. As he turned to the history of the modern state and found in Prussia of the seventeenth and eighteenth centuries a model, he grew more and more to believe in the value of a strong monarchy and a well-trained bureaucracy. He saw them as standing above party and class politics in the interest of the whole, reconciling opposing social forces, regulating economic conditions, and carrying out considered reforms. In his writings on Prussia he was able to show just how the eighteenth-century state had done these things, step by step gaining control over the towns, building the standing army, regulating the cloth manufacture and trade, developing a tax system. Although Schmoller realized the violence of the class struggle of his own day, saw the clash of interests in politics, and counted on the rise of a strong capitalistic group, he thought the state could cope with all these and restore harmony. He knew from history that the state of the past had often abused its power, and he realized the need for interstateism. Yet he believed that *Sitte* would restrain *Macht-*

politik and was even already bringing about internationalism at some points, notably in commerce. He supported all the new techniques for state power—protectionism, a navy, colonies, and foreign trade—as dictated by *raison d'état;* and he had no fear, apparently, that they would get out of hand. Even the outbreak of war in 1914 did not shake his faith that the state would survive and possibly begin a better life than before.[27]

It was Schmoller's belief in the supremacy of political power which dictated the nature of his periodization of history. Each period—that of the family group, of the village, mark, town, territorial state, modern state—appeared to him as differentiated from the preceding and subsequent periods by the nature of the political organization which obtained.

Closely connected with his devotion to the state, especially to the characteristics of the old Prussian regime, was the love which Schmoller bore to the German people. Both led him to an almost exclusive interest in internal history, as did likewise his sensitiveness to the need for reform. To preserve the security of his people and to promote their good through the time-proved medium of the state constituted his goal, and hence set the materials with which he must work. It is interesting to note that even his essays on Bismarck dealt only with Bismarck's social and economic position and importance.[28] Schmoller's appreciation of the German people and their history contributed, no doubt, to an understanding of historical individuality. Although he was less precise in detail than the best of historians should be, this lack was due to his eagerness to generalize; he grasped the individuality of an institution or of an age as few before him. The love of German character also contributed to the bitterness with which Schmoller denounced socialism. He became convinced that there must be a German solution for the social ills of his country which would leave intact the German institutions he admired. The internationalism of the Marxists was anathema to him, just as Manchesterism was; neither seemed "just" in accordance with German ethics.

It is clear that, in spite of his views in 1848 and 1870, Schmoller had very little of the liberal in him. He cannot be labeled, because he avoided dogma in favor of the view which seemed to him historically sound. Hence, in approaching his social ideas, he may seem, at first and in comparison with Treitschke in his attack on Schmoller,[29] extremely progressive; but actually the pattern of his entire social philosophy was a variegated one. The key to this pattern lies in the following words:

Our social ideal must not consist in democratic form but in the economic and moral uplift of our lower classes. To this end a certain measure of democracy is necessary; but it is not the main thing, if Germany is to remain at her peak. More important is it—or we should better say, so it seems to us—that monarchy and bureaucracy retain the leadership as the strong backbone of the state to lead us to victory in foreign affairs, to restore at home peace between capital and labor, organized industry and organized unions, and to maintain what has been restored. One-sided political control by organized labor would be a still greater misfortune than that of the cartels. But both would mean class victory with class hegemony.[30]

As Schmoller was not an individualist, so he was not a democrat. He did not deny the historical value of democracy and still found it desirable for certain peoples or places, but in Germany it was not the solution dictated by tradition. Rather, the Prussian state and the Prussian kings had always been friends and allies of the lower classes and could not desert them; but, at the same time, this monarchy had known how, through the army and bureaucracy, to win over the aristocracy which it had once had to conquer.[31] It would be a mistake to do away with this carefully evolved machinery by means of which alone class struggle could be reduced or abolished and the welfare of all made more secure. Schmoller did not see man in the mass as having ever decided epoch-making events, and eventually he opposed universal suffrage. He regarded parliamentary government as a form of class rule, with now one class, now another, in control of the majority. It was in line with his entire philosophy that he should oppose Marxian socialism, but it was as much so that he should wish the state to take every practicable step to make more just the income of the proletariat and to raise the moral level. His goal was always the greater national unity, endangered, he knew, by socialism but capable of preservation through blood, language, common values, and institutions—bonds which he thought made in the end for stronger nationalism than technical ones. Schmoller's realistic historism made him face the fact of class struggle, just as his reading of history led him to believe in the possibility of spiritual growth. This very emphasis upon the ethical force in culture was the foundation stone of Schmoller's social-reform program. Both the men who made the program, as well as those for whom it was to be made, should have moral stature.

Schmoller avoided working out a theory of social justice to oppose to liberalism or socialism. He did not know how, in detail, he would carry out all that he proposed; but he thought it best to attack the nearest problem and proceed from there, keeping always in the foreground the need for practicable measures suited to the day and age. Schmoller was a social activist, and in the seventies at the time of the *Sendschreiben an Treitschke* the list of needs was large and Schmoller's lust for battle great. In later life there are signs that Schmoller felt the strong state created by Bismarck to be the best "carrier and executor of the social progress of mankind."[32] Schmoller may never have realized the ascendancy of the Bismarckian social policy; but it is certain that the Verein after the seventies lost in influence and that Schmoller's social-ethical goal was never reached.

In considering Schmoller's method of historical research and the application of this method to political economy, special attention will be given to the essay on mercantilism and its historical importance, one of Schmoller's best and most famous studies in the history of Prussia in the eighteenth century, and to his use of this and similar material in the treatment of tariff policy in the *Grundriss*. Here Schmoller is using the historical approach to illuminate a matter of importance to the Second Reich.

In his essay on mercantilism Schmoller set out with the assumption that a phenomenon like mercantilism could only be grasped in its historical setting. It was his point of view that if a free-trader examined mercantilism in the light of his own theory of trade he would necessarily find disadvantages predominating, while a protectionist would find only advantages, and neither would be able to contribute to an understanding of the institution in its functional relationship to the culture of which it formed a part. Schmoller, therefore, made it his task to provide this understanding, first, by examining the economic character of the seventeenth and eighteenth centuries when mercantilism obtained. In accordance with his theory of the primacy of political power, he asserted that "in all phases of economic development a leading and controlling role in the economic field falls to one or the other political organ of the group,"[33] and he expounded a theory of stages of culture based on stages of political development. For each stage Schmoller correlated the economic life of the group with the political life.[34] He drew upon published material for the prehistorical, ancient, and medieval stages (developed more in the *Grundriss* than in the essay on mercantilism); but, as he approached the period which he was emphasizing, he used primary sources. The group was handled as a whole, for Schmoller saw society operating as such, and the beginnings in one stage of phenomena characteristic of a subsequent stage were brought out to indicate the way of growth of an institution. Each successive stage stood forth as a cultural advance, and Schmoller assumed that spiritual forces had exercised a greater force in each notable forward step; but he did not make precise this point. He did not show what part *Sitte* played and what part economic necessity played in the effort, for example, to suppress the egoism of town organization for wider economic co-operation. Schmoller likewise correlated technical progress with the political and economic changes, pointing out, for the first time known to the writer, the part taken by geographical and technical discovery in forcing the building of the modern national state. As is to be expected, the modern state examined is Prussia; and her mercantilism, as developed by the margraves of Brandenburg and the kings of Prussia in the seventeenth and eighteenth centuries was that described. The analysis of the building of a powerful political unit by means of an economic system, mercantilism, and of the perfecting of this economic system by the political power has been done with magnificent strokes. The picture of Prussia was set off against other states, illustrating Schmoller's use of the comparative method which is frequently found in his Prussian studies. Generalizations were made on the merits and demerits of the system, and the points at which it broke down were indicated, for Schmoller did not deny that mercantilism, at least in its exaggerated form in international commerce, proved a deterrent to world-progress. This admission opened the way for Schmoller to show at a future date the historical place of liberalistic free trade, as he demonstrated the place of mercantilism in the eighteenth century.

In this analysis there was no new and clearer definition of mercantilism. The value of the essay lay in the method, whereby mercantilism was regarded as *Staatsbildung*, and, therefore, as taking its place in promoting culture. The liberating and creative forces in mercantilism were revealed in contradiction to the view that mercantilism was restrictive. The greatest lack in Schmoller's analysis was adequate consideration of the social classes and groups which profited by the system. Had he applied his criterion of justice, he might have made more complete the understanding of the nature of mercantilism and the need for change. This fault is one which too great emphasis on the state may easily produce. Yet the essay advanced the understanding of an important institution to a point which modern research has scarcely passed.[35]

Mercantilism is treated many times in several aspects in the *Grundriss*, but especially in the section dealing with the history of tariff policy. In this section tariff policy was traced back to the practice of prehistoric, ancient, and medieval times, with extensive reference to the mercantilistic town economy of the Hansa cities, to the territorial principalities of 1500–1700, and to the mercantilistic states of the seventeenth and eighteenth centuries. Considerable attention was paid to England's mercantilistic practices and their result in creating English imperial power. Against this picture Schmoller set that of Germany and Prussia, ending with Prussia's turn to power politics and economics. "Without the policy, the wars and mercantilism, Prussia would never have secured in Germany," Schmoller concluded this section, "a firm hold against East, South, West, and North. In the eighteenth or nineteenth century our fatherland would have been divided, like Poland, by the other great powers."[36] A treatment of free trade follows. As has been suggested, Schmoller has not failed to give this movement its historical setting, and he has recognized that it was made necessary by the abuses of mercantilistic practice; but he did not accept free trade, because he saw it as weakening the state. Hence he readily found sympathy for protectionism, the spread of which in less industrially developed states he considered healthy. He accepted the new *Machtpolitik*, however, and could not escape the implications of this for tariff policy, a dilemma which he does not squarely face; but he does understand—and this is one of the products of both his method and his wisdom—that other forces than the purely economic ones were and are at work in molding tariff policy.

Schmoller then drew his conclusions for present-day policy. His historical summary of tariff policy led him to the teaching that free trade and protection were not matters of principle.[37] They were only interchangeable means for promoting the welfare of the state. The tariff policy of a country should be based on a careful survey of domestic resources and an understanding of foreign competition. Everything, he argued, depended on a well-regulated system, and the means for achieving such a system were improving and would improve. He believed that the common interest was drawing special interests more and more under control, so that "the means of tariff policy are improving, being refined, humanized." Individual states, he warned, must strive toward internationalism; and he hoped that a public better informed by him would have a care for this, as well as for a tariff policy more clearly based on the economic welfare of the whole nation. Even so, he expected a long period of international struggle before the state system should have reached a level upon which peace would be possible. Man must endeavor to bring moderation and intelligence into play and so shorten the period of struggle.

Is the historical method as Schmoller handles it successful in laying the foundation for a theory of tariff policy? No one will deny that Schmoller has used sufficient historical material and has managed this material well. In so long a survey he has not been able to use primary sources extensively, but his bibliography was very large. He has not had time to sharpen his analysis in the essay on mercantilism, nor even to go so far in discussing the relation of the political power to economic systems other than the mercantilistic. But he has suggested the complicated nature of the fixing of tariffs. He has been able neither to let the material speak for itself nor to lead the reader logically into a statement of theory of tariff policy. At every turn Schmoller's philosophy, values, and assumptions are evident, while he ends largely with advice and expressions of faith. He does not ignore any clearly undesirable aspects of an institution—as judged by his own standards; but he believes that human understanding, *Sitte*, and *Recht* are improving and will correct these aspects. He has not advanced a new policy—for example, a new departure in tariff systems—but merely a more wisely administered combination of old systems. He has placed great confidence in improved techniques without indicating how these are to have their effect in counteracting established forces. Might they not be so revolutionary as to compel a complete change of political system, as he suggested was the case in the eighteenth and nineteenth centuries? Or might not the administrative personnel deteriorate rather than improve? What if the national state, whose interest is the determining factor for Schmoller, is as an institution itself destroyed? The whole theory would fall, and there would be no tariff policy, either as given by Schmoller or to be arrived at anew on the basis of his material. What if the modern state, by its very nature and contrary to Schmoller's faith, should remain torn by groups of interests and unable to devote itself to the common welfare? All these and many more questions arise. It cannot be said that the method is at fault, for another might have used the method otherwise. But it must be said that Schmoller has not succeeded in arriving at economic theory on the basis of historical material. He has succeeded in arriving at good advice, even practicable advice; but it is advice closely linked with the time in which it is given and specifically for Germany, as Schmoller intended it.[38] His historical analysis is still superior to his economic synthesis.

It is not fitting in this essay to sum up Schmoller's work as an economist and economic theorist. Students continued to carry on the historical method of economic study, but even in his lifetime many turned from Schmoller or went beyond him. The *Weltwirtschaftliches Archiv* was established (1913) as one means of promoting a counterinfluence to the historical approach to economics, and a former student of Schmoller has confirmed to the writer the opinion of the *Archiv*'s editor that the historical school did more to delay the development of sound economic theory in Germany than any other one force. Schmoller died in 1917 before he could witness the collapse of the political system on which he had staked his reform program. After his death little was said in praise of him until the late thirties, when the occasion of the centenary of his birth aroused new interest in his work.[39] The best of these studies, however, serve chiefly to indicate the tremendous methodological and philosophical problems with which Schmoller wrestled rather than the finality with which he settled them: "Schmoller is a milestone and not the goal." In giving up the theory of the ideal type of the older economic school Schmoller gave up the clarity and precision of that theory without being able to set up against it a sharply etched "anschauliche" theory. A great wealth of material was presented, but the material served only to illustrate the older theory, for there was no new point of departure, no new line of thought in Schmoller's work on economic theory.[40]

Too severe a criticism of Schmoller as a theorist will cause one to overlook much which makes him valuable to the historian. In his effort to present reality in its complexity he took a necessary step toward greater objectivity. The effort to check accepted theory or belief against experience and to explain it thus constituted another needed step, and one which Schmoller carried further than Roscher or Knies. His effort to delineate the complexity of reality by making use of the findings and methods of other disciplines places him among the first of modern social scientists. His success in grasping the historical individuality of an institution or an age can only be the envy of the historian of any century. His understanding of the relation between the state and economic and social life had never before been equaled. Nor did appreciation of the total culture, as one sees it in the *Grundriss*, ever before find such brilliant expression. Only by spending some time with Schmoller's work can one fully realize how much he possessed and made use of the historical point of view.

It is this historical point of view which is best understood by the "historical method of economics." Schmoller was not a trained historian, although he understood the mechanics of historical research sufficiently. Even if he had been so trained, it is clear that he could not have used historical techniques alone to write the *Grundriss*.[41] What is more nearly his case is that (1) Schmoller proposed for himself and for his students and successors a long line of historical monographs on economic institutions which would furnish economists with more material than they could observe for themselves; (2) he then made—and hoped others would—use of such material, that is, of facts, to illustrate and criticize existing institutions and theories, but in addition to this illustrative material he employed as tools what he had learned from his study of history—a sense of becoming, of change, a feeling for individuality, and the understanding of group activity, by which in the *Grundriss* he interpreted his facts and gave new emphases. Instead of the cross-sectional analysis of an institution, Schmoller preferred the long-time or vertical view, because his was primarily a historical point of view, with feeling for process uppermost, rather than a sociological one. Schmoller's "younger historical school" of economics was actually a school of realism in which the historical approach or historism was well developed. After a long period of rationalism, it placed again the emphasis upon empiricism. But Schmoller did not intend, certainly not after about 1895, to neglect synthesis. His own account of his method of teaching, whether history or economics, gives a clue to his true point of departure: (a) to make whatever he is describing live before the eyes of the students, and (b) to present the complexity of a phenomenon so that a student may appreciate as nearly as possible its true nature. This complexity might confuse some but was better than laying down a law which made things seem simple.[42]

Schmoller's contributions to Prussian history should not be omitted in a summary of his work. If colleagues and successors of his in economics have been critical, the reverse is true in the field of his historical work, where only admiration reigns.[43] This is due to the fact that, whatever his shortcomings, Schmoller innovated so much that the profession cannot but feel gratitude toward him. One needs only to recall that administrative history had hardly been touched upon before Schmoller; that in a decade of work he opened archival sources for this and produced some of the most stimulating pages ever yet written in the field—pages on army reform, on tax and tariff reforms, on absolutism in the eighteenth century. The organization of the *Acta Borussica* alone might stand as a sufficient monument to Schmoller, but in addition he was a member of the commission which published *Urkunden und Aktenstücke zur Geschichte des Grossen Kurfürst* and was responsible for an extension of this publication into internal and financial materials. The *Forschungen* and the Verein für Geschichte der Mark Brandenburg under his stimulus did their part likewise in contributing to sound internal history and documentary publication. It has been objected that Schmoller buried himself in the seventeenth and eighteenth centuries when he would not have dared explore his own age so thoroughly. Opposed to this criticism is the fact that Schmoller purposely attacked modern times instead of the ancient or medieval fields, seeking the roots of institutions of the nineteenth century and in time comparing conditions. One of the most valuable of his studies is that dealing with the towns under Frederick William I.

Both the romanticists and the liberals had waxed sentimental in their support of town liberties; but Schmoller's researches soon showed another side to the town of the middle ages and of the sixteenth and seventeenth centuries. His reconstruction of the reforms for the towns was in itself a masterly piece of historical effort, for the procedure had been different in almost each case, and Schmoller was content only when he had examined the instructions and had followed through their execution. He felt repaid, however, in that he presented a brilliant example of the growth of state power over local autonomies, showing the care and patience needed by the central power for such work. He could make his research valuable because he knew what questions he wished to answer, why he was working. If he acquired the epithet of "Borusser" because he became so strong an admirer of Prussia, it is to his credit that he saw much at fault in his own age and took upon himself the responsibility of understanding why this was so and what were the more perfect prototypes of these faulty institutions. Nor can one forget that, although Schmoller never lost interest in and contact with Prussian history, he turned more and more to the wider field of western European culture. Yet, his greatest contribution to historical studies lies in the Prussian field.[44]

What of Schmoller's success in the third of his roles, that as a statesman and reformer? Certainly, Schmoller played it with the same energy and devotion as he did those of economist and historian, paralleling his time in the classroom and seminar with hours spent on public commissions and in conference. If there were any egoistic reasons for Schmoller's interest in reform, they did not outweigh his sincere concern for the general welfare. Knowing this, one wonders why he should not have become a policy-determining figure, even outside academic halls. Why should the administrators in whom he had such confidence not have adopted his goals and used his techniques for achieving them? Why should the Verein have lost, rather than gained, steadily in prestige? The answer seems to lie in part with an interesting circumstance—interesting for historians, at least. It was Schmoller's interest in the problems of his own age and in the future of his country which governed his interest in both history and economics. But these latter interests ultimately determined the views he held toward his age, robbing him, in ways almost too subtle to analyze, of sufficient force to inspire reform. It has been mentioned that he grew to accept the Bismarckian social solution rather than his own, possibly without realizing it. Thus he, like the bourgeois citizens whom he criticized, came to feel something of the complacency of the Second Reich. His historical study confirmed his faith in existing and traditional institutions, and he did not wish any radical change. The necessary adjustments were made in part through a turn to *Machtpolitik*. Schmoller concurred in this turn, while reiterating the need for internal reform. He, who had always appreciated the value of great men in the state, seems to have made little distinction between Bismarck and his successors, trusting men like Bülow to carry out reform. He, who understood the social conflicts of his age, in the midst of his faith in man and history failed to understand the full force of the proletarian movement or the bitter meaning of the proletarization of the lower middle class. Schmoller became a shade too secure, a compromiser, not a leader of the new. His cardinal virtue, however, is that he exerted himself, that he kept abreast of contemporary problems, either examining them himself or stimulating members of the *Verein* to do so, that he knew himself a responsible member of the national and international community.

Schmoller does not create an impression of a passionate man who was moved to reform by love of humankind.[45] He seems rather to have looked always about with the practiced eye of a trained bureaucrat who takes the measure of his problem and sets confidently to work upon it. In this the difference between Schmoller and Friedrich Naumann, whose democratic teaching Schmoller scorned, is striking. History cannot choose the men who serve her, and those who write of these men must rest content if now and again they record valuable services where no sympathetic personality is to be found. Schmoller poured his sympathy, his love, his charm, his consideration for others, his religion, into his work, where all are transmuted into sincere workmanship, faith in human endeavor, patriotism, and a broad understanding of historical process. Werner Sombart said of Schmoller at his death (July 1, 1917):

This was Gustav von Schmoller's faith, this did he make living in us [his students]: the conviction that knowledge which does not fulfil these conditions, which is not fundamental, which does not have its roots in the mother-earth of philosophy and history, is only a utilitarian knowledge [*Zweckwissen*], a technical knowledge [*Fachwissen*], a technology, but has no right to the honorable name of science.[46]

NOTES

1. See Erich Rothacker, "Historismus," *Schmollers Jahrbuch für Gesetzgebung, Verwaltung und Volkswirtschaft im Deutschen Reiche*, LXII (1938), No. 4–6, 4 ff. See also Joseph Schumpeter, "Gustav von Schmoller und die Probleme von Heute," *Schmollers Jahrbuch*, L (1926), No. 3, 1–52; also Schmoller's own preface to his *Zur Sozial- und Gewerbepolitik der Gegenwart* (Leipzig, 1890).

2. In *Umrisse und Untersuchungen zur Verfassungs-, Verwaltungs- und Wirtschafts-geschichte* (Leipzig, 1898), pp. 562–627. This collection of essays gives an excellent idea of Schmoller's historical work.

3. One should read in this connection the essay of Ernst Troeltsch, "Das neun-zehnte Jahrhundert," *Aufsätze zur Geistesgeschichte und Religionssoziologie, gesammelte Schriften*, IV (Tübingen, 1925), 614 ff. Schmoller wrote of Bismarck: "In short, each person, even the greatest, has the shortcomings of his virtues, and each is a child of his age and of its ideas, a product of his course of life" (*Charakterbilder* [Munich and Leipzig, 1913], p. 45).

4. See *Reden und Ansprachen bei Gustav Schmollers 70. Geburtstag* (1908), *passim;* Carl Brinkmann, *Gustav Schmoller und die Volkswirtschaftslehre* (Stuttgart, 1937), pp. 11–16.

5. *Reden und Ansprachen*, p. 47. See Waldemar Mitscherlich, *Die Lehre von den beweglichen und starren Begriffen erläutert an der Wirtschaftswissenschaft* (Stuttgart, 1936), where the opinion is expressed that Schmoller's emphasis on process, development, and growth goes back to an early understanding of Darwinism.

6. *Charakterbilder*, pp. 141–89.

7. *Reden und Ansprachen*, p. 49.

8. Quoted by Brinkmann, pp. 20–21. The essay appeared in *Zeitschrift für die gesamte Staatswissenschaft*, XVI (1860), 461–716.

9. *Handwörterbuch der Staatswissenschaften* (4th ed.), article on Schmoller by Meitzel.

10. Werner Sombart, *Die drei Nationalökonomien* (Munich and Leipzig, 1930), p. 154. Sombart holds that Schmoller was correct in his view but that he could not adequately demonstrate it.

11. Preface of the *Grundriss der Volkswirtschaftslehre* (Leipzig, 1908), I, v–vi, where Schmoller says that he was always interested in philosophy and psychology. Volume

I of the *Grundriss* was reviewed by E. R. A. Seligman in *Political science quarterly*, XV (1900), 728–32.

12. *Literaturgeschichte der Staats- und Sozialwissenschaften* (Leipzig, 1888), p. 75. Reviewed by E. R. A. Seligman, *Political science quarterly*, IV (1889), 543–45.

13. *Ibid.*, p. 6.

14. Ernst Troeltsch, *Der Historismus und seine Probleme, gesammelte Schriften* (Tübingen, 1922), III, 420 ff.

15. Max Weber, "Roscher und Knies und die logischen Probleme der historischen Nationalökonomie," *Schmollers Jahrbuch*, XXVII (1903), 1181 ff.; XXIX (1905), 1323 ff.; XXX (1906), 81 ff.; Thorstein Veblen, "Gustav Schmoller's economics," *Quarterly journal of economics*, XVI (1901–2), 69 ff.

16. The first of the three essays appeared in *Württemberger Jahrbücher*, 1862, Heft 2; the second in brochure form, Frankfurt, 1862; the third in *Zeitschrift für die gesamte Staatswissenschaften*, Vol. XIX (1863).

17. Schmoller's part in the work of the Verein and the great scientific achievements of the organization are monuments to Schmoller and to the century. The monographs published by the Verein are too often overlooked. Cf. also Albion W. Small, *Origins of sociology* (Chicago, 1924), chaps. xv, xvi.

18. Strassburg, 1879.

19. *Umrisse und Untersuchungen*, pp. 457 ff.

20. For further details on these matters see Brinkmann, pp. 115–16.

21. Cf. *Reden und Ansprachen, passim*.

22. P. vi.

23. Cf. Paul Menzer, "Gustav von Schmollers Lehre von der Entwicklung," *Schmollers Jahrbuch*, LXII (1938), No. 4–6, 82 ff. The quotation from the *Grundriss* is given by Menzer, p. 87.

24. *Grundriss*, II, 678.

25. "Die Gerechtigkeit in der Volkswirtschaftslehre," *Zur Sozial- und Gewerbepolitik der Gegenwart* (Leipzig, 1890), pp. 204 ff. See also *Über einige Grundfragen des Rechts und der Volkswirtschaft: ein offenes Sendschreiben an Herrn Professor Dr. Heinrich von Treitschke* (Jena, 1875), *passim*.

26. *Zur Sozial- und Gewerbepolitik*, p. 246.

27. Franz Boese, "Aus Gustav von Schmollers letztem Lebensjahrzehnt," *Schmollers Jahrbuch*, LXII (1938), No. 4–6, 372.

28. "Vier Briefe über Bismarcks sozialpolitische und volkswirtschaftliche Stellung und Bedeutung," *Charakterbilder*, pp. 27–77.

29. Heinrich von Treitschke, "Der Sozialismus und seine Gönner," *Preussische Jahrbücher*, XXXIV (1874), 67 ff., 248 ff., and "Die gerechte Verteilung der Güter," *ibid.*, XXXV (1875), 409 ff.

30. Quoted by Wiese, "Aristokratie und Demokratie bei Gustav von Schmoller," *Schmollers Jahrbuch*, LXII (1938), No. 329. Schmoller's constant fear was that one class would control instead of the neutral state.

31. *Grundriss*, II, 519 ff.; "Der deutsche Beamtenstaat," *Schmollers Jahrbuch*, XVIII (1894), 712 ff.

32. *Charakterbilder*, p. 74. Cf., also, Friedrich Meinecke, "Drei Generationen deutscher Gelehrtenpolitik," *HZ*, CXXV (1921–22), 248–83.

33. *Umrisse und Untersuchungen*, p. 2.

34. Such a *Stufenlehre* was new to economics and, as can readily be appreciated, helped to relate economics to the total culture.

35. Heckscher, the contemporary student of mercantilism, works from a different point of view but hardly from a different conception of mercantilism.

36. *Grundriss*, II, 599.

37. *Ibid.*, pp. 647 ff. Cf. speech in the Verein in 1879, "Der Übergang Deutschlands zum Schutzzollsystem," *Zur Sozial- und Gewerbepolitik*, pp. 166 ff.

38. Arthur Spiethoff, "Die allgemeine Volkswirtschaftslehre als geschichtliche Theorie: die Wirtschaftsstile," *Schmollers Jahrbuch*, LVI (1932), No. 2, 51 ff.

39. Carl Brinkmann, published in 1937; and the double number of *Schmollers Jahrbuch* so often quoted above, *Gustav von Schmoller und die deutsche geschichtliche Volkswirtschaftslehre*, ed. Arthur Spiethoff (Berlin, 1938), *Schmollers Jahrbuch*, LXII 1938), No. 4–6.

40. Cf. Spiethoff, "Gustav von Schmoller und die anschauliche Theorie der Volkswirtschaftslehre," *Schmollers Jahrbuch*, LXII (1938), No. 2, 16 ff.

41. Georg Weippert, "Gustav von Schmoller im Urteil Wilhelm Diltheys und Yorck von Wartenburgs," *ibid.*, pp. 64 ff. Dilthey makes this distinction between historical research and the historical point of view, which both he and Yorck recognized as quite different things. The historical point of view is Germany's contribution to history, not antiquarianism (*ibid.*, p. 69).

42. *Grundriss*, I, vi.

43. Cf. *Reden und Ansprachen, passim*, especially the testimony of Breysig and Koser. See also, Fritz Hartung, "Gustav von Schmoller und die preussische Geschichtsschreibung," *Schmollers Jahrbuch*, LXII (1938), No. 4–6, 277 ff.

44. It is interesting to know that William II declined to make Schmoller director of the Prussian state archives because of his interest in social history. This failure to attain one of the highest honors accorded to the historian of Prussian history must have hurt Schmoller, especially in view of his devotion to the Hohenzollerns and to their history.

45. In his essay on Bismarck, Schmoller said that a man with work to do could not have a heart for everyone (*Charakterbilder*, p. 33).

46. Quoted in *Schmollers Jahrbuch*, LXII (1938), No. 2, 2.

XX

HENRI SÉE (1864–1936)

HAROLD T. PARKER*

THE movement of modern, scientific—shall we say, university?—historical scholarship began later in France than in Germany. When Ranke started his seminar in Berlin in 1833, French history was still the province of nonprofessionals like Augustin Thierry and Guizot. Only when in Germany members of the second generation of historical scholarship —pupils of Ranke, like Waitz and Giesebrecht—were doing their mature work, did instructors in France during the closing years of the 1860's begin to give courses on historical method and to write monographs after the German model. Among this group of instructors were many competent scholars and teachers—Monod, Luchaire, Lavisse, and others—but the prophet of the movement was Fustel de Coulanges. In an age when Michelet was still living to resurrect a somewhat imaginative past, and Guizot and Taine were still imposing their systematizing minds upon the facts, Fustel naturally emphasized the careful study of the documents. "The best historian is he who follows the sources most closely." Historical reality, he furthermore observed, was complex, and it was the duty of the historian to lay it bare and to explain it in all its complexity.

Among the later pupils of Fustel de Coulanges, and hence among the members of the second generation of French historical scholarship, was Henri Sée.[1] Like Fustel de Coulanges, Sée, until he left to take his first position, was a Parisian, that is, a Parisian in everything except birth. He was born in the small town of Saint-Brice, a few miles north of Paris, on September 6,

* Instructor in history, Duke University.

1864.[2] But his childhood and youth—his growing years—were spent in Paris, and he attended the Lycée Henri-Quatre and then the Sorbonne. When it came time to select the subject for advanced work he considered choosing philosophy but, after some hesitation, decided for history. (As we know little of the early career of Sée, the reader in these first paragraphs must imagine for himself the hopes and fears and intellectual life which lie behind each sentence.) In history, at the Sorbonne, his teachers were Lavisse, Luchaire, Monod, and Fustel de Coulanges. As has already been suggested, the latter left the deepest and longest impression. From Fustel, Sée apparently gained insight into method, faith in the value of history and of scholarship, and a certain vision of how history should be written. From all his teachers he learned mastery of his tools. When, at the age of twenty-three, he was ready to start on his thesis he could read Medieval Latin and Old French, decipher the script of late medieval documents, and critically analyze and weigh a text.

For his thesis Sée had selected a topic in the late medieval field: Louis XI and his relations with the towns. At that time (in the 1880's), the history of the towns and of municipal organization in France during the middle ages had been fairly thoroughly surveyed down to the fourteenth century; but the story of the decline of communal liberties during the fourteenth and fifteenth centuries had been neglected and the relations of Louis XI to the towns studied only with respect to one municipality.[3] In preparation he explored documents at the Archives Nationales and Bibliothèque Nationale, visited the departmental archives of Hérault, Gironde, and Haute-Garonne, worked in the municipal archives of Dijon, Lyon, Perpignan, Toulouse, Angoulême, Poitiers, and Orléans, and gathered and then wrote up his material. The thesis was published in 1891, defended by Sée in his examination for the doctorate in March, 1892. The documentation was thorough; the treatment of the subject complete, or nearly so. Reviewing it in the *Revue historique*, Monod wrote: "The thesis of M. Henri Sée on *Louis XI et les villes* marks an important progress in our knowledge of the reign of Louis XI. . . . . If his work

remains incomplete, uncertain, and contradictory on certain
points, it is, nevertheless, interesting, new, and written in a very
attractive manner; which is not a slight merit in such a subject."[4]
On the whole a favorable review, although, of course, no author
is ever pleased.

In 1893, at the age of twenty-nine, Sée was appointed by the
University of Rennes, in Brittany, as *chargé du cours* (in 1897
appointed professor) on modern and contemporary history. He
took up his duties in October and immediately assumed the
threefold task of teaching, research, and the direction of the research of his students. As a teacher, he gave courses first on political ideas in France in the seventeenth and eighteenth centuries
and later on the history of French commerce and industry under
the Old Regime and on the history of the agrarian regime in
modern Europe. As a supervisor of research, he "initiated" his
students, as he indicated, into "good critical method" and tried
to "direct them toward the history of Brittany, and especially
toward the economic and social history of the province, hitherto
too neglected."[5] It is true that before the arrival of young Sée
at Rennes, and before he had time to win influence, there had
appeared each year in the provincial Breton revues a number of
articles on local history. But these articles (although all dealing
with Brittany) were scattered in subject matter according to the
personal interests of amateur investigators and were often merely
of antiquarian or genealogical interest.[6] Sée had his students
work on topics like "Beggary and poor-relief in Brittany during
the eighteenth century," "The *corvée* on the highways and the department of roads and bridges in Brittany during the eighteenth
century," "The condition of the peasants in the district of
Rennes according to the parish *cahiers*"[7]—that is on topics whose
results could be woven into a general history of Brittany or would
help form the basis of a general social and economic history of
France. So successful was Sée in organizing research that in
1906, after years of teaching at Rennes, he could write: "More
and more numerous are those monographs which deal with the
institutions and the economic and social history of Brittany.

There has certainly been progress in the organization of historical research;"[8] and Camille Bloch could remark that "as professor, indeed, M. Henri Sée has created at the University of Rennes a real school of modern Breton history."[9] Furthermore, as Sée's reputation grew, the archivists and nonprofessional investigators in Brittany came to ask him for direction of their study. Aided by Sée's advice, these, too, produced articles and monographs on local history which were of value to the general historian. In this fashion, by Sée's quiet work and influence in a province, the history of France was enriched.

Sée himself, in his own investigations, was a tireless worker. During the first eight years of his stay at Rennes he pursued research along three separate lines: the political history of Britanny, with a monograph on *Les états de Bretagne au XVIe siècle;*[10] the intellectual history of the Old Regime, with three articles on the political ideas of Diderot, Fénélon, and Saint-Simon; finally, the broad subject of the rural classes and the manorial regime in medieval France, and here, as a preliminary to a larger book, he published two regional studies, *Études sur les classes serviles en Champagne du XIe au XIVe siècle,*[11] and *Études sur les classes rurales en Bretagne au moyen âge.*[12] In each of the studies of these eight years (except for the one on the servile classes of Champagne, where it was unnecessary), Sée displayed the ability and also the intelligence to utilize, to exploit, and to turn to account the documents which lay within his reach. This first period of research at Rennes was closed in 1901 by the publication of his large volume on *Les classes rurales et le régime domanial en France au moyen âge.*[13] Except by Molinier in the *Revue historique,* whose praise was reserved, the book was acclaimed by reviewers: "one of the most important that has been written on the agrarian regime of the middle ages, and one of the most conscientious"; "fills a gap . . . . in an excellent manner"; "it was a very difficult task to which M. S. set himself some years ago; he has completed it admirably."[14]

During his second decade at Rennes, Sée, observing the need of regional studies on the condition of the rural classes under the

Old Regime, devoted himself to the history of the Breton rural classes from the sixteenth century to the Revolution. So, while he continued to work on the political ideas of the Old Regime, he spent most of his own time—long hours, days, weeks, months, and years—in the archives of the departments of Brittany, poring over the manuscripts of the seigniories (manors), the ancient eighteenth-century tax rolls, the reports of the intendants, the *cahiers* of the parishes of 1789. The information thus acquired was used by Sée in a number of articles on the eighteenth-century agrarian regime in Brittany and France, in a long monograph on *Les classes rurales en Bretagne du XVᵉ siècle à la Révolution*,[15] and in the preparation (in collaboration with André Lesort, archivist of the department of Ille-et-Vilaine) of a thickly annotated edition of the *Cahiers de doléances de la sénéchaussée de Rennes pour les états-généraux de 1789*.[16] With the appearance of the monograph and of the edition of the *cahiers*, the reviewers, on the whole, were again favorable. The edition of *cahiers* was spoken of as "valuable."[17] Of the monograph, the pro-royalist A. Roussel objected that Sée had painted too dark a picture of the condition of the peasants under the Old Regime,[18] but no other reviewer expressed that opinion. By most, *Les classes rurales en Bretagne* was praised highly: "a vast tableau of social history," "a capital monograph," "not only an excellent work but a model," "this book greatly honors him who wrote it."[19]

One reviewer turned from the book to the author and gives us a glimpse of the personal qualities of Sée. Camille Bloch wrote of Sée as "a modest scholar whose writings and conversation reveal solid erudition, rare breadth of view, a noble disinterestedness in pursuing long researches . . . . a tireless worker."[20] And it does seem that throughout his life Sée was moved to continuous study by a disinterested desire to advance knowledge of the past and was supported by an underlying faith in the value of history and of scholarship. In his personal relations he was always courteous and kind. One who knew him long wrote: "An unbearable feeling to him was, I would not say to have wronged anyone, for such a thing can scarcely be imagined, but to have been, even in the smallest of things, a cause of inconvenience or annoyance."[21]

During the war of 1914—those days of grimness—Sée, except for a few book reviews, published nothing. Shortly after the war a severe illness left him not strong enough to continue teaching, and in 1920 he resigned as professor at the University of Rennes, accepting the title of "professeur honoraire." At the age of fifty-six, and with a fragile body, it might well seem that he had reached the end of his career. Nevertheless, the succeeding sixteen years, until his death in 1936, proved in scholarly publication to be the most productive of his life. During the 1890's he had published eight articles and two books; during the 1900's, ten articles and three books; and during the 1910's, six articles and the edition of the *cahiers*. During the 1920's he published one hundred and thirty-six articles and fourteen books; during the 1930's (to 1936), thirty-two articles, three books, and an annotated translation of the travels of Arthur Young. The articles after 1920 were, it is true, usually shorter than those which had appeared before then, and the books were also briefer and of a general, more synthetic character.[22] To them, however, must be added his "Bibliographical bulletin of economic and social history," which from 1925 to 1935 appeared in the *Revue historique* and in which each year he classified and carefully summarized from forty-five to sixty-seven books and from seventy-eight to ninety-one articles—not to speak of individual book reviews, perhaps ten to twenty annually. All this work was accomplished by living somewhat apart in his residence, Bois-Rondel, and by watching his health day after day, with his wife aiding him in protecting his time and in creating a serene atmosphere conducive to scholarly work.

In this maze of publication Sée again worked steadily along three main lines: the intellectual history of the Old Regime, with three books on French political ideas in the seventeenth and eighteenth centuries; the agrarian history of Europe, with the publication of an *Esquisse d'une histoire du régime agraire en Europe aux XVIIIe et XIXe siècles*[23] and of occasional articles on the history of agriculture in France, as from time to time he discovered new material; and finally, more especially during this period, the history of French commerce and industry in the seventeenth and eighteenth centuries, on which he published numerous books and articles. His work on economic and social history culminated in the preparation of a general economic history of France from the fall of Rome to the war of 1914. As Sée could not find a French publisher, this was published in German, under the title *Französische Wirtschaftsgeschichte*.[24] Volume I appeared in 1930; Volume II, in 1936. In addition, in the 1920's he also became interested in the method and philosophy of history. There followed on the subject many articles and four books: *Matérialisme historique et interprétation économique de l'histoire*,[25] *Science et philosophie de l'histoire*,[26] *Évolution et révolution*,[27] and *Science et philosophie d'après la doctrine de M. Émile Meyerson*.[28] Finally, he published several articles on issues of current importance: the League of Nations, capitalism in the United States, Bernard Shaw and capitalism. With the appearance of these various books in the last fifteen years of his life Sée's reputation spread beyond the boundaries of France. In Germany, Belgium, Holland, England, and the United States, among professional modern European historians he became a well-known and a respected writer.

When viewing Sée's life as a whole, it is seen that he followed the career of a typical scholar. He attended a *lycée*, pursued advanced studies at a university, obtained a Doctor's degree, entered instruction, taught, pursued research, directed the research of others, and, after long years of teaching, retired—in Sée's case, somewhat earlier than is usual. In the changing character of his scholarly investigation he also passed through those stages which many a scholar has experienced. Starting out in one field, in this case the middle ages, he moved in his research to the field in which he was teaching—modern European history. Starting out with using the documents that could be found in the central archives, he turned to the local documents which lay within his reach and to subjects concerning the region in which he resided. Starting out with an almost exclusive devotion to specialized investigation, to the ignoring in publication (although not in teaching or in conversation) of general syntheses, philosophical questions, and current world-happenings, Sée in later life turned to the publication of general surveys of broad subjects—the syntheses of his own previous investigations, of years of meditation, and of wide reading of the monographs of others. Matured, furthermore, by observation of past and present experience and by reflection, he came to feel he had something of value to say on the state of the nation and the world; and, made more sure by age, he expressed his views in several articles. Finally, in his later years he turned to philosophize about the nature of history.

In one respect, perhaps, his life differed from that of many scholars: his career had been singularly complete. Not only had he engaged in every type of scholarly activity—the preparation and publication of editions of documents, of specialized monographs, general syntheses, and philosophical disquisitions— but he had also been able to round out nearly every task. During the 1890's he was working largely on the history of the rural classes and the manorial regime in the middle ages. That work was completed in 1901 with the publication of *Les classes rurales et le régime domanial en France au moyen âge*. During the 1900's the long years of investigation of the agrarian history of Brittany in early modern times had been brought to a successful conclusion, with the publication in 1906 of *Les classes rurales en Bretagne* and in 1909–12 of the *cahiers*. The twenty-seven years of teaching at Rennes on the political ideas in France during the seventeenth and eighteenth centuries, on the agrarian regime in modern Europe, and on the history of French commerce and industry in the seventeenth and eighteenth centuries had been summarized in a number of books published shortly after his retirement in 1920. The articles written in his later life on the philosophy of history had been used in the composition of four long essays on philosophical subjects. An entire life devoted to the economic and social history of France had been summarized in the *Französische Wirtschaftsgeschichte*, the last volume of which reached Sée a few weeks before his death. Doubtless, at the end there were still plans to be carried out, projects to complete, a French edition of his *Französische Wirtschaftsgeschichte* to prepare, for he died while working; but, on the whole, it had been granted to him that he should finish nearly everything he had begun.

In the course of his life Sée worked in five fields: medieval history, the agrarian history of Brittany, the intellectual history of the Old Regime, the economic history of France, and the philosophy of history. And as the nature and quality of his achievement was different in each field, it is necessary to consider briefly and objectively his accomplishment in each one. But it must, in addition, be realized that as we examine his achievement we are also (except in the first paragraph on the medieval field) discussing his abilities as an editor of documents, a writer of monographs, of syntheses, and finally of philosophical disquisitions.

In the field of medieval history Sée's contribution included monographs on the condition of the rural classes in the middle ages in Champagne and Brittany, and a longer work on the manorial regime and the rural classes in all of medieval France. The latter book was based on the few regional monographs then existing and on a wide sampling of medieval charters and chartularies. It traces the various transformations of the French manorial regime from the late Roman Empire to the fourteenth century and describes in great fulness its characteristics during the period of high feudalism. The book is marked by a calm mastery of the material. Although Sée himself in the preface referred to his work as a provisional synthesis, after forty years it still remains the standard account.

Of the other fields in which Sée worked, three were new: the agrarian history of Brittany, the intellectual history of the Old Regime, and the economic history of France. From the standpoint of relative permanence, the danger of working in a new field is that one's work will be only provisional, soon superseded by later research. In Breton agrarian history, one source which Sée used in his monographs and articles was the *cahiers* of grievances which each peasant parish drew up when in 1789 it participated in the election of the estates-general. As we have seen, when Sée's work became known, the Commission de Recherche et Publication des Documents relatifs à la Vie économique de la Révolution authorized Sée and André Lesort, archivist of the department of Ille-et-Vilaine, to publish the *cahiers* of the *sénéchaussée* of Rennes, which once embraced a large section of Brittany. The resulting four-volume publication was one of the larger contributions of Sée to agrarian history and gives us the opportunity to examine his skill as an editor.

When Sée and Lesort undertook their task a number of editions of *cahiers* from other regions of France had already been published, and previous editors and the commission mentioned above had already partly worked out a method of publication. It had already been decided that the complete *cahier* should be published; that it should be published from an authentic text, either from the original *cahier* or from a copy certified by the president of the assembly which had adopted it; and that each *cahier* should be preceded by a short notice giving the location of the parish or town, its population, taxation totals, and distribution for *capitation*, *vingtièmes*, and *fouages*, brief description of chief agricultural and industrial products, and finally a summary of the minutes of the meeting, including a list of those present. In all this—publication of complete *cahier*, use of authentic text, notice preceding each *cahier*—Sée and Lesort followed previous editors.

In addition, one editor, Camille Bloch, had discovered that in the *bailliage* of Orléans *cahiers* emanating from assemblies having the same president were often similar and sometimes identical, and in publication he had grouped the *cahiers* by assemblies having the same president.[29] Furthermore, certain other editors, especially Émile Bridrey, had attempted, somewhat casually, to check by other documents the accuracy of the *cahiers*.[30] On these two points, Sée and Lesort perfected the method of their predecessors. Like Bloch, they grouped their *cahiers* by assemblies having the same president. But, where Bloch had not attempted the analysis of the interrelationships of dependence within each group, Sée and Lesort, by comparing the dates of the assemblies and the language of the cahiers, were able in a brief notice at the top of each group to point out not only which was the first *cahier* but also how the others were interrelated (or related to some general model *cahier*), and they sometimes arrived at relationships as complex as the following:

> The assemblies of all the parishes of this group consisting of the marquisate d'Épinay and of the barony of Nétumières had the same president, François-Gilles Guyot du Brossay, *procureur fiscal* of the marquisate d'Épinay and of the barony of Nétumières and of the jurisdiction of Bremanfany. The *cahier* of *Landavran* (March 29) is independent of the others; that of *Cornillé* (April 2) follows very closely that of *Saint-Jean-sur-Vilaine* (March 31) and directly inspires those of *Marpiré* and of *Champeaux*, both of April 3 and whose text is identical; that of *La Chapelle d'Erbrée* (April 5) was profoundly influenced by those of Cornillé and of Marpiré, and it is the latter which inspired the only two articles which form the *cahier* of *Erbrée* (April 4). We have joined to this group the *cahier* of *Mondevert* (April 2) *tréve* d'Erbrée, which was adopted in an assembly presided over by J.-B. Hevin . . . . ; this *cahier* has no analogy with the preceding ones.[31]

Furthermore, while Bloch was content to indicate in a remark or two where copying had occurred and where variants existed, Sée and Lesort followed the copying word for word and brought out by italics where a *cahier* followed a general model or another *cahier* of the group, and by the absence of italics where it was independent or deviated, if only for a word or phrase. Finally, whereas previously only casual, general attempts had been made to check the accuracy of the *cahiers*, Sée and Lesort sought, as far as possible, to check the accuracy and truth of each item of each of their four hundred *cahiers*. For this purpose they ransacked a wide drift of material: the papers of the Breton clergy, the seignorial manuscripts, the archives of the intendance, estates, and parlement of Brittany, documents of the central government, brochures of 1788 and 1789, and a long list of books. The information thus secured was placed in the notes. When a *cahier* mentioned the *corvée* (work on the king's highway), the task of that parish is given; the tithe, the amount and distribution for that parish; certain seignorial dues, the amount and character of dues paid in that locality, and so on.

Preceding the four volumes of *cahiers* is an introduction, in which Sée and Lesort describe their method. To be read in conjunction with the introduction is an article by Sée,[32] which, penetrating, subtle, and acute, removes any doubt that Sée could analyze documents critically.[33] Taken as a whole, the four volumes of *cahiers* probably constitute one of the finest examples of editing in the modern field; and, as one studies it, one cannot help but be profoundly moved by the spirit—the ideal of careful workmanship and the faith in the value of scholarly endeavor— which the work embodies.

In the field of Breton agrarian history Sée's chief monograph— indeed, the chief monograph of his life—was *Les classes rurales en Bretagne du XVIᵉ siècle à la Révolution.* The book is a long one— five hundred and nineteen large pages—and depicts in detail the organization of property in Brittany, the characteristics of the seignorial regime (a chapter apiece—twelve in all—to each of the twelve obligations of the peasant to the seignior), the different types of farm lease, the burden of royal fiscality, the backward farming methods and attempts to improve them, and finally the material and moral condition of the peasantry. Sée paints a rather dark picture of the seignorial regime, and in the conclusion he rises to a quiet eloquence:

> It can be understood, therefore, why the discontent of the Breton peasants had been so keen when the Revolution opened, why their irritation had manifested itself with such sharpness in their parish *cahiers.* . . . . They had suffered too much from the exploitation which, for so many centuries, had weighed upon them, to follow blindly the masters whose yoke they had just recently detested.[34]

The book is obviously the product of daily and prolonged contact with the manuscript sources. The description is always clear and full. Nevertheless, it has been objected that the documentation is insufficient and that Sée has painted a darker picture of the condition of the rural classes than the facts would warrant.[35] As this is Sée's chief monograph, it might be well to examine the charge and to scrutinize his methods of handling evidence.

Two defects may be noted at once. The controversial section of the book on the seignorial regime is based largely on the archives of various seigniories in Brittany. For the entire province Sée examined and used the archives of fifty-five seigniories, two baronies, one castellany, eight abbeys, and five commanderies.[36] Necessarily, this is a sampling of the material, for, as Sée himself notes, there was an "immense number" of seigniories in Brittany. But unnecessarily, of the seventy-one sets of documents examined, fifty-two, or nearly three-fourths (73 per cent), come from a single department of Brittany, the department of Ille-et-Vilaine; the other fourth, from the other four departments.[37] Furthermore, in the book itself, of the illustrative examples used in the description of the seignorial regime in Brittany, 88 per cent are taken from the seigniories and abbeys of this department of Ille-et-Vilaine.[38] This concentration of evidence and of example from a single section of Brittany assumes that the seignorial regime of that section was typical—like that of the other sections.[39] The assumption may be correct. It has, of course, been checked by the examination of nineteen sets of documents from the other departments and in the chapter on the abuses of the regime by a use of the *cahiers* from these departments. But the failure to check it by, or to base the book on, an even wider sampling constitutes a weakness.

Strangely enough, furthermore, for a historian who was so thorough, Sée in the book itself does not cite all the evidence on which each general conclusion is based. His practice is to make a general statement concerning the regime, the sentence usually containing the word "often" or "frequently," and then to add in illustration an example, or two or three examples, of particular seigniories. "*Lods et ventes* [one-eighth of sale's price to the lord when property was sold] were very profitable for the seignior, as the accounts show very clearly. Consult, for example . . . . "; then follow the figures for two seigniories.[40] "Often for each *péage* or *trépas*, there existed a tariff of dues which the differ-

ent classes of merchandise had to pay. Here is, for example.
. . . ."[41] Each example is footnoted to the set of documents from
which it is taken, but seldom are additional instances mentioned
in the note. To write, as Sée does, that "often," "most often,"
"frequently," such and such a thing was true, and then to cite an
example, does not always carry conviction, especially when the
generalization concerns all Brittany and when the words "often"
and "frequently" suggest a rather casual method of working.[42]
To illustrate is not to prove, and Sée's method of arranging the
evidence is really a method of description and not a method of
proof.

This does not necessarily mean that the book is a bad book or
that the conclusions are wrong. But the somewhat casual method
of working, plus the fact that Sée was a liberal who approved of
the society which developed out of the Revolution and condemned the society of the Old Regime, raises the question: Did
Sée, in working with the documents and in arriving at general
statements, see (that is, did his mind register) as typical only those
instances which were in accord with his bias?[43] While it is impossible to answer this for most of his particular, detailed generalizations, nevertheless he arrived at five general conclusions concerning the seignorial regime in Brittany; and these may be
tested, and one verified in detail.

He concluded: (1) In Brittany, of those manorial charges
which had been at the center of the system, the *taille personnelle*
and the *corvée* (work on the lord's land) had in most cases disappeared, the seignorial dues in money were now usually insignificant, and only the dues in kind were still of some value to the
lord.[44] (2) In addition, however, there existed a large number
of miscellaneous dues and obligations: *lods et ventes, rachat* (a
year's revenue when property was inherited), local tolls, the
obligation of the peasant to use the lord's mill and pay the price
set by his miller, and others.[45] (3) Furthermore, in the administration of the system abuses occurred: millers were fraudulent;
frequent and expensive legal acknowledgment (*aveux*) of their
obligations was required of the peasants; injustices prevailed in

the collection of dues to the benefit of the seignior; extraordinary *corvées* were demanded; seignorial justice was employed to maintain seignorial usurpation; the seignior's agents were hard, pitiless, and unjust.[46] (4) Finally, during the second half of the eighteenth century the seigniors—anxious to increase their revenue —revived old rights which had fallen into disuse, reintroduced old measurements, and, in general, tightened up the seignorial regime at every point.[47] (5) The accumulation of dues and obligations weighed very heavily on the peasants, although perhaps not as heavily as one might suppose;[48] but it was the abuses and spirit of the administration which rendered the regime insupportable.[49] Together the dues and abuses constituted "une très dure exploitation."[50]

On points (1), (2), and (4), the evidence—always assuming a representative sample—is sufficient; besides, point (1) is against Sée's bias. Point (3), and hence the second half of point (5), that abuses in the administration of the regime existed, were common, and weighed heavily, rests on those few rural *cahiers* of the departments of Morbihan, Loire-Inférieure, and Finistère, which Sée believed actually represented the views of the peasants.[51] The conclusion thus reached may be checked indirectly by an examination of Sée's edition of the *cahiers* of the *sénéchaussée* of Rennes, which once comprised a large section of the other two Breton departments. An examination of that edition reveals that the *cahiers* were a reliable source in their statement of fact. Although Sée and Lesort had been unable to check most of the individual items of the *cahiers*, a reading of their notes reveals that in every case where an item could be verified it turned out to be accurate or true.[52] On the basis of probability, therefore, if a *cahier* said that an abuse existed, it almost undoubtedly did. Furthermore, an inspection of the rural *cahiers* themselves reveals that, of the six abuses mentioned by Sée, five (all except the demand for extraordinary *corvées*) were mentioned rather frequently in the *cahiers*,[53] and hence he was justified in concluding that these abuses were common, widespread, and existed in the majority of the seigniories.

But that the demand for the extraordinary *corvée* was a wide-spread abuse cannot be demonstrated. And from the *cahiers* it is also difficult to prove any quantitative or qualitative statement concerning the severity of the seignorial regime. When, therefore, Sée in his general conclusion implied that the abuses weighed heavily on the country population (granted that they were exasperating, vexatious, and a burden) and that the entire regime constituted "une très dure exploitation," I take it that, overimpressed by the violence of certain *cahiers*, he was swept by his bias and perhaps by his eloquence beyond what the evidence would warrant, and it may be somewhat beyond reality. But even this remark grants the validity of most of his conclusions.

The qualities and characteristics of *Les classes rurales en Bretagne* are typical of Sée's other monographs and of the great mass of articles which he wrote on the medieval, agrarian, commercial, and industrial history of France. As a writer of monographs, Sée used the best possible sources, usually manuscript; he analyzed these sources critically; and in his description his mind followed the documents on the whole without distortion, except when bias intervened, which was infrequently. His chief defect was to move a little too rapidly from the particular case to the general conclusion—from the documents of a single department to conclusions regarding all Brittany, from a few *cahiers* mentioning the extraordinary *corvée* to a general seignorial demand for extraordinary *corvées*, from the methods of a single business firm in Brittany to methods of all firms in western France. This slight haste may mean that an occasional, detailed generalization is erroneous and that a general conclusion has to be modified. But, on the whole, the excellence of his judgment is such that, although he uses fewer documents than a modern historian would consider requisite, his general conclusions are usually valid.

Turning, now, to Sée's works in other fields, the field of intellectual history of the Old Regime, when Sée entered it in the 1890's, was still new, and consequently he wrote at a time when it could still be considered scholarly to treat of men and topics which were important, before scholars in this worked field had to retreat to the obscure and minute. He wrote, therefore, a series of articles on the political ideas of Fénélon, Saint-Simon, Voltaire, Condorcet, and on related subjects. After the war these articles, with additional material, were brought together in two books: *Les idées politiques en France au XVIIe siècle*[54] and *L'évolution de la pensée politique en France au XVIIIe siècle*,[55] intended as an introduction to the field.[56] In the two books, through six large divisions, the history of political ideas is followed from the culmination of the absolutist doctrine (Bossuet) through the reaction against absolutism (Fénélon and Saint-Simon), the growth of liberal doctrine (Voltaire), and the growth of democratic doctrine (Rousseau), to the appearance of the reformers (Helvétius and Holbach) and the formation of the Revolutionary doctrine. Under each division the writers representing each doctrine or tendency are discussed, a chapter to each writer; under the liberal doctrine, for example, a chapter each to Montesquieu, D'Argenson, and Voltaire.

The broad movement of political ideas during this period, the influence of events on this movement, and the relationship of each author to the general trend are traced with astonishing clarity. But the treatment of the individual writers is less satisfactory. Sée went to each author, read his major works, and then described the author's thought logically—described, for example, Voltaire's ideas on religion, on freedom of thought, on individual liberty, on the rights of man, on political liberty, a section to each major conception. The resulting chapters are neither penetrating, profound, nor subtle. There is, of course, the danger of being more subtle than the matter requires or than truth of description and explanation will stand; but in intellectual history Sée is never in that danger. In the chapters, furthermore, any chronological development of the author's thought is ignored; the influences which helped to shape his life and thinking and the influence which the author himself had on others are largely neglected. In extenuation it must be remembered that these books were intended as an introduction, but even as an introduction they must be supplemented.

In the field of economic and social history Sée's contribution included a mass of articles on the commercial and industrial history of Brittany in the seventeenth century—articles notable chiefly for the skill with which Sée selected topics of value to general French history and gave significance to local detail and for the exploitation of the papers of old commercial and business firms to describe the business techniques of the Old Regime and the commerce of Old-Regime France with Spain and Portugal to the south and with Holland and the Baltic states to the north. Sée's contribution also included five works of a general, more synthetic nature: *La France économique et sociale au XVIIIe siècle*,[57] a static description of the society of the Old Regime; *L'évolution commerciale et industrielle de la France sous l'ancien régime*,[58] the development of French commerce and industry from 1600 to the Revolution; *La vie économique et sociale de la France sous la monarchie censitaire (1815–48)*;[59] *Les origines du capitalisme moderne*,[60] a brief history of European capitalism from the Renaissance; and finally the two-volume *Französische Wirtschaftsgeschichte*. In all these works of synthesis Sée displayed similar qualities: mastery of an almost unbelievable amount of secondary, monographic literature, including naturally the results of his own investigations; an ability to give the material a strong, intelligent organization, which yet weaves in all the factors and circumstances involved; a singular balance and objectivity of temper which gives each subject or factor its due; and a certain caution in presenting the results as tentative, a willingness to point out that here and there are possible problems on which further research is needed. The style, it is true, is seldom exciting, and there appears a slight liberal bias against the mercantilistic-corporative regime;[61] but otherwise it is difficult to find any flaws in these books. As a writer of syntheses, Sée was much more successful in economic, than in intellectual, history. Of the individual works, the *Französische Wirtschaftsgeschichte* impresses by the mass of its learning and by the strong clarity of its organization. But for deftness in weaving into a chronological account a variety of materials and factors, for skill in use of the comparative method—of the comparative history of capitalism in Italy, Holland, France, and England, and in the colonies—to demonstrate that everywhere increasing commerce has been the fundamental factor behind the rise of capitalism and changes in its form, for quiet pointing of this central theme, yet for many-sided presentation of a complex development, *Les origines du capitalisme moderne* is a little masterpiece.

Through his writings on economic history there runs a philosophy, a certain view of historical reality which Sée developed more thoroughly in his four books on the philosophy of history.[62] As a scholar, Sée was primarily interested in understanding the past. In his view the reality with which the historian deals is infinitely complex: institutions, events, the action of individuals, economic phenomena, political phenomena, social phenomena, and intellectual phenomena, all intermingled, acting upon each other, and changing both individually and as a whole from year to year. So complex is this reality that it is impossible to establish, as in the physical sciences, mathematical relations among the facts—impossible, that is, to formulate scientific laws or to use the past to predict the future. In this respect, history is not, and cannot be, a science. It is also impossible in history to gain information through experiment or even through direct observation of reality. The historian can know the past "only by the trace which exists in monuments and especially in documents," and many of these traces have been lost and have dropped out altogether.

Nevertheless, a science (according to Sée, who is here following a philosopher of science whom he admired, E. Meyerson) not only formulates laws but also seeks to explain reality in terms of causes and conditions, and it is Sée's hope that in this latter respect history may become a science. The task of the historian is then twofold. In monographs he is to examine the traces which have come down, by careful study to penetrate into every corner of reality, and to *describe* it in detail. In syntheses, he will try to *explain* the course of history. But explanation is difficult. There are so many possible causes of an event—some of them fundamental factors or tendencies, others casual, individual, even acci-

dental. Change or evolution does not take place in a straight line
or at an even rate; over a period of years, perhaps, in a given
society, there are certain fundamental tendencies, but these are
obscured by surface extremes and reactions. How to discern
what are fundamental factors and fundamental tendencies and
to be sure that one's discernment is correct?

Sée was convinced that the use of the comparative method was
the solution. A comparison of different societies existing at the
same time or in the same stages of development would bring out
which causes were fundamental and which accidental or peculiar
to a time and place.[63] Thus, comparison of the rise of capitalism
in Italy, Germany, Holland, England, and France reveals that
increasing commerce was the fundamental factor in the growth of
capitalism and in changes in its form, with the presence of Jews,
the Puritan spirit, and increase of land values operating only in
certain cases.[64] A comparison of the societies of England and
France in the eighteenth century reveals those fundamental differences—the extraordinary growth of capitalism and the absence of the seignorial regime in England, the contrary in
France—which explain why their agrarian regimes diverged, in
England toward large proprietorship, in France toward small
peasant ownership.[65] Furthermore, a comparison of the same
society at different times will reveal which tendencies of development in the society have been fundamental and relatively permanent and which surface and transient.[66] In this manner history
might truly hope to become a science.[67]

In his philosophy Sée naturally gave a more specialized attention to the influence of economic phenomena. In his long essay
on *Matérialisme historique et interprétation économique de l'histoire* he
criticized Marx's doctrine that economic phenomena condition
and determine all other historical facts and explain them. The
doctrine, in Sée's opinion, is an abstraction—it will not fit all the
facts; historical reality is too complex to be explained by a single,
inflexible, unilateral hypothesis; finally, other phenomena react
on economic phenomena, and there is interaction.[68] Nevertheless, as an economic historian, Sée, in his own works and to use his

own words, granted to economic conditions "a preponderant influence."[69] They had affected in a dominant way the evolution
of the seignorial regime,[70] the formulation of governmental economic policy,[71] the division of society into social classes, and the
strength and aspirations of each class.[72] Furthermore, economic
phenomena themselves are less disturbed than other types by
events and the action of powerful individuals.[73] By the mere
effect of their mass they can balk or render vain any human
efforts, whether of maintenance or reform, which run counter
to the main economic trend. In the eighteenth century the force
of steadily increasing commerce burst the bonds of the mercantilistic system of colonial regulation. In the face of that force the
efforts of Spanish and English statesmen to maintain that system
were fruitless.[74] The efforts of well-intentioned, capable French
administrators under Louis XV and Louis XVI to improve
French agriculture by promoting the partition of common lands
were rendered sterile by the force of things—the backward methods of agriculture and the lack of capital in the hands of the peasants. After 1840, when these conditions were changed, the proposed reform went through smoothly, almost automatically.[75] The
force of economic phenomena thus sweeps men down courses
whose broad tendencies they do not see or, if vaguely aware, down
which they sometimes have no desire to go. Although Sée ac-
knowledges that the action of individuals and of legislatures often
exercises an important and beneficent influence on economic
phenomena (the abolition of the seignorial regime, for example),[76]
his works convey a sense of fatalism which he probably did not
intend.

Sée's philosophy was neither profound nor original. Most of
its elements were borrowed: the complexity of historical reality
from Fustel de Coulanges; the observation that history is based
on traces left by the past, from Langlois and Seignobos; the division of causes into fundamental and casual, accidental, even irrational, from Cournot and Meyerson; the comparative method
from Fustel, Seignobos, and perhaps Pirenne. But in borrowing,
Sée more or less unconsciously chose those elements which were in

accord with his spirit and experience, and he fused them into a logical whole. The result was a good, personal working philosophy which, except for the praise of the comparative method, most scholars probably hold today and which, hence, seems commonplace. Sée's merit, first, was to think out for himself into a logical, coherent whole what remains with most scholars half-formed suppositions. Second, his merit was that he actually applied the comparative method fruitfully in three of his books.[77] His optimistic view that the comparative method will make history a science may be criticized; and his use of information gained from the fields of sociology and economics has been condemned. But certainly in history, where it is so easy to give the answers and to assume that they are correct, no tool should be overlooked which will render our judgment more precise and accurate, or any knowledge ignored, no matter from what field, that will enlarge our understanding of the past.

A few general considerations concerning Sée's style and biases remain to be noticed. Sée wrote at different levels of style, depending on the type of work he was doing. In his notices of books he was content with unremarkable comment ("very interesting," a "conscientious study," "documentation insufficient," or "the author could have been more impartial") and with a clear but unremarkable summary apparently written as the words fell off the pen. The articles are at a higher level: abrupt, vigorous, sometimes argumentative, but with the organization, although present, not always clear. In the monographs and books the thought has thickened out and become fuller; there is calm mastery of the material, quiet pointing of the theme; the organization is strong and clear. It is a style that can partly be defined by negatives. Sée did not have the type of mind that thinks in pictures, sees in details; he thought in terms of broad general ideas and institutions. The style, therefore, lacks vividness, the flash of illuminating brief quotation or detail, although the mass of description is often clear and full and not without cumulative effect. Brilliance and epigram are also wanting; there is scarcely a quotable phrase. Positively, its qualities are economy and flexibility (the prose fits the material like a glove, there is neither too much nor too little), a clarity which allows the subject to be seen completely but without vividness, and (at its best) a quiet vigor, rising at times to a quiet eloquence. It is a style well adapted to the impersonal, intellectual presentation of the subject, to Sée's scholarly code that in a work which is attempting to establish and present the truth the author's personality should be withdrawn, and the subject be allowed to stand by itself.[78]

Sée, however, was not only a scholar, trying to be objective; he was also a Frenchman with certain political and economic views local to his time and place, and these influenced his work. Well known is Freeman's phrase: "History is past politics." Less familiar is the sardonic version of his dictum that "history is present politics," that as the present situation changes, the interests and emphases of historians change, and new biases develop. Sée's work represents this tendency in several ways. In a world which seemed to be dominated by economic facts, it was natural for historians, including Sée, to discover that economic facts had been important in the past and to work out their history. Furthermore, in the struggle of opinion under the Third Republic as to the desirability of a republican and democratic form of government, Sée, for a scholar, took a fairly active part. He was a member of the Ligue des Droits de l'Homme (roughly corresponding to the American Civil Liberties Union), and he wrote its history.[79] He ardently approved of the democratic society in which he lived,[80] and that approval apparently affected, on certain points, his writing of history. Thus, whatever may be the merit of the questions at issue, it was probably because he was a liberal that he condemned the abuses of the Old Regime, held a dark view of the condition of the eighteenth-century peasants, defended the *philosophes*,[81] rejected the (Cochin) conspiracy theory of the Revolution,[82] and praised the Revolution itself as "the greatest transformation which humanity has ever known."[83] Had he been an aristocrat, he probably would have taken the other side.

Sée was not only a liberal, he was also a French patriot; and his national feeling occasionally colored (although it probably did not distort) his view of history. In his praise of France as a rural democracy;[84] in his treatment of nineteenth-century economic history to show that, while England and Germany expanded industry excessively at the expense of agriculture, France retained a well-balanced economy;[85] and in the concluding passage of *La France économique et sociale au XVIIIᵉ siècle*, written shortly after the war of 1914: "One can still, in a certain measure at least, apply to present-day France the words of Chaptal, in 1817: 'Of all the nations of Europe, it is still France which, reduced to its own resources, would experience the least privation' "[86]—in all these passages there shines through, restrained and strong, a love of France. In fairness to Sée it is well to note, however, that his biases are never extreme—they seem quite reasonable to a liberal mind—and they do not affect the great mass of his scholarly writing.[87]

Viewing Sée's achievement as a whole, it is seen that it is important more for its mass of description and explanation than for its suggestiveness. Save for his insistence that the nature of the medieval domain itself will explain all the characteristics of the manorial regime, and his agrarian hypothesis that small peasant ownership in France may paradoxically be explained by the persistence of the seigniorial regime which protected the rights of the peasant over the land, while in England the weakening of the regime left the peasant unprotected—save for these, Sée has no brilliant theories to propose. Nevertheless, the mass of his work in medieval, agrarian, and economic history (excepting, that is, his excursions into intellectual history and into the philosophy of history) was marked by a high level of excellence. This was true whether he was working as an editor of documents, a writer of monographs, or an author of syntheses. Only as a philosopher of history was he unoriginal and somewhat commonplace.

The central fact about Sée—his work and his life—was not that he was a Frenchman or a liberal but that he was a scholar.

The fundamental assumption of historical scholarship—that it is important to get the record straight—he accepted without question. "Accept" perhaps implies on the part of Sée a greater awareness of the assumption than was actually the case. With him it was less a formal intellectual tenet consciously held than an underlying understanding which was part of his growth and being. The second assumption of historical scholarship, that it is possible to get the record straight, he accepted less unconsciously and less naïvely. As a practical investigator, he was aware that the historian works by inference from traces of the past to a complex reality, and he quoted with approval Renan's phrase that history was "une petite science conjectural."[88] Nevertheless, like his master Fustel, he believed that it was possible, even by conjecture, to get the record straight if one used scholarly methods—that is, if one would analyze the documents critically—and if in description and explanation one would allow one's mind to follow these documents without distortion. These two assumptions—the importance and the possibility of getting close to historical reality by scholarly methods—were the foundations upon which he built his work.

So quiet and unobtrusive in his case was the excellence of the product, that one is apt to miss Sée's other central quality. But the trait which distinguished Sée (I would not say from other scholars) as a worker in history was intelligence—a broad, general, objective intelligence. It was intelligence which led him in four separate cases—Louis XI and the towns, the agrarian history of Brittany, the intellectual history of the Old Regime, and the general economic history of France—to perceive that here were wide-open fields for investigation with a multitude of documents available. It was intelligence, once the study had begun, that enabled him to discern—even in a new field, and even where others would have been smothered or confused by documentary and narrative detail—to discern what were the broad outlines of the subjects.[89] And the very defect of his monographs—his tendency to move a little too rapidly from the particular case to the general conclusion—was caused by an excess of intelligence (that is, not enough), by an ability to see rapidly the possible relation of each detail to the general plan or conception.

But even the most excellent and intelligent of scholarly work is only provisional and gradually disappears from view unless preserved from oblivion by the grace of style. Even during his lifetime Sée's conclusions were being slightly modified by investigations of others. In the medieval field he was compelled to acknowledge that his insistence that the nature of the medieval domain would explain all the characteristics of the manorial regime had been too exclusive: seignorial justice might have come from the dismemberment of the justice of the Carolingian state as well as from the nature of the domain, peasant use of common lands might have been derived in some regions from primitive, peasant communal ownership as well as from the custom of renting the use of the forest from the seignior.[90] As a large number of regional monographs and articles have appeared since Sée published his book on the manorial regime, it is perhaps already time for another general account. In French agrarian history his numerous articles on the attempted partition and enclosure of the common lands in the eighteenth century were superseded by the more thorough studies of Marc Bloch,[91] which, while confirming Sée's general conclusion, corrected statements of detail. In economic history his general syntheses were already being supplemented and whittled away.[92] In time, if interest in economic history continues, new syntheses will be needed. Perhaps of all of Sée's work his edition of the *Cahiers* and his chief monograph on *Les classes rurales en Bretagne* are most likely to possess relative permanence.

With his usual objectivity Sée apparently foresaw the fate that was to be his. Speaking of Renan, Sée wrote: "What does it matter, then, that the results of his work have since been supplemented, corrected, surpassed? It is the destiny of all scientific work."[93] But writing of Quicherat, a scholar who investigated the trial of Joan of Arc, Sée observed that, although his works have been forgotten and are no longer read except by specialists, the results have been incorporated in the fabric of science.[94] It may be inferred that, in describing Renan and Quicherat, Sée was also thinking of his own work.

With his estimate of himself we would agree, although we would word it somewhat differently. In the field of history Sée was not a Marx, that is, an outsider who by his theories radically alters the interpretation of the past, or a Gibbon, who produces a literary masterpiece, or a Ranke or a Fustel de Coulanges, teachers who influence generations of scholars. In brief, Sée was one of those who are significant not for their personal achievement and influence but for their humble but important participation in a broader movement—in this case, the movement of modern scholarship. In so far as modern scholarship has been of value and significance in modern civilization, the work of Henri Sée has its importance.

NOTES

1. In preparing this article I am indebted to Miss Katherine Hall, of the University of Chicago Libraries, for securing additional material that was neither in Chicago nor in Washington; to Mr. Harold Schultz, of Duke University, for locating a bibliography of the works of Sée; and to Mr. Richard Hooker, of the Central Y.M.C.A. College, Chicago, for copying a large number of references.

2. The biographical details of the following account of Sée's life are taken, unless stated otherwise, from A. Rébillon, "Nécrologie et bibliographie des travaux de Henri Sée," *Annales de Bretagne*, XLIII (1936), 2–11. A complete bibliography of Sée's writings is given in *ibid.*,12–33. This paper is based on the items listed in that bibliography, except Nos. 22, 34, 41, 54, 66, 67, 70, 71, 99, 112, 114, 115, 116, 118, 119, 136, 138, 159, 174, 183, 190, 193, which were articles in magazines that could not be obtained.

3. *Louis XI et les villes* (Paris, 1892), pp. vii–ix.

4. XLIX (1892), 352, 354.

5. "Le travail d'histoire en province: la Bretagne (année 1902)," *Revue d'histoire moderne et contemporaine*, V (1903–4), 43.

6. *Ibid.*, pp. 42–43; "Le travail d'histoire en province: la Bretagne (année 1903)," *ibid.*, VI (1904–5), 184; "Le travail d'histoire moderne en province: la Bretagne (années 1904–1905)," *ibid.*, VIII (1906–7), 44.

7. "Le travail d'histoire en province: la Bretagne (année 1903)," *ibid.*, VI (1904–5), 185.

8. "Le travail d'histoire moderne en province: la Bretagne (années 1904–1905)," *ibid.*, VIII (1906–7), 44.

9. *La Révolution française*, LI (1906), 380.

10. Paris, 1895.

11. Paris, 1895.

12. Paris, 1896.

13. Paris, 1901.

14. Reviewed by A. Molinier in *RH*, LXXVI (1901), 357–60; by "C. D." in *Revue d'économie politique*, XV (1901), 423; by Paul Darmstädter in *HZ*, LXXXVIII (1902), 314; by Ph. Sagnac in *Revue d'histoire moderne et contemporaine*, II (1900–1901), 670.

15. Paris, 1906.

16. 4 vols.; Paris, 1909–12.

17. Reviewed by Étienne Dejean in *La Révolution française*, LVIII (1910), 272–79; by Marcel Marion in *Revue d'histoire moderne et contemporaine*, XIV (1910), 98.

18. *Revue des questions historiques*, LXXXI (1907), 685–87.

19. Reviewed by Henri Hauser in *RH*, XCV (1907), 365–66; by Ph. Sagnac in *Revue d'histoire moderne et contemporaine*, VIII (1906–7), 362; by Jean Lorédan in *Revue des études historiques*, LXXII (1906), 645. See also reviews by Camille Bloch in *La Révolution française*, LI (1906), 367–80; by Paul Darmstädter in *HZ*, XCIX (1907), 162–65; by "T. F. T." in *EHR*, XXII (1907), 400–401.

20. *La Révolution française*, LI (1906), 380.

21. Rébillon, *loc. cit.*, p. 9; see also, on his kindness, Léon Cahen's review of Sée's *Franzosische Wirtschaftsgeschichte* (Vol. II) in *Revue d'histoire moderne*, XIII (1938), 301–2.

22. These figures are based on the bibliography of Sée's writings in *Annales de Bretagne*, XLIII (1936), 12–33.

23. Paris, 1921.

24. Jena, 1930 and 1936.

25. Paris, 1927.

26. Paris, 1928.

27. Paris, 1929.

28. Paris, 1932.

29. "Les cahiers de paroisses de 1789," *RH*, CIII (1910), 298; "L'œuvre de la Commission des Documents relatifs à la Vie économique de la Révolution française (1904–1910)," *ibid.*, CVI (1911), 321. See also Bloch's edition of the *Cahiers du bailliage d'Orléans*.

30. "Les cahiers de paroisses de 1789," *RH*, CIII (1910), 303. See also Émile Bridrey's edition of the *Cahiers du bailliage du Cotentin*, especially I, 70–71.

31. Sée and Lesort, *Cahiers de doléances de la sénéchaussée de Rennes* (Paris, 1909–12), I, 246. An even more complex interrelationship is found on p. 543 of the same volume.

32. "La rédaction et la valeur historique des cahiers de paroisses pour les états-généraux de 1789," *RH*, Vol. CIII (1910). See also "Les cahiers de paroisses de la Bretagne en 1789," *La Révolution française*, XLVI (1904), 487–513.

33. The question, of course, arises: How much of the excellence of the work was due to Sée and how much to Lesort? Doubtless, both contributed. But, after reading Sée's two critical articles on the *cahiers* (see preceding note) and comparing them with the introduction to the *Cahiers*, it is my impression that much of the critical value of the edition was due to Sée. In any case, Sée's French edition of the *Voyages de Arthur Young* (Paris, 1931), with critical introduction and notes, proves that, even when working alone, Sée was a skilful editor, probably unsurpassed by any scholar of his generation.

34. *Les classes rurales en Bretagne*, p. 519.

35. In review of the book by A. Roussel in *Revue des questions historiques*, LXXXI (1907), 685–87.

36. *Les classes rurales en Bretagne*, pp. xii–xiv.

37. *Ibid.*

38. The seignorial regime is described on pp. 77–240. The examples which appear in those pages both in text and footnotes and which were taken from the manuscripts of the seigniories, baronies, castellannies, abbeys, and commanderies have been counted and distributed by departments. Of the 247 examples which appear, 217 were taken from the department of Ille-et-Vilaine, 13 from Loire-Inférieure, 11 from Côtes-du-Nord, 4 from Finistère, and 2 from Morbihan.

39. Or it may assume that the agricultural population of the department of Ille-et-Vilaine was three times the total for the other four departments. If that was the assumption, which I doubt, it was incorrect. See the census figures and deductions which may be drawn from them in the *Grande encyclopédie* under "Ille-et-Vilaine," "Côtes-du-Nord," "Finistère," "Loire-Inférieure," and "Morbihan."

40. *Les classes rurales en Bretagne*, p. 114.

41. *Ibid.*, pp. 137–38. See also pp. 78, nn. 1, 6; 81, n. 2; 84; 85; 87, n. 2; 88, n. 2; 90; 95; 105; 110; 115; 117, n. 1; 131 and n. 5; 133 and n. 1; 135–37; 138–39; 144–46; 151–52; 155–56; 163–67; 169; 172; 175; 188.

42. Probably the documents of all the seigniories are not sufficiently complete on all the points to render a statistical study possible. But, as Sée does give a large number of figures, it probably would have been better on important points, such as the increase in the rent of the mills or on the amount of the tithe, to have said, "Of the fifty-eight seigniories we have studied from all regions and of all types, we have figures on the rent of the mill over a period of years for nine; of these, all nine show a decided increase during the latter third of the eighteenth century"—and then to have cited the evidence for those nine.

43. There is also, of course, this problem: In his description did he yield to the literary temptation to select for illustration the clearest, most telling examples, which, however, in their cumulative effect would probably give a sharper and perhaps a darker picture than the mass of documents would warrant?

44. *Ibid.*, pp. 92, 96, 97, 102–3, 109, 508–9.

45. *Ibid.*, pp. 110, 112, 130, 137, 144, 149, 175, 509–10.

46. *Ibid.*, pp. 105–6, 112, 121–22, 125–26, 129, 181, 183–97, 205–6, 510–11.

47. *Ibid.*, pp. 204–7, 240, 511.

48. *Ibid.*, p. 181.

49. *Ibid.*, pp. 181, 196.

50. *Ibid.*, p. 505.

51. *Ibid.*, pp. 179, 183–97.

52. See the notes to Sée and Lesort. There are one or two exceptions to accuracy.

53. Of the 336 rural *cahiers* in the *sénéchaussée* of Rennes, frauds of millers were mentioned by 31 per cent; abuses in the collection of dues, by 36 per cent; expensive *aveux*, by 24 per cent; harsh, unjust seignorial agents, by 33 per cent; complaint of seignorial justice, by 20 per cent; demand for extraordinary *corvées*, by 20 per cent. But many of these *cahiers* emanated from assemblies whose presiding officer was a

seignorial official and who perhaps influenced the assembly to omit mention of abuses. To eliminate this factor of seignorial influence, it is necessary to compare the *cahiers* issuing from assemblies whose president was a seignorial official with those coming from assemblies without such a president. Of the 210 *cahiers* from assemblies with a seignorial official as president, frauds of millers were mentioned by 24 per cent; abuses in collection of dues, by 29 per cent; expensive *aveux*, by 17 per cent; harsh, unjust seignorial agents, by 27 per cent; complaint of seignorial justice, by 15 per cent; demand for extraordinary *corvées*, by 18 per cent. Of the 96 *cahiers* from assemblies without a seignorial official, frauds of millers were mentioned by 45 per cent; abuses in collection of dues, by 48 per cent; expensive *aveux*, by 34 per cent; harsh, unjust seignorial agents, by 43 per cent; complaint of seignorial justice, by 30 per cent; demand for extraordinary *corvées*, by 26 per cent. Presumably, if no seignorial officials had presided, the latter percentages would apply to all the rural *cahiers*.

These last percentages may still seem low; but it must be recalled (1) that silence of a *cahier* does not necessarily mean that the abuse did not exist; (2) that nearly every *cahier* speaks of the abuse it mentions as common, existing not only in its own parish but also in the surrounding country; (3) that it sometimes happens that one parish of a given seigniory mentions an abuse while other parishes from the same seigniory will be silent—in that case, it could probably be assumed (except for the frauds of millers) that the abuse mentioned by one parish should probably have been mentioned by the other parishes; (4) finally, that in most cases we still cannot be sure we have eliminated entirely all seignorial or bourgeois influence which might have kept out the mention of abuses. In twelve parishes, however, we can tell either from the minutes of the meeting or from the *cahier* itself that there was a definite rejection of seignorial influence or that the *cahier* was read to the assembly and approved by it. In these twelve cases, where we can be fairly sure that the *cahier* approximated more closely the wishes of the assembly, undisturbed by outside influence, frauds of millers are mentioned by 58 per cent; abuses of collections, by 67 per cent; expensive *aveux*, by 58 per cent; harsh, unjust seignorial agents, by 83 per cent; complaint of seignorial justice, by 92 per cent; extraordinary *corvées*, by 33 per cent. Altogether the evidence would probably justify the conclusion I have drawn.

54. Paris, 1923.

55. Paris, 1925.

56. His *Les idées politiques en France au XVIIIe siècle* (Paris, 1920) was largely a collection of extracts from the leading writers.

57. Paris, 1925.

58. Paris, 1925.

59. Paris, 1927.

60. Paris, 1926.

61. *La France économique et sociale*, pp. 106–8, 128–29; *L'évolution commerciale et industrielle de la France sous l'ancien régime* (Paris, 1925), pp. 78–80, 106, 108–9.

62. The key passages which contain Sée's general philosophy of history are the following: *Les origines du capitalisme moderne*, pp. 189, 196; *Matérialisme historique et interprétation économique de l'histoire*, 84, 124, 127; *Science et philosophie de l'histoire*, 79, 80–81, 84–85, 92, 96, 97, 101, 110, 116, 118, 122, 128–30, 135–36, 140, 141–42, 145 (n. 2), 150–51, 154, 173–74, 178, 223, 235, 254–55, 293, 350, 366, 394; *Science*

et philosophie d'après la doctrine de M. Émile Meyerson, pp. 158, 161; *L'évolution commerciale et industrielle de la France sous l'ancien régime,* p. 373; "L'évolution commerciale et industrielle de la France sous l'ancien régime," *Revue de synthèse historique,* XXXV (1923), 89; "Remarques sur l'évolution du capitalisme et les origines de la grande industrie," *ibid.,* XXXVII (1924), 67; "La division de l'histoire en périodes à propos d'un ouvrage récent," *ibid.,* XLII (1926), 66, 67; "Remarques sur le concept de causalité en histoire," *ibid.,* XLVII (1929), 21; "La mémoire et l'étude de l'histoire," *La psychologie et la vie,* I (1927), 6–7; "De l'intuition en histoire," *ibid.,* III (1929), 115–16; "Interprétation d'une controverse sur les relations de l'histoire et de la sociologie," *Archiv für Sozialwissenschaft und Sozialpolitik,* LXV (1931), 90–92, 95; "Les idées de M. Paul Valéry sur l'histoire," *Mercure de France,* CCXXXIV (1932), 309–10; "Remarques sur la méthode en histoire économique et sociale," *RH,* CLXI (1929), 94, 96; "Taine, historien," *Grande revue,* CXXVI (1928), 640; "Les cadres d'une histoire économique de la France dans ses relations avec l'histoire générale et la science économique," *Revue d'économie politique,* XLIII (1929), 50; "L'activité commerciale de la Hollande à la fin du XVIIᵉ siècle," *Revue d'histoire économique et sociale,* XIV (1926), 204; "Un type de document: le livre de raison d'un parlementaire breton au XVIIIᵉ siècle," *Annales d'histoire économique et sociale,* III (1931), 237.

63. *Science et philosophie de l'histoire,* pp. 142–43; "De l'intuition en histoire," *La psychologie et la vie,* III (1929), 115.

64. *Les origines du capitalisme moderne,* pp. 30, 34–35, 42.

65. *Ibid.,* pp. 173–74; *La France économique et sociale,* pp. 4–5, 13–14; "L'évolution du régime agraire en Angleterre depuis la fin du moyen âge," *Revue de synthèse historique,* XXXVIII (1924), 55, 79–82.

66. *Science et philosophie de l'histoire,* pp. 142–43, 232–33; "Remarques sur la méthode en histoire économique et sociale," *RH,* CLXI (1929), 94; "Interprétation d'une controverse sur les relations de l'histoire et de la sociologie," *Archiv für Sozialwissenschaft und Sozialpolitik,* LXV (1931), 99–100. This comparison (of the same society at different times) will disclose, Sée was convinced after the study of four major revolutions, that in a revolution the only reforms which survive into the period of stabilization are those which continue the fundamental tendencies of evolution of the society in question. The reforms which have gone beyond that evolution constitute a surplus which is temporarily lost, although it may influence later generations and thus lead to further evolution. See *Évolution et révolution,* pp. 245–51; "Remarques sur le concept de causalité en histoire," *Revue de synthèse historique,* XLVII (1929), 22–23.

67. "La méthode comparative," *Revue de synthèse historique,* XXXVI (1923), 46.

68. *Matérialisme historique et interprétation économique de l'histoire,* pp. 77–86, 124; "Remarques sur la méthode en histoire économique et sociale," *RH,* CLXI (1929), 96–97. See also *La France économique et sociale,* pp. 6–7, 185–86; *Esquisse d'une histoire du régime agraire* (Paris, 1921), pp. 271–72; *La vie économique et les classes sociales* (Paris, 1924), pp. 1–2; *Les origines du capitalisme moderne,* p. 3.

69. *Science et philosophie de l'histoire,* p. 129.

70. *Les origines du capitalisme moderne,* pp. 12, 173–74; *Les classes rurales et le régime domanial en France au moyen âge,* pp. viii, 259, 615, 626.

71. *L'évolution commerciale et industrielle de la France sous l'ancien régime,* pp. 1–2.

72. *Ibid.*, p. 3; *La vie économique et les classes sociales,* pp. 1–2, 123–24, 227–28; *La France économique et sociale,* pp. 6–7, 140, 182, 185; *Les origines du capitalisme moderne,* pp. 178–80, 183–87.

73. *Science et philosophie de l'histoire,* pp. 232–33; *Matérialisme historique et interprétation économique de l'histoire,* p. 120.

74. *L'évolution commerciale et industrielle de la France sous l'ancien régime,* pp. 1–2, 237–38; *Les origines du capitalisme moderne,* pp. 127–28; *La France économique et sociale,* pp. 121–22.

75. *La vie économique et les classes sociales,* pp. 1, 24, 119–21; *La France économique et sociale,* pp. 5–6; "Les forêts et la question du déboisement," *Annales de Bretagne,* XXXVI (1924–25), 23; "Notes sur les foires en France et particulièrement sur les foires de Caen au XVIIIe siècle," *Revue d'histoire économique et sociale,* XV (1927), 383.

76. *La vie économique et les classes sociales,* p. 121; *La France économique et sociale,* p. 6, 176–77.

77. *Esquisse d'une histoire du régime agraire en Europe au XVIIIe et XIXe siècles; Les origines du capitalisme moderne; Évolution et révolution.*

78. It is well to point out that Sée could write in other manners. In *La France économique et sociale,* which was written for popular consumption, the style is swifter and simpler, even epigrammatic. His biography of *Bertrand du Guesclin* (Paris, n.d.), for young people, is written with considerable charm in the "juvenile" style. In an article for the *Bulletin of the Business Historical Society* of Boston (translated as "Les armateurs de Saint-Malo au XVIIIe siècle," *Revue d'histoire économique et sociale,* XVII [1929], 29) the opening paragraph contains a vivid and imaginative description of the port of Saint-Malo. He is capable of irony; but curiously enough—it is a trait revealing of his kindness—he exercises it only on the dead, on Bossuet, Victor Hugo, on the old École Normale Supérieure, and uses it only in familiar essays, never in scholarly works (see *Science et philosophie de l'histoire,* p. 14; "Le Cromwell de Victor Hugo et le Cromwell de l'histoire," *Mercure de France,* CC [1927], 6; "Fustel de Coulanges," *ibid.,* CCXVIII [1930], 514). Equally revealing is the fact that Sée, in reviewing works of scholarship, never praised or criticized a book for its style. The chief questions he asked were: Is it conscientious? Is it impartial? Is it true? For him the subject and truth were everything; and apparently he believed that in a scholarly work stylistic brilliance and intrusion of the author's personality were out of place; clarity and intelligence were enough.

79. *Histoire de la Ligue des Droits de l'Homme (1898–1926)* (Paris, 1927).

80. *Ibid.,* pp. 12–13.

81. "Histoire des idées politiques, France, XVIIe et XVIIIe siècles," *Revue de synthèse historique,* VI (1903), 239–40; "Les idées politiques de Diderot," *RH,* LXV (1897), 57, 60; "Condorcet, ses idées et son rôle politique," *Revue de synthèse historique,* X (1905), 32.

82. *La vie économique et les classes sociales,* p. 172; *Science et philosophie de l'histoire,* pp. 99–100, 344–45.

83. *Les idées politiques en France au XVIIIe siècle,* p. 254. Sée also had the liberal's tolerance for revolutionary violence—when it had occurred in the past. Thus, after describing from court records the Breton peasant uprisings in 1790, the burning of seigniorial records, the looting of wine cellars of the chateaux, the smashing of furniture, etc., Sée concludes: "The peasants were working unconsciously at a great deed

of human emancipation. The witnesses' stories of pillage, drunkenness, thefts do seem to have a character rather common. But from these humble episodes dates a new era in the history of humanity" ("Les troubles agraires en Haute Bretagne [1790–1791]," *Bulletin d'histoire économique de la Révolution* [1920–21], p. 256; see also *La France économique et sociale*, p. 154).

84. "La France, démocratie rurale: son influence et son rôle en Europe," *Scientia*, XXXIII (1923), 205, 213.

85. *La France économique et sociale*, p. 187.

86. *Ibid.*, p. 188.

87. Sée himself could not see that any of his work was affected by his sympathies, and hence, like most historians who are convinced of their impartiality, he sometimes seems naïve. Thus, in defending the *philosophes* against the charges of Taine that they were "creators of abstractions," Sée wrote: "It seems that a careful, truly scientific study of their doctrines would re-establish the reality of things and set forth the grandeur of the work accomplished by these thinkers, who, if they had been only creators of abstractions, would not have been able to contribute so powerfully to the founding of modern society." It is certainly reassuring to know in advance that a scientific study of the subject will confirm your prejudices. (Quotation taken from Sée, "Histoire des idées politiques, France, XVIIe et XVIIIe siècles," *Revue de synthèse historique*, VI [1903], 240.)

88. "De l'intuition en histoire," *La psychologie et la vie*, III (1929), 116; "Remarques sur la concept de causalité en histoire," *Revue de synthèse historique*, XLVII (1929), 25; *Science et philosophie d'après la doctrine de M. Émile Meyerson*, p. 155.

89. His intelligence, furthermore, enabled him, as witnessed in his bibliographical bulletins for the *Revue historique*, to see the whole field of world social and economic history and to notice where his work fitted in.

90. *Les classes rurales et le régime domanial en France au moyen âge*, pp. 120–23, 311–15, 434–35, 490–525; "Recent work in French economic history," *Economic history review*, I (1928–29), 141; *La vie économique et les classes sociales*, p. 54; *Les classes rurales en Bretagne*, p. 118.

91. "La lutte pour l'individualisme agraire dans la France du XVIIIe siècle," *Annales d'histoire économique et sociale*, II (1930), 329–83, 511–56; Sée, "Bulletin bibliographique sur l'histoire économique et sociale," *RH*, CLXVIII (1931), 346–47.

92. See the bibliographical notes of Robert Schnerb at the end of each chapter of the posthumous French edition of Vol. I of Sée's *Französische Wirtschaftsgeschichte*. See also, for a minor point, P. Harsin, "De quand date le mot 'industrie?' " *Annales d'histoire économique et sociale*, II (1930), 235, 239; Sée, "Bulletin bibliographique sur l'histoire économique et sociale," *RH*, CLXV (1930), 137.

93. *Science et philosophie de l'histoire*, p. 380. See also *ibid.*, pp. 284–85; "Fustel de Coulanges," *Mercure de France*, CCXVIII (1930), 520.

94. *Science at philosophie de l'histoire*, p. 365. See also "La philosophie d'histoire d'Ernest Renan," *RH*, CLXX (1932), 48.

XXI

CHARLES SEIGNOBOS (1854——)

GORDON H. McNEIL*

PROFESSOR SEIGNOBOS enjoys today an international reputation which is perhaps unique among contemporary historians. His name is certainly well known to students of modern history. During a long career he has written more than his share of excellent historical works; he has made contributions to pedagogy, to the study of historical method, the social sciences, and the philosophy of history. Yet it must be admitted that his work, as a whole, has not been outstanding. He has founded no new school of history; his theories of method and historical philosophy lack the originality that characterizes the work of other disciples of Clio; and his reputation rests, in large part, on the pecuniarily satisfying but transitory fame of the writer of successful textbooks. There is a more enduring basis for his reputation to be found in the significance of his historical writings, in their qualities which are typical of his period in the history of France and Europe. In this his background was naturally an important factor.

Michel-Jean-Charles Seignobos was born September 10, 1854, at Lamastre, a small market village in the highlands of southern France near Lyon.[1] In religion his family was not Roman Catholic, as are the great majority of his countrymen, but had been Calvinist since the days of the Huguenots in the sixteenth century. Furthermore, it belonged to the liberal party in the French Protestant church. Thus his religious background was not a stern "fundamentalism" but a "modernist" creed, similar to that of the English Deists of the eighteenth century and the American

* Instructor in history, Denison University.

Unitarians, rejecting both the Trinity and the divinity of Christ. That was the exceptional part of his background, which was not to be without influence when he came to write about the church in his various works. Otherwise his milieu was typical. His father was a *propriétaire*, a member of the independent landowning class that was and remains the backbone of the French nation, and Seignobos grew up in an agricultural community which economically and socially belonged to the end of the eighteenth, rather than to the nineteenth, century. His parents were prosperous enough to send him and his older brother in 1863 to nearby Tournon, where they lived with an old servant while attending the *lycée* in that town. This was during the Second Empire; French education had yet to be reformed, and his "very mediocre" teachers left him with a great deal of liberty, which he spent in reading what pleased him. After eight years he finished his studies at the *lycée* and passed the examinations.

That was in 1871. His father had been elected that same year to the National Assembly, which had been called to decide the future of a France decisively defeated by the armies of Germany. The son followed him to Paris, planning to continue his studies in one of the special faculties, there being, as yet, no regular course at the Sorbonne. He knew that he was not prepared for admission to the École Normale; so he began the study of law at the École de Droit. After one year, having found such studies "vain," he withdrew to enter the Lycée Louis-le Grand and prepare for the École Normale competitive examinations, which he finally passed successfully in 1874. Here his professors included Fustel de Coulanges, one of the most famous medievalists of the day, and Ernest Lavisse, who helped him greatly in his career and with whom he later became very closely associated. During his three years as a *normalien* Seignobos also began to serve, as he says, an "apprenticeship" in the realities of political life through his father, who sat in the chamber of deputies with the moderately liberal Left Center during the first ten years of the Third Republic, an apprenticeship which was of value later when he was to write the political history of the period.[2] During these years of widening experience he developed friendships with Mallarmé, Anatole France, and others of the Parnasse literary group.

He received the agrégation with the highest honors from the École Normale in 1877, and the way lay open for him to enter the French School of Athens. But having no particular interest in archeology, he accepted, instead, a governmental grant for a two-year study of German higher education, offered to him through the influence of Professor Lavisse. The France of the Third Republic believed that the German educational system had been an important factor in the victory of 1870–71, and the French authorities wished to study and copy it. Seignobos studied first at Göttingen. From there he went to the University of Berlin, where Ranke and Sybel were still teaching, and then to Leipzig and Munich, where he made the acquaintance of the world of the opera, returning to France by way of Heidelberg.

There had been no precedent for such grants for foreign study and observation, but Seignobos soon became used to pedagogical pioneering. On his return to France in 1879 he was appointed *maître de conférences* at the University of Dijon, a rank hitherto unknown in the French educational system. There were, as yet, few regularly enrolled students in the French universities, where public lectures were still the chief offering; and the young instructor spent his spare time in the archives of the medieval dukes of Burgundy at Dijon, doing research for his doctoral thesis, which earned him a *docteur ès lettres* in 1882. The following year he returned to Paris, to initiate at the Sorbonne still another academic rank, that of Privatdozent, supposedly copied from the German system. The position was, in fact, ambiguous; yet he held it for seven years—the first and last of that title. Then, after a period during which he served as professor of historical pedagogy, he became in succession *maître de conférences, professeur-adjoint*, and *professeur*.

Although now retired, Professor Seignobos continues to lecture at the Sorbonne, on history and the social sciences and, at the beginning of each year, on historical method. The writer had the pleasure of hearing him during the year 1938–39 and can attest

the quality and interest of his lectures—even on such a presumably dry and uninteresting topic as the methods and procedures of
historical research. There he sat, a small and slight figure, with
traditional beard, wing collar, and frock coat, striking the table
with his hand for emphasis as he lectured with a verve and enthusiasm that was scarcely expected from a man of eighty-four.[3]

Successive generations of university students have come under
the influence of Professor Seignobos during the six decades of his
teaching career; and, although he has never taught at the secondary-school level, he has influenced an even larger number of
younger students through his many textbooks. The first was a
two-volume *Histoire de la civilisation*, published in 1885–86,[4]
which was written for secondary girls' schools—for special textbooks had to be prepared for the weaker sex then. This was followed by three books which went through many editions, the
Histoire narrative et descriptive of the ancient Orient, Greece, and
Rome.[5] Even wider in scope was the subsequent series of textbooks covering the ancient, medieval, and modern fields for the
sixth to the first classes. They were written for the revised system
of secondary education which was introduced in 1902 and have
been widely used in the French schools since that date.[6] Mention, too, should be made of his various Sorbonne lectures which
have been published in the *Revue des cours et conférences* since 1893.
Professor Seignobos has made other contributions to French education as well. There was the published report of his study of
German universities, which turned out to be a rather harsh criticism of the teaching of history in the German schools. Prussianism and Hegelianism (one of his pet dislikes) had perverted German education, and he objected to much of the German theory
and practice. But since 1871 there had been a return to the pure
science; and France, he reported, had much to learn from Germany.[7] During the early years of the present century, while the
French educational system was being reorganized, he was a frequent contributor to various journals, writing articles on methods and practices in historical pedagogy both at home and
abroad.[8]

Yet it is on his work as a historian rather than as a pedagogue that the fame of Professor Seignobos is most solidly based. He received his education in an age when historical scholarship was concentrated on the ancient and medieval periods, and it was in this *Zeitgeist* that he wrote his doctoral thesis, *Le régime féodal en Bourgogne jusqu'en 1360.*[9] This study of medieval feudalism was confined to Burgundy because, as he said, it was a region small enough to be studied thoroughly, it was typical of the feudal regime as a whole, and there were abundant sources in the Dijon archives.[10] Unlike most theses, this was a broad institutional study, embracing the political, economic, and social aspects of the feudal regime over a period of centuries. The influence of his teacher at the École Normale, Fustel de Coulanges, can perhaps be seen in the emphasis he gave in discussing feudal institutions to the continuity from Roman times. Interesting, too, is the thesis that feudalism was an improvement over the Roman system which it replaced; that what was harsh and brutal in medieval society was a remnant which had come down from imperial Rome.

That was a detailed study, based in large part on manuscript sources, and in the best traditions of historical research. Significantly, he was to do little more work of that type, and his reputation as a historian is founded, instead, on broader studies, which, although thoroughly scholarly, are still largely syntheses of the research done by others as well as by himself. In the early 1890's Ernest Lavisse and Alfred Rambaud began their co-operative *Histoire générale du IV*e *siècle à nos jours;* and their young colleague Seignobos joined them as one of the founders of the series, becoming director of the project when Lavisse later entered the government. He himself contributed several sections. That on the feudal regime, drawn in part from his detailed work on Burgundy, has been widely used in the United States in translation.[11] It was a very good, factual summary of the subject, but this time there was no mention of the special thesis of the earlier work on the continuity of institutions from Roman times. In the same volume he wrote a chapter on the Crusades, in which the role of the church and religion was presented from the purely rational point of view;[12] and in a later volume he wrote on the revolution of 1848 and its aftermath in France, and on the Third Republic.[13]

The latter chapter reflected an interest in recent and contemporary history which was now to occupy all his attention, except for the general-survey textbooks already mentioned, and an interest which was to gain for him his chief fame as a historian. Actually, his position in the field had already been established with the publication of the *Histoire politique de l'Europe contemporaine* in 1897,[14] a work that was very well received by the reviewers and was honored by the Academy. He had lectured for a number of years on the period of European history since the Treaty of Vienna, and this volume was a natural product of those courses. The tangled web of nineteenth-century history, with its almost unmanageable mass of source material, was not easy to trace, particularly as he allowed himself practically no perspective of time, bringing the account up to almost the moment of writing. Although the work is factual to a fault, the organization is excellent. The internal development of each of the countries is traced separately in detail, with the international story, minus the unessential military and diplomatic events, left for independent treatment at the end. Such an arrangement has much to recommend it; yet the story it tells is fragmentary at best, and thirty years later, when Seignobos wrote again on European history, the system of organization was quite different from that used in this book. As the title reads, this is a political history, but those nonpolitical factors which have influenced political events are discussed at length. By and large, it is not the result of firsthand research, being based, for the most part, on many other detailed studies. No one man could have done the necessary research to write the whole story, and the imposing quantity of sources on nineteenth-century Europe had dissuaded French historians from writing anything but elementary textbooks on the subject. There are extensive bibliographies at the end of each chapter, but otherwise the mechanics of scholarly writing are lacking. Yet the facts are correct, the conclusions sound, and the whole work thoroughly historical.

Not the least of the book's merits are its objectivity and fairness. Although he wrote as a Frenchman and as a non-Catholic, it would be hard to take exception to his presentation of church affairs and the development of the German Empire. Particularly good is the analysis of the development of democracy in England during the century, for which he credited the "non-English," the Scotch, the Irish, the Welsh, and the political leaders from the northwest counties.[15] In one paragraph he gave a penetrating summary of the main thread of French political and institutional development since the Revolution.[16] The German trend was not so clearly seen; yet one cannot blame a writer in 1897 for failing to perceive what many observers today cannot recognize—the inevitability of some form of German dominance of central Europe. The concluding chapter is a well-thought-out essay summarizing from the supranational, European point of view the main political trends of the nineteenth century. All in all, the book possesses merits which made it a classic, and it remains today probably the best study of the period.

The nineteenth century, and particularly the history of France, was now Seignobos's chosen field, and this one-volume survey was followed by detailed studies, chiefly on the revolution of 1848, published as articles in various reviews during the pre-war years.[17] The definitive result of this research, however, was again a survey, published after the war of 1914 in the co-operative *Histoire de France contemporaine*, edited by Lavisse. Seignobos contributed three volumes—*La révolution de 1848, le Second Empire (1848–1859)*, *Le declin de l'Empire et l'établissement de la Troisième République (1859–1875)*, and *L'évolution de la Troisième République (1875–1914)*[18]—as well as a chapter in the final volume, "L'action de la guerre sur la vie française."[19] Again the subject is a broad one, the history of France from the revolution of 1848 to the war of 1914. It was a period through a large part of which he had lived himself, and more than once he drew on personal knowledge or observation for his material. But these volumes were based on extensive research, not only in the earlier chapters which covered the period on which he had already published articles, but in the later parts as well.

It would be difficult to summarize this work, for it presents the history of France for the period—political, military, diplomatic, economic, social, and intellectual—and there is no outstanding originality of interpretation. But it is a presentation that has yet to be equaled. The major part is political history; yet some of the most successful sections concern the economic and social development of the nation, notably the chapter "La société française" in the first volume.[20] The geographical distribution of political parties is explained in detail,[21] and he shows a keen awareness of the importance of class distinctions in political life.[22] There are hints of a dislike of doctrinaire socialism[23] and of the Comte de Chambord, the royalist standard-bearer during the 1870's.[24] An obvious liking for the Third Republic and a dislike for its opponents, which included the church, can also be seen;[25] and there is a slight French prejudice in the discussion of the story of Alsace in 1870–71.[26] But such evidence of bias is hardly worth mentioning; and, as in the *Histoire politique*, the objectivity maintained throughout these volumes is noteworthy.

Contemporary political problems had also come to occupy Professor Seignobos's attention. Such an interest, presaged in his several works on political history, was to have been expected from the son of a delegate to the National Assembly and member of the chamber of deputies. Through his father he had observed at first hand the political life of the Republic—the personal interests, the ways of getting things done, and the very real difference between political theory and practice. Combining his observation with research, he wrote many articles, which were published in French, German, English, and American journals.[27] Some of these were semihistorical, such as one of the first on the separation of powers, in which the historical background of the doctrine and its practice was portrayed,[28] and another on the political evolution of Italy since 1860. The great majority dealt with France and French political problems, both of internal affairs and of international relations. Some of the best were concerned with contemporary electoral questions, the geographical distribution of parties, and the significance of certain elections.

Before 1914 he had written on Franco-German relations and on the conflict between Austria and Serbia. With the outbreak of the war of 1914 his attention was turned to this subject almost exclusively; and, like his colleagues in the other warring countries, he devoted his talent to the writing of articles designed to bolster the national *esprit*. In 1915 a long essay, entitled "1815–1915," was published in the *Revue de Paris*, and later was issued separately in a series of war pamphlets.[29] The reader will find here a fairly good summary of the diplomatic history of this century between two great wars, with the interpretation to be expected under such circumstances (he speaks, for instance, of the "childish psychology" of the Germans), coupled with a rather idealistic view as to the final outcome and the eventual peace. This was followed by an analysis of some articles by the German historian Delbrück in the *Preussische Jahrbücher* during the pre-war years.[30] In these articles, which were quoted extensively by Seignobos, this "intelligent Prussian" (the implication is that his intelligence was exceptional) expressed his dislike of the extreme nationalism and potentially dangerous foreign policy of the Empire and predicted a German defeat. Once that defeat had been accomplished, there came from Seignobos's pen articles on such subjects of current interest as the League of Nations, the past and future of Italy, the new Latvian state, Constantinople, the downfall of aristocracy in eastern Europe, Franco-German relations, and the possibility of converting Germany to the ways of peace.[31]

Closely allied to historical narrative and political science has been the interest of Professor Seignobos in the problems of methodology in history and the social sciences. This field of study has always interested him, he writes, and his investigation and study of comparative methodology has taken him into the realm of philosophy and the natural sciences. In 1887 he published an article on the psychological basis of historical knowledge in the *Revue philosophique*,[32] and a decade later the theories advanced there were stated again in the *Introduction aux études historiques*, which he wrote with Charles V. Langlois.[33] There had been

other studies of historical method, notably Bernheim's *Lehrbuch;*
but the *Introduction,* subsequently translated into English, has had
a wide circulation and soon became one of the standard handbooks. Scientific method in research had advanced by leaps and
bounds during the century, largely as a result of German scholarship. Yet it remained for two Frenchmen to publish the best
summary and explanation of the method thus developed, in
which the practical aspect is dominant and in which the successive steps in historical research and writing are explained in detail.

The book is not specifically concerned with philosophies of history; but Seignobos, in the sections written by him, discussed at
length the psychological and philosophical problems of historical
knowledge, as well as the question of causation. He insisted that
history is subjective, inasmuch as it deals with written documents which, considering the obvious shortcomings of language
as a means of communication, are by their nature subjective; and
he distinguished it from the other sciences, which are concerned
with the analysis of real objects. The problem is stated thus:
"Facts which we did not see, described in language which does
not permit us to represent them in our minds with exactness,
form the data of history."[34] Time and again he pointed out to
the reader the necessity of a healthy skepticism and the pitfalls
that face the uncritical historian who accepts his sources at face
value. Thus his approach to the problems of method is that of
shrewd common sense, enlightened by experience and theory but
rejecting all metaphysical formulas, Hegelian or otherwise.

The interest of Seignobos in methodological problems was not
limited to the field of history and pedagogy. He gave a series of
lectures at the Collège Libre des Sciences Sociales, the first part
of which was drawn from the *Introduction aux études historiques* but
the second part of which was a discussion of historical method and
its relation to the social sciences.[35] In this he pointed out the
necessity of the historian's method for the various social sciences,
which must gather facts from the past (and therefore use the various techniques of the historian), as well as from the present, by

direct observation. He reviewed the methodological problems of social history and the related topic of collective action. This book was followed by a number of articles on specific problems. In the first of these, "Les conditions pratiques de la recherche des causes dans le travail historique,"[36] he stated clearly his theory— or rather lack of a theory—of causation, cautiously maintaining that historical knowledge was in too rudimentary a state to assimilate its methods with the natural sciences. Causation in history, he wrote, by the very nature of the material at hand, could not be treated as the philosopher or sociologist would have it, for history deals with sources which are incomplete at best and with facts which are unique, no two being alike. After still another essay, "L'inconnu et l'inconscient en histoire," he went even farther afield in the last article, "La méthode psychologique en sociologie," in which he criticized the Comtian school, which rejected psychological, subjective observation and insisted that *phénomènes de conscience* are an integral part of social phenomena and, as such, could not be neglected by the social scientist.[37]

Since his formal retirement Professor Seignobos has continued to give courses at the Sorbonne, and from time to time he has presented broad historical surveys. From the latter type of course have come in the last decade two small volumes on the history of France and the history of Europe. The first of these, a *Histoire sincère de la nation française*,[38] is the better of the two. His particular interest had always been the history of his own nation, and here he gave his personal, frank interpretation of the evolution of the French people, with a hint of patriotism that had been rigorously excluded from his other writings on his country's history. It is only a summary, an *esquisse*, of the complete story; and the style is deliberately simple. This book is an interesting illustration of the problems of emphasis in any history. He explained in the introduction that some political events have been decisive in French history, and these were discussed, while those without influence were ignored.[39] Similarly, the details of cultural history, he wrote, are foreign to the story of a people; and he consistently focused attention on the masses of the people and on the social

history aspects of the narrative. Yet intellectual history was included as well—when it had influenced social history. He adhered to these principles of selection quite successfully, and the
book is an organic unit of political, social, economic, and cultural history—an ideal often proclaimed but rarely achieved.

It was his intention, utilizing the mass of material that historians had accumulated, to explain for the lay reader the origins
and historical development of contemporary France. His long
life of study and teaching was turned to good account, and the
entire book reveals the hand of one who knows the subject intimately. Beginning with the dawn of history in France (the sections on anthropology are particularly well done), the thread
of continuity to the present was kept clearly in mind throughout
the book—for example, in the discussion of the early and pagan
survivals in contemporary Christianity,[40] or when he suggested
that the Gallic tribal divisions have been perpetuated in the departmental boundaries of today.[41] In this book, as in his other
writings, there is an emphasis on comparative etymology which
adds both to the interest and to the understanding of the developments portrayed. Seignobos had returned from Germany with a
belief that institutional history should be emphasized, only to reject it later. Yet here, as in some of his other volumes, there is a
strong emphasis on the story of institutions, particularly in the
sections on the medieval and early modern periods and in the
story of the church. No American enthusiast of socioeconomic
history could object to the space devoted to that phase of history
in this book, particularly in the treatment of recent economic
changes. By the beginning of the nineteenth century, Seignobos
wrote, the evolution of France had been practically completed;
yet he fully recognized the importance of recent and contemporary economic changes which have yet to exert their full effect.[42]

The success of this book led to a much more ambitious project,
an *Essai d'une histoire comparée des peuples de l'Europe*,[43] a work in
many respects similar to the *Histoire sincère de la nation française*.
This, also, is a study dealing primarily with the larger develop-

ments and the masses, rather than with the unimportant, if picturesque, details about their rulers, and tracing the transformations that the peoples of Europe have undergone to arrive at the
present. The style and presentation are simple and straightforward, enlivened only rarely with such observations as: "Literature has continued to be produced in the same form and spirit,
divided between the necessity of pleasing the public and the desire to astonish it."[44] Writing in 1938, he saw an impending conflict between the opposing forces of totalitarianism and liberalism, which, aggravated by economic depression, boded no good
for the future of Europe.[45]

This book was not so successful as the *Histoire sincère de la nation
française*. Perhaps he was aware of this, for he had entitled it an
Essai d'une histoire, and he admitted that it was even more rash a
project than the preceding book. Actually, there were almost insurmountable difficulties. In fewer pages than the number used
for the history of France alone, he attempted to narrate the history of a continent. True, he told the story of Europe, keeping
the narrative consistently on the European plane, instead of discussing each of the various nations in turn, as he had in the
Histoire politique; and, on the whole, the experiment was successful. A good balance between interpretation and detail was
usually maintained; yet sometimes the details, particularly when
drawn from minor countries, bog down the story and leave the
narrative fragmentary. At times the generalizations are far-
fetched, as when he tried to show a unity in the period 1648–60
in European history which was nonexistent.[46] On the other hand,
he sometimes failed to note common factors which did exist. In
listing the oppressed nationalities in recent times, Ireland and
certainly Alsace-Lorraine should have been included in the list.[47]
Yet, when all is said, this most recent of his works remains the
most original and interesting of them all.

Such a long and active career is perhaps ample justification for
the reputation which Seignobos holds today among contemporary historians. Age alone would entitle him to his position, for he
was born during the early years of the Second Empire, and his

career as a historian and teacher has extended over six decades. Froude, in spite of grave faults in his work, lived to see his reputation as a historian bolstered by age and the mere quantity of his pen's output; while Seignobos has written only good history, and few historians have done good work in so many fields. Yet the significance of his work lies less in the intrinsic quality and value of his writings than in their representative character.

The best of recent historical tradition is represented in his work. He began to write when historical scholarship was breaking away from belles-lettres; and he was aware, perhaps to a fault, of the shortcomings of the historian who emphasized the artistic aspect of his work to the detriment of the purely scientific and historical.[48] Believing that there was an almost inevitable conflict between the two, he deliberately avoided any literary flavor in his own books, and they are noteworthy for their simple and clear style and vocabulary.

The period of his early years demanded scientific scholarship in the German tradition; and he was trained in that, contributing his share to the literature of research. Even in his works of synthesis he showed a fine respect for his sources, admitting it freely when there were lacunae and stating, whenever necessary, his inability to come to a conclusion on a disputed point. The tradition of his generation also set objectivity as an ideal, and his adherence to that ideal has been admirable. Wiser than some, he admitted the impossibility of maintaining complete objectivity, and he stated frankly in one of his earlier works his personal bias.

Having adopted the tone of a scientific treatise, I have had no occasion for display of personal feelings toward any party or nation. I have, indeed, a preference for a liberal, unclerical, democratic, Western government; but I have a conscience too, and it has saved me, as I think, from the temptation to distort or ignore phenomena that are personally distasteful to me. If I am deceived in this, the reader is aware of the direction in which it is possible that I have had a leaning.[49]

One can see here and there in his writings a reflection of his preference for a liberal and lay society. His religious background had been Protestant and extremely liberal, and in his recent books he has written just a bit cynically about medieval Catholicism and the medieval fear of hell-fire which still exists.[50] As a liberal and democrat, his sympathies were naturally with the Third Republic in France and with democracy abroad,[51] and he has further declared his belief in the utility of history as a valid instrument for political training in a lay democracy.[52] Otherwise, there is scant evidence in his writings of either this bias or of an excessive patriotism—no mean feat when one realizes that he wrote in a period when patriotism and the principle of a lay democracy were still a subject of violent discussion in France. His preference for liberalism and democracy has not taken him far from the accepted meaning of those terms during the early years of the Third Republic, and he has written critically of doctrinaire socialism in theory and in practice.

He rejected the economic interpretation of history as being fragmentary at best;[53] and he has likewise criticized other interpretations, such as the geographical and the institutional (to which he once adhered).[54] Yet he has continued to make use of these and other approaches to history on occasion. He might be listed as belonging to the political school of history. That has been his major interest, and in his last two books he has insisted on the fundamental importance of political events.[55] But, as we have seen, other interpretations have not been ignored, and throughout his work the approach has been eclectic rather than one-sided. Perhaps he can be assigned to a school of "accidental determinists." In the conclusion of the *Histoire politique de l'Europe contemporaine* he claimed that the political evolution of nineteenth-century Europe had been determined by the events of 1830, 1848, and 1870—events for which no general causes may be found.[56] Similarly, when he wrote on the problems of methodology and theory, again reflecting the interests of his generation, he avoided favoring any particular theory of causation; and when he wrote history he either gave the simplest and most immediate cause for an event or, more often than not, left it unexplained. All of which is in the best tradition of recent historiography.

Practice, if not theory, among historians also requires an occasional glance beyond both the past and the present, and Sei-gnobos has from time to time ventured to predict the future. Eight years before the Russian Revolution of 1905 he suggested that the Russian autocracy was approaching a change;[57] and, as we have seen, he had envisioned an impending conflict between liberalism and totalitarianism. But he also predicted on the eve of the war of 1914 that there would be no conflict between France and Germany, which cured him of making rash predictions.[58]

Students, however, step in where professors fear to tread. At the moment of writing, it is possible that the liberal, lay, demo-cratic government and society that Seignobos has preferred and which he saw come into being in France during his lifetime will, as the result of the third conflict between France and Germany that he has witnessed, give way to a new regime which will bring forth a different ideal and interpretation of history. For we are told that history must be re-written by each new generation in terms of its own ideals. Yet, even if that were to take place, Seignobos's work would remain one of the best expressions in the field of historiography of the ideals and standards of the par-ticular society for which he wrote—a society liberal but not radi-cal, rational, and critical of outworn modes and ideas, yet hesitant to venture on untrodden paths. Therein lies the true significance of the work of Charles Seignobos.

NOTES

1. The biographical material in this essay is taken from a five-page autobio-graphical sketch which Professor Seignobos very kindly sent to the author.

2. According to one writer, Seignobos in his youth had little respect for the republicans of this period, preferring the Orleanist faction of the monarchist party (Pierre Leguay, "M. Seignobos et l'histoire," *Mercure de France*, LXXXVIII [1910], 37).

3. It is interesting to compare this description of Professor Seignobos with one published thirty years ago, which came to the author's attention after this paper was written. The similarity is striking (*ibid.*, p. 36).

4. *Histoire ancienne de l'Orient, des Grecs, histoire des Romains, le moyen âge jusqu'a Charlemagne* (Paris, 1885); *Le moyen âge depuis Charlemagne, la Renaissance et les temps modernes, periode contemporaine* (Paris, 1886). There is a complete list of Professor Seignobos's publications, both books and articles, in J. Letaconnoux (ed.), *Études de*

politique et d'histoire (Paris, 1934), which is a collection of selected articles by Professor Seignobos.

5. *Histoire narrative et descriptive des anciens peuples de l'Orient* (Paris, 1890); *Histoire narrative et descriptive de la Grèce ancienne* (Paris, 1891); *Histoire narrative et descriptive du peuple romain* (Paris, 1894).

6. *Cours d'histoire Ch. Seignobos* (9 vols.; Paris, 1902–4).

7. "L'enseignement de l'histoire dans les universités allemandes," *Revue internationale de l'enseignement*, Vol. I (1881), reprinted in Letaconnoux, pp. 64–108.

8. Letaconnoux, pp. vii–viii and *passim*.

9. Paris, 1882. The supplementary thesis was entitled *De indole plebis romanae apud T. Livium*.

10. P. viii.

11. "Le régime féodal de ses débuts à la fin du XIIIᵉ siècle," in E. Lavisse and A. Rambaud (eds.), *Histoire générale du IVᵉ siècle à nos jours* (Paris, 1893), II, 1–67.

12. "Les croisades," *ibid.*, pp. 294–351.

13. "La révolution de 1848 et la réaction en France," *ibid.*, XI (1899), 1–37; "La Troisième République," *ibid.*, XII (1901), 1–51.

14. *Histoire politique de l'Europe contemporaine, évolution des partis et des formes politiques, 1814–1896* (Paris, 1897).

15. *Ibid.*, p. 90.

16. *Ibid.*, p. 96.

17. Letaconnoux, pp. xii–xiv.

18. Vols. VI–VIII (Paris, 1921).

19. IX (Paris, 1921), 485–504.

20. VI, 341–420.

21. VI, 158–85.

22. VII, 346 and *passim*.

23. E.g., VIII, 236–37.

24. VII, 376 and *passim*.

25. E.g., VIII, 33–34.

26. VII, 253.

27. Letaconnoux, pp. xii–xiv.

28. "La séparation des pouvoirs," *Revue de Paris*, I (1895), 709–32, reprinted in Letaconnoux, pp. 183–208.

29. Reprinted in Letaconnoux, pp. 209–40.

30. "Les inquiétudes d'un Prussien intelligent," *Revue de Paris*, II (1916), 752–76, reprinted in Letaconnoux, pp. 241–68.

31. Letaconnoux, pp. xiii–xv.

32. "Les conditions psychologiques de la connaissance en histoire," *Revue philosophique*, XXIV (1887), 1–32, 168–97.

33. Paris, 1898.

34. *Introduction to the study of history*, trans. G. G. Berry (London, 1898), p. 221.

35. *La méthode historique appliquée aux sciences sociales* (Paris, 1901).

36. *Bulletin de la Société Française de Philosophie*, May 30, 1907, reprinted in Letaconnoux, pp. 26–59.

37. *Journal de psychologie*, IV (1907), Nos. 6–7, reprinted in Letaconnoux, pp. 3–25.

38. *Histoire sincère de la nation française, essai d'une histoire de l'évolution du peuple français* (Paris, 1933). The English translation appeared a year before the original edition (*The evolution of the French people*, trans. Catherine Alison Phillips [New York, 1932]).

39. *Histoire sincère de la nation française*, p. x.

40. *Ibid.*, pp. 63, 68–70.

41. *Ibid.*, p. 19.

42. *Ibid.*, pp. 488–89.

43. Paris, 1938. The English edition is entitled *The rise of European civilization*, trans. Catherine Alison Phillips (New York, 1938).

44. *Essai d'une histoire comparée des peuples de l'Europe*, p. 466.

45. *Ibid.*, p. 469.

46. *Ibid.*, pp. 275–77.

47. *Ibid.*, pp. 404–5.

48. "L'histoire," in L. Petit de Julleville (ed.), *Histoire de la langue et de la littérature française des origines à 1900*, VIII (1899), 305–10.

49. *A political history of Europe since 1814*, trans. S. M. Macvane (New York, 1898), p. x.

50. See, e.g., *Essai d'une histoire comparée des peuples de l'Europe*, p. 466.

51. In 1922, when a friend, admitting that he had misjudged the potentialities of a militant Fascism, said to Professor Seignobos: "It was stupid of me to have quoted Napoleon in writing of Mussolini, 'One can do everything with bayonets except sit on them,' " he replied: "Yes, yes, but you can make others sit on them !"

52. "L'enseignement de l'histoire comme instrument d'éducation politique," *Conférences du Musée Pédagogique, 1907, l'enseignement de l'histoire* (Paris, 1907), pp. 1–24, reprinted in Letaconnoux, pp. 109–32.

53. "Que reste-t-il de vivant dans le marxisme?" *Les enquêtes du Temps*, Aug. 27, 1933, reprinted in Letaconnoux, pp. 391–96; *Histoire de France contemporaine*, VIII, 236–37; *La méthode historique appliquée aux sciences sociales*, pp. 312–15.

54. See, e.g., *Essai d'une histoire comparée des peuples de l'Europe*, p. 3.

55. *Ibid.*, p. vi; *Histoire sincère de la nation française*, p. x.

56. P. 805. In spite of criticism, he maintained substantially the same thesis in the revised edition of 1926 (II, 1223).

57. *Histoire politique de l'Europe contemporaine*, p. 584.

58. "Que reste-t-il de vivant dans le marxisme?" *loc. cit.*, p. 396.

XXII

HAROLD TEMPERLEY (1879–1939)

MARGARETA FAISSLER*

THE period between 1919 and 1939 was an extraordinarily favorable one for the study of diplomatic history. Rich new materials, popular interest, the belief that an understanding of past wars could help to eliminate future conflicts, all served to attract able students to the investigation of diplomatic problems. Among the foremost of these students was Harold William Vazeille Temperley. He is entitled to a high place in English and international historiography not only because of the quality of his scholarship but also because of the number and variety of his interests. As teacher and organizer of historical studies, and even as soldier and diplomat, he performed distinguished services; and as editor and writer he was among the first of his generation.

By experience, interest, and temperament Harold Temperley was singularly well suited to his chosen profession. In the first place, he had a thoroughly academic background.[1] He was born in Cambridge on April 20, 1879, the son of a fellow and mathematical tutor of Queen's College. He was educated at Sherborne, one of the smaller public schools, and later at King's College, Cambridge (B.A., 1901; M.A., 1906), where a distinguished record and the winning of prizes bore witness to his inclinations and his ability. "As an undergraduate historian he would strike out a rich line on occasion [one of his teachers reported later]— exuberant with learning already, though not always entirely accurate, not always quite disciplined in form."[2] In 1905, after a brief period as lecturer at Leeds, he returned to Cambridge as

* Teacher of history, Roland Park Country School, Baltimore, Md.

fellow of Peterhouse, and during all the vicissitudes of the rest of his life he retained his connection with his college. In 1930 he became university professor of modern history, and in 1938 he was elected master of Peterhouse. He died on July 11, 1939.

Of equal importance with his academic experience were his two favorite avocations, reading and travel. He was a voracious reader of English and foreign literatures. Wherever he went he carried a book in his pocket, usually a book of poetry. Even in his university days a walking companion complained that it was necessary to restrict him to a single literary quotation a kilometer. Hungarian and especially Serbian legends and folk literature interested him particularly, and he illuminated his reading of them by seventeen journeys to eastern Europe—the first in 1905. A knowledge of the Balkan languages enabled him to converse with Serbian, Rumanian, and Hungarian peasants in their own tongues. He was at hand to witness many important events in the Balkans—among them the Turkish revolution of 1908, the last public appearance of Abdul Hamid in 1909, and the Albanian revolt in 1910. Nor did he escape without personal adventures, of which he recounted endless lively stories.

Another important part of Temperley's experience was his career in the Near East as soldier and diplomat. When war broke out in 1914 he became captain in the Fife and Forfar Yeomanry, and he served in the campaign of the Dardanelles until he contracted some kind of eastern fever, from the effects of which he never wholly recovered. He returned to England for a time to work in the intelligence branch of the war office, where his already extensive knowledge of the Balkans was most useful. In 1918 he was again in military service as a general staff officer at Saloniki with the rank of major. During this period he was so constantly moving about that, as he afterward declared, he slept in fifty-nine beds in seventy-six nights. After the armistice and again after the signing of the peace treaties he was employed on military missions in Yugoslavia and Hungary, in the course of which he had numerous hazardous experiences. One night he was attacked in a blockhouse near Pech in Old Serbia and was forced to defend himself with an ax. In 1920, as assistant military attaché at Belgrade, he submitted a White Paper on conditions in Montenegro, which reveals his own interest in a united South Slav state.[3] He attended the Paris Peace Conference and participated in the drawing of some of the eastern frontiers; later he represented Great Britain on the Albanian frontiers commission.

As a man, Temperley was known for the enthusiasm and warmth of his nature. His abounding vigor of personality was reflected in his physical habits and his ample build. In his earlier days he played Rugby football, and he always kept up the habit of swimming and of making boating excursions on the Cam. As a young man, at least, he made himself somewhat ridiculous in the eyes of his critics by the headlong manner in which he threw himself into everything he did. He never lost his wholehearted enthusiasm, and to the end of his life his loud voice and his hearty laugh represented to his friends both the generosity of his nature and a certain lack of conventionality. For the forming of deep personal relationships he had a peculiar gift. He was married twice, both times very happily. His first wife, Gladys Bradford, whom he married in 1913, was herself a historian. After their marriage she published a biography of Henry VII. She died in 1923, leaving one son. In 1929 he married a cousin, Dorothy Vazeille Temperley, a woman of charm, who made his home a most hospitable place. His friends were legion, both in England and abroad. They included such persons as the Serbian sculptor Mestrovich, and King Alexander of Yugoslavia. Temperley's own easy manner made him at home with the great. Everyone who was his friend found him unswervingly loyal and ready for endless unobtrusive deeds of kindness. On the other hand, he was sometimes unduly censorious of others. He had rigid standards of conduct for himself, and he demanded that others conform to those same standards. To him, things were either right or wrong, and he could not tolerate wrongdoing in others any more readily than in himself. In the sum of his personality, however, intolerance was well outweighed by humanity.

These personal qualities and his particular experiences made him successful in a number of fields. In the first place, he was a notable teacher.[4] He was interested in younger people—in the students, in his younger colleagues, and even in small children, who adored him. To his students he imparted not only the zest and imagination with which he approached historical problems but also his own lofty ideals of craftsmanship. He was successful both in his lectures to undergraduates and in the directing of research. Indeed, he helped make Peterhouse known for the excellence of its historical teaching. From the first he wielded an important influence, and in his later years a dominating one, in the Cambridge historical faculty; and he brought historical studies, especially those relating to nineteenth-century diplomacy, to a high degree of excellence.

Temperley's influence was not, however, limited to Cambridge, for it was soon felt outside the university and outside England as well. He was active in the Historical Association, for example, and served on its editorial board, edited its *Annual bulletin*, and was instrumental in persuading the association to form affiliations with local societies to promote the study of local history.[5] He was a fellow of the British Academy. The extensiveness of his foreign professional connections was a salient fact of his career. In 1911 he was invited to Harvard University for a semester, and there he began an acquaintance with Americans which was continued in 1924 when he was a guest of the American Historical Association at its annual meeting and in 1936 when he lectured at Stanford. He was also deeply interested in the International Congress of Historians, of which he was president from 1933 to 1938. Among his contributions to its vitality were a journey around the world in its interests and the organization of an English national committee. The latter task was a particularly difficult one because of the age and independence of the universities and the historical societies. He also inaugurated the idea of special commissions for the study of particular geographical regions, of which he helped establish two, one for the Near East and the other for the Far East. These accomplishments and his own attainments as a historian brought him recognition abroad. He was decorated by Rumania, Poland, and Serbia and was a corresponding member of many foreign learned societies.

But, valuable as were Temperley's services as teacher and organizer, his greatest contributions to historical study were undoubtedly his editorial work and his own writings. A scrutiny of his titles reveals the versatility of his interest and talent and the course of his development as a historian.

Until the war he experimented in various fields. His first book, published in 1905, when he was twenty-five years old, was the small *Life of Canning*,[6] in which he attempted to present a well-rounded picture of his subject and to discuss domestic policy quite as fully as foreign policy. In 1910 he published a second volume, *Senates and upper chambers*,[7] describing the practices of upper chambers in the dominions, the United States, and other countries in relation to the reform of the house of lords. Meantime he had written five sections in the *Cambridge modern history*,[8] dealing with domestic or imperial history, 1687–1832. Before the outbreak of the war he also published at least ten other articles on a variety of subjects. Three of them discussed diplomatic problems,[9] and three others were on the subject of Hungary.[10]

The best of this early work is still of value, and most of it is very creditable. In thoroughness of research and clarity of organization, in narrative power and beauty of phrase, it is, however, far inferior to his later writing. It was the war and the subsequent political change in Europe which gave him firsthand experience of military operations and diplomacy and an increased intimacy with the Near East and which furnished his later work in his two chosen fields of diplomatic and Near Eastern history with such unsurpassed authority.

Before the war began, however, he had nearly completed two studies, one on diplomacy and one on Serbia. In 1915 he published *Frederick the Great and Kaiser Joseph*,[11] in which he used hitherto unexploited English sources for the War of the Bavarian Succession. Here, for the first time, he showed his real power in dealing with diplomatic and military materials. He may have exaggerated the importance of his new sources,[12] but he produced a coherent, analytical, and extremely readable little volume. In 1917 he brought out a *History of Serbia*,[13] still a most useful book for Western readers, in which he traced and interpreted the story of Serbia's long past. Thus, at the very moment when fortune offered him the most valuable experiences of his life, he began to devote himself to those two fields of study for which his talent, his interests, and his wartime adventures best fitted him.

At Paris in 1919 it was determined by members of the English and American delegations that a history of the Peace Conference should be written at once. Temperley was chosen editor, and the British Institute of International Affairs undertook the publication of the *History of the Peace Conference of Paris*.[14] Temperley himself wrote nine chapters. The history is much more than an account of the activities of the conference, for the background for each of the problems dealt with at Paris is very fully and carefully explained. It could not but suffer from the nearness to events and the bias of the writers, which Temperley actually encouraged them to reveal.[15] It is, however, an invaluable record of Anglo-American impressions of the conference, much of it written by actual participants. Temperley himself was a firm believer in the worth of such contemporary records to later and undoubtedly more disinterested historians.[16]

Beginning with 1923, Temperley renewed his study of Canning with seven articles,[17] which culminated in the publication of two books: an edition of the *Unpublished diary and some political sketches of Princess Lieven*[18] and the *Foreign policy of Canning*.[19] A comparison of the exhaustive, authoritative, readable *Foreign policy of Canning* with the earlier *Life of Canning* is not only a most interesting exercise in historical method but also a most revealing means of studying Temperley's own growth as historian and writer. The book begins with the death of Castlereagh and covers the last five years of Canning's life. Canning's policy developed, so Temperley maintained, through two phases. In the first, from 1822 to 1825, the great minister was hampered by lack of support and sometimes by active opposition from George IV; by the beginning of the second, in 1826, he had, through his extraordinary influence over parliament, press, and people, won over the king and

made "the triumph of his policy and system . . . .world-wide."[20]
One-third of the book is devoted to the first phase. Here Canning
is shown breaking with the Concert of Europe, the value of which
Castlereagh himself had begun to doubt; failing to prevent the
French invasion of Spain; but successfully opposing a very real
French threat to Spanish possessions in America. American co-
operaition, which he wanted if it could be had on his own terms,
was not forthcoming; and the Monroe Doctrine, with its implied
American monopoly of the new world, was not entirely to his
liking. In other respects his success was greater, and he was able
to recognize the new Latin-American states, to establish the independence of Brazil, and to restore British influence in Portugal.
Before considering the second phase of Canning's policy Temperley inserts several interesting chapters on the minister's personality, on his relations with the king, the foreign office, the
press, and public opinion. The second half of the book is devoted
to the last two years, 1826–27, a period when Canning was in
actual control both at home and abroad. During these years he
was able to destroy the Neo-Holy Alliance and to substitute for
it Anglo-Russian co-operation in the Greek question. He intervened in Portugal to frustrate the designs of Austria and Spain.
Then for his Hundred Days he played with skill an unusually
difficult part as prime minister.

Before the *Foreign policy of Canning* was in print Temperley became involved in another large undertaking. In 1924 the British
government determined to issue a collection of diplomatic documents similar to the German publication *Die grosse Politik der
Europäischen Kabinette, 1871–1914*. Dr. G. P. Gooch and Temperley were selected as editors. The preparation of *British documents
on the origins of the war, 1898–1914*,[21] which ran to eleven volumes,
was a tremendous task. The work cannot be thoroughly tested by
anyone, since an adequate judgment would necessitate the reading of all that the editors rejected as well as what they printed.
The skill and fundamental honesty of the editors have, however,
been taken for granted by both English and American reviewers,
and the series has been of the highest value to historians.

In 1938 Temperley made further capital out of his great editorial labors. In collaboration with Professor Lillian M. Penson, who had assisted with the later volumes of the *British documents*, he published a book called *Foundations of British foreign policy*, containing documents, many previously unpublished, illustrating British foreign policy from 1792 to 1902, and furnishing careful editorial introductions to each. The same authors also brought out simultaneously a most useful explanatory bibliography of nineteenth-century British Blue Books, which they called *A century of diplomatic Blue Books, 1814–1914*.[22]

Meanwhile Temperley had found time to write probably his best, certainly his most characteristic, work, *England and the Near East: the Crimea*.[23] It was preceded by some nine journal articles on the Eastern question.[24] The book was planned as part of a trilogy on England's relation to the Near East from the death of Canning to 1878. Certainly along with the *Foreign policy of Canning* and—because of its subject—the *History of Serbia*, it is his most valuable work. A second volume was well toward completion when he died, and it is much to be regretted that he did not live to finish it and to write the final volume.

In *The Crimea* Temperley picks up the threads of England's relations with the Ottoman Empire precisely at the point where he dropped them at the end of the *Foreign policy of Canning*, that is, at the battle of Navarino. The book begins with a careful and sympathetic account of the reforming activities of Sultan Mahmud II. Then the diplomatic relations between the great powers and Turkey during the reign of Mahmud are analyzed. The picture of Palmerston and of the development of his attitude toward the Turkish problem is particularly interesting. Temperley characterizes him as "the greatest personality in British foreign policy between Canning and Disraeli,"[25] but he shows that Palmerston was an opportunist, while Canning acted on preconceived principles carefully thought out before any concrete steps were taken. The story of the Mehemet Ali is also, to a considerable extent, the story of Palmerston, who had learned to fear Russia but who was, nevertheless, determined that the Ottoman Empire should not fall before its rebellious vassal. The years

after the fall of Mehemet Ali were by no means easy ones for the
Sick Man. The disheartening story of the double failure to reform is told—the failure of the Turks to reform themselves and
the failure of Stratford de Redcliffe to goad them on to reform.
Although the trouble in the Lebanon was settled somewhat successfully with the help of the powers, the uprisings in Bosnia and
Montenegro were disturbances in the European calm which
were not without influence on the origins of the Crimean War.
The last section of the book is devoted to a detailed account of the
diplomatic background of that war, an account which is especially interesting because of the analysis of Stratford de Redcliffe,
who receives less blame than is sometimes accorded him for the
outbreak of hostilities.

The list of books already mentioned by no means exhausts
Temperley's work. Besides other books, which will be mentioned
later, he wrote, in collaboration with Professor A. J. Grant, a
textbook, largely political and diplomatic, *Europe in the nineteenth
century*.[26] Altogether his articles and pamphlets number over
sixty. In spite of the repetitious use of some materials they discuss a wide variety of subjects. He wrote on the sculpture of
Malvina Hoffman and of Mestrovich,[27] on the supernatural element in history,[28] and on the new constitution in India.[29] In addition to this long list of books and articles, he found time to edit
the *Cambridge historical journal* (1923–27) and to act as member of
the Historical Manuscripts Commission, to which he was appointed in 1928. Before his death he had planned the *Cambridge
modern history*, new series, to which he had written an introduction;
and he had had his influence on the plans for the *Cambridge history of Poland*.

Temperley was not the founder of a new school of historical investigation, nor was he the exponent of any avowed philosophy
of history, either original or ready-made. He had, however, well-
formulated views on the methods and value of historical studies.
These views are to be found scattered through his writings and in
his own practices. Once only did he make a considerable declaration of faith as historian, and that was in his inaugural address

as university professor in 1930,[30] which is well worth reading not only as a statement of Temperley's own convictions but also for the wise advice it offers to all students of history.

A key to the understanding of Temperley's attack on historical problems may be found in the following sentence from his *Selected essays of J. B. Bury:*[31] "Science and Art have found a meeting ground in History today."[32] Much of Temperley's attitude toward historical studies is implied in those few words.

On the scientific side he staunchly repudiated the notion that history is a science in the sense of those "old scientific historians, who regarded men as engines and progress as mechanical."[33] On the other hand, he was devoted to accuracy and untiring in his effort to give his writing the closest possible approximation to scientific dependability.

He had a passion for sources. He wrote directly from the original materials and insisted upon exhausting all the materials which he considered pertinent to his subject. He was constantly to be found in the archives, not only in London but in Paris, The Hague, Berlin, and Vienna as well.[34] Nor was he satisfied with the official documents. He demanded all the available private papers.

It is . . . . by a comparison of private with official records that truth is obtained, not by an examination of one or the other. It is that comparison which Lord Acton regarded as the crucial test of a man's conduct. But a comparison . . . . must be exhaustive and, I fear, also exhausting. None the less, a man becomes a historian only in proportion as he gets cumulative effects from masses of documents and relates them to broader issues. There is an immense difference between reading sixty percent. and ninety percent. of the materials which concern you. It is a difference between relying on selections made by others, and making your selections for yourself. It is the difference between appreciation and mastery of your subject. Should you wish to understand a statesman, read all that he spoke and wrote, not selected speeches or writings. Master his parliamentary speeches, his published, his secret despatches, and his private letters. Then you will have four separate checks on his policy, his conduct, and veracity, and all supplied by himself. The whole man is the authentic man. The statesman thus revealed is his own critic. The historian has his mind enlarged and his senses sharpened by the completeness of knowledge. With these keys in his hand even a dullard may open locks by which even a genius has been foiled.[35]

That Temperley himself fully conformed to his own rigorous standards is clearly shown in the bibliographies and notes of the *Foreign policy of Canning* and *The Crimea*. The *British documents on the origins of the war* also reflect his views on this subject, for they are notable for including private letters and minutes. When some public protest was made against the printing of such materials, Gooch and Temperley warmly defended their policy.[36]

Most of Temperley's editorial work was devoted, of course, to putting before the public important, unexpurgated, hitherto unpublished documents. His own books were also well furnished with long quotations from the sources and with appendixes in which unpublished documents were printed in full. Such materials were intended primarily for the better information of the general reader and for his protection against the author's particular bias. Temperley would insist, of course, that the serious research worker, and particularly the young student receiving his training,[37] should consult all the documents and not printed excerpts.

With all his tremendous knowledge and his determination to exhaust the available materials, it is to be noted, however, that Temperley was still a specialist. There were some kinds of sources which he scarcely touched. He made no real effort to investigate economic conditions. In *The Crimea* the reader is given almost no specific information about the commercial basis for the relation between England and the Ottoman Empire. In the *Foreign policy of Canning*, to cite another instance, Temperley ascribes to Canning's diplomatic skill the sympathetic relations between England and the South American states, and he makes no particular investigation of the economic side of that relationship. He was simply not greatly interested in the impact of social and economic questions upon the problems of diplomacy. He investigated and took into careful consideration the importance of military developments, and in that field his own experience stood him in good stead. The psychological and personal factors he studied with especial care, as will be noted presently. Otherwise history was to him the record of past politics. He studied and understood English party history and wove domestic and foreign policy together with skill. Primarily, however, he was a diplomatic historian and perhaps more of a specialist in that field than he himself realized.

Once the original materials were collected, Temperley was well aware of the human element involved in their interpretation. He demanded of himself and of others the greatest possible objectivity. His own writings were equable in spirit, and he labored to make them so, for he was remarkable for a lack of rancor in his judgments both of past events and of those of his own day.[38] Particularly in such a task as the editing of the *British documents* was objectivity important. The editors themselves were well aware of that problem. Volume III and later volumes carry the statement that the editors would have felt compelled to resign if their judgment of what must be printed to give a full and accurate account were challenged by anyone. Dr. Gooch says that "in maintaining this attitude to the end Temperley was a tower of strength";[39] and Professor Penson makes the following statement: "Few things brought out more surely the fighting spirit that was always behind Professor Temperley's genial humanity than any suggestion, from whatever quarter, that suppressions were possible in this series."[40] He was disturbed at the efforts of governments and of persons of wealth to control the study of history through the establishing of chairs in universities. "Poor Clio—so long injured and neglected—has at last been dragged into the market place with a noise of cymbals and of shouting. For history as a whole this popularization is unlikely to be good, to research it may actually be fatal."[41]

But with all his determination to be dispassionate Temperley was convinced that complete impartiality was out of the question. "Not only do we repudiate the ideal of Ranke that history should be colourless, new and impartial. We do not even suggest that it is desirable."[42] Since he believed it to be impossible for any human being to interpret the past without prejudice, he thought that it was desirable for the historian to reveal his own bias to his readers as clearly as possible. In that way the reader could make the necessary corrections in the writer's point of view.[43]

When the historian has studied all the available materials, interpreted them as objectively as possible, and safeguarded his reader as fully as possible against any lack of objectivity, he has, in Temperley's view, fulfilled the scientific part of his duty. There remains his duty as an artist. Temperley thought of history as an art because of the importance he attached to imaginative power and because of the possibility of presenting historical findings in an artistic way.

Perhaps the most original of Temperley's ideas was his conception of the value of imagination in the study of history. "Bury . . . .," he wrote, "speaks of 'sympathetic imagination,' and 'psychological imagination' as necessary to the interpretation of the past. And this kind of sympathy or imagination can hardly be purely scientific. Indeed there are undoubtedly cases in which the truth can only be ascertained by methods which are not purely scientific."[44] Temperley believed in the continuity of the present with the past and in the possibility of so projecting the imagination into the past that the past may be viewed with some of that reality with which we see the present. The imaginative power to which he referred was not exactly of the same sort as that employed by the novelist. He thought that the methods of Carlyle, Macaulay, and Froude were dangerously literary. "These methods, magnificent as they are, are essentially those of the lightning flash. And all lightning is blinding as well as illuminating. History so often requires not a flash, but a steady and constant ray of light."[45] On the other hand, there were such writers as Ranke, Gierke, and Stubbs who scarcely attempted to stimulate the "literary emotions" at all.

Yet surely no one would deny to any of these a gift of that imagination without which no true history can exist. . . . . The power of discovering and establishing the truth, of piecing together and forming a coherent theory out of apparently unrelated scraps of evidence, is one of the greatest a historian can possess. It is a faculty demanding insight of the highest kind, it is a kind of constructive detective work.[46]

On another occasion he put the same idea in another way:

> [The historian is] not only a chemist, judging by calculation and tests, but a detective endowed with that "finer feeling for moral evidence" which Gibbon thought of such importance to historians. He must be more human than scientist, for he deals with human records and feelings, that is, with uncertainties.[47]

This imaginative insight could, so Temperley believed, be cultivated in various ways. Travel was, he thought, of first importance.[48] Undoubtedly, his own travels were of great advantage to him, especially in his work on the Near East. From the first page, *The Crimea* has life and color which is rarely to be found in serious historical writing. In his introduction to Marczali's *History of Hungary* his firsthand knowledge of the geography of the country stands him in good stead.[49] Passage after passage in the *History of Serbia* is made vivid by his own acquaintance with the people and their twentieth century customs.

Historical insight could also, in Temperley's opinion, be developed by the reading of imaginative writings. His own extensive reading is apparent in all that he wrote. His works abound in literary references. He also had a great interest in the historical novel. In 1929 he wrote a pamphlet for the Historical Association on *Foreign historical novels*.[50] In 1931 he edited a little book which he called *Scenes from modern history by great imaginative writers*.[51] It contained excerpts from works of avowed fiction. "The principle of selection was to choose nothing which is not good literature as well as good history."[52] That the selections could be good history was quite possible from Temperley's point of view because he believed that the imaginative writer often approaches historical truth more closely than the academic historian.[53] He included a portion of Victor Hugo's *Quatre-vingt-treize*. In the introduction to that piece he makes the following defense of it:

> The conversation . . . . is wholly fictitious in one sense, for Danton, Robespierre and Marat never conferred together as represented. It is true to history in another for had they done so, their views would have been pretty much as here given. No historian in such short compass gives us as good an idea of the gross manly breadth of Danton, of the feline caution of Robespierre, or of the insane suspicions of Marat. Victor Hugo was always the most learned of writ-

ers, and here, with an immense wealth of corroborative detail, he draws a picture of the new Republic in its struggle with old Europe.[54]

Temperley himself ventured near to the field of historical romance by helping Laurence Gilliam prepare four radio broadcasts: one in 1934 on the outbreak of the war of 1914, one in 1935 on the Jubilee, a third in 1936 on Kitchener, and a fourth in 1937 on the Russian Revolution of 1917.[55] But, for all his delight in historical fiction, he demanded that imaginative works should be acknowledged as such. He saw danger in those indeterminate works which masquerade as history but which are actually in part fiction. He spoke particularly of Lytton Strachey's *Elizabeth and Essex*, which, so he said, employed imaginative methods which historians must disapprove. "If works like this are avowed fiction, it is well enough; if they are professed history it is very bad."[56]

Temperley's theories about historical imagination led him to make extensive use of certain sources which are unusual. In his study of the Near East he employed songs and legends with which he had become familiar in his travels and his reading. From such materials he thought he could come to understand the spirit of the peoples of eastern Europe and so to comprehend what he considered to be a powerful motivating force back of their political actions. In his lecture "Bulgarian and other atrocities, 1875–8," for example, he leans heavily upon the poems of the Serbian poet Shobaich to explain the timing of the revolt in Herzegovina.

He made careful investigations of the personalities of the great political figures whose careers he described. He was fond of studying and interpreting their portraits, which he often used to illustrate his books. For instance, he says the following of Frederick the Great:

The portraits we see of him differ so amazingly from one another that it is difficult to believe that they are those of the same man, and that fact is no bad index to his strange personality. . . . . From the hard satiric lines, from the iron-bound jaw, from the air of ruthless energy pervading his face, we can read a hundred confirmations of his bitter jests against religion, of his revolting meanness towards old friends, of his cold brutality towards one of his brothers and many of his veterans.[57]

The great leaders of the past were alive to him, and he contrived to make them come alive for his readers. In his earlier days he was a hero-worshiper, as may be seen in the *Life of Canning*, where Canning is the hero and Castlereagh the villain. As long as he lived, he defended Canning against all attack, not only in books and articles but even in the columns of the *Times*.[58] On the other hand, he moderated his harsh opinion of Castlereagh.[59] A good example of his study of personality is to be found in his article "Stratford Canning and the origins of the Crimean War," in which he uses his acquaintance with Stratford Canning's character to argue against the legend that Canning fomented the Crimean War.

A final and very important aspect of Temperley's belief that history was a meeting-ground of science and art was his love of good historical style. He believed that history should be made to appeal to a wide audience. The monographic article was for the scholar, and it should be printed with all the scholarly apparatus of complete documentation. It was suited to the elucidation of minute technical questions. Longer works should be written in such a way that they could be understood and enjoyed by the layman. In deference to this principle he put the bulk of his notes in the back of his books. *The Crimea*, of which over a quarter is made up of notes and appendixes, has only seventeen footnotes in the first hundred pages.

His own style was increasingly lucid and pleasing. At first he strove too hard for effect, and his efforts to be clever were often only irritating. Sometimes he strained his sentences to use figures which were cumbersome and inept, and even in his later writings he overworked a fondness for antithetical words, phrases, and ideas. Such a sentence as the following was typical of his youthful manner: "[He] added alike to his distress and his happiness by marrying a beautiful and penniless girl of eighteen."[60] His later work was, however, beautifully phrased. The figurative ornament that had cost him a struggle in his earlier years became a natural part of his style, which he used with force and vivid effect. Even his best productions were not without an occasional awkward or obscure sentence; but, in general, the excellence of his writing is one of the notable features of his work.

In organization he also had considerable skill. The complicated materials of his mature works were marshaled with perfect mastery. He wove his facts into a bold pattern, carefully relating the details to the whole so that the most confused diplomatic maneuvers became comprehensible. A sense of narrative, a perception of the dramatic quality of historical developments, which was one of his most telling powers as a writer, often enabled him to unravel his story with the vividness and ease of a novel.

The Crimea, his last original work, is, as he hoped it would be, a worthy "contribution towards the art of history"[61] and is, in fact, the very pattern of what he considered to be good history. In it he wove into a single narrative the two stories he was most competent to tell—the story of the Ottoman Empire and that of England's relations to the Sublime Porte. It would be difficult to say whether his long hours of exhaustive research or his acquaintance and sympathy with the Near East stood him in better stead. His style is to be seen in its fullest development.

But if history was to Temperley both science and art, it had also a moral purpose. He believed that the study of the diplomatic problems to which he devoted so much of his life would help eventually to break down those nationalist legends which he considered to be important causes of wars. As a step in the direction of international amity, he collaborated with Alfred Coville in editing *Studies in Anglo-French history*,[62] an outgrowth of a conference between English and French historians held in London in 1933 and in Paris in 1934. In 1934 he helped organize and became the first president of the New Commonwealth Institute, which was devoted to research in international relations with the ultimate purpose of furthering international security and justice between nations. The hopes which prompted him to these activities were well expressed in his inaugural address as university professor:

Acton tells us that "knowledge has prevailed over opinion"; Trevelyan, that "each year there is less ground for the perpetual misrepresentation employed by

creed, class, and race." Here we have traces of authentic victories which have
been won over stubborn foes and on stricken fields. They have been won over
armies as innumerable as they were reported to be invincible; and over mental
states against which even the gods had hitherto fought in vain. The Anglo-
Saxon race has sacrificed its patriotic ideals on the altar of truth. English-
speaking historians have gradually destroyed the patriotic belief that our Saxon
ancestors were democratic and that our parliament was a unique, or even a
legislative institution. American historians are slowly causing the American
people to give up the belief that George III was a tyrant and to admit that
economic, as well as political, motives supplied fuel to the revolutionary
ardour. These conversions of public opinion to common sense make us hope
that one day history will prevail over public opinion. But it is not enough that
England and America have begun to adjust their historical differences. Further
victories remain to be won. We should work and work towards the age when
France and Germany will do so. That end is certainly far off.[63]

This, then, was Temperley's ultimate purpose—to put before
English readers the truth about the past and about other countries and to assist historians in other countries to do the same
thing for their peoples, with the hope that such truth would have
a beneficent influence upon international relations. He realized
that the struggle in which he engaged was a long one and that
very few results could be expected in his own lifetime. He did
not doubt the ultimate success of the struggle, however, and he
did not cease to play his part in it.

It was his opinion, also, that the past had very concrete lessons
to teach the present. A study of past institutions could, he believed, often throw light on those of today.[64] He was interested in
the events of the day at home, and he took an even greater interest in foreign affairs.[65]

From his reading of history and his general experience he developed some lifelong political convictions which he employed as
a standard by which to judge the past and the present. His doctrines were, to be sure, by no means extraordinary or even particularly original. On the whole, he shared the beliefs of the society in which he moved. He was convinced of the excellence of
the democratic form of government, although his democracy was
of no radical sort,[66] and of the high importance of a democratic
relation of the parts of the British Empire to one another. In his

opinion the development of the colony into the dominion was one of England's chief glories.[67] In brief, he heartily approved the form of government which had developed in England and the British Empire in the last hundred years.

He also admired British foreign policy. He might and did criticize it in detail, but in general he approved it. In the introduction to *Foundations of British foreign policy* there is the following statement:

> Despite opposed parties, and even opposed policies, the continuity of ideas in British diplomacy is striking. . . . . The balance of power, the sanctity of treaties, the danger of extending guarantees, the value of non-intervention, the implications of what Castlereagh called "a System of Government strongly popular and national in its character" were understood by all.[68]

It was that fundamental policy which Temperley admired and to which he accorded indirect approval time after time in those pages in which he set forth the details of British diplomacy.

In post-war Europe he saw the greatest hope in the League of Nations. In *The second year of the League*[69] he summarized the League's activities during the year and left no doubt as to his own approval of its purposes and his high hopes of its success. Any attack on the prestige of the League aroused his bitter disapproval.[70] In fact, he believed that he saw in the League the full flowering of the policies of Canning, which his own studies had taught him to admire so sincerely.

It is difficult to assign to Temperley a place among historians. Unquestionably, he had a wide influence in his own day through the great range of his activities—his writing and editing, his teaching, and his international connections. His energy made its impress in so many different places and on so many different groups of people that, had he written nothing, his death would have been widely felt.

Unquestionably, also, he made a valuable contribution to historiography. He himself said that great history is the product of ceaseless, incredibly arduous labor. The task of "the great historian whose first aim is to advance knowledge" is endless.

Such a historian can quote a dozen printed or little-known sources for each of his major statements. What such a historian gives us is not abundance but certainty of information. By these methods he has removed some doubts forever, he has done some work which will never need be done again. That is one road to immortality, and a very good one.[71]

Certainly, in his most important articles, in *Frederick the Great and Kaiser Joseph*, in the *Foreign policy of Canning*, and in *The Crimea*, he walked a little way along that road; and some of his findings will stand unchallenged. Moreover, his work on the Near East opened to English readers and English scholars materials which would not otherwise have been available to them. His editorial work, supported by his colossal knowledge and his firsthand experience, will be of use to students as long as the diplomacy of the nineteenth and twentieth centuries is of interest to anyone. Finally, his method of writing, his insistence upon style, and his precept and example in the matter of imagination in historical study are valuable. Whether he will find important followers only the future can tell.

On the other hand, it probably can never be argued that Temperley's work marked a turning-point in historiography. His interest in diplomatic history made him but one—although a distinguished one—of a large group of able students. Diplomatic history would have been studied during his lifetime, and in much the same way, whether he had written and edited or not. Moreover, at the very moment of his death those ideals for which he labored were subject to the most severe attack. For his personal peace of mind it is well that he did not live to see September, 1939, when those international hatreds which he hoped could be softened by the disinterested findings of scholars were again let loose in all their fury. He died at the end of an epoch—an epoch of which he himself was a characteristic product. What will be the ultimate influence of his work and of the work of contemporary historians of similar interests and hopes can be determined only when it is clear what will be the next developments in historical writing and in international relations.

NOTES

1. Most of this biographical material is taken from the numerous memorial articles which appeared at the time of Temperley's death. The fullest is by G. P. Gooch, "Harold Temperley," in *Proceedings of the British Academy*, XXV, 355–93. Others of particular value are in the London *Times*, July 12, 1939, p. 16, and in *History*, N.S., XXIV (1939), 121–24, the latter written by Professor Lillian M. Penson. See also *Times literary supplement* (London), July 15, 1939, p. 422; *New York Times*, July 12, 1939, p. 19; *Bulletin of the International Committee of Historical Sciences*, XI (1939), Part III, 273–74; *Cambridge review*, Oct. 14, 1939, p. 11; *Cambridge historical journal*, VI (1939), No. 2, p. 123; *AHR*, XLV (1939–40), 261. For other valuable information I am indebted to Mrs. Harold Temperley, Dr. Waldo G. Leland, Professor Roger B. Merriman, and Professor Bernadotte E. Schmitt.

2. *Times* (London), July 12, 1939, p. 16.

3. "Report on political conditions in Montenegro," Cmd. 1123, Misc. No. 1 (1921). The report is dated Oct. 12, 1920.

4. *Times* (London), July 12, 1939, p. 16; July 13, p. 18; *Cambridge review*, Oct. 14, 1939, p. 12.

5. *Times* (London), Jan. 8, 1926, p. 8; Penson, *loc. cit.*, p. 123.

6. London, 1905. Reviewed by E. D. Adams, *AHR*, XI (1905–6), 389. G. P. Gooch (*loc. cit.*) summarizes all Temperley's books and some of his articles.

7. London, 1910. Reviewed, *Spectator*, CV (1910), 751.

8. Cambridge, 1902–12. In Vol. V Temperley wrote: chap. x, "The revolution and the revolution settlement in Great Britain: (1) England, 1687–1702," and chap. xv, "Party government under Queen Anne"; in Vol. VI: chap. ii, "The age of Walpole and the Pelhams"; in Vol. X: chap. xviii, "Great Britain, 1815–1832"; and in Vol. XI, of which he was a subeditor: chap. xxvii, "Great Britain and her colonies: (1) The new colonial policy."

9. "Later American policy of George Canning," *AHR*, XI (1905–6), 779–97; "Causes of the War of Jenkins' Ear, 1739," *Transactions of the Royal Historical Society*, 3d ser., III (1909), 197–236; "Relations of England with Spanish America, 1720–1744," *American Historical Association reports, 1911*, I, 229–37.

10. "Maurus Jokai and the historical novel," *CR*, LXXXVI (1904), 107–14 (the same article also appeared in *Living age*, CCXLII [1904], 412–18); "Racial strife in Hungary," *Westminster review*, CLXIX (1908), 1–12; "Introductory essay on the earlier history of Hungary," in H. Marczali, *Hungary in the eighteenth century* (Cambridge, 1910). The last was particularly valuable.

11. London, 1915. Reviewed by C. G. Robertson, *EHR*, XXX (1915), 554, and by S. B. Fay, *AHR*, XX (1914–15), 846.

12. *EHR*, XXX (1915), 554.

13. London, 1917; 2d ed., 1919. Reviewed by W. Miller, *EHR*, XXXII (1917), 589, and by R. J. Koerner, *AHR*, XXIII (1917–18), 136.

14. 6 vols.; London, 1920–24. A series of reviews by C. Seymour appeared in the *American historical review* beginning with Vol. XXVI (1920–21). See also R. C. Binkley, "Peace conference history," *JMH*, I (1929), 608.

15. *History of the peace conference of Paris*, IV, vii–viii.

16. See his letter to the *Times* (London), Feb. 21, 1928, p. 17.

17. "Documents illustrating the reception and interpretation of the Monroe Doctrine in Europe, 1823–4," *EHR*, XXXIX (1924), 590–93; "French designs on Spanish America in 1820–5," *ibid.*, XL (1925), 34–53; "Canning and the conferences of the four allied governments (1823–1826)," *AHR*, XXX (1924–25), 16–43; "Princess Lieven and the protocol of 4 April 1826," *EHR*, XXXIX (1924), 55–78; "Canning, Wellington, and George the Fourth," *ibid.*, XXXVIII (1923), 206–25; "British policy in the publication of diplomatic documents under Castlereagh and Canning" (with C. K. Webster), *Cambridge historical journal*, I (1923–25), 164–69; chap. ii in Ward and Gooch (eds.), *Cambridge history of British foreign policy* (Cambridge, 1923), Vol. II. His "Later American policy of George Canning" has already been mentioned. After the publication of the *Foreign policy of Canning* he wrote two more articles: "Instructions to Donzelot," *EHR*, XLI (1926), 583–87, and the essay on "George Canning" in F. G. C. Hearnshaw (ed.), *Political principles of some notable prime ministers of the nineteenth century* (London, 1926).

18. London, 1925.

19. London, 1925. Reviewed by D. Perkins, *AHR*, XXXI (1925–26), 317, and by R. B. Mowat, *EHR*, XLI (1926), 610.

20. P. 229.

21. London, 1926–38. The series is reviewed in *AHR* in a number of articles by S. B. Fay, beginning in Vol. XXXII; in *JMH* in a similar series by R. J. Sontag beginning in Vol. II; and in *EHR* by R. B. Mowat beginning in Vol. XLIV.

22. Both books published in Cambridge. They are reviewed together by E. L. Erickson, *JMH*, XI (1939), 390, and by R. B. Mowat, *EHR*, LIV (1939), 142. The *Foundations of British foreign policy* is also reviewed by W. P. Maddox, *AHR*, XLIV (1938–39), 892; and the *Century of diplomatic Blue Books* by S. F. Bemis, *AHR*, XLV (1939–40), 144.

23. London, 1936. Reviewed by B. E. Schmitt, *JMH*, IX (1937), 94; H. L. Hoskins, *AHR*, XLII (1936–37), 329; G. P. Gooch, *Spectator*, CLVI (1936), 624; W. Miller, *EHR*, LI (1936), 534.

24. "The Bulgarian and other atrocities, 1875–8, in the light of historical criticism," *Proceedings of the British Academy*, XVII (1931), 105–46; "Disraeli and Cyprus," *EHR*, XLVI (1931), 274–79; "The Treaty of Paris of 1856 and its execution," *JMH*, IV (1932), 387–414, 523–43; "Last phase of Stratford de Redcliffe, 1855–8," *EHR*, XLVII (1932), 216–59; "British secret diplomacy during the Palmerstonian period," *Mélanges de Halvdan Koht* (Oslo, 1932), pp. 274–94; "British policy towards parliamentary rule and constitutionalism in Turkey, 1830–1914," *Cambridge historical journal*, IV (1933), 156–91; "Alleged violations of the Straits convention by Stratford de Redcliffe," *EHR*, XLIX (1934), 657–72; "Stratford de Redcliffe and the origins of the Crimean War," *ibid.*, XLVIII (1933), 601–21; XLIX (1934), 265–98; "New light on Russia's policy in regard to the Eastern question, 1876–8," *CR*, CXLVIII (1935), 554–61.

25. P. 59.

26. London, 1927; 5th ed. (*Europe in the nineteenth and twentieth centuries*), London, 1939.

27. "Malvina Hoffman in the East," *American magazine of art*, XX (1929), 132–37; "Mestrovich puts Wilson's ideals in medal," *New York Times*, magazine section, Jan. 18, 1925, p. 13.

28. "On the supernatural element in history," *CR*, CX (1916), 188–98.

29. "New chapter in India," *Spectator*, CLVIII (1937), 571, 612.

30. *Research and modern history* (London: Macmillan & Co., Ltd., 1930). Quotations from this work are made with the permission of the publisher.

31. Cambridge, 1930.

32. P. xxx.

33. *Ibid.*, p. xxix.

34. Penson, *loc. cit.*, p. 122.

35. *Research and modern history*, pp. 13–14.

36. *Times* (London), Nov. 21, 1932, p. 13; Nov. 22, 1932, p. 13; Dec. 1, 1933, p. 15.

37. *Research and modern history*, p. 11.

38. See the supplementary chapter in Grant and Temperley, *Europe in the nineteenth and twentieth centuries*, where Temperley speaks with understanding of the problems of Germany.

39. Gooch, *loc. cit.*, p. 355.

40. Penson, *loc. cit.*, p. 122.

41. *Research and modern history*, p. 4.

42. *Ibid.*, p. 18.

43. *Senates and upper chambers*, p. x.

44. *Selected essays of J. B. Bury*, p. xxix.

45. *Research and modern history*, p. 8.

46. *Ibid.*, p. 9.

47. *CR*, CX (1916), 190.

48. *Research and modern history*, pp. 9–10.

49. See, e.g., p. xxi.

50. "Historical Association leaflet," No. 76 (London, 1929).

51. London, 1931.

52. Foreword.

53. *Foreign historical novels*, p. 7.

54. *Scenes from modern history*, p. 119.

55. Gooch, *loc. cit.*, p. 392; *Times* (London), July 12, 1939, p. 16.

56. *Foreign historical novels*, p. 5.

57. *Frederick the Great and Kaiser Joseph*, pp. 17–18.

58. See his letters to the *Times*, Oct. 16, 1909, p. 3; Dec. 27, 1923, p. 6; Jan. 8, 1924, p. 8; Apr. 6, 1925, p. 15; Oct. 25, 1927, p. 15.

59. See his judgments of Castlereagh in the *Foreign policy of Canning, passim*.

60. *Life of Canning*, p. 18.

61. *The Crimea*, p. xxx.

62. Cambridge, 1935.

63. *Research and modern history*, pp. 19–20.

64. *Senates and upper chambers*, pp. v–vii.

65. See his articles "The new chapter in India," *Spectator*, CLVIII (1937), 571–72, 612–13, and "Palestine report," *Nineteenth century and after*, CXXII (1937), 129–39; and his letters to the *Times*, May 1, 1922, p. 10; Oct. 12, 1922, p. 13; June 27, 1923, p. 13; Sept. 17, 1923, p. 8; Sept. 17, 1935, p. 15.

66. See his article "Referendum," *EHR*, VII (1910–11), 368–79, in which he argues against the institution. See also his ideas on the reform of the house of lords, *Senates and upper chambers*, chap. v. In his later years his views were similar to those here expressed (*Foreign policy of Canning*, p. 224).

67. *Cambridge modern history*, XI, 754–66; *Victorian age in politics* (Cambridge, 1928), pp. 16–17.

68. P. xxvii.

69. London, 1922.

70. Note his attitude toward the settling of the Corfu incident, *Times* (London), Sept. 17, 1923, p. 8; Grant and Temperley, *Europe in the nineteenth and twentieth centuries*, p. 686.

71. *Research and modern history*, p. 6.

INDEX

Historical personages and episodes (e.g., Napoleon, Peter the Great, the Terror, Crimean War) discussed by writers of the several essays are not listed.

Abbott, W. C., 150

Acton, Lord, 511

Adoratsky, V. V., 452

Aegidi, L. K., 106

Aksakov, S. T., 337

Alas, Leopoldo, 3, 17

Alonso Sánchez, B., *Fuentes de la historia española*, 19

Altamira, Rafael (*John E. Fagg*), birth, 1; education, 2; professor at Oviedo, 2; other interests, 3–5; patriotic activities, 5–7; tour of Latin America, 12–13; member of the Permanent Court of International Justice, 13; activities in old age, 16; personality, 16
Arte y realidad, 17; *Bibliographie d'histoire coloniale: Espagne*, 18; *Constituciones vigentes* ... , 18; *Cuestiones de historia del derecho y de legislación comparada*, 13; *Cuestiones hispano-americanos*, 18; *Cuestiones modernas de historia*, 1, 19; *De historia y arte*, 1; *Derecho consuetudinario* ... , 19; *La enseñanza de la historia*, 1, 4; *Escritos patrióticos*, 18; *España en América*, 18; *España y el programa americanista*, 18; *La guerra actual y la opinión española*, 18; *Historia del derecho español*, 18; *Historia de España y de la civilización española*, 1, 8, 11, 13–14; *Historia de la propiedad comunal*, 1, 13, 19; *La huella de España en América*, 18; *Manuel de historia de España*, 18; *Mi primera campaña*, 17; *Mi viaje a América*, 18; *La política de España en América*, 18; *Psicología del pueblo español*, 1, 6; *Rice Institute pamphlet*, 19; *La sociedad de las naciones*, 18; *Temas de historia de España*, 1; *Ultimos escritos americanistas*, 18
Editor: *Revista crítica de historia y literatura españolas, portuguesas, y hispano-americanas*, 2
Translation: *Fichte's Reden an die deutsche Nation*, 6
His historical method, 14; nature of his *Historia de España*, 8–10; pessimism

about the future, 16–17; philosophy of history, 16; qualifications as a historian, 7; style, 14–15; views on the importance of history in the contemporary world, 15; work as legal historian, 13; work in Hispanic American history, 11–12; estimate, 17

Althoff, Friedrich, 104, 124

American Historical Association, 12, 278, 498

Amherst College, 383

Andler, Charles, 255

Arndt, W., 218

Arneth, A. von, 270

Ashington, Frances (Lady Firth), 132

Ashley, Sir William, 274

Ashley, Sir William (*Janet L. Mac-Donald*), birth, 21; education, 22–24; professor at Toronto, 21; at Harvard, 21, 34, 35; at Birmingham, 21, 33, 35, 39; academic honors, 38; war work and knighthood, 39; last years and death, 39–40
Books: *The adjustment of wages*, 35; *The bread of our forefathers*, 20, 39, 40–41; *The Christian outlook; sermons of an economist*, 22; *The early history of the English woolen industry*, 26; *The economic organization of England*, 38; *Edward III and his wars, 1327–1360*, 26; *Introduction to English economic history and theory*, 20, 26, 28–29, 31, 38; *James and Philip van Artevelde*, 26; *The progress of the German working classes*, 36–37; *Surveys: historic and economic*, 23, 31, 33; *The tariff problem*, 36–37
Contribution to: *Essays introductory to the study of English constitutional history*, 26
Articles: listed, 33
Editor: *British dominions*, 35; *British industries*, 35
Contributions, 27; his historical concepts, 24–25, 34; interest in economic history, 25; its application to politics, 36–37; estimate, 21, 42